THE EARLY AND MIDDLE BRONZE AGE IN THE CENTRAL BALKANS

I dedicate the book to my dear friends and colleagues who are unfortunately no longer with us,
Jovica Stankovski (1949–2020) and Alexandru Szentmiklosi (1971–2019)

THE EARLY AND MIDDLE BRONZE AGE IN THE CENTRAL BALKANS

Aleksandar Bulatović

OXBOW | books
Oxford & Philadelphia

Published in the United Kingdom in 2025 by
OXBOW BOOKS
81 St Clements, Oxford OX4 1AW

and in the United States by
OXBOW BOOKS
1950 Lawrence Road, Havertown, PA 19083

Paperback Edition: 979-8-88857-207-8
Digital Edition: 979-8-88857-208-5 (epub)

A CIP record for this book is available from the British Library

Library of Congress Control Number: 2025935374

Printed in the United Kingdom by Short Run Press
Typeset in India by DiTech Publishing Services

For a complete list of Oxbow titles, please contact:

UNITED KINGDOM
Oxbow Books
Telephone (0)1226 734350
Email: oxbow@oxbowbooks.com
www.oxbowbooks.com

UNITED STATES OF AMERICA
Oxbow Books
Telephone (610) 853-9131, Fax (610) 853-9146
Email: queries@casemateacademic.com
www.casemateacademic.com/oxbow

Oxbow Books is part of the Casemate Group

Front cover: Gold jewellery from the burial of the inhumed deceased at the site of Svinjarička Čuka near Lebane, SE Serbia - photo by Felix Ostmann, Austrian Archaeological Institute of Austrian Academy of Sciences, Vienna

The Publisher's authorised representative in the EU for product safety is Authorised Rep Compliance Ltd., Ground Floor, 71 Lower Baggot Street, Dublin D02 P593, Ireland.
www.arccompliance.com

Contents

Copyright acknowledgements

Original drawings after:
Grčki-Stanimirov 1996: Figs 2.3 and 2.4/1–6; M. Garašanin 1973: Fig. 2.4/7–8; Stojić and Jacanović 2008: Figs 2.10/1–3, 2.15/1–5, 3.2/7–17, 3.4/19–20, 3.7/15; Krstić *et al.* 1986: Fig. 2.12; Nikolić and Kapuran 2001: Fig. 2.19; Stojić and Čađenović 2006: Figs 2.43/5–7, 3.9/17–23, 3.10/2–13, 3.12; Alexandrov 2007: Fig. 2.44; Alexandrov 1998: Fig. 2.45; Stojić, Cerović 2011: Fig. 3.7/13; Stojić 1989: Fig. 3.10/21; Kapuran 2014: Figs 3.20/23–27, 3.21/10–11, 3.25/21–27, 3.28/12, 15–26; Kapuran *et al.* 2014: Figs 3.20/14–22, 3.21/1–9, 3.23/6–17, 3.24, 3.25/1–20, 3.28; Kapuran *et al.* 2020: Figs 3.26, 3.27, 3.34/13–21; Kapuran and Škundrić 2009: Fig. 3.28/1–11; Peković and Jevtić 2007: Fig. 3.28/13–14; Kapuran *et al.* 2022: Figs 3.30, 3.31; Filipović 2022: Fig. 3.34/6; Stojić and Ilijić 2011: Fig. 3.34/22; Milojević and Kapuran 2023: Fig. 3.35; Stojić and Jocić 2006: Figs 3.39/1–4, 3.47/12; M. Garašanin *et al.* 1971: Fig. 3.49/1–2, 10; Mitrović and Filipović, in preparation: Fig. 3.49/3–9; D. Garašanin 1954: Fig. 3.49/11 and Filipović and Milojević 2015: Fig. 3.49/13.

Drawings by Jelena Antić based on:
Antonović 2014: Figs 2.15/16–19, 2.20/1–5, 2.24/1–3, 2.26/1–4, 3.7/12, 3.34/1–3; Vranić 1991: Fig. 2.13; Vukmanović and Radojčić 1996: Fig. 2.15/20, 3.7/14, 3.13/9; Todorović 1967: Fig. 2.14/1–4; Svilar 2007: Figs 2.16, 2,17/1–14; Stojić 1986: Figs 2.17/15–22, 2.18, 2.20/6; Garašanin, M. and Garašanin D., 1958: Figs 2.21/9–16, 2.22/5–7; Garašanin, M. and Garašanin D., 1962: Fig. 2.21/15–16; Dmitrović 2002: Fig. 2.22/22–24; Dmitrović 2003: Fig. 2.22/17; Dmitrović 2004: Fig. 2.23/6; Dmitrović 2005: Figs 2.22/18–21, 2.24/6; Dmitrović 2015: Figs 2.22/14–16, 2.23/1, 3–4; Zotović 1985: Figs 2.22/1–4, 2.23/2, 9–10, 15; Nikitović 1994: Fig. 2.23/7; Nikitović 1996: Fig. 2.22/8–9; Nikitović 2000: Fig. 2.22/10–13; Nikitović 2003: Fig. 2.23/5; Stojić and Nikitović 1996: Fig. 2.22/10–13; Antonović and Dimić 2017: Fig. 2.23/16–20; Garašanin 1983: Fig. 2.24/4; Popović *et al.* 1986: Fig. 2.25/7–8; Radojčić 2005: Fig. 2.25/9–16; Mitrevski 2016: Fig. 2.31; Jevtić 1999: Fig. 2.42; Radojčić 2013: Figs 3.1, 3.2/1–6, 3.3, 3.7/1–11; Tasić 1984: Fig. 3.4/1–18; Bogdanović 1986: F igs 3.8, 3.9/1–16, 3.13/11–23; Čađenović 2000: Fig. 3.9/17–23; Stojić 1992: Fig. 3.10/1; Stojić 1998: Figs 3.10/15–17, 3.34/7; Stojić 1980: Figs 3.10/13, 3.13/10; Stojić 2011: Fig. 3.11; Krstić *et al.* 1972: Fig. 3.13/1–8; Ljuština and Dmitrović 2009: Figs 3.14, 3.15; Dmitrović 2009: Figs 3.16, 3.18/2–9; Lazić 2007: Figs 3.16, 3.18/2–9; Jovanović 1971: Fig. 3.21/12–13; Vukmanović, Popović 1986: Fig. 3.22; Srejović and Lazić 1997: Fig.3.33/14–28; Jovanović and Janković 1990: Fig. 3.34/4; Jevtić 1975: Fig. 3.39/10–11; Sanev 1999: Figs 3.46, 3.47/1–10 and Srejović 2002: Fig. 3.48.

Maps on Figs 1.1, 3.19, 3.56. and pls 4, 14, 16–19, 25, 28–29 were provided courtesy of M. Milinković, and Fig. 2.14/5–14 courtesy of D. Milanović.

Remaining figures were made by the author.

Foreword

One of the foremost duties of an archaeologist should be to provide the most accurate interpretation of certain social phenomena from the past, as far as current state-of-the-art conditions allow. This task becomes increasingly challenging the further one delves into the past, particularly in prehistory – a period of human life devoid of written documents.

In the search for as many arguments as possible to achieve a satisfactory interpretation, archaeologists often rely on data from others and adopt hypotheses from other scholars without fully verifying their credibility, especially when their opinions align. This 'scholarly path' often takes a winding, even erroneous direction which can be dangerously detrimental to the pursuit of archaeological truth and to properly uncovering events from the ancient past. Despite numerous challenges, such as the lack of significant data from the central Balkans or insufficient research in certain regions, this book aims to bring the lives of the Bronze Age communities who inhabited this area closer to the reader.

What does it mean to define a certain period of the past within a specific territory, especially when dealing with deeper history before the use of writing? Historical sources, while useful, are often narcissistic, malicious, dismissive of one side of an event's participants, or prone to exaggeration, depending on the origin of the source or the historian's stance toward the event. Such sources often burden history with biased interpretations or pretentious and subjective representations of certain events. Therefore, even historical sources are not a completely reliable path to true information from the past, except, perhaps, in descriptions of everyday life, where the data are largely authoritative, as they are less encumbered by the political views and biases of the historian.

Are we, without historical sources, insightful and scientifically responsible enough to free ourselves from the constraints of modern geopolitical boundaries and reveal the lives of our distant ancestors in their true light, devoid of contemporary political burdens that weigh down the sciences? The concept of cultural-historical archaeology assumes that a population within a specific territory, sharing similar spiritual and material cultural characteristics that distinguish them from other, more-or-less similar populations, is defined by the conventional terms 'culture' or 'cultural group'. These terms, surprisingly, remain in use today, likely to the astonishment of archaeologists inclined toward more theoretical views of archaeology, due to the lack of a differently conceived approach. Did territorial boundaries exist between these populations and, if they did, were they clear and inviolable? How did these communities perceive them? How did they communicate before the advent of writing and what languages did they speak? How similar was the genetic code of individuals within a prehistoric community that modern archaeologists have defined as belonging to the same cultural group, and how, and to what extent, did this change based on cultural transmission and mutual contact?

Archaeology, in collaboration with many other scientific disciplines, has been attempting to provide answers to these questions for decades, though it seems that more reasonable questions have been raised as a result. Today, thanks to the interdisciplinary approach to the issues and uncertainties of the distant past, much to the joy of many archaeologists, answers to these unknowns are gradually emerging.

The last study of the Bronze Age in the central Balkans was published over four decades ago, as part of one of the greatest publishing undertakings of Yugoslav archaeology *Prehistory of the Yugoslav Lands* (Serbo-Croatian: *Praistorija Jugoslavenskih Zemalja*). While this was an unparalleled publication at the time, much has changed since its release. Numerous excavations and various types of research, along with a wide range of analyses, have been conducted since, significantly enriching and advancing our understanding of the communities of that period in these areas. Of particular importance for studying the Bronze Age are the recent discoveries of copper-smelting workshops from the first quarter of the 2nd millennium BC in Timok Valley, and the identification of significant quantities of cassiterite in the waterways on the southern slopes of Mount Cer in western Serbia, from which tin was extracted to make bronze objects in the Late Bronze Age.

These developments were the main motivation for writing this book, which employs a multi-disciplinary approach, based primarily – as much as possible – on the results of various exact analyses, including AMS dating, palaeobotanical and archaeo-zoological analyses, chemical-physical and isotopic analyses of metal finds, and Bayesian modelling of sets of absolute dates. All of this was done while simultaneously observing the past through the prism of cultural groups, or 'cultures'.

Finally, I would like to thank Milorad Stojić who, in many ways, introduced me to the world of archaeology and sparked my interest in the Bronze Age, as well as my long-time friend and colleague Aleksandar Kapuran, and my dear colleagues Radu Băjenaru, Marc Vander Linden and Sonja Vuković for their assistance, advice, and support. I am also grateful to colleagues Vojislav Filipović, Ognjen Mladenović, Petar Milojević, Aleksandar Aleksić, Dragan Milanović, and everyone else who contributed to the realisation of this book. Special thanks are due to the Fritz Thyssen Foundation for funding the dating of 25 samples; the Atlas Project at the Department of Archaeology and Classical Studies, Stockholm; and the Ministry of Culture of the Republic of Serbia for funding AMS analyses of certain samples from the site of Velika Humska Čuka. I am also indebted to Brooklyn College and colleagues Arthur Bankoff and Wayne Powell for providing results on copper and tin isotope analyses, a few of which was used in the book; the Pusta Reka Project; the Austrian Archaeological Institute; and many others.

This book is partly a result of the project *THE FLOW – Interactions–Transmission–Transformation: Long-distance connections in Copper and Bronze Age of the Central Balkans, funded by the Science Fund of the Republic of Serbia* (IDEAS Program, Grant No. 7750074).

For any errors or omissions, the author alone is responsible.

1

Introduction

1.1 Natural characteristics of the region

As pointed out by J. Cvijić more than a century ago, the Balkan Peninsula has a strategic position as a geographic and geological medium between Europe and Asia (Cvijić 1922, 9). Such a nature of the Balkan Peninsula can be observed throughout prehistory and especially in times of the first farmers and Metal Ages, yet it remains relevant during the historic and modern times. The interest in the Balkan Peninsula reaches back to the Antique, when historians and geographers considered that the peninsula is divided by a high mountain range from east to west, or from the Black Sea to the Alps (Cvijić 1922, 5). That was more than a geographical division, as it was a political division that divided the region into the civilised south and the barbaric north. Such a misleading geomorphological view of the Balkan Peninsula prevailed until the 19th century, a time when the proper geomorphological characteristics of the Balkan Peninsula were defined.

The idea of the central Balkans as a separate geographical entity was highlighted by J. Cvijić at the beginning of the 20th century. He considered it as a territory between the Iskar River in the east and the Dinarides and Pindus in the west. Its central part is represented by the Morava and Vardar basins. In the north, its borders are marked by the Danube and Sava rivers, and the Aegean coast acts as a southern border. According to J. Cvijić, the geomorphological characteristics of the Balkan Peninsula allow a separation into the Aegean area and the continental block. The continental block is further divided into three areas: eastern (Balkan), central (Morava-Vardar), and western (Dinarides-Pindus) (Cvijić 1922, 29–34).

The separation of such a geo-social region of the Balkan Peninsula proved justified, particularly in the cultural and historical sense, as the given territory represented a compact cultural unity during several different periods of prehistory. This primarily refers to its central part, between the Sava and Danube in the north, the upper course of the Vardar and the Pčinja river in the south, the course of Drina in the west, and the southern reaches of the Carpathians and the Stara Mountain in the east.

The given territory represents the geographical focus of the book. In order to provide a solid interpretation and increase comprehensibility, and due to the different cultural and historical development of certain geographic regions through different phases of the Bronze Age, the territory is divided into five geographic zones (Fig. 1.1):

1. Peri-Pannonian Zone (Srem, Mačva, lover course of the Great Morava River, Braničevo, Stig – the so-called peri-Pannonian rim)
2. Great Morava Basin and Šumadija
3. Western Serbia (Jadar, Rađevina, Azbukovica, West Morava Basin, Drina, and Lim regions)
4. Timok Basin and Đerdap Region
5. Southern Serbia (South Morava Basin, Kosovo and Ras region) with Middle Pčinja Basin and Skopje Basin.[1]

The territories between the Iskar River and the southern slopes of the Carpathians and the Stara Mountain, meaning the Vardar Basin, and the regions between the Drina River and Dinarides, between the Pindus and the upper course of the Vardar River, will not be analysed to the same degree as the regions above even though they are likewise within the central Balkans. However, those territories will certainly be taken into consideration, since they display significant socio-cultural connections with the main geographical regions discussed in this book. In a geopolitical sense, the book will address the territory of present-day Serbia south of the Sava and Danube rivers, and the northern part of the present-day Republic of Northern Macedonia which are,

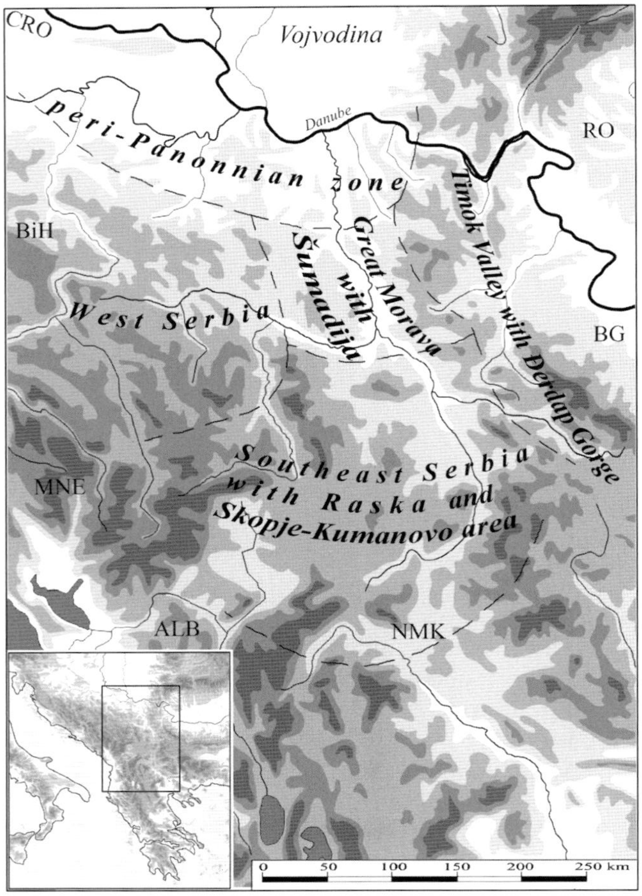

Figure 1.1. Map of the central Balkans with geographical zones referred to throughout this book.

in fact, the major components of the central Balkans. Other geographic zones of the central Balkans will be discussed secondarily.

The central Balkans can be observed as a geomorphological unit intersected with several major watercourses, mostly oriented north–south/south–north (Iskar, Ogošta, Lom, Timok, South Morava, Great Morava, Drina, Vardar, etc.) and few oriented west–east/east–west (Nišava, Pčinja, Jablanica, West Morava, etc.). These major watercourses are particularly important since the fringes of their valleys and basins represented crucial natural communications during prehistory. Minor watercourses served as connections between the major ones, as a sort of 'alternative communication route'. Although the region in question is marked by seemingly insurmountable natural barriers, such as the Carpathian Mountains which, in fact, divide the region, numerous river courses acted as a connection that surpassed those barriers. Of particular importance valley is marked by the low and easily surmountable Preševo Plateau, which facilitates the communication route connecting the Pannonian and Aegean basins, meaning Southeastern and Central Europe (Marković and Pavlović 1995, 86). Judging by the number of prehistoric and Bronze Age sites, another major natural communication route that connected the central Balkans with Thrace and Asia Minor followed the valleys of Nišava and Maritsa rivers.

Another communication route, frequently utilised in the past and nowadays forgotten due to the taming of Grdelica Gorge in the last century, was the Veternica valley, which connected the Leskovac Basin with the Vanje-Bujanovac Basin. Timok Basin, which connects the Nišava and Danube regions through the valleys of Malčanska, Svrljiški Timok, Beli Timok, and Timok rivers, is an important corridor of communication between the southern and northern parts of eastern Serbia or the Timok Valley. Numerous additional important communications are known, which will be discussed in chapters focused on different geographic zones of the central Balkans.

Climate represents the key factor for the development of vegetation and soil types of a particular region (Pavlović *et al.* 2017, 31), and have always acted as important aspects regarding the selection of settling locations. The climate of the central Balkans can generally be considered continental, the so-called Central European climate, although with different conditions in certain areas (Pontic climate in the Negotin Valley, Mediterranean climate in the Vardar Region). The climate is mostly dependent on the geomorphological characteristics of the region and, due to the large area that the study region covers, as well as significant altitude differences some of the regions are characterised by harsh (mountainous regions in the southern and eastern Serbia) or mild climate (Aleksandrovačka Župa, Metohija, etc.).

Different vegetation zones in the region, marked by the representation and distribution of forests, grasslands, and meadows, are determined by climate and soil types, without taking into account the anthropogenic influence, which intensified from the Neolithic. Several vegetation zones are represented in Serbia, from steppes, lowland forests, hilly and mountainous areas, Sub-Mediterranean forests, and low-growing vegetation, to Boreal forests and formations of moorlands (Pavlović *et al.* 2017, 41). For example, vegetation plays an important role in the formation of soil types, especially vertisol. In the past, the vertisol was covered with alder and ash forests, and nowadays it is covered with oak forests (Hungarian and Austrian oaks), which affected the transformation of the soil (Pavlović *et al.* 2017, 123). This is a fine example of the gradual transformation of soil during a long time period, which makes it hard to identify soil types with certain archaeological locations and their original soil types. An example of the frequent change in soil quality through time is the study conducted in central Hungary (a River Valley), where chernozem represents the main soil type. During the Early–Middle Holocene, the brown forest soil was primarily transformed into a grassland soil or chernozem, with a high percentage of organic matter. However, during the Early Bronze Age, the valley was occupied by grasslands formed on loess slopes, with forests on the fringe of the flood-prone part of the lowland, and such representation remained almost the same during the Middle Bronze Age. However, between 1200 and 1100 BC, there were significant soil erosions and the formation of channels and, starting from 1100 BC, peat soil was formed within the flood-prone part of the valley, grasslands were expanding, and types and density of forest changed. The expansion of arable land starts during the Iron Age and later periods (French 2010, 43–49, table 2.1). Regarding the soil types, soils with higher salinity were of utmost importance for the maintenance of livestock and the sustainability of biodiversity. Therefore, such soils were also important for the selection of locations for settlement in prehistory.

With regard to temperature, the region belongs to the meso-thermal climate zone, with a median temperature above 10°C during the warmest months, and above –3°C during the coldest months (Pavlović *et al.* 2017, 31). The highest average temperature during a year, 11–14°C, is recorded in the transitional zone between the Pannonian Plain and the mid-mountainous portion of the region (peri-Pannonian zone). The lowest average temperature, between 0 and –3°C (Pavlović *et al.* 2017, fig. 3.1), is recorded in high mountainous zones of southwestern Serbia. The same can be pointed out for precipitation, with the lowest precipitation in the transitional zone and the Morava Region and the highest in the mountainous areas of southwestern and southeastern Serbia (Pavlović *et al.* 2017, 33, fig. 3.2).

The crucial factors for the formation and evolution of soils are climate, geomorphological structure of the terrain, geological substrates, vegetation, and soil flora and fauna (Pavlović *et al.* 2017, 25). within the central balkans, meaning the territory of serbia without vojvodina, soil types are mostly represented by dystric cambisol, dystric leptosol, and eutric cambisol on loess, as well as vertisol, eutric cambisol on limestone, planosols and luvisols. alluvial soil (fluvisol) is distributed only within valleys of major rivers (Danube, Sava, Great Morava, Mlava, Timok, Nišava, South Morava, West Morava, etc.) (Protić *et al.* 2005, 297–298). Chernozem, as one of the most productive soils, is represented mostly in Vojvodina (Srem, Banat, and Bačka), and south of the Sava and Danube its representation is limited to eastern Serbia, on the right bank of the Danube, between Kladovo and Radujevac (Pavlović *et al.* 2017, 50).

As a natural phenomenon, wind forms through uneven heating of air on the ground, which causes vertical and horizontal differences in atmospheric pressure. As a such, wind can have quite an unfavourable impact on the quality of lifeways and even endanger human lives. However, the wind has certain favourable characteristics, such as faster soil drying following massive rainfall and floods. Several permanent winds are persistent in the territory of Serbia. 'Košava' blows from the east, from the Carpathians, and penetrates into the Danube Region, the Morava Region up to the Nišava Basin, southern Vojvodina, and western Serbia. The northwestern wind ('Severac') blows in Vojvodina, and the western wind from the Drina River affects western Serbia (*Serbian Encyclopedia* 2013, 320). Additionally, there are numerous local low-intensity winds. However, it seems that in the past wind was less troublesome to humans than nowadays, as humans were more resistant to possible natural disasters and the effects on their everyday life compared to modern times in urban surroundings. This is observable on a number of sites inhabited during several prehistoric periods and which are constantly exposed to strong gusts of wind, especially during autumn and spring. For example, the site of Velika Humska Čuka near Niš, almost continuously inhabited from the Early Eneolithic to the medieval period, is under strong and constant influence by the northwestern wind, which is particularly prominent during the autumn and winter. Similar/y, the site of Bubanj in Niš is constantly exposed to strong wind, yet has a vertical stratigraphy from the Early Neolithic to the Iron Age. Gradina in Svinjište near Preševo represents another similar case, although the excavations have detected the remains of a wooden fence with a stone foundation which might have served as a windshield. Numerous examples from the central Balkans point to the fact that the selection of settlement location was not significantly dependent on the wind or on the possibility of different natural conditions in the central Balkans. The less likely option would indicate significant human impact on nature, strength, and direction of the wind, which is, however, a characteristic of the modern age. The vigorous 'Košava' wind that blows from the Carpathian-Balkan area towards Šumadija, Niš Basin to the south, Vojvodina Region, and especially in the area of Požarevac and west of the Iron Gates, is described by Jovan Cvijić at the beginning of the 20th century (Cvijić 1922, 35). The data indicate that the direction and intensity of the 'Košava' wind have not changed in the past century. The study conducted by Gavrilov *et al.* (2017) confirms the persistence of winds in the area since the beginning of the Holocene.

The Bronze Age coincides with the Subboreal climatic period, a dry and warm period with temperatures on average 2°C higher than previously, that lasted from the beginning of the 3rd to the mid-1st millennium BC (Dukić 2006). In Central Europe, climate during the Bronze Age was dryer and warmer up to the Late Bronze Age (Br D), when it became more humid (Bouzek 1994). In the territory of Bohemia, several climatic oscillations which caused significant social and economic changes have been registered. These oscillations were particularly emphasised around the mid-4th millennium, during the second half of the 3rd, at the end of the 2nd, and the beginning of the 1st millennium BC (Cilek 1997). According to H. Todorova, the 5th millennium is marked by a climate crisis that caused the complete depopulation of the Balkans during the Early Eneolithic (Todorova 2007), which is confirmed by the results of excavations of period-related sites in Serbia and Bulgaria. Further, Todorova considers that, due to the mentioned climate crisis, the bearers of the Early Bronze Age (the final quarter of the 4th and the first half of the 3rd millennium BC according to Bulgarian chronology) were not of autochthonous origin, but rather newcomers to the Balkans (Todorova 2007, 5). In western Bulgaria, which is part of the central Balkans, the palaeo-botanical data indicate that the climate was humid and warm post-5250 BC which led to the expansion of fir forests around 2500 BC with beech forests represented in the higher mountains where, together with fir and hornbeam, they remained dominant up to around 700 BC (Božilova and Tonkov 2007). Such data are in accordance with the interpretation proposed by Todorova.

A major climate change occurred at the end of the 3rd millennium (2200–2000 BC), represented by a temperature maximum. This climate change had catastrophic consequences for the inhabitants of the Balkans, although not to the same degree as the aforementioned climate oscillation of the 5th millennium BC. It did not cause the complete collapse of Bronze Age cultures but rather a significant collapse in settlement systems at the beginning of the 2nd millennium BC. In the following period, the temperature steadily dropped and remained moderated until 1500 BC, then further dropped, up to 800 BC (Božilova and Tonkov 2007). Significant climate changes during the given period have been recorded in Russia, Ukraine, and Moldavia. In southwestern Russia, the temperature dropped significantly around 4500 BP (about 2500 BC), forests were displaced towards the south, and the lake levels dropped. This caused the disappearance of farming communities and the appearance of a nomadic population (Krementski 1997, 367). N. Gerasimenko likewise points to a complete decline of forests in Ukraine due to droughts and the reduction of humus soil between 2500 and 1700 BC (Gerasimenko 1997).

W. J. Burroughs considers that the Bronze Age climate change was affected both by natural variables and volcanic eruptions (Burroughs 2005, 251–252). Traces of volcanic activities dated to 2354 cal BC, 1627 cal BC, and 1159 cal BC, have been recorded within ice caps in Greenland and the Antarctic. The first date is connected with the eruption of Hekla in Iceland which could, according to the chronology, have caused climatic change. The second date is connected with the Santorini eruption which could have been either the cause, or one of the causes, for the temperature drop around 1500 cal BC. However, some authors highlight that natural factors were not the only cause of major social change during the Bronze Age. Hence, S. Manning considers that one of the main factors in the collapse of Aegean civilisation at the end of the 3rd century BC was the denudation of soil caused by intensified plough farming, which is evident through traces of utilisation of plough in settlements of the EH II period (Manning 1997, 151–152).

Periods of major changes in climate that occurred during the transition between the 3rd and the 2nd millennium BC, volcanic eruptions, and the intensification of anthropogenic changes, played significant roles in the formation, origin, and development of European Bronze Age cultures, and acted as important factors that should not be overlooked in the definition of the origin of the material and spiritual culture of communities that inhabited the central Balkans. Insufficient and superficial research of sites in the central Balkans, without palaeo-botanical, osteological, pollen, and other analyses, do not allow for a more significant interpretation of the climatic conditions in the central Balkans during the Bronze Age.

One of the most important natural characteristics of the central Balkans is its mineral resources, especially regarding copper ores as one of the most important resources during later prehistory and the Metal Ages, utilised since the 6th millennium BC. The mineral resources of the region represent the result of fissures and masses of eruptive rocks with precious mineral deposits, of which the largest is located within the so-called Timok Eruptive Area, where the earliest copper mines have been recorded (Jovanović 1971; 1995; Borić 2009).

Besides copper, other metals were utilised during the Bronze Age, such as gold, silver, and tin. Gold deposits are often connected with the gold-bearing rivers of Timok (Cvijić 1922, 38), Pčinja, and Pek (Trifunovski 1964, 14; Bulatović and Stankovski 2012, 15; Kapuran *et al.* 2014, 20, 21, with cited literature). Placer gold deposits, originating from the Timok andesite massive, which could have been exploited during prehistory have also been registered within the alluvium of Crni Timok River, Borska River, and Zlotska River (Bulatović *et al.* 2013, 16, with cited literature). Gold is also found in Lece, near Medveđa, within the Pčinja Region, Zletovo-Kratovo mountains, etc (Trifunovski 1964, 14). A large number of toponyms indicate that small quantities of gold (*Zlat* in Serbian) were exploited throughout the region (Zlatokop, Zlatica, Zlatno Brdo, Zlot, etc). However, gold objects were scarce during the Bronze Age in this region and the archaeological remains that would indicate metallurgical processes and the technology of their production have not been recorded so far.

Similarly, silver deposits are common in the central Balkans (southern Serbia, Timok Eruptive Area, Kosovo, Azbukovica, etc.), yet silver objects are apparently less represented than gold ones during the Bronze Age appearing rather regularly during the proto-historic period, while exploitation of silver is primarily connected with the Roman period.

The question of tin deposits in the region has recently been brought to light once again. Namely, potential tin deposits within the Cer and Jadar regions and the Bukulja Mountain have been the subject of discussion for several decades (Muhly 1985; Durman 1997; Harding 2000) resulting in the initiation of the international Jadar Project, from 2011, by the Institute of Archaeology in Belgrade and the Brooklyn College in New York, USA. The most important result of this project is the detection of significant amounts of the tin ore cassiterite in alluvial deposits of the southern slopes of the Cer Mountain, in the vicinity of a large Late Bronze Age mound necropolis of Paulje, which yielded numerous finds of bronze jewellery, weaponry, and other objects (Gligorić 2014; Bulatović *et al.* 2017). Experiments that included the simple sieving of cassiterite using sieving pans and sieve by several persons were conducted on a number of occasions in Milinska River on the slopes of Cer Mountain. Depending on the number of persons, season, and water levels, as well as the characteristics of the watercourse (calm or spate), different amounts of cassiterite were collected. On an early summer day during the spate season, a small team of 4–5 persons collected cassiterite which produced a sufficient amount of tin for the production of a medium-sized bronze pin. These results, and the similar fingerprinting of isotopes Sn-120 and Sn-124 from Milinska River and bronze objects from the Paulje necropolis, re-affirmed the idea that Bronze Age communities in the region utilised tin from placer deposits for the production of bronze (Mason *et al.* 2016).

1.2 History of research of Bronze Age sites in the central Balkans

One of the first travel writers of modern history who marked and sketched and therefore preserved portable and immobile antiques of the central Balkans from oblivion, was Felix Kanitz. He was the first to document bronze jewellery and weaponry from Serbia and described the so-called Kličevac Idol, one of the most attractive Bronze Age figurines, which unfortunately disappeared during the havoc of the First World War (Kanic 1985).

Early archaeological interests were focused on Western Serbia, which is understandable since the area was known for a large number of easily detectable Bronze Age mounds. Therefore, at the end of the 19th century, Mihailo Valtrović, Đoko Jovanović, and Sima Trojanović published the first results of excavations of those mounds. Nowadays, these publications are particularly important, since most of the documentation and finds from those excavations are lost (Valtrović 1893, 75–97).

At the beginning of the 20th century, M. Vasić published finds from several sites of the Žuto Brdo culture within the Serbian Danube Region and finds from the excavations at the site of Tilva Roš near Bor, which he attributed to the Copper or Bronze Age (Vasić 1904, 597; 1914, 1–93). Further, he published finds from the multi-layered site of Gradac in Zlokućane near Leskovac, also attributed to the Bronze Age (Vasić 1911).

During 1930s, the region was visited by an archaeological expedition from Harvard University, USA, led by Vladimir Fewkes. The team recorded numerous prehistoric sites, of which some were attributed to the Bronze Age (Bubanj near Niš, Pavlovac near Vranje, a number of sites on the Danube's bank, etc.) (Fewkes 1933; 1935, 11–13; Bulatović *et al.* 2013, 7). The expedition encouraged local archaeologists, which resulted in the intensification of archaeological activity during the 1930s, and led to the initiation of a number of excavations throughout Serbia. The excavations were conducted in the vicinity of Niš, at Velika Humska Čuka by Miodrag Grbić in 1934, and at the site of Bubanj in the following year, led by Adam Oršić-Slavetić (Oršić-Slavetić 1936; 1940). In the same years, Miodrag Grbić excavated the Bronze Age settlement at the site of Milića Brdo in Ljuljaci in the Šumadija Region (Grbić 1956, 19–20; Vulić and Grbić 1937), while the Harvard expedition led by V. Fewkes registered a large number of 'Early Bronze Age' necropolises within the West Morava Basin (Fewkes 1935).

The period during and after the Second World War was marked by a short suspension in excavations. However, the noticeable expansion of archaeological research in Serbia occurred during the 1950s, which resulted in the continuation of previous excavations and the initiation of a number of new ones.

Within the Đerdap Region, a necropolis of cremation burials attributed to the Žuto Brdo group at the site of Glamija, and the mound necropolis in Brusnik, were excavated in 1957 and 1958 (Galović 1961; Krstić 1971, 173–174; 2003), and the necropolis of cremation burials at Pesak in Kladovo, likewise attributed to the Žuto Brdo group, was excavated slightly later (Cermanović-Kuzmanović 1960, 185–191; Srejović 1960a, 59–60).

Excavations at the site of Milića Brdo in Ljuljaci in Šumadija Region were revisited (Garašanin 1973, 359, 360). Within Western Serbia, in Grotnica and Jančići near Čačak, and Belotić and Bela Crkva near Krupanj, Bronze Age mound necropolises were being excavated (Garašanin and Garašanin 1958, 17–50; 1962, 47–68; 1967, 5–30; Dmitrović 2016, 17).

Within the South Morava Region, excavations were being continued at the sites of Velika Humska Čuka and Bubanj, led by Milutin Garašanin. Based on the results of those excavations, he defined the Copper and Bronze Age culture of the South Morava Valley and hence named it the Bubanj-Hum culture, which became widely accepted within the scientific domain (Garašanin 1957; 1958).

The period is also marked by large-scale rescue excavations of sites in the Iron Gates, which were continued during the 1980s when several Late Bronze Age settlements and necropolises with cremation burials were excavated

(Velesnica, Kladovo, Korbovo, etc.) (Bulatović *et al.* 2013, 68–71, 91–93, 109–120, and cited literature).

The excavations in Kosovo and Metohija were primarily focused on Neolithic sites, yet during the late 1950s Dragoslav Srejović registered the necropolis of cremation burials in Donja Brnjica, which became the eponymous necropolis for the Early Iron Age culture (Srejović 1960b, 83–135).

The research of Bronze Age sites during the 1950s–60s culminated in two large exhibitions and catalogues: *Bronzano doba Srbije* (*Bronze Age of Serbia*) and *Praistorijske kulture Pomoravlja* (*Prehistoric Cultures of the Morava Region*). Further, in 1973, M. Garašanin published his capital work *Praistorija na tlu SR Srbije* (*Prehistory in the territory of the Socialist Republic of Serbia*), in which he analysed and provided a cultural and chronological definition of prehistoric groups in the territory of Serbia (Krstić *et al.* 1972; Garašanin *et al.* 1971; Garašanin 1973).

In the following decades, large-scale excavations were often conducted with foreign partners, which resulted in the so-called golden age of prehistoric archaeology in Serbia, especially regarding the excavation of Neolithic sites. Regarding the Bronze Age, the period is marked by excavations at the site of Novačka Ćuprija with Brooklyn College from New York. These excavations were realised within the scientific project 'The Morava Valley Project in Yugoslavia' (Bankoff and Winter 1982), which resulted in a study of the Late Eneolithic and Early Bronze Age in the territory of Southeastern Europe (Bankoff and Winter 1990).

In the territory of Eastern Serbia, B. Jovanović excavated the Trnjane necropolis near Bor (Jovanović and Janković 1990), and the team from the Centre for Archaeological Research of the Faculty of Philosophy conducted excavations at several sites in the region – Banjska Stena, Magura, Zvezdan, etc. Based on the results of those excavations, D. Srejović and M. Lazić defined the new Bronze Age group – the Gamzigrad cultural group (Srejović and Lazić 1997). Within the Sava Region, excavations of the renowned tell site Gomolava were continued during the1970s and '80s. Besides other periods, the site yielded a cultural layer from the Bronze Age, marked as horizon IV (Tasić 1988). Some 60 km downstream of Gomolava, in the vicinity of the Sava and Danube confluence, excavations were conducted on a large Bronze Age necropolis in Karaburma. The results of those excavations were published soon after and represented a significant source of data for the burial rites in the area between the Middle Bronze Age and the Early Iron Age (Todorović 1977).

The unfortunate period of Civil War in the former Yugoslavia and sanctions against Serbia during the first half of the 1990s resulted in the withdrawal of foreign partners and the excavations of Bronze Age sites in Serbia were completely abandoned. However, the period is characterised by intensified activities in terms of exhibitions and conferences, as well as the publication of previous excavations. Therefore, several important volumes were published in this period, such as *Arheologija istočne Srbije* (*Archaeology of Eastern Serbia*) and *Bor i okolina* (*Bor and its Surroundings*), which collected the results of all archaeological research in that region (Lazić 1997; 2004). The two-volume publication *Arheološko blago Kosova i Metohije* (*Archaeological Treasures of Kosovo and Metohija*), with the text volume comprising comprehensive papers by renowned archaeologists and the accompanying catalogue of the exhibition from the Gallery of the Serbian Academy of Sciences and Arts in 1998, collected all of the results of major archaeological research in Kosovo (Tasić 1998), to the joy of numerous archaeologists whose research was focused on the southern parts of the central Balkans.

Archaeological excavations of prehistoric sites were once again intensified at the beginning of the 21st century, although to a lesser degree compared to the previous decades. The exceptions were rescue archaeological excavations which were conducted on the routes of highways towards Sofija and Skopje, where several Bronze Age settlements and necropolises were excavated (Perić and Bulatović 2016; Prodanović-Ranković 2017). Large-scale excavations of Late Bronze Age sites within the South Morava Region were conducted at the site of Hisar in Leskovac (Stojić 2001), and small-scale excavations were conducted in partially contemporaneous sites of Gradina in Svinjšte and Gradište in Končulj (Bulatović 1999; 2000). The rescue archaeological excavations on the route of the Niš-Skopje Highway resulted in the discovery of an Early Bronze Age necropolis comprising cremation burials in Ranutovac (Bulatović *et al.* 2016a; Bulatović 2020). Cultural layers and finds from the Bronze Age were recorded on several sites during theese rescue excavations (Bulatović 2014; Bulatović *et al.* 2016b).

In addition to the rescue archaeological excavations, the team of the Institute of Archaeology in Belgrade and the National Museum in Niš re-initiated the systematic excavation of the remaining portion of the site of Bubanj (Bulatović and Milanović 2020) (Pl. 1), and the excavations at the site of Velika Humska Čuka, which are still ongoing (Bulatović and Milanović 2015). Excavations were also continued at Mediana in Niš, where several residential structures from the Late Bronze Age and the Transitional Period were recorded (Bulatović 2008).[2]

Simultaneously, within the Lower Pčinja Region, systematic archaeological excavations were conducted at the site of Tatikev Kamen in Kokino and resulted in the discovery of an Early Bronze Age observatory and a large ritual area utilised during all of the phases of the Bronze Age (Stankovski 2002; 2010) (Pl. 2). These excavations constituted something of a follow-up on the excavations of Bronze Age sites in the region in the 1980s–90s at the sites of Pribovce in Lopate and Dve Mogili in Pelince (e.g. Sanev 1999; Georgievski 1994; Trajkovska 1995; 2003), which provided the first data on the Bronze Age in this region. The large-scale rescue excavations at the site of Kale in Skopje between 2007 and 2012, among others, yielded a cultural layer from the Early and Late Bronze Age, therefore complementing the Bronze Age data from excavations at Lopate, Kokino, and Pelince (Mitrevski 2013; 2016).

These excavations within the South Morava and Pčinja regions, spurred A. Bulatović and J. Stankovski to create a synthesis of the genesis and development of the Bronze Age in the region, which was published in 2012 (Bulatović and Stankovski 2012).

Within the last decade, research on Bronze Age sites has been intensified in the territories of the Timok Valley and eastern Serbia. Following the discovery of a metallurgical workshop for copper smelting at the site of Ružana, the Institute of Archaeology in Belgrade and the OREA Institute from Vienna (former Institute for Oriental and European Archaeology, current Austrian Archaeological Institute) conducted excavations at the Middle Bronze Age necropolises in Trnjane and Hajdučka Česma, and the period related settlements in Trnjane and Čoka Njica (Kapuran *et al.* 2020). With the same partner, and the National Museum in Leskovac, the Institute of Archaeology in Belgrade has been conducting systematic archaeological excavations at the multi-layered prehistoric site of Svinjarička Čuka near Lebane since 2018, within the *NEOTECH* project. The site yielded cultural layers from the Early Neolithic, all phases of the Eneolithic and the Bronze Age, and the Iron Age (Horejs *at al.* 2018; 2019).

In western Serbia, within the valleys of West Morava and Jadar rivers, excavations were conducted on mound necropolises of the Late Bronze Age (Nikitović *et al.* 2002; Gligorić 2014; Dmitrović 2016; Bulatović *et al.* 2017). One such necropolis was also excavated in the village of Bukovac in Podgorina region (Filipović 2008). Additionally, in collaboration with the Brooklyn College from New York and the Jadar Museum from Loznica, the Institute of Archaeology in Belgrade conducted significant research on the subject of exploitation of cassiterite by Late Bronze Age populations of the region and the provenance of tin from the southern slopes of the Cer Mountain based on the isotopic analyses, all within the international 'Jadar' project (Huska *et al.* 2014; Mason *et al.* 2020).

The rescue archaeological excavations of sites endangered by the construction of the Ruma–Loznica Highway and the Požarevac–Golubac Motorway in 2021–2023, resulted in the discovery of several sites from the Early and Middle Bronze Age, such as Adžine Njive in Klenak near Šabac, Cigansko Brdo in Bratinac near Požarevac, and Marjansko Brdo in Majilovac near Veliko Gradište. All these sites are quite important for the study of the Bronze Age within the peri-Pannonian zone of the Balkan Peninsula.

Finally, project 'Arheološka građa Srbije' should be highlighted within this short overview of archaeological research on Bronze Age sites, which most certainly does not include all the research. The project was initiated in 2006 by M. Stojić from the Institute of Archaeology in Belgrade with a goal of publishing all the unpublished prehistoric collections from museums in Serbia, therefore making the publicly available. Fortunately, this ambitious project was successful, and since 2006, a total of ten volumes have been published in collaboration with the local museums, with the 11th volume in preparation (Stojić and Čađenović 2006; Stojić and Jocić 2006; Bulatović 2007; Stojić and Jacanović 2008; Bulatović and Jović 2010; Stojić and Cerović 2011; Stojić and Ilijić 2011; Bulatović *et al.* 2013; 2017; Kapuran *et al.* 2014).

1.3 Chronology and periodisation of the Bronze Age in the central Balkans

The term Bronze Age was introduced into different disciplines that research the past of humankind in order to mark the period of its development characterised by utilisation of a new metal – bronze – an alloy of the known metal copper and a new material, either tin or some other mineral. Certainly, the existence and utilisation of bronze objects do not represent a decisive factor for marking the period as a Bronze Age. There are, however, numerous other aspects of the period, such as the social and economic organisation of communities, the appearance of a writing system in the eastern Mediterranean, contacts and connections between continental Europe and the Aegean and Mediterranean, and others. The period is usually regarded as a 'Crucial phase' of the development of European prehistory (Harding 2011, 327).

From the end of the 19th century and throughout the 20th century, several chronological systems have been applied in European archaeology, each serving researchers to provide a better determination of different periods within the Bronze Age. Those systems differ in certain specifics and characteristics, which are more-or-less marked by major changes in spiritual or material culture. Such divisions were often unclear and focused only on certain geographic regions, which caused those divisions to be short-lived and locally used, or sometimes proved wrong with new archaeological finds. The first chronological systems, of which some are still in use, were relative in nature, and based on the stratigraphy of indicative sites and the typology of archaeological finds. Out of various chronological systems, certainly, the ones postulated by Montelius, Dechelette, and Reinecke remain the most relevant. The periodisation proposed by Montelius was published in 1885 and primarily focused on Scandinavia and northern Germany. It divided the Bronze Age into six phases (period I – the initial phase of the Bronze Age; periods II and III – Early Bronze Age; periods IV and V – Late Bronze Age; period VI – Transitional Period concurrent to the development of the Developed Iron Age in the south), yet unfortunately it could not be applied to the rest of Europe (Harding 2000, 11, 12).

The most famous, as well as the most common and long-lasting chronology, which is nowadays less compatible with the existing periodisations, is the chronology proposed by P. Reinecke. According to his chronology, the European Bronze Age is divided into four phases marked as phases A, B, C, and D (Reinecke 1965). This chronological division is still in use, although with certain alterations that moved the end of the Bronze Age from phase D to early phases of the Iron Age marked as Ha A and Ha B (Harding 2011, 331).

Within Central Europe, the chronology is mostly based on absolute dates which divide the Bronze Age into Early (2200–1500 BC), Middle (1500–1300 BC), and Late (1350–750 BC) (Harding 2011, 330, 331). Kristiansen and Larsen relied on the periodisation proposed by S. Gerloff (1993, 58–102), and divided the European Bronze Age into three phases, with the first phase between 2300 and 1900 BC, the second phase between 1900 and 1600 BC, and the final third phase between 1600/1500 and 1300 BC (Kristiansen and Larsson 2005, 118–130).

If the definition of the Bronze Age would be based exclusively on the mass utilisation of tin-bronze objects, without elaborating on the lack of metallurgical and craftmanship activity on the Bronze Age sites in the central Balkans, or the lack of research in the region, it could be concluded that the Bronze Age in the study region begins during the mid-2nd millennium BC. Since there are other factors regarding the definition of the Bronze Age, as mentioned, the Bronze Age chronology of the central Balkans is mostly compatible with the European chronology.

The chronology and periodisation of the Bronze Age in the central Balkans were due to the lack of absolute dates, primarily relying on the periodisation from several decades ago, based on the relative chronology. Therefore, according to the periodisation proposed by Draga Garašanin, which is similarly based on the genesis and development of material and spiritual culture of a period, the Bronze Age of Serbia is divided into Early (Bronze Age I), Middle (Bronze Age II), and Late (Bronze Age III) (Garašanin 1967). By comparing the suggested chronology with that proposed by Reinecke which, in fact, served as a model, the Early Bronze Age in Serbia is compatible with phase Br A1, the Middle Bronze Age with phases Br A2–C, and the Late Bronze Age with phases Br C–D.

Archaeologists in Serbia mainly agree with such periodisation, although R. Vasić, as well as A. Harding, consider that the Bronze Age should be extended to phases Ha A–B according to Reinecke's chronology. Some authors, including the author of this book, closed the gap between the chronological systems by introducing a new term – the Transitional Period between the Bronze and Iron Age – which encompasses phases Ha A–B according to Reinecke's chronology, and therefore phase Ha C marks the beginning of the Iron Age (Vasić 1997; Bulatović 2009).

According to M. Stojić, who studied the cultural and chronological problems of the Bronze Age, the chronology of the Bronze Age in the Morava Region begins with the two-handled beaker culture around 2000 BC, continues with the proto-Vatin culture (1900–1700 BC), which evolves into Vatin culture during the Middle Bronze Age (1700–1400 BC), while the Late Bronze Age is marked by Paraćin and Brnjica cultural groups (Stojić 1996).

However, A. Bulatović and J. Stankovski consider that the Early Bronze Age within the Southern Morava Region is divided into two phases. The first phase, positioned around 2300 BC is marked by the so-called Bubanj-Hum III–Pelince II–III horizon. The Middle Bronze Age is marked by the Bubanj-Hum IV-Ljuljaci group (1950/1900–1500/1450 BC), and the Late Bronze Age is marked by the Brnjica group which lasted until around 1100 BC (Bulatović and Stankovski 2012, 327–331). Such chronology can be considered as relative since it relied on solely several absolute dates which were available at the moment, of which some originate from the 1970s and 1980s and display a high deviation (Coles and Harding 1979, 452: Bogdanović 1986; Krstić *et al.* 1986).

Nowadays, due to the large number of Bronze Age absolute dates from the central Balkans, the chronological framework in Serbia has significantly improved (Bulatović and Vander Linden 2017; Bulatović 2020; 2021; Bulatović *et al.* 2018; 2020; 2021; Kapuran *et al.* 2020), and enabled the division of the Bronze Age into several chronological phases with subphases, which will be further discussed.

In other parts of the Balkans, such as Bulgaria and northern Greece, the Bronze Age chronology has a slightly different definition. Primarily, according to the chronology applied in Bulgaria, the Bronze Age started during the final quarter of the 4th millennium BC, with the Ezero culture in the northeast, or Magura phase of the Coţofeni culture in the northwest of Bulgaria (Orlea–Sadovec phase according to S. Alexandrov) (Alexandrov 1995; Bojadžiev 1998), which represent the eastern portion of the central Balkans. The Middle Bronze Age starts during the final quarter of the 3rd millennium BC, and the Late Bronze Age during the mid-2nd millennium BC (Boyadziev 1995; Todorova 2003).

In Greece, the Bronze Age is divided into the Early Helladic, Middle Helladic, and Late Helladic periods. Similar to Bulgaria, the Early Bronze Age (Early Helladic) starts at the end of the 4th millennium BC and lasts until the end of the 3rd millennium BC (Manning 1995; Rutter 2001). The Middle Bronze Age lasted until the second quarter of the 2nd millennium, followed by the Late Helladic period which lasted up until around 1100 BC (Harding 2000; for Northern Greece refer to: Andreou *et al.* 1996).

In the Republic of North Macedonia, whose northern territories are part of this study, the Bronze Age is divided into Early, Middle, and Late (Mitrevski 2013), based exclusively on the relative chronology, since period related absolute dates from this territory are extremely rare (Bulatović *et al.* 2018, table 1/8; 2020, 1178, 1179).

Such discrepancies in chronological systems of different regions of the central Balkans represent a significant problem in terms of defining a uniform chronology and periodisation of the Bronze Age. Therefore, in order to synchronise chronology with Bulgaria and Greece, whose Bronze Age cultures are significantly connected to the central Balkans Bronze Age groups, a new chronology of the Bronze Age in Serbia was proposed recently. According to such chronology, the Early Bronze Age is divided into four phases: EBA 1, EBA 2, EBA 2–3, and EBA 3 (Bulatović *et al.* 2020). The EBA 1 phase is marked by the population of the Coţofeni–Kostolac culture and positioned between the end of the 33rd and the end of the 29th century cal BC. The second phase, marked by the Bubanj-Hum II group, is positioned between the third quarter of the 29th and the first quarter of the 26th century cal BC. The third phase, EBA 2–3, is positioned between the first quarter of the 26th and the beginning of the 22nd century BC (the phase is related to the peri-Pannonian zone of the Balkans, and Vinkovci-Somogyar/Belotić–Bela Crkva groups). The final phase of the Early Bronze Age is positioned between the beginning of the 25th and the mid-19th century cal BC and is marked by the Bubanj-Hum III and Armenochori groups (both groups are present solely within the Vranje–Bujanovac Basin). All presented dates are calibrated with the probability of 68.2%.

However, it must be emphasised that this chronology, whose main goal is to harmonise the chronology in Serbia with those of the Bronze Age in the surrounding areas, was based on a small number of dates and is subject to corrections that the new absolute dates will provide.

Notes

1 The characteristics of these zones will be further discussed in the following chapter.

2 The excavations directed by S. Perić remain unpublished.

Bibliography

Alexandrov, S. 1995. The Early Bronze Age in western Bulgaria: Periodization and cultural definition. In: *Prehistoric Bulgaria*, eds D. W. Bailey and I. Panayotov, 253–270. Madison WI: Monographs in World Archaeology 22.

Andreou, S., Fotiadis, M. and Kotsakis, K. 1996. Review of Aegean prehistory V: The Neolithic and Bronze Age of northern Greece. *American Journal of Archaeology* 100(3), 537–597.

Bankoff, H. A. and Winter, F. 1982. The Morava Valley Project in Yugoslavia: Preliminary report. *Journal of Field Archaeology* 9(2), 149–164.

Bankoff, H. A. and Winter, F. 1990. The Late Aeneolithic in southeastern Europe. *American Journal of Archaeology* 94, 175–191.

Bogdanović, M. (Богдановић, М.). 1986. *Љуљаци, насеље протоватинске и ватинске културе*. Крагујевац: Народни музеј, Крагујевац (National museum, Kragujevac).

Boyadziev, J. 1995. Chronology of prehistoric cultures in Bulgaria. In: *Prehistoric Bulgaria*, eds D. Bailey and I. Panayotov, 149–191. Madison WI: Monographs in World Archaeology 22.

Bojadžiev, J. 1998. Radiocarbon dating from southeastern Europe. In: *J. Harvey Gaul in Memoriam*, eds M. Stefanovich, H. Todorova and H. Hauptmann, 349–370. Sofia: J. Harvey Gaul Foundation.

Borić, D. 2009. Absolute dating of metallurgical innovations in the Vinča Culture of the Balkans, In: *Metals and Societies: Studies in honour of Barbara S. Ottaway*, eds T.L. Kienlin and B. W. Roberts, 191–245. Bonn: Universitätsforschungen zur prähistorischen Archäologie 169.

Bouzek, J. 1994. Late Bronze Age in Greece and the Balkans: A review of the present picture. *Annual of the British School at Athens* 89, 217–234.

Božilova, E. and Tonkov, S. 2007. Paleoecological evidence of the main postglacial vegetation and climate changes in southwestern Bulgaria from the Neolithic to modern times. In: *The Struma/Strymon river Valley in Prehistory*, eds H. Todorova, M. Stefanovich and G. Ivanov, 531–534. Sofia: Gerde Henkel Stiftung.

Bulatović, A. (Булатовић, А.). 1999. Градина у Љанику – градинско насеље позног бронзаног и старијег гвозденог доба. *Врањски гласник* 31–32, 7–17.

Bulatović, A. (Булатовић, А.). 2000. Налазишта брњичке културне групе у Врањско – бујановачкој и Прешевској котлини. *Гласник Српског археолошког друштва* 15–16, 23–42.

Bulatović, A. (Булатовић, А.). 2007. *Врање-културна стратиграфија праисторијских локалитета у Врањској регији*, Београд-Врање: Археолошки институт, Београд, Народни музеј, Врање (Institute of archaeology, Belgrade and National museum, Vranje).

Bulatović, A. (Булатовић, А.). 2008. Стамбени објекат из позног бронзаног доба са локалитета Медијана-сектор југ – прилог проучавању односа параћинске културне групе и брњичке културне групе. *Гласник Српског археолошког друштва* 24, 223–244.

Bulatović, A. 2009. South Morava basin in the transitional period from the Bronze to the Iron Age. *Старинар* н.с. 57 (2007), 57–82.

Bulatović, A. 2014. New finds as a contribution to the study of the Early Bronze Age in the southern part of the central Balkans. *Старинар* 64, 57–75.

Bulatović, A. 2020. *Ranutovac, an Early Bronze Age Necropolis in Southeastern Serbia*. Oxford: British Archaeological Report S2978.

Bulatović, A. 2021. Beakers with trapezoidal mouth as one of the most specific types of Middle Bronze Age vessel in the central Balkans. In: *Crafting Pottery in Bronze Age Europe*, eds V. Vučković, V. Filipović, B. Stojanović and R. Rich, 121–148. Paraćin: National Museum of Paraćin.

Bulatović, A. and Jović, C. (Булатовић, А., Јовић, С.). 2010. *Лесковац-културна стратиграфија праисторијских локалитета у Лесковачкој регије*. Београд-Лесковац: Археолошки институт, Београд, Народни музеј, Лесковац (Institute of archaeology, Belgrade and National museum, Leskovac).

Bulatović, A. and Milanović, D. (Булатовић, А., Милановић, Д.). 2015. Велика хумска чука, истраживања 2009. године – прилог проучавању стратиграфије енеолита и бронзаног доба у југоисточној Србији. *Гласник Српског* 30, 163–188.

Bulatović, A. and Milanović, D. 2020. *Bubanj, the Eneolithic and the Early Bronze Age Tell in Southeastern Serbia.* Vienna: Mitteilungen der Prahistorischen Kommission 90.

Bulatović, A. and Stankovski, J. (Булатовић, А., Станковски, J.). 2012. *Бронзано доба у басену Јужне Мораве и у долини Пчиње/Бронзено време во басенот на Јужна Морава и долината на Пчиња.* Куманово: Археолошки институт Београд и НУ Музеј,

Bulatović, A. and Vander Linden, M. 2017. Absolute dating of Copper and Early Bronze Age levels at the eponymous archaeological site Bubanj (southeastern Serbia). *Radiocarbon* 59(4), 1047–1065.

Bulatović, A., Bizjak, D. and Vitezović, S. 2016a. Early Bronze Age necropolis at the site of Meanište near Vranje. In: *Archaeological Investigations Along the Route of the E 75 Highway, 2011–2014*, eds S. Perić and A. Bulatović, 71–89. Belgrade: Institute of Archaeology.

Bulatović, A., Kapuran, A. and Milanović, D. 2016b. Metal Age finds at the site of Kovačke njive in Pavlovac near Vranje. In: *Archaeological Investigations Along the Route of the E 75 Highway, 2011–2014,* eds S. Perić and A. Bulatović, 205–219. Belgrade: Institute of Archaeology.

Bulatović, A., Filipović, V. and Gligorić, R. (Булатовић, А., Филиповић, В., Глигорић, Р.). 2017. *Лозница, културна стратиграфија праисторијских локалитета у Јадру, Рађевини и Азбуковици.* Лозница: Археолошки институт, Београд, Центар за културу.

Bulatović, A. Gori, M. and Vander Linden, M. 2018. New absolute dates as a contribution to the study of the Late Bronze Age chronology in the central Balkans. *Гласник САД* 34, 121–132.

Bulatović, A. Gori, M. and Vander Linden, M. 2020. Radiocarbon dating the 3rd millennium BC in the central Balkans: A re-examination of the Early Bronze Age sequence. *Radiocarbon* 62(5), 1163–1191.

Bulatović, A., Kapuran, A. and Janjić, G. (Булатовић, А., Капуран, А., Јањић, Г.). 2013. *Неготин, културна стратиграфија праисторијских локалитета у Неготинској Крајин.* Београд-Неготин: Археолошки институт, Београд, Народни музеј, Неготин (Institute of archaeology, Belgrade and Museum of Krajina, Negotin).

Burroughs, W. J. 20115. *Climate Change in Prehistory, the end of the Reign of Chaos*. Cambridge: Cambridge University Press.

Cermanović-Kuzmanović, A. (Цермановић-Кузмановић, А.). 1960 Нова некропола жутобрдске културе „Песак" код Корбова. *Старинар* 11, 185–191.

Cilek, V. 1997. Mid-Holocene dry spells in Bohemia, Central Europe. In: *Third Millennium BC Climate Change and Old World Collapse*, eds N. Dalfes, G. Kukla and H. Weiss, 309–320. Heidelberg: Springer.

Coles, J. M. and Harding, A. F. 1979 *The Bronze Age in Europe.* London: Methuen.

Cvijić, J. (Цвијић J.). 1922. *Балканско полуострво и јужнословенске земље.* Београд: Državna štamparija, Beograd.

Dmitrović, K. (Дмитровић, К.). 2016. *Некрополе бронзаног доба у регији Чачка/Bronze Age Necropolises in the Čačak region.* Čačak: Народни музеј, Чачак (National museum, Čačak).

Dukić, D. 2006. *Klimatologija.* Beograd: Geografski fakultet.

Durman, A. 1997. Tin in southeastern Europe? *Opvscvla Archaeologica* 21, 7–14.

Fewkes, V. 1935. Report on the 1934 summer course of the school. *Bulletin of the American School of Prehistoric Research* 11, 11–18.

Filipović, V. (Филиповић, В.). 2008. *Некрополе развијеног доба Подгорине и доњег Подриња.* Unpublished master thesis, необјављена магистарска теза, одбрањена на Филозофском факултету у Београду.

French, C. 2010. The palaeo-environments of Bronze Age Europe. In: *Organizing Bronze Age Societies* eds. T. Earle, and K. Kristiansen, 34–56. Cambridge: Cambridge University Press.

Galović, R. (Галовић, Р.). 1961. Брусник код Неготина. *Старинар* 11, 238–239.

Garašanin, D. 1967. Periodizacija bronzanog doba Srbije, *Materijali* IV, 7th Congress of archaeologists of Yugoslavia held in Herceg Novi in 1966, 203–208.

Garašanin, M. (Гарашанин, М.). 1957. Ископавања на Бубњу код Ниша. Претходни извештај за 1954–1956 годину. *Старинар* н.с. 7–8, 269–274.

Garašanin, M. 1958. Neolithikum und Bronzezeit in Serbien und Makedonien. *Bericht der Romisch-Germanischen Kommission des Deutschen* 39, 1–130.

Garašanin, M. (Гарашанин, М.). 1973. *Праисторија на тлу Србије*. Београд: Српска књижевна задруга.

Garašanin, M. and Garašanin, D. (Гарашанин, М., Гарашанин, Д.). 1958. Ископавања тумула у Белотићу и Белој Цркви (Западна Србија). *Зборник радова Народног музеја* 1, 17–50.

Garašanin, M. and Garašanin, D. (Гарашанин, М., Гарашанин, Д.). 1962. Ископавања тумула у комплексу Белотић-Бела Црква 1959. и 1960. године. *Зборник радова Народног музеја* 3, 47–68.

Garašanin, M. and Garašanin, D. (Гарашанин, М., Гарашанин, Д.). 1967. Ископавања тумула у комплексу Белотић-Бела Црква 1961. године. *Зборник радова Народног музеја* 5, 5–30.

Garašanin, M. Ajdić, R. and Dejanović, D. (Гарашанин, М., Ајдић, Р., Дејановић, Д.). 1971. *Праисторијске културе Поморавља и источне Србије*. Ниш: каталог изложбе, Народни музеј.

Gavrilov, M., Marković, S., Schaetzl, R., Tošić, I., Zeeden, C., Obreht, I., Sipos, G., Ruman, A., Putniković, S., Emunds, K., Perić, Z., Hambach, U. and Lehmkuhl, F. 2017. Prevailing surface winds in Northern Serbia in the recent and past time periods; modern-and past dust deposition. *Aeolian Research* 31(B), 117–129.

Georgievski, B. (Георгиевски, Б.). 1994. Праисториски градишта од Кумановско. *Macedoniae Acta Archaeologica* 13, 12–22.

Gerasimenko, N. 1997. Environmental and climatic changes between 3 and 5 ka BP in southeastern Ukraine. In: *Third Millennium BC Climate Change and Old World Collapse*, eds N. Dalfes, G. Kukla and H. Weiss, 371–399. Heidelberg: Springer.

Gerloff, S. 1993. Mittelmeerländische Kontakte und absolute Chronologie der Frühbronzezeit. *Praehistorische Zeitschrift,* 68(1), 58–102.

Gligorić, R. (Глигорић, Р.). 2014. *Некропола развијеног бронзаног доба у Брезјаку, Центар за културу 'Вук Караџић'*. Лозница: Музеј Јадра.

Грбић 1956 - Grbić, M. 1903. Прекласична грнчарија средњег Балкана, Старинар V–VI, Belgrade 1956, 19–20.

Harding, A. 2000. *European Societes in the Bronze Age*. Cambridge: Cambridge University Press.

Harding, A. 2011. The Bronze Age. In: *European Prehistory*, ed. S. Milisauskas, 327–404. Heidelberg: Springer.

Horejs, B., Bulatović, A., Meyer, C., Milić, B., Schneider, S., Schlöffel, M. and Stevanović, V. 2018. Prehistoric landscapes of the Pusta Reka river (Leskovac), new investigations along the Southern Morava River. *Гласник САД* 34, 23–51.

Horejs, B., Bulatović, A., Bulatović, J., Brandl, M., Burke, C., Filipović, D. and Milić, B. 2019. New insights into the later stage of the Neolithisation process of the central Balkans. First excavations at Svinjarička Čuka 2018. *Archaeologia Austriaca*, 175–226.

Huska, A., Powell, W., Mitrović, S., Bankoff, H. A., Bulatović, A., Filipović V. and Boger, R. 2014. Placer tin ores from Mt. Cer, West Serbia, and their potential exploitation during the Bronze Age. *Georchaeology* 29(6), 477–493.

Jovanović, B. 1971. *Metalurgija eneolitskog perioda Jugoslavije*. Beograd: Arheološki institut, Beograd.

Jovanović, B. (ed.). 1995. *Ancient Mining and Metallurgy in Southeast Europe*. Donji Milanovac: Archaeological Institute Belgrade and Museum of Mining and Metallurgy Bor

Jovanović, B. and Janković, I. 1990. Nekropola paraćinske grupe u Trnjanima kod Brestovačke banje. *Zbornik radova muzeja rudarstva i metalurgije u Boru* 5/6, 1–20.

Kanic, F. (Каниц, Ф.). 1985. *Србија, земља и становништво*. Београд: СКЗ.

Kapuran, A., Bulatović, A. and Jovanović, I. (Капуран, А., Булатовић, А., Јовановић, И.). 2014. *Бор и Мајданпек, културна стратиграфија праисторијских локалитета између Ђердапа и Црног Тимока*. Београд-Бор: Археолошки институт, Београд, Музеј рударства и металургије, Бор (Institute of archaeology, Belgrade and Museum of Mining and Metallurgy, Bor).

Kapuran, A., Gavranović, M. and Mehofer, M. 2020. Bronze age settlement and necropolis of Trnjane, near Bor – revision and new researche results. *Старинар* 70, 51–84.

Krementski, C. 1997. The Late Holocene environmental and climate shift in Russia and surrounding Lands. In: *Third Millennium BC Climate Change and Old World Collapse*, eds N. Dalfes, G. Kukla and H. Weiss, 351–370. Heidelberg: Springer.

Kristiansen, K. and Larsson, T. B. 2005. *The Rise of Bronze Age Society*. Cambridge: Cambridge University Press.

Krstić, D. (Крстић, Д.). 1971. Glamija. Korbovo pres de Kladovo. In: *Epoque prehistorique et protohistorique en Yugoslavie – Recherches et resultats*. Beograd: Societe archeologique de Yugoslavie, Beograd.

Krstić. D. (Крстић, Д.). 2003. *Гламија, некропола бронзаног доба у Корбову*. Београд: Народни музеј, Београд (National museum, Belgrade).

Krstić, D., Stalio, B., Garašanin, D., Galović R., Pavlović K. and Miletić M. (Крстић, Д., Сталио, Б., *Гарашанин, Д., Галовић,* Р., Павловић К., Милетић М.). 1972. Бронзано доба Србије. Београд: каталог изложбе, Народни музеј.

Krstić, D. Bankoff A., Vukmanović M. and Winter F. (Крстић, Д., Bankoff, A., Вукмановић, М., Winter, F.) 1986. Праисторијски локалитет Новачка ћуприја. *Зборник Народног музеја* 12(1), 17–63.

Lazić, M. (Лазић, М.). 1997. *Археологија источне Србије, зборник радова са научног скупа Археологија источне Србије, одржаног у Београду и Доњем Милановцу 1995.* Београд: године, Филозофски факултет у Београду, Центар за археолошка истраживања,.

Lazić, M. (Лазић, М.). 2004. Бор и околина у бронзано доба. У: *Бор и околина,* ур. М. Лазић, 101–126, Бор-Београд: Музеј рударства и металургије, Бор, Центар за археолошка истраживања Филозофског факултета у Београду.

Manning, S. W. 1995. *The Absolute Chronology of the Aegean Early Bronze Age: Archaeology, radiocarbon and history*. Sheffield: Sheffield Academic Press.

Manning, S. W. 1997. Cultural change in the Aegean c. 2200 BC. In: *Third Millennium BC Climate Change and Old World Collapse*, eds N. Dalfes, G. Kukla and H. Weiss, 149–171. Heidelberg: Springer.

Marković, J. Đ. and Pavlović, M. (Марковић, Ј. Ђ., Павловић, М.). 1995. *Географске регије Југославије*. Београд: Savremena Administracija.

Mason, A. H., Powell, W. G., Bankoff, H. A. Mathur, R., Bulatović, A., Filipović, V. and Ruiz, J. 2016. Tin isotope characterization of bronze artifacts of the central Balkans. *Journal of Archaeological Science* 69, 110–117.

Mason, A., Powell, W., Bankoff, H.A., Mathur, R., Price, M., Bulatović, A. and Filipović, V. 2020. Provenance of tin in the Late Bronze Age Balkans based on probabilistic and spatial analysis of Sn isotopes. *Journal of Archaeological Science* 122, 1051–1081.

Mitrevski, D. (Митревски, Д.). 2013. Праисторија на Република Македонија. У: *Македонија, миленијумски културно-историјски факти*, ур. Е. Димитрова, Ј. Донев, П, 83–266. Скопје: Кузман, Медиа принт Македонија и Евробалкан.

Mitrevski, D. 2016. *Skopje Fortress – Kale, from Prehistory to the Early Ancient period.* Скопје: ПНВ Публикации.

Muhly, J. 1985. Sources of tin and the beginnings of bronze metallurgy. *American Journal of Archaeology* 89, 275–291.

Nikitović, L., Stojić, M. and Vasić, R. (Никитовић, Л., Стојић, М., Васић, Р.). 2002. *Мојсиње, некропола под хумкама из бронзаног и гвозденог доба.* Чачак: Народни музеј, Чачак, Археолошки институт, Београд (National museum, Čačaka and Institute of archaeology, Belgrade).

Oršić-Slavetić, A. (Оршић-Славетић, А.). 1936. Преисторијска налазишта у околини Ниша. *Старинар* 10–11, 174–182.

Oršić-Slavetić, A. 1940. *Bubanj, eine Prähistorische Ansiedlung bei Niš.* Wien: Mitteilungen der prähistorische Kommission der Akademie Wissenchafte IV Band, Nr. 1–2, 1–42.

Pavlović, A., Kostić, N., Karadžić, B. and Mitrović, M. 2017. *The Soils of Serbia*. Heidelberg: Springer.

Perić, S. and Bulatović, A. (Перић, С., Булатовић, А.). (eds/ур.). 2016. *Археолошка истраживања на траси аутопута Е75, 2011–2014 [Archaeological Investigations along the Route of the E 75 Highway, 2011–2014].* Belgrade: Institute of Archaeology.

Prodanović-Ranković, I. (Продановић-Ранковић, И.). 2017. *Археолошка истраживања на аутопуту Е80*. Београд: Републички завод за заштиту споменика културе.

Protić, N., Martinović, I., Miličić, B., Stevanović, D. and Mojašević, M. 2005. The status of soil survey in Serbia, In: *Soil Resources of Europe*, eds R. J. A. Jones, B. Houškova, P. Bullock, and L. Montanarella, 297–315. Ispra: European Soil Bureau, Institute for Enviroment and Sustainabillity.

Reinecke, P. 1965. *Mainzer Aufsatze zur Chronologie der Bronze- und Eisenzeit*. Bonn: Habelt.

Rutter, J. B. 2001. The Prepalatial Bronze Age of the southern and central Greek mainland. Addendum: 1993–1999. In: *Aegean Prehistory: A review*, ed. T. Cullen, 148–155. Auburndale MA: *American Journal of Archaeology* Monograph 1.

Sanev, V. 1999. Pottery in favour of designating the cultural borders of the Early Bronze Age in Macedonia. In: *Macedonia and the Neighbouring Regions from 3rd to 1st Milenium* [sic] *b.c.*, ed. E. Petrova, 127–136. Skopje: Museum of Macedonia

Serbian Encyclopaedia. (*Српска енциклопедија*). 2013. *Српска енциклопедија*. Београд Матица Српска, Српска Академија наука и уметности, Завод за уџбенике, Нови Сад.

Srejović, D. 1960a. Pesak - Korbovo - Negotin, nekropola, *Arheološki pregled* 2, 59–60.

Srejović, D. 1960b. Praistorijska nekropola u Donjoj Brnjici. *Glasnik Muzeja Kosova i Metohije* 4–5, 83–135.

Srejović, D. and Lazić, M (Срејовић, Д., Лазић, М.). 1997. Насеља и некрополе бронзаног доба у Тимочкој крајини. У: *Археологија источне Србије*, 225–247. Београд: Универзитет у Београду.

Stankovski, J. (Станковски, J.). 2002. Татикев Камен – мегалитска опсерваторија и светилиште. *Музејски гласник* 7–9, 29–48.

Stankovski, J. (Станковски, J.). 2010. Прилог кон проучување на обредната практика на локалитетот Татиќев Камен, село Кокино. *Macedoniae Acta Archaeologica* 19, 115–125.

Stojić, M. 1996. Le Bassin de la Morava a l'age de bronze et a la periode de transition de l'age de bronze a celui de fer. In: *The Yugoslav Danube Basin and the Neighbouring Regions in the 2nd Millennium B.C.*, ed. N. Tasić, 247–256. Belgrade: Serbian Academy of Science and Arts.

Stojić, M. (Стојић, M.). 2001. Брњичка културна група у басену Јужне Мораве. *Лесковачки зборник* 61, 15–94.

Stojić, M. and Čađenović, G. (Стојић, M., Чађеновић, Г.) 2006. *Крушевац, културна стратиграфија праисторијских локалитета у зони става Западне Мораве и Јужне Мораве*. Београд–Крушевац: Археолошки институт, Београд, Народни музеј, Крушевац (Institute of archaeology, Belgrade and National museum, Kruševac).

Stojić, M. and Cerović, M. (Стојић, M., Церовић, M.) 2011. *Шабац, културна стратиграфија праисторијских локалитета у Подрињу*. Београд–Шабац: Археолошки институт, Београд, Народни музеј, Шабац (Institute of archaeology, Belgrade and National museum, Šabac).

Stojić, M. and Ilijić, B. (Стојић, M., Илијић, Б.). 2011. *Књажевац, културна стратиграфија праисторијских локалитета књажевачког краја*. Београд: Археолошки институт Београд, Завичајни музеј Књажевац.

Stojić, M. and Jacanović, D. (Стојић, M., Јацановић, Д.). 2008. *Пожаревац, културна стратиграфија праисторијских локалитета у Браничеву*. Београд: Археолошки институт Београд, Народни музеј Пожаревац.

Stojić, M. and Jocić, M. (Стојић, M., Јоцић, M.). 2006. *Ниш-културна стратиграфија праисторијских локалитета у нишкој регији*. Београд-Ниш: Археолошки институт, Београд, Народни музеј, Ниш (Institute of archaeology, Belgrade and National museum, Niš).

Tasić, N. 1988. Bronze- und Altere Eisenzeit auf Gomolava. In: *Gomolava I, zbornik radova sa međunarodnog simpozijuma održanog u Rumi 1986. godine, Novi Sad, 1988*, eds. M. Dalmacija, R. Samardžić, Novi Sad 47–58 Vojvođanski muzej; Novi Sad and Balkanološki institut SANU, Beograd.

Tasić, N. (Тасић, Н.). 1998. *Археолошко благо Косова и Метохије*. Београд: каталог изложбе.

Todorova, H. 2003. Prehistory of Bulgaria. In: *Recent Research in the Prehistory of the Balkans*, ed. D. V. Grammenos, 257–328. Thessaloniki: Publications of the Archaeological Institute of Northern Greece 3.

Todorova, H. 2007. Die paleoklimatische Entwicklung in VII–I Jt. vor Chr. In: *The Struma/Strymon River Valley in Prehistory*, eds. H. Todorova, M. Stefanovich and G. Ivanov, 1–6. Sofia: Gerda Henkel Stiftung.

Todorović, J. 1977. *Praistorijska Karaburma II*. Beograd: Muzej grada Beograda.

Trajkovska, L. (Трајковска, Л.). 1995. Рано бронзено светилиште кај селото Пелинце. Y: *каталог изложбе*, ур. Б. Таневски. Куманову: Народни музеј у Куманову.

Trajkovska, L. (Трајковска, Л.). 2003. Светилиште од раното бронзено доба на лок. 'Градиште' во село Пелинце кај Куманово. *Пирајхме* 2, 289–297.

Trifunovski, J. (Трифуновски, J.). 1964. *Горња Пчиња*. Београд: Srpska akademija nauka i umetnosti, Srpski etnografski zbornik, knjiga LXXVII.

Valtrović, J. (Валтровић, M.). 1893. Преисториске старине у ваљевском и подринском округу. *Старинар* 10(3–4), 75–97.

Vasić, M. M. (Васић, M. M.). 1904. Археолошка истраживања у Србији. *Српски књижевни гласник* 15(8), 593–603.

Vasić, M. M. (Васић, M. M.). 1911. Градац, преисторско налазиште латенског доба. *Глас Српске краљевске академије* 86, 97–135.

Vasić, M. M. (Васић, M. M.). 1912. Жуто Брдо, прилог за познавање културе гвозденог доба у дунавској долини, *Старинар* н.р. VI (1911), 1–93.

Vasić, R. 1997. Bronzano doba. In: *Arheološki leksikon*, ed. D. Srejović, 149–151. Beograd: Savremena administracija.

Vulić, N. and Grbić, M. 1937. Musée-Belgrade, *Corpus vasorum antiquorum* Yugoslavie No 3, Belgrade, 1–20.

2

The Early Bronze Age: Review by geographical zones of the central Balkans

In order to make it easier to follow and understand this chapter, which contains a large amount of information, in the region is divided into, and discussed first by, smaller geographical units (zones) of the central Balkans, which are defined mainly on the basis of geographical characteristics, especially orographic, but also according to the characteristics of the material and spiritual culture of the populations that inhabited them. In this sense, as stated in the previous chapter, the area of the central Balkans is divided into five geographical zones: the peri-Pannonian zone (actually the peri-Pannonian rim); the Great Morava Basin with Šumadija; western Serbia with Lim Valley; Timok Valley with Đerdap Gorge and southern Serbia with the Raška Region; The Middle Pčinja and Kumanovo and Skopje Plains (see Fig. 1.1).

Within these geographic zones, the organisation of the settlements and the architecture of the houses are first analysed, where possible, then the ritual and method of burial, as well as other aspects of spiritual culture. After that, the results of the analysis of portable finds are interpreted and, finally, based on everything presented and available absolute dates, the cultural-chronological determination of the targeted period is discussed within certain geographical zones.

2.1. The peri-Pannonian zone (so-called peri-Pannonian rim)

This zone is composed of smaller geographical regions such as Mačva, the northern part of the Great Morava Basin, the northern part of Šumadija, and Stig. Most of this geographical unit consists of lowland terrain while, to the south, it is bordered by hilly relief, marking the transition between the Pannonian Plain and the mountainous zone of Serbia's interior. In addition to its geographical features, this zone is distinguished by slightly different cultural and chronological characteristics during the Bronze Age in comparison to other zones of the central Balkans. Its western and southern borders are formed by the Drina River, followed by Mount Cer, Vlašić, and the northern slopes of the Rudnik mountains; the northern boundary is represented by the Sava and Danube Rivers, though some sites on the left bank of the Danube are included as well, while the eastern boundary is defined by the northern slopes of the Homolje Mountains.

The relief of this area is varied: the northern part is lowland while, to the east, the northern slopes of Kosmaj, Beljanica, and the Homolje Mountains cut into this region, affecting the micro-climate. The area is criss-crossed by major rivers (the Drina, Sava, Danube, Tamnava, Kolubara, Great Morava, Mlava, etc.), making it exceptionally suitable for agriculture. The hilly part of this region is rich in lead and zinc deposits (Kosmaj and Avala), and deposits of cinnabar, a mineral used in prehistory for decorating pottery, have also been discovered on Mount Avala.

2.1.1 Settlement and dwelling

This predominantly lowland geographical zone features gently undulating terrain in the south and east, which transitions into a mountainous region. Within this area, only one hilltop settlement and five lowland settlements have been recorded. Site numbers refer to Plate 4.

2.1.1.1 Hilltop settlements

1. Svileuva, the site of Kik (Stojić and Cerović 2011).

The hilltop settlement of Kik in Svileuva is located in Pocerina on the south-eastern slopes of Cer. There is no detailed information about the site itself, apart from descriptions and illustrations of the finds, which, according to Stojić and Cerović, could be attributed to the Vinkovci–Somogyvár Cultural Group (Stojić and Cerović 2011, 144, 145).

2.1.1.2 Lowland Settlements

2. Klenak, the site of Adžine Njive;[1] 3. Pančevo, the site of Donja Varoš (Grčki Stanimirov 1996); 4. Viminacium, Stari Kostolac, the site of Rit (Bulatović *et al.* 2019); 5. Viminacium near Stari Kostolac, the site of Nad Klepečkom (Kapuran *et al.* 2019a); 6. Drmno near Požarevac, the site of Nad Lugom (Stojić and Jacanović 2008); 7. Veliko Gradište, the site of Marjansko Brdo;[2] 8. Grčac near Smederevska Palanka, the site of Novačka Ćuprija (Krstić *et al.* 1986).

Lowland settlements have mostly been recorded on terraces of the Danube River at 75–77 m above sea level, such as the Donja Varoš in Pančevo, or on terraces of the Danube's tributaries at 70–85 m above sea level, such as Nad Klepečkom, Rit, Drmno in Viminacium, and Adžine Njive in Klenak (Grčki Stanimirov 1996; Stojić and Jacanović 2008; Bulatović *et al.* 2019; Kapuran *et al.* 2019b). An exception is the site Marjansko Brdo near Veliko Gradište, located on a spacious terrace of diluvial relief at the edge of a natural ravine, about 170 m above sea level,[3] and the site Novačka Ćuprija, located on the gently rolling terrain of northern Šumadija, on a plateau above a small river, at approximately 145 m above sea level (Krstić *et al.* 1986), which could be considered a lowland settlement, despite being on an elevation. The ratio of hilltop to lowland settlements in this geographical zone is 13:87.

As for the characteristics and organisation of the settlements, as well as the architecture and other features of the residential structures, little information is available from the sites mentioned. At Donja Varoš in Pančevo, the Bronze Age settlement was single-layered, with remains of above-ground and semi-subterranean structures and no overlapping of these structures was recorded. The floors of the above-ground buildings (houses) were thin, without sub-structures or traces of renovation. No other architectural remains from these structures have been discovered.

Semi-subterranean structures consisted of shallow, ellipsoid or circular pits containing fragments of profiled house daub, as well as soot and ash. One semi-sunken structure was recorded in the shape of the number 8, with dimensions of 4 × 2.4 m and a depth of 0.5 m. The ceramic material found in both the above-ground and semi-subterranean structures was identical. Based on the arrangement of the structures, the stratigraphy of the settlement, the architecture, and the portable material, the author suggested that this type of settlement corresponds to a semi-nomadic lifestyle, associated with an agricultural economy, that is, a community not yet fully stabilised in this territory (Grčki Stanimirov 1996, 69, 70).

Similar architecture has been noted in other lowland settlements in the peri-Pannonian zone. At the site Nad Klepečkom, a circular structure with a diameter of approximately 2 m and a depth of about 0.5 m was recorded, as well as a rectangular structure measuring 4.7 × 2.7 m, dug about 0.8 m into the ground. This structure contained a large amount of daub, a hearth, and a deep pit in the centre. In addition to pottery, it also contained part of a perforated stone axe, a quern-stone palette, and spindle whorls (see Fig. 2.15/8–10). A structure in the shape of the number 8 was also found at this site, with dimensions of 4.1 × 3.4 m, which was dug significantly deeper than the one in Pančevo – up to 1.6 m. Not far from this structure, an approximately rectangular pit was discovered, measuring 4.8 × 4 m, dug about 0.2–0.3 m deep, containing fragments of daub and soot in its fill, as well as polished and chipped stone and horn tools (Kapuran *et al.* 2019a, T. 7/22–26). This pit was damaged by two later burials, making it difficult to determine its original dimensions and shape (Kapuran *et al.* 2019a, 79–97).

No consistent pattern has been identified in the dimensions, orientation, shape, architecture, or spatial relationships of the structures at this site. In fact, there was a considerable distance between the structures, often several tens of metres, and differences in their orientation, dimensions, and shapes, raising the question of whether this represents a dispersed type of settlement or individual structures from different periods of the Early Bronze Age. Unfortunately, only one absolute date is available, placing one of these structures at the transition from the 3rd to the 2nd millennium BC, while the other structures have been tentatively dated to the same period based on the relatively similar characteristics of the pottery found.

The situation, at least regarding the arrangement of the structures, is somewhat different at the Rit site in Viminacium, where three shallow, dug structures were recorded, separated by only a few metres (Fig. 2.1).

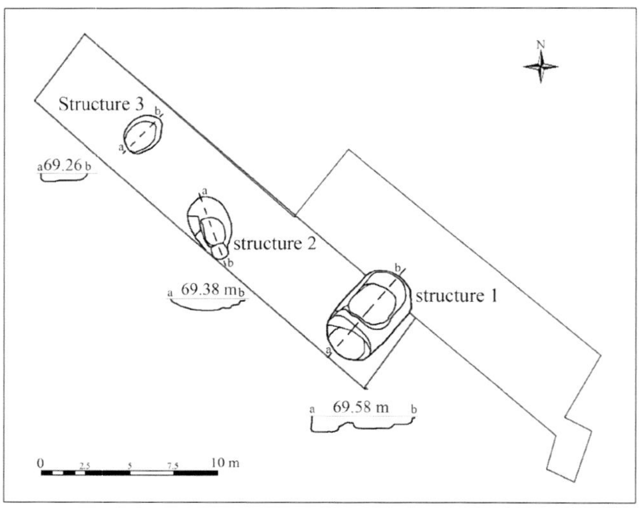

Figure 2.1. Viminacium, site of Rit, ground plan of structures 1–3.

The largest structure, an oval pit measuring 5.6 × 3.4 m (Fig. 2.1, structure 1), with two smaller pits and a bank in between, was dug to a depth of 0.9–1.2 m and likely represents a residential structure built from wattle and daub, as confirmed by the fill, which contained a certain amount of daub, as well as other portable finds (Bulatović *et al.* 2019, 59, fig. 2, T. 4/9–11). The second structure (Fig. 2.1, structure 2), located about 7 m from the first, had an oval base measuring 3.8 × 2.5 m and was dug to a depth of up to 1 m. Within the pit, at a relative depth of 0.3 m along the eastern wall, a levelled earthen bank was found, measuring 2.7 m in length and up to 0.8 m in width, which may have been used for sleeping. Daub was also found in this structure, suggesting that it had an above-ground part made of wattle and daub. The third recorded structure (Fig. 2.1, structure 3), located just 4 m from the previous one, was shallow with an oval base, measuring 2.5 × 1.8 m but the excavators did not define it as a residential structure. The only available absolute date, originating from the largest structure, indicates that this settlement (or at least this structure) is slightly younger than the dated structure at the Nad Klepečkom site (Kapuran *et al.* 2019b, 260). If we assume that the Nad Klepečkom settlement is somewhat older, and that these dates apply to the settlements and not just the individual structures they come from, it raises the question of their spatio-temporal relationship, as they are located very close to each other – about 1 km apart. The solution to this issue may lie in the fact that Nad Klepečkom is located on a ridge above the Rit site, which is on marshy terrain, with a difference in elevation of about 10 m. This information could indicate certain climatic changes at the transition from the 3rd to the 2nd millennium BC, which may have caused a drought that led the communities living on ridges and other elevations to abandon these locations and move to previously marshy areas closer to major rivers, in this case, the Mlava River.

At the Novačka Ćuprija site in northern Šumadija, which spans two flattened plateaus with slopes gently descending towards a small river, several dug-in structures were recorded, which the authors interpret as semi-subterranean dwellings or storage pits (Krstić *et al.* 1986, 33). One of these structures (pit 2) was most likely a semi-subterranean dwelling, rectangular in shape with rounded corners, measuring 4.2 × 3.5 m and dug to a relative depth of about 2.6 m. The pit's fill contained, in addition to pottery and other portable archaeological material, concentrations of daub fragments, soot, and ash, indicating the existence of an above-ground part of the structure made using wattle and daub techniques. Adjacent to this semi-subterranean dwelling was a smaller oval pit filled with various types of debris and, nearby, a regular channel 1.7 m wide was recorded, with a pit measuring 1.5 m in diameter dug from the bottom of the channel, containing a large amount of coarse daub. The authors suggested that these are the remains of another semi-subterranean dwelling (Krstić *et al.* 1986, 19). Other closed (residential) units have been noted at this site; however, they belong to the Late Bronze Age and will be presented in the second volume of this work.

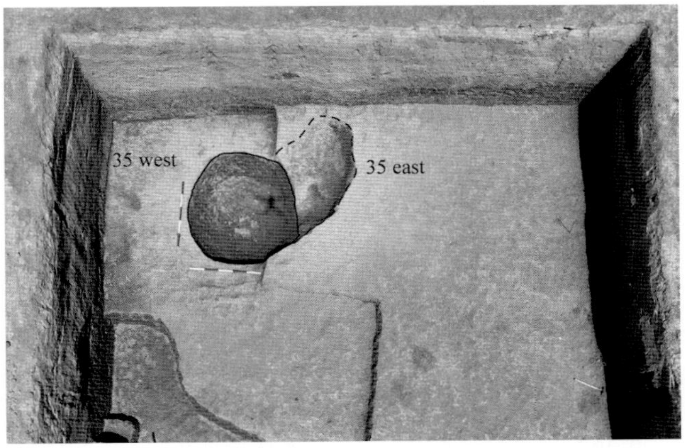

Figure 2.2. Majilovac, site of Marjansko Brdo, structures 35 west and 35 east.

At the Marjansko Brdo site near Veliko Gradište, during rescue excavations no residential structures were discovered,[4] but several pits (structures 44, 45, 12, and 35; Fig. 2.2) were found filled with pottery, animal bones, ash, and other portable finds and, in some pits, the fill had been burned.

The purpose of these pits is unclear. They were certainly used secondarily as refuse pits but their primary function remains unknown. Some contained large numbers of almost intact pottery vessels. Therefore, it is possible that these pits may have served ritual purposes. Interestingly, no remains of residential architecture were identified, except for fragmented daub found in the pits, although it is evident that the site was inhabited during this period. The explanation likely lies in the fact that only a small portion of the site was excavated, specifically the southern periphery, so it is very possible that the settlement was located on the expansive field to the north of the excavated area.

At the Adžine Njive site in Klenak, on the right bank of the Sava River, several pits containing Early Bronze Age finds were discovered but no residential architecture was identified.

2.1.2 Necropolises and burial practices

In the peri-Pannonian zone, three necropolises have been documented, each containing only one grave that dates to the Early Bronze Age. These necropolises are located in the wider area of the confluence of the Sava and Danube rivers, on the left bank of the Danube, near Kovin.

List of necropolises

9. Šljunkara in Surčin, a grave with an inhumed individual (Vranić 1991); 10. Rospi Ćuprija in Belgrade, a grave with a cremated individual in an urn (Todorović 1967); 11. Skorenovac near Kovin, a tumulus with contracted burials

(Garašanin 1973); a. Vojlovica, Rafinerija site, a tumulus with a contracted burial; b. Jabuka, Tri Humke site, a tumulus with a contracted burial; c. Pančevo, Livade site, a tumulus with a contracted burial (Koledin *et al.* 2020, 1–26).

At the Šljunkara necropolis in Surčin, located on the right bank of the Danube, only one grave from the Early Bronze Age was recorded. It contained an inhumed individual in a contracted position on their left side, oriented east–west, with the head facing west (Vranić 1991, 19, 20). The grave contained nine grave goods: eight vessels and one gold headband (diadem). The grave goods were arranged in two rows, oriented north–south, with one row placed above the head and the other below the feet (see Fig. 2.13, below). Anthropological analysis showed that the individual was a woman, aged between 25 and 30 years. The author assigned the grave, culturally and chronologically, to the beginning of the Vinkovci–Somogyvár cultural group, around 2000–1900 BC, a date that does not align with today's absolute chronology for this group. In light of new research, particularly regarding absolute chronology, this date could approximately match the material from the grave, though the finds indicate a later phase of the Vinkovci–Somogyvár group, with strong stylistic and typological elements from the Mokrin group, such as the shape of the beaker (Fig. 2.13/3) and the bowl with double handles (Fig. 2.13/5).

A necropolis from this period was also recorded at Rospi Ćuprija in Belgrade, on the slopes towards the Danube between the Mirijevo stream and Slanački road (Todorović 1956). This is a flat necropolis from multiple prehistoric periods, where the deceased were either inhumed or cremated. The only grave that could be attributed to the Early Bronze Age is grave 11, containing cremated remains placed in a large urn covered by a bowl, along with two grave goods in the form of conical bowls (Fig. 2.14/1–4). The stylistic and typological forms of the vessels suggest similarities with Pannonian Early Bronze Age groups, such as the Bell Beaker-Csepel (Glockenbecher–Csepel) or Vinkovci–Somogyvár cultural groups (Schreiber-Kalicz 1984; Kulcsár 2009).

The final necropolis, or rather a burial under a mound, from this period in the peri-Pannonian zone was documented at Skorenovac near Kovin, though little information is available and what exists is contradictory. M. Garašanin mentions a grave with a contracted burial under a mound at Skorenovac, with two vessels from the 'Baden culture' (Garašanin 1973, 202, 203) while S. Dimitrijević, citing M. Garašanin, refers to multiple contracted burials under the mound, which 'could perhaps belong to the classic phase of the Baden Culture' (Dimitrijević 1979a, 203). As a result, it is unclear whether the published vessels came from one or more graves, although M. Garašanin states that they originated from the same grave (Garašanin 1973, 193, 195, T. 40/1, 2). A beaker from the mound, and likely a small amphora (which could also belong to the Baden group; Fig. 2.4/7, 8), belongs to the so-called Novačka Ćuprija–Pančevo group, suggesting that at least one grave with a contracted burial dates to the Early Bronze Age.

At the sites Livade, Tri Humke, and Rafinerija in Pančevo and its surroundings, a single large tumulus was excavated at each location, with a central grave dug into a rectangular pit (Đorđević and Đorđević 2016). The deceased in all three central graves were laid on their backs with their legs bent to the side and covered in red ochre. Around the skull of the individual in the central grave at Vojlovica, were found silver hair rings, and similar rings were found near the grave at Livade in Pančevo, though no other grave goods were present. These graves have been dated to the 1st and early 2nd quarter of the 3rd millennium BC (Koledin *et al.* 2020). The burial practices, chronology, and grave goods identify these tumuli as belonging to the Steppe Yamnaya Culture.

2.1.3 Portable finds

The portable finds from the peri-Pannonian zone dating to the Early Bronze Age primarily consist of pottery, though several spindle whorls, copper axes (mostly chance finds), the aforementioned gold headband from the grave in Surčin, and other portable finds from closed contexts at the sites Rit, Nad Klepečkom, and Marjansko Brdo have also been recorded.

2.1.3.1 Pottery

The stylistic and typological characteristics of the pottery from this region are fairly uniform and clearly defined, particularly with regard to settlement pottery. The types of vessels represented include bowls, cups, beakers, amphorae, pots, double vessels, and pithoi.

A. BOWLS

Bowl with a semi-globular recipient and everted rim (slightly S profiled) and wide arched handles or without handles, sometimes with sharper transitions at the belly and shoulder (Type 1a), are very common in this zone (Fig. 2.3/1, 3; Fig. 2.5/5; Fig. 2.9/8; Fig. 2.10/1, 2; Fig. 2.12/5; Fig. 2.14/1). Biconical bowls with a everted rim (with sharper or softer S-profiling – Type 1b) are also well represented (Fig. 2.3/2, 5; Fig. 2.5/1–4; Fig. 2.6/6, 7, 9, 11, 17; Fig. 2.7/1, 2, 11–14; Fig. 2.8/1, 14, 15; Fig. 2.9/1–5, 7; Fig. 2.10/4; Fig. 2.11/1–7, 10, 11; Fig. 2.12/2–4, 6, 7; Fig. 2.15/2, 3). Bowls of Type 2a, which include deeper spherical or biconical bowls with a short funnel-shaped or cylindrical neck, or an S-profiled rim, are somewhat less frequent (Fig. 2.3/4; Fig. 2.8/2; Fig. 2.9/9; Fig. 2.10/11, 13; Fig. 2.13/5–8; Fig. 2.14/5; Fig. 2.15/5), while bowls of Type 3a, semi-globular with unprofiled rims or slightly thickened inner rims, are more common (Fig. 2.6/8, 16; Fig. 2.8/12, 13; Fig. 2.10/5, 9, 10, 14; Fig. 2.11/9; Fig. 2.12/1; Fig. 2.13/1; Fig. 2.14/3, 4).

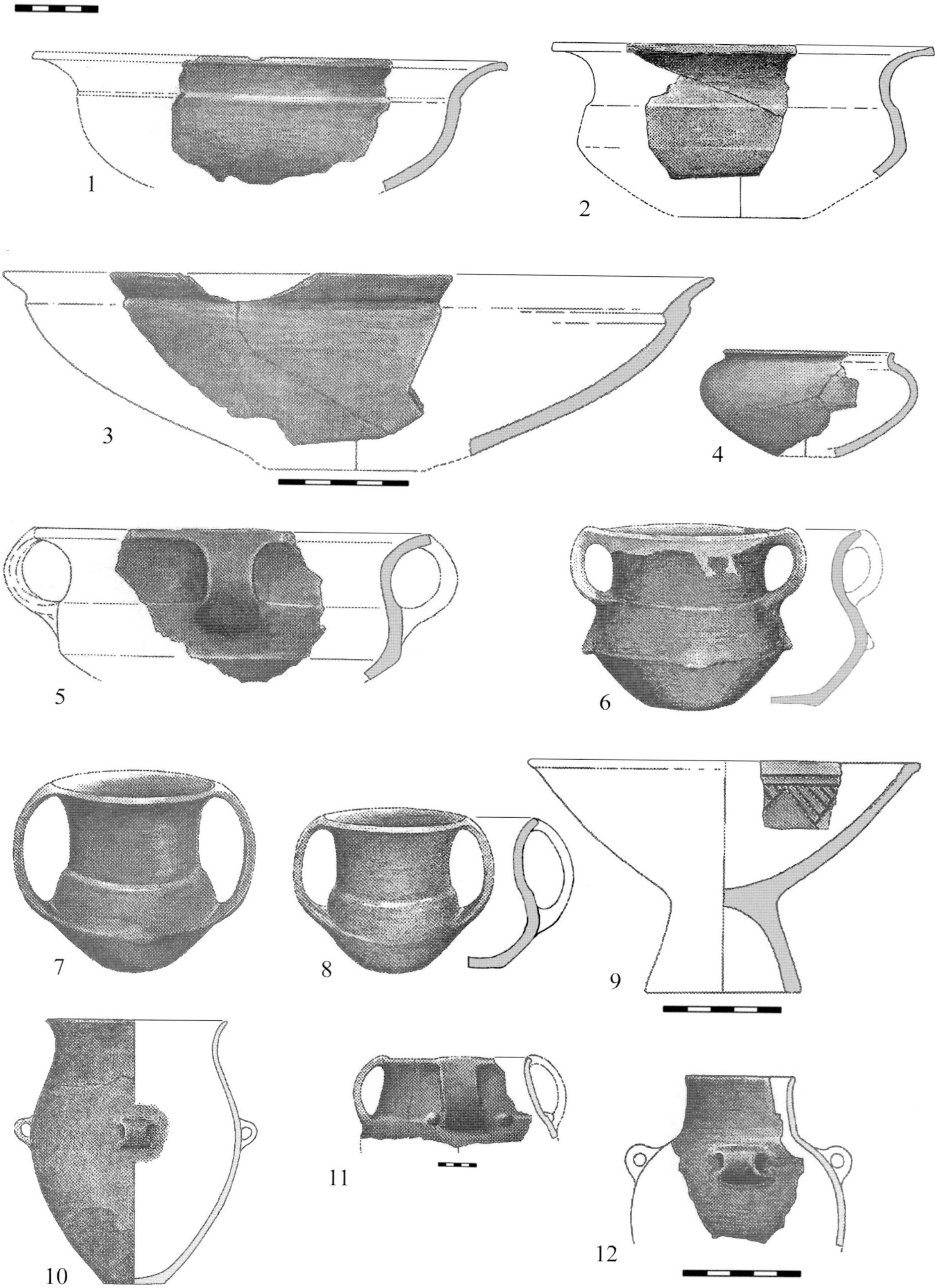

Figure 2.3. Pančevo: site of Donja Varoš.

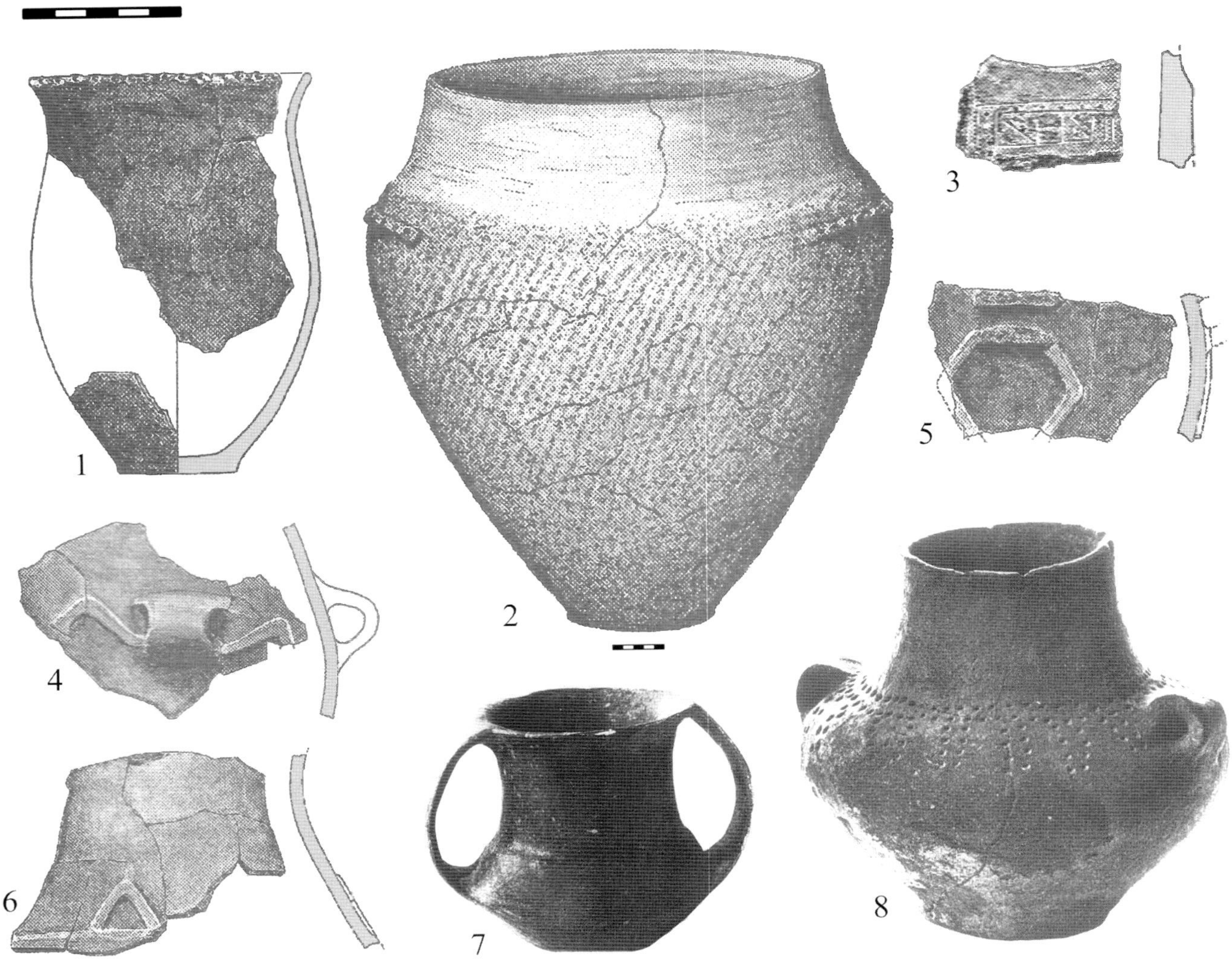

Figure 2.4. 1–6, Pančevo: site of Donja Varoš; 7–8 Kovin, Skorenovac.

These bowls are mostly undecorated, often with wide arched handles. The colour, texture, and surface treatment vary depending on the site but most surfaces are polished, with medium to fine textures.

B. CUPS

The cup type has so far been identified only at the necropolis in Surčin. It is ovoid in shape, with a short slightly funnel-shaped neck and a single handle below the rim, classified as Type 3a (Fig. 2.13/4).

C. BEAKERS

Type 1a beakers (with a slightly biconical body and a longer cylindrical or slightly funnel-shaped neck, with short handles extending from the rim to the shoulder) are only sporadically present in this zone (Fig. 2.3/6; Fig. 2.13/3). In contrast, type 1b beakers (with a slightly biconical or hemispherical body and a longer cylindrical or slightly funnel-shaped narrow neck, with long handles extending from the rim to the widest part of the belly) are more commonly found (Fig. 2.3/7, 8; Fig. 2.4/7; Fig. 2.7/15; Fig. 2.9/11, 12; Fig. 2.12/8). Type 1c beakers, with a pear-shaped form and handles extending from the rim to the shoulder without exceeding the rim or only slightly, are also documented (Fig. 2.5/7; Fig. 2.9/13; Fig. 2.15/1). Type 1e beakers, similar in form and proportion to Type 1c but with arched handles crossing over the opening of the vessel, are represented by only one example (Fig. 2.11/12).

Type 2a beakers (S-profiled, wide-mouthed with a rounded body, with two wide arched handles of ribbon cross-section, aligned with the rim or slightly exceeding it, and extending from the rim to the shoulder) have been documented at two sites (Fig. 2.5/6; Fig. 2.12/2, 10, 11). Type 3a beakers (with a slightly biconical or ovoid form and two handles that do not exceed or only slightly exceed the rim) are also present (Fig. 2.8/4, 6, 7; Fig. 2.14/6, 8, 10).

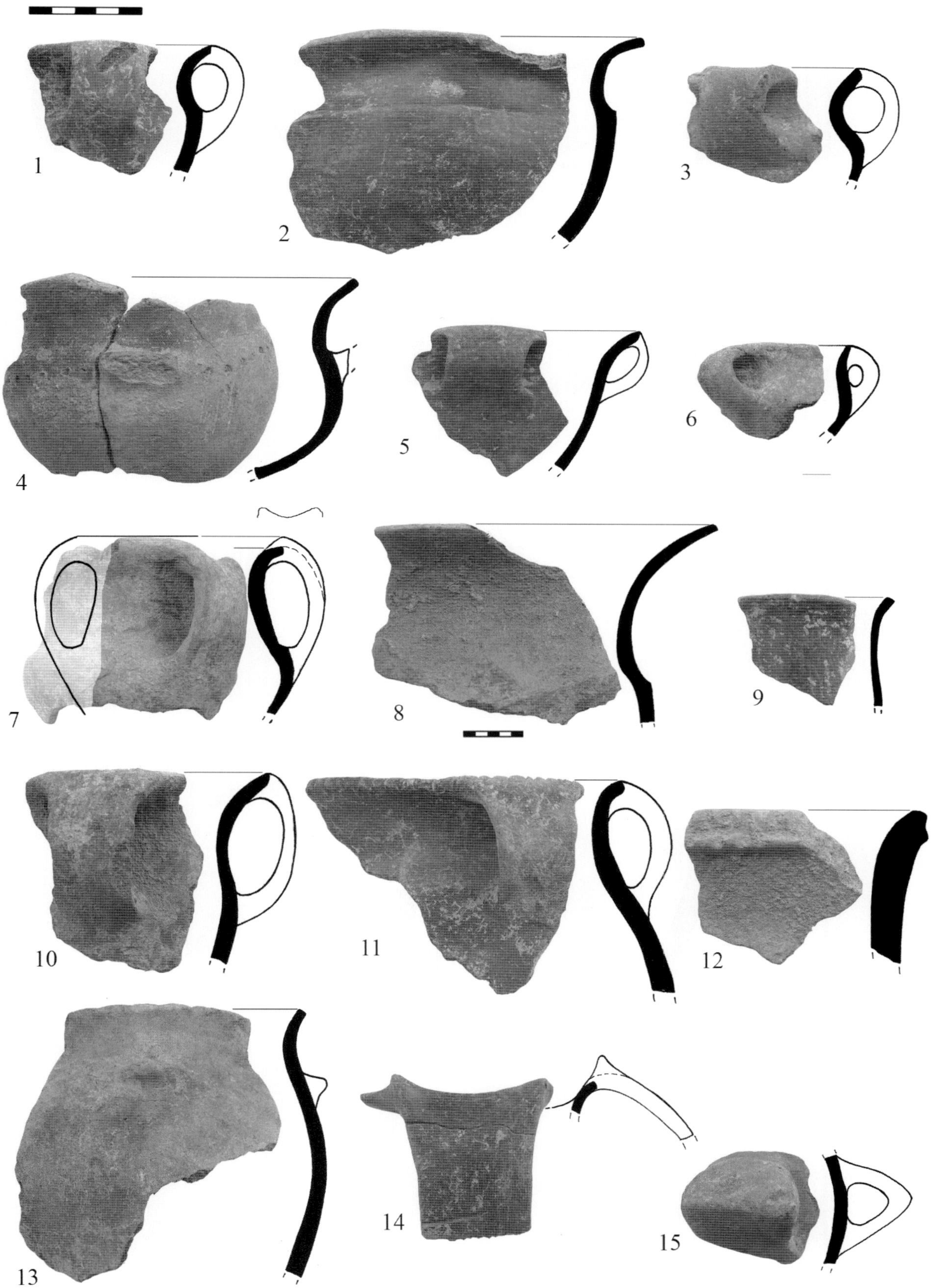

Figure 2.5. Viminacium: site of Rit, Trench 18, structure 1.

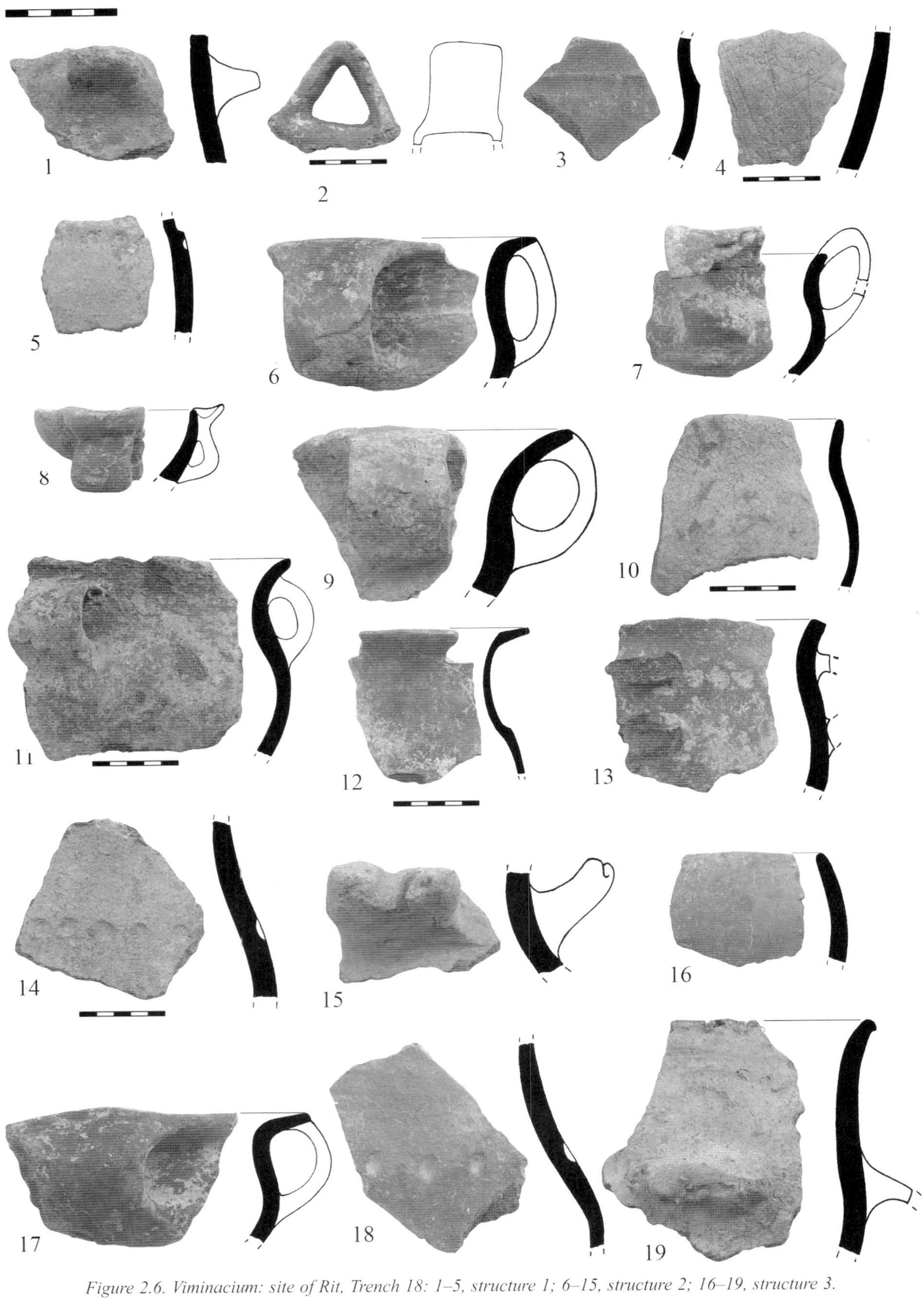

Figure 2.6. Viminacium: site of Rit, Trench 18: 1–5, structure 1; 6–15, structure 2; 16–19, structure 3.

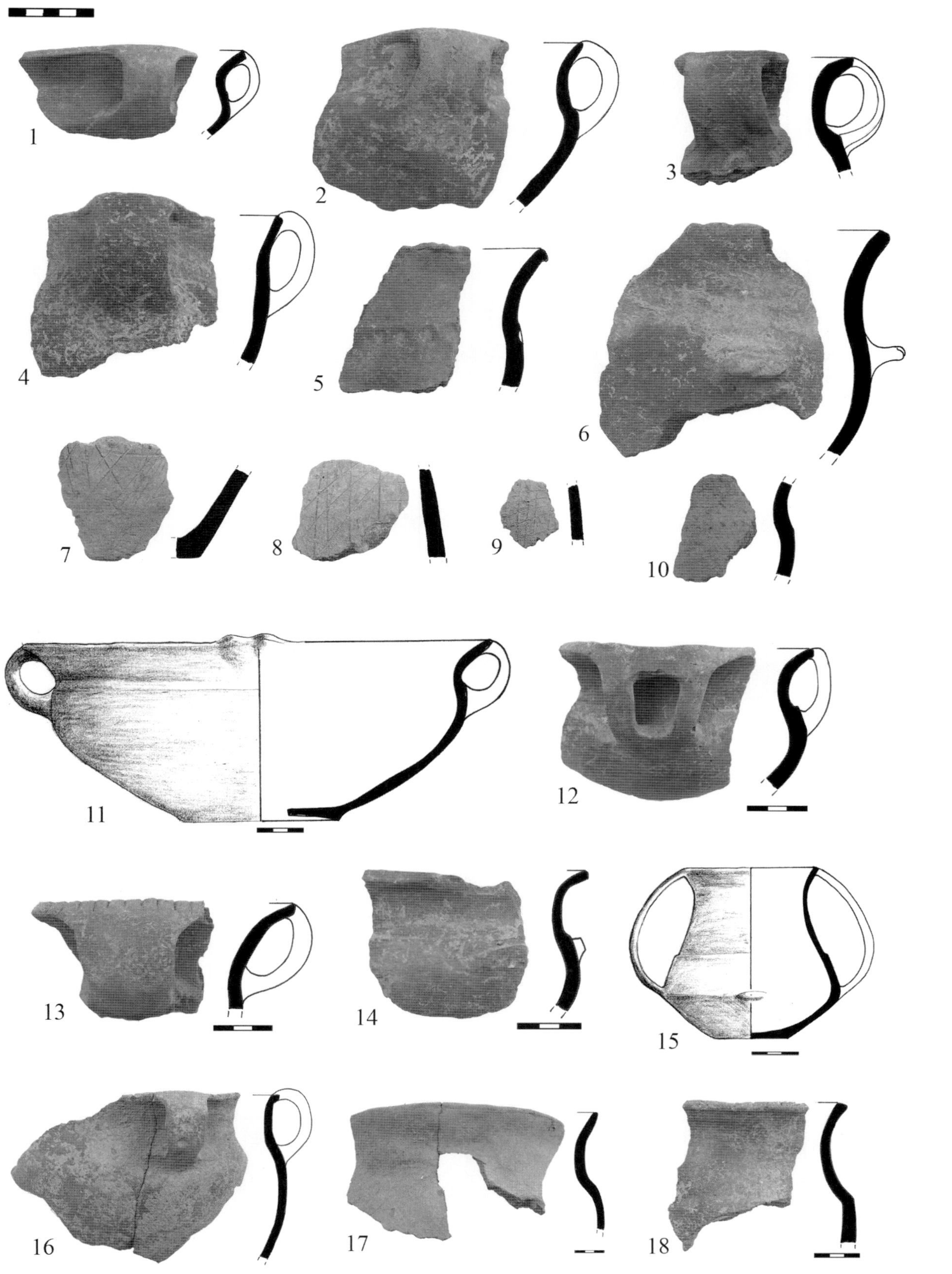

Figure 2.7. Viminacium: site of Nad Klepečkom: 1–10, Trench 77, structure 9; 11–18, Trench 69, structure 1.

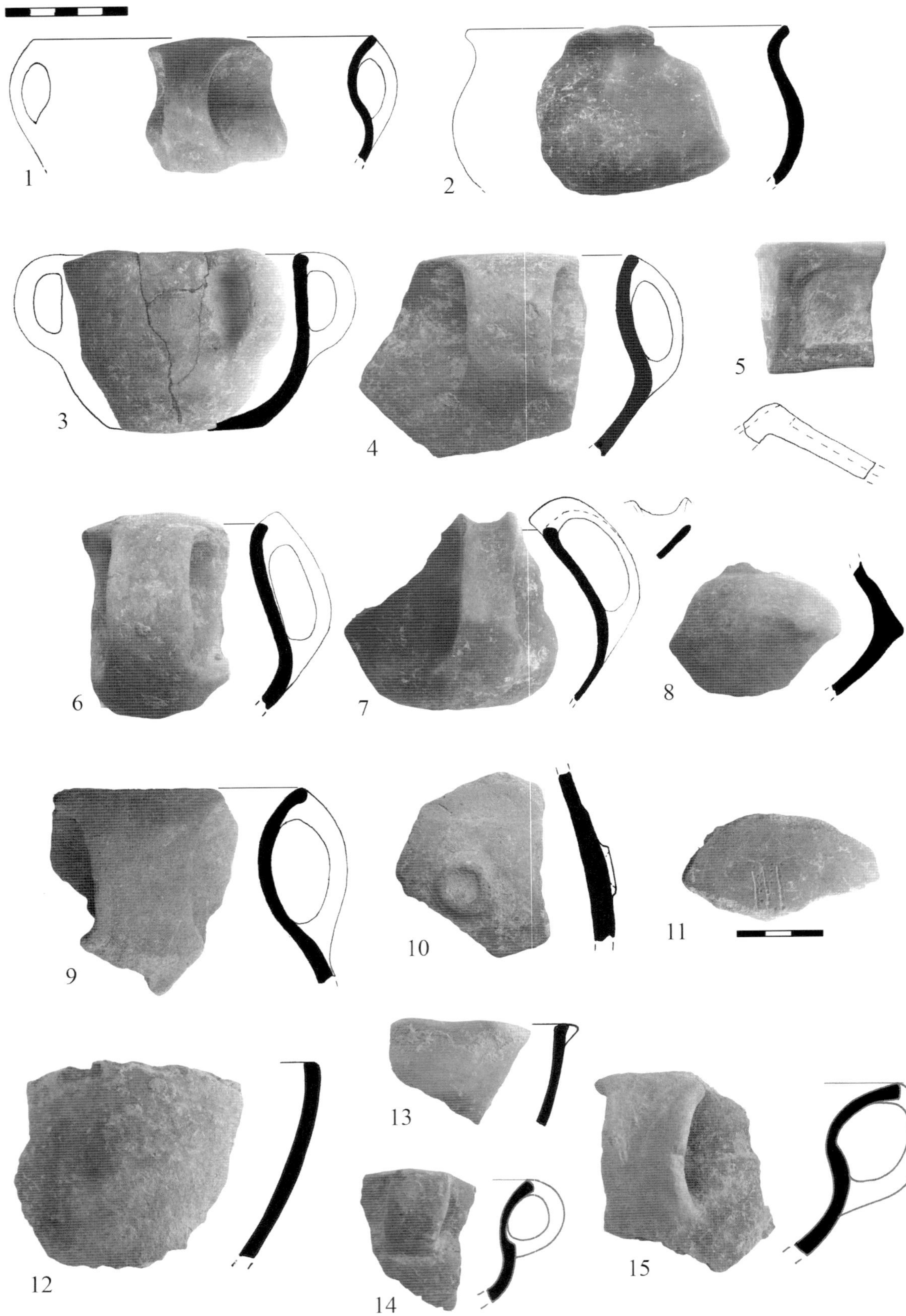

Figure 2.8. Viminacium: site of Nad Klepečkom: 1–11, Trench 79, structure 1, 12–15, Trench 77, structure 8.

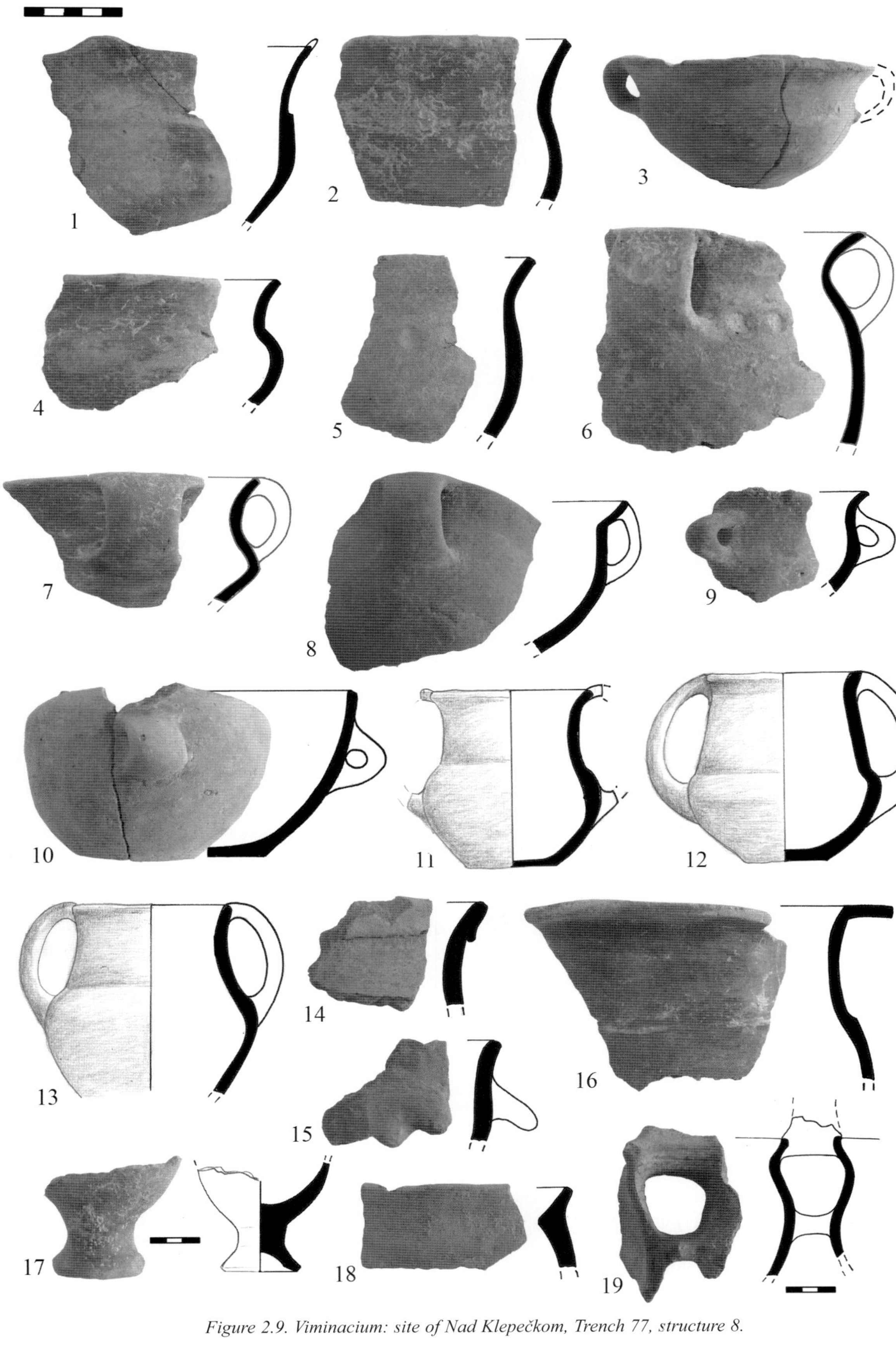

Figure 2.9. Viminacium: site of Nad Klepečkom, Trench 77, structure 8.

Type 4a beakers (with a semi-globular body on a hollow foot) are the least common (Fig. 2.3/9; Fig. 2.9/17; Fig. 2.10/12; Fig. 2.12/21).

At the Adžine Njive site in Klenak, beakers with a soft S-profile, sharply emphasised transitions, a cylindrical neck, and a flaring or obliquely expanded rim have been classified as Type 3b (Fig. 2.14/7, 9, 11). A very similar profile, but on Type 1b bowls, has been noted at the sites of Donja Varoš, Rit, Nad Klepečkom, Marjansko Brdo, and Novačka Ćuprija.

One beaker of Type 7 (a or b), characterised by a long cylindrical neck and a short, rounded body with an arched handle (or handles) connecting the belly to the area just below the rim, has been recorded in this zone (Fig. 2.10/15).

Beakers in this zone are mostly decorated with plastic ridges (Fig. 2.3/6, 7; Fig. 2.7/15), except for one example of Type 4a from Pančevo, which is decorated with the false cord technique in the form of horizontal parallel lines, beneath which hang hatched triangles (Fig. 2.3/9). Like the bowls, the beakers generally have polished surfaces and medium to fine textures.

D. AMPHORAE

Amphorae in this zone can be classified into five types:

Type 1a: are mostly ovoid in shape, with shorter or longer, often cylindrical necks, and sometimes with wide tunnel-like handles on the shoulder or belly (Fig. 2.3/10, 12; Fig. 2.4/1, 4–6, 8; Fig. 2.5/12, 13; Fig. 2.6/10, 12, 19; Fig. 2.7/5, 6; Fig. 2.9/14; Fig. 2.12/12, 18, 19; Fig. 2.14/2 – used as an urn, 13; Fig. 2.15/6).

Type 1b: another deep amphora, with an ovoid form, was also recorded (Fig. 2.11/17), and these forms are expected to become more common in the subsequent period of the Bronze Age.

Type 2a: have two arched handles connecting the rim and shoulder, similar to beakers but significantly larger in size (Fig. 2.14/11; Fig. 2.5/11; Fig. 2.7/3, 4, 16; Fig. 2.8/9; Fig. 2.9/6; Fig. 2.10/6, 7, 17; Fig. 2.12/17, 18; Fig. 2.13/2; Fig. 2.14/12).

Type 3a: are deeper vessels with wide openings and more or less everted rims. These vessels could not be assigned to a more specific type and were classified simply as amphorae (Fig. 2.5/8–10; Fig. 2.7/17, 18; Fig. 2.9/16).

Type 4a: a single example of a new Type 4a amphora, a spherical amphora with a short funnel-shaped neck and a handle on the shoulder, was found (Fig. 2.10/13).

The only decorations on the amphorae consist of plastic appliqué, such as knobs and ridges of various forms (Fig. 2.4/4–6), as well as rows of impressed dots (Fig. 2.4/8).

On some Type 1a examples, the outer side of the rim has a triangularly profile (Fig. 2.5/12; Fig. 2.9/14) or is decorated with a series of impressions (Fig. 2.4/1). Some are decorated with fingertip impressions directly applied to the vessel's surface (Fig. 2.9/6; Fig. 2.13/12). One amphora is decorated with a low plastic band featuring a row of impressions above which there are four vertical parallel incised lines. This vessel served as an urn, so it may have been treated differently for that purpose (Fig. 2.14/2).

E. DOUBLE VESSELS

Double vessels, also referred to as 'salt containers' in the literature, have been documented at several Early Bronze Age sites in the transition zone. Unfortunately, only parts of the vessels and handles have been preserved, making it impossible to establish a typology based on form (Fig. 2.9/19; Fig. 2.11/15, 16, 18; Fig. 2.12/13–15). A specific type of triangular handle, found on double vessels, has been recorded at several sites in this region (Fig. 2.6/2; Fig. 2.12/14).

F. POTS

This category includes only vessels with thicker walls, coarser textures, and surfaces decorated with plastic strips (Fig. 2.6/13; Fig. 2.11/8). It is possible that some vessels classified as amphorae, particularly Type 3a, are actually pots, but attribution is difficult because the primary difference between pots and amphorae (especially Type 3a) may lie in their function rather than their appearance.

Cooking pot, known as a *piraunos*, has been identified in one example from a pit at Marjansko Brdo, dated to the end of the Early and beginning of the Middle Bronze Age.

G. PITHOI

One example of a pithos, or large storage vessel for grain, has been recorded in this zone. It has an ovoid form with a conical neck and plastic ribs on the shoulder, featuring fingertip impressions (Fig. 2.4/2). The surface of the lower part of the vessel is roughened with *barbotine*, organised in diagonal rows.

H. HANDLES

Handles on Early Bronze Age vessels in the peri-Pannonian zone are mostly arched, wide, and predominantly ribbon-shaped or oval in cross-section, extending from the rim to the shoulder, most commonly on beakers.[5] Another type of handle, though less common, is the tunnel-like handle, which is typically wide and short (Fig. 2.14/10, 12; Fig. 2.4/4, 8; Fig. 2.5/15; Fig. 2.9/10; Fig. 2.14/2, etc.). Other recorded handle types include tongue-shaped handles and rectangular ones with a groove in the middle (Fig. 2.6/15, 19; Fig. 2.9/15), as well as the triangular handles on double vessels mentioned earlier. Characteristic are the double arched handles, where the body is divided (Fig. 2.7/12; Fig. 2.13/5), as well as the arched handle with a recipient on top (Fig. 2.6/8). Most arched handles are flat in profile but there are also examples with concave profiles (Fig. 2.5/7; Fig. 2.6/7; Fig. 2.8/7; Fig. 2.11/12, 18; Fig. 2.12/4, 8, 16).

I. ORNAMENTATION

The most common decorative techniques on this pottery include the application of plastic ridges and bands of various shapes, and the impressing of fingertip rows directly onto the fresh surface of the vessel. Plastic additions include knob- and tongue-shaped ridges (Fig. 2.3/6, 11; Fig. 2.7/15; Fig. 2.8/8; Fig. 2.15/2), mostly found on the belly of beakers or the shoulder or belly of amphorae.

Plastic strips with a rectangular cross-section (ribs) in zigzag, polygonal, or triangular shapes (Fig. 2.4/4–6; Fig. 2.12/20), mostly found on amphorae, were recorded, as well as groups of three vertical ribs (Fig. 2.15/6) and a characteristic horizontal band on Type 1a amphorae (Fig. 2.5/12). One example of a plastic circular rib was noted (Fig. 2.8/10).

Plastic appliqués on the rim of bowls were also recorded, including semicircular (sometimes double) and triangular additions (Fig. 2.7/11; Fig. 2.9/1; Fig. 2.11/9; Fig. 2.12/5). Fingertip impressions on the surface of the vessels were frequently used, with the ornament often applied to the rim, shoulder, or belly of amphorae and pots (Fig. 2.4/1; Fig. 2.5/11; Fig. 2.6/5, 14, 18, 19; Fig. 2.7/5, 10; Fig. 2.9/5, 6; Fig. 2.11/8, 19; Fig. 2.12/12; Fig. 2.15/6), as well as on the shoulder and rim of bowls (Fig. 2.5/4; Fig. 2.6/11).

Incised decoration has been recorded on several vessels, most often in the form of parallel or crossed lines (Fig. 2.6/4; Fig. 2.7/7–9; Fig. 2.14/2), often combined with punctation (Fig. 2.4/3; Fig. 2.8/11; Fig. 2.10/12; Fig. 2.12/22, 23; Fig. 2.14/4).

Less frequent techniques on this pottery include impressed decoration with a serrated tool, in the form of a horizontal band and hanging hatched triangles (Fig. 2.3/9), *barbotine* organized into diagonal lines (Fig. 2.4/2; Fig. 2.10/18), and plastic bands with fingertip impressions (Fig. 2.10/3–5, 8; Fig. 2.14/2). Rows of impressed dots forming horizontal and vertical lines appear on one amphora and a fragment of another vessel (Fig. 2.4/8; Fig. 2.14/14). Plastic ribs with a semicircular cross-section, mostly placed horizontally on the shoulder of the vessel, were also recorded (Fig. 2.10/13, 14).

It is evident that the pottery from the necropolises (Surčin, Rospi Ćuprija) is mostly undecorated, with the exception of one amphora from Rospi Ćuprija, decorated with a plastic band with fingertip impressions and incised lines, and an amphora from Skorenovac, decorated with impressed dots.

2.1.3.2 Other finds

In addition to pottery, one of the most interesting finds from this zone is a gold headband with rounded open ends and small perforations, from the grave at the Šljunkara site. The headband measures 57.8 cm in length, 1.4 cm in width, and weighs about 40 g. It is decorated along the edges with a series of small circular impressions (Fig. 2.13/9; Fig. 2.15/15).

Gold jewellery started to circulate more intensively in this region during the Early Bronze Age, as evidenced by this find and a group of gold items from roughly the same period from Bosut, Orolik, and Jászdózsa–Kapolnahalom in the northern Pannonian Basin (Majnarić Pandžić 1974; Tárnoki 2003; Popović and Radojčić 1996, cat. no. 34). A similar, copper, headband, though somewhat wider and more richly decorated, was found in grave 73 at Mokrin and is also dated to the Early Bronze Age (Girić 1971, 218, 219, T. xxii). Part of the jewellery from Orolik, attributed to the Vinkovci–Somogyvár culture, is decorated in a similar way to the diadem from Šljunkara, with punctuated lines along the edges (Majnarić Pandžić 1974, 23/1–3).

Other finds from closed contexts include items from this zone. From a deep, regular circular pit at Marjansko Brdo (structure 45), dated to the 25th/24th century cal BC, which had been dug into a Neolithic house and virgin soil, the following were found alongside pottery (Fig. 2.10): a pyramidal loom weight made of fired clay (Fig. 2.14/19), disk-shaped spindle whorls with profiled perforations in the centre (Fig. 2.14/18), part of a spoon, and anchor-shaped objects made of fired clay (Fig. 2.14/20, 16, 17). Anchor-shaped objects are known from Early Bronze Age sites in Thessaly, southern Albania, Aegean Macedonia, Ezero in Thrace, and Oltenia, as well as at Maskare near Kruševac (Roman 1976, pl. 52/7, 8; Georgiev *et al.* 1979, 406, 407, table 228; Mallory 2006, 89, ill. 43; Stojić 2011). In Ezero, two pendants of this type were found in layer VII, which, based on available dates, are attributed to the late 4th and early 3rd millennium BC (Werninger 1995, 446–449; Boyadziev 1998, 365; Nikolova 1999, 401), approximately half a millennium earlier than structure 45. Identical objects have been recorded in the III horizon at Kričani, which parallels layers 25–27 at Kastanas, dated to the Early Bronze Age (Aslanis 1985, 252, 317).

Also found in structure 45 at Marjansko Brdo was an unusual triangular object of unknown function, made from the scapula of a large mammal, with two circular perforations on one side and one perforation on the other (Fig. 2.14/15). In its shape, arrangement of perforations, and dimensions, this object resembles the earliest forms of copper daggers, suggesting it might have been used as a type of weapon, tool, or part of armour.

Another notable find is a stone axe-hammer with a slightly elongated, cylindrical-shaped back end, from a closed context at the Nad Klepečkom site. Such axe-hammers are characteristic of the Early and Middle Bronze Age in Eastern Europe but are relatively rare in this region. According to the typology of D. Antonović and A. Đorđević, this axe is most similar to Type 8 (Antonović and Đorđević 2011).

A rectangular object with concave longer edges, perforated in the centre and decorated with circular impressions on all surfaces, also stands out. Its purpose is unknown (Kapuran *et al.* 2019b, T. 6/15).

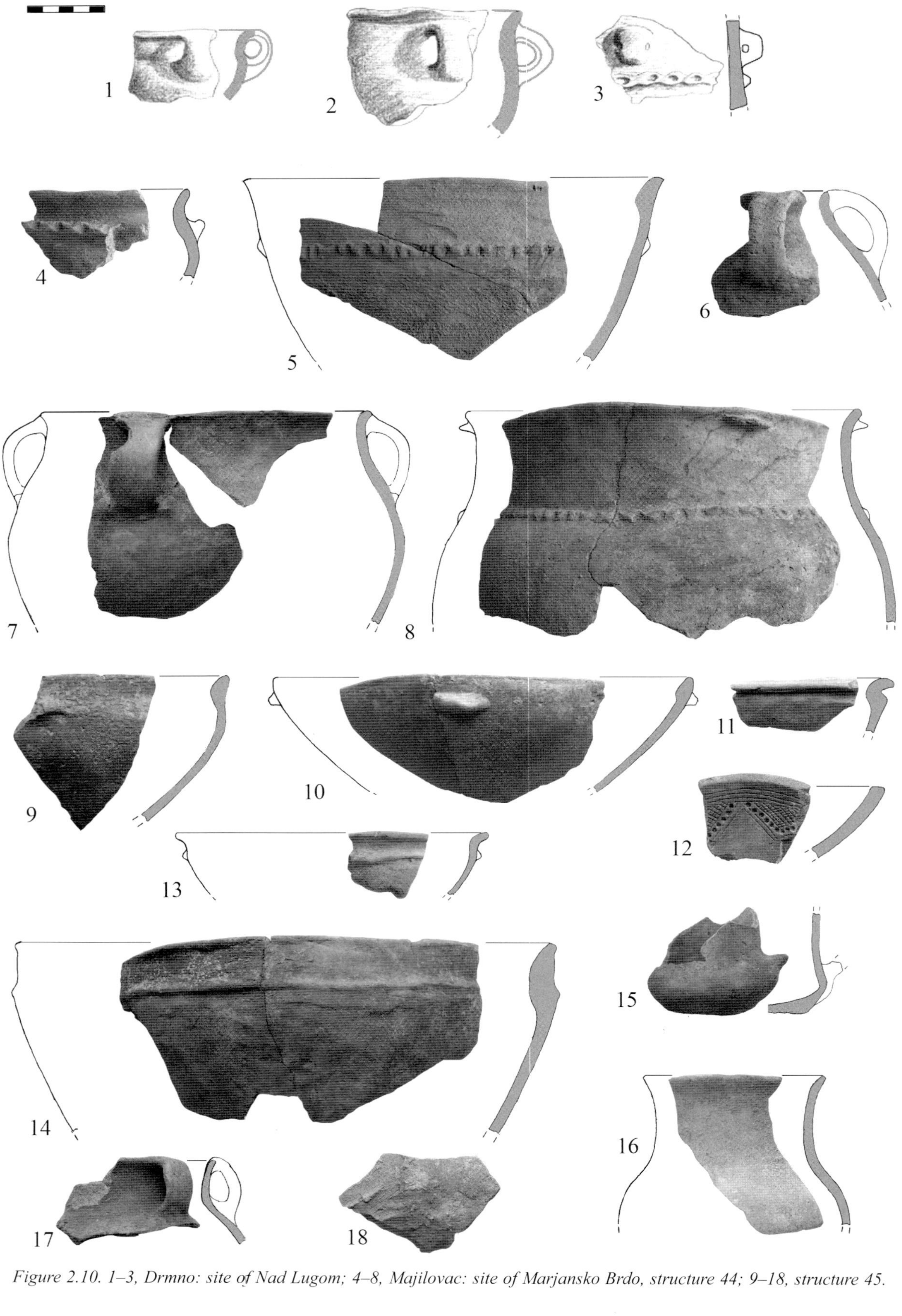

Figure 2.10. 1–3, Drmno: site of Nad Lugom; 4–8, Majilovac: site of Marjansko Brdo, structure 44; 9–18, structure 45.

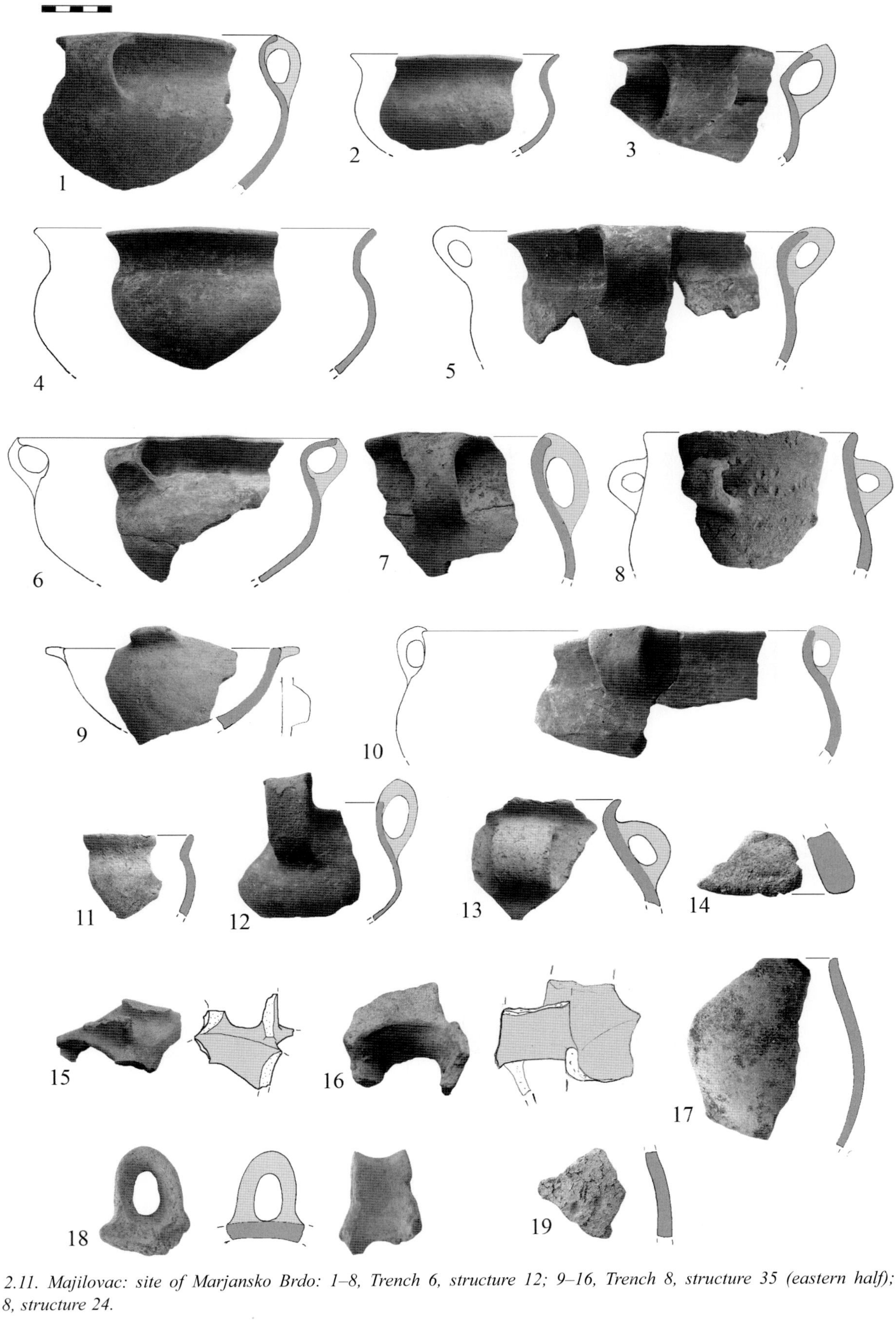

Figure 2.11. Majilovac: site of Marjansko Brdo: 1–8, Trench 6, structure 12; 9–16, Trench 8, structure 35 (eastern half); 17–19, Trench 8, structure 24.

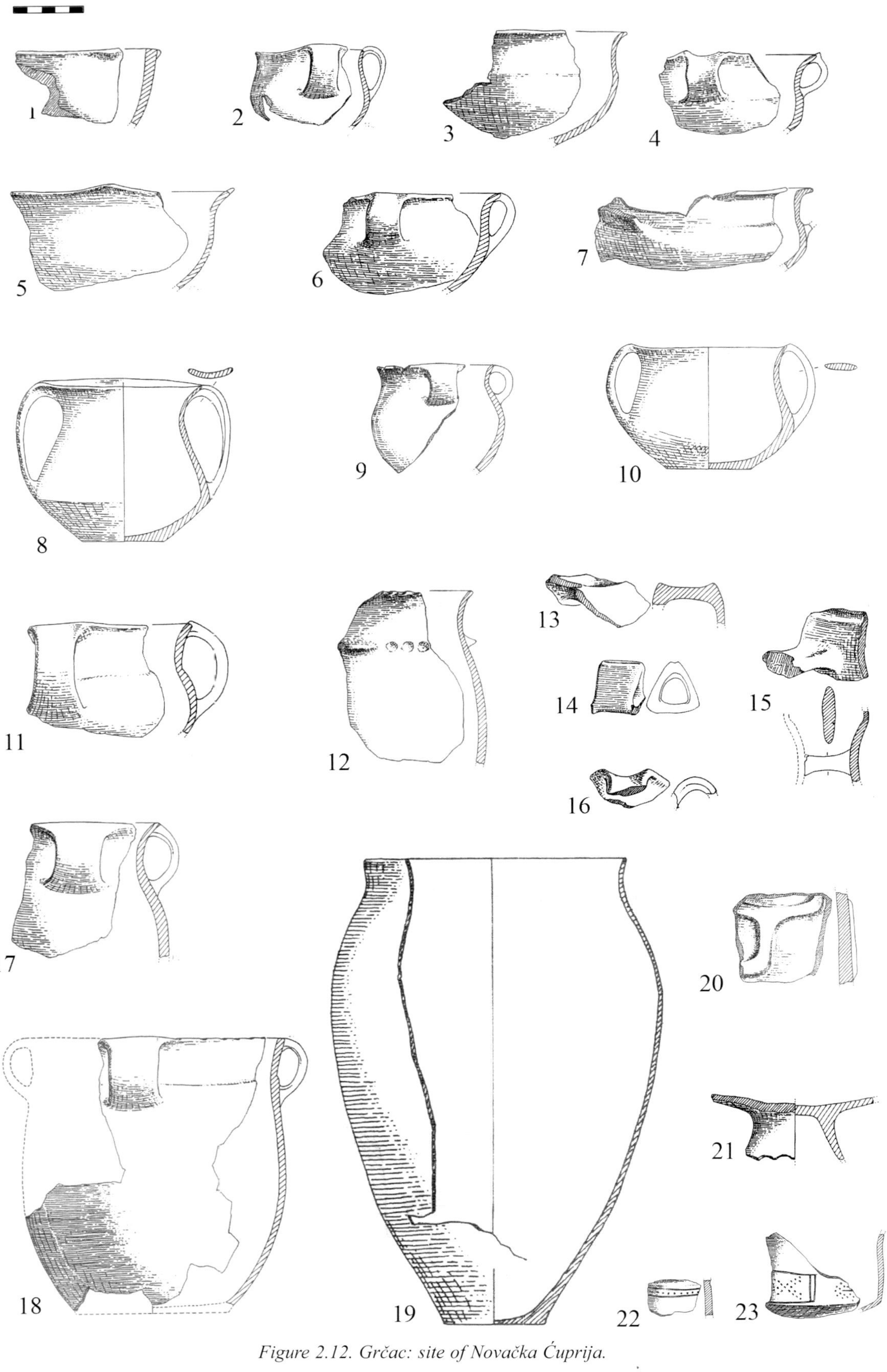

Figure 2.12. Grčac: site of Novačka Ćuprija.

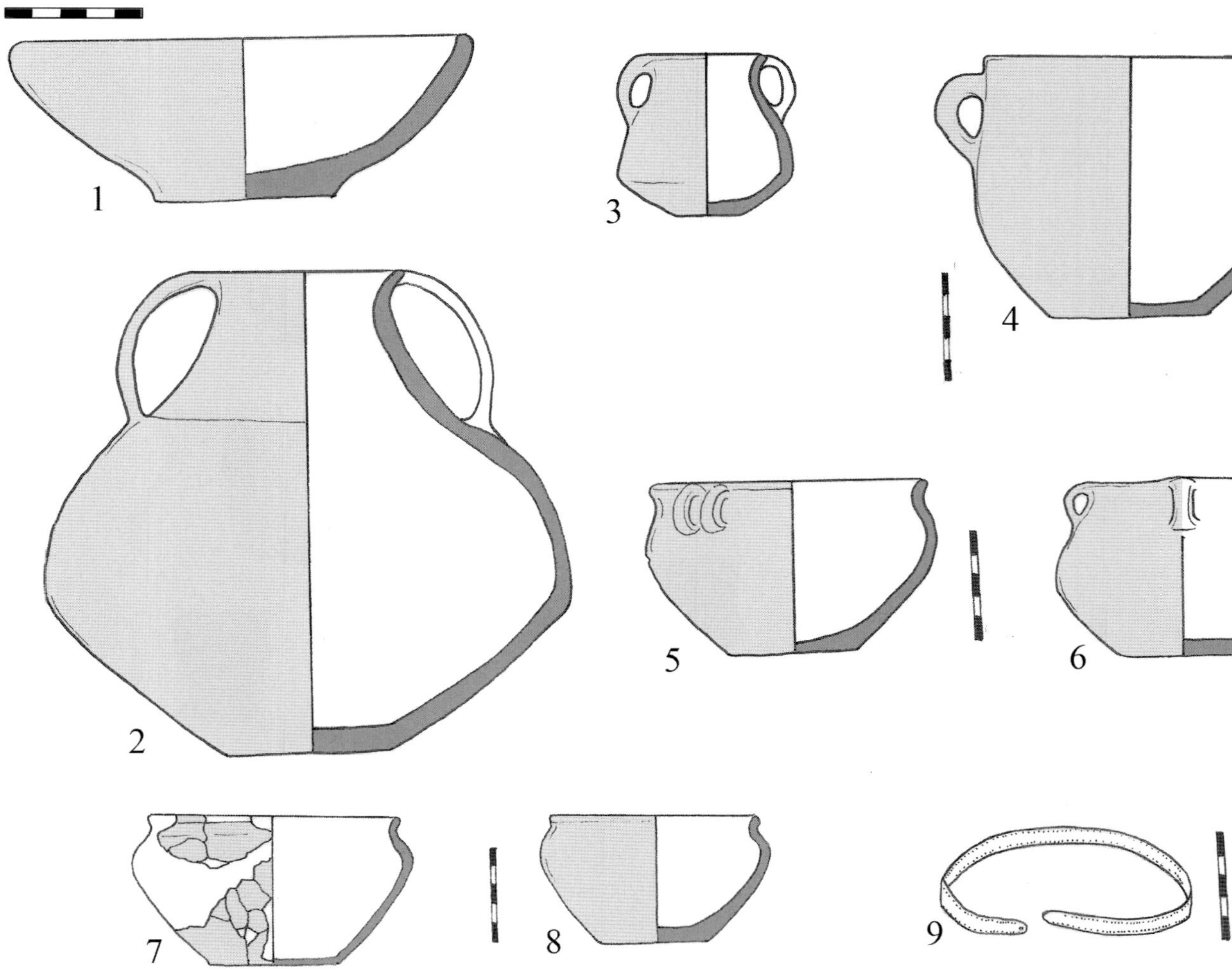

Figure 2.13. Surčin: site of Šljunkara.

Other finds from closed contexts dating to the Early Bronze Age include a biconical spindle whorl, a bone cover, and part of a quern-stone from the Rit site, as well as horn awls, biconical spindle whorls, a conical spindle whorl, a horn hoe, grinders, and a tool made from chipped stone from Nad Klepečkom. In a larger pit at Marjansko Brdo (structure 12), dated to the 20th century cal BC, in addition to a large number of pottery fragments (Fig. 2.11/1–8), horn and bone tools were discovered (Fig. 2.15/21, 22), a bone sewing needle with an eye (Fig. 2.15/23), ceramic projectiles (Fig. 2.15/24), and a copper needle with a bent tip (Fig. 2.15/25).[6]

A larger number of similar finds, such as bone tools, spindle whorls, stone axes, leg models, grindstones, and the like, were uncovered at the Novačka Ćuprija site, though they were not found in secure archaeological contexts and cannot be definitively attributed to the Early Bronze Age (Krstić *et al.* 1986, T. xvii–xix).

LIST OF SITES WITH CHANCE FINDS

12. Kličevac near Požarevac, two vessels; Batovac near Požarevac, parts of two vessels; 13. Trnjane near Požarevac, a beaker with two handles (all Stojić and Jacanović 2008); Amfiteatar, Viminacium, amphora-type vessel (Bulatović *et al.* 2019); Kovin, Kozarac-type axe; Štitar near Šabac, Kozarac-type axe; Uzveće near Šabac, Kozarac-type axe; Begaljica near Smederevo, Kozarac-type axe (all Antonović 2014); Confluence of the Drina and Sava rivers, Kozarac-type axe (Vukmanović and Radojčić 1995).

When it comes to indicative metal finds from this zone, copper axes of the Kozarac type, discovered in Kovin, Štitar, Uzveće, Begaljica, and at a site near the confluence of the Drina and Sava rivers (Fig. 2.15/16–20), are certainly noteworthy (Antonović 2014). Axes of this type, in two variants, Jasika and Baranda, are mostly found at sites in river valleys in northern and central Serbia and are absent south

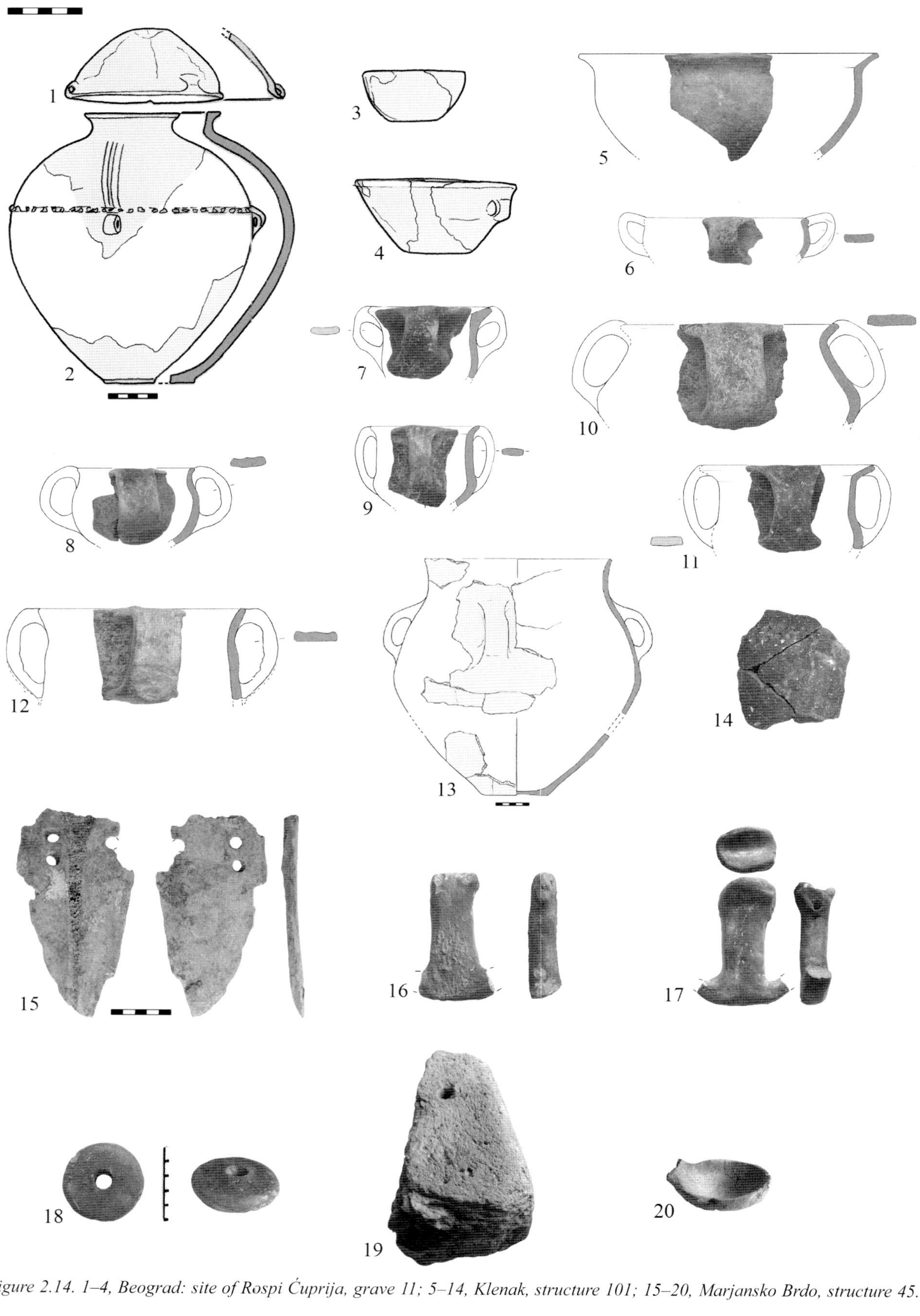

Figure 2.14. 1–4, Beograd: site of Rospi Ćuprija, grave 11; 5–14, Klenak, structure 101; 15–20, Marjansko Brdo, structure 45.

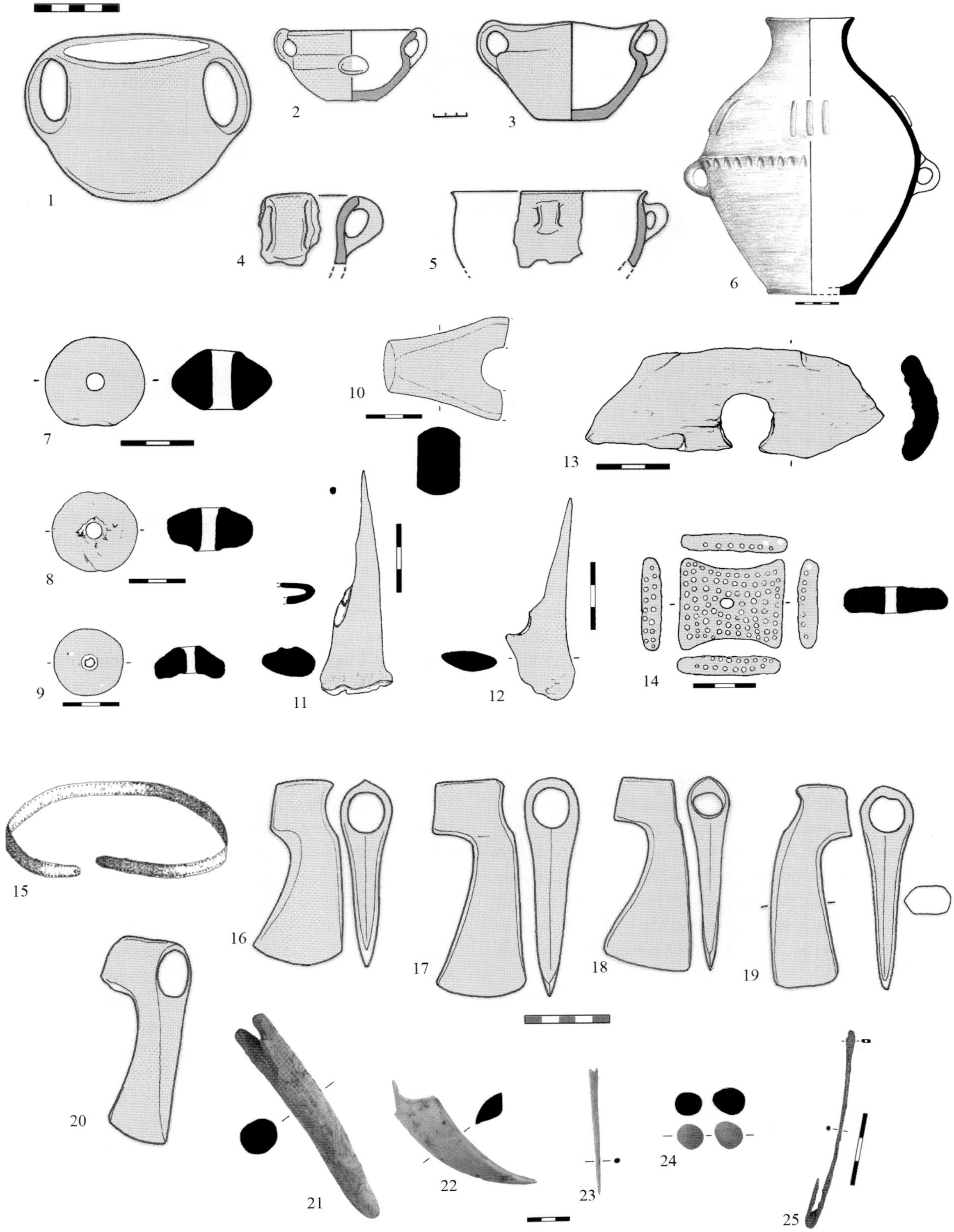

Figure 2.15. 1, Trnjane: site of Kod Groblja; 2–3, Kličevac, unknown site; 4–5, Batovac, unknown site; 6, Viminacium: site of Amfiteatar; 7, 13, Viminacium: site of Rit; 8–12, 14, Viminacium: site of Nad Klepečkom; 15, Surčin: site of Šljunkara; 16, Štitar, unknown site; 17, Uzveće, unknown site; 18, Kovin, unknown site; 19, Begaljica, unknown site; 20, Ušće Drine u Savu, unknown site; 21–25, Majilovac: site of Marjansko Brdo, structure 12.

of western Morava (Antonović 2014, 92). The distribution of these finds suggests a west-east diffusion pattern, as the number of these axes is significantly lower in this region than in the western Balkans, but noticeably higher than in the eastern Balkans. D. Antonović dates axes of this type to the end of the Eneolithic and the Early Bronze Age. This dating has been confirmed by an absolute date from grave 208 at Mokrin, which contained a Jasika variant of this type of axe (Antonović 2014, 91),[7] dating to 2200–2020 cal BC (O'Shea 1996). Most of the Kozarac axes from the peri-Pannonian zone belong to the Baranda variant, except for the axe from the confluence of the Drina and Sava rivers, which belongs to the Jasika variant. Aside from the example from Begaljica, which contains no tin but about 0.84% arsenic, most of the axes have not been analysed for their composition, so it is unclear whether they were made solely of copper or if they contain arsenic or tin.

2.1.4 Chronological and cultural attribution of Early Bronze Age finds in the peri–Pannonian Zone

The stylistic and typological characteristics of the pottery from this zone indicate a varied material culture during this period, as confirmed by absolute dates. However, most of the finds, particularly from sites in the wider area of the confluence of the Great Morava and Danube rivers, as well as the Sava and Danube rivers (Pančevo, Skorenovac, Nad Klepečkom, Rit, Marjansko Brdo, Novačka Ćuprija, and Klenak), can be attributed to the same material culture. Absolute dates from the latter four sites suggest a similar chronological framework, dating to the 21st/20th–19th centuries cal BC (see Table 1). Although dates are lacking from Pančevo and Skorenovac, the characteristics of the pottery suggest they belong roughly to the same period. The absolute date from Klenak determined structure 101 (a pit) in the last two centuries of the 3rd millennium cal BC,[8] aligning approximately with dates from Viminacium and the younger horizon of the Early Bronze Age at Marjansko Brdo. The absolute date from structure 45 at Marjansko Brdo indicates an older horizon of the Early Bronze Age in this zone, dating to the 25th/24th centuries cal BC, which is also reflected in the material culture.

The pottery from the later period of the peri-Pannonian zone, which is geographically understandable, includes elements from the Bubanj-Hum III group from the southern central Balkans (e.g., double-handled beakers with a rounded belly and wider mouth, Type 1c, and plastic appendages on the rim). It also features elements from the Mokrin group from the north (e.g., bowls of Type 1a, double-handled beakers with wide-set long handles and a sack-shaped lower part, often with small tongue-shaped handles placed upward and connected by a line separating the cone of the vessel; arched double handles; and smaller recipients on the rim or top of the handle) (Girić 1971, T. xxxii/2). Particularly significant is the double-handled beaker with small tongue-shaped plastic appliqués on the belly, connected by a line along the cone of the vessel, as this would become one of the more common types of vessels in the Vatin culture of the Middle Bronze Age. A prototype of this vessel was found at the Varoš site in Pančevo (Fig. 2.3/6).

In addition to connections with the Mokrin group, the pottery from the peri-Pannonian zone also has analogies with examples from the Mako–Kosihy–Čaka and Vinkovci–Somogyvár groups, such as the hemispherical beaker on a foot (Type 4) decorated with cord impressions, among others (Kulcsár 2009). Similar footed beakers, though decorated using different techniques, have been recorded sporadically in the southern Morava River Region (Pelince, Bubanj, Kokino). Finds from closed contexts corresponding to the stylistic and typological features of the Vinkovci–Somogyvár group have also been documented at Marjansko Brdo, including deep bowls of Type 3a with semicircular thickenings on the inner side of the rim (Fig. 2.10/5, 9, 10, 14), hemispherical bowls with sharply S-shaped profile rims (Fig. 2.10/11, 13), beakers with long cylindrical necks (Type 7) (Fig. 2.10/16), and a hemispherical beaker with an ornamented interior featuring incised lines and punctation (Fig. 2.10/12), among others (Kulcsár 2009, figs 50, 52, 54, 55, 58–62; Marković 2010, T. 2/3, T. 7/3, T. 6/6).

On the other hand, pottery from sites in this zone also exhibits some peculiarities not seen in contemporary pottery from other regions. Notably, beakers with a short biconical body and longer conical neck, with long arched handles aligned with the rim, usually ribbon-shaped in cross-section, connecting the rim and lower cone of the vessel, which constitutes only a third or even a quarter of the vessel's height (Type 1b), are unique to this zone. Several beakers with similar proportions have been recorded in the central Morava River Region, specifically in pit 2 at the Vecina Mala site in Majur (Stojić 1986, fig. 3–25). Type 2 beakers, which may also represent a characteristic of this zone, resemble beakers typical of the Bubanj-Hum III group but are shorter, stockier, and have a wider mouth. Another characteristic of the pottery from the peri-Pannonian zone could be the appearance of triangular handles with a ribbon-shaped cross-section (Fig. 2.6/2; Fig. 2.12/14), as such handles have not been documented at Bronze Age sites in other regions. Noteworthy are the narrow, cylindrical-necked, slightly rounded-bellied beakers of Type 3b from Klenak, with an everted rim (Fig. 2.14/7, 9, 11), whose profile is very similar to many Type 1b bowls (Fig. 2.3/2; Fig. 2.6/6, 12; Fig. 2.7/14, etc.), though these bowls have a much wider opening.

Based on the available absolute dates (Table 1), it is difficult to fully define the chronology of the Early Bronze Age in this zone, but enough information exists to establish a basic chronological framework. Unfortunately, the dates from Novačka Ćuprija are from the 1980s, with deviations of 100–330 years, resulting in calibrated dates with a wide range of 2860–1850 cal BC (68% probability). The remaining dates are more precise, and therefore more reliable. The oldest date from this zone is 2466–2339 cal BC (94% probability) from structure 45 at Marjansko Brdo, which featured pottery with stylistic and typological traits of the Vinkovci–Somogyvár group (Fig. 2.10). The dates from Viminacium are relatively consistent and precise, placing the Nad Klepečkom site in the period 2040–1965 cal BC (79.6% probability), and Rit in the period 1977–1907 cal BC (91.6% probability), corresponding to the second half of the 21st and the 20th century BC. Dates from Marjansko Brdo, from structures 12, 24, and 35 – eastern half – confirm the dates from Viminacium and date the younger phase of the Early Bronze Age at this site to the period from the beginning of the 20th century to the second half of the 19th century cal BC.

In any case, the first date from Marjansko Brdo can be associated with the older phase of the Early Bronze Age, while the dates from Viminacium, Marjansko Brdo, and Klenak correspond to the younger phase of the Early Bronze Age, which, based on the characteristics of the pottery, also includes the Pančevo site and probably Surčin. However, the other sites, which lack absolute dating, cannot be precisely dated with certainty.

Based on certain stylistic and typological characteristics of the pottery that are not present at Early Bronze Age sites in other regions (e.g., Type 1b and Type 2 beakers, Type 1a and 1b bowls, Type 1a amphorae, triangular handles, etc.), and for the purpose of easier and more practical interpretation, the material culture of the younger phase of the Early Bronze Age in the peri-Pannonian zone, particularly its eastern part, could be defined as the Novačka Ćuprija–Pančevo cultural group (or horizon), named after two culturally and chronologically significant sites in the northern and southern parts of this zone. This would define the final phase of the Early Bronze Age in this zone (mid-21st to mid-19th century cal BC), as will be discussed further.

The earliest sites, referring to Yamnaya culture tumuli in the vicinity of Pančevo, are dated to the first and early second quarter of the 3rd millennium BC, marking the earliest phase of the Bronze Age in this zone.

According to absolute dates and various stylistic and typological traits of the finds (mostly pottery), apart from the youngest third phase, which could be defined as the phase of the Novačka Ćuprija–Pančevo cultural group in the peri-Pannonian zone (mid-21st to mid-19th century cal BC), a slightly older second phase can also be defined. This second phase is characterised by pottery analogous to that of the Vinkovci–Somogyvár group in southern Pannonia which, based on the date from Marjansko Brdo, could be placed in the 25th/24th century cal BC. The oldest, first phase of the Early Bronze Age in the peri-Pannonian zone consists of communities with characteristics of the Yamnaya culture in the first half of the 3rd millennium cal BC.

Finally, we must briefly mention the so-called steppe tumuli documented in the wider Pančevo area, at the Livade site in Pančevo, Rafinerija in Vojlovica, and Tri humke in Jabuka. These tumuli emerged in the first half of the 3rd millennium, during and after the disintegration of Late Eneolithic cultures and before the appearance of the Vinkovci–Somogyvár group. It is possible that these communities contributed, among other things, to the disintegration of indigenous Eneolithic cultures in this region. These tumuli have steppe characteristics, which will be discussed further, and they mark a new epoch in the central Balkans – the end of the Eneolithic cultures and the beginning of the Bronze Age. For this reason, this period is determined as phase 1 of the Early Bronze Age (EBA 1), while the period marked by the dominance of the Vinkovci–Somogyvár group is defined as EBA 2, and that associated with the Novačka Ćuprija–Pančevo group communities is defined as EBA 3.

2.2 The basin of the Great Morava River with Šumadija

This geographical unit, consisting of the basin of the Great Morava River and a large part of Šumadija, encompasses the expansive valley of the Great Morava, stretching from the confluence of the South and West Morava rivers near Stalać to the mouth of the Jasenica River near Veliko Orašje, between the western slopes of the Homolje and Kučaj mountains and Beljanica to the east, and the eastern slopes of Rudnik, Juhor and Crni Vrh, as well as the Grabovac Gorge to the west (see Fig. 1.1). It comprises the Upper Great Morava Basin, the Bagrdan Gorge, and the Lower Great Morava extension.

Šumadija, in a broader sense, includes the areas between the Sava and Danube rivers to the north, the Great Morava to the east, the West Morava to the south, and the courses of the Dičina, Ljig, and Kolubara rivers to the west. The Rudnik Mountain in the central part of Šumadija is rich in copper, lead, zinc, and silver, and according to some research Bukulja contains deposits of cassiterite, the primary ore of tin (Durman 1983; 1997).

The Great Morava is the principal watercourse of the region and, together with the South Morava, forms the largest river in Serbia and one of the longest tributaries of the Danube. Flowing from south to north, its basin is one of the most important natural communication routes on the Balkan Peninsula. Among the tributaries from Šumadija and Great Morava Valley, we can mention, from north to south, the Jasenica, Rača, Lepenica, Osanica, Belica, and Lugomir rivers, while from eastern Serbia, the Resava, Ravanica, Crnica, and other smaller streams flow into it. During rainy seasons these rivers frequently flood, inundating the lowland parts of the valleys and the basin of the Great Morava, a phenomenon that evidently occurred in the past as well, as the lowland areas of the basin were almost uninhabited during the Bronze Age.

Today, Great Morava Valley serves as the primary natural transportation artery of the Balkans, characterised by fertile soil, a favourable climate, dense forests along the edges of the valley, and significant hydrogeographic potential. The situation was not significantly different in the past, so it is entirely understandable that much of this zone was inhabited and traversed by numerous populations in antiquity. The Great Morava Basin has a moderately continental climate, with somewhat harsher conditions in the hilly and mountainous regions, especially in Šumadija. The Great Morava flows through the most fertile area of the central Balkans, alongside the Vardar valley, which formed in the place of a former bay of the Pannonian Sea. As in the basin of the West Morava, Šumadija was known in more recent times for its vast forests (Rodić and Pavlović 1994, 144; Marković and Pavlović 1995, 81–85), which made these forested parts less suitable for settlement in earlier periods.

2.2.1 Settlement and dwelling

In this region with a hilly terrain intersected by the valleys of larger rivers, two hilltop settlements and eight lowland settlements have been recorded. Site numbers refer to Plate 4.

2.2.1.1 Hilltop settlements

21. Lešje, the site of Vrelo (Stojić 1989; Svilar 2007);
22. Ostrikovac, the site of Đula (Svilar 2007).

Hilltop type settlements have been documented at the sites of Đula in Ostrikovac and Vrelo in Lešje. The first is located in a dominant position on a tongue-shaped plateau of Juhor, which overlooks the valley of the Great Morava. The plateau originally covered an area of about 1 ha but it was later largely devastated by a local quarry (Garašanin and Stojić 1986, 192; Stojić 1989, 171).

The Vrelo site is situated on a plateau on the northern slopes of Mount Baba, from which the Grza valley can be surveyed up to its confluence with the Crnica. Both these hilltop settlements were, therefore, established in dominant geo-strategic positions along major natural communication routes.

2.2.1.2 Lowland settlements

23. Crnče, the site of Raskrsnice; 24. Bresje, the site of Imanje Dušana Markovića; 25. Belica, the site of Cerjak; 26. Rekovac, the site of Čičkovica (all Svilar 2007); 27. Majur, the site of Vecina mala (Stojić 1986; Svilar 2007); 28. Lukar, the site of Trnati laz (Svilar 2007); 29. Poljna, the site of Blagotin (Nikolić and Kapuran 2001); 30. Drenovac, the site of Slatina (Svilar 2007).

There is a significantly larger number of lowland settlements, most of which are located outside today's main natural communication routes of the Great and West Morava valleys. They are found in the hilly region of Levač (Rekovac, Lukar), at the foot of the eastern slopes of Crni Vrh (Crnče, Belica), and at the eastern foot of the Gledić Mountains (Poljna). Three sites are located on the periphery of the Great Morava valley, mainly on higher ground in smaller tributary valleys of the Great Morava (Majur, Bresje, Drenovac). Based on this topography, i.e., the avoidance of the valley floors of the Velika and West Morava rivers, it can be assumed that one of the main reasons for this was the significantly more intense hydrography than today. This area was marshy, as confirmed by topographic maps from over half a century ago, which illustrate the marshy nature of this zone even at that time (Map 531_2_4). The ratio of hilltop to lowland settlements in this geographical zone is 20:80.

Unfortunately, there is very little data on housing and residential or other settlement architecture, as most of these sites are known primarily from reconnaissance surveys and no archaeological excavations have been carried out at the majority of them.

At the Đula site in Ostrikovac, part of an Early Bronze Age pit dwelling with a rectangular plan and rounded corners was recorded. It was later repurposed as a refuse pit (Stojić 1989, 171). One absolute date (25th–24th century cal BC) originates from this structure, confirming its chronological placement in the Early Bronze Age, as previously established by the finds. A total of five pits from the Early Bronze Age and five from the Copper Age have been identified at the site. According to the author, the material from pits 1 and 2 mostly belongs to the Vinkovci–Somogyvár group, with sporadic finds of pottery with elements of the Vatin culture, while pits 3–5 contain exclusively Vinkovci–Somogyvár group pottery, i.e., Early Bronze Age pottery (Stojić 1989, 182). Besides pottery, the pits also contained clay, ash, animal bones, and, in pit 5, a portion of a human skull.

A similar situation was recorded at the Vecina mala site in Majur, where five pits were also discovered, three (1–3) of which belonged to the Early Bronze Age (Stojić 1986, 145–149). In these pits were found pottery – often entire vessels, mainly beakers – along with clay, soot, ash, animal bones, broken stones, river shells, and other materials. The author suggests that pit 1, which was covered with a large number of bivalve shells, had a ritual function, while the character of the other pits is not mentioned (Stojić 1986, 145).

A similar pit, with a diameter of about 2 m and a depth of about 0.7 m, identified as a refuse pit, was recorded at Blagotin, dug into the Eneolithic layer (Nikolić and Kapuran 2001).

Apart from these pits and the remains of a single pit dwelling, no other enclosed structures have been discovered at Early Bronze Age sites in the Great Morava Valley and Šumadija. The portable finds from other sites mostly come from reconnaissance surveys or are chance finds, meaning that we have virtually no data on residential architecture and settlement characteristics.

2.2.2. *Necropolises and burial practices*

No necropolises or solitary graves from the Early Bronze Age have been documented in this region. In one of the pits at Vecina mala in Majur, a portion of a human skullcap was found but this is more likely to be interpreted as part of a ritual rather than a burial practice.

Based on burial rituals in neighbouring regions, such as western Serbia and the South Morava valley, it can only be assumed that the deceased in this region were buried through inhumation.

2.2.3 *Portable finds*

The majority of the portable finds from this region in the Early Bronze Age consist of pottery. However, several copper axes have been recorded, mostly as chance finds, as well as a number of weights, ceramic spindle whorls, flint tools, and tools made from deer antler.

2.2.3.1 Pottery

The stylistic and typological characteristics of pottery from this region seem to be even more uniform than in the previous zone. The types of vessels represented include bowls, cups, beakers, amphorae, elongated narrow cylindrical (flask-like) vessels, and pots.

A. BOWLS

Semi-circular bowls with a flared rim (S-shaped profile) with wide arching handles or without them (type 1a), sometimes with sharper transitions at the belly and shoulder, have been recorded at one site (Fig. 2.19/1, 2, 4), as well as bowls of type 1b (biconical bowls with a flared rim, S-shaped profile: Fig. 2.17/12).

Only one bowl belongs to type 2a (globular or biconical deeper bowls with a short funnel-shaped or cylindrical neck) (Fig. 2.16/8), while type 3a is the most common and has been recorded at several sites (Fig. 2.16/9, 10; Fig. 2.18/8; Fig. 2.19/3).

The bowls are mostly unornamented, sometimes with wide arching handles and plastic triangular extensions on the rim (Fig. 2.16/10; Fig. 2.17/12) or horned handles on the belly (Fig. 2.18/8), and they are mostly black or brown, with fine to medium fabric and polished surfaces. A type 3a specimen from Ostrikovac is ochre in colour Fig. 2.16/9).

B CUPS

Cups have not been recorded at early Bronze Age sites in this geographical zone.

C. BEAKERS

Type 1a beakers have not been recorded in this zone, while type 1b beakers have been documented at Majur (Fig. 2.18/2, 3), and several beakers can be classified as a variant of this type with slightly shorter handles (Fig. 2.18/1, 4–7). Type 1c beakers have been found in larger numbers at Majur, with two specimens from Blagotin (Fig. 2.17/15–21; Fig. 2.19/8, 9).

Two beakers of type 2a have been recorded in this zone (Fig. 2.17/8; Fig. 2.19/5), along with several of type 3a (Fig. 2.17/3, 10, 22). One specimen has a T-shaped profiled rim, likely a survival from the previous period, the late Eneolithic (Fig. 2.17/10). Type 4a beakers have not been documented in this zone, while a type 5a beaker (funnel-shaped with two handles that do not extend beyond the rim) appears for the first time in this zone (Fig. 2.19/6).

The last type of beaker, not recorded in the previous two zones, is the gently S-shaped profile beaker, with narrow and tall proportions, and tongue-shaped or rectangular handles on the belly (type 6a) (Fig. 2.19/7).

A certain number of beakers could not be precisely typologically defined based on the illustrations and the author's description, although it seems that most belong to types 1c and 2a. In any case, these specimens will not be included in the typological statistics.

Most of the beakers are undecorated, with the exception of one type 1c specimen, which is ornamented with a plastic circular thickening with a depressed centre on the belly (Fig. 2.17/17), and another type 1c specimen decorated with a plastic nodular thickening on the belly (Fig. 2.19/8).

Beakers were made in various fabric qualities and colours, which did not depend on the type of beaker but rather on the site from which they originate. For instance, beakers from Blagotin, Bresje, Lešje, Lukar, and Majur were made with fine to medium fabric, thinner walls, and shades of grey, black, or ochre, while those from Belica, Rekovac, and Crnče were made with coarse fabric, containing small stone and sand inclusions, and appeared in shades of grey, ochre, and brown. Interestingly, Belica, Rekovac, and Crnče are located in the same micro-region, at the foot of the eastern slopes of Crni Vrh.

D. AMPHORAE

Amphorae of types 1a, 2a, and 3a have also been documented in this zone, although they are sparsely represented. A type 1a amphora, with a tunnel handle on the belly, was found in Ostrikovac (Fig. 2.16/7), while type 2a (Fig. 2.19/10, 11) and type 3a (Fig. 2.19/13) amphorae were recorded in Blagotin. No ornaments have been found on amphorae in this region.

E. ELONGATED (FLASK-LIKE) VESSELS

Only one narrow, elongated cylindrical vessel has been documented, known as a *Zylinderflasche* (cylinder flask). This form originates from the Vučedol culture and also appears in the Vinkovci–Somogyvár group (Dimitrijević 1977; Tasić 1984a). This vessel was found in Ostrikovac in a datable closed context. It is tall and narrow, with a cylindrical profile and two small tunnel handles below the rim (Fig. 2.16/11).

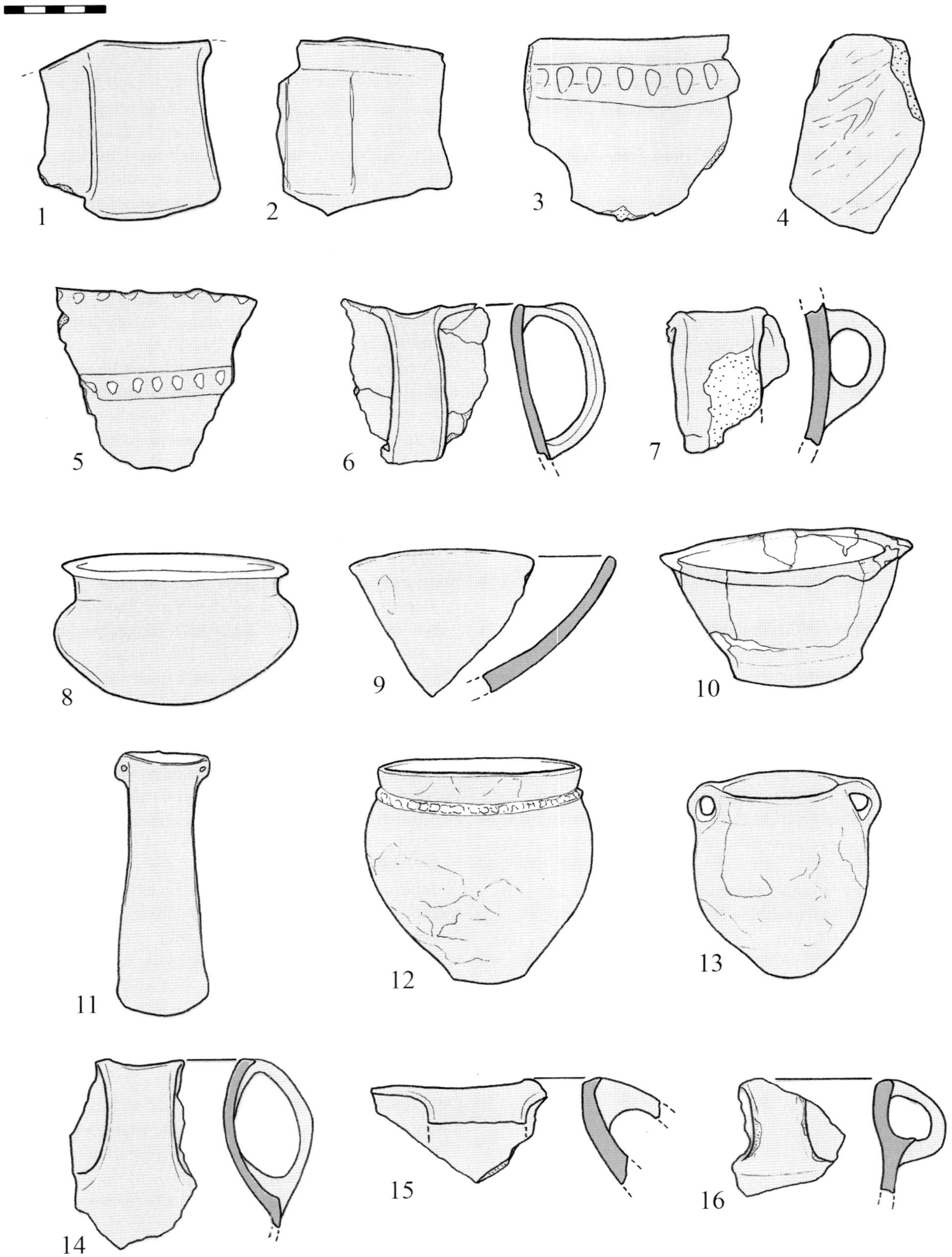

Figure 2.16. 1–5, Lešje: site of Vrelo; 6–13, Ostrikovac: site of Đula: 9, 13, pit 1; 8, 11–12, pit 3, 10 pit 5; 14–15, Crnče: site of Raskrsnice; 16, Belica: site of Cerjak.

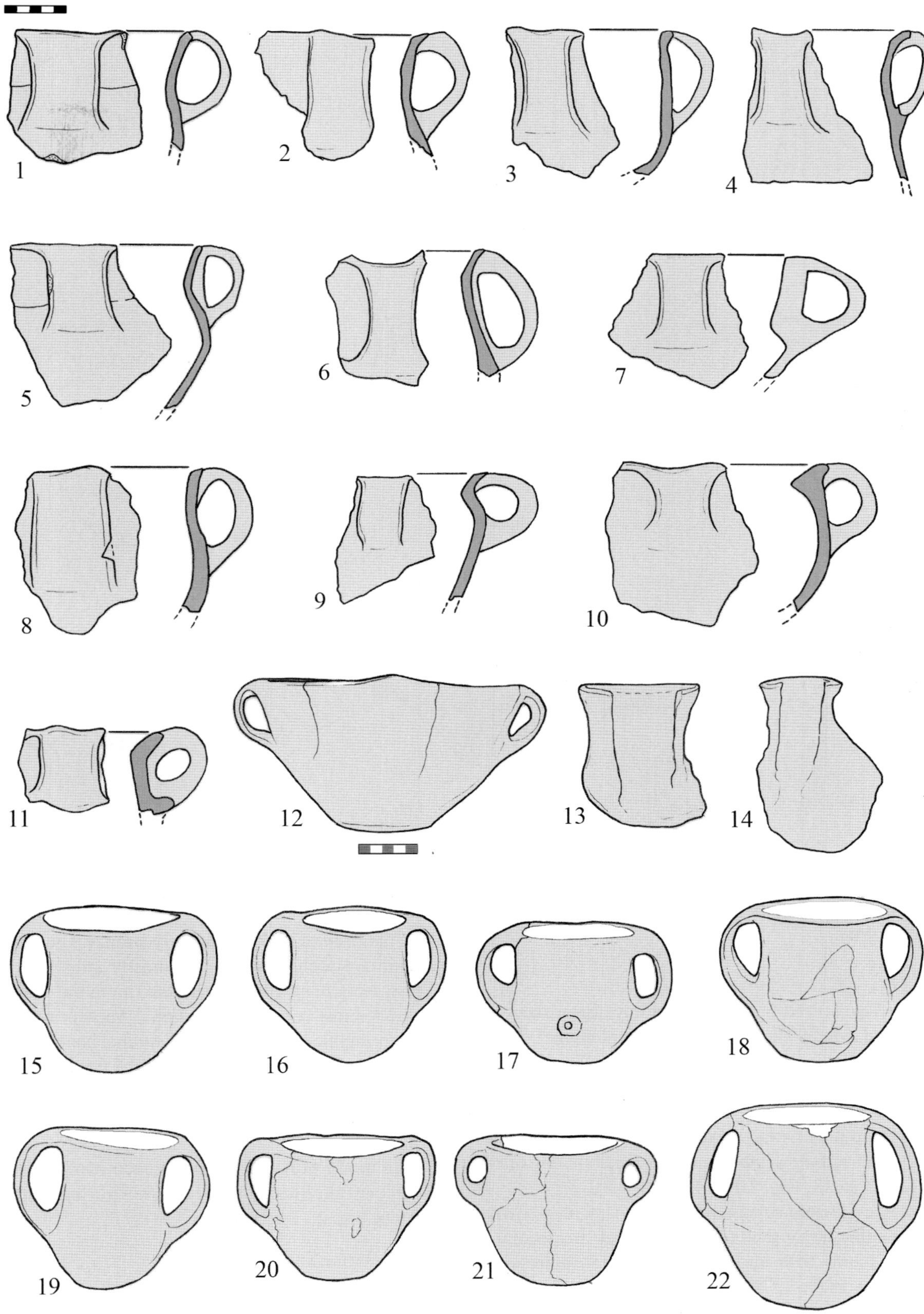

Figure 2.17. 1–5, Bresje: site of Okućnica Dušana Markovića; 6–7, Lukar: site of Trnati Laz; 8–11, Rekovac: site of Čičkovica; 12, Drenovac: site of Slatina; 13–22, Majur: site of Vecina Mala: 13–14, pit 1, 15–22, pit 2.

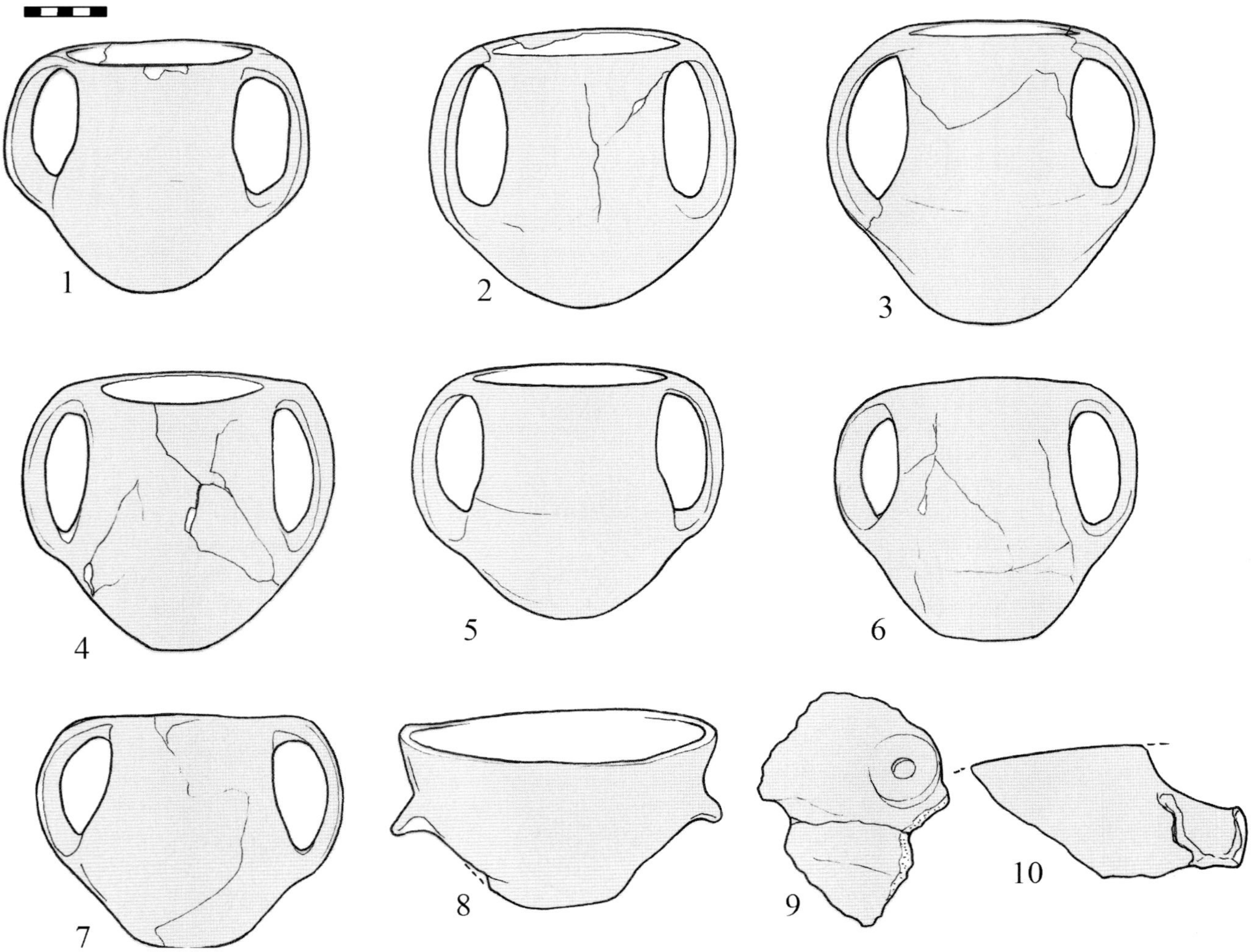

Figure 2.18. Majur: site of Vecina Mala.

It is made of medium quality fabric, with a polished surface and black colour.

F. POTS

Several well-preserved pot specimens have been recorded in this region which allowed for their typological classification. Type 1a includes ovoid, almost spherical, wide pots with a broad opening, often decorated with a plastic band with impressions (Fig. 2.16/12). Type 2a consists of narrower ovoid pots with a narrowing opening, sometimes featuring handles below the rim or on the shoulder of the vessel (Fig. 2.16/13; Fig. 2.19/14, 15).

The pots are mostly of larger dimensions, with a coarser fabric containing larger sand or pebbles. They are decorated with plastic bands with impressions or direct impressions on the fresh surface of the vessel, often along the rim (Fig. 2.19/14, 15).

No cooking pots (*piraunoi*) have been documented.

G. HANDLES

The majority of handles on Early Bronze Age vessels in this region are arched, wide, and mostly strap-like or oval in cross-section, extending from the rim to the shoulder of the vessels, most commonly beakers.[9] Another type of handle, though smaller in number, is the tunnel handle, mostly wide and short or miniature, as seen on the flask-like vessel (Fig. 2.16/7, 11), followed by tongue-shaped (Fig. 2.18/8; Fig. 2.19/3, 8) and rectangular, vertically perforated handles (Fig. 2.19/7).

As in the previous region, arched handles with convex (concave) profiles also appear, though they are rare (Fig. 2.16/6, Fig. 2.17/6, 10).

H. ORNAMENTATION

Pottery from this region is almost entirely devoid of ornamentation. The most common decorative techniques are the application of plastic bands and ribs that form various

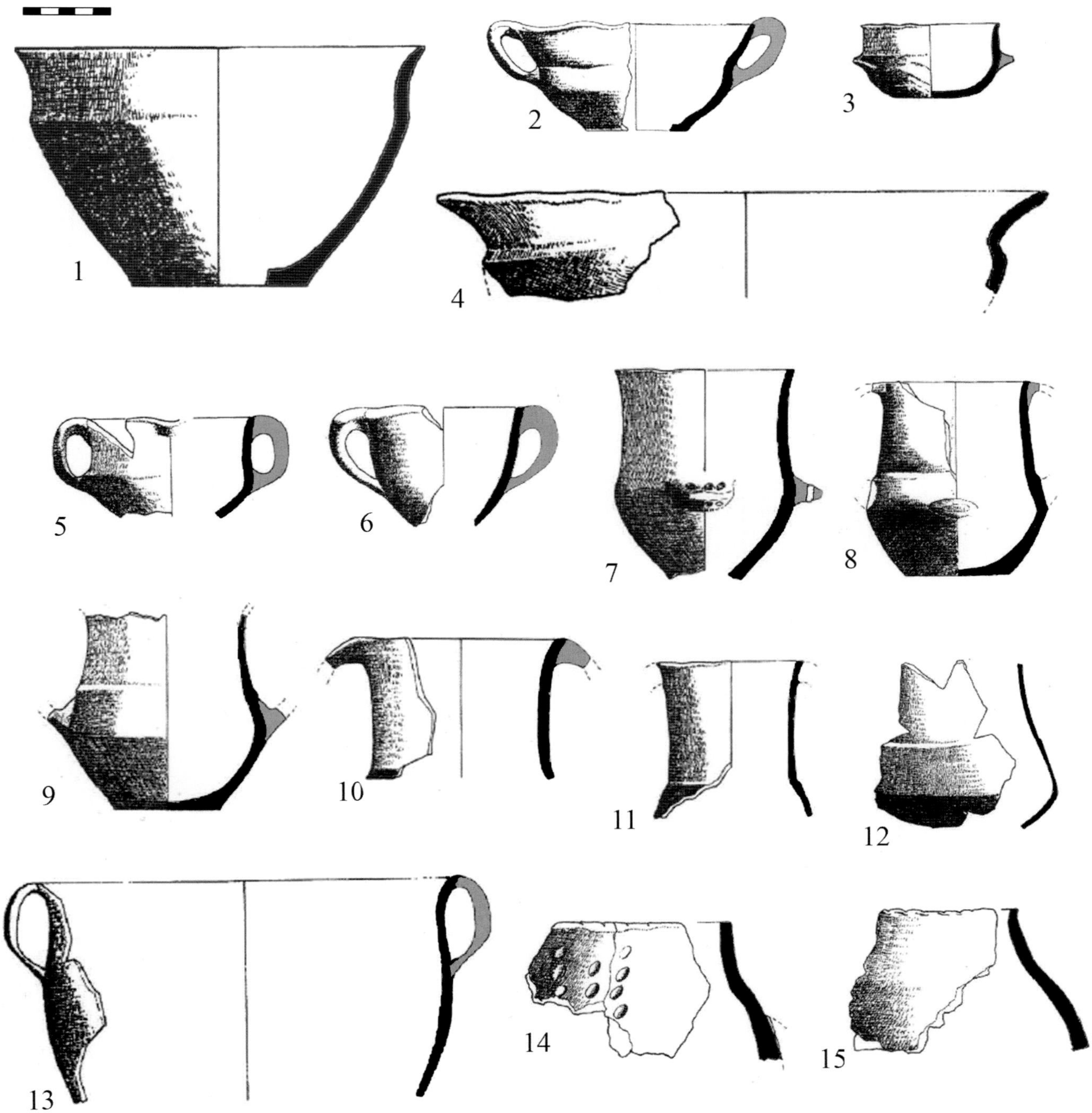

Figure 2.19. Poljna: site of Blagotin.

shapes (Fig. 2.16/3, 5; Fig. 2.18/9, 10) and the imprinting of rows of finger impressions directly onto the fresh surface of the vessel (Fig. 2.19/14, 15).

The bands, often with finger impressions, are applied primarily below the rim of the vessel, while ribs that form different shapes are mainly evident on the belly of the vessel.

Pit-like impressions are found on the rim, neck, shoulder, or belly of the vessel.

2.2.3.2 Other finds

A number of copper socketed axes have been recorded, mostly as Chance finds, along with a number of pyramid-shaped or conical weights with rounded corners (Majur and Ostrikovac), ceramic spindle whorls (Majur and Ostrikovac), flint tools (Ostrikovac), bone tools (Majur), and a tool made from deer antler (Ostrikovac).

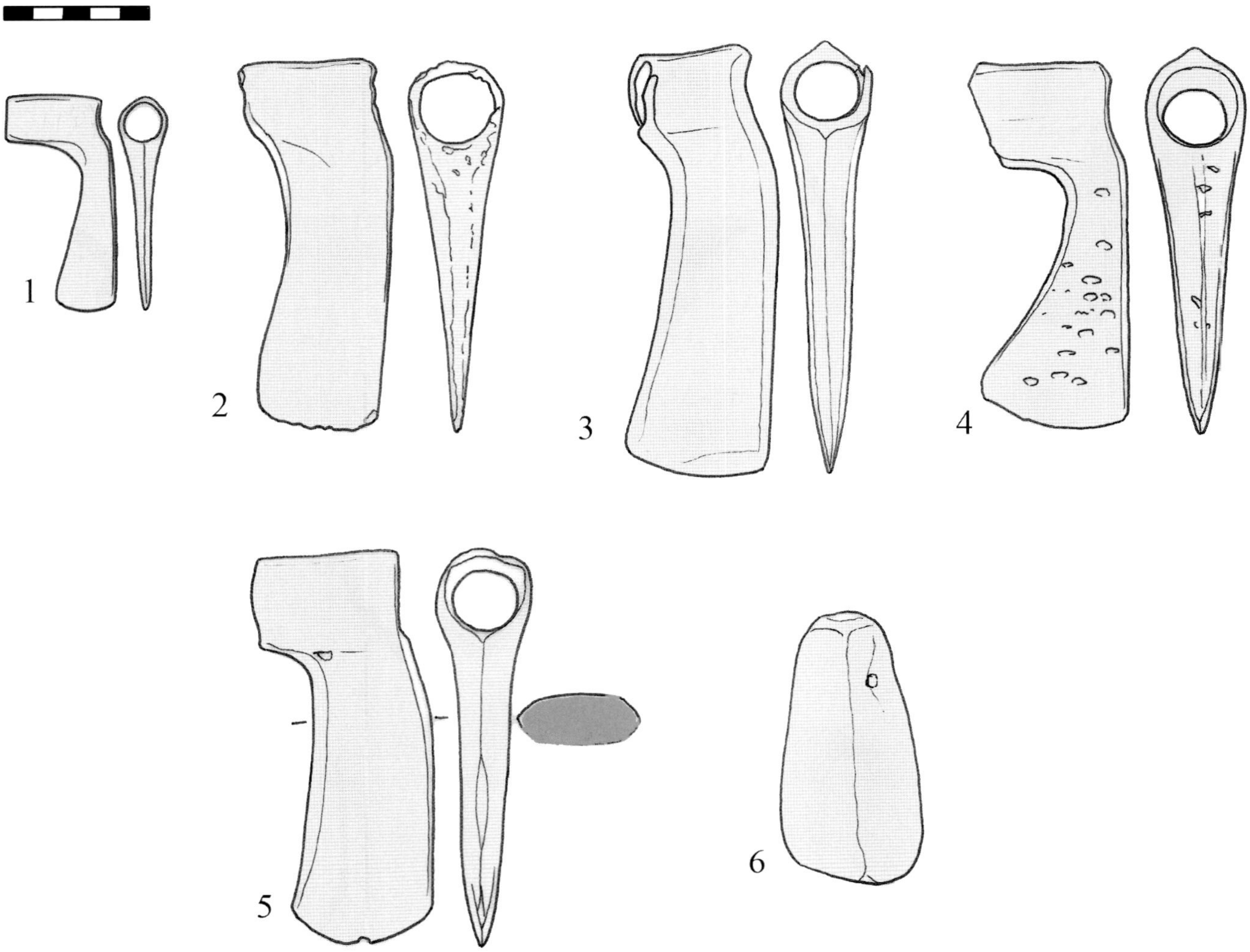

Figure 2.20. 1, Staro Selo, unknown site; 2, Vojska, unknown site; 3, Rekovac, unknown site (Čičkovica?); 4, Zakuta, unknown site; 5, Jasika, unknown site; 6, Majur: site of Vecina Mala, pit 2.

LIST OF SITES WITH CHANCE FINDS

31. Rekovac near Jagodina, Kozarac-type axe; 32. Jasika near Kruševac, Kozarac-type axe; 33. Staro Selo near Velika Plana, Kozarac-type axe; 34. Zakuta near Knić, Kozarac-type axe; 35. Vojska near Svilajnac, Lozane-type axe (all Antonović 2014).

The copper axes, mostly of the Kozarac type (Rekovac, Jasika, Staro Selo, and Zakuta) and one of the Lozane type (Vojska) (Fig. 2.20), are noteworthy. Three Kozarac-type axes are classified, according to Antonović, into a special variant named after the axe from Jasika (Staro Selo, Rekovac, and Jasika; Fig. 2.20/1, 3, 5), while the axe from Zakuta (Fig. 2.20/4) is classified into the Baranda variant (Antonović 2014).

Interestingly, the axe from Staro Selo (Fig. 2.20/1) contains 1.8% tin (Antonović 2014, 114, table 5), making it one of the earliest examples of tin bronze objects from the Early Bronze Age in the central Balkans, though in this case, it was likely an unintentional bronze (Kienlin 2010, 130).[10] The axe from Rekovac is made of copper, and the specimen from Jasika contains nearly 1% arsenic in addition to copper, while the axes from Zakuta (Fig. 2.20/4) and Vojska (Fig. 2.20/2) have not been analysed.

These sites where axes have been found are located in larger river valleys, specifically on the edges of the Great and West Morava valleys, but also in the interior beyond these valleys, on the eastern and western slopes of the Gledić Mountains, such as Rekovac and Zakuta.

2.2.4 Cultural and chronological classification of the Early Bronze Age in the Great Morava Basin and Šumadija

Only two absolute dates have been obtained from this zone, which complicates a more precise chronological definition of the communities that inhabited it. However, they are sufficient, along with the stylistic and typological characteristics of the pottery, to distinguish two distinct phases of the Early Bronze Age. The most dominant vessel type in this zone is the beaker with two handles level with the vessel's rim (type 1c), which is also the most recognisable element of the material culture of Early Bronze Age communities in this territory. It is found at almost all sites, except for Drenovac, where only one bowl from the Early Bronze Age has been recorded. These beakers are characteristic of a broader Balkan area and their distribution will be discussed in subsequent chapters. This type of beaker is particularly prevalent in the Bubanj-Hum III group of the Central Balkans, defined several decades ago by M. Garašanin (1958, 60).

Nonetheless, the stylistic and typological features of the pottery in the Great Morava Valley and part of Šumadija also display elements that can be associated with southern Pannonia, specifically the Vinkovci–Somogyvár group, such as the flask-like vessel from Ostrikovac (Fig. 2.16/11; Tasić 1984a, Taf. II/3, 4, 9, Taf. IV/15; Kulscar 2009, fig. 53). However, despite the clear Bubanj-Hum III characteristics, this pottery also shares similarities with the pottery from the adjacent peri-Pannonian zone, especially finds from Blagotin and the bowl from Drenovac. For instance, the type 1b bowl from Drenovac, with its form and plastic extensions on the rim, is very similar to a bowl from the site Nad klepečkom (Fig. 2.7/11). These extensions, in addition to the two-handled beakers, are a common element of Early Bronze Age pottery in nearly all regions of the central Balkans.

It has also been observed that type 1a bowls, which are common in the peri-Pannonian zone, are scarcely represented in this geographical zone and have only been found at the Blagotin site. These bowls are very rare in other geographical zones of the central Balkans. Ornamentation in the form of plastic circular appliqués on type 1c beakers has been noted not only in this zone (Fig. 2.17/17) but also on a vessel in the peri-Pannonian zone (Nad klepečkom; Fig. 2.8/10) and on an identical beaker in the Pčinja Basin (Kokino; see Fig. 2.38/9).

One of the two absolute dates from this zone is from pit 3 at the Đula site in Ostrikovac, where pottery with characteristics of the Vinkovci–Somogyvár group was dated to 2411–2342 cal BC (61.4% probability range), or 2470–2290 cal BC (2σ probability range), corresponding, broadly, to the second quarter of the 25th–early 23rd century cal BC or,more narrowly, from the late 25th–mid-24th century cal BC (see Table 1). This timeframe coincides with the earliest date for the Bubanj-Hum III group, but also with dates for the Belotić-Bela Crkva group of the Early Bronze Age in western Serbia. The second date comes from a pit in Majur at the Vecina mala site, where numerous type 1c beakers were found, and it is considerably later than the date from Ostrikovac. Specifically, this date places the pit approximately between the mid-23rd and mid-22nd century cal BC (70% probability), justifying the assumption that these finds are younger than those of the Vinkovci–Somogyvár group in this zone. Previously, this assumption was based primarily on analogies with finds from dated sites in other zones, particularly South Morava Basin. Thus, Vecina mala chronologically aligns with Bubanj-Hum III group sites in South Morava Basin, as indicated by the finds, especially the type 1c beakers, although some stylistic and typological features of the pottery also correspond with the Novačka Ćuprija–Pančevo group from the north. However, the chronological relationship between the Đula and Vecina mala sites and Blagotin remains unclear. Based on analogies, particularly with finds from the peri-Pannonian zone (Nad Klepečkom, Rit, Novačka Ćuprija), Blagotin could also be classified into the later phase of the Early Bronze Age, specifically the last quarter of the 3rd millennium BC.

Thus, with the available data, we can define two phases of the Early Bronze Age in this zone: an earlier phase with finds from the Vinkovci–Somogyvár group, which chronologically corresponds to the second phase in the peri-Pannonian zone, and a later phase, with finds typologically corresponding to the Bubanj-Hum III and Novačka Ćuprija–Pančevo groups, which is parallel to the third phase in the peri-Pannonian zone.

Considering the cultural-chronological relationship of the pottery from sites in the peri-Pannonian zone and Great Morava Valley, it appears that the Novačka ćuprija–Pančevo group emerged in Great Morava Valley precisely at the end of or in the final quarter of the 3rd millennium BC, as a symbiosis of the Bubanj-Hum III group and the late Vinkovci–Somogyvár group.

Although absolute dates are lacking, the tumuli at Bare and Rogojevac, based on the analogy of finds and the architecture of the graves and tumuli, most likely belong to the first half of the 3rd millennium BC and are chronologically parallel with the tumuli in the peri-Pannonian zone and western Serbia. Therefore, they could be defined as phase 1, or the earliest phase of the Early Bronze Age in the Great Morava Valley and Šumadija zone.

2.3 Western Serbia with Lim Valley

This geographical zone encompasses the regions of Jadar, Azbukovica, and Rađevina, along with the basin of the West Morava, the region of Podrinje, and a part of Lim Valley (the middle course of the Lim River) (see Fig. 1.1; Pl. 4). To the north, the zone is bordered by the Sava River, to the west by the Drina River, to the south by Zlatar, Čemerno, and Kotlenik, and to the east it borders Šumadija at Mount Rudnik.

The Jadar Region consists of a valley with a central part flattened by the valleys of the Jadar and Korenita rivers, while the rest of the valley is gently undulating. Its open terrain towards the Drina has resulted in a somewhat wetter climate than other geographical zones with more precipitation throughout the year, contributing to abundant vegetation. It is also rich in thermal mineral waters, as well as rare metallic and non-metallic ores, the most important of which are tin (cassiterite found in streams on the southern slopes of Cer) (Huska *et al.* 2014; Bulatović *et al.* 2017, 19–30) and copper (Srebrne rupe on Cer, Vragočanica), both essential for bronze production (Durman 1983; compare with: Vasiljević 1967, 133). Jadar has a moderately continental climate, with hot summers, cold winters, and clearly defined seasonal transitions (Rakičević 1997).

Azbukovica is a predominantly limestone mountain region with a rugged relief, situated between the Drina, Jagodnja, Sokol, and Povlen mountains, and is rich in lead and zinc. Rađevina is a region located between the Jadar and Obnica rivers, Medvednik, the Sokol mountains, Jagodnja, and Boranja. Surrounded by high mountains, this region is characterised by a mild, moderately continental micro-climate (Rakičević 1997). Due to its complex geological structure, it is exceptionally rich in metals such as copper, tin, mercury, lead, and zinc, some of which have been exploited since ancient times (Durman 1983; Bulatović *et al.* 2017, 29).

To the east of this zone is Rudnik, rich in malachite ore, which was exploited during the Early Bronze Age, as evidenced by research at the Prljuša site in Mali Šturac.

The West Morava Valley Region consists of the basin of the West Morava and its main tributaries: the Moravica, Skrapež, Đetinja, and Rasina rivers, as well as the Gruža, whose basin partially belongs to both Šumadija and Ibar which, along with Kopaonik, forms a distinct sub-region.

The basin of the West Morava is geologically complex, consisting of one major feature, the Ovčar–Kablar Gorge, and four basins: Požega, Čačak–Kraljevo, Vrnjačka, and Kruševac. In this book, the region of western Serbia includes only the western course of the West Morava, i.e., the Požega, Čačak–Kraljevo, and Vrnjačka basins, while the Kruševac Basin is discussed within the context of the Great Morava Valley Region with Šumadija.

The climate of the West Morava Basin is largely influenced by its position and, primarily, by the terrain, resulting in a moderately continental climate. West Morava Valley is rich in ores and thermal mineral springs, and in the past, the entire territory of the West Morava Valley was covered with dense forests (Marković and Pavlović 1995, 53–57).

The Drina Basin is a rather inaccessible area, bordered by the high mountains of Tara, Povlen, and Jagodnja to the east, and by Devetka, Javor, Javornik, and Majevica to the west. This relatively impassable area was almost uninhabited during prehistory.

Lim Valley is formed by the Lim River, which originates from Lake Plav in Montenegro, along with its tributaries. It can be divided into Upper, Middle, and Lower Lim Valley. The area covered by this study is the Lower Lim Valley, between the Jadovnik mountains to the east and Jabuka and Pobijenik to the west. This region is quite inaccessible, characterised by a narrow valley with a slight widening in the area near the confluence of the Mileševka River with the Lim, and steep slopes of the Jadovnik and Pobijenik mountains. Despite its difficult terrain, several Bronze Age sites have been recorded in this area. The region is rich in copper and it is possible that it was exploited in the past (Durman 1983).

2.3.1 Settlement and dwelling

It is interesting to note that in this region, which is exceptionally favourable for habitation due to its abundant hydrography, fertile pastures, forests, mineral wealth, and other natural resources, only one Early Bronze Age settlement has been recorded so far, despite the discovery and excavation of several necropolises with graves from this period. The settlement is located on one of the elevations of Mount Jelica, in the vicinity of the village of Grab, from which part of the West Morava Valley can be surveyed. This site comprises the remains of a large Byzantine city from the 6th century AD and, during excavations that have lasted several decades, portable finds from the Early Bronze Age have also been uncovered, leading to the assumption that these are the remains of a hilltop settlement from this period (Milinković 2002; Bulatović 2009).

The absence of settlements in this zone is most likely due to insufficient exploration of the region, as research has primarily focused on the more easily noticeable burial mounds and necropolises which tend to yield more impressive results. This suggests that, rather than a true absence of settlements, there has been a research bias toward exploring necropolises rather than settlements.

For this reason, defining the material and spiritual culture of the Early Bronze Age in this zone is largely only possible through the interpretation of finds and other data obtained from necropolis excavations.

Regarding types of dwellings, it is noteworthy that in Kovačevića (or Cerovačka) Cave in Rađevina, near Krupanj, finds from almost all periods of the Metal Age have been recorded, including artefacts typologically belonging to the Early Bronze Age (Fig. 2.23/14). This indicates the possibility that caves were also used as dwellings during this period.

2.3.2 Necropolises and burial practices

In the zone of Western Serbia with Lim Valley, 24 Early Bronze Age necropolises have been discovered, with the deceased mostly buried under tumuli and in only one case in a flat necropolis (Stapari) (Zotović 1985, 34). Both cremation and inhumation are present, with cremation slightly more prevalent. A combined ritual has also been recorded in one tumulus (Jarmovac), where both cremation and inhumation were practiced (Derikonjić 2010, 19). Site numbers refer to Plate 4.

List of necropolises

38. Belotić, the site of Šumar, Rađevina, tumuli, cremation (Garašanin and Garašanin 1958; 1962; Garašanin 1973; Filipović 2008); 39. Bela Crkva, the site of Cerik-Bandera, Rađevina, tumuli, inhumation, crouched deceased (Garašanin and Garašanin 1958; 1962; Garašanin 1973; Filipović 2008); 40. Tolisavac, unknown site, Rađevina, tumulus, inhumation, crouched deceased (Filipović 2008, 42); 41. Ražana, the site of Anište, tumuli, cremation (Garašanin 1967; Zotović 1985; Dmitrović 2015); 42. Jančići, the site of Veliko polje, tumuli, inhumation, crouched deceased (Nikitović 1996; Dmitrović 2016); 43. Jančići, the site of Dubac, tumuli, inhumation, crouched deceased (Dmitrović 2013; 2016); 44. Prijevor, the site of Ade, tumulus, cremation (Stojić and Nikitović 1996; Nikitović 2000; Dmitrović 2016); 45. Stapari, the site of Mala Gradina, flat necropolis, cremation (Zotović 1985, 34; Dmitrović 2015); 46. Vranjani, the site of Veliki Lug, tumulus, cremation (Zotović 1985; Dmitrović 2015); 47. Lučani, the site of Kruševlje, tumulus, cremation (Ikodinović 1969; Dmitrović 2016); 48. Guča, the site of Rajića brdo, tumulus, inhumation (Dmitrović 2003; 2016); 49. Lučani, the site of Suva Česma, tumulus, cremation (Dmitrović 2005; 2016); 50. Dučalovići, the site of Ruja, tumuli, inhumation, crouched deceased (Dmitrović 2002; 2016); 51. Mrčajevci, the site of Gušavac, tumulus, destroyed contexts (Ikodinović 1985; Dmitrović 2016); 52. Markovica, the site of Negrišori, tumulus, inhumation, crouched deceased (Dmitrović 2016); 53. Pilatovići, the site of Ravni Lug, tumulus, cremation (Zotović 1985, 32–33; Dmitrović 2015); 54. Krstac, the site of Ivkovo Brdo, tumulus, cremation (Nikitović 2003; Dmitrović 2016); 55. Donja Kravarica, the site of Babinjak, tumulus, cremation (Dmitrović 2004; 2016); 56. Turica, the site of Ošljevac, tumulus, no remains found (Nikitović 1994; Dmitrović 2016); 57. Višesava near Bajina Bašta, tumulus, cremation (Zotović 1985); 58. Priboj, the site of FAP, tumulus, inhumation (Garašanin 1973; Zotović 1985, 31; Derikonjić 2010); 59. Drežnik, the site of Do, tumulus, cremation (Dmitrović 2015); 61. Jarmovac, the site of Kaluđersko Polje, tumuli, combined burial rites (inhumation and cremation) (Derikonjić 2010, 19); 61. Mramorak, the site of Goleško Brdo, tumulus (Derikonjić 2010, 7).

Tumuli typically have diameters between 10 m and 20 m and heights of about 1–2 m. Exceptions include the tumuli at the Bandera–Cerik site in Bela Crkva (Tumulus 1), Gušavac in Mrčajevci, and Anište in Ražana, which have diameters exceeding 20 m (Garašanin 1973, 256; Dmitrović 2015). The tumuli are generally constructed of earth with stone being used as a construction material for the tumulus mound in mountainous areas (Dubac, Ražana). At Jarmovac, tumuli made from earth and river cobbles have been recorded (Derikonjić 2010, 19). Stone was used not only for the mound itself but also for forming a ring or mantle, as seen at the sites of Belotić-Šumar, Bela Crkva–Bandera, Ruja, Veliko polje, Ade, Do, Grotnica, Dubac, Markovica, Suva česma, and others. Stone was also used to create so-called stone cores in the centre of tumuli, as at Belotić–Šumar (Tumulus 15), Dubac, and Anište. In some tumuli, stone cists have been found, mostly containing inhumed individuals (Veliko polje, Ruja, Negrišori), while others were empty, without any remains (Ruja and Turica). At Tolisavac, in the north-western part of this zone, a tumulus was excavated containing a contracted burial placed on a 'stone bed', meaning a surface covered with stone (Filipović 2008).

Regarding the remains of cremated individuals, they were typically covered with stone constructions (Krstac, Ruja, Ražana) or placed in urns on stone platforms (Kruševlje). In some cases, a stone construction was built around the cremated remains (Grotnica, Suva česma). At Stapari, Ražana, and Vranjani, urns were enclosed by stones, and the openings of the urns were also covered with stone. In grave 6 (the central grave) in Tumulus 1 at Dubac in Jančići, a contracted burial (a man *c.* 60 years old) was found on his right side, oriented north-west to south-east, with a stone ring around the body. Traces of ochre were observed on the skull and cervical vertebrae (Nikitović 1999, 10). The grave contained no offerings and was dated to the 26th–25th centuries cal BC (Dmitrović and Molloy 2021). Another dated context from this site is grave 4 in Tumulus 2, which also contained a contracted burial of a man aged 30–35 years, similarly oriented (Nikitović 1999, 15), without grave goods, and dated to the 22nd–21st centuries cal BC (Dmitrović and Molloy 2021).

It is important to note that many of these tumuli were re-used during the Late Bronze Age, highlighting the continuity of burial practices under these monuments. Interestingly, no Middle Bronze Age burials under tumuli have been recorded, which would definitively indicate continuity of tumulus burial practices in this zone. A similar situation has been observed at the ritual site of Dve mogili in Pelince, northern Macedonia.

In the tumuli of Rađevina, the funeral pyre was placed within the tumulus and the remains of the deceased individual were left on the pyre, which was then covered with earth to form the mound (Garašanin 1973, 259). The only flat necropolis recorded is at Mala Gradina in Stapari. In the southern part of this larger necropolis, which contained graves from the Early Iron Age and the Middle Ages, several poorly preserved Early Bronze Age graves were excavated (Zotović 1985, 34). The cremated remains were placed in urns or directly on the ground with occasional offerings in the form of ceramic vessels.

In any case, throughout the territory of western Serbia, from Rađevina and Jadar in the north, across the upper West Morava Basin to Lim Valley, burial rituals and practices were very similar, with only slight regional differences regardless of the distinct geographical regions within this zone.

Grave goods in tumuli mostly consist of vessels, typically beakers with one or two handles (Bela Crkva, Ade, Kruševlje, Suva česma, Ruja, Negrišori, Pilatovići, Priboj, Vranjani, Jarmovac). However, a copper/bronze dagger was found in Tumulus 10 at Belotić (Fig. 2.24/4), and flint arrowheads or stone hammers were discovered in the tumuli at Ivkovo Brdo and Suva česma (Fig. 2.24/5, 6).

The dating of the tumuli based on calibrated AMS dates ranges from the 28th to the 20th centuries cal BC. The oldest date, from the tumulus at Veliko Polje, likely belongs to a culture with steppe traditions, although identical globular vessels, like the one from this tumulus (Fig. 2.22/5), have also been found in tumuli believed to belong to the Early Bronze Age (Mrčajevci, Belotić: Fig. 2.21/16, Fig. 2.23/1). The oldest date in this zone that unequivocally belongs to the Early Bronze Age is from the central grave of Tumulus 12 at Ruja in Dučalovići, dating to the 25th–24th centuries cal BC (Table 1). This date could be considered as a reference point for the beginning of the Early Bronze Age in this geographical zone. The available absolute dates from this zone have eliminated doubts about whether the phenomena of cremation and inhumation can be chronologically separated, as both rituals appear simultaneously, sometimes even within the same tumulus. It is worth noting that all absolute dates currently come from the upper West Morava Basin, while dates from Rađevina and Lim Valley are still lacking.

2.3.3 Portable finds

The portable finds from this zone consist mostly of ceramic vessels but also include several copper and stone objects.

2.3.3.1 Pottery

In this central Balkan geographical zone, the recorded ceramic vessels include bowls, cups, beakers, jugs, amphorae, and pots.

A. BOWLS

Semi-circular bowls with an everted rim (S-shaped profile) and wide arched handles or without handles, sometimes with sharper transitions at the belly and shoulder (type 1a), have not been documented in this zone. Biconical bowls with a everted rim (sharper or more subtle S-shaped profile – type 1b) have been discovered at Belotić, Anište, and Prljuša (Fig. 2.21/13; Fig. 2.22/1, 2; Fig. 2.23/19).

Globular or biconical deeper bowls with a short funnel-shaped or cylindrical neck (type 2a) have been recorded in one example (Fig. 2.21/4), while several globular vessels with narrow openings, without a pronounced rim, and mostly richly decorated with incised ornaments (Belotić, Mrčajevci, Jančići), have been classified as type 2b (Fig. 2.21/16; Fig. 2.22/5; Fig. 2.23/1), and are characteristic of this zone. Semi-circular or slightly conical bowls with an unprofiled rim, classified as type 3a, have been recorded at Bela Crkva and Lučani, although the Lučani specimen has a slightly pronounced rim (Fig. 2.21/9; Fig. 2.22/18).

Type 1b bowls in this zone mostly have short arched handles extending from the rim to the shoulder or belly of the vessel, and the example from Anište is ornamented with a wavy incised line and a series of dotted punctures (Fig. 2.22/1).

The bowls are mostly made of clay mixed with sand and range in quality from fine to coarse fabric. One example has a polished surface (Fig. 2.22/18). They are unevenly fired, with colours ranging from light brown to dark brown and reddish-brown.

B. CUPS

Cups are somewhat more common in this zone compared to the previous zone, where only one cup was recorded. A cup of type 3a with one handle level with the opening was recorded at Belotić (Fig. 2.21/14), and a new cup type, 2a, has also been documented in this zone, characterised by a conical profile, a wide opening, and a slightly pronounced rim, with one elongated tongue-shaped handle level with the opening (Fig. 2.21/1, 15; Fig. 2.22/17).

The cups are unornamented and made of refined clay in uneven firing colours, ranging from reddish-brown to grey. The cup from Guča (Fig. 2.22/17) has a thin polished coating.

C. BEAKERS

A gently biconical beaker with a longer conical shape and handles extending from the rim to the shoulder, classified as type 1a, has been found at the Kruševlje site in Lučani (Fig. 2.22/14). Type 1b beakers have not been recorded, while type 1c beakers (pear-shaped with handles extending from the rim to the shoulder, not exceeding or barely exceeding the opening) are relatively common (Fig. 2.22/7, 11; Fig. 2.23/4), as are type 2a beakers, which are short with a gentle S-profile, wide openings, and two arched handles level with the rim (Fig. 2.22/10; Fig. 2.23/4, 11–12, 16–18). A type 3a beaker could include those from Pilatovići (Fig. 2.23/3), Jelica, and Kovačević Cave (Fig. 2.21/3, Fig. 2.23/14), while types 5a and 6a are not documented. Type 4a beakers have been found in Ražana (Fig. 2.22/6), and an interesting globular beaker with a short, everted rim and one short arched handle on the rim, on a hollow conical foot, could represent a combination of types 3a and 4a (Fig. 2.22/5). This beaker has been classified as type 4b. A distinctive form in this zone is a special type of beaker with a globular body, a long cylindrical or funnel-shaped neck, and one or two long handles, usually strap-shaped in cross-section, classified as type 7 (7a with one handle and 7b with two handles). These beakers are the most common and are distributed throughout western Serbia (Fig. 2.21/2, 5, 10–12;

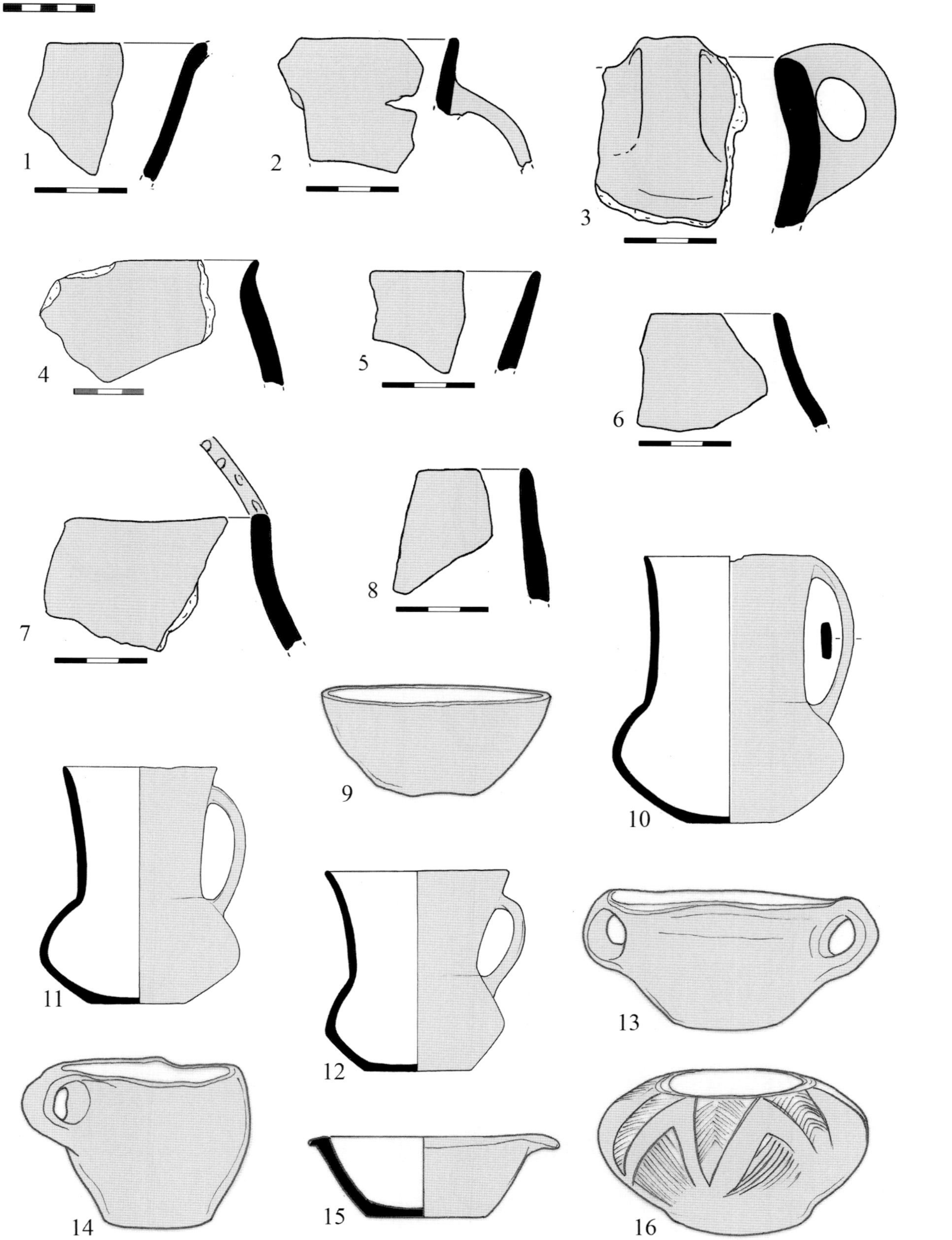

Figure 2.21. 1–8, Jelica: site of Gradina; 9–12, Bela Crkva: site of Cerik-Bandera: 9, mound I, grave 25; 10, mound I, grave 24; 11–12, mound I, group 1; 13–16, Belotić: site of Šumar: 13–14, mound XII; 15–16, mound 15.

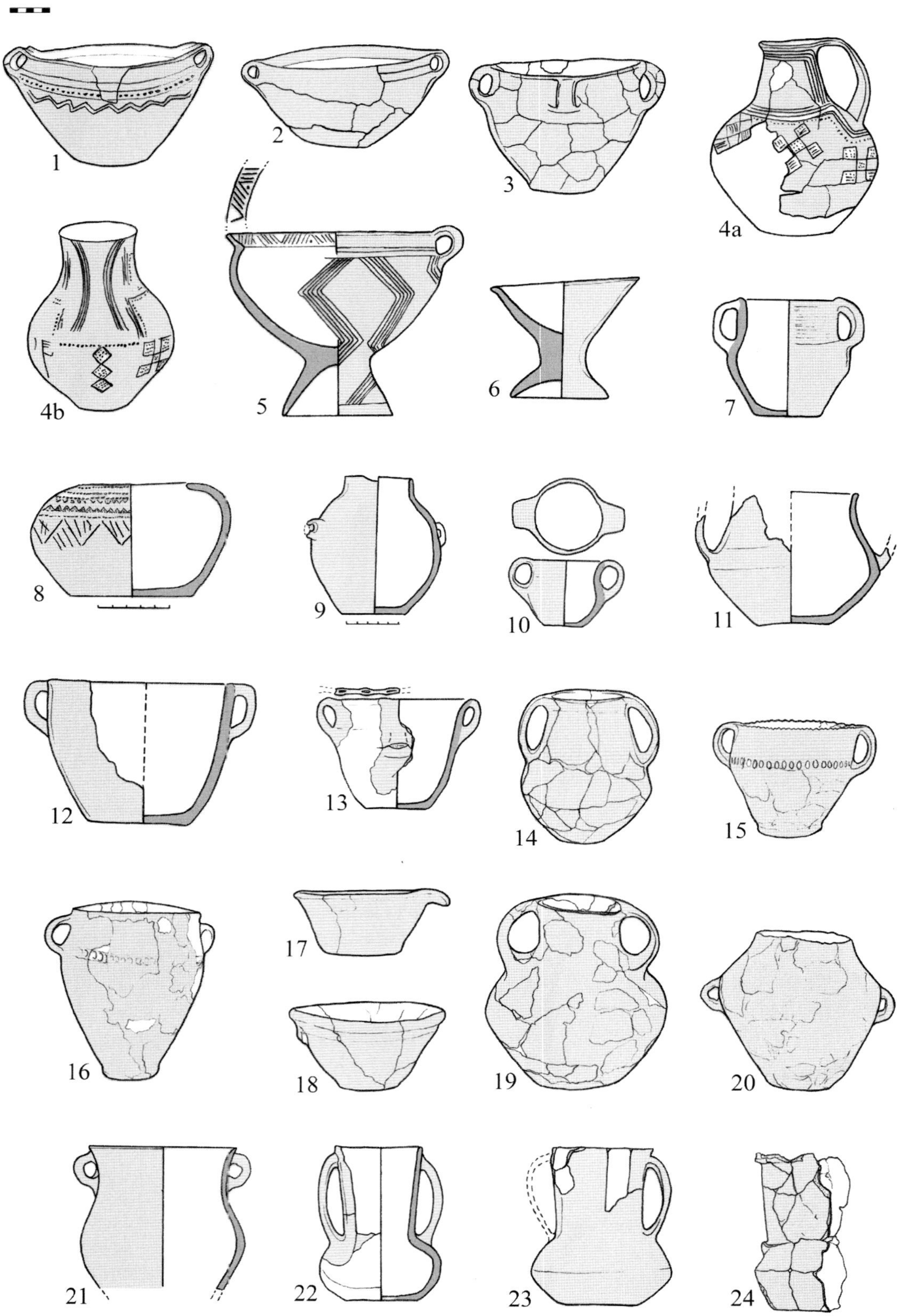

Figure 2.22. 1–7 Ražana: site of Anište: 1–4, mound I; 5–7, mound V; 8–9, Jančići: site of Veliko polje, mound I, grave 2; 10–13, Adže: site of Prijevor; 14–16, Lučani: site of Kruševlje, mound 1, grave 1; 17, Guča: site of Rajića brdo; 18–21, Lučani: site of Suva Česma, mound VII; 22–24, Dučalovići: site of Ruja: 22, mound 12, grave 1, 23, mound 13, 24, mound 10, grave 1.

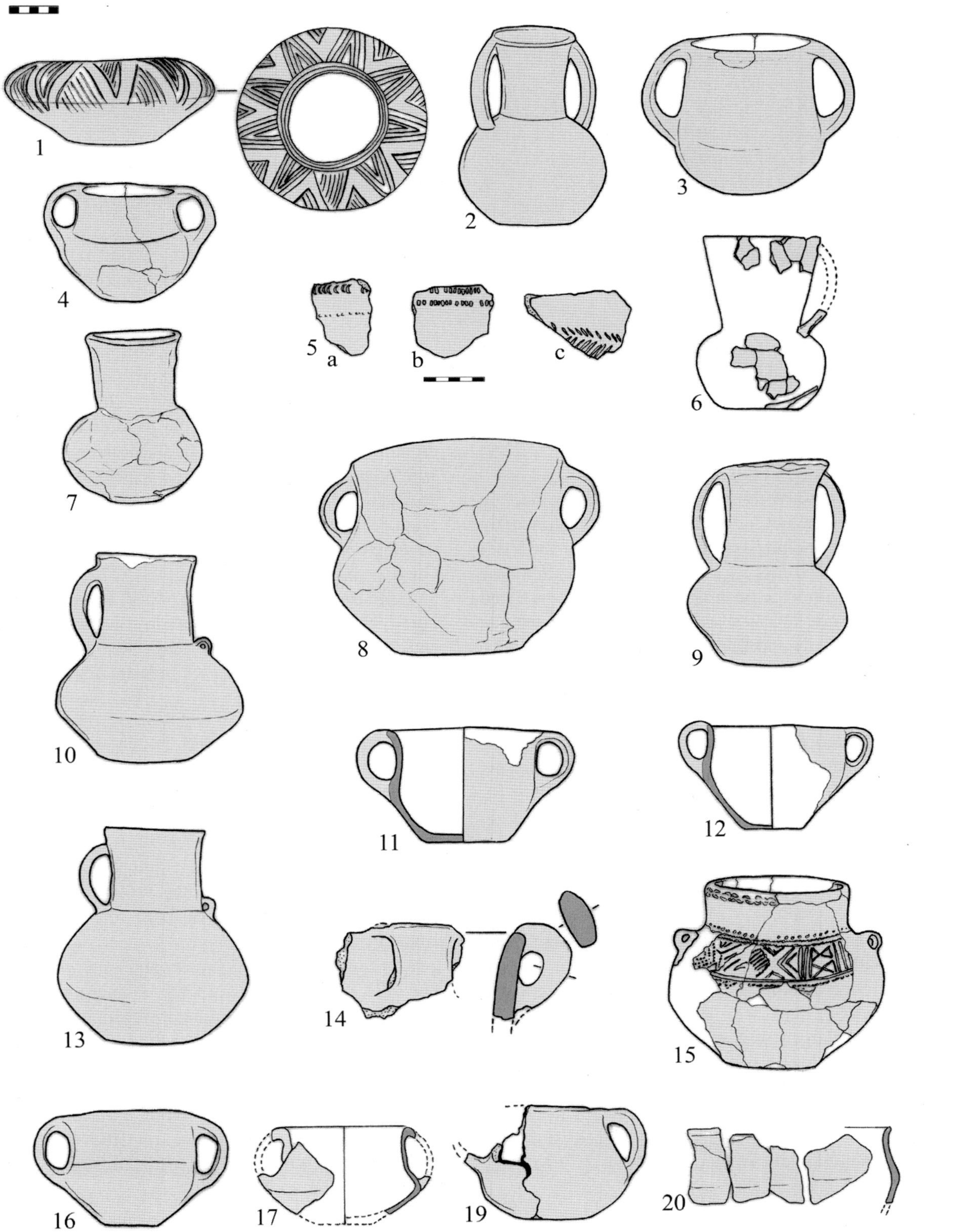

Figure 2.23. 1, Mrčajevci: site of Gušavac, mound II; 2, Markovica: site of Negrišori, mound VI; 3–4, Pilatovići: site of Ravni Lug, mound 1; 5, Krstac: site of Ivkovo Brdo, mound 1, central grave; 6, Donja Kravarica: site of Babinjak, mound II; 7, Turica: site of Ošljevac; 8, Višesava, mound; 9–10, Priboj: site of FAP, mound; 11–12, Vranjani: site of Veliki Lug; 13, Jarmovac: site of Kaluđerske Livade, mound 1, grave 2; 14, Cerje, Kovačevića pećina (Kovačević Cave); 15, Stapari: site of Mala Gradina, 16–20, Mali Šturac: site of Prljuša.

Fig. 2.22/22–24; Fig. 2.23/2, 6, 7, 9, 10, 13). Some type 7a beakers have small handles at the junction of the neck and belly, found exclusively in Lim Valley (Fig. 2.23/10, 13). Only one type 4b beaker is ornamented.

Beakers vary in firing quality and fabric. Some are of good quality, such as examples from Anište (Fig. 2.22/5), Lučani (Fig. 2.22/14), or Donja Kravarica (Fig. 2.23/6), while some still retain a polished coating (Fig. 2.22/11, 14, 22–24). Type 7 beakers from Belotić and Bela Crkva are mostly of poor quality and grey in colour. The clay is rarely purified, generally containing sand, and the firing quality is uneven, resulting in shades of brown and grey.

D. AMPHORAE

Type 1a amphorae, mostly ovoid in shape with shorter or longer cylindrical or slightly conical necks, sometimes with tunnel-shaped wide handles on the shoulder or belly, include examples from Jelica (Fig. 2.21/6, 8) and Lučani (Fig. 2.22/20). A miniature amphora from Jančići (Fig. 2.22/9) could also be included in this type.

Type 2a amphorae (with two arched handles connecting the rim and shoulder, similar to beakers but of significantly larger dimensions) include examples from Lučani and Više-sava (Fig. 2.22/19, 21; Fig. 2.23/8), while type 3a amphorae (deeper vessels with wide openings and more or less flared rims that could not be classified more precisely) include examples from Anište and Lučani (Fig. 2.22/3, 12).

This zone also includes a unique type of amphora with a globular body, a short cylindrical neck, and a wide opening, such as the example from Stapari (Fig. 2.23/15), which is richly decorated and resembles the so-called globular amphorae of Central Europe (*Kugelamphorenkultur*). This type has been classified as type 4a.

Ornamentation has been documented on only one type 4a amphora, in the form of geometric motifs created by incising, grooving, and stamping (Fig. 2.23/15).

E. JUGS

A new type of vessel appears in this zone: the jug. These are vessels with a globular, larger body, a narrower conical neck, and a longer handle that extends from the rim to the shoulder or belly of the vessel. They resemble type 7 beakers, but jugs are larger, with narrower and shorter necks, often conical in profile, unlike type 7a beakers, which have cylindrical or slightly funnel-shaped necks. Only one jug (type 1a) has been recorded in Ražana, which is brown, of good quality, and richly decorated with incised geometric motifs combined with dotted punctures (Fig. 2.22/4).

F. POTS

Pots are very rare in this zone, which is not surprising as most of the pottery comes from burial contexts and pots are not common grave goods. The pots found in tumuli are small, almost miniature (10–28 cm), of poor quality and firing. Decorations consist of horizontal plastic bands with finger impressions or rows of finger impressions directly on the upper surface of the rim. Type 1a (ovoid, almost globular, wide pots with wide openings) includes examples from Kruševlje and Prijevor (Fig. 2.22/13, 15, 16), while type 2a (narrower ovoid pots with narrowing openings, sometimes with handles below the rim or on the shoulder) likely includes a pot from Jelica (Fig. 2.21/7).

G. HANDLES

The most common handles in this zone are arched handles with a strap-shaped cross-section, mainly found on type 7 beakers, but also on other beakers, bowls, pots, and the jug (Fig. 2.21/2, 10–14; Fig. 2.22/1–5, 10–16, 19, 22–24; Fig. 2.23/2–4, 6, 9–13, 17, 18). Less common are arched handles with a wider oval cross-section, mostly on amphorae and occasionally on beakers (Fig. 2.21/3; Fig. 2.22/7, 20, 21; Fig. 2.23/8, 14, 16). Tunnel handles are found mainly on amphorae, but also on type 7a beakers, in combination with arched handles with a strap-shaped cross-section (Fig. 2.22/9; Fig. 2.23/10, 13, 15). This zone also features elongated tongue-shaped handles on the rims of cups, which have been documented outside this geographical zone only in the Đerdap Gorge region (Fig. 2.21/15; Fig. 2.22/17, Fig. 2.25/8).[11]

Handles are generally undecorated, except for that on the jug which is decorated with incised vertical lines (Fig. 2.22/4), and the tops of handles on the beaker from Ražana (Fig. 2.22/7), which are adorned with plastic nodular protrusions.

H. ORNAMENTATION

Unlike the Early Bronze Age pottery from the peri-Pannonian zone, as well as from Great Morava Valley and Šumadija, a significant number of vessels in this zone are richly decorated, primarily using techniques of incising, grooving, and stamping. Plastic bands and nodular protrusions, as well as inlays and finger impressions on the surface of the vessels, are less common.

The most common incised motifs include parallel horizontal or vertical lines, hanging hatched or inscribed triangles, rhombuses, zigzag bands, and others (Fig. 2.21/16; Fig. 2.22/1, 4, 5, 8; Fig. 2.23/1, 15). These motifs are often accompanied by rows of dotted punctures (Fig. 2.22/1, 4; Fig. 2.23/15), and sometimes the motifs are organized into metopes (Fig. 2.23/15).

Impressed motifs include rows of rectangular and crescent-shaped impressions in a tumulus at Krstac (Fig. 2.23/5a, 5b). A fragment from the same tumulus is decorated with short, opposing diagonal lines forming a herringbone pattern (Fig. 2.23/5c).

It appears, however, that this ornamented pottery is older, created under strong Eneolithic traditions, in contrast to the unornamented pottery from this zone, which has been classified in the Belotić–Bela Crkva group in the literature (Garašanin 1973, 252–268).

A type 1c beaker from Anište has a small nodular plastic protrusion at the top of the handles, where they join the rim (Fig. 2.22/7). This decoration will become widespread in the Central Balkans only in the next period, the Middle Bronze Age. On several pots, finger impressions have been noted directly on the upper surface of the rim (Fig. 2.21/7; Fig. 2.22/13, 15) or on plastic bands placed on the shoulder or belly of the pot (Fig. 2.22/16).

2.3.3.2 Other finds

Among the other finds registered in this zone, the most significant are the copper axes and the dagger, with the dagger being the only non-accidental find (Antonović 2014).

LIST OF SITES WITH CHANCE FINDS

62. Šljivovica, unknown site, Lozane-type axe (Antonović 2014, 89, nr 334, and cited literature); 63. Donja Leskovica, unknown site, Kozarac-type axe (Antonović 2014, 91, nr 342, and cited literature); 64. Ševrljuge, unknown site, Kozarac-type axe (Antonović 2014, 91, nr 350).

The most common chance finds in this zone are metal axes, specifically of the Kozarac type. They originate from the areas around Valjevo and Kosjerić (Donja Leskovica and Ševrljuge; Fig. 2.24/2, 3) and are the most frequently found type of axes from the Early Bronze Age, at least in the northern part of the central Balkans. According to D. Antonović, the axe from Leskovica belongs to the Jasika variant, while the specimen from Ševrljuge belongs to the Baranda variant. In addition to this type, a Lozane-type axe was found near Užice (Šljivovica), which is more commonly distributed in the southern central Balkans. The axes have not been analysed for composition, so it is unknown whether they are made solely of copper or contain traces of arsenic or tin.

A triangular metal dagger with three rivets was found in the central grave at the Belotić-Šumar site in Tumulus 10 (Garašanin 1973, 262). M. Garašanin notes that such daggers are known from the Periamos group and should be dated to the Br A1 phase of the Bronze Age according to Reinecke's chronology. This dating corresponds with the chronology of daggers according to Wels-Weyrauch, though the chronological placement of this type of dagger could be extended to the Br A2 phase (Wels-Weyrauch 2015).

Among the other finds, a bifacially worked flint arrowhead with a concave lower edge and a stone hammer are notable (Fig. 2.24/5, 6). Such arrowheads appear in the Eneolithic and continue into the Bronze Age, making them not particularly sensitive for chronological determination.

COPPER MINE

65. Mali Šturac, Prljuša site (Antonović and Dimić 2017, 117–137).

This is a copper malachite mine discovered on the western slopes of Mount Rudnik, on the border between the zone of western Serbia and Šumadija with Great Morava Valley, at

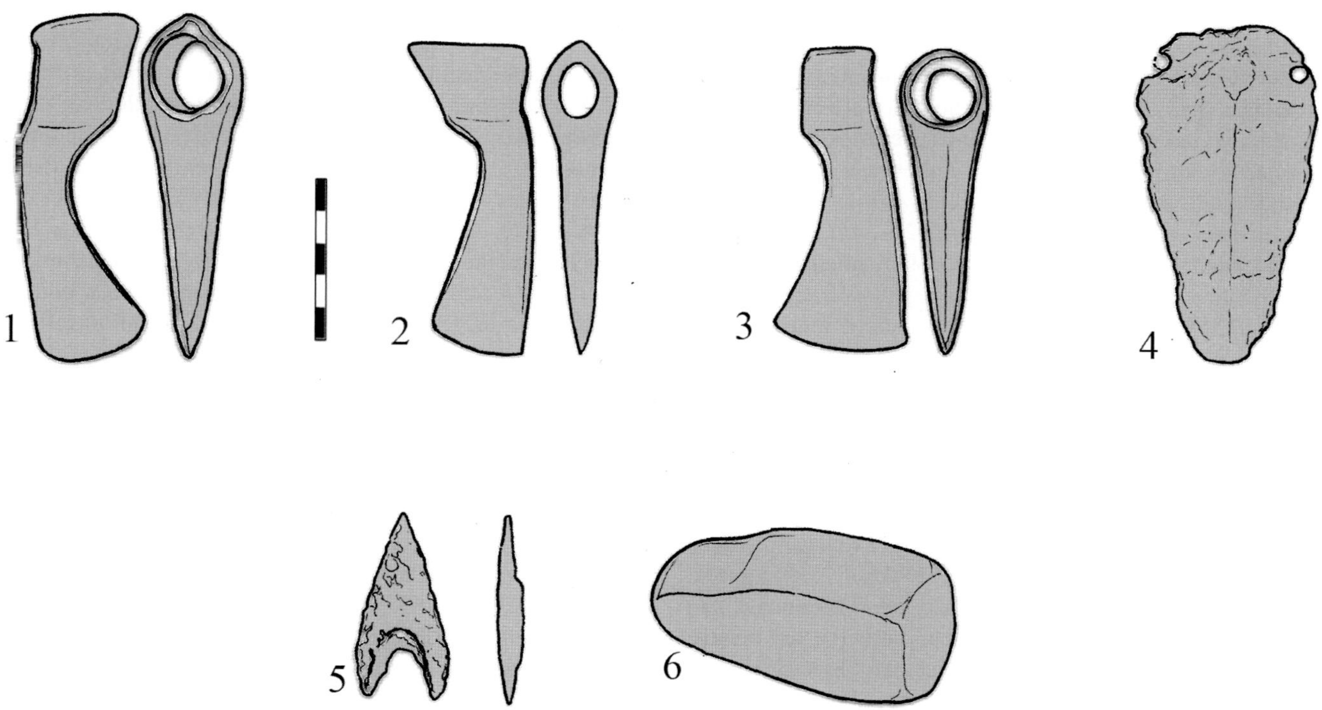

Figure 2.24. 1, Šljivovica, unknown site; 2, Donja Leskovica, unknown site; 3, Ševrljuge, unknown site; 4, Belotić: site of Šumar, mound X; 5, Krstac: site of Ivkovo Brdo; 6, Lučani: site of Suva Česma, mound VII.

an elevation of over 900 m above sea level. Several mining shafts were discovered and, in some of them, wooden constructions were found that might have supported large stone hammers (Antonović and Dimić 2017, 132, 133). During archaeological research, parts of vessels and stone hammers used for mining were also found. The mine is dated to the Early Bronze Age, possibly the second half of 3rd millennium BC. The site was used for extracting copper carbonate ore, mainly mineralised malachite, which was found in very hard rock. Therefore, these communities exploited the ore through surface mining without deep shafts (Antonović and Dimić 2017, 136–139). This method of exploitation is characteristic of the older Eneolithic period in the central Balkans, although no portable finds have been discovered at Prljuša to confirm this yet.

2.3.4 Cultural and chronological classification of the Early Bronze Age in western Serbia and Lim Valley

It is interesting to observe that the stylistic and typological characteristics of pottery, as well as burial customs, in the north (Rađevina), south (Lim Valley), and central part of this zone (upper basin of the West Morava River) are quite uniform. This suggests the existence of a unified culture that originated and developed in the western part of present-day Serbia. However, it must be noted that this assessment is based solely on burial pottery, as no Early Bronze Age settlements – except for a few sporadic finds at Jelica, which are out of context – have been identified in this zone. M. Garašanin previously defined this culture as the Belotić–Bela Crkva culture, based on the basic typological characteristics of the pottery. However, almost all these forms are also characteristic of the Vinkovci–Somogyvár group, as Garašanin himself observed (Garašanin 1973, 262–266). Despite the significant similarities between these groups, not only in ceramic finds, such as type 1b and 2a bowls (Fig. 2 21/10–13, 15, 16), type 7 beakers (Fig. 2.21/10–12, Fig. 2.22/22–24, Fig. 2.23/2, 7, 9 – especially the specific examples with small handles on the shoulder Fig. 2.23/10, 13) (Tasić 1984a, Taf. 1/1, 2, 4. Kulcsar 2009, figs 48, 50, 52, 54, 69), and amphorae types 1a, 2a, and 4a (Fig. 2.22/19–21, Fig. 2.23/8, 15) (Tasić 1984a, Taf. III/4, 5, 7; Kulcsar 2009, figs 52, 67), but also in burial customs, Garašanin still defined a new cultural group for these finds. On the other hand, N. Tasić believes this group to be a regional variant of the Vinkovci–Somogyvár culture (Tasić 1984a, 19). It should be noted that there are some differences between type 7 beakers and their parallels in the Vinkovci–Somogyvár culture (Kulcsar 2009, fig. 48). The Vinkovci–Somogyvár beakers have shorter necks and taller bodies, while the examples from western Serbia have more bulbous bodies and taller necks, but these differences are minor.

In addition to finds typical of the so-called Belotić–Bela Crkva group, or the regional variant of the Vinkovci–Somogyvár culture, elements characteristic of late Eneolithic cultures, especially the Vučedol culture, also appear in this zone. The bowls classified as type 2a are common in the pre-classical phase of the Vučedol culture (phase A), and they are often richly decorated with deep carving and incised motifs similar to those found in western Serbia (Dimitrijević 1977, Abb. 4/18–22). One such bowl has been indirectly dated to the 29th–27th centuries cal BC, in the late Vučedol culture, corresponding to the date of the grave from the tumulus in Jančići (Durman and Obelić 1989). This raises the question of whether the burials under the tumuli at Belotić (Tumulus 15) and Mrčajevci also date to this period as they contain the same type of similarly decorated bowls, or whether they represent a tradition retained into the Early Bronze Age.

Elements of the Vučedol culture could also be observed in the forms of semi-circular vessels on pedestals from Ražana, which are decorated with zigzag incised lines on the upper surface of the rim (Fig. 2.22/5) (Dimitrijević 1977, Taf. 17/2), and the zigzag band motif composed of two horizontal rows of opposing triangles, found at Belotić, Jančići, and Mrčajevci (Fig. 2.21/16, Fig. 2.22/8, Fig. 2.23/1). This motif was very common in the pre-classical phase of the Vučedol culture but became less frequent in the late Vučedol culture (Dimitrijević 1977, Taf. 3/2, 4, 5, Taf. 7/2, 3, Taf. 12/3, Taf. 13/1, Taf. 17/1). Similarly, the metope-style decoration, featuring geometric motifs such as rhombuses, rectangles, and triangles (Fig. 2.22/4, Fig. 2.23/15), is present in the classical and late phases of the Vučedol culture (phases B and C) (Dimitrijević 1977, Taf. 8/2, 3, 7, Taf. 10/2–5, 8, 9, Taf. 17/3).

A notable form, however, is the deep bowl with an S-shaped rim profile and short arched handles of strap cross-section. These are not known in the Vučedol culture but are common in the Vinkovci–Somogyvár group (Kulscar 2009, fig. 19/9, figs 48 and 50). Jugs are present in both the Vučedol and Vinkovci-Somogyvár (Kulscar 2009, fig. 19), especially in the latter, though they are mostly undecorated. The richly decorated jug from Anište seems to be a product of the Vinkovci–Somogyvár group and Vučedol traditions (Dimitrijević 1979a, taf. 8, 10–13, 16, 17).

The type 1c beaker from Tumulus 5 at Anište (Fig. 2.22/7) is typologically similar to an example from the pit at Vecina mala (Fig. 2.17/21), dated to the 23rd–22nd centuries BC. A smaller beaker on a pedestal is identical to examples from the Kokino sanctuary (Fig. 2.38/12, 17), though similar vessels are also found in the Vučedol, Mako-Kosihi-Čaka, and Vinkovci–Somogyvár groups (Dimitrijević 1979a, taf. 17; Kulscar 2009, fig. 60). The two-handled beakers, already mentioned, are certainly younger than the Vučedol culture and may correspond with post-Vučedol groups, probably no older than the mid-3rd millennium BC. Given the presence of type 1c beakers and deep S-profiled bowls, it seems that Tumuli 1 and 5 at Anište in Ražana belong to the Belotić–Bela Crkva group, and the unusual and rich ornamentation on this pottery is either a product of surviving Eneolithic traditions (with known examples from several sites, Fig. 2.21/16, Fig. 2.23/1), or this population on the western edge of Serbia maintained some connections with populations in eastern Bosnia. In eastern Bosnia, numerous finds have been classified as belonging to the Cetina group, with very similar stylistic and typological pottery features (Marović and Čović 1983, T. XXIX, T. XXXII). Another detail that connects the finds from Ražana with the Cetina group is an unpublished polished stone object in the Užice museum which closely resembles items documented in the Cetina group (Marović and Čović 1983, 215).

Even in older literature, these phenomena, which are unusual for the indigenous Belotić–Bela Crkva group, were associated with the Cetina group (Čović 1970, 17; Garašanin, M. 1983a, 474–475; Govedarica 2006, 103), which is unsurprising, as it also draws from Ljubljana and Vučedol traditions, as does the Vinkovci–Somogyvár group indirectly.

For the late Eneolithic, or steppe traditions, the decorations in the form of rows of rectangular and crescent-shaped impressions, as well as the herringbone motif from the tumulus in Krstac (Fig. 2.23/5), may be associated. This site is dated to the 26th–24th centuries cal BC (Table 1) (Bulatović *et al.* 2020).

As for the finds attributed to the so-called Belotić–Bela Crkva group, they are dated between the 25th/24th and 23rd/22nd centuries cal BC, based on dates from Lučani and Dučalovići.

Interestingly, the finds from Prijevor, which stylistically (type 1c beakers) belong to the Bubanj-Hum III group, are dated to the latest period, the 22nd–20th centuries cal BC. The finds from Pranjani and Pilatovići could also be attributed to this group, with all these sites showing evidence of cremation as the burial rite. It is worth noting that at the Paulje site in Jadar, despite numerous tumuli from the developed Bronze Age being explored, no Early or Middle Bronze Age graves have been recorded. This is particularly surprising given that the necropolis is only about 15 km from Bela Crkva. However, during the excavation of one tumulus at Paulje, a charcoal sample was AMS dated to the 20th–19th centuries cal BC, despite the absence of portable finds indicating this period. This suggests the possibility that older burials may yet be discovered in future excavations.[12]

In the western Serbia zone, a prehistoric copper mine was discovered decades ago at Prljuša on Mount Rudnik, and it is intensively researched in recent years (Jovanović 1988; Antonović and Dimić 2017). Numerous mining shafts, dated to the second half of the 3rd millennium BC, indicate that Early Bronze Age communities exploited copper at this site. The vessels found there exhibit stylistic and typological characteristics of the Bubanj-Hum III group (Fig. 2.23/16–19), with some elements typical of the Novačka Ćuprija–Pančevo group.

This zone also contains well-known copper deposits in Lim Valley (Jarmovac), Zlatar, and Cer (Srebrne rupe) (Durman 1983, 10). Although research in Jarmovac has not confirmed the use of the mine during the Bronze Age, it has been established that it was used in the Early Eneolithic (Derikonjić 2010, 7, 8).

Based on the absolute dates and various stylistic and typological features of the pottery, as well as the relatively uniform burial customs, the Early Bronze Age in this zone can be divided into three phases:

- First phase (EBA 1): Elements of Vučedol culture (28th–25th centuries cal BC), based on Eneolithic cultural traditions, particularly Vučedol and steppe cultures.
- Second phase (EBA 2): Belotić–Bela Crkva group pottery (regional variant of the Vinkovci–Somogyvár culture) and possible survivals from the previous phase (25th–22nd/21st centuries cal BC).
- Third phase (EBA 3): Finds typologically corresponding to the Bubanj-Hum III group, with certain elements from the Novačka Ćuprija–Pančevo group (22nd–20th centuries cal BC).

2.4 The Timok Region with Đerdap Gorge

The Timok Region belongs to the Carpathian–Balkan Mountain massif, one of the most significant mineral formations in Europe, which has marked the past of this area, making it known for the earliest copper mining in human history (Jovanović 1971; Durman 1983; Borić 2009). The Timok Region consists of the valleys of Svrljiški Timok, Crni Timok, Beli Timok, and Crni Timok, with the surrounding mountains, the most notable being the Homolje Mountains, Kučaj Mountains, Rtanj, Miroč, Deli Jovan, and Tresibaba (see Fig. 1.1). The region is adorned with numerous rivers, lakes, and caves, the most famous being Lazar's Cave, Rajko's Cave, and Resava Cave. In addition to copper ore, the area is rich in deposits of gold, silver, and iron, with smaller quantities of zinc and lead. In the northern part of this region, in Timok Valley and Ključ, the soil is exceptionally suitable for agriculture (luvisol), consisting of well-drained, multi-layered soil on a limestone base formed by the atmospheric effects of frost and rain on clay. In the recent past, it was recorded that the areas around Timok were covered by dense oak forests which survive only in rare enclaves.

The climate of this region is influenced by the Carpathian massif to the north, the Homolje Mountains to the west, and the orographic openness of the area toward the north-east, through which cold and dry continental air masses from the Wallachian Plain penetrate, making the summers warm and the winters cold. However, on some mountains, an alpine climate prevails, and the entire region is characterised by the Gornjak wind, which blows from the Carpathians toward the south-east, mostly during the summer (Bulatović *et al.* 2013). The orographic openness of this region toward the north-east also influenced the more intense cultural interaction of the populations that inhabited the Timok Region and the Wallachian Plain during many periods of prehistory.

2.4.1 Settlement and dwelling

Very few Early Bronze Age sites have been documented in this region. Hilltop settlements have not been registered and lowland settlements are scarce. One settlement has been documented in Đerdap Gorge, another in the mountainous region on the southern slopes of the Homolje Mountains, and a third on the banks of the Crni Timok (Kapuran *et al.* 2014). Site numbers refer to Plate 4.

List of settlements

66. Velesnica, the site of Obala-Donja Strana, lowland settlement (Vasić 1986; Bulatović *et al.* 2013; Kapuran 2014, 152); 67. Bor, the site of Kučajna, lowland settlement (Kapuran *et al.* 2011; Kapuran 2014, 97); 68. Gamzigrad, the site of Palace, lowland settlement (Kapuran 2014, 125).

The site Obala-Donja Strana in Velesnica is situated on the right terrace of the Danube, upstream from the confluence with Kamenica Stream, while Kučajna is on an east facing slope above the confluence of the Kučaj and Martinov streams near Bor. The third site is located on the river terrace of the Crni Timok, within the fortified Roman palace at the well-known ancient site of Gamzigrad–Romuliana (Kapuran 2014, 125). Unfortunately, although these sites have been excavated, there is insufficient information regarding the type of settlement or domestic architecture, as the sites are multi-layered and their stratigraphy is disturbed. Thus, traces of above-ground architecture in the form of daub have been recorded at Kučajna and Gamzigrad but it cannot be confirmed with certainty whether they belong to the Early Bronze Age horizon.

2.4.2 Necropolises and burial practices

In this geographical zone, two necropolises have been documented:
69. the site of Pesak in Vajuga (Popović *et al.* 1986); 70. the site of Glamija in Korbovo (Radojčić 2005).

At the Pesak site in Vajuga, along with an Iron Age necropolis and settlements from various prehistoric periods, one grave of an inhumed individual was discovered. The body was buried in a slightly flexed position, resting on its right side with the head turned toward the south-west (Popović *et al.* 1986). Two beakers were found in the abdominal area of the skeleton (Fig. 2.25/7, 8) and the authors note that the individual was male, aged 20–30 years.

During the excavation of the large Bronze Age necropolis at Glamija in Korbovo, an older grave containing a cremated individual was also documented. The remains were placed in an urn (Fig. 2.25/16), actually, in a smaller bowl (Fig. 2.25/11) positioned at the bottom of the urn (Radojčić 2005). The urn was covered with a larger conical bowl (Fig. 2.25/9), with five additional vessels around it (Fig. 2.25/10, 12–15). Both graves, from Pesak and Glamija, were dug into the ground without a tumulus above them, indicating flat necropolises.

2.4.3 Portable finds

Since only three settlements and two graves have been documented in this zone there are not many portable finds and most consist of ceramic vessels. In addition, four copper axes have been registered as chance finds.

2.4.3.1 POTTERY

A total of 16 vessels from the Early Bronze Age have been registered in this zone, of which only six come from settlements, while the others come from necropolises, specifically from two graves at different sites (see above).

A. BOWLS

Two bowls have been recorded, both of semi-circular form (type 3a). The larger has a broad strap handle running from the rim to the shoulder and four paired, plastic tongue-shaped projections on the rim (Fig. 2.25/9, 11).

B. CUPS

Only one cup has been registered, found in a grave at Vajuga. It is grey–brown in colour and made from clay with quartz inclusions (Fig. 2.25/8). The cup is conical in shape, with a tongue-shaped handle on the rim (type 2a), and is almost identical to examples found in tumulus graves from the Western Serbia and Lim Valley geographical zone.

C. BEAKERS

Beakers are the most numerous. Types 1a and 1b have not been documented but a fragment of a beaker from Glamija (Fig. 2.25/12) could possibly be classified as type 1c. A relatively common type is the beaker with a globular body, narrow neck, and two arched handles extending from the rim to the shoulder of the vessel (Fig. 2.25/1, 2, 14). These resemble type 1c beakers which, however, are much more squat and generally lack a pronounced neck compared to the body of the vessel. For this reason, this beaker has been classified as type 1d, and a beaker missing its handles (Fig. 2.25/13) may also belong to this type. Beakers of this type are made in shades of brown (ranging from grey–brown to reddish–brown), from refined clay or clay with fine sand, well-fired with a smoothed or polished surface.

A fragment of the base of a slightly biconical beaker with an arched, strap-shaped handle extending from the body (Fig. 2.25/12) is presumed to belong to type 1c. Another example of type 1d is a beaker with short handles and a globular body on a prominent base (Fig. 2.25/10). It is

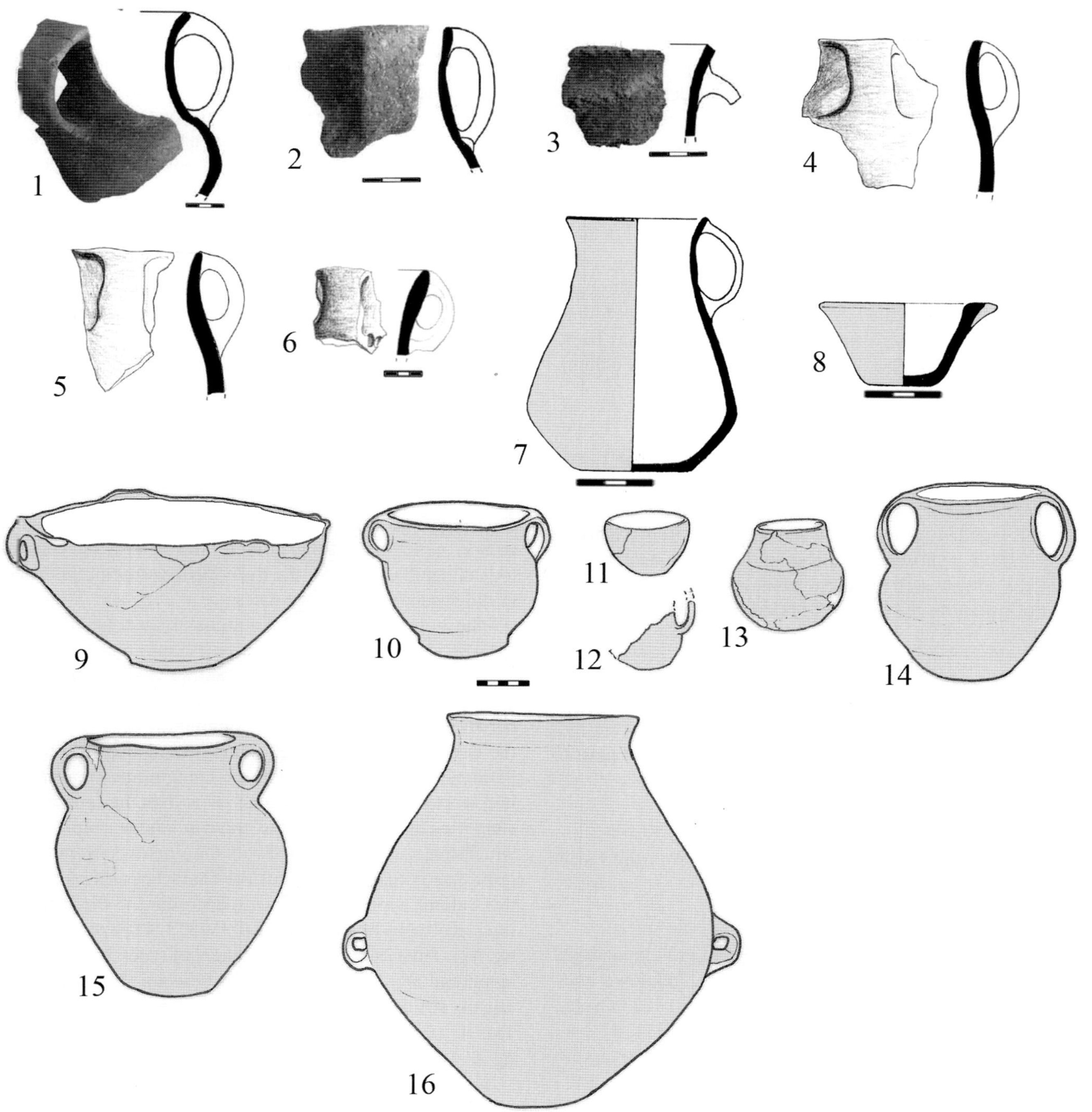

Figure 2.25. 1–3, Velesnica: site of Obala-Donja Strana; 4–5, Bor: site of Kučajna; 6, Gamzigrad: site of Carska Palata; 7–8, Vajuga: site of Pesak (grave); 9–16, Korbovo: site of Glamija (grave).

light brown in colour, with a rough surface, insufficiently fired, and made from clay mixed with coarsely granulated sand. A fragment of a vessel from Velesnica with a slightly funnel-shaped long neck and a handle below the rim, resembling type 7, could also be categorised as a beaker (Fig. 2.25/3).

D. AMPHORAE

The amphora from the grave at Glamija, with an ovoid body and two short handles on the belly (Fig. 2.25/16), belongs to type 1a. An amphora similar to a beaker but larger in size, with short handles extending from the rim to the lower part of the neck (Fig. 2.25/15), would be classified as type 2a.

Large vessels from Kučajna, with arched strap-shaped handles extending from the rim to the shoulder of the vessel (Fig. 2.25/4, 5), fall under type 3a amphorae. A fragment of a vessel with a slightly funnel-shaped neck and a short, arched handle on the neck lacks sufficient elements for precise typological classification, but it is likely to belong to type 3a amphorae (Fig. 2.25/6).

E. JUGS

In this zone, one jug has been recorded. It has a bag-shaped body, a narrow conical neck, and a slightly flared rim, with one arched handle extending from the rim to the lower part of the neck (Fig. 2.25/7). Since it differs from jugs found in the previously discussed geographical zone, it has been designated as type 2a. The jug is grey–brown in colour, with quartz inclusions.

F. HANDLES

The handles documented in this zone during the Early Bronze Age are mostly arched, placed vertically from the rim to the shoulder or belly, or just below the rim. Exceptions are the handles on the bowl and amphora from Glamija (Fig. 2.25/9, 16), which are also arched but much shorter than the others and resemble tunnel-like handles, which were common in the previous period, the Late Eneolithic.

G. ORNAMENTATION

True ornamentation is absent on the vessels from this period in Đerdap and eastern Serbia. However, the bowl from Glamija features plastic tongue-shaped projections on the rim (Fig. 2.25/9), which can be considered a form of plastic ornamentation.

2.4.3.2. Other finds

In eastern Serbia, four metal chance finds from the Early Bronze Age have been documented.

LIST OF SITES WITH CHANCE FINDS

71. Kostol, unknown site, Kozarac-type axe (Vukmanović, Radojčić 1995, cat. no. 140); 72. Boljetin, unknown site, Kozarac-type axe (Jovanović 1971, taf. 7/7); 73. Osnić, unknown site, Kozarac-type axe (Garašanin 1954, 51, taf. 34/8); 74. Laznica, unknown site, Kozarac-type axe (Garašanin 1954, 51, taf. 34/5).

All chance finds are Kozarac-type axes, found within this zone, from Đerdap (Fig. 2.26/1, 2),[13] through the Homolje mountain range (Fig. 2.26/3), to the Crni Timok (Fig. 2.26/4). The axes from Boljetin and Osnić (Fig. 2.26/2, 4) were classified by D. Antonović as the Baranda variant of the Kozarac-type axe, while those from Kostol and Laznica (Fig. 2.26/1, 3) were classified as the Jasika variant (Antonović 2014). The axe from Boljetin is made of copper with a significant admixture of arsenic (3.48%) and lead (4.76%), the axe from Kostol contains 0.72% arsenic, while the axes from Osnić and Laznica are made of copper without any significant admixtures (Antonović 2014, table 2).

Based on the distributive analysis of certain variants of the Kozarac-type axes, which are most prevalent in the Early Bronze Age in the central Balkans, no conclusive arguments can be drawn. The Jasika variant has been documented across the central Balkans, from the Danube to West Morava Valley to the south and the Drina River to the west, similar to the Baranda variant. However, the southernmost point of distribution for the Baranda variant is southern Šumadija, and the westernmost is Mačva (Antonović 2014, 90–92).

2.4.4 Cultural and chronological classification of the Early Bronze Age in the Timok Region

Unfortunately, there are no absolute dates from Early Bronze Age sites in this geographical zone, so the cultural and chronological determination relies solely on the stylistic and typological characteristics of the portable finds.[14] We know that a Kozarac-type axe, Jasika variant, from grave 208 in Mokrin has been indirectly dated to the 22nd–21st century BC (O'Shea 1996) which can, conditionally, serve as a chronological starting point for the cultural and chronological determination of the Early Bronze Age in this zone, in the absence of absolute dates.

The conical cup with a tongue-shaped handle (Fig. 2.25/8), almost identical to examples from tumulus graves in Belotić and Guča in western Serbia (Fig. 2.21/15; Fig. 2.22/17), is also indicative of the cultural connections between the Early Bronze Age communities in this zone and the bearers of the Vinkovci–Somogyvár group in southern Pannonia, as is the case with the communities that inhabited western Serbia at that time. This hypothesis is further supported by the jug from the grave in Vajuga (Fig. 2.25/7), which can also be associated with the Vinkovci–Somogyvár group, as it shares nearly all the characteristics of jugs of this culture, types I/12 and I/13, according to the typology of G. Kulcsar (Tasić 1984a, Taf. IV/3, 8, 11; Kulcsar 2009, fig. 49). The vessels, such as beakers of types 1d and 3, and amphorae of types 2 and 3 from Glamija (Fig. 2.25/1, 2, 10, 14–16), also have parallels in that group (Tasić 1984a, Taf. II/10, Taf. III/1–5, 7, Taf. IV/2, 7, 10; Kulcsar 2009, fig. 52 (tip III/2–III/6), fig. 63 (tip XI/1), fig. 67 (tip XV/1).

However, type 1d beakers also have analogies in the Mokrin necropolis. A vessel identical to type 1d beakers was found in grave 124, and a beaker of the same form, but with only one handle, was registered in grave 208 at Mokrin, which has been dated to the 22nd–21st century cal BC, along with a Kozarac-type axe (Girić 1971, T. LVI; O'Shea 1996). A similar, though somewhat more slender, beaker was found in grave 259 of the same necropolis, dated to the 20th–18th century cal BC (Girić 1971, T. LXVIII; O'Shea 1996).

The semi-circular bowl with plastic projections on the rim has no parallels in the Vinkovci–Somogyvár culture, and the

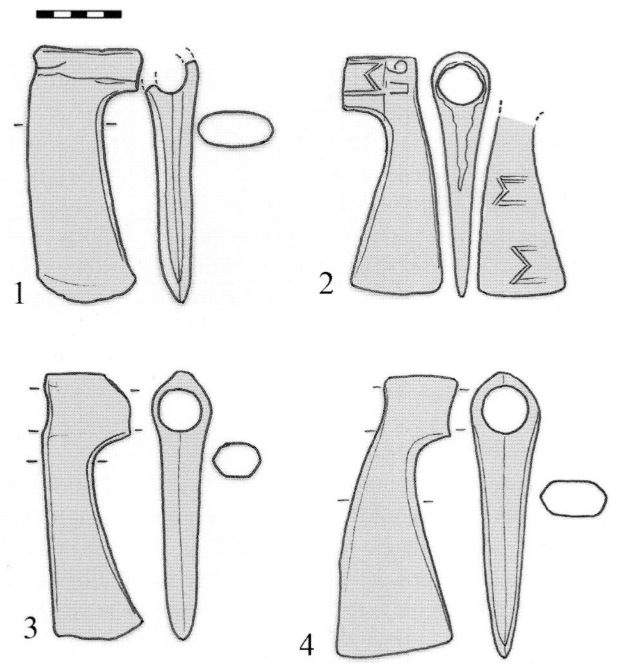

Figure 2.26. 1, Kostol, unknown site; 2, Boljetin, unknown site; 3, Laznica, unknown site; 4, Osnić, unknown site.

concept of a bowl decorated with plastic projections is foreign to the Early Bronze Age communities in neighbouring Banat (Guma 1997) as well as in Oltenia (Machnik 1991). However, these forms of bowls with plastic projections on the rim are characteristic of the Early Bronze Age in the Great Morava Valley (Fig. 2.17/12), especially South Morava Basin (Fig. 2.30/1, 10, 15, Fig. 2.33/7, 10, 11, 22, 26), as well as the Middle Bronze Age in the Timok Region (Kapuran *et al.* 2014, T. XIII/3; Kapuran 2014, T. 14/25–31). Identical plastic projections, though on S-profiled bowls, have been identified at Nad Klepečkom (Fig. 2.7/11) in Viminacium, near a structure dated to the 21st–20th century cal BC (see Table 1) In South Morava Basin, objects containing bowls with plastic projections on the rim are variously dated within the Early Bronze Age. For example, the ceramic group from Velika Humska Čuka, featuring double-handled beakers of type 1c and these bowls (Fig. 2.3/1–6), is dated to the 25th–24th century cal BC, while objects 1 and 91 at Bubanj, containing bowls with similar projections on the rim (Fig. 2.33/10, 11, 22), are dated to the 22nd–20th century cal BC (Table 1). Evidently, this form of decoration is characteristic of a longer period within the Early Bronze Age in South Morava Basin and most likely reached the Danube region through the interaction of these communities with those in the peri-Pannonian zone at the end of the Early Bronze Age.

Based on this discussion, the grave from Glamija could be tentatively dated to the last quarter of the 3rd millennium BC or the first quarter of the 2nd. The finds from Velesnica, Kučajna, and Gamzigrad likely belong to this same period.

The grave from Vajuga, however, due to its parallels exclusively with the Vinkovci–Somogyvár group (including its regional variant, the Belotić–Bela Crkva group in western Serbia), could be assumed to belong to an earlier period, possibly the third quarter of the 3rd millennium BC.

From the information presented, it is possible to hypothesise the existence of two phases of the Early Bronze Age in the Đerdap zone. The older phase, with elements exclusively of the Vinkovci–Somogyvár culture, includes the grave from Vajuga and probably Velesnica, corresponding to EBA 2 in the previous two zones. The younger phase, which contains elements of the Vinkovci–Somogyvár group as well as Early Bronze Age elements from Great Morava Valley, is also a possibility. However, this is speculative as only a small number of finds have been documented and absolute dates are lacking from which to draw more concrete conclusions.

Since only a few finds that can be attributed to the Early Bronze Age come from the Timok Region, and their stylistic and typological characteristics could also belong to the beginning of the Middle Bronze Age, the cultural–chronological picture in this region during the second half of the 3rd millennium BC remains unclear.

2.5 Southern Serbia with central Pčinja and the Kumanovo and Skopje Plains

This area encompasses the territory between Ponišavlje (Nišava Basin) in the east and the mountains of south-western Serbia, such as Zlatar, Jadovnik, and Stari Vlah, in the west, as well as between the West Morava River and the Ozren and Tresibaba mountains in the north, extending to the Skopje Plain, Gradištanska Mountain, and Osogovo Mountain in the south (see Fig. 1.1). Although this area is not geographically unified, consisting of several distinct geographic regions, it is treated as a single zone due to its similar cultural and chronological development during the Bronze Age. This zone includes southern Serbia (South Morava Basin, Ponišavlje, south-western Serbia, and Kosovo) and central Pčinja with the Skopje Plain.

South Morava Basin encompasses the basin of the South Morava River and its tributaries. The composite valley of the South Morava consists of three basins and two gorges: the Vranje-Bujanovac Basin, Grdelica Gorge, Leskovac Basin, Niš–Aleksinac Basin, and Stalać Gorge. The South Morava Basin predominantly features a moderately continental climate, although there are considerable variations due to the vastness of the region and the significant altitude differences within various parts of it. This area is rich in thermal-mineral springs and mineral resources (Rodić and Pavlović 1994, 145; Marković and Pavlović 1995, 113–121). The soil is fertile, particularly in the lowlands, such as the

Niš and Leskovac plains, the Vranje–Bujanovac Basin, the Preševo Depression, and others.

The eastern part of southern Serbia is known as Ponišavlje, which refers to the basin of the Nišava River. It is bordered to the north by the Svrljig Mountains and Vidlič, and to the south by Suva Mountain. This area consists of a composite valley made up of several basins (Pirot, Đurđevac, Dimitrovgrad, Niš, etc.), along with gorges and canyons (Ždrelo, Sićevo Gorge, Gradištanski Canyon, Mokranje Gorge, etc.). This natural communication route, connecting Great Morava Valley with the Sofia Plain and Thrace, was especially significant during the later periods of prehistory, as well as during the Roman era, as evidenced by the number of sites (Prodanović and Ranković 2017).

The south-western part of Serbia, or the Raška Region, is a mountainous area located between Zlatibor, Čemerno, Goč, the Metohija Plain, and Kopaonik, and includes the territories of the middle Ibar River Basin and the basins of the Studenica and Raška rivers.

Kosovo and Metohija is one of the most fertile regions in the central Balkans, surrounded by high mountains on all sides: Skopska Crna Gora and the Šar Mountains to the south; Mokra Gora and Kopaonik to the north and north-east; Goljak to the east; and Prokletije to the west. The territory of Kosovo is connected to south-western Serbia, or the Raška Region, through the Ibar Valley, making it probably the most significant natural communication route in prehistory between the communities in Kosovo and the Raška Region, just as it is today. This explains the similar cultural and chronological development during the Bronze Age, particularly in the Late Bronze Age.

The Pčinja Valley consists of three parts: Upper, Central, and Lower Pčinja, of which the regions of Upper and Central Pčinja are covered in this study. The upper course of the Pčinja Region is a distinctly mountainous area interspersed with smaller mountain rivers and it is connected to its central course, or the Kumanovo Plain, through a narrow gorge at Pelince. In the Upper Pčinja Region, the soil is generally poor, with fertile alluvial soil present only in the narrow zone of the Pčinja Valley. The Kumanovo Plain has a gently sloping terrain towards the south, with the most fertile parts being the alluvial plains along the Pčinja, Kumanovska River, and Kriva River, as evidenced by the numerous prehistoric settlements documented in these zones.

Geographically, the Skopje Plain is part of the Upper Vardar Valley, which merges with the Kumanovo Plain to the north-east, forming a large V-shaped plain, as one arm of Skopska Crna Gora partially intrudes from the north-west. The maximum length of this plain is about 35 km (north–south), and its maximum width is about 15 km. It is bordered by the slopes of Kozjak, Osogovo, and Gradištanska mountains to the east and south-east, and by the slopes of Jakupica and Skopska Crna Gora to the west and south-west.

The climate in this region varies depending on the orographic features and elevation, ranging from moderately continental in the lowland areas to harsher continental conditions in the mountainous areas.

As for mineral resources, aside from the Timok Region, this is one of the richest areas in terms of minerals, particularly copper and graphite, which could have been exploited during prehistory. Graphite deposits have been documented in Toplica and on Kopaonik, as well as in the vicinity of Bujanovac. Copper deposits have been registered on Kopaonik and in the northern part of Skopska Crna Gora (Durman 1983) and, according to some data, there are deposits of tin ore (cassiterite) near Bujanovac (Durman 1997).

2.5.1 Settlement and dwelling

In this zone, five hilltop settlements and 11 lowland settlements have been documented. In percentage terms, lowland settlements account for 69% of the total number of settlements, while hilltops constitute 31%. In some regions of this zone, this ratio is quite different. For example, in the Raška area, hilltops make up 100% of the settlements, while in the South Morava Basin and the upper course of the Vardar River, the ratio of hilltops to lowland settlements is 21% to 79%.

2.5.1.1 Hilltop settlements

In this zone, with its predominantly mountainous terrain, five hilltop settlements have been registered: two in the Raška area and one each in Ponišavlje, the Vardar Valley, and South Morava Basin. Site numbers refer to Plate 4.

LIST OF HILLTOP SETTLEMENTS

75. Postenje, the site of Gradina (Jevtić 1999); 76. Pazarište, the site of Gradina (Jevtić 1999); 77. Hum, the site of Velika Humska Čuka (Garašanin and Garašanin 1959; Bulatović and Milanović 2015; 2021); 78. Crvena Reka, the site of Šuplji Kamen (Bulatović and Stankovski 2012); 79. Skopje, the site of Kale (Mitrevski 2016).

In Raška, one hilltop settlement was discovered on a narrow ridge above the confluence of the Sebečevka and Raška rivers (Gradina in Pazarište), and another on a north-west to south-east oriented ridge overlooking the Raška Valley in Postenje near Novi Pazar. Both hilltops were also inhabited in the Middle Ages which significantly disturbed the prehistoric layers. Nonetheless, fragments of prehistoric pottery have been found in the archaeological layers though, unfortunately, no closed contexts were discovered. As a result, information about the architecture and living conditions during prehistory, including the Early Bronze Age, remains inaccessible for these hilltops.

The only Early Bronze Age hilltop settlement in South Morava Basin was registered on a prominent elevation on the north-eastern edge of the Niš Plain, offering a view of a large part of the Plain, as well as sections of the South

Morava and Nišava valleys. This is the site of Velika Humska Čuka, which is relatively easily accessible only from the northern side, while it is surrounded by steep limestone cliffs on the other sides. The large plateau at the top, covering almost 1 ha, was continuously inhabited from the Early Eneolithic to the Middle Ages, which negatively affected the preservation of cultural layers, particularly from the later prehistoric periods, including the Early Bronze Age. The site was excavated several times in the 1930s and 1950s, with further excavations resuming in 2014 (Bulatović and Milanović 2015).[15]

No closed contexts from the Early Bronze Age were documented at the site, except for a group of pottery with bones in the Early Bronze Age cultural layer in trench 1/15, and in later structures 9/09 and 10/09. The cultural layer from this period was therefore registered only at the top of the plateau and along the north-eastern edge of the site, despite excavations being conducted in all other parts of the plateau. This distribution of Early Bronze Age finds may suggest that the settlement from this period was located at the top of the plateau and on its northern part. Other than topographic characteristics, there is no further data about this settlement, as it was mostly damaged by the activities of later inhabitants, particularly those from late Antiquity.

There is little information about the hilltop settlement at the site of Šuplji Kamen in the village of Crvena Reka in Ponišavlje (Bulatović and Stankovski 2012, 42; Lazić 2017, 30). This settlement was located on a small dominant hill west of the Nišava River, where the Nišava comes closest to the edge of the valley. Several fragments of Early Bronze Age pottery were found at this site, but no additional data are available.

The southernmost hilltop settlement from the Early Bronze Age in this zone is located in the central part of the Skopje Plain, on a prominent elevation at the southern end of a long ridge of sedimentary sandstone on the eastern bank of the Vardar River, at the site of Kale. Like Velika Humska Čuka, this site was almost continuously inhabited from the Early Eneolithic to the Middle Ages. However, fortunately, the remains of several Early Bronze Age hearths, along with associated materials, have been preserved (Mitrevski 2016). The settlement from this period was significantly smaller than the Early Eneolithic one and was located only in the north-eastern part of the plateau. In two cultural layers from the Early Bronze Age, remains of above-ground structures and ten hearths were documented (Mitrevski 2016, 121), most of which were arranged in a north–south line, with some hearths overlapping. The hearths consist of irregular circular surfaces coated with clay, about 1 m in diameter, on a foundation of smaller river stones. One hearth, which extended under the Byzantine walls, was constructed with a foundation of ceramic fragments and river stones and, based on the amount of clay, it is assumed to have had a dome. Based on the structure of the architecture and the portable finds, mostly consisting of coarse kitchen pottery, it is assumed that this part of the settlement was used for food preparation, and post-holes indicate that the area was covered.

South of this area, an elliptical house was discovered, with post-holes along its perimeter dug into the bedrock. The southern part of the house is not preserved, while the northern part was apsidal in shape. The house was constructed using wattle and daub techniques with a packed earth floor. The author suggests that some elements of this building's architecture may have originated from the south (Mitrevski 2016, 124).

Hilltop settlements in this Central Balkan zone were mainly established along major natural communication routes, such as the valleys of the South Morava, Nišava, and Vardar rivers, or alternative routes, such as the Raška Valley on the edge of the Pešter plateau. From all these locations, large parts of the surrounding area could be surveyed, and all the sites were difficult to access and suitable for defence, which were likely important factors in the choice of settlement locations during this period for reasons that are not yet fully understood. No traces of fortifications have been documented at these settlements but, given the poorly preserved Early Bronze Age layers at these sites, the existence of defensive structures cannot be ruled out.

Of the mentioned hilltop settlements, only the settlement at Velika Humska Čuka has been absolutely dated, to the third quarter of the 3rd millennium cal BC.

2.5.1.2 Lowland settlements

Lowland settlements in this zone are significantly more numerous than hilltops, primarily located in the valleys of the South Morava and Nišava rivers, and the valleys of the South Morava's tributaries. Unfortunately, no remains of residential architecture have been documented at any of these sites. However, at certain locations such as Bubanj, Kovačke Njive, and Gradište in Davidovac, burials from this period have been discovered. The percentage ratio of hilltops to lowland settlements in this geographical zone is 31:69.

LIST OF LOWLAND SETTLEMENTS

80. Braljina, the site of Smrdan;[16] 81. Rujište, the site of Crnokalačka Bara (Tasić and Tomić 1969; Stojić and Čađenović 2006); 82. Vrtište, the site of Velika Česma (Garašanin *et al.* 1971; Stojić and Jocić 2006); 83. Novo Selo, site of Bubanj (Bulatović and Milanović 2020); 84. Glogovac, the site of Polje (Bulatović and Stankovski 2012; Lazić 2017); 85. Mala Plana, the site of Reka (Bulatović and Stankovski 2012); 86. Štulac, the site of Svinjarička Čuka (Horejs *et al.* 2018; 2019; 2022); 87. Pavlovac, the site of Kovačke Njive (Bulatović 2014; Bulatović *et al.* 2016, 205–220); 88. Davidovac, the site of Gradište (Bulatović 2014); 89. Klinovac, the site of Tri Kruške (Bulatović and

Stankovski 2012); 90. Miratovac, the site of Banjka Kaldrma (Bulatović and Stankovski 2012).

Lowland settlements in this zone are predominantly located near rivers, at the transition from alluvium to diluvium, i.e., on the first river terraces, which are slightly elevated compared to the floodplain areas of the alluvium. The majority of settlements have been documented on higher terraces along the South Morava River (Braljina, Školska Gradina, Vrtište, Bubanj, Kovačke Njive, Davidovac), but also along its tributaries, such as the Toplica River (Mala Plana), Moravica River (Miratovac), and Klinovačka River (Klinovac). A smaller number of settlements are located away from the main natural communication routes, deeper in the interior of the region, in the valleys of smaller rivers in the hilly and mountainous parts of the zone, such as the sites of Rujište, Glogovac, or Svinjarička Čuka (Stojić and Jocić 2006; Bulatović and Milanović 2020; Horejs *et al.* 2022).

Only a few of these settlements have been systematically excavated, so the quality of the data varies. The best-investigated sites are Bubanj, Kovačke Njive, and Polje, but all these sites are multi-layered, and no closed residential structures from the Early Bronze Age have been identified. The only closed contexts from this period are burials.

At the Bubanj site, during excavations from 2008 to 2014 (Pl. 1), three pits were discovered, mostly circular in shape – shallow (structures 1 and 91) or deeper (structure 20) – which likely served, at least secondarily, as refuse pits (Bulatović and Milanović 2020, 229–234). All structures are dated to the period of the 22nd–20th centuries cal BC (see Table 1). Despite detailed excavation of this part of the site, no other closed contexts were found, except for an aggregation of river cobbles with Early Bronze Age pottery (structure 75).

An Early Bronze Age burial has also been documented at the multi-layered site of Gradište in Davidovac near Vranje. The burial was approximately circular, with a diameter of about 0.7 m and a depth of about 0 2 m, filled with whole vessels, including a drum (Bulatović 2014, 61). No other finds from this period were found in the vicinity, leaving it unclear whether this was part of a settlement or a solitary burial with a special purpose, such as a ritual pit.

With these sparse and sporadic details it is difficult to draw any significant conclusions about the architecture, appearance, and organisation of settlements during the Early Bronze Age. M. Garašanin reported that fragments of daub and rammed earth floors were noted during earlier excavations in layers attributed to this period (Garašanin 1957, 270, 271), but these findings have not been confirmed by more recent excavations.

Fragments of plaster have been found at the sites of Velika Humska Čuka, Bubanj, Reka in Mala Plana, and Tri Kruške near Vranje. However, since these are multi-layered sites, it is uncertain whether this daub belongs to Early Bronze Age settlements from these locations.

Nevertheless, based on the remains of above-ground architecture at the hilltop settlement from this period at Kale in Skopje, and on the data from Bubanj as cited by M. Garašanin, it can be assumed that residential structures in the lowland settlements of the Early Bronze Age in this zone were also built using wattle and daub techniques.

Most of the other sites have been identified through survey work, except for the Smrdan site in Braljina, which was discovered during soil excavation for a brick factory in 2020.[17] This excavation opened up a large area, though it was not deep. The stratigraphy was simple, with a thin cultural layer containing numerous Early Bronze Age finds and possible late eneolithic and Middle Bronze Age finds. A bone tool fragment from the site has been dated to the 24th–23rd century cal BC, which corresponds to the stylistic and typological characteristics of the pottery from the site. Rescue excavations in 2024 revealed several pit dwellings and one larger rectangular above-ground structure with a hearth.[18]

2.5.2 Necropolises, burial practices, and ritual spaces

2.5.2.1 Necropolises

In this zone, three necropolises have been documented: 91. Rutevac, the site of Utrina, grave of an inhumed individual (Bulatović 2010); 92. Ranutovac, the site of Meanište, necropolis of cremated deceased (Bulatović 2020); 86. Štulac, the site of Svinjarička Čuka, grave of an inhumed deceased (Horejs *et al.* forthcoming).

The first necropolis is actually a single grave, discovered by chance during earthworks at the Utrina site in the lower course of the South Morava River. An inhumed individual was found, reportedly buried in an extended position on their back, with a single vessel placed near the skull (Fig. 2.37/7) (Bulatović 2010).

The necropolis at Ranutovac near Vranje, in the upper course of the South Morava River, represents a cremation necropolis with circular stone structures, 1.5–3 m in diameter (Bulatović 2020). It is situated on a higher river terrace of the South Morava, where the terrain begins to transition into the steep slopes of Mount Kukavica. During a rescue excavation in 2012, due to the construction of the Niš–Skopje highway, 21 graves were discovered in three separate segments of the necropolis. In all segments, the deceased were cremated at high temperatures on a communal pyre outside the necropolis. Each grave contained the cremated remains of one individual, usually placed directly on the ground, rarely in a vessel. Pottery was also found in the graves as grave goods, some of which had been burned along with the body. Around the remains of the deceased and the vessels, a ring of larger stones was created, and everything was covered with a structure comprising one or two layers of smaller stones.

Due to the poorly preserved and well cremated remains, anthropological analysis only determined that one individual was male, aged 20–29 (grave 3), and six other individuals were of similar age (graves 4, 5, 7, 14, 15, and 19). Analysis showed that the deceased were cremated at uneven temperatures ranging from 645° to 1200°C, and they were laid on their backs on the pyre. Absolute dates from six graves date the necropolis to the period between the 22nd and 18th centuries cal BC.

Although these necropolises are from approximately the same period (though no absolute date exists for the Rutevac grave) and they are only about 100 km apart, the necropolises in Rutevac and Ranutovac are entirely different. In Rutevac, the individual was inhumed in an extended position, while in Ranutovac, bodies were cremated and a small stone construction was erected above and around them. The stylistic and typological characteristics of the finds are also different but these will be discussed further below.

The grave at Svinjarička Čuka was discovered during research in 2023, and it is possible that it is not the only one at the site. It contained an inhumation in a crouched position on their right side, within a cist made of large stone slabs (Fig. 2.27). The grave goods included a set of gold jewellery, consisting of a hair ring (Pl. 5), a spring wire, and 35 miniature perforated cylindrical beads with bevelled edges, probably part of a necklace. The absolute date places this grave in the third quarter of the 3rd millennium BC (Horejs *et al.* forthcoming). Based on the grave goods, for which direct analogies have been found in steppe tumuli of the Yamnaya culture, from the peri-Pannonian zone to the Lower Danube, the grave can be placed culturally in phase 1 of the Early Bronze Age. This phase is more culturally, rather than chronologically, parallel to phase 1 in the previous zones.

Figure 2.27. Štulac: site of Svinjarička Čuka, grave of an inhumed individual with golden jewellery (photo by F. Ostmann).

2.5.2.2 Ritual spaces

In this geographical zone, two ritual spaces have been documented:

93. Pelince, the site of Dve Mogili, small circular stone constructions with offerings (Georgievski 1994; Trajkovska 1995; 1999; 2003; Mitrevski 2003; Bulatović and Stankovski 2012); 94. Kokino Selo, the site of Tatikev Kamen, observatory and ritual space (Stankovski 2002; 2003; 2007; 2010; Mitrevski 2003; Bulatović and Stankovski 2012).

The site Dve Mogili is located on a small elevation above the confluence of the Pčinja and Bistrica rivers on the southern periphery of the village Pelince, about 300 m south-west of the plateau where remains of Late Bronze Age and Early Iron Age settlements have been documented (Georgievski 1994; Trajkovska 1995; 2003). At the site, two larger mounds (Mogila I and II) were documented, made of soil and stones (possibly a cover). On the highest part of one of them (Mogila I), a large burnt area was discovered on bedrock, roughly circular with a diameter of about 6 m and a thickness of 0.10–0.15 m. In this burnt area, slag, a few animal bones, and ceramic fragments were found.[19] Around and beneath the burnt area, numerous groups of fragmented vessels or pottery shards were found, arranged in circular shapes, sometimes in natural rock depressions, often accompanied by other offerings besides ceramic vessels. The purpose of the burnt area is unclear, as the portable finds from the site were not burned. One explanation is that a specific type of volcanic ore, whose slag was found in the burnt area, was burned, emitting large amounts of smoke, which may have been used in fire rituals as a strong visual effect (Mitrevski 2003, 45).

Mogila II was significantly smaller and leaned against Mogila I on the north-eastern periphery, separated from it by a semi-circular stone ring. A smaller semi-circular area with a lot of ash, slag, and a few ceramic fragments was documented on Mogila II. Around the tumulus, on the north-eastern side, there was a semi-circular stone ring that probably enclosed the mound from that side (Trajkovska 1999).

About 4–5 m south-east of the burnt area on Mogila I, it was observed that the stone ring turned toward the west, as if to enclose the tumulus from the southern side. It was also noted that behind this ring, to the south, there was a depression about 3 m wide filled with soil and, beneath the soil, groups of pottery were found in the bedrock. This seems to represent the southern boundary of Mogila I and the beginning of another complex beyond the depression with very similar pit architecture. Supporting this theory is a smaller, irregularly shaped burnt area or hearth in that part of the site, in squares Г 27–28, about 12 m south of the centre of the large burnt area (Trajkovska 1999, 54). Additionally, a north–south oriented retaining wall about 4 m long was documented, securing this group of pits and the mentioned burnt area (hearth) from erosion on the steep eastern side.

Based on the architecture and layout of these pits, as well as the method of depositing ceramics and other offerings, A. Bulatović and J. Stankovski divided the entire area around the burnt area into four zones (Bulatović and Stankovski 2012, 73–85).[20]

The first zone consisted of groups of pottery beneath and immediately around the burnt area. In this zone, mostly ceramic fragments were deposited directly on the bedrock and, in some cases, they were surrounded by river pebbles. The southern part of this zone was covered with a stone layer.

The second zone consisted of pits located to the east, south-east, and south of the burnt area, seemingly outside Mogila I, or on and south of the stone ring, which likely marked the boundary of Mogila I. In this zone, the units consisted of one or more whole vessels deposited on a thin, levelled clay layer placed on the bedrock. The groups of vessels were surrounded by river pebbles and then covered with a stone layer. The units belonging to the second zone were found in squares: Б 25/26; БВ 26; В 25/26; Г 24, 25; Д 22, 25; Ѓ 22–23, 26; Е 21–23; Ж 15–22; З 15–20 and S 16.

The third zone was located to the south of zone 2, and its northern part contained the hearth. About 1 m east of the hearth was a retaining wall about 4 m long, made of several rows of stones. In this zone, mostly fragments of vessels were deposited on the bedrock and, in some pits, they were covered with a clay layer, while whole vessels were rare. In some units, new fragments of the same stylistic-typological characteristics were documented on the clay layer over the ceramic fragments. The squares with units belonging to the third zone were: А 35/36; Б 28, 34, 37; В 28, 29, 35, 37; Г 28–32.

The fourth zone consisted of several groups of pottery or pits located in the western and south-western part of this ritual space. These groups were not clearly defined or physically separated by pebbles or a clay layer, except for one group of pottery bordered by 17 slabs (square Ќ/У 24). The stylistic and typological characteristics of the ceramics in this zone are entirely different from the previous three zones. The groups of pottery or pits belonging to the fourth zone were located in squares: А 29; Ќ/У 24, Ч 32/33, Ц/Ч 34; Ц 22, 28/29; Ш/А 29, 32/33. Interestingly, fragments of pottery with the same characteristics as those from zone IV were also found on the stone cover in all zones of the sanctuary, suggesting that this zone IV pottery is younger than the other zones.

This is further supported by two absolute dates from the sanctuary, one from zone 3 (square Б 28) and the other from zone IV (square Ц 22) (Bulatović *et al.* 2018; 2020). The first date placed zone 3 in the Early Bronze Age, in the 24th–23rd centuries cal BC, while the second date placed zone 4 at the end of the Late Bronze Age, around the 12th century cal BC.

Unlike the last publication on this ritual space, we now have two absolute dates that confirm our earlier assumptions that zone 4 is much younger than the other zones, which are roughly chronologically close and continuously used during the Early Bronze Age (Bulatović and Stankovski 2012, 85). The previous publication suggested that zone 3 belonged to the end of the Early Bronze Age but the absolute date from this zone points to the developed phase of the Early Bronze Age, raising the question of whether zone 3, particularly the part with the smaller burnt area and retaining wall, is the oldest part of the ritual space. If so, the space would have expanded northward (Mogila 1, i.e., zones 1 and 2) and southward (the southern part of zone 3). In any case, the stylistic and typological characteristics of the pottery from zones 1–3 are nearly identical, indicating a similar period of use. Therefore, it can be assumed that zones 1–3 are roughly contemporaneous and belong to the Early Bronze Age and that the large burnt area is one of the younger components of this ritual space, at least younger than the pits beneath it (zone 1). However, the finds from the burnt area suggest that it also belongs to the Early, not the Late, Bronze Age, like zone 4.

It is fascinating that no material from the Middle Bronze Age was found at the site, indicating that there was no continuity of ritual activities throughout the entire Bronze Age. Instead, the communities that inhabited this region during the Late Bronze Age somehow recognised this ritual space and performed similar rituals as their predecessors had done about 1000 years earlier. Similar rituals have been documented at the Tatikev Kamen site in the Kokino Selo, 9 km east of Pelince.

The Tatikev Kamen site is located in the Kokino Selo on a prominent elevation with steep slopes, at an altitude of about 1000 m, offering a wide view of the surrounding area (Stankovski 2002). This location was not chosen by chance, as it dominates the landscape for several kilometres around. The summit consists of andesite rocks of volcanic origin with numerous channels and fissures which were suitable for interventions necessary to form a prehistoric observatory, which was part of this ritual space (Cenev 2009).

The most accessible slope of the site is the south-eastern one and a small settlement from the Early Iron Age was discovered at the top of this slope, without traces of ritual activities. Not far from the settlement, in a narrow passage about 5 m wide between two peaks, remains of surfaces with daub and Late Bronze Age finds were discovered. The entire summit (the highest part) of the north-western slope of the site is covered with ritual pits from various phases of the Bronze Age (Fig. 2.28).

On the lower of the two peaks, the so-called stone thrones were discovered: rocks carved into massive, connected seats facing north-east toward the higher peak about 20 m away. Several grooves and cuts in rock were documented on this higher peak, which served as markers for observing various astronomical phenomena. A special stone marker was also documented on the higher peak, used to mark the position of the sun on a day that could be associated with the end of the harvest. Analyses have shown that the sun passes through this marker twice a year, in mid-May and at the end of July when the harvest, which was of great importance in the ancient world, ends. On this day, the sun's rays pass through this marker and a smaller trench on the lower peak, falling directly on the throne (one of the stone seats), where it is believed a priest or elder sat (Cenev 2009, 10–11, fig. 10).

This unique archaeo-astronomical observatory could track the summer and winter solstices, the equinoxes, the minimum and maximum declination of the full moon in winter and summer, and it established a 19 year chronological cycle when the full moon appears in exactly the same place on the same date.

A flattened stone plateau on the top of the north-eastern slope, about 10 m north of the stone thrones, was used to observe the star Aldebaran, a companion of the Pleiades, a group of about 120 bright stars that have attracted the attention of skywatchers throughout history and are associated with many myths and legends (Kuzmanovska and Stankovski 2018, 35). Interestingly, the declination of Aldebaran and the equinox point coincided around 2000 BC, suggesting that the sanctuary was already established at that time, which is confirmed by numerous portable finds.

Four markers were documented at the observatory, used to observe total lunar eclipses, with each marker designed to observe this phenomenon 54 years after the previous one. Archaeo-astronomical measurements revealed that these markers were used to observe total lunar eclipses in 1917 BC, 1863 BC, 1809 BC, and 1755 BC (Cenev 2009, 9, table 2), a period confirmed by the stylistic and typological characteristics of some of the pottery from this site.

Regarding the absolute dates obtained through astronomical calculations and in the case of calculations of the Earth's axial tilt, the formation of the Kokino observatory is estimated to have occurred around the same period *c.* 1810 BC (Cenev 2002, 62).

This observatory, by the number of parameters it recorded, is one of the most significant in the ancient world. The discovery of a fragment of a large globular vessel depicting activities carried out at this site (Fig. 2.37/14),[21] convinced even the most sceptical that Kokino is indeed an astronomical observatory.

On the northern slope of the site, from the summit to the slope about 50 m below, numerous ritual units were documented. The entire area was enclosed on the northern side by a protective dry-stone wall, oriented east–west, about 80 m long (Fig. 2.28). South of the dry-stone wall, several shorter

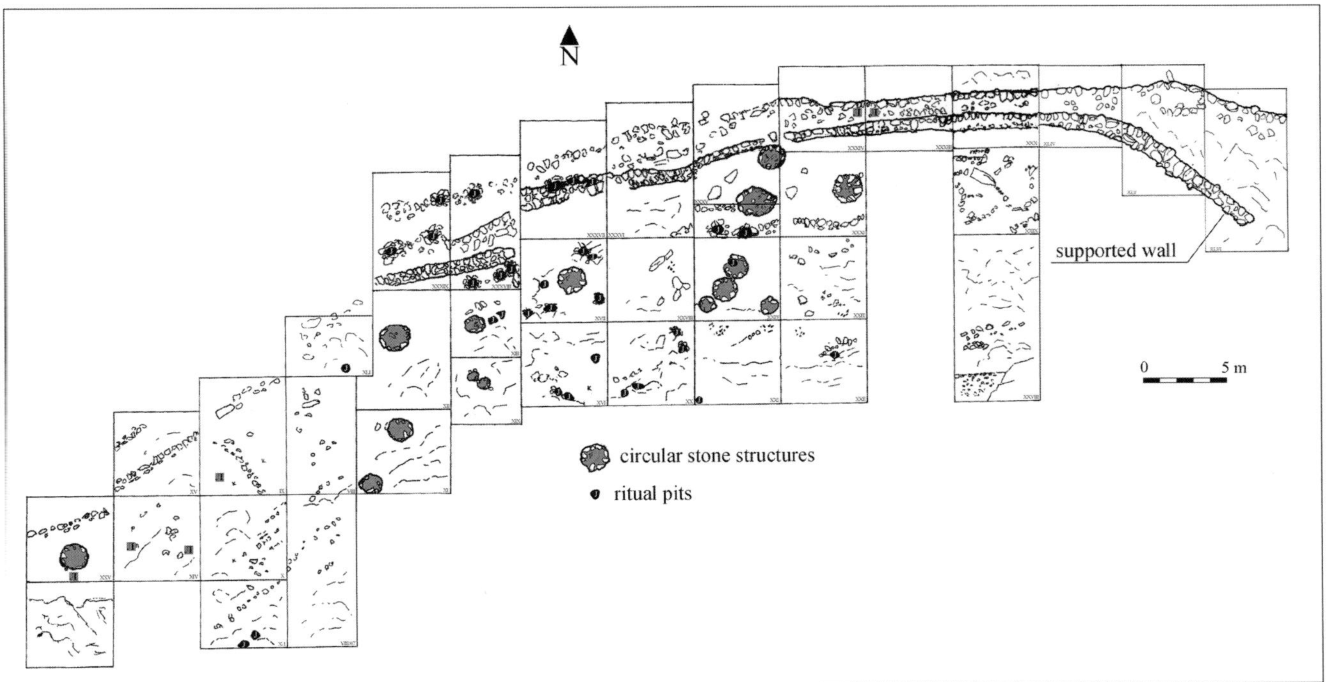

Figure 2.28. Kokino: site of Tatikev Kamen, ground plan of the ritual place on the northern slope of the site.

dry-stone walls of varying widths were documented, made of 2–3 rows of stones, likely to prevent soil erosion and maintain the stability of the ritual units, forming several platforms.

On these platforms, two types of units were documented: ritual pits and circular stone structures. The pits were dug into the ground or formed in the fissures of the bedrock, filled with offerings in the form of whole ceramic vessels or fragments, as well as objects made of baked clay, stone, or bronze. The circular stone structures had a diameter of 0.5–2 m, made of broken stone, and typically covered offerings placed on the ground or in a rock fissure. The structure consisted of a circular ring and a covering of larger stones, filled with smaller stones. The only difference between the pits and the stone structures is that the pits had no stone construction, or only a few stones marked the edge of the pit; both were then covered with soil and small stones, giving them the appearance of small tumuli. In some units the offerings were covered with a stone slab and clay.

Groups of pottery were also found without pits or circular structures, placed directly on the ground or rock. These ritual units were used for offerings to deities for various purposes, aimed at ensuring the well-being and prosperity of the donor and their loved ones.

Several objects made of baked clay were found at the site, including a human leg, a fragment of a bench (chair), and anthropomorphic and zoomorphic figurines. The choice of these offerings was presumably related to the specific wishes of those making the offerings.

The discovery of a funnel in a beaker in one pit (Fig. 2.29) suggests certain chthonic rituals involving libations, or the offering of liquid sacrifices. Based on the stylistic and typological characteristics of the ceramics, most of the ritual units date to the Early Bronze Age, while finds from the Middle and Late Bronze Age are mostly from

Figure 2.29. Kokino: site of Tatikev Kamen, a funnel inside a beaker on the bottom of the pit (detail), remains of some libation ritual?

layers or disturbed units, making their attribution difficult. Almost no animal bones were found at the site, except in a few cases where they were in such poor condition that they were unsuitable for dating. Due to the lack of organic samples, there are no absolute dates from this site, except for those obtained from archaeo-astronomical analyses.

2.5.3 Portable finds

2.5.3.1 Pottery

The largest number of Early Bronze Age settlements has been recorded in this zone, which has resulted in a significant number of ceramic vessels being found. Only a few indicative and typical examples are presented here. The percentages of various types of vessels are not entirely precise but give an approximate sense of their relative abundance.[22]

New vessel types, such as askoi and so-called ember containers, appear in this zone, as well as other new elements that distinguish it, particularly in terms of pottery.

A. BOWLS

The most common type of bowl in this zone is the semi-circular bowl, mostly with an unprofiled rim (type 3a), found in all regions of the zone but most prevalent in the south, in the upper South Morava Basin, Upper Pčinja, and the Skopje Plain (Fig. 2.30/2, 6, 13; Fig. 2.31/3, 5–8, 11, 13; Fig. 2.32/2, 3, 5, 12; Fig. 2.33/13, 14, 22, 23, 26, 29; Fig. 2.34/2, 20; Fig. 2.35/1; Fig. 2.36/8, 9, 17; Fig. 2.37/4–6, 18; Fig. 2.38/4, 7, 16, 17; Fig. 2.39/2, 4; Fig. 2.40/1, 5; Fig. 2.41/1, 16, 18, 19; Fig. 2.42/1, 11). These make up almost half of the bowls (around 47%) in this zone. The second most common type is a variant of the previous bowl, a semi-circular form with an inward-curving upper part or rim (type 3b), accounting for about 21%, and similarly most frequent in the southern part of this zone (Fig. 2.30/15, 16; Fig. 2.33/7, 10, 11; Fig. 2.36/10; Fig. 2.37/9–11; Fig. 2.38/5; Fig. 2.40/10, 13; Fig. 2.41/4–7, 23; Fig. 2.42/12, 14).

Types 1b (Fig. 2.31/10, 12; Fig. 2.34/3, 4; Fig. 2.35/4; Fig. 2.36/11; Fig. 2.40/2; Fig. 2.42/2) and 2a (Fig. 2.30/1; Fig. 2.31/4; Fig. 2.32/1, 13; Fig. 2.35/2, 3, 14; Fig. 2.37/8) are equally represented, with about 10% and 8%, respectively, and are more prevalent in the southern part of the zone. The least common types are 3c (Fig. 2.30/10; Fig. 2.32/4; Fig. 2.36/1; Fig. 2.39/1, 3; Fig. 2.42/13; Fig. 2.43/7), 1a (Fig. 2.31/1, 2; Fig. 2.32/14; Fig. 2.34/1; Fig. 2.38/6), and 4a (Fig. 2.32/3, 11; Fig. 2.39/14, 15), which together make up about 15%, and are evenly distributed throughout all regions of this zone.

B. CUPS

Cups are not common in this zone but still appear to be more frequent here than in other zones and they are found in all types. The most numerous are type 1a cups (semi-circular with a handle extending high above the rim), making up more than half of the cups in this zone (Fig. 2.31/15; Fig. 2.35/23; Fig. 2.36/2, 12, 13, 15; Fig. 2.37/2; Fig. 2.38/2).

Cups labelled as types 4a (Fig. 2.35/17, 25) and 4b (Fig. 2.35/21; Fig. 2.39/5; Fig. 2.42/5) are characteristic only of the far south and south-west of this zone. Together, they account for about 33%, while type 3b cups, found only in the ritual space at Pelince (Fig. 2.39/18; Fig. 2.41/9), make up about 13% of all cups. Conical cups have not been documented in this zone.

C. BEAKERS

Beakers are found in many different types, with type 1c being the most numerous, accounting for about 42% (Fig. 2.30/3, 4, 8, 9, 12; Fig. 2.31/16, 19; Fig. 2.33/1–3, 6, 15, 24; Fig. 2.34/5; Fig. 2.35/7; Fig. 2.37/15; Fig. 2.38/3, 9; Fig. 2.39/6, 8, 10; Fig. 2.40/15, 16; Fig. 2.43/5–7). These are equally represented throughout the zone, from the lower course of the South Morava in the north to the Skopje Plain in the south, except in the Raška Region, where ceramic finds are scarce. This type of beaker is the most common type in the central Balkans during the Early Bronze Age and remained in almost unchanged form throughout the entire Bronze Age, with handles becoming higher and extending across the vessel's opening over time.

The next most common type is 1e (about 15%), characteristic mainly of the southern part of this zone (Fig. 2.31/16, 17; Fig. 2.35/18, 20; Fig. 2.36/3, 14, 20; Fig. 2.37/1, 3), followed by type 4a (11.5%) (Fig. 2.31/20; Fig. 2.33/27; Fig. 2.35/22; Fig. 2.37/12, 17; Fig. 2.38/15; Fig. 2.41/22). Types 1d (Fig. 2.39/7; Fig. 2.40/7; Fig. 2.41/2, 3), 2a (Fig. 2.31/18), 5a (Fig. 2.41/8), 7c (Fig. 2.37/16; Fig. 2.39/9, 11–13), and 8 (Fig. 2.35/9; Fig. 2.40/3) have been documented exclusively in the southern part of the zone, i.e., in Upper Pčinja and occasionally in the Skopje Plain, together making up about 21%.

Types 3a (Fig. 2.30/5, 7), 6a (Fig. 2.37/7), and 7b (Fig. 2.33/28), on the other hand, have been registered only at sites in the northern part of the zone, i.e., in the lower South Morava. However, these beakers are very rare, accounting for only 7% of the total number of beakers presented.

D. AMPHORAE

Compared to bowls and beakers, amphorae are not a widely represented type of vessel in the Early Bronze Age in the central Balkans, and the same applies to this zone. The most common type of amphora in this zone is type 1a (Fig. 2.31/22; Fig. 2.33/18; Fig. 2.36/5, 16; Fig. 2.40/9, 11), predominantly found at southern sites in the zone. All other types of amphorae, such as 2a (Fig. 2.32/9; Fig. 2.40/12), 3a (Fig. 2.40/8), and 4a (Fig. 2.35/5), have been found exclusively at sites in the southern part of this zone, i.e., in the upper South Morava or Upper Pčinja.

E. DOUBLE VESSELS

As in the peri-Pannonian zone, double vessels have also been documented in this zone, but only one example was found, in the necropolis at Ranutovac (Fig. 2.35/15). Interestingly, it was found in the grave completely vitrified, having clearly been burned at high temperatures, suggesting it burned on the pyre together with the deceased, whose remains were placed in the grave along with the vessel (Bulatović 2020).

F. ASKOI

This type of vessel has been documented only in this zone, in the southern part, i.e., in the upper South Morava and Skopje Plain (Fig. 2.31/21; Fig. 2.35/19). This is not surprising geographically, as such vessels are characteristic of the Aegean region.

G. EMBER CONTAINERS

These unusual vessels have been documented only in this zone, at the necropolis of cremated burials at Ranutovac (Fig. 2.35/4; Fig. 2.36/4, 25) and at the ritual space at Kokino. A total of five such vessels were found in the necropolis and one in Kokino which, however, is attributed to the Middle Bronze Age (Bulatović and Stankovski 2012; Bulatović 2020). The vessels in Ranutovac were found in later graves dated to the first quarter of the 3rd millennium, which could already be chronologically assigned to the Middle Bronze Age according to the Bronze Age chronology of the central Balkans. This necropolis is the northernmost site where such vessels have been found as they are characteristic of ancient Macedonia, a region inhabited during the Early Bronze Age by communities of the so-called Armenochori group (Bulatović 2013).

These vessels, based on their appearance and location, have been defined as ember containers, though their exact purpose is unclear. It is speculated that they may have been used as a type of censer (Bulatović 2013, 7; Gori 2015, 117–120).

It is difficult to generalise about the fabric, colour, and surface quality of vessels in this zone for several reasons. This zone contains the largest number of Early Bronze Age sites, resulting in an extremely high number of vessels and the quality of published information is uneven. For this reason it is possible to speak about these characteristics based on a certain number of sites, which fortunately are located in different regions of this zone, so this information can be treated as a reference for other nearby sites.

For example, at the Smrdan site in Braljina, the vessels are mostly smoothed or rough-surfaced, with colours ranging from reddish, through dark grey, to black. At Bubanj, in structures 1 and 91 from the Early Bronze Age, the pottery has equally smoothed and polished surfaces, regardless of vessel type, and the colour is mostly dark grey, dark brown, or black. The pottery from Velika Humska Čuka is similar to that from Bubanj but mostly brown in colour, including some ochre tones. In Davidovac, in the 'ritual' pit, the pottery is polished or smoothed and fired in shades of black–ochre or grey–dark brown. The ceramic drum from the pit is black, with a well-polished exterior and interior surface. Thus, at all the settlements mentioned, the situation is similar: the pottery is generally smoothed or polished, regardless of vessel type, while pots have rough or smoothed surfaces and are reddish or light brown in colour.

The situation at the Ranutovac necropolis and the ritual spaces in Kokino Selo and Pelince is somewhat different. In Ranutovac, there is a higher proportion of cups compared to other vessel types and at the aforementioned sites, suggesting that this type of vessel was more prevalent in funerary rituals. Other vessel types, such as askos, double vessels, and ember containers (censers), which are rare or absent at other sites, also appear here. The pottery is exclusively polished or smoothed, and rough vessels are absent, which is expected for a necropolis. The pottery lacks a slip and is fired in shades of reddish, grey, ochre, or brown. Chemical–physical analyses of the composition of the pottery from this necropolis revealed that it was made from local clay from a nearby deposit at Beli Šanac in Suvi Do, about 2 km west of the necropolis (Gajić-Kvaščev *et al.* 2020).

The outer surface of the pottery from the ritual space in Pelince is mostly polished, with some polished examples (beakers), whether bowls, cups, beakers, or amphorae. Only sporadically are some amphorae and pots smoothed. As in Ranutovac, there is a higher proportion of cups compared to settlement assemblages, as well as a large percentage of pottery fired in shades of red, which may indicate a specific choice of pottery colour for offerings. In addition to red, shades of brown, grey, and black were also documented.

At the ritual space in Kokino Selo, a higher number of cups were also documented, along with reddish pottery, although not to the extent seen in Pelince. However, here too, the pottery is mostly polished, which may suggest more careful treatment or selection of pottery with better quality surfaces intended for offerings. In addition to reddish pottery, brown, grey, ochre, and black pottery was also recorded.

H. HANDLES

The most common type of handle is the arched handle, usually of ribbon-shaped, but sometimes oval cross-section, found primarily on beakers but also on bowls. These handles are evenly distributed throughout the entire geographic zone, from the Raška Region in the west to Ponišavlje in the east (Fig. 2.30/3–9, 12; Fig. 2.32/8–10; Fig. 2.33/2–9, 14, 15, 24, 28, 29; Fig. 2.34/3–5, 8, 9; Fig. 2.42/2, 3, 18), and to the upper course of the South Morava and Skopje Plain in the south (Fig. 2.31/3, 13, 15–22; Fig. 2.34/23; Fig. 2.35/1, 4, 5, 11, 14, 17, 18, 20, 21, 23; Fig. 2.36/2, 3, 10–15, 20; Fig. 2.37/1–3, 11, 15–17; Fig. 2.38/1–3, 7–9, 11, 14, 15; Fig. 2.39/6–13, 16, 17; Fig. 2.40/3, 7, 12, 15, 16; Fig. 2.41/2, 3, 6, 8, 19, 23).

It has been observed that these handles rarely extend above the opening of the beaker in the northern part of this zone while, in the southern part, a greater number of beakers with handles extending above the vessel's opening were noted. However, it is unclear whether this difference is due to geographical distribution or a chronological distinction.

Occasionally, these handles have a concave cross-section, as seen in examples from Braljina, Bubanj, and Ranutovac (Fig. 2.32/9; Fig. 2.33/10; Fig. 2.37/1), which will become one of the distinguishing characteristics of material culture in the Middle Bronze Age, particularly in the northern Balkans.

Tunnel-shaped handles are also numerous in this zone, typically of ribbon-shaped (Fig. 2.31/4, 14; Fig. 2.35/10, 13, 22, 25; Fig. 2.36/5, 16; Fig. 2.37/9; Fig. 2.40/5, 9–11; Fig. 2.41/1), oval (Fig. 2.30/11; Fig. 2.31/1; Fig. 2.35/19; Fig. 2.37/18; Fig. 2.42/8, 9, 11), or concave cross-sections (Fig. 2.33/10). Tongue-shaped handles are also quite common and many are vertically perforated or decorated with finger impressions along the rim (Fig. 2.31/5–7, 11, 23, 24; Fig. 2.32/12, 15, 18; Fig. 2.34/10; Fig. 2.35/27; Fig. 2.36/7, 19, 24; Fig. 2.38/5; Fig. 2.39/15; Fig. 2.41/15; Fig. 2.42/1, 10). Rectangular-shaped handles are rare but are found throughout the entire territory of this zone (Fig. 2.32/16, 17; Fig. 2.34/25; Fig. 2.35/12; Fig. 2.37/7; Fig. 2.39/14; Fig. 2.40/2).

I. ORNAMENTATION

When it comes to the ornamentation of pottery, this geographic zone has the highest occurrence of decorated ceramics among all zones in the central Balkans. The most common forms of ornamentation are incising and applying plastic additions to the rim, or protrusions on the vessel's body. Also present are puncturing and grooving, as well as imprinting rows of punctate impressions (fingerprints) or incised notches directly onto the surface, along with the application of plastic bands or ribs.

Among incised motifs, the most frequent are zig-zag lines (Fig. 2.30/2, 14; Fig. 2.33/12; Fig. 2.38/10, 11; Fig. 2.40/14–16) and triangles (Fig. 2.33/19, 27; Fig. 2.35/16; Fig. 2.37/13; 33/8, 15), often combined with punctate impressions (Fig. 2.33/19, 27; Fig. 2.35/16; Fig. 2.38/8). Other incised motifs include nets (Fig. 2.30/13, 14), horizontal and vertical lines (Fig. 2.32/15, 18; Fig. 2.33/20; Fig. 2.38/15), occasionally filled with inlays (Fig. 2.32/16; Fig. 2.33/27, 30; Fig. 2.41/10), which sometimes form zig-zag or straight bands filled with triangles, punctate impressions, or incised lines reminiscent of late eneolithic pottery (Fig. 2.38/12, 13; Fig. 2.40/6). One fragment features an incised rectangular motif combined with punctate impressions (Fig. 2.33/30), and ceramics decorated with wavy lines have also been documented (Fig. 2.37/14; Fig. 2.38/14).

Of particular interest is a fragment of a large globular vessel decorated with multiple wavy lines, above and below which several sun motifs are depicted (Fig. 2.37/14). This fragment illustrates ancient astronomical activities at the Kokino site. The motif is intriguing as it comes from

Tatikev Kamen, a site that served as a kind of prehistoric observatory for observing the positions of the sun and moon. The depiction of several suns and wavy lines, which likely represent the horizon of mountains or hills, or perhaps stone markers, appears to describe the activities occurring at this site during the Early Bronze Age. Unfortunately, only part of this composition has survived, so it is impossible to recognise any actual positions of the sun in relation to the surrounding terrain of the site. Nonetheless, it seems that the incised representation is more symbolic than realistic, but in any case, it confirms, along with all other astronomical parameters, that this was a prehistoric observatory.

Incised ornamentation is also the most visually striking, especially when filled with inlays. Interestingly, these ornaments have been found mainly in the north (Bubanj, Velika Humska Čuka, Braljina) at settlement sites while, in the south, they are exclusively associated with ritual spaces in Kokino Selo and Pelince, and are not found in settlements.

One of the most common decorative techniques, not only in this geographic zone but also across all zones in the central Balkans, is the application of plastic additions to the rims of vessels, especially bowls. These additions can be triangular (Fig. 2.30/1; Fig. 2.32/3; Fig. 2.33/10, 11, 22; Fig. 2.36/9; Fig. 2.37/4; Fig. 2.38/17; Fig. 2.41/6, 19), semi-circular (Fig. 2.30/10; Fig. 2.31/8; Fig. 2.32/4; Fig. 2.33/26; Fig. 2.34/17, 20, 21, 22; Fig. 2.36/12; Fig. 2.37/5, 10, 11; Fig. 2.38/7; Fig. 2.42/11), fan-shaped (Fig. 2.30/15; Fig. 2.33/7; Fig. 2.35/1; Fig. 2.38/1, 5; Fig. 2.39/3; Fig. 2.40/10; Fig. 2.41/5), or rectangular (Fig. 2.41/1, 4, 18). It is noteworthy that rectangular additions are the least common and were found mainly in the southern part of the zone (Pelince), while the others are more-or-less evenly distributed across the entire zone.

In addition to plastic additions on the rim, pottery were also decorated with this technique in other forms, such as vertical (Fig. 2.33/1; Fig. 2.36/6, 7; Fig. 2.38/3; Fig. 2.41/23) and horizontal ribs (Fig. 2.33/1, 21; Fig. 2.38/18), crescent-shaped ribs (Fig. 2.38/6), wart-shaped protrusions (Fig. 2.31/2, 9, 12; Fig. 2.34/13; Fig. 2.37/13; Fig. 2.41/22; Fig. 2.42/12), or button-like additions (Fig. 2.36/1; Fig. 2.38/9; Fig. 2.40/9). These decorations are found throughout the entire geographic zone.

Puncturing is also a fairly common ornamentation technique, often used in combination with other techniques, most commonly incising. The punctures can be dot-like (Fig. 2.33/12, 19, 27, 30; Fig. 2.35/16; Fig. 2.38/8, 12, 13; Fig. 2.41/10, 17), slanted (Fig. 2.32/15; Fig. 2.41/20), or oval (Fig. 2.32/6; Fig. 2.39/19; Fig. 2.40/14; Fig. 2.42/4).

In addition to the above, the technique of applying fingertip impressions directly to the surface of the vessel is also fairly common in this zone where it is used to decorate the rims (Fig. 2.32/5, 12; Fig. 2.41/14; Fig. 2.42/16), bodies (Fig. 2.34/24, 25), necks (Fig. 2.35/8), just below the rims (Fig. 2.38/19; Fig. 2.40/8; Fig. 2.41/13), and is especially common along the outer edges of handles (Fig. 2.31/6, 23, 24; Fig. 2.32/19; Fig. 2.41/15; Fig. 2.42/10, 17). It has been noted that this ornament is used throughout this zone, from the South Morava and West Morava basins to the Skopje Plain.

Finger impressions and vertical notches on plastic bands on rougher vessels are also very common, as in nearly all prehistoric periods in the central Balkans (Fig. 2.30/17; Fig. 2.40/8, 9; Fig. 2.41/12, 21; Fig. 2.42/6). Rows of notches along or just below the rim, directly on the surface of the vessel, have been documented mainly in South Morava Basin (Fig. 2.33/17, 23, 25, 29; Fig. 2.34/18).

Grooving is a sporadically used technique, as seen on fragments from Pelince with circular concentric grooves (Fig. 2.39/20–22) or a vertical groove on a handle from Pazarište (Fig. 2.42/2). One example is decorated with an ornament in the form of lines in various directions (Fig. 2.32/17), known as the *Besenstrich* ornament.

2.5.3.2 Other and chance finds

Among the notable finds are a percussion instrument, specifically a drum found in a pit in Davidovac (Fig. 2.35/6), and numerous items made of copper, polished and chipped stone, bone, antler, and baked clay.

LIST OF SITES WITH CHANCE FINDS

95. Lozane, the site of Biljurski Rid, two axes of the Lozane type (Fig. 2.43/2, 3) (Ercegović-Pavlović and Kostić 1988, 18, fig. 125; Bulatović and Jović 2010, 228); 96. Leskovac, the site of Hisar, an axe of the Lozane type (Fig. 2.43/1) (Garašanin and Ivanović 1958, 42; Ercegović-Pavlović and Kostić 1988, 18; Bulatović and Jović 2010, 200–201); 97. Gornji Matejevac, unknown site (Fig. 2.43/4);[23] 98. Rutevac, the site of Školska Gradina, three beakers of type 1c (Fig. 2.43/5–7) (Stojić and Čađenović 2006, 313–314, cat. 1–4);[24] 99. Konopnica, unknown site, a bowl of type 3b with two handles (Fig. 2.43/8) (Bulatović and Jović 2010, 195); 100. Pločnik, unknown site, a beaker of type 1c (Fig. 2.43/9) (Stojić and Jocić 2006); 101. Bacijevce near Surdulica, unknown site, a stone axe with flanges (Fig. 2.43/22) (Bulatović 2007).

In this geographic zone, three axes of the Lozane type have been documented, two of which were found at Biljurski Rid near Bojnik (Fig. 2.43/2, 3) and one at Hisar in Leskovac (Fig. 2.43/1), both in the same region, approximately 25 km apart. This type of axe has been recorded predominantly in this zone, specifically in South Morava Basin, with one example each found in Great Morava Valley (zone 2) and western Serbia (zone 3). Chemical analyses are available for the specimens from Lozane and Hisar, revealing that they were made of copper with a small percentage of arsenic, though not enough to classify them as arsenical bronze

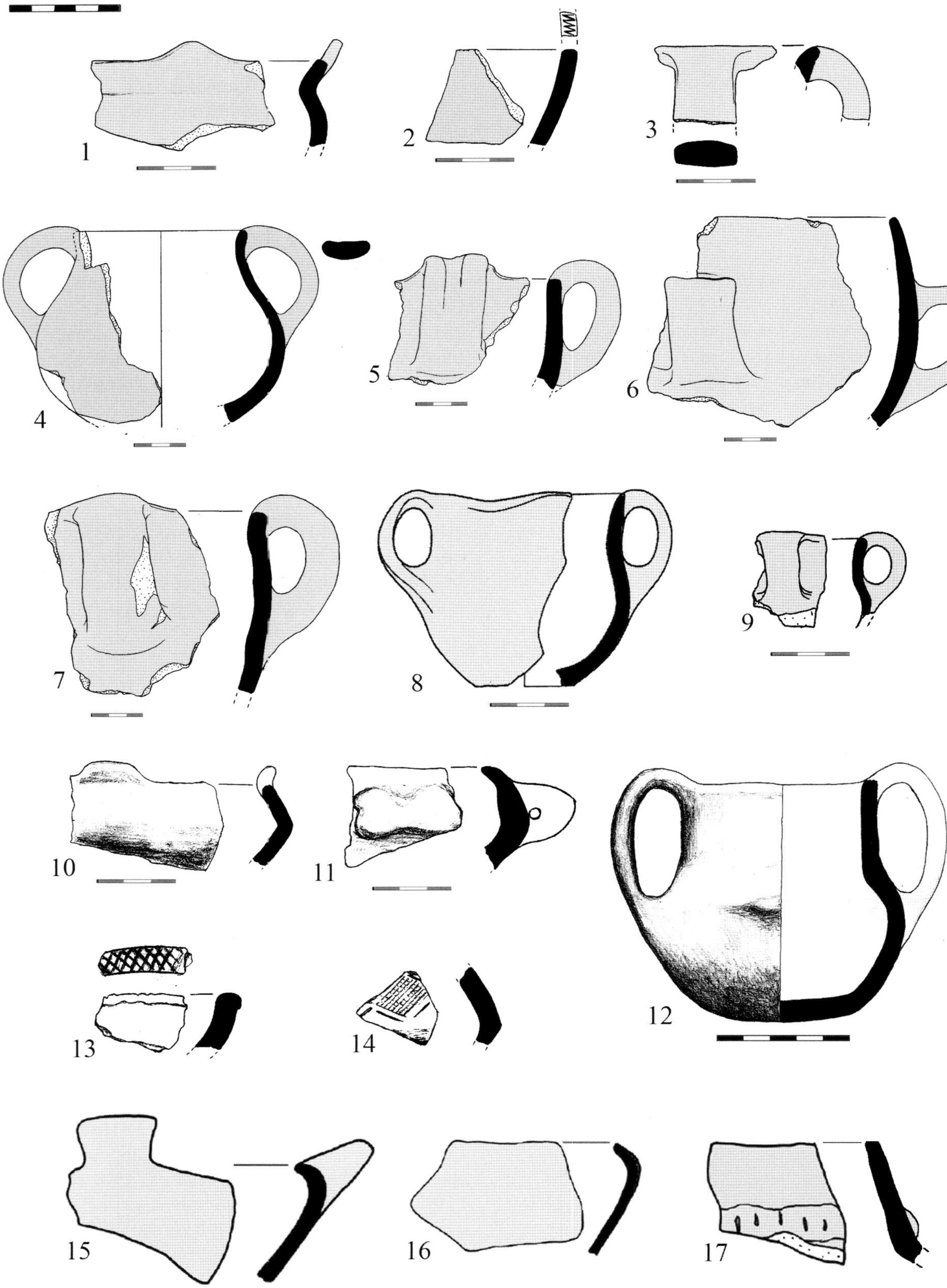

Figure 2.30. Hum: site of Velika Humska Čuka: 1–7, Trench 1/15, pottery accumulation; 8–9, previous finds; 10–14, Trench 1/09, structure 10; 15–17, Crvena Reka: site of Šuplji Kamen.

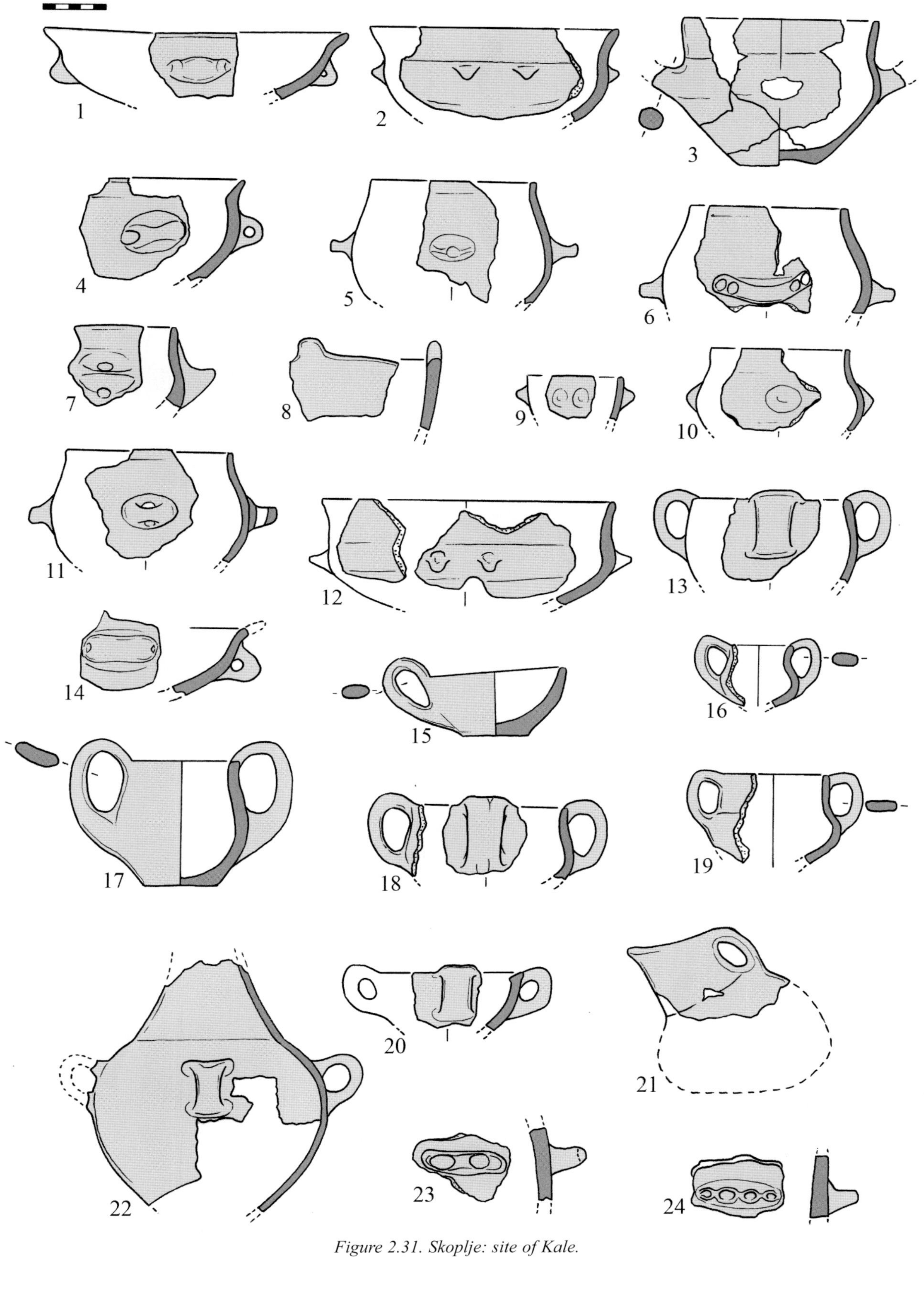

Figure 2.31. Skoplje: site of Kale.

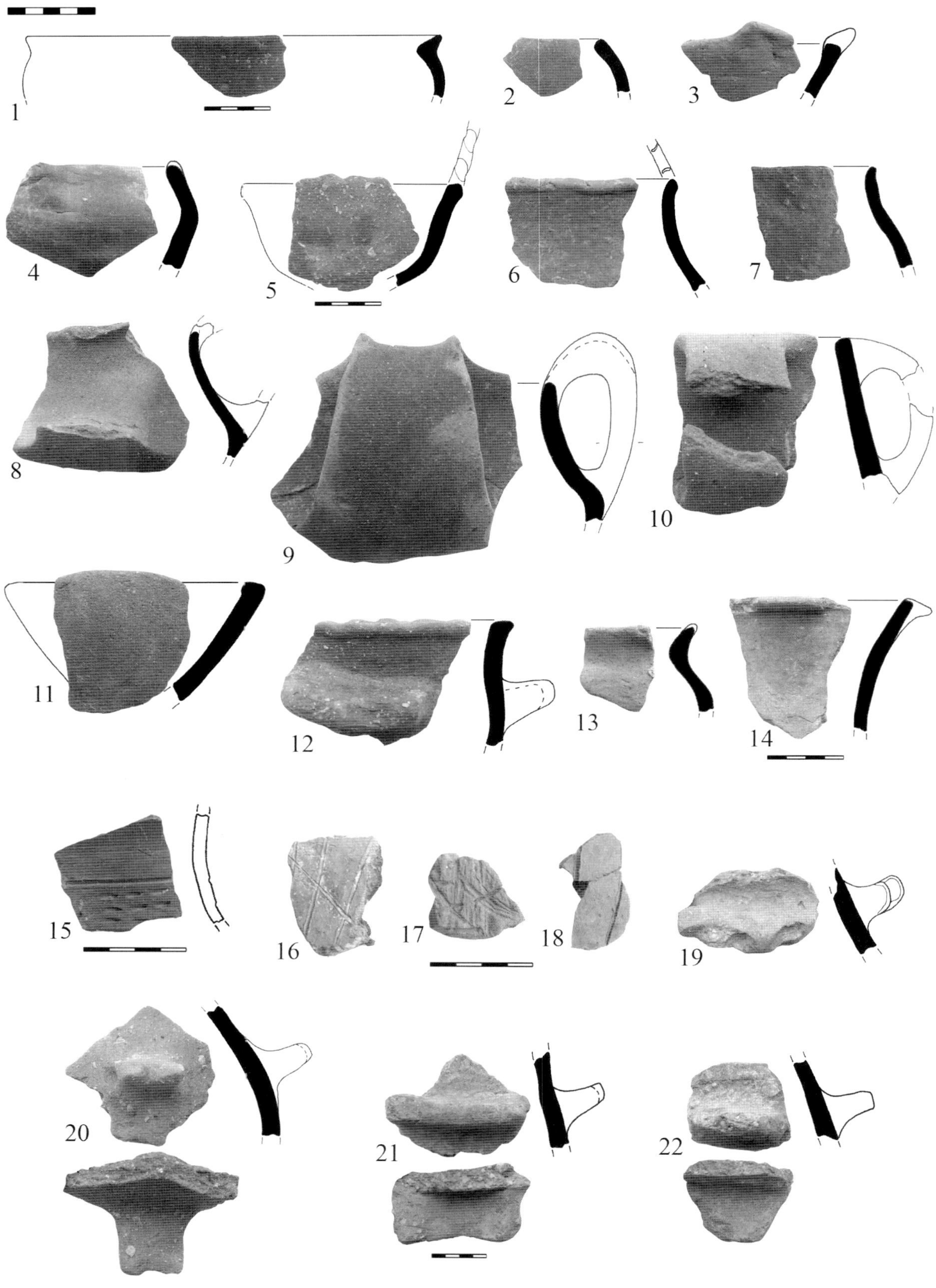

Figure 2.32. Braljina: site of Smrdan.

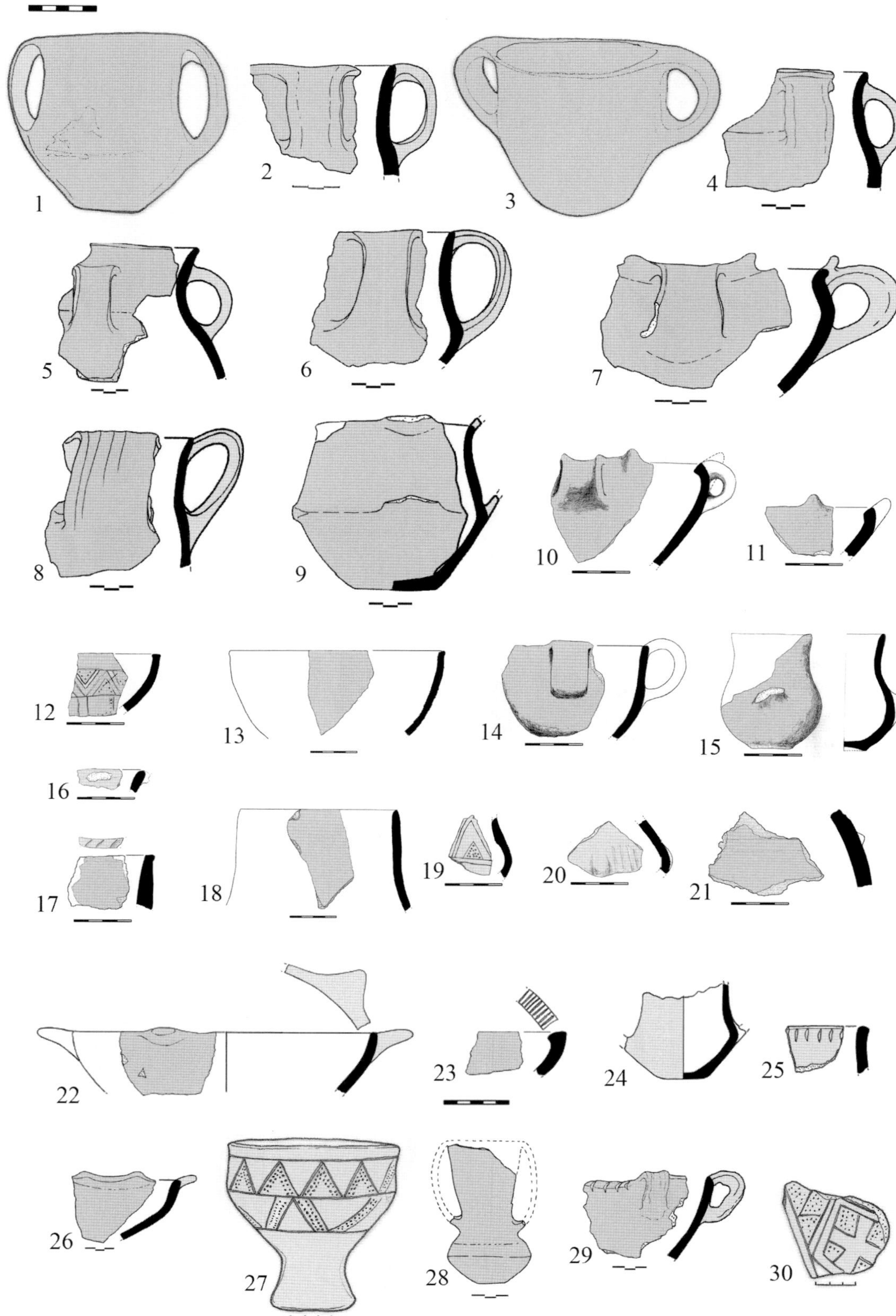

Figure 2.33. 1–2, Rujište: site of Crnokalačka Bara; 3–9, Vrtište: site of Velika Česma; 10–30, Novo Selo: site of Bubanj: 10–21, structure 1; 22–25, structure 91; 26–30, the old excavations.

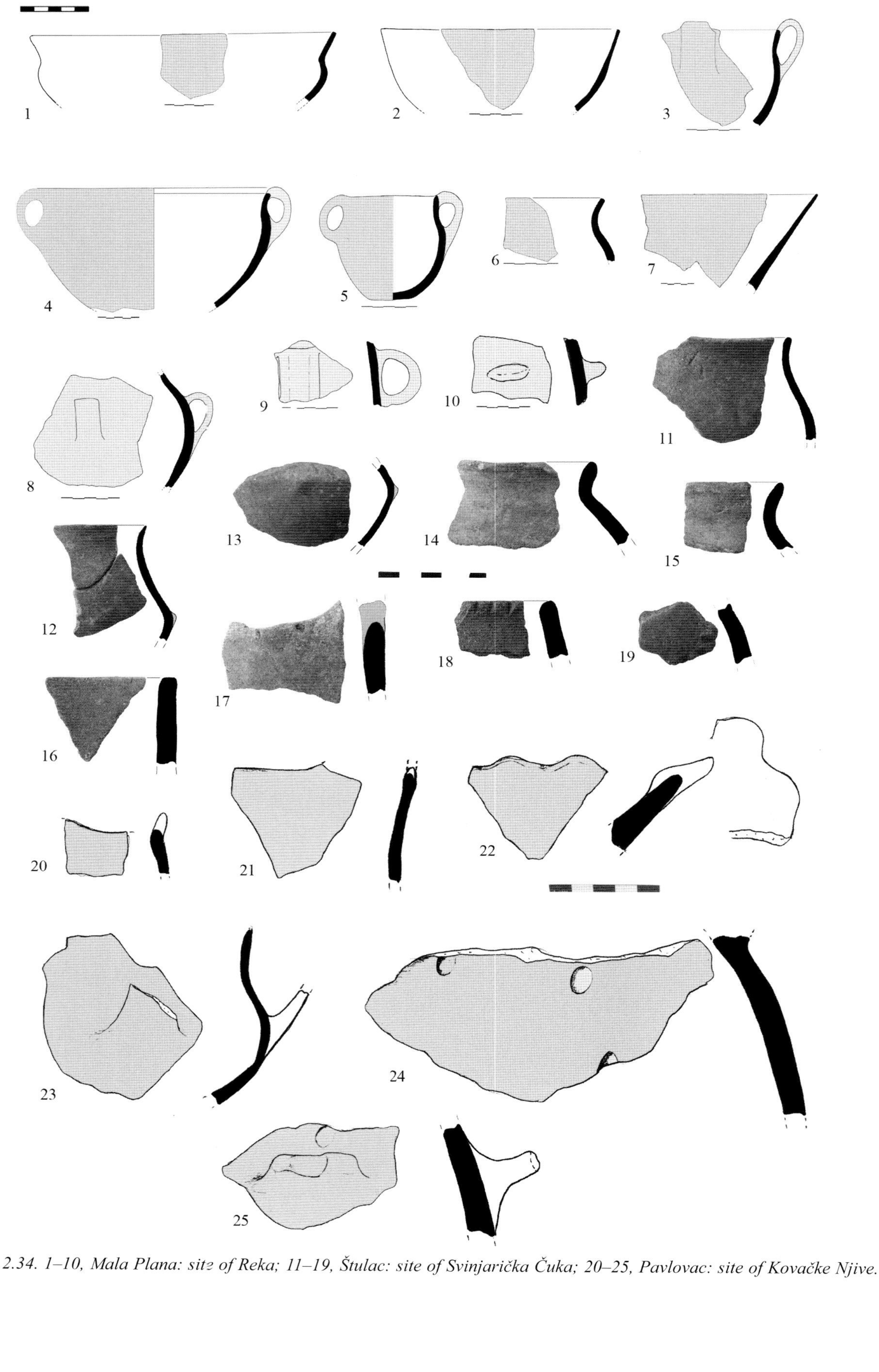

Figure 2.34. 1–10, Mala Plana: site of Reka; 11–19, Štulac: site of Svinjarička Čuka; 20–25, Pavlovac: site of Kovačke Njive.

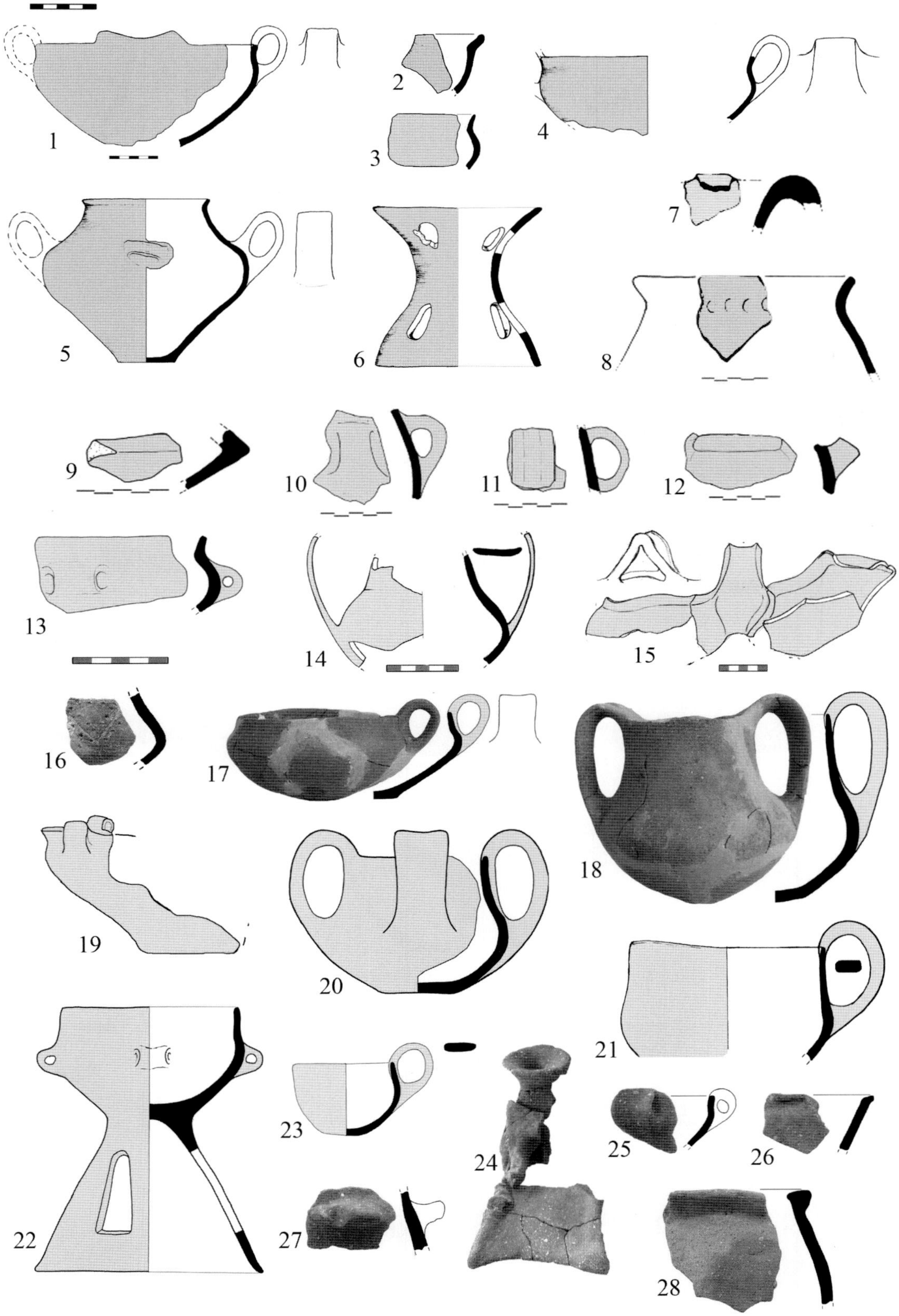

Figure 2.35. 1–6, Davidovac: site of Gradište; 7–8, Klinovac: site of Tri Kruške; 9–11, Miratovac: site of Banjka-Kaldrma; 13–28, Ranutovac: site of Meanište: 13–16, grave 1; 17–19, grave 3; 20–21, grave 5; 22, grave 6; 23, grave 10; 24, grave 12; 25–28, grave 14.

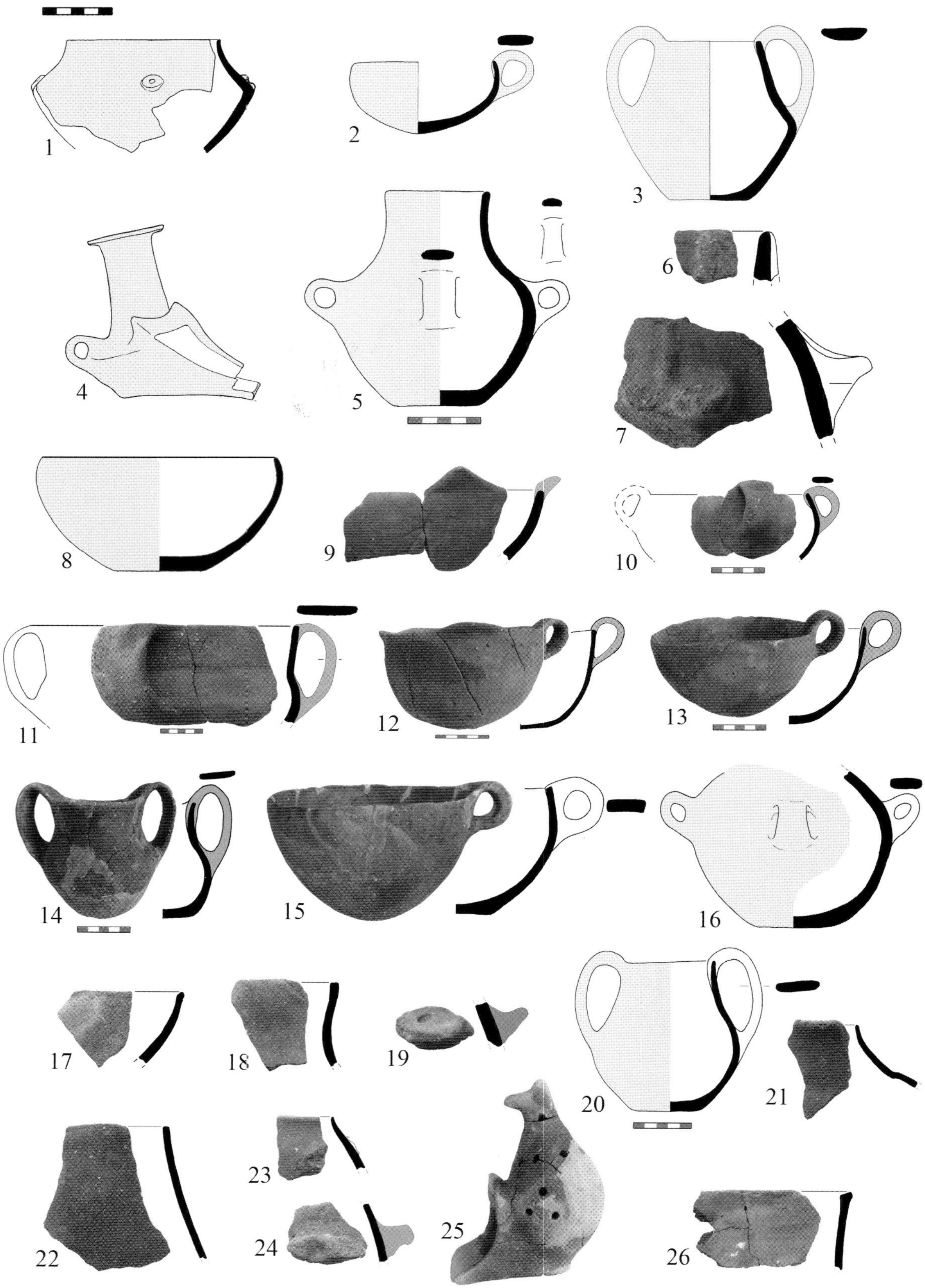

Figure 2.36. Ranutovac: site of Meanište: 1–4, grave 7; 5–7, grave 15; 8–14, grave 17; 15–19, grave 19; 20–26, grave 20.

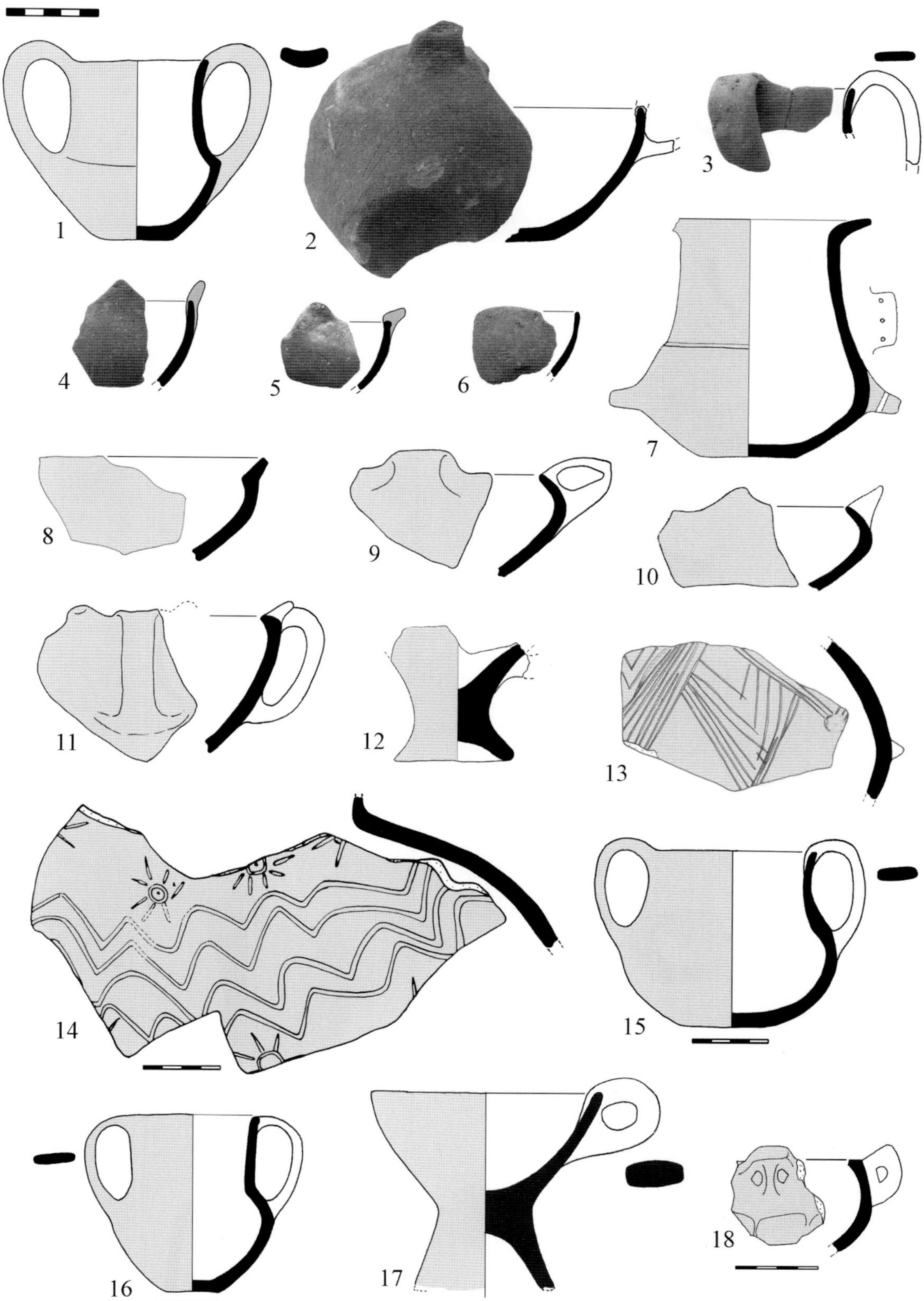

Figure 2.37. 1–6, Ranutovac: site of Meanište: 1–3, grave 21; 4–6, grave 22; 7, Rutevac: site of Utrina; 8–18, Kokino: site of Tatikev Kamen: 8–14, Trench 33, inner side of the support wall 2, pottery accumulation; 15–17, Trench 21, pottery accumulation 2; 18, cultural layer of the Early Bronze Age.

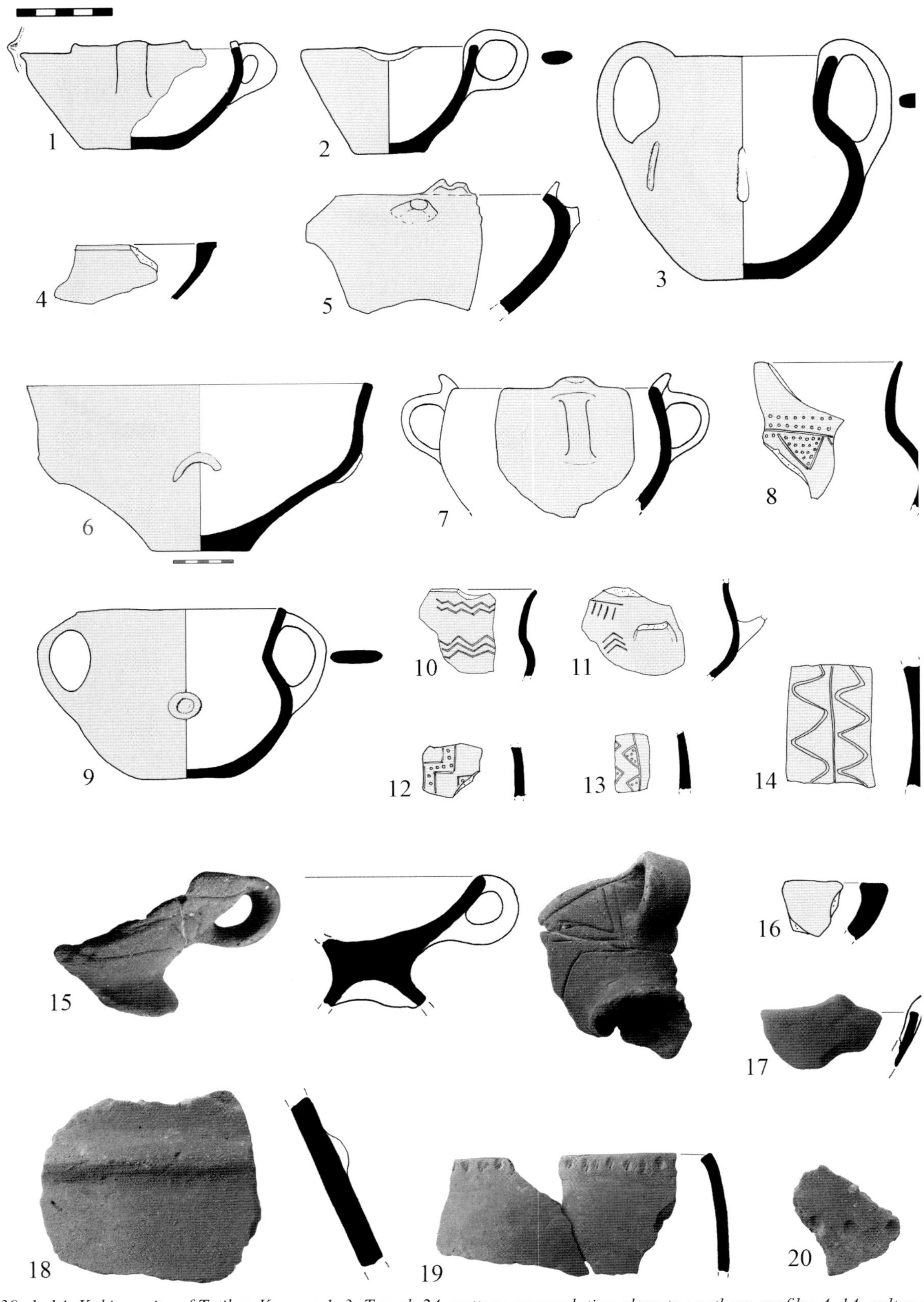

Figure 2.38. 1–14, Kokino: site of Tatićev Kamen: 1–3, Trench 24, pottery accumulation close to northern profile; 4–14, cultural layer; 15–20, Pelince: site of Dve Mogili, zone 3, square Б28.

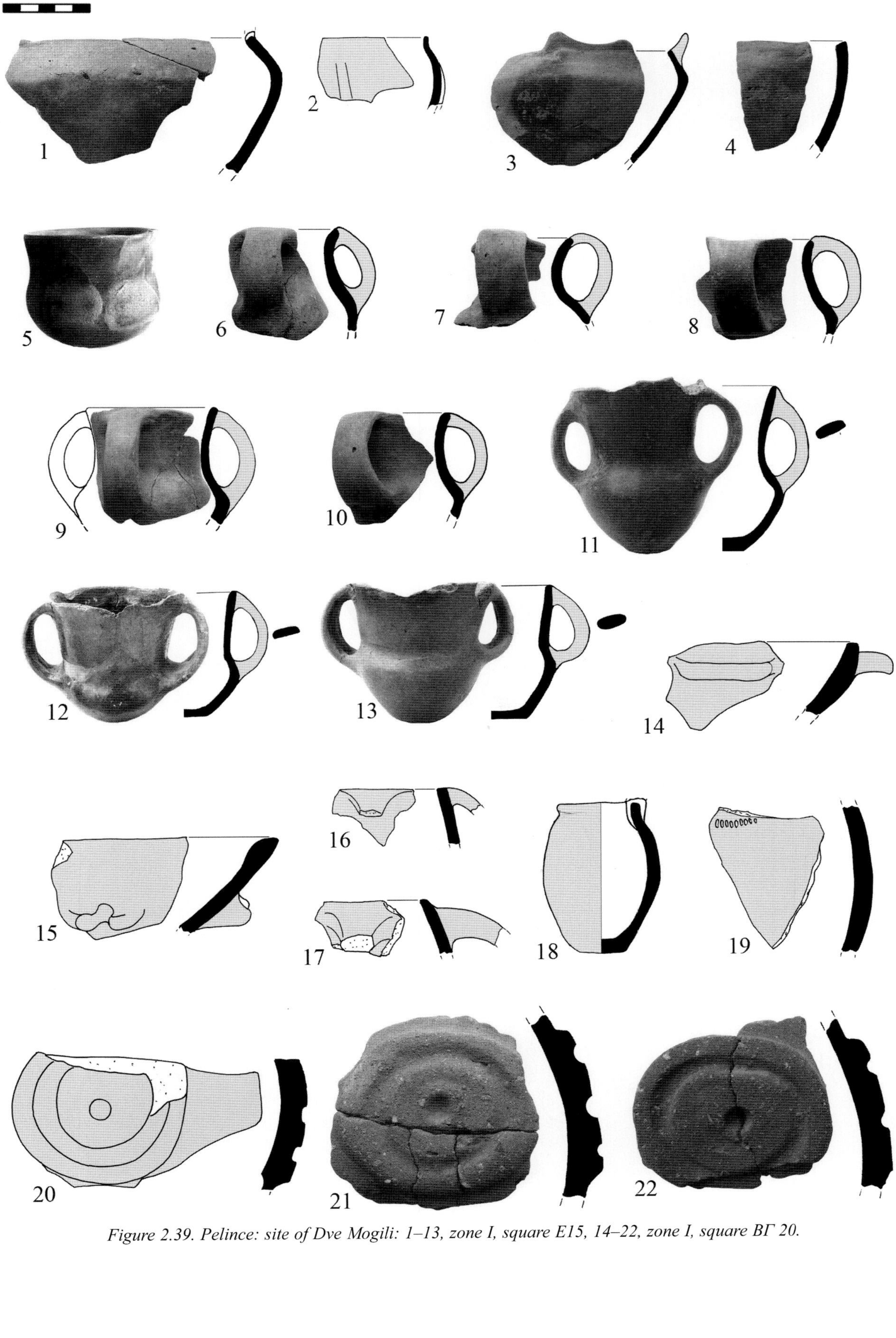

Figure 2.39. Pelince: site of Dve Mogili: 1–13, zone I, square E15, 14–22, zone I, square BΓ 20.

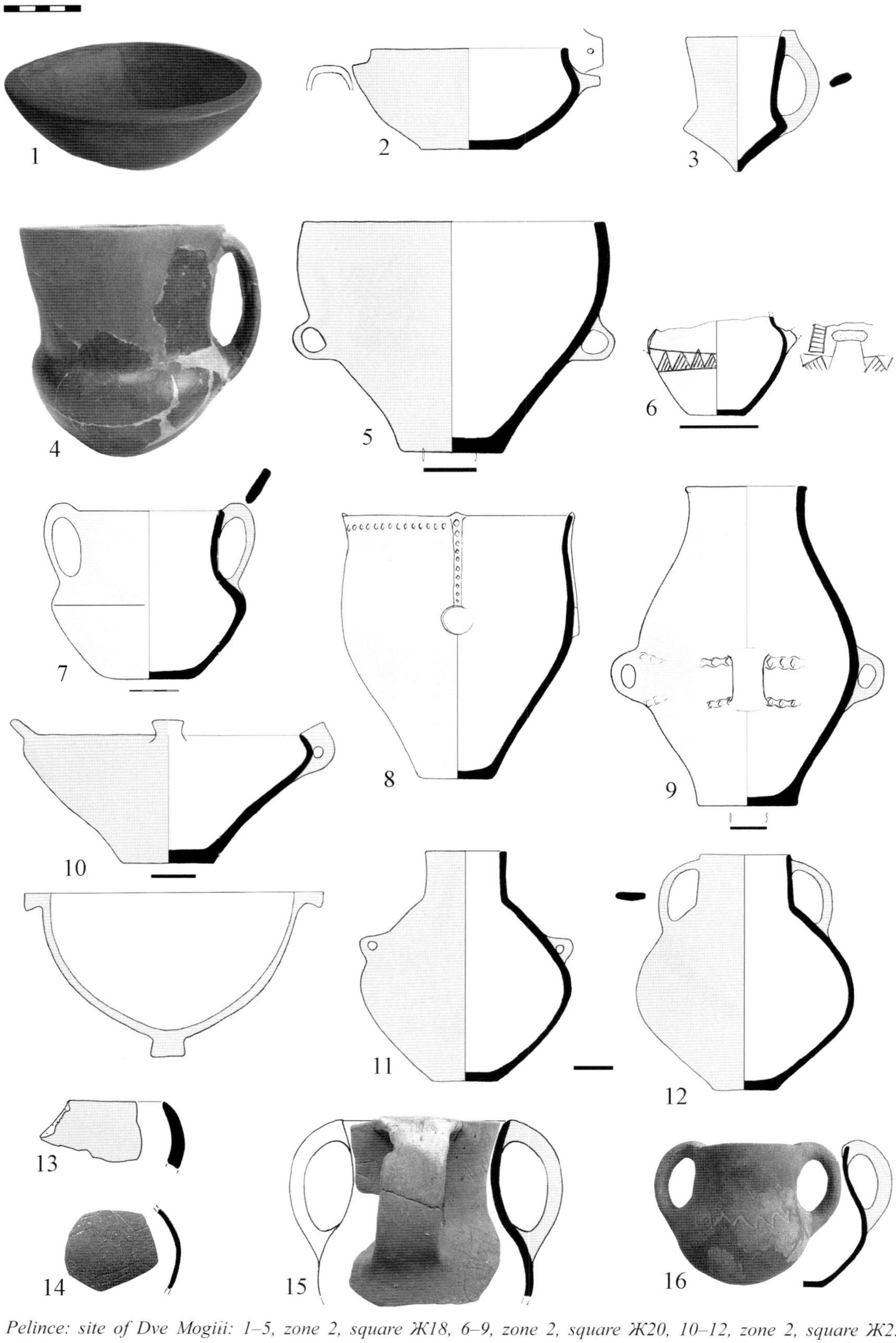

Figure 2.40. Pelince: site of Dve Mogiii: 1–5, zone 2, square Ж18, 6–9, zone 2, square Ж20, 10–12, zone 2, square Ж22, 13–16, zone 2, square Д22.

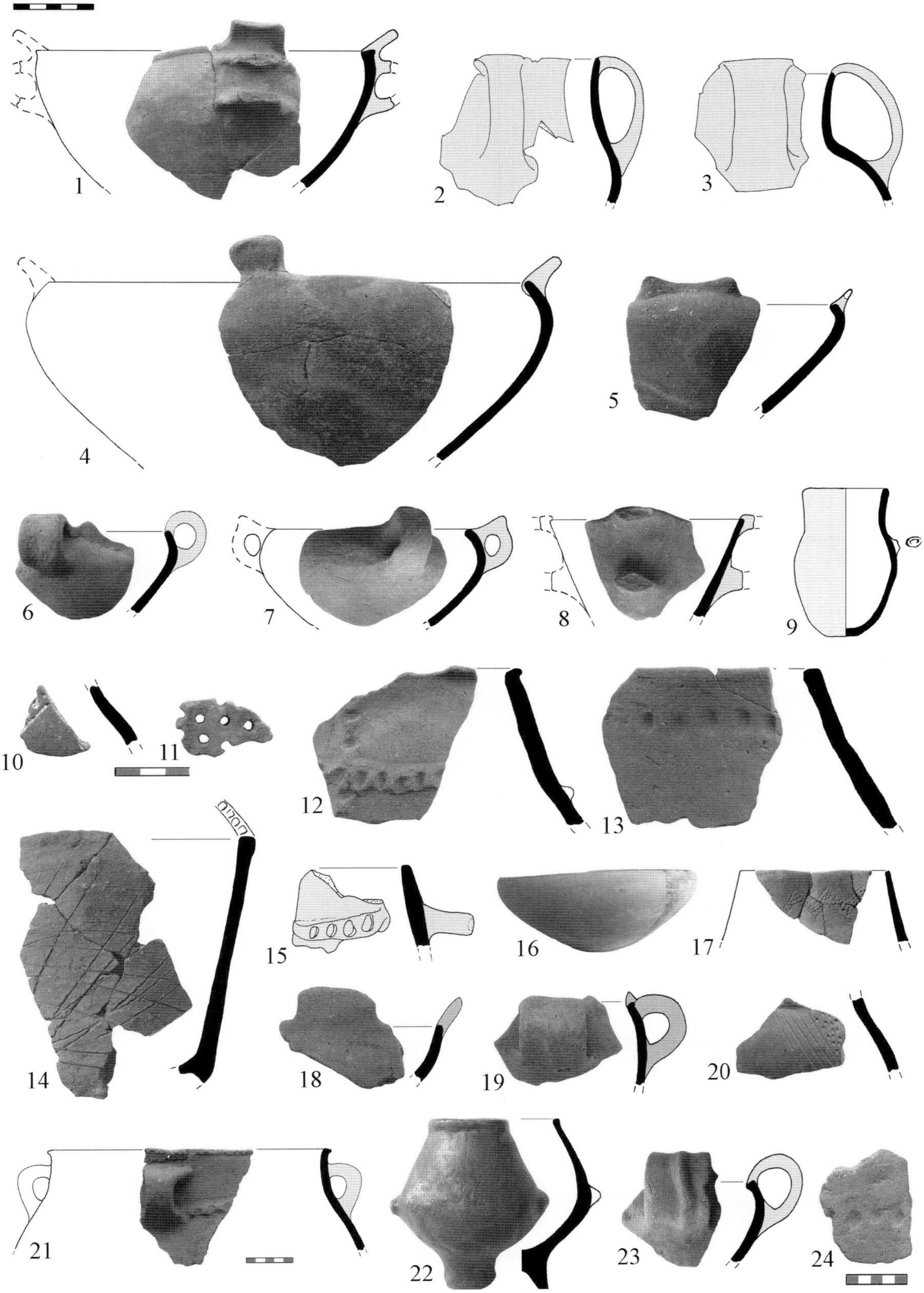

Figure 2.41. Pelince: site of Dve Mogili, zone 3: 1–3, square Г 28, 4–5, square Г 29, 6–13, square Г 31–32, 14–15, square B 37, 16–17, square B 28–29, 18–21, square AБ 35–36, 22, square Б 34, 23–24, square БВ 35.

(Antonović 2014, table 5). Interestingly, isotopic analysis of copper (^{65}Cu) was performed on the axes from Lozane, yielding values of –0.70 and –0.25 (Powell *et al.* 2017), corresponding approximately to Balkan sulphide copper deposits (Powell *et al.* 2018).

From an unknown site in Gornji Matejevac near Niš, a triangular dagger with a damaged rivet plate was found, displaying remnants of two perforations on its sides (Fig. 2.43/4). The dagger is flat and very thin, with gradually bevelled edges, lacking a pronounced rib. It is 108 mm long, with a rivet plate width of 38 mm at its widest point, and a maximum thickness of 1.6 mm below the rivet plate. The dagger corresponds to the *Safferstetten* type according to the Wels-Weyrauch typology, dating to the Early Bronze Age or the late phase of the Bell Beaker culture (Wels-Weyrauch 2015, 45, 46). An almost identical dagger was found in Odaia Turcului, Muntenia (Bajenaru 2014, fig. 66/2). The gold jewellery from the grave at Svinjarička Čuka matches examples (particularly the hair ring) from the tumuli of the Yamnaya culture in the Lower Danube region (Đorđević and Đorđević 2016; Alexandrov 2021).

At the sites in Rutevac and Pločnik, beakers of type 1c and a bowl of type 3b (from Konopnica) were recorded as random finds and later donated to museums. This type of beaker is characteristic of the Early Bronze Age in the central Balkans and is especially popular in this zone, while type 3b bowls are evenly distributed across all zones. These sites were revisited but no additional material from this period was found, thus they were classified as random finds. From Bacijevce near Surdulica comes a perforated stone axe with

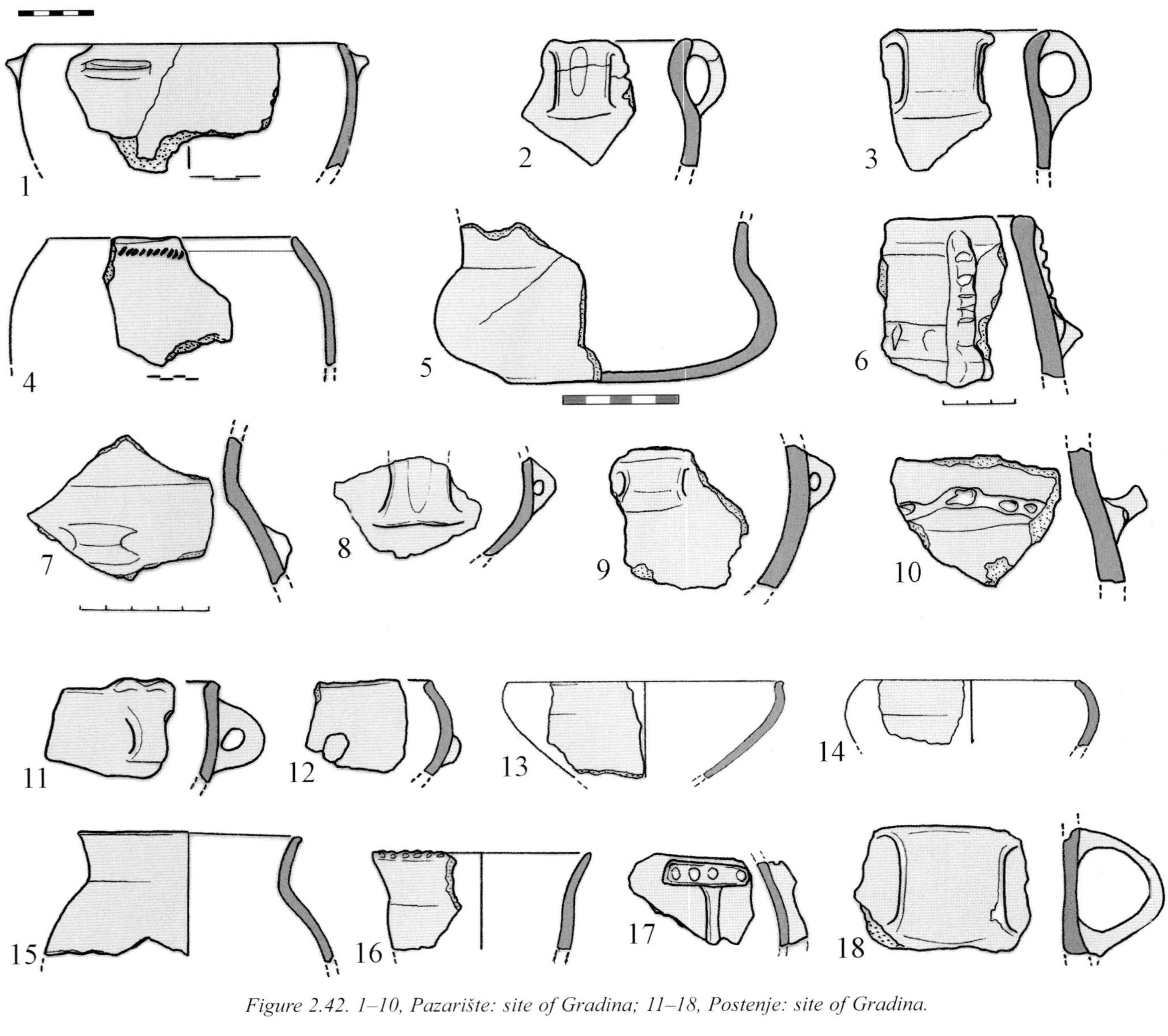

Figure 2.42. 1–10, Pazarište: site of Gradina; 11–18, Postenje: site of Gradina.

side flanges resembling wings (Bulatović 2007, 84). According to Antonović and Đorđević's typology, this specimen corresponds to a combination of types 7 and 8, with type 8 being particularly characteristic of the Early Bronze Age in the western Balkans (Antonović and Đorđević 2011, 60–61).

The stone axe from grave 3 in Ranutovac (Fig. 2.43/21) is a typical representative of type 5 according to Antonović and Đorđević, also documented at the site of Milića Brdo in Ljuljaci, dating to the end of the Early and the Middle Bronze Age (Antonović and Đorđević 2011, 59). Grave 3, from which the specimen in Ranutovac originates, has been dated to the 22nd–21st centuries cal BC.

An interesting find is the torso of an anthropomorphic female figurine from a ritual pit in square G 29 in Pelince (Fig. 2.43/10), found together with type 3 and 3a bowls and type 2 amphorae (or type 1c beakers), all characteristic finds of the Early Bronze Age in this zone (Bulatović and Stankovski 2012, LVII/66–68, as well as unpublished finds in Bulatović and Gjorgievski in prep.). Similar figurines have been documented at the settlement of Troy I, Razkopanica, and in horizons IIIa–b at Malič (Blegen *et al.* 1950, fig. 216/35–165; Prendi 1978, T. IV/8; Detev 1981, fig. 26/6). The figurines from the Transdanubian culture share a similar depiction of the body and arms, though they are richly decorated without the plastic emphasis on the breasts (Garašanin, D. 1983, T. LXXII/3). Another interesting find is a long, pointed object made of baked clay, resembling a wedge, from a ritual pit in square Ž 22 in Pelince, found together with type 3a bowls, type 1 and 2 amphorae, and a spindle whorl (Bulatović and Stankovski 2012, T. LV/43–45, as well as unpublished finds in Bulatović and Gjorgievski, in prep.). The shape of the object suggests it had some ritual function, possibly of a chthonic nature.

Apart from these finds, biconical, globular, and spool-shaped spindle whorls (Fig. 2.43/11–15), clay weights (Fig. 2.43/17), as well as tools made of bone, antler, chipped, and polished stone (Fig. 2.43/19, 20, 23–26), were recorded at Early Bronze Age sites in this zone. The purpose of a flat, rectangular, perforated object made of baked clay with a bent lower part (Fig. 2.43/16), found in Pelince in square D 22, together with type 1c beakers and a type 3a bowl, is unknown. Similar objects have not been documented in the literature, so it is assumed that it was either part of a vessel or tool, or it served some ritual purpose.

2.5.4 Cultural and chronological framework of the Early Bronze Age in the South Morava Basin, Kosovo, and the Pčinja Valley

Given that this geographical zone is the most extensive, it is not surprising that its material culture is not entirely uniform. First, based on absolute dates, the Early Bronze Age begins and proceeds similarly to other zones in the central Balkans. The oldest date comes from the house at Velika Humska Čuka, dated to the 28th/27th century cal BC, corresponding to the EBA 1 phase in the peri-Pannonian zone and western Serbia. The next date is from a group of pottery in the Early Bronze Age cultural layer at Velika Humska Čuka, which currently places the beginning of EBA 2 at the 25th–24th century cal BC. The end of the Early Bronze Age in this zone is defined by dates from Bubanj (21st–20th century cal BC) and Ranutovac (20th–19th century cal BC) (see Table 1). Thus, these dates chronologically define the Early Bronze Age in this zone between the 28th/27th and the 20th/19th centuries cal BC, roughly spanning from the early second quarter of the 3rd millennium to the end of the last quarter of the 3rd millennium and the beginning of the 2nd millennium cal BC.

Regarding the portable finds in this zone, particularly ceramics, there are no significant differences in the stylistic and typological characteristics between the pottery group from Velika Humska Čuka and the youngest dated group at Bubanj, both of which are located in the same region, the middle course of the South Morava River. However, noticeable differences appear between the stylistic and typological elements of pottery from similarly dated sites in different regions of this zone. For example, Bubanj and the Ranutovac necropolis are dated to approximately the same period, the last quarter of the 3rd millennium cal BC, although some graves at Ranutovac are slightly younger. While the forms and ornaments of pottery at Velika Humska Čuka and Bubanj are nearly identical, despite several centuries separating their dated contexts, the pottery from Ranutovac show some stylistic and typological differences from contemporaneous ceramics at Bubanj. One immediately apparent difference is that the handles of beakers at Ranutovac extend above the rim by a quarter or even a third of the handle's height and these beakers are slim (type 1e), whereas the beakers at Bubanj are mostly squat and the handles are either level with the rim or slightly extend beyond it (type 1c). Another difference is the presence of vessel types such as askoi, ember containers (censers?), and percussion instruments (drums) in Ranutovac, which are absent in the northern part of the zone.

Interestingly, however, the ceramics from some sites even further south of Ranutovac are nearly identical to those from the north of this zone. This ceramic assemblage is characterised by bowl types 3a, 3b, 3c, beaker types 1c, 4a, and 8a, amphorae type 1a, as well as ornaments in the form of plastic attachments on the rim, incised lines often combined with punctures, and rows of fingertip impressions directly on the vessel surface. These elements are common throughout this entire zone but it seems that this ceramic group predates the necropolis at Ranutovac.[25] For example, the ritual site at Pelince in the Pčinja Valley, which contains ceramics that stylistically and typologically correspond to the pottery from the northern part of the zone, is dated to the 24th–23rd centuries cal BC, while the oldest dated grave in Ranutovac is placed in the 22nd–21st centuries cal BC. Unfortunately,

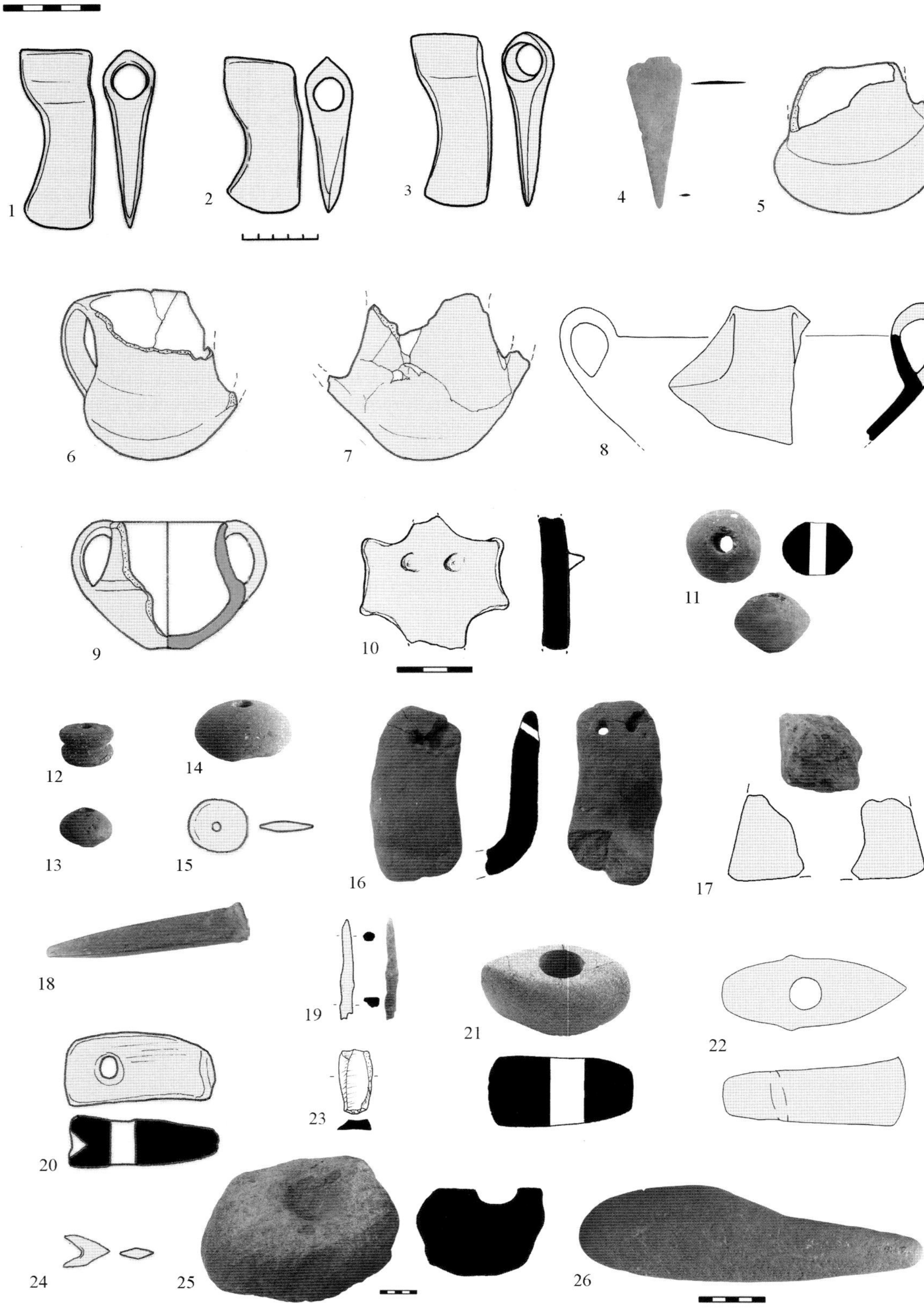

Figure 2.43. 1, Leskovac: site of Hisar, 2–3, Lozane: site of Biljurski Rid; 4, Gornji Matejevac, unknown site; 5–7, Rutevac: site of Školska Gradina; 8, Konopnica, unknown site; 9, Pločnik, unknown site; 10, 12–14, 16, 18, 26, Pelince: site of Dve Mogili: 10, square G 29; 12, square D 25; 13, square Ž 21; 14, square G 28; 16, square D 22; 18, square Ž 22; 26, square D 15; 11, 17, 19, 23, Braljina: site of Smrdan; 15, 20, 24, Skopje: site of Kale: 21, 25, Ranutovac: site of Meanište: 21, grave 3; 25 grave 16; 22, Bacijevce, unknown site.

many southern sites in this zone with identical ceramic forms, such as Davidovac, Pavlovac, Kokino, and others, have not been dated but, based on ceramic analogies, they align more closely with finds from Pelince than with those from Ranutovac.

As mentioned earlier, the situation in the northern part of this zone is different, as there is almost no variation in material culture throughout the second and third phases of the Early Bronze Age (approximately the second half of the 3rd millennium cal BC). The only potential difference is that the latest dated context in the north (structure 1 at Bubanj, 21st/20th century cal BC) features a handle with a concave cross-section (Fig. 2.33/10), which also appears at the end of the Early Bronze Age in the northern Balkans and becomes characteristic of the subsequent period, the Middle Bronze Age.

According to its typological elements, the ceramics of the older phase in the southern part of the zone and the entirety of the pottery from the northern part would belong to the Bubanj-Hum III group, which was defined over half a century ago by M. Garašanin, though based on pottery from only a few sites (Garašanin 1958). However, A. Bulatović, including broader analogies, has more precisely defined this manifestation as the Bubanj-Hum III–Pelince–Pernik cultural phenomenon, due to the remarkable similarity of Early Bronze Age material culture from sites in present-day western Bulgaria (west of the Iskar River), the South Morava and Nišava basins, and the Pčinja Valley (Bulatović 2011; Bulatović and Stankovski 2012), which will be further discussed in the following chapter.

In the Raška Region, on the far west of this zone, although there are few finds it is clear that the stylistic and typological characteristics of the pottery differ from those of other zones in the Central Balkans. Primarily, there are elements that suggest certain survivals from the preceding Eneolithic period, such as the bulbous recipient cup (Fig. 2.42/5) or broad tunnel handles (Fig. 2.42/7, 9), as well as elements characteristic of this entire geographical zone (zone 5), such as bowl types 3b and 3c and plastic attachments on the rim (Fig. 2.43/11). On the other hand, the bowl of type 1b from Pazarište has a deep, wide fissure along the axis of the handle, which strongly resembles the handles from the site Nad Klepečkom (Fig. 2.7/12) and the Mokrin necropolis (Girić 1971, T. II/5, T. IV/1, T. VIII/10, T. XI/1, etc.). Some vessels, such as the low, wide-bodied beaker (Fig. 2.43/5), resemble the beakers of type 7, characteristic of the Belotić–Bela Crkva group.

Zone 5 is also notable for its copper axes with shaftholes, which appear to be the most widespread copper tools in the Early Bronze Age on the central Balkans. Although only three examples have been documented in this zone, all are of the Lozane type, while the Kozarac type predominates in other central Balkan zones, with only one other example of the Lozane type found in Great Morava Valley and western Serbia (Vojska and Šljivovica) (Antonović 2014). The gold jewellery from the grave at Svinjarička Čuka is likely the oldest gold find from the Bronze Age in the Central Balkans. Ongoing compositional analyses will reveal more about its origins, given that identical hair ornaments were found in tumuli of the Yamnaya culture in north-western Bulgaria (Alexandrov 2021, fig. 12/4), and identical silver ornaments were discovered in Yamnaya culture graves in Vojlovica and Pančevo (Đorđević and Đorđević 2016, 21, 22).

Based on the data presented, it seems that the development of the Early Bronze Age in the southern part of this geographical zone, similarly to some other zones of the Central Balkans (such as western Serbia), could be viewed in three chronological phases. The earliest phase would correspond to finds from sites with elements indicating an Eneolithic tradition, such as Velika Humska Čuka and Svinjarička Čuka. This phase would have occurred during the second and early third quarters of the 3rd millennium cal BC. The second phase, which could be dated according to the dates from Pelince, as well as from Velika Humska Čuka and Braljina, to the period between the 25th/24th and 23rd/22nd centuries cal BC, would include all the sites except Bubanj, Skopje Kale, and Ranutovac (along with the later phase at Kokino). These latter sites would belong to the youngest phase, which marks the end of the Early Bronze Age and the beginning of the Middle Bronze Age (22nd/21st–19th centuries cal BC). This youngest phase is culturally defined by the Bubanj-Hum III group in the northern part of the zone, while in the southern part of the zone, in the Vranje–Bujanovac Valley and Skopje and Kumanovo Plains, this phase is characterised by the communities of the Armenochori group.

2.5.5 Early Bronze Age sites in western Bulgaria and their cultural and chronological relationship with sites in the South Morava Basin and Upper Pčinja

The territory of present-day western Bulgaria, specifically the area west of the Iskar and Struma rivers, was geographically defined by J. Cvijić as part of the central Balkans (Cvijić 1922, 29–34). This is supported by the material culture of the region which, in many periods of prehistory, closely resembled the cultures of the Timok Valley, the Pčinja Valley, and South Morava Basin. Numerous scholars have pointed out the cultural similarities between these regions during the Bronze Age (Garašanin 1983b, 720; Alexandrov 1998, 225, 226; Nikolova 1999, 227; Mitrevski 2003, 44, 45; Bulatović 2011), with some even defining the culture in this area during the Early Bronze Age as uniform. For instance, L. Nikolova identified this culture as Bubanj III–Pernik (Nikolova 1999, 233), likely referring to the Bubanj-Hum III culture defined decades earlier by M. Garašanin, which included the territory of modern south-western Bulgaria. On the other hand, A. Bulatović connected the cultures of the

Early Bronze Age in South Morava Basin and the Struma Valley with those in the Pčinja Valley, ultimately defining this cultural complex as Bubanj-Hum III–Pelince–Pernik (Bulatović 2011, 69; 2014, 68; Bulatović and Stankovski 2012, 328–331).

When examining representative sites that characterise this culture in western Bulgaria, it is evident that many have not been thoroughly excavated. Instead, they were discovered through surface surveys or as chance finds. Nevertheless, a number of representative sites have been selected to illustrate the material cultural similarities between this region and the central Balkans.

Among the hilltop sites, the best-researched ones west of the Iskar River include Bagačina in Stalijska Mahala and the site in Jakimovo. To the west of the Struma River, Pekljuk and Krakra in Pernik are notable.

LIST OF SITES IN WESTERN BULGARIA (PL. 4)

a. Stalijska Mahala; b. Jakimovo; c. Pekljuk; d. Pernik; e. Kondofrei; f. Đakovo; g. Separeva Banja

2.5.5.1 Bagačina site

Bagačina is an elevated site, approximately 40 m above the high terrace of the Lom River, a few kilometres south of its confluence with the Danube. Excavations took place during the 1980s, with the main publications focusing primarily on the Thracian ritual space (Bonev and Aleksandrov 1996). It was not until 2007 that the cultural layers from the Bronze Age were published (Alexandrov 2007). The article presents Bronze Age material according to the chronology used in Bulgaria, which includes the Coţofeni group from the end of the 4th millennium, alongside material from the so-called Glina IV group (Early Bronze Age in Serbian chronology) and the Verbicioara group (Late Bronze Age in Serbian chronology).

The ceramic finds associated with the Glina IV group primarily consist of bowls of types 1a, 2a, 3a, 3b, 3c, and 4a (Fig. 2.44/1–9), beakers of types 1c and 8a (Fig. 2.44/10–12), and amphorae of types 1a and 2a (Fig. 2.44/13–15) (Alexandrov 2007, 227, pl. vii–xii). Some of the bowls of types 1a and 2a have T-shaped profiled rims or rectangular and fan-shaped plastic attachments on the rim (Fig. 2.44/1, 2, 4–6, 11), decorated with incised patterns, such as fine mesh or a series of short vertical strokes (Fig. 2.44/1, 5). Some bowls feature incised decorations on the upper cone or on the interior (Fig. 2.44/7, 9). The amphorae are decorated with geometric motifs or barbotine (Fig. 2.44/13, 14).

Bowls of type 3b and 3c also appear at Bubanj in Layer V, with decoration similar to examples from Bagačina (Fig. 2.44/9). However, it is unclear if they belong to the lower part of the layer, which corresponds to the Bubanj-Hum II group, or to the upper part, attributed to the Bubanj-Hum III group (Bulatović and Milanović 2020, 219–234, figs 214, 218). At Velika Humska Čuka, a type 3b bowl with a rectangular plastic attachment adorned with incised mesh and stamped circles was found in Structure 6A, which has been dated to the 27th–26th centuries cal BC (68.5% probability; see Table 1). Based on the stylistic and typological characteristics of the pottery, it has been assigned to the Bubanj-Hum II group (Bulatović *et al.* 2020, 1168, table 1, fig. 2/16–18). This structure also contained type 3a bowls (Fig. 2.46/3, 4, 6), one of which had a T-profiled rim (Fig. 2.46/5), similar to examples from Bagačina (Fig. 2.44/2). Additionally, tunnel handles, a survival from the previous period, were found in both Velika Humska Čuka and Bagačina (Fig. 2.44/8; Fig. 2.46/14, 15). Based on these analogies, the cultural layer at Bagačina could be similarly dated to the second quarter of the 3rd millennium.

However, it is uncommon, at least at sites in Ponišavlje and the South Morava Valley, for type 1c and 8a beakers to appear alongside these stylistic and typological elements. The elements mentioned correspond to the Bubanj-Hum II group, while beakers of types 1c and 8 are characteristic of the subsequent phase of Bronze Age development, i.e., the Bubanj-Hum III group. Two possibilities arise: either there are two sub-layers within the Early Bronze Age III cultural layer at Bagačina, or the Early Bronze Age development in this region followed a different trajectory than in South Morava Basin and the Pčinja Valley, with Bubanj-Hum II elements persisting until the appearance of type 1c and 8 beakers (i.e., Early Bronze Age III in Bulgarian chronology, or Early Bronze Age in Serbian chronology). A third, less likely possibility is that type 1c and 8 beakers appeared earlier in this region than in the south. The earliest reliable date for type 1c beakers comes from Velika Humska Čuka, dating to the third quarter of the 3rd millennium cal BC.

Shallow bowls resembling plates with incised lines on the inner side (Fig. 2.44/7) and amphorae decorated with barbotine (Fig. 2.44/15) resemble vessels found in the Vinkovci-Somogyar group and the slightly older Makó-Kosihy-Čaka group (Kulcsár 2009, figs 27–30, 32–36, 59, 60, 64). The bowl from Bagačina has a slightly rounded thickened inner rim, similar to a bowl found in Pelince (Fig. 2.39/15). Based on these ceramic analogies, if we assume that these are contemporary pottery, the layer at Bagačina could be chronologically placed at the end of the second and beginning of the third quarter of the 3rd millennium. The stylistic and typological features of the pottery suggest a cultural mixture of the Glina group with inland Balkan groups (Bubanj-Hum II, Bubanj-Hum III–Pelince–Pernik) and the southern Pannonian Region (Vinkovci–Somogyvár).

2.5.5.2 Krakra Site, Pernik

The next site that can be attributed to the Bubanj-Hum III group is Krakra in Pernik. Situated on a dominant elevation above the Struma River, at a point where the river sharply changes its course from north to west, the site is located on a spacious oval plateau, oriented north-east to south-west, with an elevation of over 40 m above the Struma River. Due

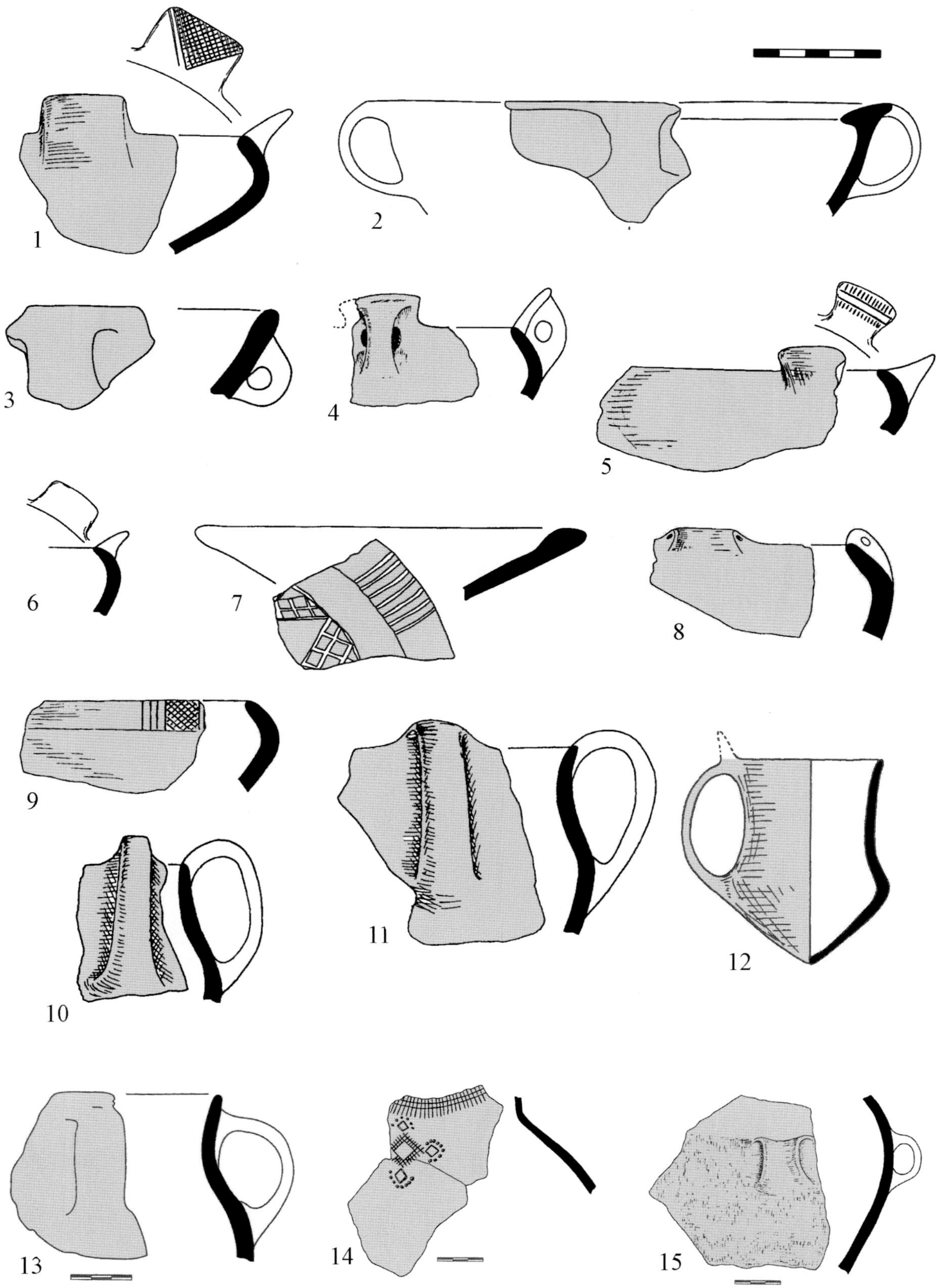

Figure 2.44. Stalijska mahala: site of Bagačina.

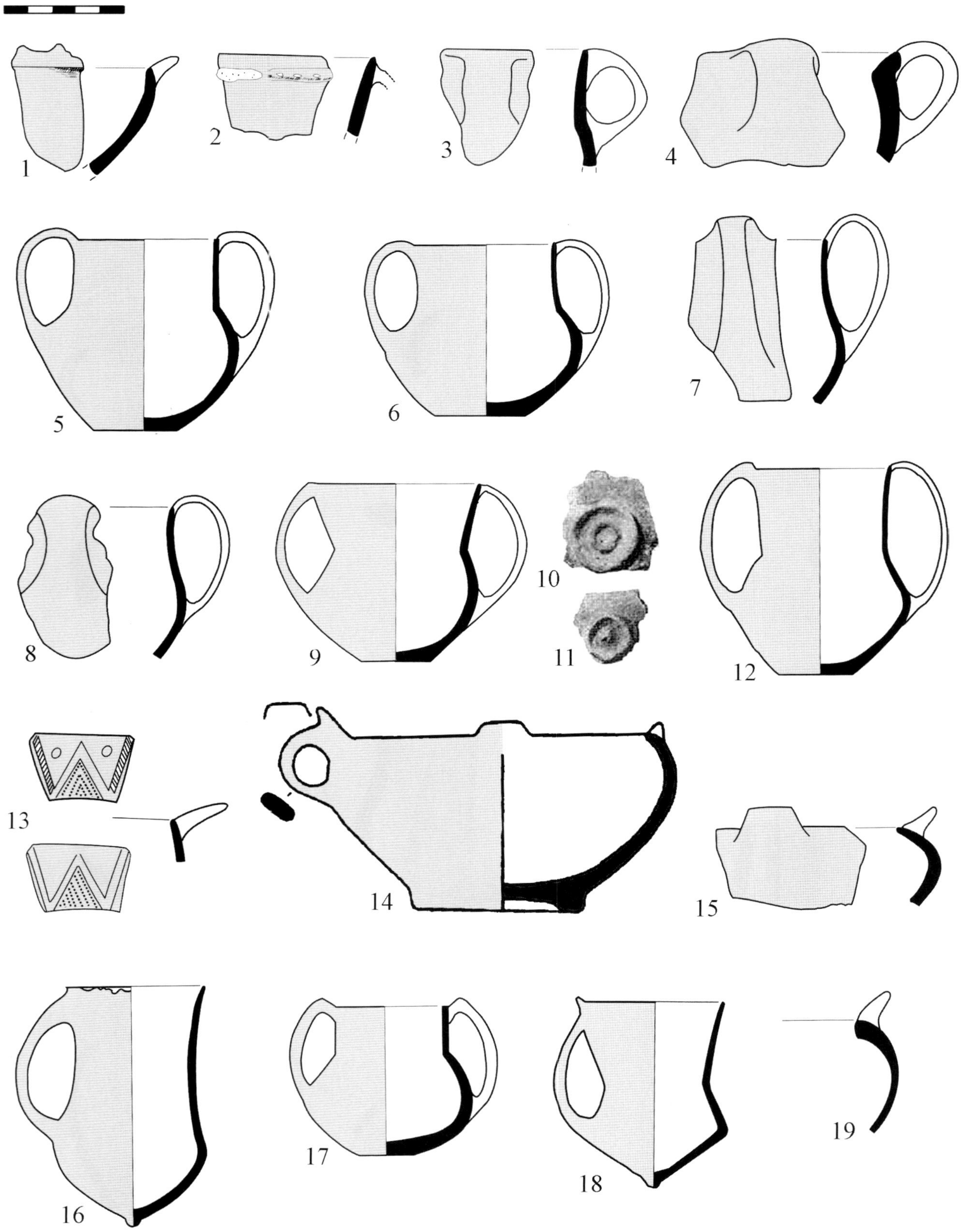

Figure 2.45. 1–3, Jakimovo; 4–11, Pernik; 12, 13, Kondofrei; 14–16, Đakovo; 17, Separeva banja; 18, Sadovec; 19, Pekljuk.

to its favourable position, Krakra was continuously inhabited from prehistory through the Hellenistic and Roman periods and into the Middle Ages (Ovčarov 1981, 11–51). The site was intermittently excavated between 1960 and 1979. Prehistoric settlement layers were identified on the north-eastern part of the plateau, covering an area of about 0.5 ha. In addition to a substantial cultural layer from the Early Neolithic, a layer from the Early Bronze Age, corresponding to the end of the Eneolithic and the Early Bronze Age in Serbian chronology, was also recorded.

Finds from the Early Bronze Age, according to Serbian chronology, include beakers of type 1c (Fig. 2.45/5–8) and type 7c (Fig. 2.45/9) (Alexandrov 1998), as well as bowls of type 2a (Fig. 2.45/4), and decorations in the form of plastic concentric ribs (Fig. 2.45/10, 11), which are also noted at sites from this period in Ponišavlje and the Pčinja Valley (Fig. 2.39/20–22) (Bulatović and Stankovski 2012, T. XIII/4). The beakers from Krakra are identical to those found at Bubanj-Hum III sites in the valleys of the Velika and South Morava rivers, as well as the Pčinja Valley, which was one of the primary reasons for unifying these cultures under the same term as those in Great Morava Valley and the Pčinja Valley.

Other hilltop sites in western Bulgaria, such as Pekljuk and Jakimovo, also reveal pottery with similar stylistic and typological features, including semi-circular bowls (types 3a and 3b) with plastic attachments on the rim (Fig. 2.45/1, 19) and beakers of types 3a (Fig. 2.45/3) and 7c (Fig. 2.45/2).

Lowland sites in western Bulgaria with Early Bronze Age pottery resembling those from Great Morava Valley and the Pčinja Valley include Kondofrei and Đakovo, both located in the Struma Valley, as well as the site of Separeva Banja, from which several chance finds have been recovered. From Kondofrei, a beaker of type 1c and a bowl of type 3a with a fan-shaped plastic attachment on the rim were found (Fig. 2.45/12, 13), while Đakovo yielded bowls of type 3b with plastic attachments on the rim and a beaker of type 8a (the so-called Junacite type, with one handle). Separeva Banja produced a single beaker of type 1c (Fig. 2.45/17).

In terms of stylistic and typological characteristics, the pottery from all of these sites in western Bulgaria bear varying degrees of similarity to those found in South Morava Basin and the Pčinja Region. Moreover, it is observed that the ceramics exhibit similarities with local cultural groups of the Early Bronze Age, such as the late Glina-Odaia Turcului-Montenouru Ic4 and Junacite groups, while also displaying influences from the south, specifically from the Armenochori group (Alexandrov 1998, 230, 231).

These cultural similarities between the communities inhabiting the Struma Valley and the broader territory of western Bulgaria, on the one hand, and those in South Morava Basin and the Pčinja Region during the Early Bronze Age (roughly the second half of the 3rd millennium BC), on the other hand, have led to the perception of this territory as part of a broader cultural complex, albeit with its regional specificities. The term Bubanj-Hum III–Pelince II–III Complex was first introduced over a decade ago to define the culture of this geographic zone (Bulatović 2011; Bulatović and Stankovski 2012, 327–330). A few years later, following new research results in the South Morava Valley and the Pčinja Region, A. Bulatović refined the term, naming the cultural–chronological phenomenon in western Bulgaria, South Morava Basin, eastern Serbia, and north-eastern Macedonia as the Bubanj-Hum III–Pelince–Pernik Complex, incorporating western Bulgaria into the broader cultural framework (Bulatović 2014, 68).

The cultural similarity in these neighbouring geographical regions can be explained by the area's geographical characteristics. It comprises several plains and valleys (e.g., the Sofia Plain, Leskovac Plain, Vranje–Bujanovac Valley, Skopje Plain, Niš Plain) and the Serbian–Macedonian mass of mountains intersected by river valleys and basins, which served as natural communication routes between the lowlands to the east and west. The Nišava Valley, along with the Pčinja and Jerma valleys, are among the most prominent natural corridors. These mountainous areas surrounded by plains and valleys evidently suited the needs of these Early Bronze Age communities, which developed a highly similar, almost uniform culture. Shared stylistic and typological elements of this culture include double-handled beakers, semi-circular bowls of types 3b, 3c, and 4a (often with various forms of plastic attachments on the rim, most commonly rectangular), double-handled beakers of types 1c, 3a, and 8a, amphorae of types 1a and 3a, and more.

The lack of absolute dates and necropolises for these communities hinders a complete definition of their culture, particularly in terms of spiritual characteristics and a more precise absolute chronology.

2.6 Discussion on the Early Bronze Age in the central Balkans

As mentioned, the Central Balkans occupy a geostrategic position as a geographical intermediary between Europe and Asia, a role that has been evident from the earliest history up to the modern era. The central Balkans comprise a partly compact region of diverse terrain: plains in the north, transitioning to hilly and then mountainous terrain towards the south. This geographical diversity contributed to the independent development of several distinct cultural groups which, due to the orogeographic features of the terrain, were nonetheless connected and had varying degrees of interaction, depending on the historical period. In contrast, the Pannonian Plain, an entirely orographically open geographical entity surrounded by the Carpathians, was home to the material culture of numerous cultural groups that existed in this area during the Bronze Age. In the Central Balkans, only a few distinct cultural groups can be identified during the Bronze Age, although elements of neighbouring cultural

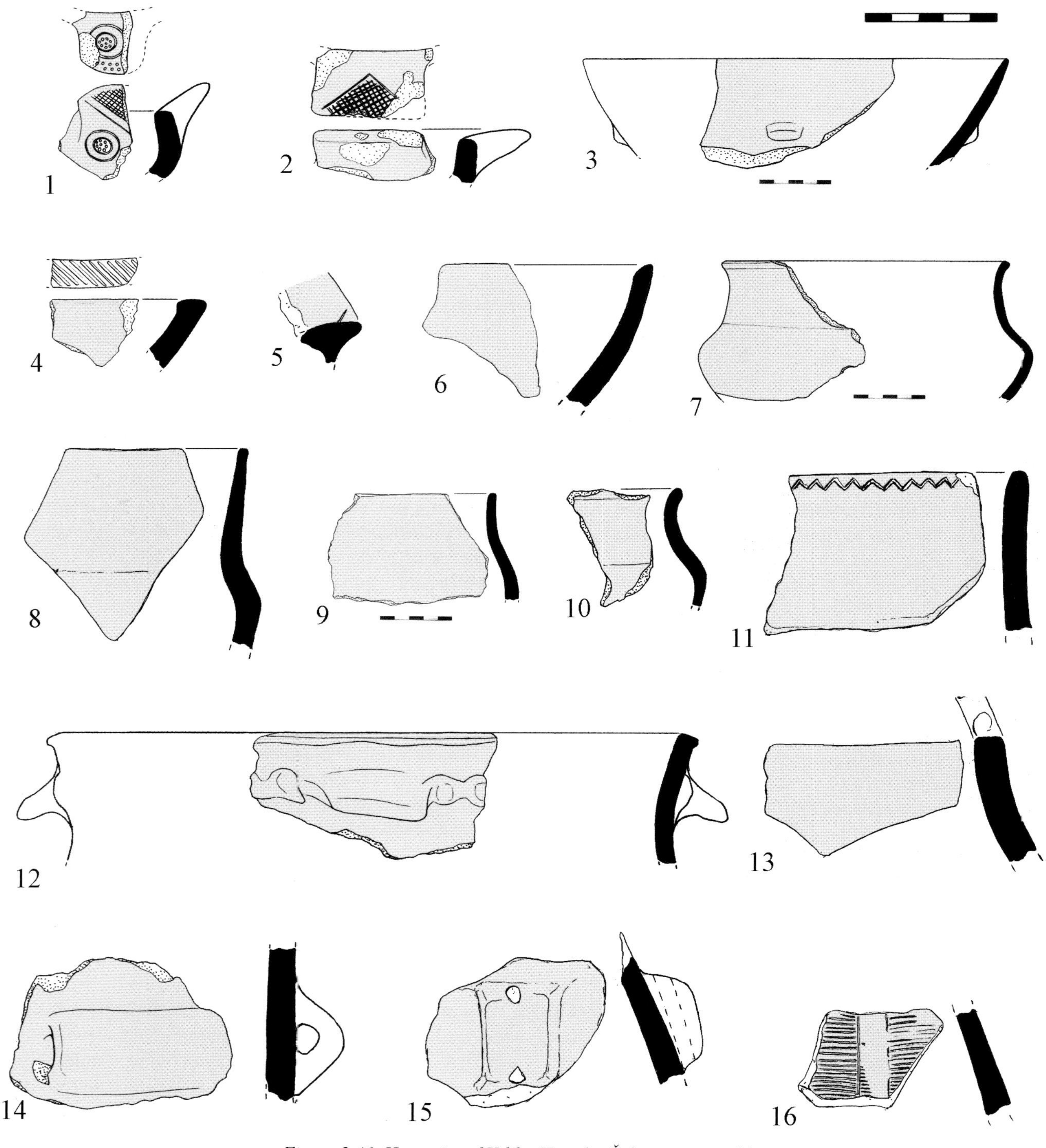

Figure 2.46. Hum: site of Velika Humska Čuka, structure 6A.

groups are also evident, further indicating certain cultural interactions during that time.

The diversity of the terrain provided the communities that inhabited it during the Bronze Age with a range of living conditions, from plains suitable for agriculture and fishing to mountainous areas ideal for livestock farming, hunting, and the exploitation of mineral resources in regions rich in ore deposits. For this reason, the analysis of the material and spiritual culture of Bronze Age communities in the central Balkans, in the previous section of this book, was conducted through five separate geographical micro-regions. In the following pages, a more detailed analysis of the material and spiritual culture of all the communities will be presented, where the results of the analyses from all geographical zones are synthesised, along with the inter-relationships between the populations that inhabited them.

2.6.1 Sites, topography, settlements, and dwelling structures of the Early Bronze Age in the central Balkans

The analysis of the topography of Early Bronze Age settlements in the central Balkans led to a somewhat expected conclusion: the number of hilltop settlements increases from north to south, or from lowland to mountainous terrain. The highest number of hilltop settlements was recorded in the fifth and southernmost zone (southern Serbia, northern Macedonia, and the Raška Region), where five hilltop settlements were identified, while the fewest were recorded in the first, peri-Pannonian zone, and the third (western Serbia), with only one hilltop settlement in each (Kik in Svileuva and Jelica near Čačak).[26] The exception is the Timok Region, where no hilltop settlements were recorded. However, this area is not particularly relevant, as very few lowland settlements have been recorded there, and it is unclear whether the two documented settlements even belong to the Early Bronze Age.[27]

Most of these settlements were established along important communication routes, on the edges of larger river valleys such as the Great Morava (Ostrikovac), Nišava (Crvena Reka and Velika Humska Čuka), Vardar (Kale), and West Morava (Jelica). Occasionally, they were also found along smaller, perhaps alternative, routes, such as the valleys of Grza (Lešje) or Raška (Postenje and Pazarište). This pattern was also observed in western Bulgaria, where hilltop settlements were built above major rivers, such as Lom (Stalijska mahala), Cibrica (Jakimovo), and Struma (Pernik). Thus, it appears that a similar model of settlement construction was employed across the central Balkans during the Early Bronze Age, regardless of cultural affiliation, geographical area, or the degree of cultural development during this period. Defensive architecture was not observed on hilltops, except at the site of Kale in Skopje, which, according to portable finds, could belong to the very end of the Early Bronze Age and the Middle Bronze Age.

Far more lowland settlements were recorded than hilltops, with 29 lowland settlements and nine hilltops, giving a ratio of 24:76 across the central Balkans (Pl. 6).

The analysis of settlement architecture and dwelling structures showed that the remains are sporadic, mostly destroyed by later activity, and unreliable for making significant conclusions, particularly in certain zones. As a result, comparing architecture between zones is almost impossible. The best-preserved residential architectural remains were found in the peri-Pannonian zone during Early Bronze Age 3, consisting of above-ground and semi-subterranean dwellings, as well as pit houses. The above-ground structures had thin floors without sub-structures (Pančevo), while the semi-subterranean dwellings were composed of ellipsoid or circular pits with remains of walls made of wattle and daub (Pančevo, Nad Klepečkom, Rit, Novačka Ćuprija). Rectangular above-ground structures dug about 0.8 m deep and built using wattle and daub, with a deep pit and a hearth in the centre (Nad Klepečkom), were also recorded. Additionally in this zone, structures with a figure-eight foundation were identified (Pančevo, Nad Klepečkom).

Some structures were dug deeply into the ground, with above-ground portions made of wattle and daub (Nad Klepečkom, Rit, Novačka Ćuprija), and could be classified as pit houses. No furniture was found, but earthen benches inside some structures (Rit) may have served as sleeping areas. In almost all these structures, along with pottery, items made of stone, bone, fired clay, and other materials intended for everyday use were discovered. The arrangement of three semi-subterranean structures in a row at the Rit site (see Fig. 2.1 above) could illustrate the spatial organisation of dwellings within the settlement. If all three structures served as dwellings, it could be said that the residential buildings at the Rit site were arranged in a north-west to south-east line about 6–8 m apart, although the varying dimensions and structure of these buildings do not fully support this hypothesis.

A similar semi-subterranean above-ground rectangular structure, but with rounded corners, was excavated in the Great Morava valley at the hilltop settlement of Đula (Early Bronze Age 2). An ellipsoid house, dug into the sub-soil and with an above-ground portion made of wattle and daub, similar to houses from the peri-Pannonian zone in Early Bronze Age 3 (Pančevo, Nad Klepečkom, Rit, Novačka Ćuprija), was recorded at the Skopje Kale. Based on these remains, it can be said that residential architecture was similar throughout the central Balkans, whether in hilltops or lowland settlements, at least in the zones where such information is available.

In addition to the few remnants of residential architecture, numerous pits filled with various contents were recorded at almost all Early Bronze Age sites. These could be classified as waste pits, at least in terms of their secondary use. At the Skopje Kale, remains of ovens with clay floors and sub-structures made of river pebbles and traces of domes were also found. At the Smrdan site in Braljina, several pit houses and one larger rectangular above-ground structure made of wattle and daub were excavated.[28]

There is insufficient data on the spatial arrangement of residential structures within settlements, except for the Rit site, where three dwellings were found in a row. However, an interesting phenomenon concerning the spatial arrangement of lowland settlements was noted. Specifically, at the large ancient site of Viminacium near Požarevac, in the peri-Pannonian zone, two Early Bronze Age settlements were identified in close proximity: the Nad Klepečkom, located on a ridge and dated to the second half of the 21st and the first half of the 20th centuries cal BC, and Rit, located about 10 m lower on a waterlogged river terrace, with identical stylistic-typological pottery dated to the second half of the 20th century cal BC. This spatial and temporal relationship between the settlements might indicate a change in the settlement pattern in this micro-region over a short period, possibly triggered by certain climatic changes but, unfortunately, we only have a single date from each of the two sites, and the sites have since been destroyed by surface mining, making it impossible to verify this hypothesis. Also, more detailed research at these sites is impossible, as they have been completely destroyed by the large Drmno surface mine.

A similar settlement pattern, i.e., the use of different habitats of smaller dimensions, ranging from semi-subterranean to subterranean structures and above-ground houses, was also observed in the Pannonian Plain, within the Vinkovci–Samogyvár cultural group (Kulcsár 2009, 265–268), as well as across the European continent. However, it was noted that structures with circular or ellipsoid foundations were generally smaller than above-ground rectangular houses (Harding 2000, 24–28), referring in this case to the elongated narrow houses characteristic of Central Europe and Scandinavia (Harding 2000, 38–53).

Somewhat different Early Bronze Age houses were recorded in eastern Pannonia, between the rivers Mureș and Tisza, in the settlements of the Mureș/Moriș group. Here, long above-ground houses, up to 14 m in length, with mud walls and internal hearths, were recorded. According to Whitelaw, these hearths reflect a desire for privacy in the preparation and storage of food (Whitelaw 1983, 48–66; O'Shea 1996, 43), although the presence of hearths inside the house could also be a response to the strong winds that often blow in this area. This example shows that there was no unified settlement pattern or dwelling structure; rather, environmental factors, the availability of local resources, and socio-economic relations within the settlement likely influenced these aspects.

In addition to lowland and hilltop settlements, one cave with Early Bronze Age finds (Cerovačka or Kovačevića Cave) was recorded. Caves are known to have served as temporary or occasional shelters during the Metal Ages in the Balkans. However, European caves, particularly Mediterranean ones according to A. Harding, primarily served as ritual sites and only occasionally as shelters (Harding 2000, 54, 55).

2.6.2 Necropolises, burials, and ritual practices

The available data indicate that the burial rites in the Early Bronze Age of the central Balkans were varied, even within the same geographical zone or phase. Flat necropolises with inhumation burials, where the deceased were placed in a flexed position on their side, have been discovered in the peri-Pannonian zone (Šljunkara), Đerdap (Pesak), and south-eastern Serbia (Svinjarička Čuka). Flat necropolises with cremation burials, where the remains were placed in urns or directly on the ground, have also been documented in the peri-Pannonian zone (Rospi Ćuprija), Đerdap (Glamija), western Serbia (Stapari), and the South Morava Valley (Ranutovac). Burials under tumuli were recorded in western Serbia, with both inhumation and cremation graves present, and one tumulus even exhibited a bi-ritual burial practice (Jarmovac). Tumuli were also found in the peri-Pannonian zone, with inhumations in a flexed position (Skorenovac).

This evidence suggests that a mixed burial ritual appears in all zones, except in the Great Morava Basin with Šumadija, where no necropolises have been recorded. The exceptions are the tumuli at Rogojevac and Bare, which belong to the first phase of the Early Bronze Age; this will be discussed in more detail in the following chapters. The mixed burial rituals are most evident in the peri-Pannonian zone, which exhibits the greatest variety.

However, only a small number of these necropolises have been dated, making it difficult to establish any chronological distinctions between burial rites. For instance, necropolises in western Serbia, dated to the Early Bronze Age, whether cremations or inhumations (Dubac, Jančići; Krstac, Ivkovo Brdo; Dučalovići, Ruja; Lučani, Suva Česma, etc.), indicate that both rites were used simultaneously, at least from the end of the Early Bronze Age 1 phase.

A certain pattern can be tentatively observed only in the far south of the central Balkans, in the fifth geographical zone. Here, a grave with an inhumed body in a stone cist, without a tumulus, was dated to the third quarter of the 3rd millennium cal BC (Svinjarička Čuka), while a flat necropolis with cremated bodies (Ranutovac) was dated to the last quarter of the 3rd millennium and the beginning of the 2nd. These examples might suggest that skeletal graves existed before cremations in this area during the Early Bronze Age, but with data from only two necropolises, this hypothesis should be approached with caution.

The ritual life of the inhabitants of the central Balkans in the Early Bronze Age can be gleaned from the so-called ritual pits, which have been recorded at many Early Bronze Age sites in this region. The best examples are the so-called ritual spaces in southern central Balkans, at Pelince and Kokino, which consist of dozens of these pits.

The spiritual life of prehistoric people is most clearly seen through the rituals they practised during their lifetime. However, from this temporal distance, it is challenging to identify and classify these practices as definitively ritualistic. One of the most visible examples are ritual pits, dedicated to a deity or higher power, intended to appease them and secure the safety, health, food, and general survival of the community. This ritual can be traced back to the earliest times, perhaps even as early as the Palaeolithic, and certainly from the Neolithic period up to the present day (Bulatović 2015; 2018).

These so-called special purpose pits are sometimes difficult to define with certainty or distinguish from pits of other purposes, especially when found outside organised ritual spaces. They often contain whole offerings in the form of vessels and other household items and they are frequently filled with plaster, animal bones, and occasionally human bones or parts of skulls. At the sites of Tatikev Kamen and Dve Mogili in northern Macedonia, a large number of shallow pits were recorded, often partially carved into bedrock, containing various offerings. At Tatikev Kamen, retaining walls were discovered, which prevented the area with the pits from sliding due to the steep terrain. At Dve Mogili, a similar situation was observed but, in addition to the retaining walls, a large circular hearth was discovered in part of the 'open-air sanctuary', i.e., the ritual space, around and beneath which ritual pits were located. These pits received special treatment, as most were lined with moistened clay before offerings were placed inside or were enclosed with stone. Interestingly, material from both the Early and Late Bronze Age was definitively identified at both sites, while Middle Bronze Age finds were fewer at Kokino and their presence in Pelince is questionable.

Apart from the ritual pits, Tatikev Kamen also features a so-called megalithic observatory, where important dates related to the movements of the sun, moon, and Pleiades were observed by the community, accompanied by ritual ceremonies in which a specific member of the community (leader, priest, etc.) was illuminated on a stone throne located on the stone plateau. For all these reasons, this mountain was considered sacred and was not inhabited during the Bronze Age.

The fact that an Early Iron Age settlement was recorded on the northern slope of this site, with no ritual pits from this period present in the area, indicates the arrival of a new era – the Iron Age. The communities of this era had a different religious perception and they did not consider Tatikev Kamen 'sacred' nor used it for astronomical or ritual purposes.

2.6.3 Typology of Early Bronze Age ceramic vessels in the central Balkans

In order to easily comprehend the utilisation and distribution of ceramic vessels of the Bronze Age communities in a certain region, it is necessary to determine the typology

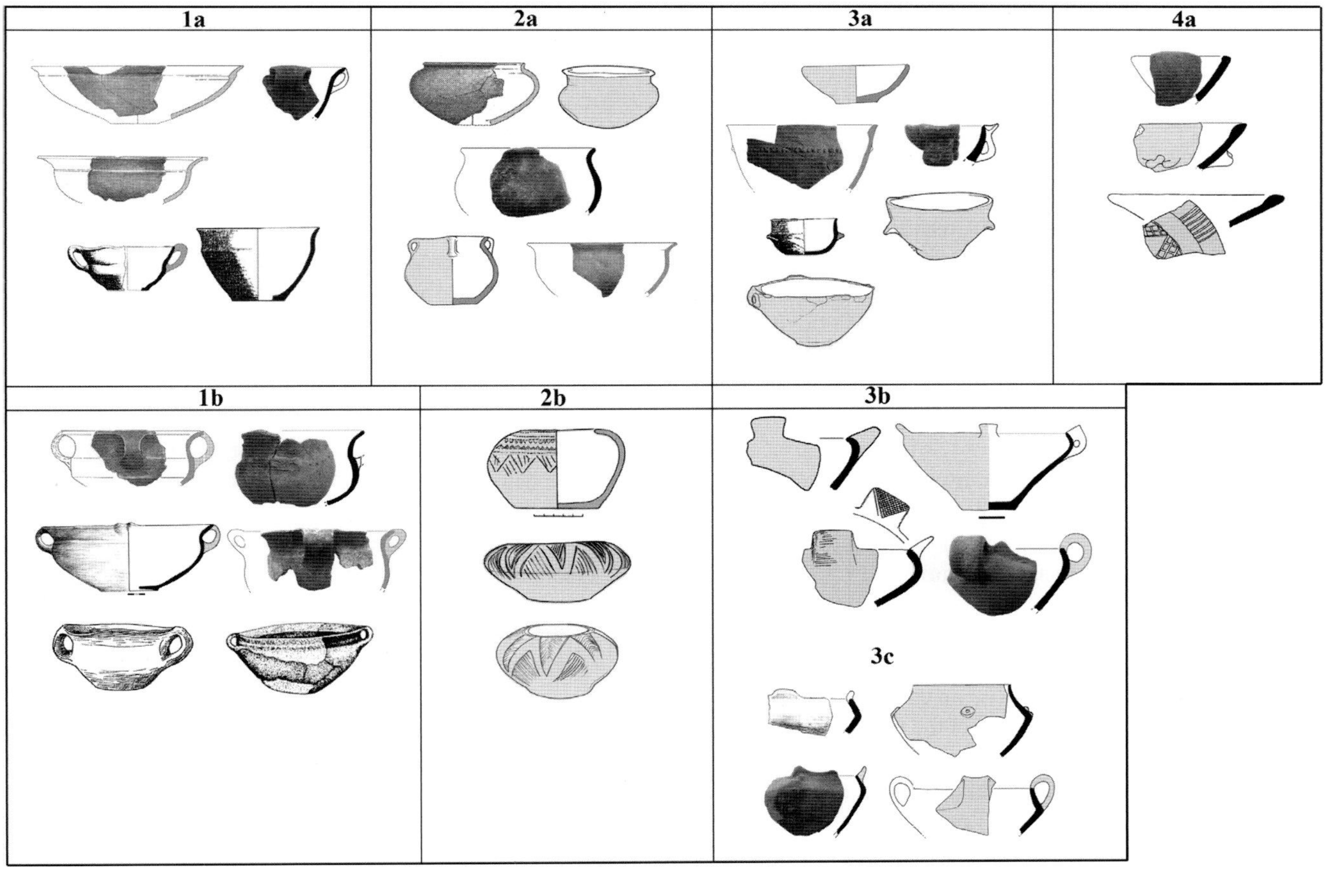

Figure 2.47. Early Bronze Age bowls in the central Balkans.

of ceramic inventory. The typology is based on form and shape, manner of production, decoration, proportions of certain parts of the vessel, and other indicative characteristics.

The ceramic vessels represented during the Early Bronze Age in the central Balkans can be divided into bowls, cups, beakers, amphorae, jugs, flask-shaped vessels, pots, pithoi, and lids, as well as certain vessels of a specific function, such as ember containers, askoi, and double-vessels (Figs 2.47–2.52).

2.6.3.1 Bowls (Fig. 2.47)

Type 1a: bowl with a semi-globular recipient and everted rim (slightly S-profiled), with or without wide arched handles, sometimes of emphasised transition on the belly and the shoulder.

Type 1b: biconical bowl with everted rim (slightly or sharply S-profiled)

Type 2a: globular or biconical deep bowl with short funnelled or cylindrical neck, often with a short, everted rim.

Type 2b: sub-type is represented by deep globular bowl with a narrow mouth, without emphasised rim, and usually lavishly decorated.

Type 3a: semi-globular bowl with flat rim, sometimes represented by a sub-type with a semi-circularly thickened inner side of the rim

Type 3b: semi-globular or slightly biconical bowl with an inverted upper portion or the rim.

Type 3c: biconical bowl.

Type 4a: shallow conical bowl, similar to plate.

2.6.3.2 Cups (Fig. 2.48)

Cups are divided into three types:

Type 1a: semi-globular cup, usually with one arched handle that connects the rim and the belly of the vessel.

Type 2a: conical cup, usually with one elongated tongue-shaped handle in line with the mouth of the vessel.

Type 3a: ovoid cup with a short and slightly funnelled neck and one handle connecting the rim and the shoulder.

Type 3b: narrow and high ovoid cup, sometimes with a funnelled neck.

Type 4a: slightly biconical cup, sometimes with a short cylindrical neck and a handle that surpasses the rim.

Type 4b: deep ovoid or slightly bicanonical cup with one handle that surpasses the rim

2.6.3.3 Beakers (Fig. 2.49)

Type 1: pear-shaped or slightly biconical beaker with two small handles ribbon-like in cross-section which do not surpass the rim and connect the rim and the shoulder or belly of the vessel. This type has five variants.

Type 1a: beaker with the slightly biconical recipient and long cylindrical or slightly funnelled neck, with shorth handles that connect the rim and the shoulder of the vessel.

Type 1b: beaker with slightly biconical or semi-globular recipient and long cylindrical or slightly funnelled neck, with long handles which connect the rim and the widest portion of the vessel belly.

Type 1c: stubby, wide beaker, slightly pear-shaped, with handles that connect the rim and the shoulder and do not or slightly surpass the rim

Type 1d: beaker with globular recipient, narrow neck, with two handles that connect the rim and the shoulder of the vessel. Similar to type 1c, which is stubbier and does not have an emphasised neck in comparison to the belly.

Type 1e: similar to type 1c, slightly slenderer and the handles significantly surpass the rim, for a quarter or even a third of the height of the handle.

Type 2a: S-profiled beaker with a wide mouth and belly, with two arched handles of ribbon-like cross-section, which are in line with the rim or slightly surpass it. The handles connect the rim and the shoulder of the vessel.

Type 3a: Slightly biconical or ovoid beaker with two handles that are in line with the rim or slightly surpass it.

Type 3b: slightly S-profiled beaker, with emphasized form, cylindrical neck, everted or bevelled rim, with two handles, sometimes on a short foot.

Type 4a: beaker with semi-globular recipient on a hollow foot.

Type 4b: beaker with globular or biconical form with emphasized profiled rim and an arched handle that connects the rim and the shoulder or belly of the vessel.

Type 5a: funnelled beaker with two handles in line with the rim.

Type 6a: slightly S-profiled beaker, with narrow and high proportions, and tongue-shaped or rectangular handles on the belly.

Type 7: beaker with the globular recipient, long cylindrical or slightly funnelled neck, with one or two long handles, usually ribbon-like in cross-section, which start from (or below) the rim and connect on the vessel shoulder (sub-type 7a with one handle, and 7b with two handles). Type 7c is a beaker with a long funnelled neck, wide mouth, and globular recipient, with two long handles that connect the rim and the shoulder of the vessel.

Type 8: beaker with long cylindrical or slightly funnelled neck, with emphasized biconical recipient, and one or two narrow handles that connect the rim and the belly of the vessel, known as the 'Junatzite' type (type 8a is with one handle).

2.6.3.4 Amphorae (Fig. 2.50)

Amphorae are divided into five types:

Type 1a: ovoid amphora with short or long cylindrical neck, sometimes with wide tunnelled handles on the shoulder and the belly.

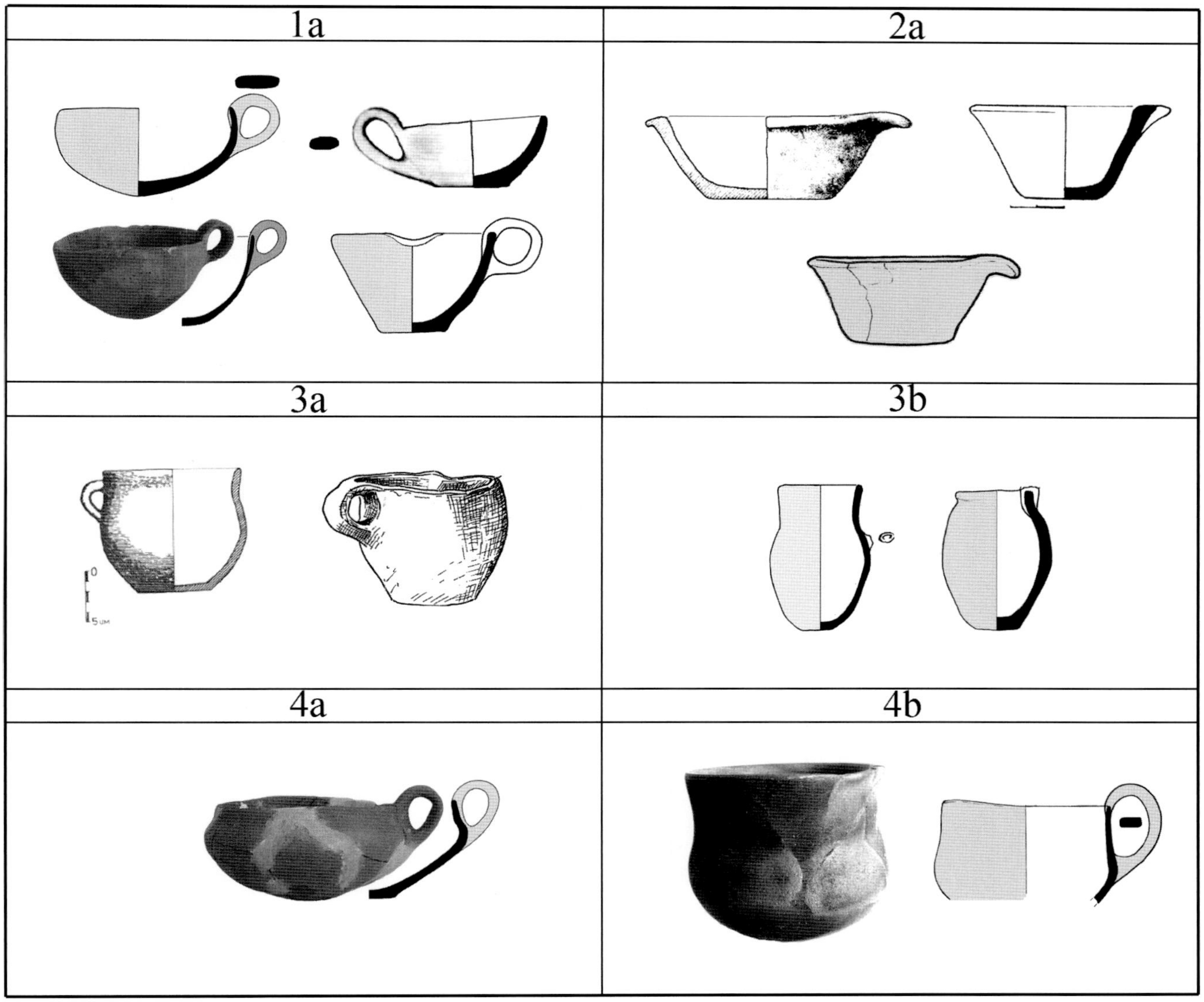

Figure 2.48. Early Bronze Age cups in the central Balkans.

Type 1b: deep ovoid amphora with a short bevelled or flat rim.
Type 2a: deep pear-shaped or barrel-shaped vessel with a short cylindrical or slightly funnelled neck, usually with two arched handles that connect the rim and the shoulder of the vessel. Similar to beakers, although taller and larger.
Type 3a: deep vessel with a wide mouth, more or less everted rim. Such vessels are categorised as amphorae due to the fact that specific type could not be determined.
Type 4a: short amphora with an ovoid, biconical or globular recipient, wide belly, short cylindrical or slightly funnelled neck, usually with two or more handles on the shoulder and belly.

2.6.3.5 Flask-shaped vessels (Fig. 2.51)

Within the study region, only one narrow elongated vessel, the so-called flask-shaped vessel has been recorded, marked by the term *Zylinderflaschen*.

2.6.3.6 Jugs (Fig. 2.51)

Jugs attributed to Type 1a are vessels with a large globular recipient, narrow conical neck, and a long handle that connects the rim and the shoulder or belly of the vessel. Such vessels are similar to beakers of Type 7, although jugs are larger, and their neck is narrower, shorter, and often conical.

Jugs with a sack-shaped recipient, conical neck, and slightly everted rim, with a long, arched handle that connects the rim and the lower portion of the neck, are marked as Type 2a.

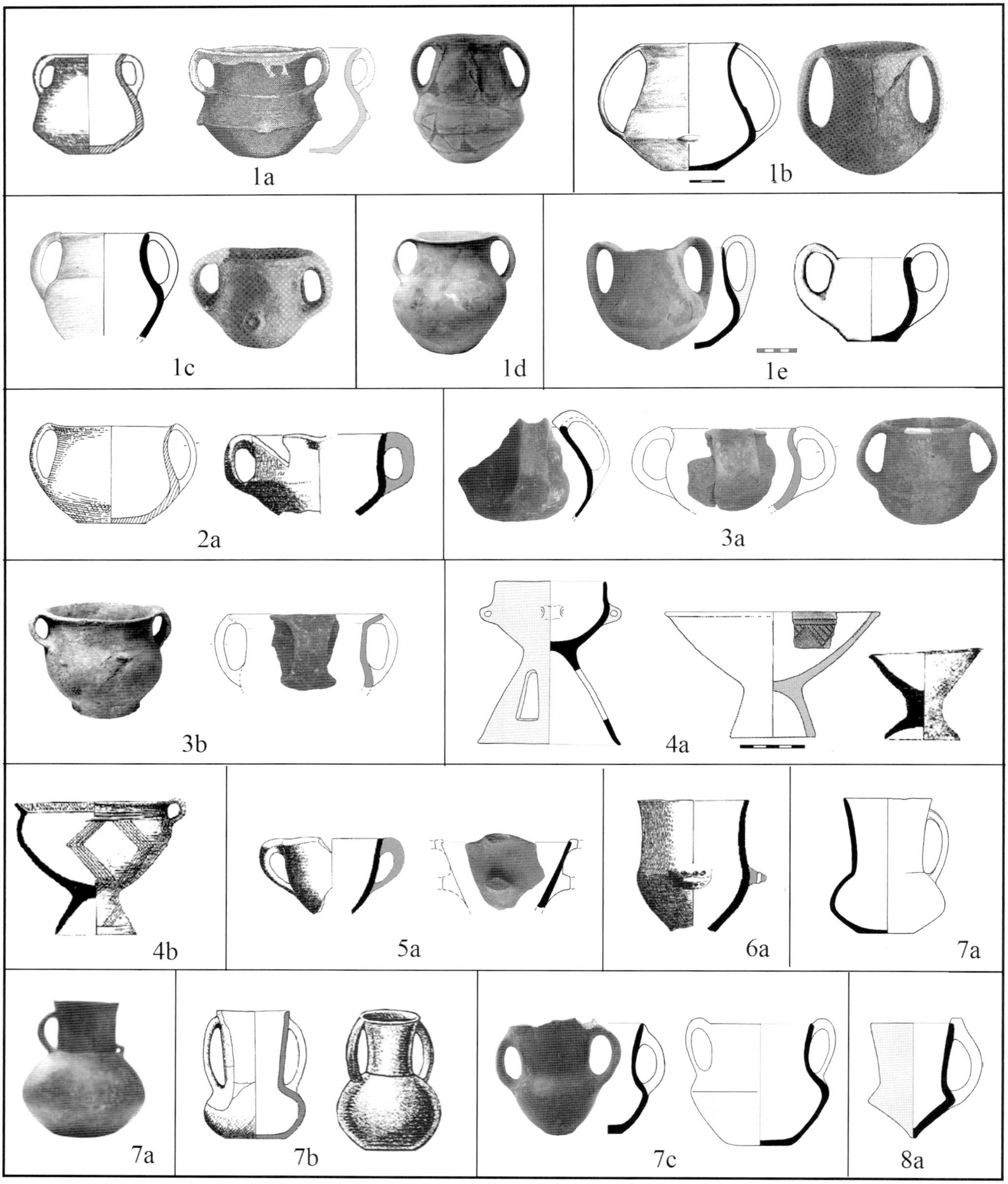

Figure 2.49. Early Bronze Age beakers in the central Balkans.

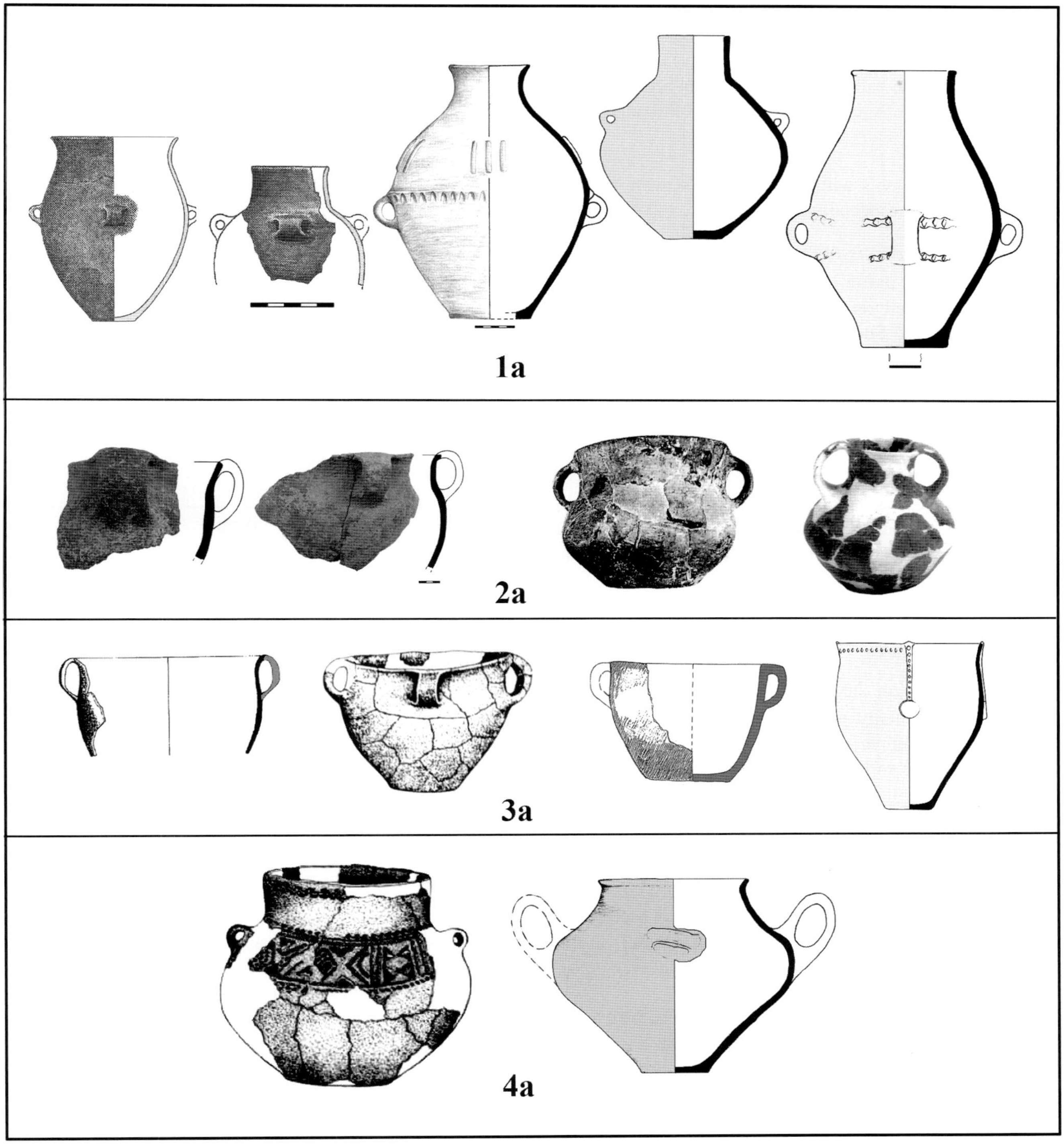

Figure 2.50. Early Bronze Age amphorae in the central Balkans.

2.6.3.7 Pots

This group of vessels is comprised of vessels with thick walls, coarse ware and surfaces, decorated with modelled bands. It should not be excluded that some of the vessels attributed as amphorae, especially Type 3, are in fact pots. Such attribution is difficult since often the only difference between pots and amphorae (especially regarding Type 3) is their function rather than form.

Pots are divided into two types:

Type 1a: ovoid, almost globular pot with a wide mouth, often decorated with modelled band with finger impressions.

Type 2a: ovoid narrow pot with a narrowing mouth, sometimes with handles below the rim or on the shoulder of the vessel.

Cooking pots, the so-called *pyraunoi* have not been recorded at the Early Bronze Age sites in the central Balkans.

2.6.3.8 Pithoi

Pithoi are large vessels with thick walls that were utilised as storage vessels, especially for grains.

2.6.3.9 Double-vessels (Fig. 2.51)

Double-vessels, or the so-called 'salt-vessels' in literature, have been recorded on a number of Early and Middle Bronze Age sites. Such vessels are comprised of two recipients similar to semi-globular cups, which are connected by a modelled 'bridge' on the belly and a larger one on the rim, which transforms into a massive arched or triangular handle.

2.6.3.10 Ember containers (Fig. 2.51)

These unusual vessels have been recorded only in the south of the central Balkans, within zone 5. Such vessels usually have two mouths, one in front and one on the upper side, and possess a small handle for carrying. The upper mouth is often shaped as a chimney or a funnel, and the front mouth is shovel shaped. One such vessel is made in the shape of a bird, possibly a dove.

2.6.3.11 Askoi (Fig. 2.51)

Ovoid and horizontally positioned vessels with a handle and mouth on the upper side. Such vessels possibly imitate leather bags as the earliest form of the recipient.

2.6.3.12 Handles

Handles can represent a quite indicative element for the cultural and chronological attribution of the vessel and therefore should be treated as an important part of the vessel.

According to the form, shape, and cross-section of handles from Early and Middle Bronze Age vessels in the central Balkans, those can be divided into several types, sub-types, and variants.

The most represented type are arched handles which can have a ribbon-like, rectangular, oval, circular, rhomboid, triangular, and other cross-section. Arched handles are those whose length surpasses the width and form an arch. Such handles can be positioned on any part of the vessel but usually connect the rim and the shoulder or the belly of the vessel. The second type are tunnelled handles, which are also arched in form, with different cross-sections, usually ribbon-like, and their height is less than the width.

The next type are tongue-shaped handles, modelled in the shape of a tongue, flat in the root and rounded at the edge. Such handles are usually horizontally positioned on the belly, or sometimes on the vessel rim. Tongue-shaped handles sometimes have a split upper portion.

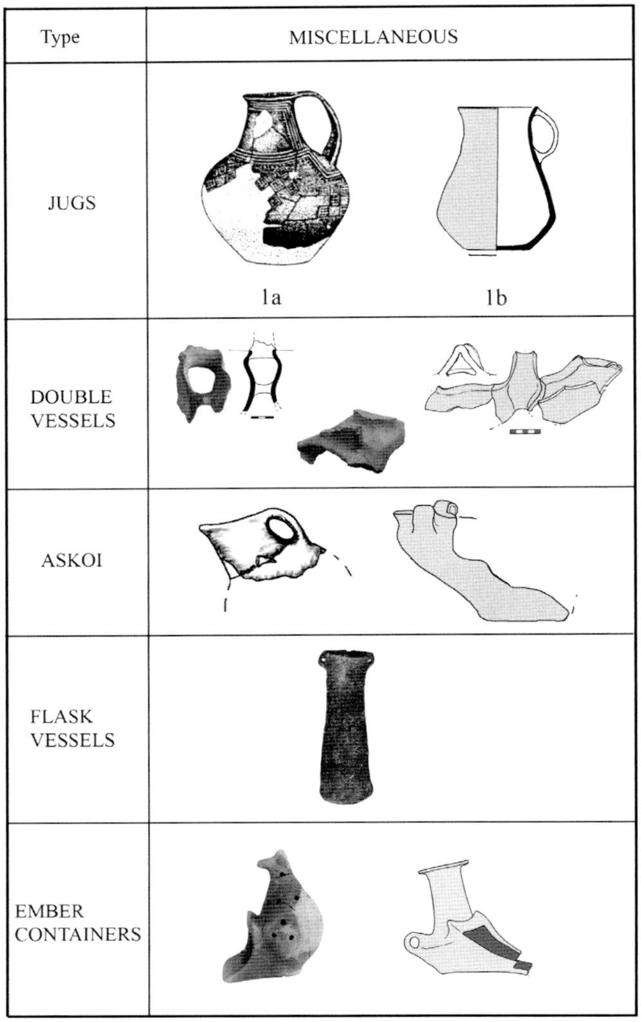

Figure 2.51. Early Bronze Age pottery in the central Balkans, miscellaneous.

Rectangular handles have a flat root and rectangular top. Such handles can also possess a split upper portion.

Triangular handles are quite rare and recorded on several Early Bronze Age sites in the central Balkans. Those are vertically positioned handles with ribbon-like cross-section bent on the top to form a triangle (usually on double-vessels).

2.6.4 Subsistence and economy

The fundamental human instinct is the drive for survival and the primary concern is to protect oneself from danger and secure food and water. By the Bronze Age, the procurement of food had become a routine activity for humans, inherited through hundreds of generations. This began with foraging for food in nature, followed by hunting wild animals during the Palaeolithic, as a result of survival instincts, and continued in the Neolithic with the domestication of wild animals and plants to ensure food was readily available.

Based on archaeo-zoological analyses from several Early Bronze Age sites in the Central Balkans, it is possible to create a picture of the economy and subsistence strategies of this period. However, palaeo-botanical analyses from this era are exceedingly rare, limited to samples from two structures at the Bubanj site and one grave at Ranutovac. Although scarce, the samples from Structures 1 and 91 at Bubanj indicate that during the last quarter of the 3rd millennium cal BC, einkorn and emmer wheat (*Triticum monococum* and *T. dicoccum*) were used, with einkorn being more frequent. Additionally, barley (*Hordeum vulgare*), cornelian cherry (*Cornus mas*), bitter vetch (*Vicia ervilia*), and bedstraw (*Galium spurium*) (Filipović 2020, 339–370) were also utilised. In Grave 3 at Ranutovac, located in the South Morava Valley and dated to the first half of the 21st century BC, seeds of einkorn wheat were found.

As mentioned, faunal data from Early Bronze Age sites in the central Balkans are much more numerous, particularly from the peri-Pannonian geographical zone. In two roughly contemporaneous pits at the Marjansko Brdo site (Structures 44 and 45), one of which was radiocarbon-dated to the third quarter of the 3rd millennium cal BC, remains of domestic cattle (*Bos taurus*) (64%), sheep/goat (*Ovis/capra*) (12%), domestic pig (*Sus scrofa domesticus*) (16%), and dog (*Canis familiaris*) (8%) were identified (Pl. 7). At the same site in the subsequent period, the last quarter of the 3rd millennium cal BC, in Structures 12, 24, and 35, the percentage of sheep/goat increased (58%), while cattle significantly decreased (26%), and the percentage of pig remained the same (16%) (Pl. 8). River mussels of the genus *Unio* were noted in both periods, with only one example found in the earlier period, but 12 specimens in the structures from the later period.[29]

Not far from Marjansko Brdo, at the Viminacium sites of Nad Klepečkom (21st/20th centuries cal BC) and Rit (20th century cal BC), the percentages of species were nearly identical. At Nad Klepečkom, domestic cattle accounted for 48%, while at Rit it was 42%; sheep/goat accounted for 13% and 17%, respectively; domestic pig 18% and 19%; dog 3% at both sites; horse (*Equus caballus*) 1.5% and 3%; and red deer (*Cervus elaphus*) 10.5% and 8%, respectively. Wild cattle (*Bos primigenius:* Aurochs) and roe deer (*Capreolus capreolus*), along with wild boar (*Sus scrofa*), were recorded only at Nad Klepečkom, at small percentages (1.5% and 3%, respectively), while badger (*Meles meles*) was recorded only at Rit (8%). A significant quantity of *Unio* mussels was found at Nad Klepečkom (Pls 9 and 10) (Vuković and Marković 2019, 232–238).

In the southern part of the same geographical zone, at Novačka Ćuprija, during roughly the same period, in the Early Bronze Age contexts and layers, sheep (*Ovis aries*) accounted for 3.2%, goat (*Capra hircus*) for only 0.2%, unidentified sheep/goat for 24.8%, with domestic cattle 39%, pig (*Sus scrofa domesticus*) 24.8%, dog 3%, horse (*Equus caballus*) 1.9%, red deer 0.2%, roe deer 0.2%, brown hare (*Lepus capensis*) 1.7%, and polecat (*Mustela putorius*) 0.2%. Additionally, a considerable amount of *Unio* river mussels was recorded (Pl. 11) (Greenfield 1986).

Palaeo-zoological data from Early Bronze Age sites in eastern and western Serbia and the Great Morava Valley and Šumadija regions are lacking. The next available data come from the southernmost geographical zone, the South Morava Basin, specifically from the Bubanj site near Niš. In the older excavations from the 1950s, the faunal distribution at Bubanj was as follows: cattle accounted for 43%, sheep/goat 10%, pig 7%, red deer 21%, with small percentages of horse and some wild animals also noted (Pl. 12) (Bökönyi 1990).

During the new excavations at Bubanj from 2008–2014, two closed contexts from the Early Bronze Age were recorded (Structures 1 and 91, 22nd–20th centuries cal BC). In Structure 1, the remains of two cattle individuals, one domestic pig, one wild boar, one deer, and one wild cat were found, along with several *Unio* shells (Bulatović and Stankovski 2012, 63). A horse bone dated to the 21st/20th centuries cal BC was found in one deep pit from the Early Bronze Age layer (Structure 20), extending to the level of the Early Eneolithic (Bulatović and Stankovski 2012, 64).

According to J. Bulatović, who analysed the fauna from the new excavations at Bubanj but did not differentiate between samples from the Bubanj-Hum II group (the first phase of the Early Bronze Age in the central Balkans, second quarter of the 3rd millennium BC) and the Bubanj-Hum III group (the second phase of the Early Bronze Age, i.e., the last quarter of the 3rd millennium BC), domestic cattle accounted for 30.1%, wild cattle for 0.6%, domestic pig 15.5%, wild boar 3.8%, sheep 7.2%, goat 1.9%, sheep/goat 24.1%, dog 4.7%, horse 0.1% (three individuals), red deer 7.1%, roe deer 1%, with small percentages of bear, wolf, fox, badger (0.1% each), wild cat and beaver (0.2% each), and hare (0.3%) (Pl. 12) (Bulatović J. 2020).

During the third quarter of the 3rd millennium at the Marjansko Brdo site, cattle dominated with over 60%, followed by pig, sheep/goat, and dog. Interestingly, the representation of animal species differed at the end of the 3rd millennium cal BC at the Rit, Nad Klepečkom, and Marjansko Brdo sites, which are less than 10 km apart. While the species distribution at Rit and Nad Klepečkom was very similar, with cattle accounting for over 40%, as it did at Marjansko Brdo during the third quarter of the 3rd millennium (64%), by the end of the millennium at Marjansko Brdo, sheep/goat dominated with almost 60%. Domestic pig was represented similarly across all three sites, with approximately 16–19%.

It seems that hunting did not play a significant role in the economy of the communities at Marjansko Brdo during the second half of the 3rd millennium. In contrast, at the Rit and Nad Klepečkom sites, a certain percentage of wild animals such as deer, badger, and wild boar suggests

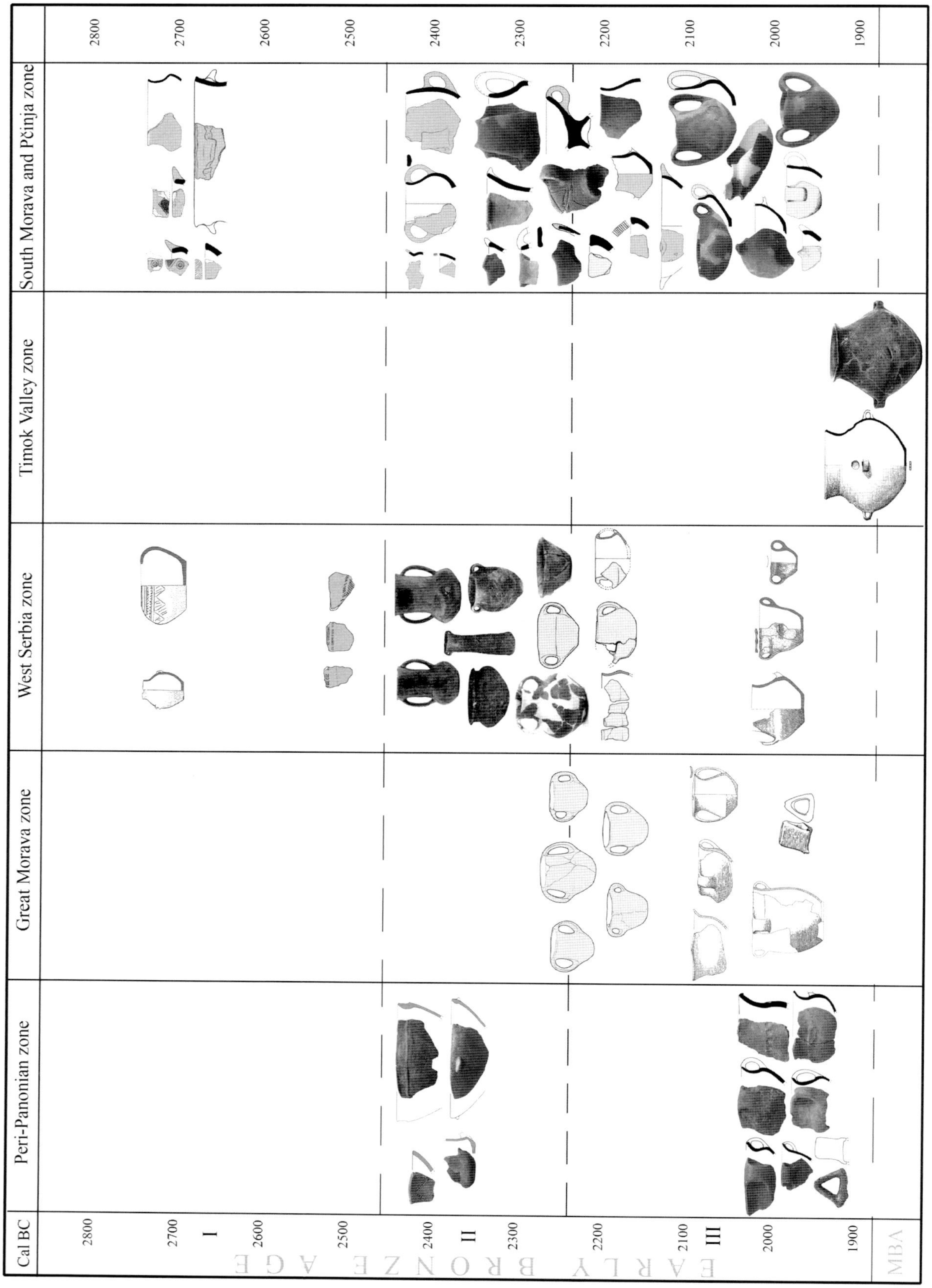

Figure 2.52. Chronology of Early Bronze Age pottery in the central Balkans.

that hunting was practised during this period. Cattle also dominated at Novačka Ćuprija and Bubanj, followed by sheep/goat and pig, though wild animals were much more prevalent at Bubanj (about 17%) than at Novačka Ćuprija (2.3%), in similar proportions as at Nad Klepečkom (16.5%) and Rit (16%).

From this limited data, it can be said that a similar subsistence strategy was evident across all the aforementioned zones during the Early Bronze Age, particularly in the last quarter of the 3rd millennium cal BC. However, there were certain differences at the level of individual settlements rather than regions or zones. In addition to animal husbandry and agriculture, hunting was practised in both the northern and southern parts of the Central Balkans. During this period, river *Unio* mussels were used in diets, more likely for feeding domestic animals than humans, which is expected given that most of the sample sites are located near major rivers. This period also marks the first confirmed presence of domestic horses (*Equus caballus*) at multiple sites.

2.6.5 The appearance of the domestic horse in the central Balkans

The remains of horses (*Equus caballus*) first appeared in this region during the latest phase of the Early Bronze Age, across various zones at the following sites: Nad Klepečkom (21st/20th centuries cal BC), Rit (20th century cal BC), Novačka Ćuprija (29th–18th centuries cal BC (Table 1), and Bubanj (21st/20th centuries cal BC).

While most of the dates are fairly precise, those from Novačka Ćuprija, particularly, show a high degree of standard deviation and are thus not chronologically reliable. The older date, from Pit 2 where several horse bones were found, has a standard deviation of 300 years, yielding a range of 2860–1765 BC (68% probability), corresponding to a broad chronological range from the 29th to the 18th centuries cal BC. In contrast, the second date, from Pit 1 where horse bones were also found, is more precise, giving a range of 2160–1850 BC (68%), which statistically most likely falls in the second half of the 21st and the first half of the 20th centuries cal BC. The date from Pit 2 is about two centuries older in BP dates, so statistically, it could potentially be accepted as the earliest evidence of horses in the central Balkans, but only within a broader chronological spectrum, perhaps in the last quarter of the 3rd millennium BC.

On the other hand, horse bones discovered at Bubanj during earlier excavations could be even older, as the samples were combined from Late Eneolithic and Early Bronze Age layers and the horse bones themselves were not dated (Bökönyi 1990). H. Greenfield also mentions the Crkvina site in Šumadija as an Early Bronze Age site where the remains of a domesticated horse were recorded but, without absolute dates or adequate archaeological material, this finding cannot be chronologically confirmed (Greenfield 2006, 230). A quantity of horse bones was found at Feudvar site in Vojvodina in the Early Bronze Age layer but the layer is not dated (Becker 1991).

The history of human–horse relations stretches far back into the past. In central and northern Europe, as well as in the region between the Dnieper and Volga rivers, wild horses (*Equus ferus ferus*) which are ancestors of domestic horses survived the Late Pleistocene and humans continued to hunt them during the Neolithic, though primarily as wild animals and in a marginal role (Mallory 2006, 209). In the Late Atlantic, between 5500 and 3750 cal BC the horse population increased in central and western Europe, probably as consequence of increased landscape opening by Neolithic and Eneolithic communities (Sommer *et al.* 2011). Although it has long been assumed that horses were originally domesticated in Central Asia within the Botai culture (Outram *et al.* 2009), more recent evidence suggests that Botai horses are not the ancestors of domestic horses (Taylor and Barron-Ortiz 2021, with references cited), but rather that domestic horses from the Eurasian steppes where they were domesticated spread to Europe in the last quarter of the 3rd millennium BC (Librado *et al.* 2024). They suggest that the modern domestic horse lineage emerged around 2200 BC, and that domestication began no earlier than around 2700 BC, coinciding with the population expansion from Eurasia into Europe.

In the Near East and the Balkans, however, these early horse species are nearly absent, making these Early Bronze Age finds of domesticated horses the first evidence of horses in the central Balkans. In the Carpathian Basin, at the Csepel–Hollandiut and Csepel–Haros sites, which belong to the Csepel–Bell Beaker culture, a large quantity of horse bones was recorded, with percentages exceeding 60% compared to other domestic animals (Bökönyi 1978, 35). These sites date to the middle or third quarter of the 3rd millennium cal BC, representing a unique case of a site with such a high percentage of horses which, according to the author, had not been recorded in any culture in the Carpathian Basin before. A similar situation was observed at several sites in Ukraine, which were centres of horse domestication, leading the author to hypothesise that domestication also occurred at these two sites, without horse imports from the east, i.e., from the western Eurasian steppes. According to data from nearly half a century ago, horse remains were found in the Carpathian Basin at the sites of the Nagyrév culture (over 15%), Zók culture (below 1%), Kisapostag culture (slightly above 1%), and Vatya culture (over 2%) (Bökönyi 1978, 42), all dating to the last quarter of the 3rd millennium and the beginning of the 2nd millennium cal BC (Szabó 2019).

If it is accepted that the domesticated horse appeared in Europe around 2200 BC, as suggested by Librado *et al.* (2024, 819–825), then its appearance in the Central Balkans at the end of the 3rd millennium is relatively early.

However, since these archaeo-zoological analyses were conducted over 50 years ago, there is no data on the genetic lineage of the horses. The earliest known horse of the so-called DOM2 lineage (modern domestic horse), genetically close to specimens from the western Eurasian steppes, appeared in Bohemia (Holubice) and the lower Danube region (Gordinești II) during the 22nd–20th centuries cal BC (Librado *et al.* 2021, 634–636; Niskanen 2023, 57, 58). Evidence of overlap between the DOM2 lineage from the western Eurasian steppes and local varieties (?) (non-DOM2) is indicated by a specimen from the Dunaújváros–Kosziderpadlás site (2140–1977 cal BC) (Niskanen 2023, 58), which does not belong to the DOM2 lineage.

Interestingly, remains of a local horse variety (non-DOM2) were recorded in Thrace at the Kirklareli-Kanligecit site (2466–2306 cal BC), whose ancestry overlaps 70% with the DOM2 horses from Ukraine, 20% with the horse from Hungary (Dunaújváros–Kosziderpadlás), and 10% likely originates from Anatolia (Niskanen 2023, 58). Around 2000 BC, a different imported horse lineage appeared in Anatolia, distinct from the local wild horses before domestication. These patterns of change suggest that the domesticated horse arrived in Anatolia, likely via the Caucasus, during the Bronze Age (Guimaraes *et al.* 2020, 6).

Surprisingly, the data from Greece iare sporadic and quite outdated. J. Mallory notes that some scholars believe that the development of Greek civilisation was influenced not only by internal factors but also by an external stimulus in the form of a group of newcomers during the Middle Helladic period (after 2000 BC) who introduced horses and chariots, swords and shields, as well as status-based tumulus burials (Mallory 2006, 89, 208).

The data cite above suggest that the Carpathian Basin was likely the region that mediated the importation of domesticated horses into the central Balkans. Unfortunately, the horse remains from the central Balkans lack genetic information to determine whether they belonged to the DOM2 lineage or some local variety (which is highly unlikely), which would greatly help resolve questions regarding the direction of domesticated horse movement in southeastern Europe. It should be emphasised that the understanding of the initial domestication of horses is indeed still unclear.

In any case, based on current information, this sudden appearance of domesticated horses at several sites in the central Balkans during roughly the same period (21st/20th centuries cal BC), with a significant distribution along the main natural communication routes of the Balkans – through the valleys of the Danube, Great Morava, and South Morava – suggests certain socio-cultural changes. These changes likely involved intensive interactions between the local population of the central Balkans and communities that had already domesticated horses, probably from the Carpathian Basin. More on these changes in material culture will be discussed in the subsequent sections of the book.

2.6.6 Mining and metallurgy

Since the Eneolithic period, copper mining and metallurgy have been among the more important economic activities or crafts, which, depending on the region, persisted in varying degrees into the Bronze Age. During this time, the use of arsenical copper emerged, followed shortly by tin bronze.

In South-eastern and Central Europe, pure copper (from oxidised ores) was eventually replaced by arsenical copper, which was easier to work with and provided better mechanical properties (improved casting capabilities, better malleability, and greater strength, among others). Since arsenical copper contains less than 2% arsenic, it is not considered an alloy but a derivative resulting from the smelting of copper ore that contained arsenic minerals (Kienlin 2010, 18). Interestingly, this type of copper, with a high arsenic content, which is stronger than pure copper, was used in Eneolithic cultural groups for making daggers, while axes, which required greater strength, were made from copper with lower arsenic content. It is believed that the colour of the copper played a decisive role in its selection, as copper with more arsenic had an attractive silver hue. Therefore, it was used to make prestige items like daggers, while axes, being merely tools, were made from other types of copper. It was not until the Early Bronze Age that arsenical copper was replaced by 'fahlore' copper and other varieties obtained from sulphide copper ores (Kienlin 2010).

Unlike arsenical copper, tin bronze, with a tin content exceeding 2–3%, is considered a true alloy. There are, however, several instances of 'unintentional' alloys of copper and tin minerals which, when smelted, produced 'accidental' tin bronze but with a low tin content, below 2% (Kienlin 2010, 129).

While copper deposits are relatively widespread, tin deposits are very rare, with the most famous being in the Erzgebirge in Saxony and Bohemia, Cornwall in England, as well as deposits in the Iberian Peninsula, France, Tuscany, and Sardinia. However, the prehistoric exploitation of these latter sources is questionable. The closest documented tin deposit to the central Balkans used in prehistory (but only in the Late Bronze Age), is Mount Cer in western Serbia (Durman 1997, 10; Huska *et al.* 2014; Mason *et al.* 2016).

Tin was likely extracted from alluvial deposits in rivers that carried tin oxide minerals (Kienlin 2010, 133). Bronze was produced either by directly smelting copper and tin minerals together or by adding tin oxide to molten copper under reducing conditions. In many parts of the Old World, bronze did not immediately replace copper and both were used concurrently for a period. M. Pare describes this gradual adoption of bronze as 'a cultural choice, not a product of technological determinism' (Pare 2000, 25). From around 3000 BC in the Near East and the Aegean, tin bronze began to be used sporadically, mostly for prestige items, and by the mid-3rd millennium its use became common in these regions (Kienlin 2010, 130).

Regarding the earliest confirmed tin mining, primarily of cassiterite, the oldest example comes from Kestel in present-day south-eastern Turkey, dating to 2874–2133 cal BC (Yener *et al.* 1989; Huska *et al.* 2014, 478). At this site, traces of cassiterite were found on the inner rim of a vessel, indicating that smelting furnaces made of fired clay were used in the tin reduction process.

Early tin mining is also known from Deh Hosein in present-day western Iran, radiocarbon dated to the 18th–16th centuries cal BC. Based on lead isotope analyses of Luristan bronzes and some bronze objects from the southern Persian Gulf, which match tin from Deh Hosein, it is highly likely that this mine was in use as early as the 3rd millennium BC (Nezafati *et al.* 2009, 227).

In this context, it is noteworthy that the lead isotope analysis of copper from a knife found at Velika Gruda (modern-day Montenegro, south-western Balkans), dating to the first half of the 3rd millennium cal BC, suggests that the rise in tin bronze metallurgy in the Aegean was likely driven by copper and tin imported from the distant East, such as Central Asia (Kienlin 2010, 130). B. Govedarica dates this tumulus as early as around 3000 BC (Govedarica 2021, 12). The Asian origin of the raw materials for the Velika Gruda knife indicates where the tin came from during this period and explains why so few tin bronze objects have been found in the Balkans during this time.

An extremely interesting finding comes from bronze items in Layer IV at Sitagroi in north-eastern Greece, culturally and chronologically associated with the Baden group (Renfrew 1971; Sherratt 1986, 429–445). These items contained 5.9% and 3.2% tin respectively, and later bronze finds from Layer Va contained 3.4% and 8.1% tin (Durman 1997, 12; McGeehan-Liritzis and Gale 1988, 216). J. Muhly (1985) highlights that the finds from Layer IV at Sitagroi may be the earliest examples of fully developed bronze in the Old World. However, it is intriguing that this information is rarely mentioned in more recent publications dealing with the topic (Harding 2000; Pare 2000; Kienlin 2010).

Tin bronze sporadically appears in the Early Bronze Age in the Balkans. A. Durman (1997, 12, table 1/4) mentions a find of full tin bronze (7.23% tin) at the Vinkovci–Hotel site in a layer belonging to the Late Vučedol and Early Vinkovci–Somogyvár culture. Durman observes that an 'inexperienced' smelter managed to add tin but not separate the iron from the alloy. In any case, copper metallurgy in the Vučedol culture has long been confirmed (Čović 1976; Durman 1983). This suggests that the 3rd millennium BC in the Balkans was a period of experimentation with metallurgy and interaction between the metallurgical knowledge and skills of populations in the Balkans and Central Europe. It is curious that later works on this subject do not mention this find (Harding 2000; Pare 2000; Kienlin 2010).

Another 'controversial' find is a bronze sheet made of tin bronze containing 11.7% tin (by weight) from a Late Neolithic context (*c.* 4650 BC) at the Pločnik site in south-eastern Serbia, which was recently published (Radivojević *et al.* 2014). The composition of the item is not disputed but the relevant context of the find has been contested, even by co-director of the excavations, D. Šljivar (2015, 232). However, M. Radivojević *et al.* (2014, fig. 6) mention several tin bronze objects from the Eneolithic period found in Bulgaria and Serbia, suggesting the possibility of tin bronze being present in the Balkans earlier, before the Bronze Age. This could explain the composition of the Kozarac-type axe from Staro Selo, which contains tin.

In the Balkans and modern-day Romania, the widespread use of high-tin bronze is reliably attested only from the Middle Bronze Age (Pare 2000, 12–16). A similar situation is recorded in Slovakia and the northern Alpine region, where tin bronze became more widely used but not until 1900/1800 cal BC (Kielnin 2010, 130). The beginnings of tin bronze metallurgy in Central Europe are still unclear, but many agree that the Únětice culture may have been the centre of early tin bronze production and the development of advanced casting techniques (Kielnin 2010, 131). This would mean that bronze halberds and daggers with solid-cast handles appeared before 2000 BC in the Únětice culture. Interestingly, this region had a strong metallurgical tradition, known for the exploitation of sulphide copper ores ('fahlore-type copper') and the occasional occurrence of low-tin bronze dating back to the Neolithic, according to regional periodisation.

From the information presented, it can be concluded that the transition to tin bronze in Central and South-eastern Europe was a gradual process that was completed in the 2nd millennium BC. Tin bronze was used somewhat earlier in Western Europe, as early as 2200–2000 BC (Pare 2000, 26, fig. 1.14; Kielnin 2010, 130). It is also possible that tin bronze reached Central Europe from the British Isles (Kielnin 2010, 131). Another recent model of the distribution and spread of tin bronze suggests that it first appeared in the Aegean and then spread northward through the Adriatic and Istria to the Alps and Central Europe (Hänsel 2002).

In the Central Balkans, evidence of copper carbonate ore exploitation during the Early Bronze Age was found at the Prljuša site in Mali Šturac, where the mineral malachite was primarily extracted. However, the malachite was cotnained in very hard rock, so these communities exploited the ore using surface mining methods, without deep mining shafts (Antonović and Dimić 2017, 136). This type of exploitation is characteristic of the older Eneolithic in the central Balkans. Although no portable finds from the Eneolithic have been discovered at Prljuša, Early Bronze Age pottery has been found, that matches pottery from central Balkans sites from the second half of the 3rd millennium BC.

A recently published study indicates that after a boom in copper exploitation during the Early Eneolithic in the central Balkans, a so-called 'Copper Hiatus' occurred during the Late Eneolithic, when copper was scarcely mined. Exploitation resumed during the Bronze Age but in a completely different way. During the Early Eneolithic, surface oxidised copper ore (mainly malachite) and some sulphide ore were used (Powell *et al.* 2017). In the Bronze Age, sulphide copper ores were predominantly utilised. These conclusions are based on δ^{65} copper isotope analyses of 120 copper or bronze finds from the Balkans, dating to the Eneolithic and Bronze Age. The δ^{65} copper isotope values in surface oxidised ores are significantly higher than in deep sulphide ores. However, in some Bronze Age items, the δ^{65} copper isotope values are also high (Powell *et al.* 2017, table 1), which could be explained by the use of oxidised ore, perhaps from Prljuša, which was definitely exploited in the Early Bronze Age, or from another, as-yet-undiscovered mine where oxidised ore may have been exploited during this period.

Although traces of copper ore exploitation have been found, evidence of copper metallurgy from this period has not been recorded. The first traces of metallurgy appear in the following period, which will be discussed in the chapter on the Middle Bronze Age.

The analysed metal finds from the central Balkans in the Early Bronze Age are mostly made of copper. However, it should be noted that not many metal finds have been discovered across the large territory of the central Balkans, and the physical-chemical composition of most of these items has not been analysed.

In total, 25 complete or nearly complete metal items have been recorded in this region, one of which is a gold bracelet from a grave at Šljunkara (Fig. 2.15/15 above). Of the remaining 24 items, 14 have had their chemical-physical composition analysed, revealing that eight are made of pure copper, six of copper with an arsenic content of 0.5–1.1%, and one contains a high arsenic content of around 3.5%.

Thus, items made from so-called arsenical copper appear in small numbers during this period, mostly with a very low arsenic percentage, below 1%. The item with the highest arsenic content in the central Balkans during the Early Bronze Age is a Kozarac-type axe from Boljetin, with 3.48% arsenic and 4.76% lead (Antonović 2014). Interestingly, all other items made from arsenical copper are also Kozarac-type axes, from Begaljica (0.84%), Jasika (around 1%), and Kostol (0.72%) – If items with less than 1% arsenic can even be classified as arsenical copper. One Kozarac-type axe from Staro Selo in the Great Morava Valley Region contains 1.8% tin, so it could be defined as unintentional tin bronze, since true bronze alloys require at least 2–3% tin content (Kienlin 2010, 129). A dagger from Gornji Matejevac also contains around 1.1% arsenic, supporting the argument that not only axes were made from arsenical copper.

A pin found in a pit at Marjansko Brdo (Structure 12) and dated to the 20th century cal BC is made from pure copper, without any tin or arsenic content. This indicates that at this site, in the peri-Pannonian zone, the production of arsenical copper or tin bronze had not yet been mastered at that time.

In neighbouring Vojvodina, the situation is slightly different, as tin bronze appears as early as the first half of the 19th century cal BC. This is evidenced by a dagger from Grave 232 at Ostojićevo, dated to this period, which contained 6.6% tin (O'Shea *et al.* 2019; Milašinović *et al.* forthcoming). There is also a bronze find from the Mokrin necropolis, a pin with 2.1% tin and 2.8% arsenic,[30] from Grave 119, which is undated but likely older than Grave 232 (Girić 1971, 98, T. XXXV; O'Shea 1996, 37, table 3.1). This would suggest that this pin was made of accidental bronze rather than a deliberate bronze alloy, especially given its high arsenic content.

The most common metal finds in the central Balkans during the Early Bronze Age are axes with perforated shafts, specifically Kozarac and Lozane types, with the Kozarac type being much more prevalent (Pl. 15). Kozarac-type axes have been discovered mostly at sites in the northern half of the central Balkans, across the first four zones, excluding South Morava Basin, Raška, and northern North Macedonia (Pl. 14). Lozane-type axes have been recorded in South Morava Basin (three examples) and one example each in western Serbia and Great Morava Valley.

Kozarac-type axes are found in two variants, Jasika and Baranda, and are mostly from sites in the river valleys of northern and central Serbia. They do not appear south of the West Morava. The distribution of these axes suggests a west–east direction of spread, as their numbers in these areas are much lower than in the western Balkans but noticeably higher than in the eastern Balkans (Antonović 2014, 92). This is further supported by the distribution of these axes in the western Balkans, where they are mainly found in northern Croatia and northern Bosnia, and sporadically along the Adriatic coast (Žeravica 1993, 22–27, Taf. 50). D. Antonović dates these axes to the end of the Eneolithic and Early Bronze Age, a dating confirmed by the absolute date of Grave 208 at Mokrin, which is 2200–2020 cal BC. In addition to other items, a Jasika variant of the Kozarac-type axe was found in this grave (O'Shea 1996). Most of the Kozarac-type axes from the peri-Pannonian zone belong to the Baranda variant, except for the axe from the confluence of the Drina and Sava rivers, which belongs to the Jasika variant.

Interestingly, V. Klochko (2020, 325) considers Kozarac–Stublo and Baniabic-type axes as markers of Indo-European migration into Central and Eastern Europe. This could also be said for Kozarac-type axes in the central Balkans, where they have been found in greater numbers, mainly in regions where tumuli have also been documented, although they are most often associated with local production in the Vučedol culture.

In addition to copper axes, two daggers have been discovered in the central Balkans. One was found as a chance find in the Nišava Valley at Gornji Matejevac and the other in a skeleton grave in Tumulus 10 at Belotić in western Serbia. The first was made of copper, with an arsenic content of around 1.1%,[31] while the chemical-physical composition of the second dagger has not yet been analysed. The dagger from Belotić, with three rivets, is of a type known from the Perjamos group, and M. Garašanin dates it to the Br A1 phase (Garašanin 1973, 262). Wels-Weyrauch suggests a similar dating for this type of dagger but considers that it may be slightly later, placing it in the Br A2 phase (Wels-Weyrauch 2015).

The dagger from Gornji Matejevac corresponds to the *Safferstetten*-type according to the Wels–Weyrauch typology and could be dated to the Early Bronze Age, specifically to the late phase of the Bell Beaker culture (Wels-Weyrauch 2015, 45, 46).

In any case, it seems that daggers reached this area through interactions between the Central Balkan population and their neighbours in Pannonia but on the other side according to the dagger from Odaia Turcului (Bajenaru 2014, fig. 66/2), however, it is also possible that the daggers reached this area through east–west interactions. When it comes to Kozarac-type axes it seems that they arrived through interactions with populations to the east, possibly involving population movements, first from east to west, and later from north to south.

In Europe, gold in the Early Bronze Age, crafted using gold-sheeting techniques, was a method already in use during the Early Eneolithic, as seen at the Varna necropolis and other Eneolithic sites (Harding 2000, 229). In the Carpathian Basin during the Early Bronze Age gold was used to make prestige items such as cups, discs, as well as massive bracelets and axes. These items may have reached the Carpathian Basin, specifically southern Pannonia, but clearly did not spread further south.

Gold items in the central Balkans are extremely rare, even in the previous period, the Late Eneolithic. Known finds include gold items from the tumulus at Bare in Šumadija (Srejović 1963, 47; 1976, T. IV), a chance find from Kumane near Golubac (Stojić and Jacanović 2008, 172, fig. 87), and a recent discovery consisting of a gold hair ring with direct analogies in the Bulgarian Danube region (Alexandrov 2009, 10–12, fig. 1), as well as a gold spring wire and several small perforated gold beads. These items were found in a grave with a contracted individual in a stone cist at Štulac near Lebane, south-eastern Serbia, dated to the 25th–24th centuries cal BC.[32] An identical gold hair ring was found in a grave of the Yamnaya culture at Chudomir in north-western Bulgaria (Alexandrov 2021, fig. 12/4), which could provide parallels for the origins of the jewellery in the Štulac grave. An identical silver hair ring was found in a Yamnaya culture grave at Vojlovica, dated to the first quarter of the 3rd millennium cal BC (Đorđević and Đorđević 2016, 21, 22).

There are also hoards of gold items from Velika Vrbica and Stari Kostolac but these are more likely dated to the beginning of the Late Bronze Age (Garašanin 1954, 10; Stojić and Jacanović 2008, 272, fig. 130).

As for the gold band from Šljunkara in Zemun, a similar but wider and more richly decorated copper headband was found in Grave 73 at Mokrin, also dating to the Early Bronze Age (Girić 1971, 218, 219, T. XXII). Part of the gold jewellery from Orolik, assigned to the Vinkovci–Somogyvár culture, is decorated in a similar manner to the diadem from Šljunkara, with punctuations along the edges of the item (Majnarić Pandžić 1974, 23/1–3).

Other gold finds from this period have also been recorded, but it is evident that most of them are concentrated in Pannonia (a group of gold finds from the Vinkovci–Somogyvár group at Bosut, the Jászdózsa–Kapolnahalom tell, etc.) (Majnarić Pandžić 1974; Popović and Radojčić 1996, cat. no. 34; Tárnoki 2003), so it is unclear whether their absence in the central Balkans is due to insufficient exploration of the interior of the region or if gold items simply did not reach this area in larger numbers for some reason.

The lack of gold items in the central Balkans during the Early Bronze Age could also be interpreted as a sign of possible socio-cultural changes compared to the previous period, the Late Eneolithic, or as stagnation in the movement of populations from the east through the Danube region. It was likely this population movement that brought gold jewellery into the interior of the Balkans earlier, during the Late Eneolithic and the earliest phase of the Early Bronze Age in the central Balkans.

2.6.7 The cultural and chronological picture of the central Balkans in the Early Bronze Age: material and spiritual culture and relations with neighbouring groups

The material culture of the Early Bronze Age in the central Balkans cannot be described as uniform, yet the populations of all geographical zones were connected in some way, both with each other and with neighbouring and more distant regions such as the Carpathian Basin, the Aegean, Thrace, and the Lower Danube. The material culture in this region largely depended on the geographical characteristics of the area, as the five regions examined in this study each have their own specificities, as discussed in the introductory chapter.

Based on the characteristics of portable finds, mainly pottery, and absolute dating, the Early Bronze Age in the central Balkans can be divided into three cultural-chronological phases.

2.6.7.1 The oldest phase of the Early Bronze Age (EBA 1) (Pl. 16)

The cultural characteristics of the oldest phase of the Early Bronze Age in the northern part of the central Balkans are rooted in the cultural traditions of Eneolithic communities, mainly the steppe tumuli of the Yamnaya culture, followed by the Vučedol culture. In the southern part, these traditions are based on the Coţofeni–Kostolac culture in interaction with communities from western Bulgaria. This phase includes tumuli from Vojlovica, Jabuka, and Pančevo in the peri-Pannonian zone, as well as tumuli from Bare and Rogojevac in Šumadija, and tumuli in Jančići and Krstac in western Serbia. The remains of a house at Velika Humska Čuka, belonging to the Bubanj-Hum II group, which developed on the foundations of the Coţofeni–Kostolac group, and the grave of a flexed burial at Svinjarička Čuka also belong to this phase. Although chronologically this grave belongs to Phase 2, the hair ring found in the grave is characteristic of Yamnaya graves in the Danube region, including the tumulus at Vojlovica (Đorđević and Đorđević 2016; Alexandrov 2021), so from a cultural perspective, this grave is assigned to the first phase. This phase likely also includes a horizon at the Stalijska Mahala site in north-western Bulgaria, as well as Yamnaya tumuli from the same region (Todorova 2003, 299).

A. Tumuli in the Central Balkans

The burial practices of the Vinkovci–Somogyvár group (Kulscar 2009, 269–275), which were bi-ritual, were reflected in the Balkans through mixed burial practices, predominantly inhumation (Vajuga, Bela Crkva, Dučalovići, etc.), but also cremation (Belotić, Rospi Ćuprija, Krstac, Lučani) (Kulcsár 2009, 269–275). It is interesting that tumuli are rare in the Vinkovci–Somogyvár group in the Carpathian Basin and are mostly associated with the peripheral areas of this region (Kulscar 2009, 269–272). In contrast, in the Belotić–Bela Crkva group, tumuli were the usual form of burial, whether for inhumation or cremation. This suggests that this burial practice was not adopted from the Vinkovci–Somogyvár group but rather from a population that used tumuli as a burial method in the previous period, namely the Late Eneolithic. Known tumuli in the Central Balkans that may belong to the oldest phase of the Early Bronze Age include those from Bare and Rogojevac in Šumadija, as well as previously dated tumuli in southern Banat near Pančevo, dated to 3000–2600 cal BC (Koledin *et al.* 2020), just before the appearance of Vinkovci–Somogyvár elements in this area. These tumuli likely belonged to the Yamnaya culture bearers, who expanded into the Balkans from the east, through the Danube region (Alexandrov 2023, fig. 1), possibly diluting their steppe origins and customs as they mixed with the indigenous population.

At the Veliko Polje site in Jančići near Čačak in western Serbia, a tumulus was investigated with a core consisting of a layer of soil with ash and clumps of red earth, which may have represented ochre (Dmitrović 2016, 58–61). In the centre of the tumulus, the grave of a contracted individual with two vessels was found, one of which resembles Vučedol vessels and is decorated in this style (Fig. 2.22/8). Almost identical vessels were classified by S. Dimitrijević as part of the Kostolac group, specifically Phase B1 of the Vučedol group, suggesting that these vessels were inherited from the Eneolithic, from the Lengyel and Baden cultural groups (Dimitrijević 1977, 5, 29, Abb. 4/19–22).

Since tumuli as a form of burial were not previously used, the tumulus at Veliko Polje in Jančići, whose central grave is dated to the 29th–27th centuries cal BC (Table 1), appears to be the oldest dated tumulus in the interior of the central Balkans. There are the tumuli at Bare and Rogojevac, as well as a tumulus with ochre and charcoal in the central part of the tumulus, without a burial, in north-western Serbia, in Tolisavac. Also known is a tumulus with cremated individuals without an urn in north-western Serbia at the site of Banjevci and, according to the pottery, these tumuli have been assigned by M. Garašanin (1986, 69) to the earliest phase of the Baden complex (Boleraz–Černavoda III group). However, none of these tumuli has been dated. Another tumulus from western Serbia at the Dubac site in the same village is noteworthy, not for its date (26th–25th centuries cal BC), but for the traces of ochre recorded on the skull and cervical vertebrae of the contracted individual (Dmitrović 2016, 67). Ochre was also recorded in several other tumuli in western Serbia, including Donje Kravarice, Turica (Dmitrović 2016), and Tolisavac and Banjevci (Garašanin 1986, 69). Two of these tumuli with ochre traces are in the same village of Jančići, at the Dubac and Ravnine sites. It is interesting that the tumuli at Veliko Polje and Dubac, where ochre was found, are dated quite early (28th–27th centuries BC and 26th–25th centuries cal BC), while other tumuli with ochre unfortunately remain undated.

It is also noteworthy that at the Dubac site, a tumulus dated to the 21st century cal BC was investigated, unfortunately without grave goods, indicating a continuity of burial under tumuli in this micro-region from the Late Eneolithic to the end of the Early Bronze Age. This case study best illustrates how the tumulus burial method was adopted from the Late Eneolithic, likely from a population still maintaining steppe customs from the Yamnaya culture, and how it persisted throughout the Early Bronze Age. It is also known that this burial method continued to be used in the region into the Late Bronze Age (Dmitrović 2016, 207–211; Bulatović *et al.* 2017, 53–61 with cited literature). Steppe influences on the Early Bronze Age culture of western Serbia were highlighted by Garašanin and Garašanin (1962, 61), who linked spherical bowls with narrow openings (type 2b) to necropolises with tumuli in eastern Slovakia, where such vessels were found alongside corded ware pottery.

The question arises as to why the Belotić–Bela Crkva group, a local variant of the Vinkovci–Somogyvár group, thrived only in western Serbia, extending from the Sava River in the north to the Lim River in the south. In other words, why did this cultural group expand from the Sava and Danube regions only through western Serbia and down the Danube valley, while almost completely bypassing or rarely using the Great Morava Valley and eastern Serbia?

The answer may lie in the distribution of sites from the previous period, the Eneolithic, when this territory was much more sparsely inhabited than other zones of the Central Balkans. After the Neolithic and the Vinča culture, when this zone was relatively densely populated, the Eneolithic saw western Serbia being almost uninhabited, except for sporadic sites belonging to the late Bubanj-Hum I or Salcuţa IV groups (Tasić 1979, map 2; Bulatović *et al.* 2017, 42–50; Kapuran *et al.* 2018, 77–83, figs 7.1. and 7.3). A similar situation was recorded in the Late Eneolithic, during the Kostolac group period (Dimitrijević 1979a, map 4; 1979b, map 6; Nikolić 2000, 8, 39–44; Kapuran *et al.* 2018, 77–83, fig. 7.5). The reasons why this territory remained almost uninhabited during the Eneolithic are unknown. It can be assumed that this predominantly mountainous area, located outside the main natural communication routes of the central Balkans, was left to nature, possibly overgrown with dense forests, while the lower part along the West Morava River was waterlogged since this area is still frequently waterlogged today, especially during rainy seasons, and the river often floods the first terrace.

At the same time, during the Eneolithic, all other geographical zones of the central Balkans were relatively densely populated, likely because they were natural corridors for community movements, which at that time were primarily in a north–south direction. Thus, the Timok Region hosted communities of the Coţofeni–Kostolac group, which moved south from Oltenia and Transylvania, reaching South Morava Basin and, in a transformed form, Macedonia and the northern shores of Aegean Greece (Kapuran and Bulatović 2012, 77, 78). South Morava Basin was also inhabited throughout the Eneolithic, although the area south of the Grdelica Gorge was almost uninhabited during the Late Eneolithic (Bulatović 2007, 31–33, map 3). The reason for this was likely the impassable terrain through or around the gorge, as settlements from this period have been recorded in Kosovo (Tasić 1998b), which was clearly part of the main southern route beyond the Leskovac plain.

B. Steppe incursions (?) in the central Balkans

The under-population of western Serbia during the developed Eneolithic period provided fertile ground for the incursions of steppe populations, who could have easily reached western Serbia from southern Banat and eastern Srem. Several tumuli containing burials in a stretched or slightly contracted position, within rectangular graves with traces of ochre, have been investigated in Banat, eastern Srem, and eastern Bačka (Koledin *et al.* 2020). It seems that these movements in the central Balkans were likely limited by the Bagrdan Gorge, as no tumuli from this period have been recorded south of it. The question arises as to whether this was due to the natural barrier or the fact that Great Morava Valley was relatively densely populated by the late Kostolac group at the end of the 4th and in the first half of the 3rd millennium cal BC. It is also possible that both factors contributed to keeping steppe communities away from central and South Morava Basin. Certainly, the open orography of the terrain allowed for this direction of tumuli expansion from the east, as the terrain was flat and open along the Danube and Sava rivers, and then southward through the valleys of the Great Morava and possibly Lepenica and Gruža rivers, toward western Serbia (Pl. 16).

When it comes to tumuli, steppe populations, and the central Balkans, the first question to address is whether we are dealing with migrations and the presence of steppe populations in these areas or whether the local population adopted steppe burial customs? It seems that before the appearance of tumuli, the population in this area was closely related to communities of the Vučedol culture, at least judging by the flat necropolis with cremated burials in Stapari, where a typical late Vučedol urn was found (Fig. 2.23/15) (Dimitrijević 1979a, taf. 18/4, 5, 7, 10, 11). Cremated burials of the Vučedol culture were also discovered in Batajnica and Vojka, but these were under tumuli, with the urn placed on the pyre in the central part of the mound (Dimitrijević 1979b, 285). According to Dimitrijević, the practice of tumuli burials in Pannonia was inherited from the earlier Baden cultural group, while cremation was considered a southern Balkan custom (Dimitrijević 1979b, 286). It is evident that tumuli as a form of burial were adopted relatively early in western Serbia, as in the tumulus in Jančići is already dated to the end of the first quarter of the 3rd millennium cal BC. However, it is possible that burials under tumuli and in flat necropolises were practised simultaneously for some time. According to Horváth *et al.* the earliest tumuli in western Serbia, which established the chronology of the steppe culture in the Carpathian Basin, correspond chronologically to Period IV (2900/2800–2500/2400 cal BC), during which the horizon in the Carpathian Basin was under strong Catacomb culture influences (Horváth *et al.* 2013, 171, 172).

In this horizon, at least in the Carpathian Basin, steppe communities were still present, while in the final Period V (Late Pit Grave effect – 2500/2400–2200/2000 cal BC), the actual presence of Pit Grave populations disappears. This could also be applied to western Serbia, although it is not certain whether there was any foreign (steppe?) population even during Period IV. To determine their possible presence in western Serbia, all available information must be analysed.

The tumuli in Banat and eastern Bačka are larger than the possible 'steppe' tumuli in western Serbia, which could be explained by the different terrain configurations and geological characteristics of the plain compared to the mountainous area of western Serbia. When referring to 'steppe' tumuli in western Serbia, we mean those dated to the first half of the 3rd millennium cal BC, containing inhumations with traces of ochre and no grave goods, attributed to the Belotić–Bela Crkva group. These include Tumulus 1 at the Veliko Polje site in Jančići and Tumulus 1 at the Dubac site in the same village. These tumuli are smaller in size (*c.* 13 m in diameter and 0.5–1 m in height) with a central core of stone or loose soil containing traces of ash and charcoal. In the case of Veliko Polje, ochre was found in the central core (pyre), while at Dubac, it was found on the neck and skull of the deceased. The tumulus at Rogojevac in Šumadija is also small, measuring 13.5 × 1.5 m, with two chambers in the central part made of limestone slabs, each containing one inhumed individual lying on their back with bent legs, both sprinkled with ochre (Srejović 1976, 118–121).

At Bare, near Rogojevac, two tumuli were discovered, although one does not conform to the patterns of steppe tumuli, as it contains a cremated individual (Tumulus 2). Tumulus 1 at Bare is somewhat larger, measuring 25 × 1.4 m, with an inhumed individual in a stretched position with a dislocated skull, placed on a central platform made of yellow clay. The grave goods included three vessels and gold jewellery on the chest of the deceased (Srejović 1976, 122–126). The tumuli at Rogojevac and Bare have not been dated but they can be relatively chronologically placed in Period IV of the steppe culture chronology, according to Horváth *et al.* (2013) The two tumuli at Bare, which are of similar size and construction but feature different burial rituals, may represent the best example of the socio-cultural picture of the central Balkans at that time. Srejović notes that Tumulus 2 with a cremated individual, although of identical construction to Tumulus 1, is younger due to the cremation of the deceased and the spherical jug, which resembles the still-developing form of Vinkovci–Somogyvár or Belotić–Bela Crkva ceramic production. He also points out that a fragment of pottery decorated with concentric circles resembles the Vučedol culture, comparing this tumulus to those at Vojka and Batajnica (Srejović 1976, 127).

The pottery from the tumulus at Ivkovo Brdo in Krstac, in the West Morava Valley, is identical to the decorated pottery from Tumulus 1 at Bare (Fig. 2.23/5a, b) (Srejović 1976, T. IV/2), and this grave has been dated to the 25th century cal BC, suggesting that Tumulus 1 at Bare could be dated to the middle of the 3rd millennium BC. In the tumulus at Ivkovo Brdo, a cremated individual was also buried, as in Tumulus 2 at Bare, and it is known that bi-ritual burials were practised at this time, so Tumulus 2 at Bare could also be dated to the same period.

Regarding the tumulus at Rogojevac, it exhibits all the characteristics of steppe culture (the position of the deceased, ochre, chambers) so, in this case, there are enough arguments to consider the presence of a foreign (steppe) community in this area. Similarly, the tumuli in Jančići, at Veliko Polje and Dubac, indicate the steppe origin of the population buried there, as they contain contracted individual burials, ochre is present, one grave contains a vessel of Vučedol origin, and the dating of both tumuli (28th–27th and 26th–25th centuries cal BC) points to a time before the formation of the Belotić–Bela Crkva group. On the other hand, the tumuli at Bare, while not having many steppe features except for ochre in one tumulus (Tumulus 2), do not appear to be younger. The buttons from the jewellery set in Tumulus 1 are identical to those found in the Vinkovci–Somogyvár group hoard at Bosut (Popović and Radojčić 1996, cat. no. 34), so it cannot be said that these belong to the steppe population.

The other tumuli in western Serbia culturally and chronologically correspond to the Belotić–Bela Crkva group, but they are undoubtedly partly a product of the steppe population tradition. Although they belong to the Belotić–Bela Crkva group, from the third quarter of the 3rd millennium cal BC, they often contain cremated burials or cenotaphs, and some tumuli still exhibit traces of ochre or its imitation (Dubac; Jančići, Ravnine; Turica, Ošljevac; Donja Kravarica, Babinjak). Some tumuli also have a central stone core (Dubac, Belotić, Anište) (Dmitrović 2015, 100, 101, 135, 190), possibly a survival of the central chamber from steppe tumuli.

In addition to tumuli as an element of foreign culture, some vessels with uncertain cultural attribution have been found in western Serbian tumuli. These are richly decorated vessels with incised and punctuated elements from the Anište site in Ražana, from Mounds 1 and 5 (Fig. 2.22/1, 4, 5). Some authors have mentioned similarities between these vessels and the Cetina group (Čović 1970, 17–18; Govedarica 2006, 103), while others have considered them part of the Vinkovci–Somogyvár culture with ornaments resembling the Kotorac–Cetina group (Garašanin M 1983a, 474, 475). We agree with the opinion of most colleagues that these vessels are the product of the local population but were made under the influence of interactions with neighbouring communities, especially those in eastern Bosnia (Govedarica 2006, 104; Dmitrović 2015, 63). These contacts with eastern Bosnia are also reflected in other finds discovered in western Serbia, characteristic of eastern Bosnia, namely the Cetina group, such as unusually shaped objects made of polished stone (Marović and Čović 1983, 215).

Perhaps the southernmost echo of steppe elements in the Central Balkans is the gold jewellery found in the grave of a contracted individual at Svinjarička Čuka near Lebane. Although the individual was not buried under a tumulus, the jewellery is characteristic of Yamnaya culture graves in the Serbian and Bulgarian Danube regions.

According to absolute dating, the time when the Belotić–Bela Crkva group inhabited the central Balkans would be the 25th– 23rd centuries cal BC, marking the end of the oldest phase (EBA 1) and the beginning of a new phase (EBA 2) in the development of the Early Bronze Age in the central Balkans.

2.6.7.2 Phase 2 of the Early Bronze Age in the central Balkans (EBA 2) (Pl. 17)

This phase in the peri-Pannonian zone is marked by specific finds at sites such as Marjansko Brdo, Kik in Svileuva (Stojić and Cerović 2011, 144, 145, T. CXXXI–CXXXII), and grave 11 at Rospi Ćuprija. Culturally, it aligns with the Vinkovci–Somogyvár group, whose stylistic and typological ceramic traits are present. This group's population inhabited the western and southern Carpathian Basin, with its core area between the Danube, Drava, and Little Alföld (Kulscar 2009, fig. 39). In addition to dense occupation in the core region, a significant number of settlements and necropolises have been found downstream along a narrow belt following the Danube, in today's Croatia and Serbia, indicating the natural communication routes along which this group interacted with the populations of the northern central Balkans.

Interestingly, Vinkovci–Somogyvár ceramics, besides being widespread along the Danube in the peri-Pannonian zone (Marjansko Brdo, Rospi Ćuprija), also extended further downstream towards the Iron Gates, where a grave containing this type of pottery was found at Vajuga. These ceramics also reached further south into western Serbia and sporadically into Great Morava Valley (Pl. 17). The easternmost example of this group, although just a few kilometres from Vajuga, could be the settlement at Ostrovul Corbului, where P. Roman identified a cultural horizon with double-handled beakers and finds reflecting influences from the Somogyvár–Vinkovci–Rosia group (Roman 2006, 459). Vessels with Vinkovci–Somogyvár group characteristics, specifically its western Serbian variant, the Belotić–Bela Crkva group, were also found at a necropolis of inhumation burials at Verbiţi in Oltenia (Machnik 1991, 17), further extending this group's interconnections eastward.

The southernmost trace of this northern 'incursion' might be a grave at Rutevac in South Morava Basin, where earthworks uncovered a grave with a supine inhumation and a vessel with rectangular perforated handles, resembling Vinkovci–Somogyvár group ceramics (Kulscar 2009, pls. 6, 7; pl. 21/9). This find also shares similarities with Bell Beaker complex burials, where such grave types are known (Schreiber-Kalicz 1984, T. XXXVI/12; T.XLIII/7, T.XLV/2–3; Metzinger-Schmitz 2004, abb. 32/2, 3; 34/3, taf. 7/10). In western Serbia, a regional variant of the Vinkovci–Somogyvár group, known as the Belotić–Bela Crkva group (Garašanin and Garašanin 1958), co-existed, sharing many identical stylistic and typological elements while incorporating some local characteristics.

According to absolute dating, the Vinkovci–Somogyvár group in the south-western Carpathian Basin, where settlement density is highest, existed before the mid-3rd millennium cal BC (2600–2500 BC) (Kulscar 2009, 230–232; Kiss *et al.* 2015, fig. 5). In Croatia and Slovenia, south of this core region, the group is somewhat younger, dating to the 25th/24th centuries cal BC (Kalafatić 2006, 21–24), and it is youngest in Great Morava Valley (24th century cal BC; Table 1). In western Serbia, dates for the Belotić–Bela Crkva group are approximately the same or slightly younger (25th/24th–24th/23rd centuries cal BC) than those in Slavonia. The Vinkovci–Somogyvár group date from Marjansko Brdo in the peri-Pannonian zone, which places the group at 25th/24th century cal BC, suggests that interactions between populations in the Serbian Danube region and the group's core area in the western Carpathian Basin were dynamic and intense. These cultural characteristics (and possibly populations) rapidly spread southward into Croatian and Serbian Danube regions and then into Great Morava Valley, while the population in western Serbia had already embraced this group by the 25th/24th century cal BC, adapting it slightly to local traditions.

This intense cultural transmission is also reflected in the appearance of daggers and possibly horses in the central Balkans. There were known horse breeding centres in the Csepel variant of the Bell Beaker culture in the mid-3rd millennium BC, and its pottery shares many stylistic similarities with Vinkovci–Somogyvár pottery found in the central Balkans (Schreiber-Kalicz 1984, T. XXXI–XLI). Another piece of evidence supporting these interactions is a typical bell-shaped beaker decorated in the Bell Beaker style, found at the site of Đula in Ostrikovac in Great Morava Valley, with other examples discovered at Petrovaradin and one at the necropolis of Ostojićevo (Koledin 2008, 35–60; Milašinović *et al.* forthcoming).

Based on available data, these changes in the peri-Pannonian zone, western Serbia, and partially in Great Morava Valley, did not affect the other geographical zones of the central Balkans, except for the Iron Gates, where a lone grave of an inhumed individual from this group has been found. According to G. Kulcsár (2009, 269), a single grave of this group has been recorded somewhat further east of Đerdap, in Verbiţa in Oltenia. Simultaneously, with the Vinkovci–Somogyvár group, whose communities inhabited the peri-Pannonian zone and part of the Great Morava Basin, communities defined as the Bubanj-Hum III–Pelince–Pernik group lived in South Morava Basin. This group emerged from the Bubanj-Hum II group (these elements are particularly visible in pottery at Braljina, Kokino, Pelince, and others) and interacted with communities from northern Macedonia and western Bulgaria (Garašanin 1973, 168–190). The earliest date for this group comes from Velika Humska Čuka (25th/24th century cal BC), confirming its chronological parallel with the Vinkovci–Somogyvár group in the north. Unlike other geographic zones of the central Balkans, this group, except in its southernmost areas (Skopje and Kumanovo Plains and Vranje–Bujanovac Basin), developed unimpeded until the Middle Bronze Age. Even then, it remained one of the most significant cultural substrates of the new Bubanj-Hum IV–Ljuljaci group but this group will be discussed in more detail in the section of the book on the Middle Bronze Age.

Returning to the beginnings of this group around the middle of the 3rd millennium cal BC, characteristic pear-shaped beakers with two handles aligned with the rim appear, serving as a key typological feature of the BH III–Pelince–Pernik group. This feature would later be adopted by many communities in the central Balkans with slight variations.

A. TWO-HANDLED BEAKERS

The phenomenon of two-handled (double-handled) beakers has been discussed by numerous authors for decades, but the lack of absolute dating left conclusions incomplete, and their origins remain unknown. Intriguingly, this form of beaker did not exist in the central Balkans during the Middle and Late Eneolithic, although very similar forms with two handles aligned with the rim were one of the fundamental elements of the Early Eneolithic Bubanj-Hum I cultural group (Garašanin 1973, 164–215), which persisted during the second half of the 5th millennium cal BC and possibly into the first quarter of the 4th millennium cal BC – at least 1200 years before the appearance of this type of beaker in the Early Bronze Age (Bulatović and Vander Linden 2017; Bulatović *et al.* 2018). It is known, however, that after the Bubanj-Hum I group, communities from the foreign Chernavoda III–Boleráz–Baden culture arrived in the Middle Eneolithic during the third quarter of the 4th millennium cal BC (Bulatović and Milanović 2020, 185–193), settling at Bubanj and other sites in South Morava Basin. The relationship between these two groups is not clear, although some Bubanj-Hum I elements, such as bowls with inverted rims (but not two-handled beakers), were found in Chernavoda III–Boleráz–Baden pits. This phenomenon can also be explained by the intrusion of these bowls from the Early Neolithic layer into which they were embedded.

In any case, even if the population of the Chernavoda III–Boleráz–Baden group adopted two-handled beakers, by the last quarter of the 4th millennium cal BC, the dynamic and mobile Coţofeni–Kostolac group had taken over dominance at this site and across the region (Kapuran and Bulatović 2012; Bulatović and Milanović 2020, 193–219), with no sporadic finds from the BH I group, including the two-handled beakers. Thus, the potential theory that the origin of the two-handled beakers dates from the Early Eneolithic is not supported, as such ceramic forms are absent for at least a millennium between the disappearance of the BH I group and the emergence of the Bubanj Hum III–Pelince–Pernik group.

There is also a little chance that the Early Eneolithic population withdrew into the highland regions of the southern Morava mountains during the third quarter of the 4th millennium and then returned a millennium later but this possibility is scientifically unsubstantiated. Nonetheless, the fact remains that these beakers existed in the Early Bronze Age in the Balkans, particularly in a region that belonged to Eneolithic cultures where very similar two-handled beakers, so-called *kantharoi*, were characteristic, such as Bubanj-Hum I–Sălcuţa–Krivodol and Kodžadermen–Gumelniţa–Karanovo VI.

Interestingly, in the Belotić–Bela Crkva group of the Early Bronze Age in western Serbia, two-handled beakers also appear, but with the handles placed below the rim. Besides the different handle placement, these beakers also exhibit different shapes, with slender cylindrical necks and short, rounded bodies. Since the material culture of this group is based on the Vinkovci–Somogyvár group, we searched for this ceramic form there and found only one similar vessel from Somogyvár-Kupavárhegy, which G. Kulcsár believes originated in the Balkans (Kulcsár 2009, 292).

Since this form of beaker is not characteristic of the Vinkovci–Somogyvár group, it likely arrived in the Belotić–Bela Crkva group through interaction with the local central Balkan population and it is possible that this group contributed to the creation of this ceramic form.

These beakers appear, in greater or lesser numbers and in various variants (Figs 2.49, 2.52), during approximately the same period (mid–late 3rd millennium cal BC) across all regions of the central Balkans, including southern Pannonia, northern Greece, south-eastern Albania, and eastern Bosnia (Čović 1983, fig. 13/5–7; Prendi and Bunguri 2008, tab. VII; Bulatović 2022, 90–92). However, all these beakers, according to the available absolute dates, are younger than the earliest date for a type 1c beaker from Velika Humska Čuka (2454–2344 cal BC, probability 68.2%) and an almost identical date for a type 7b beaker from a Belotić–Bela Crkva group tumulus at Dučalovići (2455–2348 cal BC, probability 68.2%).

Given these currently earliest dates for two-handled beakers, as well as the Eneolithic traditions that may have revived in this region after many centuries, it is assumed that the two-handled beaker's homeland during the Early Bronze Age was the central Balkans. Namely, there is a hypothesis about the persistence of certain ideas or behavioural patterns for a long time in the mythical consciousness of human communities through so-called mythical thinking (Levi-Strauss 1977; Cassirer 1985). Conversely, the emergence of two-handled beakers might not be attributed to cultural or spiritual conditions, aesthetics, or the desire for symmetry in the population that produced them, but rather to changes in the community's economy or other shifts that may have influenced the existence of this ceramic form.

This type of beaker is known in Eastern Europe, in the Bylopotok group of western Ukraine, as well as in the Jedynec group between the Dniester and Prut rivers (Gimbutas 1965, figs 299–302; Machnik 1991, fig. 10), though in much smaller numbers than in the central Balkans. These beakers are also recorded in the Costişa culture of central

Moldova, dating to the end of the 3rd and the beginning of the 2nd millennium cal BC (Bolohan 2003, 206, pl. 5; Vasilescu 2013, table I/7–9), although they look much more like two-handled Mokrin-type beakers (Popescu 2010, fig. 1/1–6).

Similarly, beakers found in the Monteoru group, phases Ic4–Ic3, date to the final third of the 3rd and early 2nd millennium cal BC (Motzoi-Chicideanu and Sandor-Chicideanu 2015, table I/7–9), slightly younger than their appearance in the central Balkans and also resemble Mokrin beakers (Popescu 2010, fig. 1/7). Thus, eastern Europe is rejected as the possible origin of the two-handled beakers, though their presence suggests cultural contacts between the central Balkans and eastern European communities, whether direct or indirect. These contacts may have been spurred by a climatic crisis that struck south-western Russia, Ukraine, and Moldova in the mid-3rd millennium BC, causing a drop in temperatures, forest retreat to the south, declining lake levels, and the loss of fertile soil layers (Krementski 1997, 367; Gerasimenko 1997).

These beakers, particularly type 1c, along with other stylistic and typological elements in ceramics, such as pedestal beakers decorated with incised lines (type 4a), Junacite-type beakers (type 8), biconical bowls with plastic additions on the rim (type 3c), (Fig. 2.30/1, 3, 4, 8, 15; Fig. 2.33/1, 3, 6–12, 22, 27; Fig. 2.37/11, 15, 16; Fig. 2.38/1, 5, 9; Fig. 2.39/3, 8–13, etc.) are characteristic of a cultural phenomenon evident across a vast area that included modern-day western Bulgaria, the southern Morava Basin, and north-eastern North Macedonia. This cultural phenomenon was initially named the Bubanj-Hum III–Pelince–Pernik horizon (Bulatović 2011, 69), and later the Bubanj-Hum III–Pelince–Pernik culture or group (Bulatović 2014, 68). Unfortunately, absolute dates for this cultural phenomenon are scarce. From the territory of Macedonia, there is one date from the site of Pelince, which dates this group to the 24th/23rd centuries cal BC, and another, mentioned earlier, comes from Velika Humska Čuka, which is slightly older and dates this group to the 25th/24th centuries cal BC. There are also several dates from Svinjarička Čuka, which belong to this Early Bronze Age phase, while dates from Bulgaria are missing.

In eastern Serbia, apart from the Đerdap Region, where a grave of a contracted inhumation burial of the Vinkovci–Somogyvár group has been recorded at Vajuga and a cremated burial at Glamija, which might be dated slightly later, to the end of the Early Bronze Age or perhaps even the Middle Bronze Age, sites from the Early Bronze Age are almost absent. Finds from Kučajna and Gamzigrad are not exclusively characteristic of the Early Bronze Age and may belong to the beginning of the Middle Bronze Age (Fig. 2.25/4–6). It is unclear why Early Bronze Age sites are recorded in all other geographic zones of the central Balkans, as well as neighbouring regions such as Đerdap, Great Morava Valley, and western Bulgaria, but not in the Timok Region. Across from Đerdap, in Oltenia, Early Bronze Age sites have been recorded (Ostrovul Corbului), which appear to represent a mixture of cultural phenomena of the Glina group and Bubanj-Hum III–Pelince–Pernik (Gogaltan 1996, T. VIII/2, 4, 5, 8; Roman 2006, fig. 8). However, thanks to the stratigraphy at Ostrovul Corbului, it is known that the cultural layer with two-handled beakers of the Armenochori–Bubanj III–Vecina mala-type, as named by P. Roman, lies between the late Coţofeni group layer and the Gornea-Orleşti layer (Roman 2006, 459). Since there are no absolute dates, only relative chronology is available, and if it is known that the late Coţofeni group is dated to EBA Ib, and Gornea–Orleşti to EBA III, the horizon with these beakers could belong to EBA II, that is, the Mako–Glina IV horizon, or more likely, the Ostrovul Corbului horizon with certain Somogyvár–Vinkovci–Roşia influences (Gogaltan 1996, 45–47). These aforementioned influences from the northern Balkans may point to the direction of interconnections between the communities of the central Balkans and Oltenia, via the Vinkovci–Somogyvár groups in Great Morava Valley and the Danube, reaching Đerdap. This is also confirmed by finds from the necropolis in Varbita, which exhibit characteristics of the Vinkovci–Somogyvár, or rather the Belotić–Bela Crkva group (Machnik 1991, 17). This could explain the depopulation of the Timok Region in the Early Bronze Age, but the question remains as to why it was uninhabited in that period and excluded as a natural communication route in all interconnections in the central Balkans.

In north-western Bulgaria, sites have also been recorded which, according to Todorova, belong to the Early Bronze Age culture characteristic of south-western Romania and Serbia, while the sites in south-western Bulgaria are part of the Bubanj-Hum III culture (Todorova 2003, 299, 300). It is noted that the Timok Region was surrounded on all sides by sites of the Bubanj-Hum III (–Pelince–Pernik) group, making it unclear why Early Bronze Age sites are missing in this relatively large and relatively well-researched region. This puzzle is even greater considering that in the subsequent period, starting from the second half of the 2nd millennium BC, a cultural group existed in the Timok Region that was formed predominantly on the basis of the Bubanj-Hum III–Pelince–Pernik group. In this group in the Timok Region, however, unlike the previous Early Bronze Age phase, one of the main characteristics is the cremation of the deceased, raising the intriguing question of the origin of this funerary ritual in the central Balkans.

Two-handled beakers, albeit in a slightly different form and with handles extending above the vessel's rim (type Ie: Fig. 2.49), have also been recorded at sites of the Armenochori group in northern Greece and Albania (Heurtley 1939, figs 320–349; Maniatis and Ziota 2011, fig. 8; Gori 2015), which are dated to a somewhat later period than when these beakers appeared in the central Balkans (Maniatis and Ziota 2011, table I). Nearly identical beakers have been recorded in Horizon I at Ezero, Horizons I–II at Djadovo, as well as in Horizons Junacite III and Razkopanica V, and these horizons chronologically approximately correspond to the last third of the 3rd millennium cal C (Detev 1981, fig. 37; Leštakov 1992, 18, 44, fig. 4/m, 17/e; Boyadziev 1995, table 5; Nikolova 1999, 226, 227, fig. 10.2).

The form of the two-handled beaker already appears in Troy II (third quarter of the 3rd millennium cal BC), but in a very stocky shape with small handles located below the rim (Blegen *et al.* 1950, fig. 370a/A29; compare the dating in Blum 2016), similar to our type IIa, though with handles above the opening. It is only from Troy III that beakers with two handles, extending above the opening, emerge, but these differ from the Balkan examples as they have a profiled base (Blegen *et al.* 1951, fig. 154a/A37).

From this brief spatio-temporal analysis of two-handled beakers, it can be said that they originate across a wider region of the Balkans, probably in the third quarter of the 3rd millennium, although it is not possible to pinpoint definitively a narrower area. However, based on absolute dates and distribution, it seems that their place of origin would likely be the central Balkans.

B. THE EMERGENCE OF CREMATION PRACTICES IN THE CENTRAL BALKANS

Cremation as a burial practice has been known since the Mesolithic and was also documented during the Neolithic in Greece and Central Europe (Srejović 1997, 394, 395). During the Eneolithic period, this method of treating the deceased was adopted by certain cultural groups in the Carpathian Basin, such as Baden, Coţofeni–Kostolac, and Vučedol (Dimitrijević 1979a, 201–205; 1079b, 285; Nikolić 2000, 46–47; Trautmann 2006). Some scholars associate the custom of cremation with the rise of metallurgy, arguing that this technological advancement led to significant changes in the economic and spiritual life of communities (Jovanović 1976, 140). However, as previously mentioned, the phenomenon of cremation pre-dates metallurgy and is often observed in conjunction with inhumation (bi-ritual burials within the same necropolis or tumulus). It is also possible that the advent of metallurgy prompted more substantial economic and social changes in certain local populations, contributing to the rise of cremation practices (Bulatović 2020, 78).

Cremation can be more accurately defined as a custom associated with a smaller community, such as a single settlement or even an individual, rather than as a deeply ingrained religious belief passed down through strict vertical cultural transmission. Cremation as a burial practice reflects the lifestyle, economy, environment, emotions, and possibly mythical thinking of a community or individual, rather than a rigid, unchangeable religious doctrine ((Bulatović 2020). Therefore, when analysing the spiritual culture of a community, more attention should be given to reliable indicators such as burial customs and practices.

Although the custom of cremation was already known in neighbouring areas during the Eneolithic period, the earliest dated cremation grave found in the central Balkans was found under a tumulus with a stone cist at the site of Ivkovo Brdo in Krstac, western Serbia, dated to 2570–2400 cal BC (68.2%) (Table 1). Only fragments of pottery were discovered in the grave, decorated with incised rows of notches, similar to the pottery from tumulus 1 in Bare, without artefacts linking it to the Belotić–Bela Crkva group, suggesting that this tumulus likely pre-dates that group. Cremation was practised in a bi-ritual manner and, based on the dated tumuli at Veliko Polje and Krstac, a similar situation existed in western Serbia before the Belotić–Bela Crkva group emerged.

Regarding cremation graves, it is important to mention the tumuli with cremation deposits and traces of ochre in north-western Serbia (Tolisavac, Banjevci), which M. Garašanin dates to the developed Eneolithic (Garašanin 1986, 69). Perhaps the earliest cremation grave was discovered at the Mala Gradina necropolis in Stapari, where a typical Vučedol vessel (Fig. 2.23/15) was found. This vessel corresponds to the ceramic production of the late Vučedol culture (Dimitrijević 1979a, Taf. 18/4, 5, 7, 10, 11), indicating that this grave, though not absolutely dated, may be the oldest example of cremation in the central Balkans, further suggesting a potential direction from which this practice reached the interior of the Balkans.

From the peri-Pannonian zone comes a cremation burial in an urn from the flat necropolis at Rospi Ćuprija, whose ceramic finds link it to the Vinkovci–Somogyvár group. Cremation as a burial practice appeared in South Morava Basin only in the 22nd century cal BC (Ranutovac), while the earliest occurrence in Greece among dated necropolises with cremation deposits is Xeropigado, dating from the 23rd to the 19th century BC (Maniatis and Ziota 2011, 461). In eastern Serbia, specifically in the Timok Region, cremation became the exclusive burial rite only after the 20th century BC, during the Middle Bronze Age. There is an older cremation grave at Glamija but based on the finds it likely belongs to the very end of the Early Bronze Age or the beginning of the Middle Bronze Age.

Thus, it appears that the custom of cremation arrived in the central Balkans from the north, from the Carpathian Basin, certainly by the mid-3rd millennium BC, and likely even earlier. The tumuli in Tolisavac and the flat necropolis in Stapari suggest that since the Eneolithic period, at least in western Serbia, there were both flat necropolises and those with tumuli, as well as bi-ritual burials.

Although cremation appeared much later in South Morava Basin, this burial custom did not spread from western Serbia but rather from the south, from northern

Greece, as evidenced by the architecture of the necropolis in Ranutovac (Bulatović 2020). This custom also spread to the Timok Region, again from the south via South Morava Basin, as indicated by the appearance of these necropolises, which are identical to the Ranutovac necropolis, rather than from western Serbia.

These data are crucial for understanding the patterns and intensity of interactions between the populations of the central Balkans and neighbouring communities during the Late Eneolithic and Early Bronze Age. This insight helps to predict more accurately the formation of cultural groups in the subsequent period in which cremation became the dominant burial practice.

2.6.7.3 Phase 3 of the Early Bronze Age in the central Balkans (EBA 3) (Pl. 18)

By the 22nd century cal BC, non-local elements associated with the Armenochori group had already reached South Morava Basin. The Armenochori group originated in north-western Greece, south-eastern Albania, and Pelagonia. This cultural shift is supported by multiple dates from the Meanište necropolis in Ranutovac near Vranje, which situate this necropolis between the 22nd and 19th centuries cal BC. The ceramic finds from all graves belong to the Armenochori group, with sporadic inclusions from the Bubanj–Hum III–Pelince–Pernik group elements (Fig. 2.36/9; Fig. 2.37/4, 5) (Bulatović 2020). Almost all the finds from the Lopate and Skopsko Kale sites, which date to the end of the Early and the beginning of the Middle Bronze Age, also belong to the Armenochori group, as do some finds from the sanctuary in Kokino Selo. Based on the mix of foreign (Armenochori) and local (Bubanj–Hum III–Pelince–Pernik) ceramics, it is suggested that the population of the Armenochori group migrated into the southern Morava valley from the south, indicating direct migration rather than mere cultural transmission. Supporting this is the defensive architecture observed at Skopsko Kale, hinting at social disruptions in the late 3rd and early 2nd millennia BC (Pl. 18).

It is interesting that all the ceramics from the Ranutovac necropolis were made from local clay sourced from the nearby village of Suvi Do (Gajić Kvaščev *et al.* 2020, 112), which is still used in pottery making today. This fact, along with the absolute dates, suggests that this population remained in the region long enough to identify and exploit local resources. This long-term presence indicates a gradual, non-aggressive settlement, as opposed to violent invasions characterised by rapid and destructive actions. The Armenochori group not only brought material cultural changes but also spiritual transformations. Instead of skeletal burials commonly seen in Early Bronze Age central Balkans (western Serbia, Đerdap, and the skeletal grave in the stone cist at Svinjarička Čuka in south-eastern Serbia), cremation practices appeared in the Middle Bronze Age in the Timok Region, where most necropolises have been investigated. After the 20th century BC, cremated remains were buried in urns (in Ranutovac, they were mostly placed directly on the ground), then surrounded by circular stone structures that, when joined, formed so-called 'stone fields'. This burial practice was also observed at the Early Bronze Age necropolis in northern Greece at Sykia in Chalkidiki (Asouchidou *et al.* 1998; Asouhidou 2012, 383–390). However, this necropolis is roughly dated to the first half of the 3rd millennium BC (Asouchidou *et al.* 1998, fig. 8), making it likely older than the Ranutovac necropolis.

On the other hand, this population movement from south to north may have displaced local groups from the lower Pčinja and upper South Morava rivers towards the north. At this time, significant changes in material culture are evident in Great Morava Valley and western Serbia. For instance, at the Vecina Mala site in Great Morava Valley, a pit was discovered containing numerous vessels, primarily type 1c beakers typical of the Bubanj–Hum III–Pelince–Pernik group. The pit was dated to the 23rd/22nd century cal BC, while a context with Vinkovci–Somogyvár pottery at Ostrikovac, just 2–3 km away from Vecina Mala, was dated to the 25th/24th century cal BC. This illustrates the cultural changes that occurred in the 24th–23rd centuries cal BC. Similar shifts were observed at the Ada site in Prijevor, western Serbia, where a cremation grave under a tumulus contained pottery matching the stylistic and typological characteristics of the Bubanj–Hum III–Pelince–Pernik group. This grave was dated to the 21st/20th century cal BC (Table 1), suggesting that the population of the West Morava valley underwent a cultural transformation, adopting Early Bronze Age ceramic forms typical of South Morava Basin (Fig. 2.22/10–13).

Another argument regarding possible population movements from the south to the north of the Balkan Peninsula at the end of the Early Bronze Age could be the oilseed plant *Lallemantia iberica*, which was used in northern Greece already in earlier prehistory and discovered at Feudvar in larger quantities in the remains of a Bronze Age house (Reed 2016, 208). In any case, although there were population movements from the south to the north, as is unequivocally indicated by changes in material and spiritual culture, this population from the south stopped somewhere in the area of the Vranje-Bujanovac Basin. It created the Middle Bronze Age culture in Macedonia (Pelagonian group/Armenochori), and probably in the Vranje-Bujanovac Basin. D. Mitrevski (2013, 179–181) thus cites the site of Tumba–Radobor as a representative and the best-researched site from the Early and Middle Bronze Age in Macedonia, stating that it is likely that the Pelagonian group–Armenochori from the Early Bronze Age continued its existence in this area during the Middle Bronze Age. In the territory north of the Grdelica gorge, however, on the basis of the Bubanj–Hum III–Pelince–Pernik group, with certain sporadic elements of the Armenochori group, the Bubanj-Hum III group persisted, named so because in EBA 3 its territory was reduced only to part of the Great Morava Valley north of the Grdelica gorge and part of West Morava Valley. Unfortunately, data for western Bulgaria during this period are lacking, while in northern Macedonia communities of the Armenochori group existed.

In Macedonia, particularly in Pelagonia and the Skopje and Kumanovo Plains, Early Bronze Age elements were dominated by the Armenochori group. Unfortunately, there are no absolute dates to establish the chronological relationship between these sites and the Ranutovac necropolis, which is the only dated site. The only dated Early Bronze Age site in Macedonia is Pelince in the central Pčinja Region, which generally belongs to the Bubanj–Hum III–Pelince–Pernik group and is dated to the 24th/23rd century cal BC. Based on this date and the earliest date from Ranutovac, it can be cautiously suggested that the population movements and interactions between the Vranje–Bujanovac Basin, the Kumanovo–Skopje Region, and the Armenochori group occurred between the 24th/23rd and 22nd/21st centuries cal BC. These interactions certainly operated in both directions, as pottery with elements characteristic of the Bubanj–Hum III–Pelince–Pernik group has been recorded at settlements of the typical Pelagonian–Armenochori group in Pelagonia (Mitrevski 2013, fig. 56). Such elements include bowls with applied plastic attachments on the rim, bowls with handles joined by a rectangular plastic addition to the rim, two-handled beakers with handles slightly extending above the rim, among others (Fig. 2.30/1, 15, Fig. 2.33/7, 10, 11, 26; Fig. 2.34/22; Fig. 2.40/7, 10, etc.).

Interestingly, the Middle Bronze Age culture in eastern Serbia shares burial practices similar to those in southern Serbia, but also exhibits a common ceramic element, namely double-horned plastic attachments (Fig. 3.23/7–10; Fig. 3.25/9; Fig. 3.26/1, 2, 9, 10; Fig. 3.27/25, etc.), which are also found in the Vatin group of the Middle Bronze Age in the peri-Pannonian zone (Fig. 3.1/3; Fig. 3.4/6–8). These examples suggest that from the late 3rd and early 2nd millennia BC, there were intensive interactions between the population of the central Balkans and that of southern Balkans, including the Vardar Region and possibly Pelagonia.

In the last quarter of the 3rd millennium cal BC, a new cultural group, the Novačka Ćuprija–Pančevo group, emerged in the peri-Pannonian zone and Šumadija, evolving from the earlier Vinkovci–Somogyvár group, with intense interactions with the Great Morava Valley population. This group was named after the eponymous sites of Novačka Ćuprija in Grčac, Šumadija, and Donja Varoš in Pančevo, southern Banat. M. Ljuština (2022, 42) accepts the name Pančevo-Donja Varoš group, as proposed by N. Tasić (2004, 27), but considering that finds with similar characteristics have also been recorded at the site of Novačka Ćuprija, on the southern periphery of the peri-Pannonian zone, in Šumadija, and that this site was excavated before the Donja Varoš site, this study proposes the name Novačka Ćuprija–Pančevo group, as this designation not only includes the eponymous sites but also illustrates the territory in which the group existed. The characteristic ceramic inventory of this group includes beakers with a mildly biconical or hemispherical body and a long cylindrical or slightly flared narrow neck, with long handles extending from the rim to the most prominent part of the belly (type 1b), type 2 beakers, hemispherical bowls with everted rims and wide arched handles (type 1a), biconical bowls with flared rims (type 1b), ovoid amphorae with short or long cylindrical necks, often with triangular handles of strap cross-section (Fig. 2.6/2; Fig. 2.12/14), and others. This group retains some elements from the local Vinkovci–Somogyvár group (Fig. 2.3/3, 9; Fig. 2.10/5, 9–14, 16; Fig. 2.12/21) while adopting characteristics from the slightly younger Perjamoš (Maroš or Mokrin) group from northern Banat (Fig. 2.7/12; Fig. 2.13/3, 5) and elements originating from the south, such as the 1c type beakers (Fig. 2.5/7; Fig. 2.9/13; Fig. 2.15/1). Another potential argument for the population's interaction with the north, particularly the Carpathian Basin, is the significant remains of domesticated horses found at sites associated with this group (Rit, Nad Klepečkom, Novačka Ćuprija). However, there is a possibility that this animal may have appeared earlier during the Vinkovci–Somogyvár group.

One of the more prominent indicators of intense contact between the populations from the south and north of the Balkans is the presence of double vessels, which appear both in the Ranutovac necropolis (Fig. 2.35/15) in grave 1, dated to the 19th century cal BC, and in the Novačka Ćuprija–Pančevo group (Fig. 2.6/2; Fig. 2.9/19; Fig. 2.11/15, 16, 18; Fig. 2.12/13–15) at site 1 at Rit, dated to the 20th century cal BC (Podzuweit 1979, Taf. 25/N). It is uncertain in which geographical zone these vessels first appeared. The prevailing assumption is that they originated in the south since double vessels were known from Troy and Thermi while, in the north, they do not appear until the end of the Early Bronze Age. According to available absolute dates, the Novačka Ćuprija–Pančevo group can be chronologically placed in the 21st–20th centuries cal BC and the appearance of the Vatin culture, i.e., the 19th/18th centuries cal BC. Territorial evidence suggests that this group occupied the peri-Pannonian zone south of the Danube and the southern Danubian part of Banat, with its western boundary at Kosmaj and Avala, and possibly the Drina River, and its eastern boundary at Đerdap and the Homolje Mountains.

As mentioned earlier, Great Morava Valley, after the Vinkovci–Somogyvár group, around the 23rd/22nd century cal BC, was inhabited by populations with stylistic and typological elements from the Bubanj-Hum III group, which expanded from the south, alongside elements from the north. Central Great Morava Valley and Šumadija, therefore, functioned as a buffer zone between the Bubanj-Hum III group in the south and the Vinkovci–Somogyvár group, and later the Mokrin group in the north.

The northern part of South Morava Basin likely belonged to the Bubanj-Hum III group by the 24th century BC (Braljina), if not earlier. Consequently, the population in the peri-Pannonian zone and central part of Great Morava Valley during the 23rd/22nd centuries cal BC, if not before, had as its southern neighbour the Bubanj-Hum III group, which significantly influenced the formation of the Novačka Ćuprija–Pančevo group. This influence is evident at the sites of Novačka Ćuprija, Mali Šturac, and Vecina Mala, the oldest and southernmost sites of this group. A context at the Novačka Ćuprija site has been dated to between the 29th and 18th centuries cal BC, albeit with a wide variability of 330 years (Table 1) which, according to the BP date, corresponds to the 23rd/22nd centuries cal BC. This pushes the upper boundary of the Novačka Ćuprija–Pančevo group back by about a century. Date from Vecina Mala, showing ceramic stylistic-typological features from the Bubanj-Hum III group as well as from the northern groups mentioned earlier, suggest that the genesis of the Novačka Ćuprija–Pančevo group began at the start of the last quarter of the 3rd millennium cal BC, from which point it expanded northwards, evolving into the characteristic forms of this group. Future absolute dates from the peri-Pannonian zone may reveal that the group developed synchronously across its entire territory.

The least known regions of the central Balkans during the Early Bronze Age are Raška and Kosovo. While no sites from this period have been identified in Kosovo, two hilltop sites have been found in the Raška Region. These sites may or may not indicate instability in this region during the Early Bronze Age. The stylistic-typological characteristics of the ceramics point to a mixture of different elements, ranging from traditional Eneolithic forms (Fig. 2.42/4, 7, 9, 13, 14) to those resembling the Vinkovci–Somogyvár or Belotić–Bela Crkva group (Fig. 2.42/2, 3, 5). This suggests that the population in this area had contact with the latter group, while the presence of hilltop settlements may indicate that these interactions were not always peaceful.

Notes

1 Unpublished, publication in preparation. Rescue excavations at this site were conducted in 2021–2022. I take this opportunity to thank the head of works, D. Milanović, for providing the data and illustrations.

2 Unpublished. Protective research was conducted in 2022 and 2023. The publication is in preparation.

3 Protective excavations at this site were conducted in the spring of 2023, and the results have not yet been published.

4 Rescue research along the route of the Danube Corridor (due to the construction of the motorway) was carried out by the Archaeological Institute in the spring of 2023.

5 In a random sample of vessels, where care was taken to ensure that all characteristic vessels were represented in the same proportion as they appear at the sites, loop handles were present in the Early Bronze Age in the transitional zone at around 75%, tunnel handles at about 13%, and all other types were represented at less than 5% each.

6 I would like to thank M. Gajić-Kvaščev from the Vinča Institute of Nuclear Sciences for the XRF analysis of the needle.

7 On the other hand, Radu Bajenaru, EBA axe expert believes that the axe does not belong to the Kozarac type since it has an elongated butt (pers. comm.).

8 I would like to thank D. Milanović, the project director at the Adžine Njive site in Klenak, for the oral information. The publication on the research results is in preparation. The sample dating was carried out by M. Marić through the RACOLNS project, funded by the Science Fund of the Republic of Serbia, under the PROMIS program.

9 See n. 5.

10 Namely, according to some authors, for fully developed bronze, there should be at least 2–3% tin.

11 Through the statistical analysis of the handles, it was observed that arched handles with a ribbon-shaped cross-section are represented by 72%, arched handles with an oval cross-section by about 15%, tunnel-shaped by about 8.5%, and elongated tongue-shaped by about 4.5%.

12 The vessel from the grave belongs to the so-called Brezjak group of the Late Bronze Age. I extend my thanks to my colleague R. Gligorić from the Jadar Museum in Loznica for providing the date.

13 The incised ornaments on the axe from Boljetin are of recent origin.

14 The oldest date from this zone is 22nd–20th century cal BC (pers. comm., excavation authors) and it originates from a grave at the Hajdučka česma site near Bor. However, this date is based on a sample of charcoal, so considering that the other dates from this necropolis are significantly younger, this date must be taken with caution, as it is possible that it is a case of the so-called 'old wood effect'.

15 The first excavations were carried out by M. Grbić with local archaeologists; the excavations in the 1950s were led by M. Garašanin, while contemporary research is being conducted in cooperation between the Archaeological Institute and the National Museum in Niš.

16 The site was discovered during earthworks for the needs of a brick factory, and the finds were collected from the excavation. The cultural layer is not thick, so it appears that the settlement is single-layered, or it may involve horizontal stratigraphy. The AMS result of a sample from a bone artefact (Fig. 2.43/19) indicated that it belongs to the Early Bronze Age, although the finds, with their stylistic and typological features, also resemble the Middle Bronze Age. Unpublished.

17 The exploitation of the land was halted by the Institute for the Protection of Cultural Monuments in Niš. I thank A. Aleksić for the information.

18 I am grateful to the directors of the research, A. Aleksić from the Institute for the Protection of Cultural Monuments, Niš, and A. Kapuran from the Institute of Archaeology, Belgrade, for the information provided.

19 The animal bones were not preserved, so it was not possible to obtain absolute dates for the pyre.

20 After the publication of this book (Bulatović and Stankovski 2012), a larger number of ceramics finds from this site were discovered in the Kumanovo Museum, a small portion of which is presented in this book (Fig. 2.38–2.41), while the majority will be presented in the forthcoming monograph on this site (Bulatović and Gorgievski, in prep.).

21 More details about the fragment are provided in the chapter on pottery.

22 The percentages refer to the illustrated finds on the plates, selected to provide an approximate representation of the actual distribution of forms and ornaments in this zone.

23 A chance find. I thank S. Milivojević from Gornji Matejevac for providing the photograph and information.

24 It was later established that beaker No. 3 originates from a grave at the Utrina site in Rutevac (Bulatović 2010). Milojević and Trajković Filipović mention the findspot of these beakers as Terrace 1, which could likely correspond to the location of Školska Gradina (Milojević and Trajković-Filipović 2017, 153).

25 The elements are common to the entire zone, except for the Raška area, where the situation is somewhat different, which will be discussed separately.

26 In this context, the settlement of Kik in Svileuva could rather be termed an elevated settlement, rather than a true fortified settlement, which implies a difficult-to-access approach.

27 Based on the stylistic and typological characteristics of these few finds, these sites may also belong to the beginning of the Middle Bronze Age.

28 The site was excavated in 2024. I extend my gratitude for the data to co-directors A. Aleksić from the Institute for the Protection of Cultural Monuments in Niš and A. Kapuran from the Institute of Archaeology, Belgrade. The publication is in preparation.

29 I thank D. Grujić from the Archaeological Institute, Belgrade, for the analysis and provided results. A publication with detailed results of analyses is under preparation.

30 I extend my gratitude for the data to W. Powell from Brooklyn College, New York, USA.

31 I extend my gratitude for the XRF analysis to M. Gajić Kvaščev and V. Andrić from the Vinča Institute of Nuclear Sciences.

32 This find, based on the absolute date, belongs to the third quarter of the 3rd millennium cal BC. An article is in preparation.

Bibliography

Alexandrov, S. 1998. Pottery of the Early Bronze Age in western Bulgaria. In: *J. Harvey Gaul in Memoriam*, eds M. Stefanovich, H. Todorova and H. Hauptmann, 223–233. Sofia: J. Harvey Gaul Foundation.

Alexandrov, S. 2007. Bronze Age materials from Bagacina (northwest Bulgaria). In: *Prae, in honorem Henrieta Todorova.* eds M. Stefanovich and C. Angelova, 103–129. Sofia: Bulgarian Academy of Science.

Aleksandrov, S. 2009. (Александров, С.) Украшения за коса от злато и србро през бронзовата епоха в Северна Блгария, *Археология*, год. L, кн. 1–2, София, 7–20.

Alexandrov, S. 2021. Fourth/third millennium bc barrow graves in north-east Bulgaria (120 years of investigations). In: *Yamnaya Interactions*, eds V. Heyd, G. Kulscár and B. Preda-Bălănică, 271–314. Budapest: Archaeolingua 44.

Alexandrov, S. 2023. More about a particular group of Early Bronze Age barrow graves in hocker position from north-east Bulgaria. In: *Steppe Transmissions, The Yamnaya Impact on Prehistoric Europe*, eds B. Preda Balcanica and M. Ahola, 135–162. Budapest: Archaeolingua 45.

Antonović, D. 2014. *Kupferzeitliche Äxte und Beile in Serbien.* Stuttgart: Prähistorische Bronzefunde 9(27).

Antonović, D. and Dimić, V. 2017. Copper ore exploitation at the site of Prljuša on Mali Šturac. In: *Studije arheotehnologije, eksploatacija sirovina od praistorije do srednjeg veka*, eds S. Vitezović and D. Antonović, 117–142. Beograd: Srpsko arheološko društvo.

Antonović, D. and Đorđević, A. (Антоновић, Д., Ђорђевић, А.). 2011. Типологија перфорираног каменог оруђа из Србије. *Зборник Народног музеја* 20(1), 47–69.

Aslanis, I. 1985. *Kastanas, die Fruhbronzezeitlichen Funde und Befunde.* Berlin: Wissenschaftsverlag Volker Spiess.

Asouhidou, S. 2012. The Early Bronze Age burial mound at Kriaritsi–Sykia (central Macedonia, Greece). In: *Ancestral Landscapes, Burial mounds in the Copper and Bronze Ages (Central and Eastern Europe-Balkans-Adriatic-Aegean, 4th–2nd millennium B.C.*, eds E. Borgna and S. Müller-Celka, 383–390. Lyon: Travaux de la Maison de l'Orient et de la Méditerranée 58

Asouchidou, S., Mantazi, D. and Tsolakis, S. 1998. Tafikos tymvos P.E.H. sto Kriaritsi Sykias, N. Chalkidikis. Thessaloniki: *To Archaiologiko Ergo sti Makedonia kai sti Thraki* 12.

Bajenaru, R. 2014. *Sfârşitul Bronzului timpuriu în regiunea dintre Carpaţi şi Dunăre.* Cluj-Napoca: Editura Argonaut.

Becker, C. 1991. Haustierhaltung und Jagd in der Frühen Bronze – und Eisenzeit in der Vojvodina – Erste Rezultate zu Tierknochenfunde aus Feudvar. *Bericht der Römisch-Germanischen Kommission* 72, 178–190.

Blegen, C., Caskey, J., Rawson, M. and Sperling, J. 1950. *Troy: General introduction the first and second settlements.* Princeton NJ: Princeton University Press.

Blegen, C., Caskey, J. and Rawson, M. 1951. *Troy: The third, fourth, and fifth settlements.* Princeton NJ: Princeton University Press.

Blum, S. 2016. The final stages of the Early Bronze Age at Troy: Cultural development, chronology, and interregional contacts. In: *Early Bronze Age Troy: Chronology, cultural developments and interregional contacts*, eds. E. Pernicka, S. Ünlüsoy and W. E. Blum, 89–122. Bonn: Habelt.

Boyadziev, J. 1995. Chronology of prehistoric cultures in Bulgaria. In: *Prehistoric Bulgaria*, eds D. Bailey and I. Panayotov, 149–191. Madison WI: Monographs in World Archaeology 22.

Bojadžiev, J. 1998. Radiocarbon dating from southeastern Europe. In *J. Harvey Gaul in Memoriam*, eds M. Stefanovich, H. Todorova and H. Hauptmann, 349–370. Sofia: J. Harvey Gaul Foundation.

Bökönyi, S. 1978. The earliest waves of domestic horses in East Europe. *Journal of Indo-European Studies* 6(1–2), 17–76.

Bökönyi, S. 1990. Prehistoric animal remains from Bubanj-Hum at Nis. *Старинар* н.с. 40–41, 89–95.

Bolohan, N. 2003. Recent discoveries belonging to Early/Middle Bronze Age in Central Moldavia. *Arheologia Moldovei* 26, 195–206.

Bonev, A. and Alexandrov, G. (Бонев, А., Александров, Г.). 1996. *Багачина, Селище от късната каменно-медна епоха и тракийски култов център (III-I хилядолетие пр. Хр.).* Монтана.

Borić, D. 2009. Absolute dating of metallurgical innovations in the Vinča Culture of the Balkans. In: *Metals and Societies: Studies in honour of Barbara S. Ottaway*, eds T.L. Kienlin and B. W. Roberts, 191–245. Bonn: Universitätsforschungen zur prähistorischen Archäologie 169.

Bulatović, A. (Булатовић, А.). 2007. *Врање-културна стратиграфија праисторијских локалитета у Врањској регији,* Београд-Врање: Археолошки институт, Београд (Institute of archaeology, Belgrade).

Bulatović, A. 2009. South Morava basin in the transitional period from the Bronze to the Iron Age. *Старинар* н.с. 57 (2007), 57–82.

Bulatović, A. (Булатовић, А.). 2010. Рутевац и околина у праисторији. У: *Историја Поморавља и два века од Варваринске битке*, ур. С. Мишић, 35–44. А. Крушевац: Шемјакин, Историјски архив.

Bulatović, A. 2011. Relations between cultural groups in the Early Bronze Age in southeastern Serbia, western Bulgaria and northeastern Macedonia. *Archaeologia Bulgarica* 15(2), 59–72.

Bulatović, A. 2013. Oven models from Early Bronze Age settlements in central and southern parts of the Balkan Peninsula. *Archaeologia Bulgarica* 17(1), 1–13.

Bulatović, A. 2014. New finds as a contribution to the study of the Early Bronze Age in the southern part of the Central Balkans. *Старинар* 64, 57–75.

Bulatović, A. (Булатовић, А.). 2015. Феномен праисторијских ритуалних јама, неколико примера са централног Балкана. *Старинар* н.с. 65, 7–35.

Bulatović, A. 2018. Ritual pits in the central Balkans – the continuity of spiritual practice. In: *Giving Gifts to God: Evidences of votive offerings in the sanctuaries, temples and churches*, ed. D. Georgievski, 57–66. Kumanovo: National Institution Museum of Kumanovo.

Bulatović, A. 2020. *Ranutovac, an Early Bronze Age Necropolis in Southeastern Serbia.* Oxford: British Archaeological Report S2978.

Bulatović A. 2022. Хоризонти средњег и позног енеолита и раног бронзаног доба на локалитету Бубањ, *Бубањ, праисторијско насеље и некропола из Новог века / Bubanj, die vorgeschichtliche Siedlung und die Neuzeitliche Nekropole / Bubanj, Agglomération Préhistorique et Nécropole de l'Époque Moderne*, eds. A. Bulatović, D. Milanović, T. Trajković-Filipović, 57–103, Археолошки институт, Београд, Народни музеј, Ниш, Београд-Ниш.

Bulatović, A. and Jović, C. (Булатовић, А., Јовић, С.). 2010. *Лесковац-културна стратиграфија праисторијских локалитета у Лесковачкој регије.* Београд-Лесковац: Археолошки институт, Београд, Народни музеј, Лесковац.

Bulatović, A. and Milanović, D. (Булатовић, А., Милановић, Д.). 2015. Велика хумска чука, истраживања 2009. године – прилог проучавању стратиграфије енеолита и бронзаног доба у југоисточној Србији. *Гласник Српског* 30, 163–188.

Bulatović, A. and Milanović, D. 2020. *Bubanj, the Eneolithic and the Early Bronze Age Tell in Southeastern Serbia.* Vienna: Mitteilungen der Prahistorischen Kommission 90.

Bulatović, A. and Milanović, D. 2021. The cultural and chronological context of sites of Bubanj and Velika Humska Čuka near Niš (southeastern Serbia) and their significance for understanding the emergence and development of the Central Balkans Eneolithic. *Циркумпонтика/Circumpontics* 2021(5), 36–64.

Bulatović, A. and Stankovski, J. (Булатовић, А., Станковски, Ј.). 2012. *Бронзано доба у басену Јужне Мораве и у долини Пчиње/Бронзено време во басенот на Јужна Морава и долината на Пчиња.* Куманово: Археолошки институт Београд и НУ Музеј,

Bulatović, A. and Vander Linden, M. 2017. Absolute dating of Copper and Early Bronze Age levels at the eponymous archaeological site Bubanj (southeastern Serbia). *Radiocarbon* 59(4), 1047–1065.

Bulatović, A., Filipović, V. and Gligorić, R. (Булатовић, А., Филиповић, В., Глигорић, Р.). 2017. *Лозница, културна стратиграфија праисторијских локалитета у Јадру, Рађевини и Азбуковици.* Лозница: Археолошки институт, Београд, Центар за културу.

Bulatović, A., Gori, M. and Vander Linden, M. 2018. New AMS dates as a contribution to the absolute chronology of the Early Eneolithic in the central Balkans. *Старинар* н.с. 68, 19–32.

Bulatović, A. Gori, M. and Vander Linden, M. 2020. Radiocarbon dating the 3rd millennium BC in the Central Balkans: A re-examination of the Early Bronze Age sequence. *Radiocarbon* 62(5), 1163–1191.

Bulatović, A., Jovičić, M. and Milovanović, B. 2019. Horizont ranog bronzanog doba na lokalitetu Rit/Early Bronze Age horizon at the site of Rit. In: Kapuran *et al.* (eds) 2019b, 57–79.

Bulatović, A., Kapuran, A. and Janjić, G. (Булатовић, А., Капуран, А., Јањић, Г.). 2013. *Неготин, културна стратиграфија праисторијских локалитета у Неготинској Крајини*, Београд-Неготин: Археолошки институт, Београд, Музеј Крајине, Неготин.

Bulatović, A., Kapuran, A. and Milanović, D. 2016. Metal Age finds at the site of Kovačke njive in Pavlovac near Vranje. In: *Archaeological Investigations Along the Route of the E 75 Highway, 2011–2014,* eds S. Perić and A. Bulatović, 205–219, Belgrade: Institute of Archaeology.

Bulatović, J. 2020. Preliminary report on animal bones from Bubanj. In: *Bubanj, the Eneolithic and the Early Bronze Age tell in southeastern Serbia*, eds A. Bulatović and D. Milanovic, 329–338. Vienna: Mitteilungen der Prahistorischen Kommission Band 90.

Cassirer, E. (Kasirer, E.). 1985. *Filozofija simboličkih oblika–drugi deo, Mitsko mišljenje.* Teoria: Novi Sad.

Cenev, G. (Ценев, Г.). 2002. Мегалитска опсерваторија во Кокино, *Музејски гласник* 7–9, 49–68.

Cenev, G. 2009. The role of the Kokino megalith in the life of the Bronze age agricultural community. In: *The Role of Astronomy in Society and Culture*, eds D. Valls-Gabaud and A. Boksenberg, 1–15. Cambridge: Cambridge University Press

Cvijić, J. (Цвијић, Ј.). 1922. *Балканско полуострво и јужнословенске земље.* Београд: Državna štamparija, Beograd.

Čović, B. 1970. Ornamentisana keramika ranog bronzanog doba u tumulima zapadne Srbije i istočne Bosne. *Članci i građa za kulturnu istoriju istočne Bosne* 7, 15–21.

Čović, B. 1976. Metalurška djelatnost vučedolske grupe u Bosni. *Godišnjak* 13, 105–115.

Čović, B. 1983. Regionalne grupe ranog bronzanog doba. In: *Praistorija jugoslavenskih zemalja* 4, ed. A. Benac, 114–190. Sarajevo: Akademija nauka i umjetnosti BiH.

Derikonjić, S. (Дерикоњић, С.). 2010. *Трагом јармовачких рудара. каталог изложбе.* Прибој: Завичајни музеј, Прибој.

Detev, P. 1981. Le tell Razkopanica. *Cultures préhistoriques en Bulgarie, Известия на Археологическия институт* 36, 141–188.

Dimitrijević, S. 1977. Zur Frage der Genese und Gliederung der Vučedoler Kultur in dem Zwischenstromlande Donau-Drau-Save. *Vjesnik Arheološkog muzeja u Zagrebu* 10–11(1), 1–114.

Dimitrijević, S. 1979a. Badenska kultura. In: *Praistorija jugoslavenskih zemalja* 3, ed. A. Benac, 183–234. Sarajevo: Akademija nauka i umjetnosti BiH.

Dimitrijević, S. 1979b. Vučedolska kultura i vučedolski kulturni kompleks. In: *Praistorija jugoslavenskih zemalja* 3, ed. A. Benac, 267–342. Sarajevo: Akademija nauka i umjetnosti BiH.

Dmitrović, K. (Дмитровић, К.). 2002. Резултати археолошких исраживања праисторијске некрополе под хумкама на локалитету Руја у Дучаловићима. *Зборник радова Народног музеја* 32, 5–22.

Dmitrović, K. (Дмитровић, К.). 2003. Хумка из раног бронзаног доба на локалитету Рајића брдо код Гуче. *Зборник радова Народног музеја* 33, 5–9.

Dmitrović, K. (Дмитровић, К.). 2004. Праисторијска некропола под хумкама на локалитету Бабињак у Доњој Краварици. *Зборник радова Народног музеја* 34, 9–20.

Dmitrović, K. (Дмитровић, К.). 2005. Резултати истраживања хумке на локалитету Сува чесма у Лучанима. *Зборник радова Народног музеја* 35, 35–49.

Dmitrović, K. (Дмитровић, К.). 2013. Резултати истраживања хумке VII на локалитету Дубац у Јанчићима на Каблару, *Зборник радова Народног музеја* 43, 7–17.

Dmitrović, K. (Дмитровић, К.). 2015. Сахрањивање у културама бронзаног доба у западном Поморављу, (partially published doctoral dissertation) делимично објављена докторска дисертација одбрањена на Одељењу за археологију Филозофског факултета у Београду.

Dmitrović, K. (Дмитровић, К.). 2016. *Некрополе бронзаног доба у регији Чачка/Bronze Age Necropolises in the Čačak region*, Čačak: Народни музеј, Чачак.

Dmitrović, K. and Molloy, B. 2021. A contribution to the Early Bronze Age chronology of the region of the West Morava river, Serbia. In: *Graves, Cenotaphs and Votive Deposits of Weapons in Europe, Bronze and Iron Ages*, eds V. Sirbu, C. Schuster and D. Hortopan, 49–64. Targu Jiu: Editura MAIASTRA.

Durman, A. 1983. Metalurgija vučedolskog kulturnog kompleksa. *Opvscvla Archaeologica* 8, 1–87.

Durman, A. 1997. Tin in southeastern Europe? *Opvscvla Archaeologica* 21, 7–14.

Durman, A. and Obelić, B. 1989. Radiocarbon dating of the Vučedol culture complex. *Radiocarbon* 31(3), 1003–1009.

Đorđević, J. and Đorđević, V. (Ђорђевић, J., Ђорђевић, В.). 2016. *Ливаде код Панчева, средњовековна црква и некропола на енеолитској хумци.* Панчево: Народни музеј, Панчево.

Ercegović Pavlović, S. and Kostić, D. (Ерцеговић-Павловић, С., Костић, Д.). 1988. *Археолошки споменици и налазишта лесковачког краја*, Београд: Археолошки институт, Београд, Народни музеј, Лесковац.

Filipović, D. 2020. A glimpse of Eneolithic plant economy at the site of Bubanj in Serbia. In: Bulatović and Milanović 2020, 339–370.

Filipović, V. (Филиповић, В.). 2008. Некрополе развијеног доба Подгорине и доњег Подриња (unpublished master thesis) необјављена магистарска теза, одбрањена на Филозофском факултету у Београду.

Gajić-Kvaščev, M., Andrić, V. and Vuksanović, M. 2020. Characterization of Early Bronze Age pottery fragments from the Meanište site in the village of Ranutovac near Vranje, Serbia, In: Bulatović 2020, 111–121.

Garašanin, D. (Гарашанин, Д.). 1954. *Каталог метала* I. Београд: Народни музеј.

Garašanin, D. 1967. Periodizacija bronzanog doba Srbije, *Materijali* IV, 7th Congress of archaeologists of Yugoslavia held in Herceg Novi in 1966, 203–208.

Garašanin, D. 1983. Transdanubijska (južnopanonska) grupa s inkrustiranom keramikom. In: *Praistorija jugoslavenskih zemalja* 4, ed. A. Benac, 536–540. Sarajevo: Akademija nauka i umjetnosti BiH.

Garašanin, M. (Гарашанин, М). 1957. Ископавања на Бубњу код Ниша. Претходни извештај за 1954–1956. *Старинар* н.с. 7–8, 269–274.

Garašanin, M. 1958. Neolithikum und Bronzezeit in Serbien und Makedonien. *Bericht der Romisch-Germanischen Kommission des Deutschen* 39, 1–130.

Garašanin, M. (Гарашанин, М.). 1973. *Праисторија на тлу Србије. Београд*: Српска књижевна задруга.

Garašanin, M. 1983a. Vinkovačka grupa. In: *Praistorija jugoslavenskih zemalja* 4, ed. A. Benac, 471–475. Sarajevo: Akademija nauka i umjetnosti BiH.

Garašanin, M. 1983b. Bubanj-Hum III grupa. In: *Praistorija jugoslavenskih zemalja* 4, ed. A. Benac, 719–722. Sarajevo: Akademija nauka i umjetnosti BiH.

Garašanin, M. (Гарашанин, М.). 1986. Крупањ и Рађевина у праисторијско и римско доба. In: *Рађевина у прошлости*, ур. Р. Михаљчић, 57–109 Београд: Skupština Opštine Krupanj.

Garašanin, M. and Garašanin, D. (Гарашанин. М., Гарашанин, Д.). 1958. Ископавања тумула у Белотићу и Белој Цркви (Западна Србија). *Зборник радова Народног музеја* 1, 17–50.

Garašanin, M. and Garašanin, D. (Гарашанин. М., Гарашанин. Д.). 1959. Нова ископавања на Великој Хумској Чуки код Ниша. *Старинар* 9–10, 243–254.

Garašanin, M. and Garašanin, D. (Гарашанин, М., Гарашанин, Д.). 1962. Ископавања тумула у комплексу Белотић-Бела Црква 1959. и 1960. *Године. Зборник радова Народног музеја* 3, 47–68.

Garašanin, M. and Ivanović, V. (Гарашанин, М., Ивановић, В.). 1958. *Праисторија лесковачког краја.* Лесковац: Библиотека Народног музеја у Лесковцу.

Garašanin, M. and Stojić, M. (Гарашанин, М., Стојић, М.). 1986. Ђула у Остриковцу – градинско насеље из металног доба. *Гласник Српског археолошког друштва* 3, 192–194.

Garašanin, M. Ajdić R. and Dejanović D. (Гарашанин М., Ајдић Р., Дејановић, Д.). 1971. *Праисторијске културе Поморавља и источне Србије.* Ниш: каталог изложбе, Народни музеј.

Georgiev, G., Merpert, N., Katincharov, R. and Dimitrov, D. (Георгиев, Г., Мерперт, Н., Катинчаров, Р., Димитров, Д.) (eds). 1979. *Езеро, раннобронзовото селище.* София: Българската Академия на науките.

Georgievski, B. (Георгиевски, Б.). 1994. Праисториски градишта од Кумановско. *Macedoniae Acta Archaeologica* 13, 12–22.

Gerasimenko, N. 1997. Environmental and climatic changes between 3 and 5 ka BP in southeastern Ukraine. In: *Third Millennium BC Climate Change and Old World Collapse*, eds N. Dalfes, G. Kukla and H. Weiss, 371–399. Heidelberg: Springer.

Gimbutas, M. 1965. *Bronze Age Cultures in Central and Eastern Europe.* The Hague: Mouton.

Girić, M. 1971. *Mokrin – nekropola ranog bronzanog doba, Mokrin I.* Kikinda–Beograd: Arheološko društvo Jugoslavije.

Gogaltan, F. 1996. About the Early Bronze Age in the Romanian Banat. In: *The Yugoslav Danube Dasin and the Neighbouring Regions in the 2nd millennium b.c.*, ed. N. Tasic, 43–68. Belgrade-Vršac: Serbian Academy of Sciences and Arts.

Gori, M. 2015. *Along the Rivers and Through the Mountains.* Bonn: Habelt.

Govedarica, B. 2006. Keramika cetinskog tipa u unutrašnjosti zapadnog Balkana i problem kulturno-istorijske interpretacije praistorijskih nalaza. *Godišnjak 35/entar za balkanološka ispitivanja* 33, 95–114.

Govedarica, B. 2021. Monumental tumuli from the area of Montenegro and the issue of the continuity of the cult place (Part I – Example of prehistoric princely tombs). *New Antique Doclea* 12, 35–82.

Greenfield, H. 1986. Summary report on the vertebrate fauna from Novačka ćuprija. *Зборник Народног музеја* 12(1), 63–74.

Greenfield, H. 2006. The social and economic context for domestic horse origins in southeastern Europe. In: *Horses and Humans: The evolution of human-equine relationships*, eds S. Olsen, S. Grant, A. M. Choyke and L. Bartosiewicz, 221–244. Oxford: Archaeopress.

Grčki-Stanimirov, S. 1996. Pančevo-'Donja Varoš' – horizont der Ersten Siedlungen der Frühen Bronzezeit im Südlichen Banat. In: *The Yugoslav Danube Dasin and the Neighbouring Regions in the 2nd millennium b.c.*, ed. N. Tasic, 69–80. Belgrade-Vršac: Serbian Academy of Sciences and Arts.

Guimaraes, S., Arbuckle, B., Peters, J., Adcock, S., Buitenhuis, H., Chazin, H., Manaseryan, N., Uerpmann, H. P., Grange, T. and Geigl, E. M. 2020. Ancient DNA shows domestic horses were introdused in the southern Caucasus and Anatolia during the Bronze Age. *Science Advanced* 6, 1–10.

Gumă, M. 1997. *Epoca bronzului în Banat – The Bronze Age in Banat.* Timişoara: Editura MIRTON Timisoara.

Hänsel, B. 2002. Stationen der Bronzezeit zwischen Griechenlend und Mitteleuropa. *Bericht der Romisch-Germanischen Kommission* 83, 69–97.

Harding, A. 2000. *European Societes in the Bronze Age.* Cambridge: Cambridge University Press.

Heurtley, W. A. 1939. *Prehistoric Macedonia.* Cambridge: Cambridge University Press.

Horejs, B., Bulatović, A., Meyer, C., Milić, B., Schneider, S., Schlöffel, M. and Stevanović, V. 2018. Prehistoric landscapes of the Pusta Reka river (Leskovac), new investigations along the Southern Morava River. *Гласник САД* 34, 23–51.

Horejs, B., Bulatović, A., Bulatović, J., Brandl, M., Burke, C., Filipović, D. and Milić, B. 2019. New insights into the later stage of the Neolithisation process of the Central Balkans. First excavations at Svinjarička Čuka 2018. *Archaeologia Austriaca*, 175–226.

Horejs, B., Bulatović, A., Bulatović, J., Burke, C., Brandl, M., Dietrich, L., Filipović, D., Milić, B. Mladenović, O., Schinnerl, N., Schroedter, T. and Webster, L. 2022. New multi-disciplinary data from the Neolithic in Serbia. The 2019 and 2021 excavation at Svinjarička Čuka. *Archaeologia Austriaca* 103, 175–226.

Horejs, B., Bulatović, A., Brandl, M., Dietrich, L., Milić, B., Mladenović, O., Waltenberger, L. and Webster, L. forthcoming. First highlights of a new site for analyzing the prehistoric Balkans: Svinjarička Čuka in Serbia. *Antiquity, Project Gallery.*

Horváth, T., Dani J., Petö, A., Pospieszny, L., and Svingor, E. 2013. Multidisciplinary contributions to the study of Pit Grave Culture Kurgans of the Great Hungarian Plain. In: *Transition to the Bronze Age, Interregional Interaction and Socio-Cultural Change in the Third Millennium BC Carpathian Basin and Neighbouring Regions*, eds V. Heyd, G. Kulscár and V. Szeverényi V., 153–179. Budapest: Archaeolingua 30.

Huska, A., Powell, W., Mitrović, S., Bankoff, H. A. Bulatović, A., Filipović V. and Boger, R. 2014. Placer tin ores from Mt. Cer, West Serbia, and their potential exploitation during the Bronze Age. *Georchaeology* 29(6), 477–493.

Ikodinović, M. (Икодиновић, М.). 1969. Заштитно ископавање хумке у Лучанима. *Зборник радова Народног музеја* I, 3–15.

Jevtić, M. 1999. Early Bronze Age Hillforts in the Novi Pazar Area. In: *Macedonia and the Neighbouring Regions from 3rd to 1st milenium* [sic] *b.c.*, ed. E. Petrova, 73–85. Skopje: Museum of Macedonia

Jovanović, B. 1971. *Metalurgija eneolitskog perioda Jugoslavije.* Beograd: Arheološki institut.

Jovanović, B. 1976. Obredi sahranjivanja u kostolačkoj grupi. *Glasnik Centra za balkanološka ispitivanja* 13, 131–141.

Jovanović, B. (Јовановић, Б.). 1988. Прљуша – Мали Штурац: праисторијски рудник бакра и горског кристала на Руднику. *Зборник радова Народног музеја* 18, 5–12.

Kalafatić, H. 2006. Žarni grob vinkovačke kulture s lokaliteta Vinkovci-Duga ulica 40. *Prilozi Instituta za arheologiju u Zagrebu* 23, 17–28.

Kapuran, A. 2014. *Praistorijski lokaliteti u severoistočnoj Srbiji.* Beograd: Arheološki institut.

Kapuran, A. and Bulatović, A. (Капуран, А., Булатовић, А.). 2012. Праисторијски локалитети у долинама Сврљишког Тимока, Трговишког Тимока и Белог Тимока. *Гласник Српског археолошког друштва* 28, 107–132.

Kapuran, A., Bulatović, A. and Jovanović, I. (Капуран, А., Булатовић, А., Јовановић, И.). 2011. Насеља раног неолита у Тимочкој Крајини и залеђу Ђердапа, *Старинар* н.с. 60, 19–36.

Kapuran, A., Bulatović, A. and Jovanović, I. (Капуран, А., Булатовић, А., Јовановић, И.). 2014. *Бор и Мајданпек, културна стратиграфија праисторијских локалитета између Ђердапа и Црног Тимока.* Београд-Бор: Археолошки институт, Београд, Музеј рударства и металургије, Бор.

Kapuran, A., Bulatović, A. and Danković, I. 2019a. Horizonti bronzanog doba na lokalitetu Nad Klepečkom/Bronze Age horizons at the site of Nad Klepečkom. In: Kapuran *et al.* 2019b, 80–141.

Kapuran, A., Bulatović, A., Filipović, V. and Golubović, S. (eds). 2019b. *Viminacijum u praistoriji/Viminacium in Prehistory.* Beograd: Arheološki institut.

Kapuran, A., Bulatović, A. and Milanović, D. 2018. Settlement pattern changes during the Central Balkans Copper Age. In: *Communities in Transition*, eds S. Deitz, F. Mavridis, Ž. Tankosić and T. Takaoglu, 77–88. Oxford: Oxbow Books.

Kienlin, T. 2010. *Traditions and Transformations: Approaches to Eneolithic (Copper Age) and Bronze Age metalworking and society in Eastern Central Europe and the Carpathian Basin.* Oxford: British Archaeological Report S2184.

Kiss, V., Fábián, S., Hajdu, T., Köhler, K., Kulscár, G., Major, I. and Szabó, G. 2015. Contributions to the relative and absolute chronology of the Early and Middle Bronze Age in western Hungary based on radiocarbon dating of human bones. In: *Bronze Age Chronology in the Carpatian Basin*, eds R. Németh and B. Rezi, 23–36. Târgu Mureş: Editura Mega.

Klochko, B. 2020. Metal axes of the Kozarac-Stublo type from Carpathian-Volhynia metallurgy center of Willow leaf of Ukrainian corded ware culture circle and its connections to Danubian region. *Slovenská Archeológia Supplementum* 1 (eds A. Kozubova, E. Makarova, M. Neumann), 317–326.

Koledin, J. 2008. Prilog poznavanju rasprostranjenosti zvonastih pehara. *Рад музеја Војводине* 50, 33–60.

Koledin, J., Bugaj, U., Jarosz, P., Novak, M., Przybyla, M., Podsiadlo, M., Szczepanek, A., Spasić, M. and Wlodarczak, P. 2020. First archaeological investigations of barrows in the Bačka region and the question of the Eneolithic/Early Bronze Age barrows in Vojvodina. *Praehistoriche Zeitschrift* 2020, 1–26.

Krementski, C. 1997. The Late Holocene environmental and climate shift in Russia and surrounding lands. In: *Third Millenium BC Climate Change and Old World Collapse*, eds N. Dalfes, G. Kukla, and H. Weiss, 351–370. Heidelberg; Springer.

Krstić, D., Bankoff, A., Vukmanović, M. and Winter, F. (Крстић, Д., Bankoff, A., Вукмановић, M., Winter, F.). 1986. Праисторијски локалитет Новачка ћуприја. *Зборник Народног музеја* 12(1), 17–63.

Kulcsár, G. 2009. *The Beginnings of the Bronze Age in the Carpathian Basin.* Budapest: Varia Archaeologica Hungarica 23.

Kuzmanovska, O. and Stankovski, J. 2018. Cult practise and calendars of Kokino sanctuary. In: *Giving gifts to God: Evidences of votive offerings in the sanctuaries, temples and churches*, 31–36. Kumanovo: NU Muzej.

Lazić, M. (Лазић, M.). 2017. Археолошко рекогносцирање трасе Аутопута Е80 и подручја Просторног плана инфраструктурног коридора Ниш – граница Бугарске, *Археолошка истраживања на аут*, 21–79. Републички завод за заштиту споменика културе Београд, Belgrade.

Levi Strauss, K. 1977. *Strukturalna antropologija.* Zagreb: Alethia.

Leštakov, K. (Лещаков, K.). 1992. Изследования върху бронзовата епоха в Тракия I. сравнителна стратиграфия на селищните могили от ранната бронзова епоха в югоизточна България. *Годишник на софийския университет „Св. Климент Охридски"* 84–85, 5–119.

Librado, P., Khan, N., Fages, A., Kusliy, M. A., Suchan, T., Tonasso-Calvière, T. *et al.* 2021. The origins and the spread of domestic horses from the Western Eurasian steppes. *Nature* 598(28), 634–640.

Librado, P., Tressières, G., Chauvey, L., Fages, A., Khan, N., Schiavinato, S. *et al.* 2024. Widespread horse-based mobility arose around 2200 BCE in Eurasia. *Nature* 631(8022), 819–825.

Ljuština, M. (Љуштина, M.). 2022. *Изазови средњег бронзаног доба: ватинска култура и балкански суседи.* Београд: Филозофски факултет.

Machnik, J. 1991. *The Earliest Bronze Age in the Carpathian Basin.* Bradford: Bradford University.

Majnarić Pandžić, N. 1974. Der Goldenfund aus Orolik bei Vinkovci. *Archaeologia Iugoslavica* 15, 21–26.

Mallory, J. 2006. *Indoevropljani, zagonetka njihova podrijetla.* Zagreb: Školska knjiga.

Maniatis, Y. and Ziota, C. 2011. Systematic ^{14}C dating of a unique Early and Middle Bronze Age cemetery at Xeropigado Koiladas, West Macedonia, Greece. *Radiocarbon* 53(3), 461–478.

Map 531_2_4: Karta 531_2_4, Vojnogeografski institut 1970, R 1:25 000.

Marković, J. Đ. and Pavlović, M. (Марковић, J. Ђ., Павловић, M.). 1995. *Географске регије Југославије.* Београд: Savremena Administracija.

Marković, Z. 2010. Prilog proučavanju vinkovačke culture. *Prilozi Instituta za arheologiju u Zagrebu* 27, 33–50.

Marović, I. and Čović, B. 1983. Cetinska kultura. In: *Praistorija jugoslavenskih zemalja* 4, ed. A. Benac, 191–232. Sarajevo: Akademija nauka i umjetnosti BiH.

Mason, A. H., Powell, W. G., Bankoff, H. A. Mathur, R., Bulatović, A., Filipović, V. and Ruiz, J. 2016. Tin isotope characterization of bronze artifacts of the central Balkans. *Journal of Archaeological Science* 69, 110–117.

McGeehan-Liritzis, V. and Gale, N. H. 1988. Chemical and lead isotope analyses of Greek Late Neolithic and Early Bronze Age metals. *Archaeometry* 30(2), 199–225.

Metzinger-Schmitz, B. 2004. Die Glockenbecherkultur in Mähren und Niederösterreich. (Unpublished dissertation) Dissertation zur Erlangung der akademischen Grades, Saarbrücken Universität.

Milašinović, L., Kapuran, A. and Bulatović, A. forthcoming. Stari Vinogradi – Bronze Age Necropolis in Ostojićevo (Kikinda). *Starinar* 74.

Milinković, M. 2002. Die byzantitinische Höhenanlage auf der Jelica in Serbien: ein Beispiel aus dem nördlichen Illiricum des 6 Jh. *Старинар* н.с. 51, 71–132.

Milojević, P. and Trajković-Filipović, T. (Милојевић, П., Трајковић-Филиповић, T.). 2017. *Праисторијска налазишта у Алесиначкој котлини.* Алексинац: Завичајни музеј/Ниш: Народни музеј.

Mitrevski, D. 2003. Prehistory in Republic of Macedonia-F.Y.R.O.M. In: *Recent Research in the Prehistory of the Balkans*, ed. D. V. Grammenos, 13–72. Thessaloniki: Archaeological Institute of Northern Greece.

Mitrevski, D. (Митревски, Д.). 2013. Праисторија на Република Македонија. Y: *Македонија, миленијумски културно-историјски факти*, ур. Е. Димитрова, J. Донев, П. Кузман, 83–266. Скопје: Медиа принт Македонија и Евробалкан.

Mitrevski, D. 2016. *Skopje Fortress – Kale, from Prehistory to the Early Ancient Period.* Скопје: ПНВ Публикации.

Motzoi-Chicideanu, I. and Sandor-Chicideanu, M. 2015. Cateva date noi privind chronologiaculturii Monteoru. *Mousaios* 20, 9–53.

Muhly, J. 1985. Sources of tin and the beginnings of bronze metallurgy. *American Journal of Archaeology* 89, 275–291.

Nezafati, N., Pernicka, E. and Momenzadeh, M. 2009. Introduction of the Deh Hosein ancient tin-copper mine, western Iran: Evidence from geology, archaeology, geochemistry and lead isotope data. *TÜBA-AR* 12, 223–236.

Nikitović, L. (Никитовић, Л.). 1994. Праисторијска хумка у селу Турици код Гуче и њен значај у раном бронзаном добу Драгачева. *Зборник радова Народног музеја у Чачку* 24, 29–39.

Nikitović, L. (Никитовић, Л.). 1996. Праисторијска хумка на Великом пољу у Јанчићима код Чачка. *Зборник радова Народног музеја у Чачку* 26, 25–30.

Nikitović, L. (Никитовић, Л.). 1999. Резултати истраживања праисторијске некрополе на локалитету Дубац у Јанчићима на Каблару. *Зборник радова Народног музеја у Чачку* 29, 5–21.

Nikitović, L. (Никитовић, Л.). 2000. Праисторијска хумка на локалитету Аде у селу Пријевору. *Зборник радова Народног музеја у Чачку* 30, 5–11.

Nikitović, L. 2003. Krstac-Ivkovo Brdo, nekropola sa humkama iz bronzanog doba. In: *Sahranjivanje u bronzano i gvozdeno doba*, eds N. Bojović and M. Vasić, 11–21. Narodni muzej, Čačak, Arheološki institut, Beograd.

Nikolić, D. 2000. *Kostolačka kultura na teritoriji Srbije*. Beograd: Filozofski fakultet Beograd, Centar za arheološka istraživanja.

Nikolić, D., and Kapuran, A. (Николић, Д., Капуран, А.). 2001. Слој енеолита и раног бронзаног доба на Благотину. У: *Археолошки локалитети Крушевца и околине*, ур. Н. Тасић, Е. Радуловић, 159–171. Крушевац-Београд: Народни музеј, Крушевац, Балканолошки институт САНУ, Београд.

Nikolova, L. 1999. *The Balkans in Later Prehistory, Periodization, Chronology and Cultural Development in the Final Copper and Early Bronze Age (Fourth and Third Millenia BC)*. Oxford: British Archaeologica Report S791.

Niskanen, M. 2023. The prehistoric origins of the domestic horse and horseback riding. *Bulletins et Memoires de la Societe d'Anthropologie de Paris* 35(1), 54–73.

O'Shea, J. 1996. *Villagers of the Maros, A Portrait of an Early Bronze Age Society*. New York: Springer.

O'Shea, J., Parditka, G., Nikodemus, A., Kristiansen, K., Sjögren, K.-G., Paja, L., Pálfi, G. and Milašinović, L. 2019. Social formation and collapse in the Tiza-Maros region: Dating the Maros Group and its Late Bronze Age successors. *Antiquity* 93(369), 604–623.

Outram, A. K., Stear, N. A., Bendry, R., Olsen, S., Kasparov, A., Zaibert, V., Thorpe, N. and Evershed, R. P. 2009. The earliest horse harnessing and milking. *Science* 323(5919), 1332–1335.

Ovčarov, D. (Овчаров, Д.) (ed.). 1981. *Перник, Праисторически селища (V–II хил. пр. н.е.),* Перник, том I, Поселищен живот на хълма Кракра от *V* хил.пр.н.е. до *VI в. на н.е.* София: Българска Академия на науките, Археологически институт и музей, София.

Pare, C. F. E. 2000. Bronze and the Bronze Age. In: *Metals Make the World Go Round: The supply and circulations of metals in Bronze Age Europe*, ed. C. F. E. Pare, 1–38. Oxford, Oxbow Books.

Podzuweit, C. 1979. *Trojanische Gefäßformen der Frühbronzezeit in Anatolien, der Ägäis und angrenzenden Gebieten*. Mainz am Rhein: Philipp von Zabern.

Popescu, A. D. 2010. Deliberate destruction of pottery during the Bronze Age – a case study. In: *Signa Praehistorica, Studia in honorem magistri Attila László, septuagesimo anno*, eds N. Bolohan, F. Măţău and F. A. Tencariu, 213–228. Iasi; Universitatea "Alexandru Ioan Cuza", Facultatea de Istorie, Centrul interdisciplinar de studii Arheoistorice; Academia Română, Institul de Arheologie Iaşi and Muzeul National secuiesc Sfântu Gheorghe.

Popović, D. and Radojčić, N. (Поповић, Д., Радојчић, Н.). 1998. *Градина на Босуту*, каталог изложбе. Шид: Галерија Сава Шумановић.

Popović, P., Vukmanović, M. and Radojčić, N. 1986. Fouilles de sondage sur la localite Vajuga-Pesak. *Đerdapske sveske* 3, 168–182.

Powell, W. G., Mathur, R., Bankoff, H. A., Mason, A. H., Bulatović, A., Filipović, V. and Godfrey, L. 2017. Digging deeper: Insights into metallurgical transitions in European prehistory through copper isotopes. *Journal of Archaeological Science* 88, 37–46.

Powell, W., Mathur, R., Bankoff, A. H., John, J., Chvojka, O., Tisucká, M., Bulatovic, A. and Filipovic, V. 2018. Copper isotopes as a means of determining regional metallurgical practices in European prehistory: A reply to Jansen. *Journal of Archaeological Science* 93, 216–221.

Prendi, F. 1978. L'age du Bronze en Albanie. *Iliria* 7–8, 5–71.

Prendi, F. and Bunguri, A. 2008. *The Early Bronze Age in Albania.* Prishtine: The Albanological studying Center, The Institute of archaeology

Prodanović-Ranković, I. (Продановић-Ранковић, И.). 2017. *Археолошка истраживања на аутопуту Е80.* Београд: Републички завод за заштиту споменика културе.

Radivojević, M., Rehren, T., Kuzmanović-Cvetković, J. and Jovanović, M. 2014. Why are there tin bronzes in the 5th millennium bc Balkans?. In: *Archaeotechnology: Studying technology from prehistory to the Middle Ages*, eds S. Vitezović and D. Antonović, 235–356. Belgrade: Serbian Archaeological Society.

Radojčić, N. (Радојчић, Н.). 2005. Гроб из раног бронзаног доба са некрополе Гламија у Корбову. *Зборник Народног музеја* 18(1), 115–121.

Rakičević, T. (Ракичевић, Т.). 1997. Климатски услови. In: *Монографија општине Лозница*, ур. З. Јовичић, 62–78. Лозница-Београд: Српско географско друштво, Географски факултет, Географски институт "Јован Цвијић" САНУ.

Reed, K. 2016. Archaeobotanical analysis of Bronze Age Feudvar. In: *Die Archäobotanik, Feudvar III*, eds H. Kroll and K. Reed, 197–292. Würzburg: Würzburg University Press.

Renfrew, C. 1971. Sitagroi, radiocarbon and the prehistory of south-east Europe. *Antiquity* 45, 275–282.

Rodić, D. and Pavlović, M. (Родић, Д., Павловић, М.). 1994. *Географија Југославије* 1. Београд: Савремена администрација.

Roman, P. 1976. *Cultura Cotofeni.* Bucuresti: Editura Academiei RSR.

Roman, P. 2006. Preuves concernant les mouvements ethnoculturels de l'est á l'ouest et du sud au nord, dans la haute période de l'age du bronze, résultées des recherches faites á Ostrovul Corbului, In: *Homage to Milutin Garašanin*, ed. N. Tasić, 455–468. Belgrade: Serbian Academy of Sciences and Arts.

Schreiber-Kalicz, R. 1984. Komplex der Nagyrev-Kultur. In: *Kulturen der Fruhbronzezeit des Karpatenbeckens und Nordbalkans*, ed. N. Tasić, 133–190. Beograd: Institue for Balkan Studies.

Sherratt, A. 1986. The pottery of Phases IV and V: The Early Bronze Age. In: *Excavations at Sitagroi, a Prehistoric Village in Northeast Greece* 1, eds C. Renfrew, M. Gimbutas and E. S. Elster, 429–476. Los Angeles CA: Cotsen Institute of Archaeology.

Šljivar, D. (Шљивар, Д.). 2015. Осврт на нове податке о локалитетима Беловоде и Плочник у Старинару 64. *Старинар* н.с. 65, 229–232.

Sommer, R. S., Benecke, N., Lõugas, L., Neile, O. and Schmölcke, U. 2011. Holocene survival of the wild horse in Europe: A matter of open landscape? *Journal of Quarternary Science* 26(8), 805–812.

Srejović, D. 1963. Bare, Kragujevac – praistorijske humke. *Arheološki pregled* 5, 46–47.

Srejović, D. 1976. Humke stepskih odlika na teritoriji Srbije, Godišnjak XIII. *Centar za balkanološka ispitivanja* 11, 117–129

Srejović,, D. 1997. *Arheološki leksikon.* Beograd: Savremena administracija.

Stankovski, J. (Станковски, J.). 2002. Татикев Камен – мегалитска опсерваторија и светилиште. *Музејски гласник* 7–9, 29–48.

Stankovski, J. (Станковски, J.). 2003. Три мегалитни споменици во кумановскиот регион. *Пирајхме* 2, 229–262.

Stankovski, J. (Станковски, J.) (ed.). 2007 *Кокино, тврдина на сонцето*, каталог изложбе. Куманово: Национална установа Музеј Куманово.

Stankovski, J. (Станковски, J.). 2010. Прилог кон проучување на обредната практика на локалитетот Татићев Камен, село Кокино. *Macedoniae Acta Archaeologica* 19, 115–125.

Stojić, M. (Стојић, М.). 1986. Праисторијско насеље Вецина мала у Мајуру код Светозарева. *Старинар* н.с. 37, 145–152.

Stojić, M. (Стојић, М.). 1989. Праисторијско налазиште Ђула у Остриковцу код Светозарева. *Balcanica* 20, 171–183.

Stojić, M. 2011. Maskare, Bedem Site. Contribution to the research of foundations of cultures: of ostrikovac and two-handled beakers. In: *Златното пето хилядолетие*, ред. Я. Бояджиев, С. Игнатова, 313–327. София: Българска Академия на науките, Национален Археологически институт с Музей.

Stojić, M. and Cerović, M. (Стојић, М., Церовић, М.). 2011. *Шабац, културна стратиграфија праисторијских локалитета у Подрињу.* Београд–Шабац: Археолошки институт, Београд, Народни музеј, Шабац.

Stojić, M. and Čađenović, G. (Стојић, М., Чађеновић, Г.) 2006. *Крушевац, културна стратиграфија праисторијских локалитета у зони става Западне Мораве и Јужне Мораве.* Београд–Крушевац: Археолошки институт, Београд, Народни музеј, Крушевац

Stojić, M. and Jacanović, D. (Стојић, М., Јацановић, Д.). 2008. *Пожаревац, културна стратиграфија праисторијских локалитета у Браничеву.* Београд: Археолошки институт Београд, Народни музеј Пожаревац.

Stojić, M. and Jocić, M. (Стојић, М., Јоцић, М.). 2006. *Ниш-културна стратиграфија праисторијских локалитета у нишкој регији.* Београд-Ниш: Археолошки институт, Београд, Народни музеј, Ниш.

Stojić, M. and Nikitović, L. 1996. Ada in Prijevor bei Čačak – Beitrag zur der Bronzezeit im Moravagebiet und im serbischen Donaugebiet. *Старинар* н.с. 47, 205–212.

Svilar, M. 2007. Početak bronzanog doba u Pomoravlju. (Unpublished master's thesis) neobjavljen master rad odbranjen na Odeljenju za arheologiju Filozofskog fakulteta Univerziteta u Beogradu.

Szabó, G. 2019. Problems with the periodization of the Early Bronze Age in the Carpathian Basin in light of the older and recent AMS Radiocarbon data. *Archeometriai Mühely* 14(2), 99–116.

Tárnoki, J. 2003. The expansion of the Hatvan Culture. In: *Hungarian Archaeology at the Turn of the Millennium*, eds Z. Visy, M. Nagy and Z. Kiss, 145–148. Budapest: Ministry of National Cultural Heritage and Teleki László Foundation.

Tasić, N. 1979. Bubanj-Salcuta-Krivodol kompleks. In: *Praistorija jugoslavenskih zemalja* 3, ed. A. Benac, 87–114. Sarajevo: Akademija nauka i umjetnosti BiH.

Tasić, N. 1984a. Die Vinkovci-Kultur In: *Kulturen der Fruhbronzezeit des Karpatenbeckens und Nordbalkans*, ed. N. Tasić, 15–32. Beograd: Institue for Balkan Studies.

Tasić, N. 1984b. The Eneolithic. In: *The Archaeological Treasures of Kosovo i Metohija, from the Neolithic to the Early Middle Ages*, ed. N. Tasić, 88–115. Belgrade: Serbian Academy of Sciences and Arts.

Tasić, N. 2004. Historical picture of development of Bronze Age cultures in Vojvodina. *Старинар* н.с. 53–54, 23–34.

Tasić, H. and Tomić, E. 1969. *Crnokalačka bara, naselje starčevačke i vinčanske kulture.* Kruševac-Beograd: Narodni muzej, Kruševac, Arheološko društvo Jugoslavije.

Taylor, W. T. T. and Barrón-Ortiz, C. I. 2021. Rethinking the evidence for early horse domestication at Botai. *Scientific Reports* 11(7440).

Todorova, H. 2003. Prehistory of Bulgaria. In: *Recent Research in the Prehistory of the Balkans*, ed. D. V. Grammenos, 257–328. Thessaloniki: Publications of the Archaeological Institute of Northern Greece 3.

Todorović, J. (Тодоровић, J.). 1956. Праисторијска некропола на Роспи Ћуприји. *Гласник музеја града Београда* 3, 27–62.

Todorović, J. (Тодоровић, J.). 1967. Праисторијске некрополе у Ритопеку. *Старинар* 17, 153–162.

Trajkovska, L. (Трајковска, Л.). 1995. Рано бронзено светилиште кај селото Пелинце. Y: *каталог изложбе*, ур. Б. Таневски. Куманово: Народни музеј у Куманову.

Trajkovska, L. (Трајковска, Л.). 1999. Градиште-Пелинце, истражување на секторот Две Могили. *Macedoniae acta archaeologica* 15, 47–61.

Trajkovska, L. (Трајковска, Л.). 2003. Светилиште од раното бронзено доба на лок. 'Градиште' во село Пелинце кај Куманово. *Пирајхме* 2, 289–297.

Trautmann, I. 2006. The Significance of Cremation in Early Neolithic Communities in Central Europe. Unpublished PhD thesis, Erberhard-Karls-Universität Tübingen.

Vasić, R. 1986. Compte-rendu des douilles du site prehistorique a Velesnica 1981–82. *Đerdapske sveske* 3, 264–285.

Vasilescu, T. 2013. O dată ^{14}C de la Năeni-Zănoaga, Cetatea 1. *Studii de Prehistorie* 10, 171–187.

Vasiljević, M. (Васиљевић, М.). 1967. Топографија археолошких налазишта и споменика у Подрињу. *Годишњак историјског* архива 5, 121–156.

Vranić, S. 1991. A grave from the Early Bronze Age found at Šljunkara near Zemun. *Starinar* 42, 19–26.

Vukmanović, M. and Radojčić, N. (Вукмановић, М., Радојчић, Н.). 1995. *Каталог метала* II., Београд: Народни музеј.

Vuković, S. and Marković, D. 2019. Ostaci životinja iz horizonata mlađe praistorije na lokalitetima Nad klepečkom i Rit. In: Kapuran *et al.* 2019b, 223–248.

Wels-Weyrauch, U. 2015. *Die Dolche in Bayern.* Frankfurt am Main: Prahistorische Bronzefunde 6(15).

Weninger, B. 1995. Stratified ^{14}C dates and ceramic chronologies: Case studies for the Early Bronze Age at Troy (Turkey) and Ezero (Bulgaria). *Radiocarbon* 37(2), 443–456.

Whitelaw, T. 1983. People and space in hunter-gatherer camps: A generalising approach in ethnoarchaeology. *Archaeological Review from Cambridge* 2(2), 48–66.

Yener, K. A., Özbal, H., Kaptan, E., Pehlivan, A. N. and Goodway, M. 1989. Kestel: An Early Bronze Age source of tin ore in the Taurus mountains, Turkey. *Science* 244(4901), 200–203.

Zotović, M. 1985. *Arheološki i etnički problemi bronzanog doba zapadne Srbije.* Beograd: Savez Arheoloških društava Jugoslavije.

Žeravica, Z. 1993. *Äxte und Beile aus Dalmatien und anderen Teilen Kroatiens, Montenegro, Bosnien und Herzegowina.* Stuttgar: Prähistorische Bronzefunde 9(18).

Plate 1. Ranutovac, site of Meanište: cremation necropolis, excavation in 2012.

Plate 2. Hum, site of Velika Humska Čuka: excavation in 2019.

Plate 3. Novo Selo, site of Bubanj: after excavation in 2014.

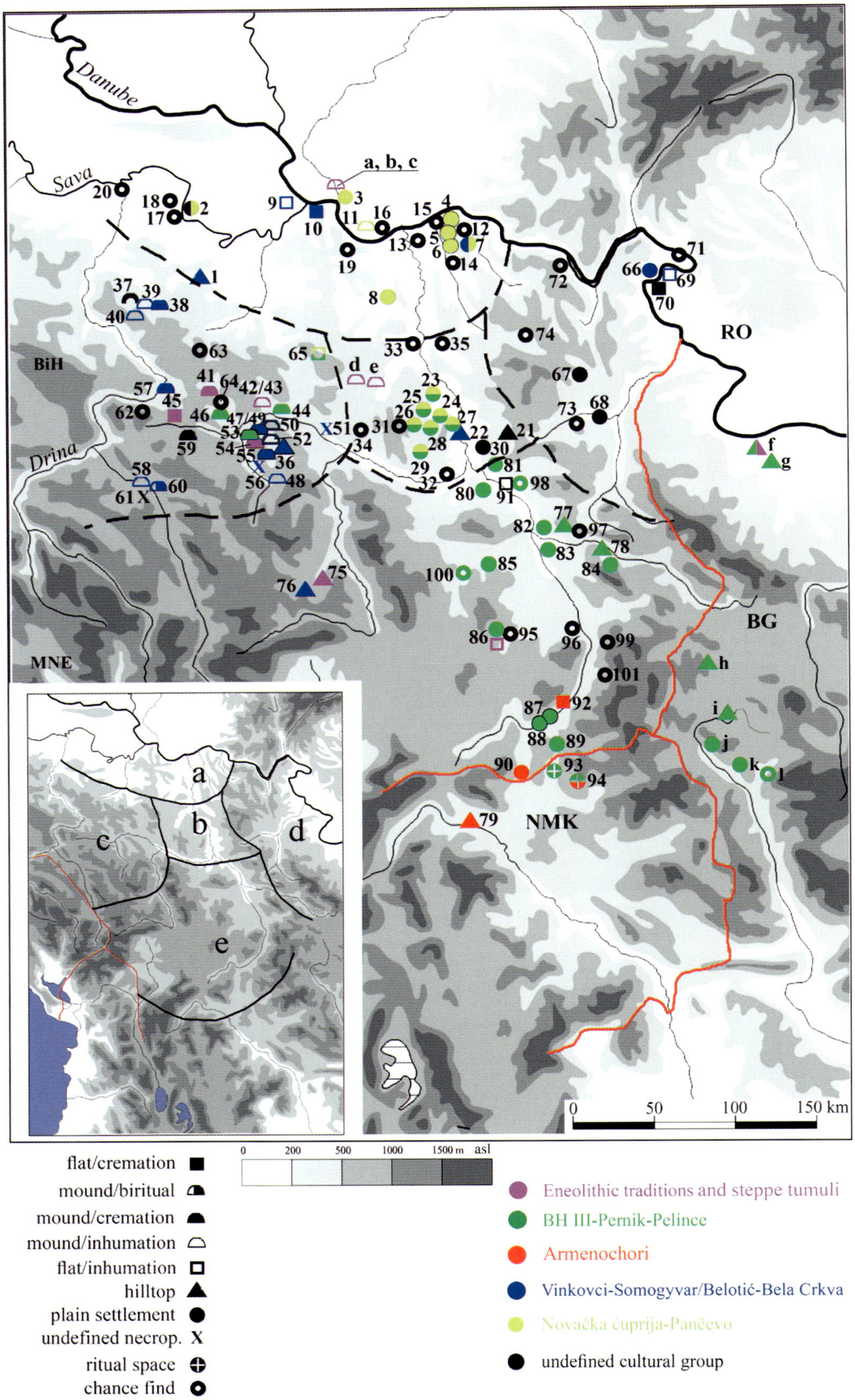
Danube
Sava
Drina
a, b, c
BiH
MNE
RO
BG
NMK
0 50 100 150 km
a
b
c
d
e
0 200 500 1000 1500 m asl
flat/cremation
mound/biritual
mound/cremation
mound/inhumation
flat/inhumation
hilltop
plain settlement
undefined necrop.
ritual space
chance find
Eneolithic traditions and steppe tumuli
BH III-Pernik-Pelince
Armenochori
Vinkovci-Somogyvar/Belotić-Bela Crkva
Novačka ćuprija-Pančevo
undefined cultural group

Plate 4 (opposite). Early Bronze Age sites in the Central Balkans.

Peri-Pannonian zone: 1. Svileuva, site of Kik; 2. Klenak, site of Adžine njive; 3. Pančevo, site of Donja Varoš; 4. Viminacium, site of Rit; 5. Viminacium, site of Nad Klepečkom; 6. Drmno, site of Nad Lugom; 7. Majilovac, site of Marjansko Brdo; 8. Grčac, site of Novačka ćuprija; 9. Surčin, site of Šljunkara; 10. Beograd, Rospi ćuprija; 11. Skorenovac near Kovin; 12. Kličevac unknown site; 13. Batovac, unknown site; 14. Trnjane, site of Kod Groblja; 15. Viminacium, site of Amfiteatar; 16. Kovin, unknown site; 17. Štitar, unknown site; 18. Uzveće, unknown site; 19. Begaljica, unknown site; 20. Ušće Drine u Savu, unknown site.

Basin of the Great Morava River with Šumadija: 21. Lešje, Vrelo; 22. Ostrikovac, Đula; 23. Crnče, Raskrsnice; 24. Bresje, Okućnica Dušana Markovića; 25. Belica, Cerjak; 26. Rekovac, Čičkovica; 27. Majur, Vecina Mala; 28. Lukar, Trnati Laz; 29. Poljna, Blagotin; 30. Drenovac, Slatina; 31. Rekovac, unknown site; 32. Jasika, unknown site; 33. Staro Selo, unknown site; 34. Zakuta, unknown site; 35. Vojska, unknown site.

Western Serbia with Lim Valley: 36. Jelica, Gradina; 37. Cerje, Cerovačka Pećina; 38. Belotić, Šumar; 39. Bela Crkva, Cerik-Bandera; 40. Tolisavac, unknown site; 41. Ražana, Anište; 42. Jančići, Veliko Polje; 43. Jančići, Dubac; 44. Prijevor, Ade; 45. Stapari, Mala Gradina; 46. Vranjani, Veliki Lug; 47. Lučani, Kruševlje; 48. Guča, Rajića Brdo; 49. Lučani, Suva Česma; 50. Dučalovići, Ruja; 51. Mrčajevci, Gušavac; 52. Markovica, Negrišori; 53. Pilatovići, Ravni Lug; 54. Krstac, Ivkovo brdo; 55. Donja Kravarica, Babinjak; 56. Turica, Ošljevac; 57. Bajina Bašta, Višesava; 58. Priboj, FAP; 59. Drežnik, Do; 60. Jarmovac, l Kaluđersko Polje; 61. Mramorak, Goleško Brdo; 62. Šljivovica, unknown site; 63. Donja. Leskovica, unknown site; 64. Ševrljuge, unknown site; 65. Mali Šturac, Prljuša.

Timok Region with Đerdap Gorge: 66. Velesnica, Obala-Donja Strana; 67. Bor, Kučajna; 68. Gamzigrad, Antička Palata; 69. Vajuga, Pesak; 70. Korbovo, Glamija; 71. Kostol, unknown site; 72. Boljetin, unknown site; 73. Osnić, unknown site; 74. Laznica, unknown site.

Southern Serbia with central Pčinja and the Kumanovo and Skopje Plains: 75. Postenje, Gradina; 76. Pazarište, Gradina; 77. Hum, Velika Humska Čuka; 78. Crvena Reka, Šuplji Kamen; 79. Skoplje, Kale; 80. Braljina, Smrdan; 81. Rujište, Crnokalačka bara; 82. Vrtište, Velika Česma; 83. Novo Selo, Bubanj; 84. Glogovac, Polje; 85. Mala Plana, Reka; 86. Štulac, Svinjarička Čuka; 87. Pavlovac, Kovačke Njive; 88. Davidovac, Gradište; 89. Klinovac, Tri Kruške; 90. Miratovac, Banjka Kaldrma; 91. Rutevac, Utrina; 92. Ranutovac, Meanište; 93. Pelince, Dve Mogili; 94. Kokino Selo, Tatikev Kamen; 95. Lozane, Biljurski Rid; 96. Leskovac, Hisar; 97. Gornji Matejevac, unknown site; 98. Rutevac, Školska Gradina; 99. Konopnica, unknown site; 100. Pločnik, unknown site; 101. Bacijevce, unknown site.

Steppe mounds in the Central Balkans: a. Vojlovica, Rafinerija; b. Jabuka, Tri humke; c. Pančevo, Livade; d. Bare, Pored puta za Grivac; e. Rogojevac, Dvorište Osnovne Škole.

Early Bronze Age sites in western Bulgaria: f. Stalijska mahala; g. Jakimovo; h. Pekljuk; i. Pernik; j. Kondofrei; k. Đakovo; l. Separeva Banja.

Inset: a. peri-Pannonian zone; b. Basin of the Great Morava River with Šumadija; c. Western Serbia and Lim Valley zone; d. Timok Region with Đerdap Gorge; e. Southern Serbia with central Pčinja and the Kumanovo and Skopje Plain.

Plate 5. Golden Noppenring *from grave with inhumed burial at the site of Svinjarička Čuka in Štulac.*

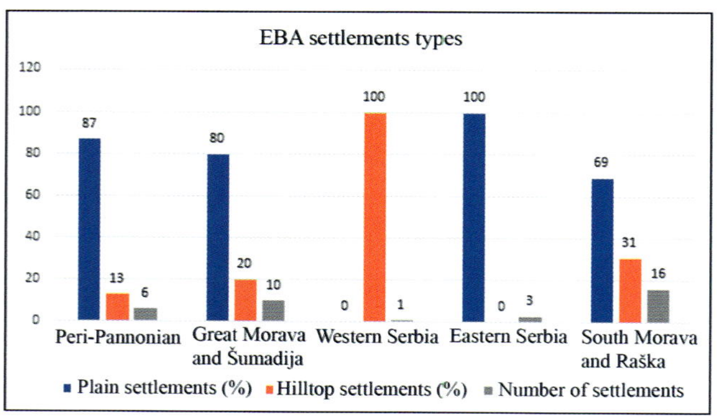

Plate 6. Types of Early Bronze Age settlements.

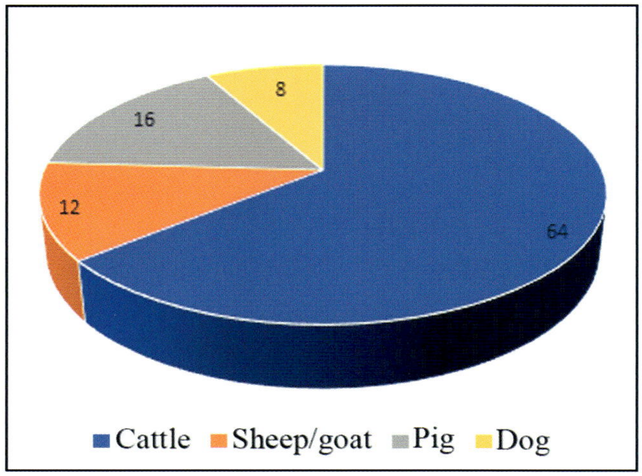

Plate 7. Marjansko Brdo site: utilisation of animal species in the 3rd quarter of the 3rd millennium cal BC (courtesy of D. Grujić).

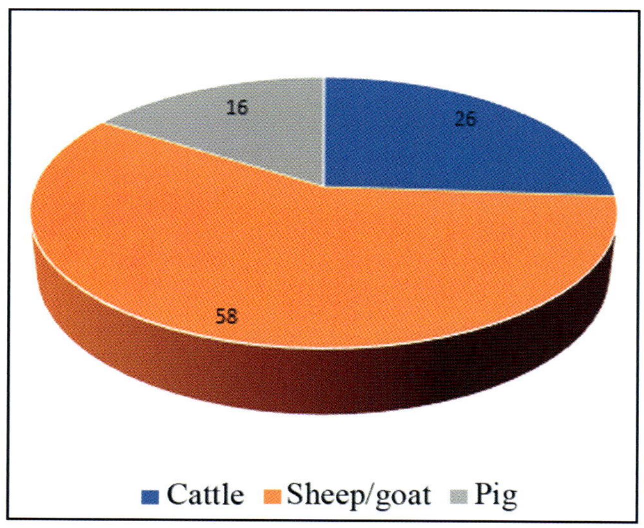

Plate 8. Marjansko Brdo site: utilisation of animal species in the 4th quarter of the 3rd millennium cal BC (courtesy of D. Grujić).

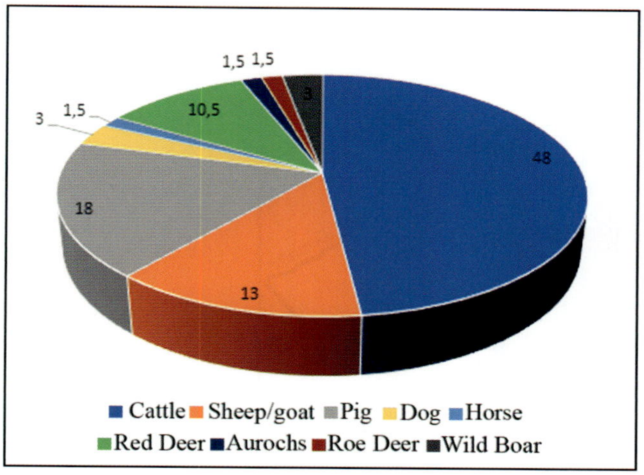

Plate 9. Viminacium, site of Nad Klepečkom: utilisation of animal species (based on Vuković and Marković 2019).

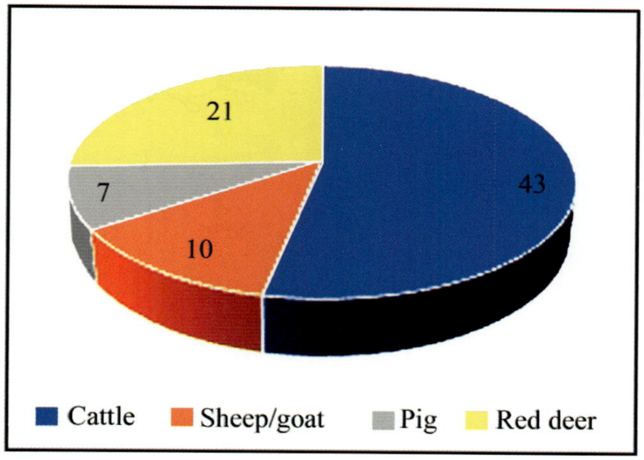

Plate 12. Bubanj site: utilisation of animal species (after Bökönyi 1990).

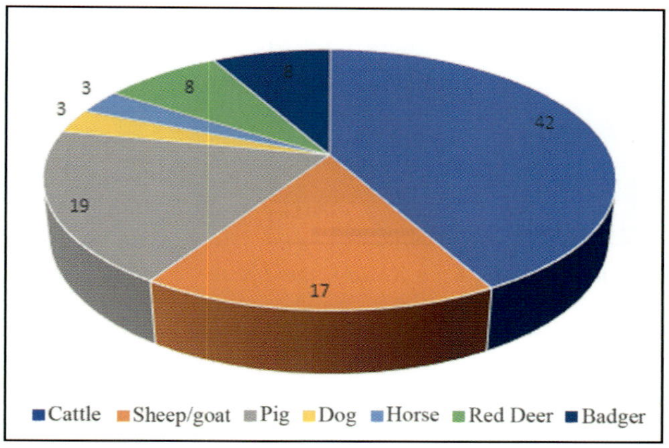

Plate 10. Viminacium, site of Rit: utilisation of animal species (based on Vuković and Marković 2019).

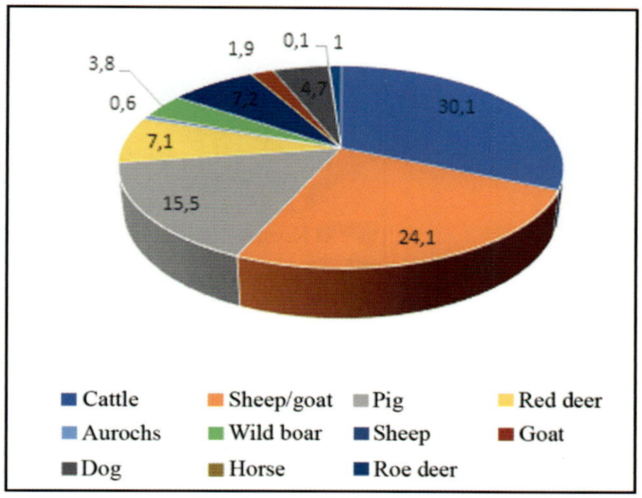

Plate 13. Bubanj site: excavations 2008–2014, Late Eneolithic and Early Bronze Age structures and layers (after Bulatović 2020).

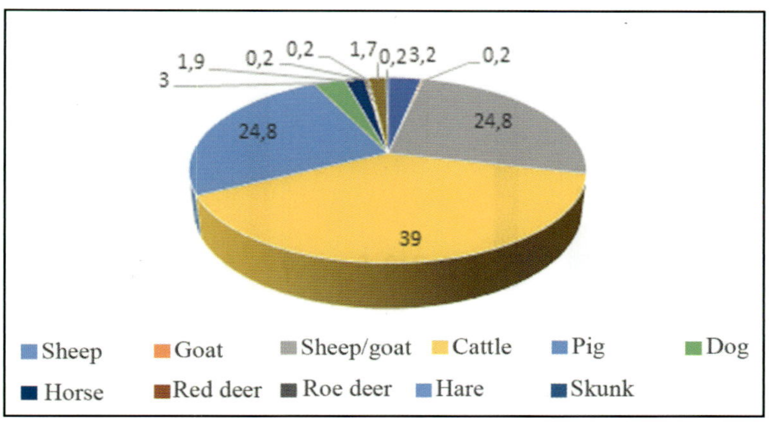

Plate 11. Novačka Ćuprija site: utilisation of animal species (based on Greenfield 1986; 2006).

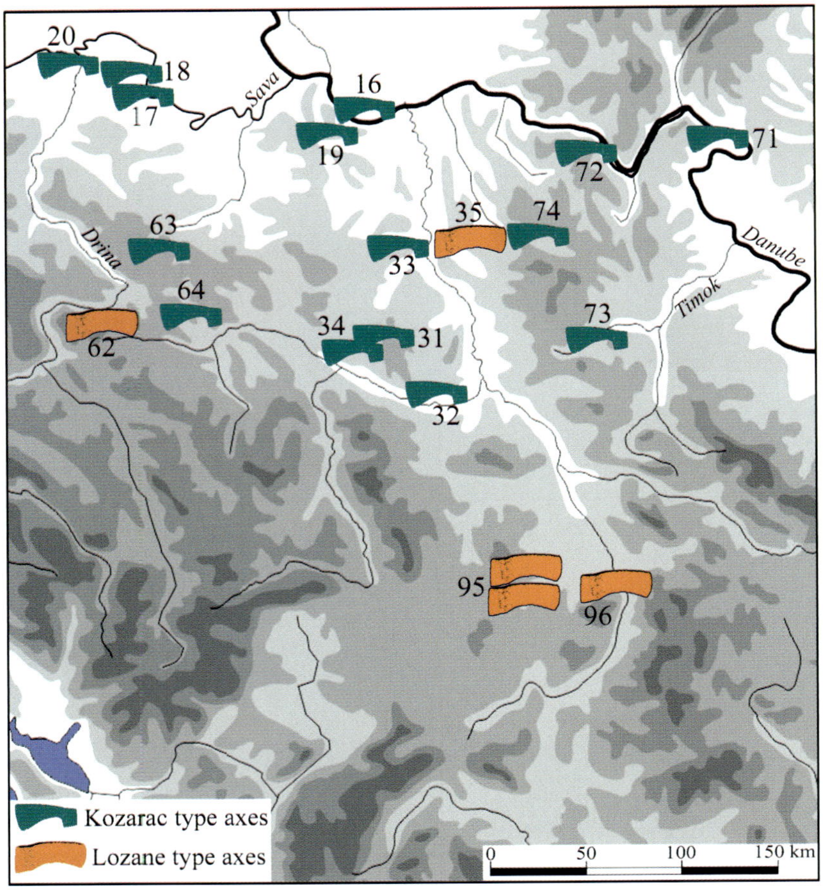

Plate 14. Distribution of Early Bronze Age axes in the central Balkans, types Kozarac and Lozane.

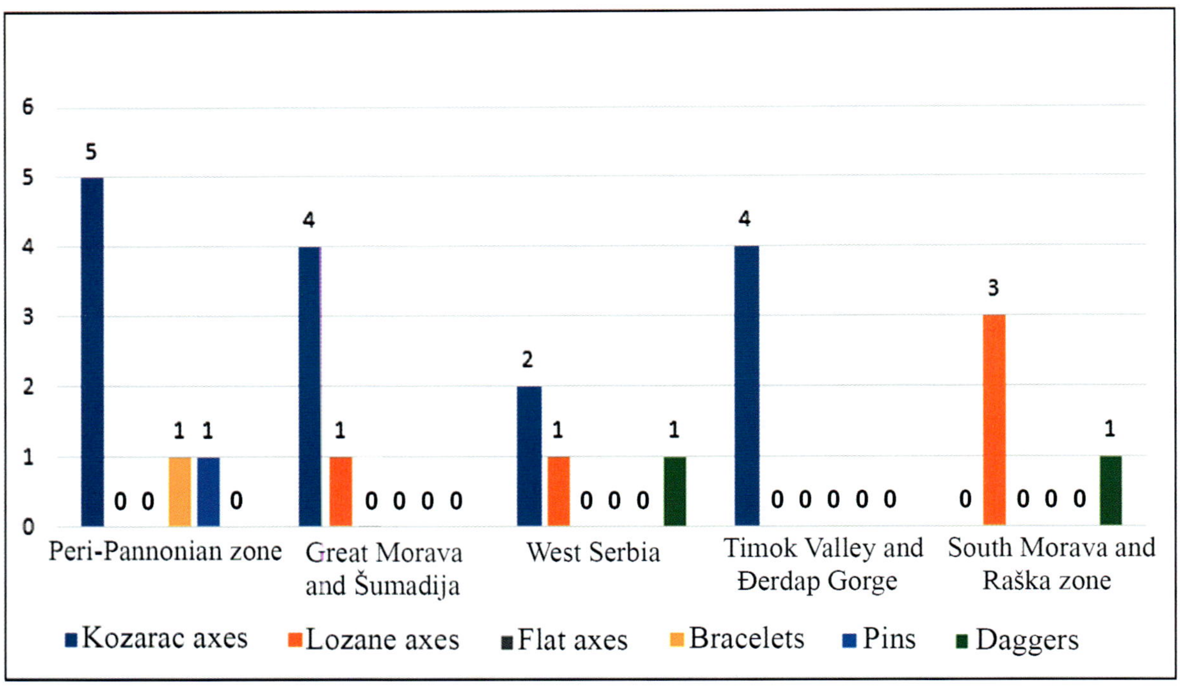

Plate 15. Early Bronze Age metal finds in the central Balkans.

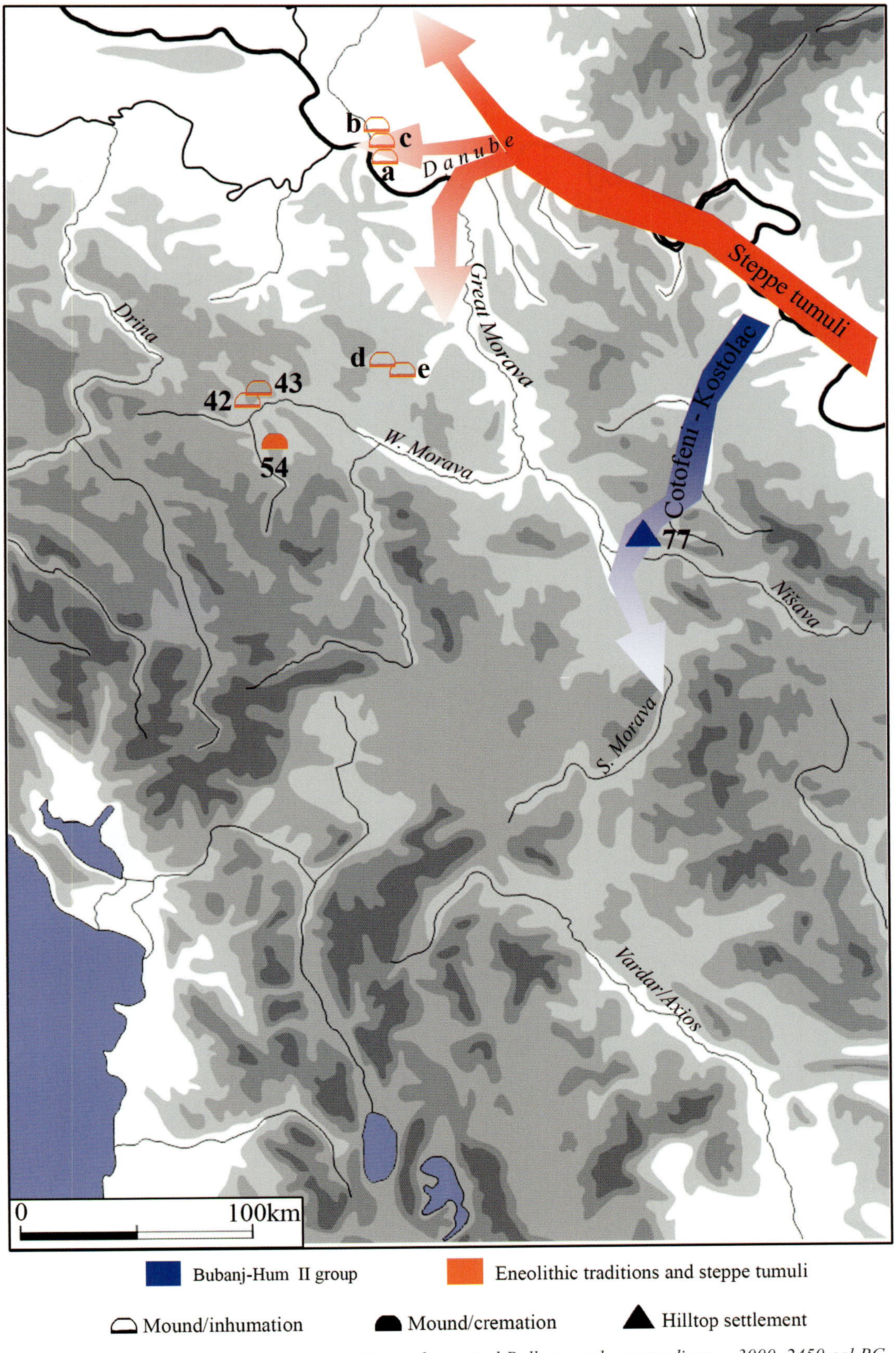

Plate 16. Cultural transmission of communities in the central Balkans and surroundings c. *3000–2450 cal BC.*

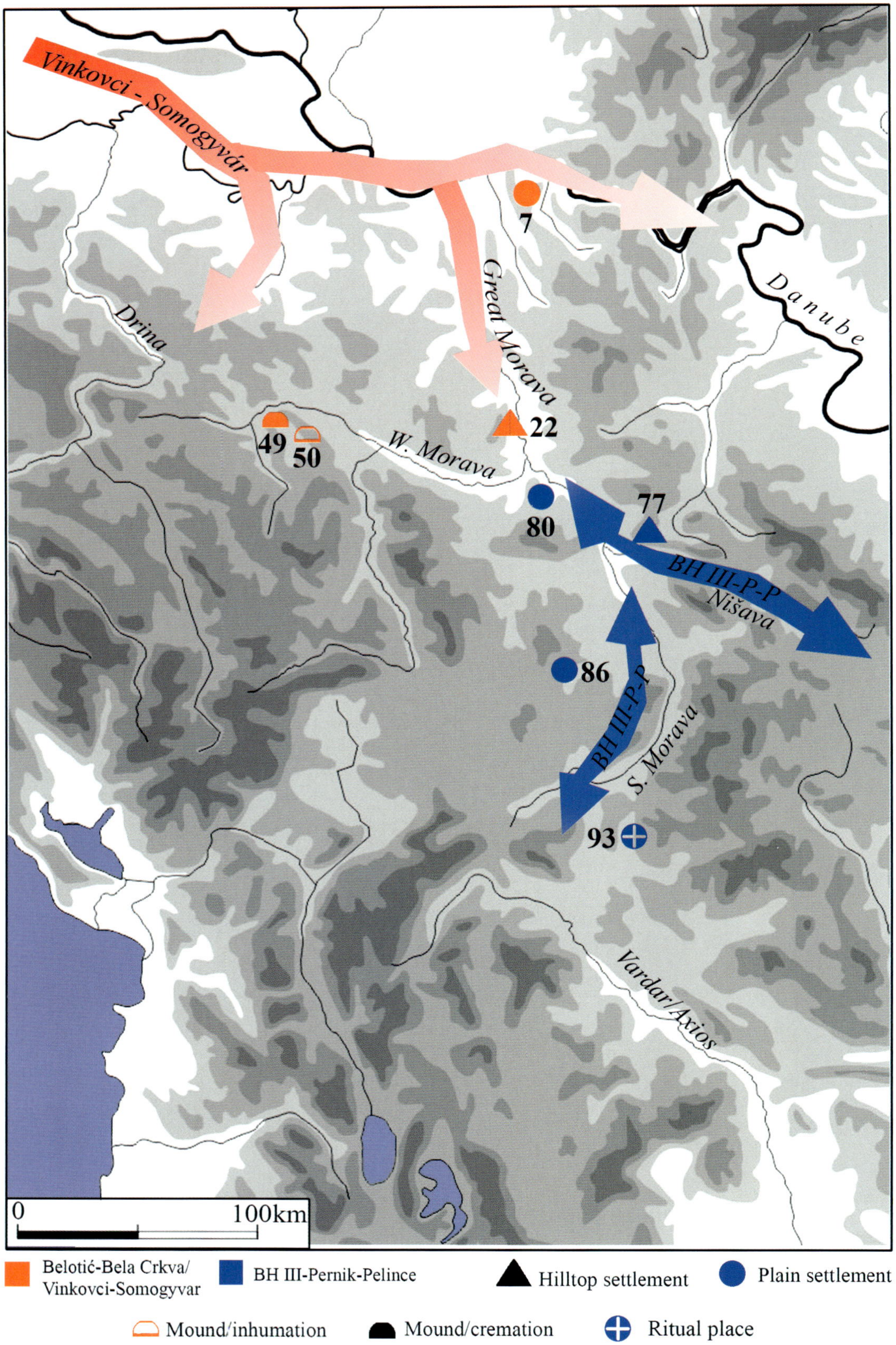

Plate 17. Cultural transmission of communities in the central Balkans and surroundings c. *2450–2250 cal BC.*

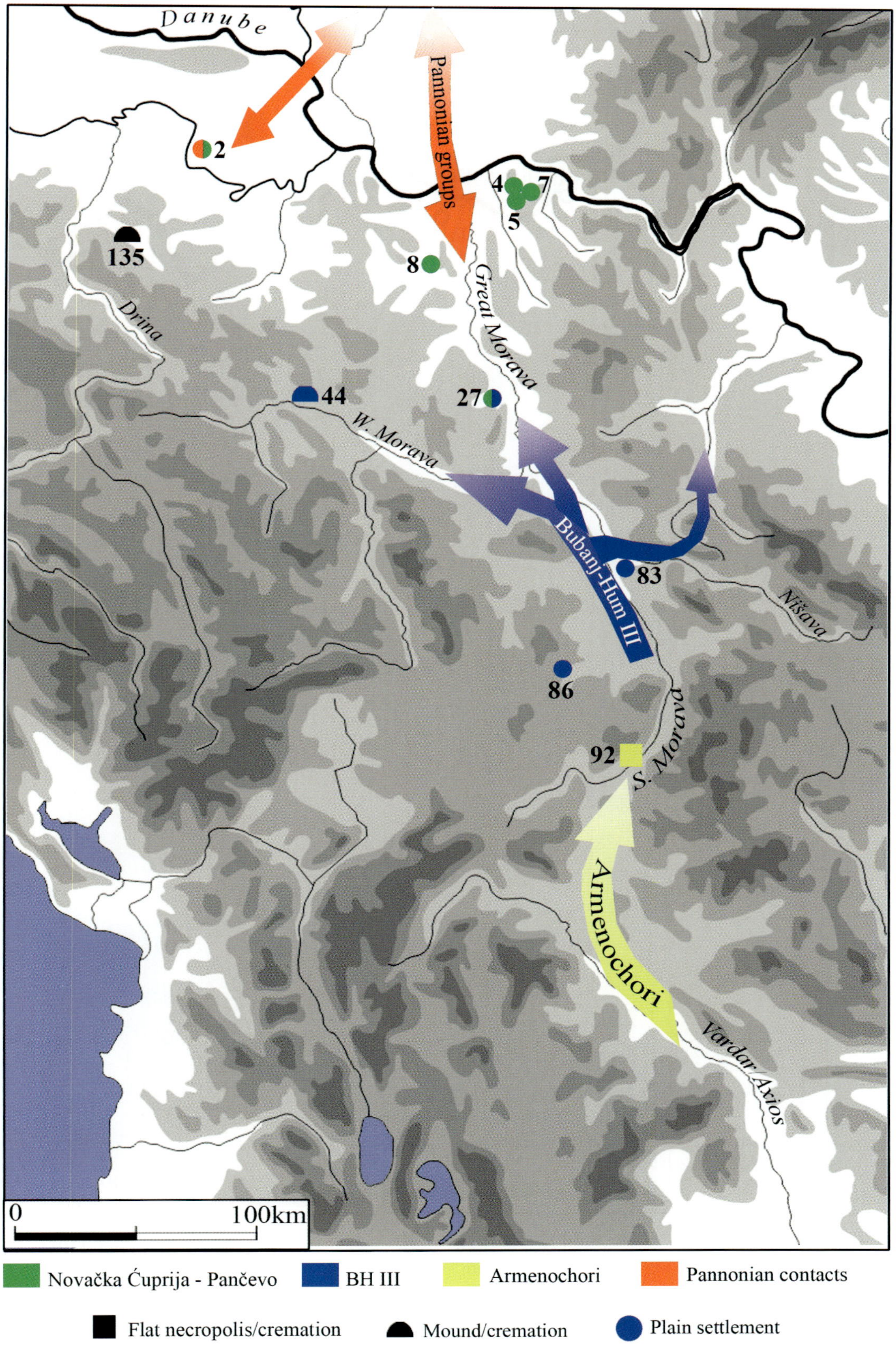

Plate 18. Cultural transmission of communities in the central Balkans and surroundings c. *2250–1900 cal BC.*

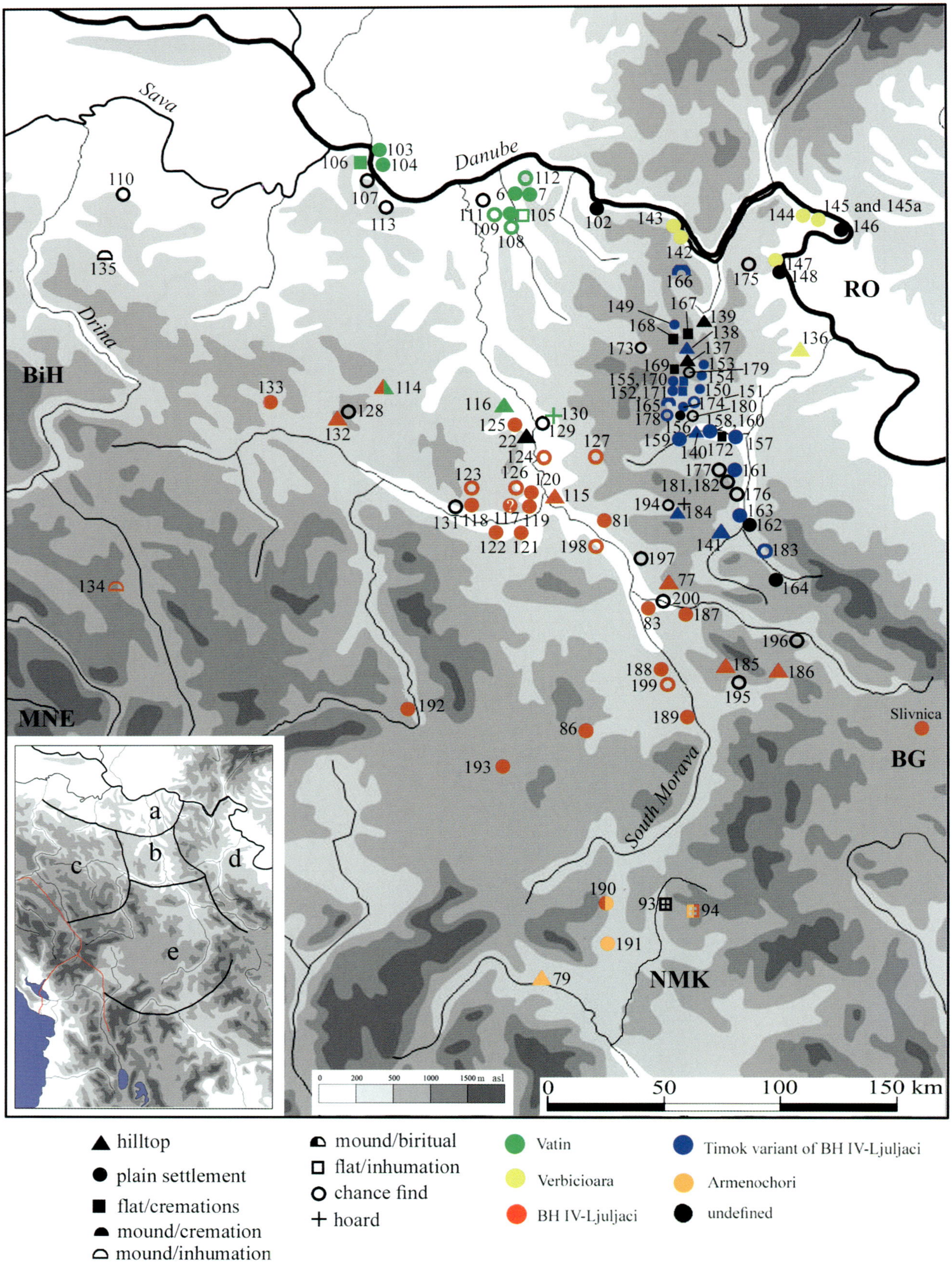
Sava
Danube
Drina
South Morava
BiH
MNE
RO
BG
NMK
Slivnica
a
b
c
d
e
0 200 500 1000 1500 m asl
0 50 100 150 km
hilltop
plain settlement
flat/cremations
mound/cremation
mound/inhumation
mound/biritual
flat/inhumation
chance find
hoard
Vatin
Verbicioara
BH IV-Ljuljaci
Timok variant of BH IV-Ljuljaci
Armenochori
undefined

Plate 19 (opposite). Middle Bronze Age sites in the central Balkans.

Peri-Pannonian zone: 102. Golubac, the site of Ušće Tumanske Reke; 103. Vojlovica, the site of Najeva Ciglana; 104. Omoljica, the site of Zlatica; 6. Drmno, the site of Nad Lugom; 105. Bratinac, Ciganško Brdo; 7. Majilovac, Marjansko Brdo; 106. Vinča, Belo Brdo; 107. Ritopek, unknown site; 108. Bratinac, unknown site; 109. Požarevac, Živinarska Farma; 110. Bela Reka, Popovača; 111. Petka, unknown site; 112. Kurjače, unknown site; 113. Begaljica, unknown site.

Basin of the Great Morava River with Šumadija: 114. Ljuljaci, Milića brdo; 115. Stalać, Gologlava; 116. Novo Lanište, Gradac; 22. Ostrikovac, Đula; 117. Marenovo, Đerđelin; 118. Stragari, Reka; 119. Šanac–Bošnjane, Skela–Kolarac; 120. Maskare, Bedem; 121. Kruševac, Lazarev Grad; 122. Globoder, Ivlje; 81. Rujište, Crnokalačka Bara; 123. Poljna, unknown site; 124. Paraćin, Gloždak; 125. Svetozarevo, Sarina međa; 126. Orašje, unknown site; 127. Lešje, Baba; 128. Borač, unknown site; 129. Dražmirovac, unknown site; 130. Trućevac, unknown site; 131. Medveđa, unknown site.

Western Serbia with Lim Valley: 132. Ostra, Sokolica; 133. Gornja Gorevnica, Slatina; 134. Jabuka, Savin lakat; 135. Brezjak, Paulje

Timok Region with Đerdap Gorge: 136. Mokranjske stene, Potkapina; 137. Bor, Čoka Kazak; 138. Bor, Čoka Njica; 139. Tanda, Mali Vizak; 140. Gamzigradska Banja, Banjska Stena; 141. Podvis, Bolvan; 142. Dobra, Padina; 143. Dobra, Gospođin Vir; 144. Kladovo, Donje Butorke; 145. Mala Vrbica, Livade; 145a. Mala Vrbica, Konopište; 146. Rtkovo, Glameja; 147. Brza Palanka, Obala Kod Crkve; 148. Brza Palanka, Egeta-Blok III; 149. Mali Krivelj, Valja Mare–Ciglana; 150. Banjsko Polje, Ružana; 151. Brestovačka Banja, Selište; 152. Brestovačka Banja, Hajdučka česma; 153. Čoka Kormaroš; 154. Bor, Kučajna; 155. Brestovačka Banja, Trnjane; 156. Brestovac, Dubrava; 157. Zvezdan, Njive na ulazu u Zvezdan; 158. Gamzigrad, Bazilika III; 159. Metovnica, Kot 1; 160. Gamzigrad, Potoci; 161. Grlište, Osenje, Na trasi gasovoda; 162. Knjaževac, Kadijski krst; 163. Knjaževac, Boševo-Tina; 164. Kalna, Bojčin; 165. Zlot, Zlotska pećina (Lazareva pećina); 166. Majdanpek, Kapetanova pećina; 167. Bor, Kriveljski Kamen; 168. Šoka lu Patran; 169. Brestovac, Borsko Jezero; 170. Brestovačka Banja, Trnjane; 171. Brestovačka Banja, Hajdučka Česma; 172. Zaječar, Magura; 173. Žagubica, Straža; 174. Brestovac, unknown site; 175. Urovica, Valja mare; 176. Koželj, unknown site; 177. Tromeđa Lenova, Leskovca and Gornje Bele Reke, Trasa gasovoda; 178. Podgorac, Strmljeno; 179. Bor, unknown site; 180. Džanovo polje, unknown site; 181. Gornja Bela Reka, Suvi Peć; 182. Gornja Bela Reka, Česma; 183. Kamenica, unknown site.

Southern Serbia with central Pčinja and the Kumanovo and Skopje Plains: 184. Sokobanja, Popovica; 77. Hum, Velika Humska Čuka; 185. Semče, Pusto Semče; 186. Gornje Krnjino, Česma–Provalija; 79. Skoplje, Kale; 83. Novo Selo, Bubanj; 187. Niš, Medijana; 188. Čekmin, Kučište; 189. Bobište, Izvorište–Sastanci; 190. Trnava, Trnavska Reka; 191. Lopate, Pribovce; 86. Štulac, Svinjarička Čuka; 192. Karagač, Valač; 193. Donja Brnjica; 94. Kokino Selo, Tatikev Kamen; 93. Pelince, Dve Mogili; 194. Sokobanja, unknown site; 195. Štrbovac, Čuka; 196. Staničenje, unknown site; 197. Lipovac, Lipovački Grad; 198. Vitkovac, unknown site; 199. Kaštavar, Groblje Novo; 200. Niš area, unknown site.

Inset: a. peri-Pannonian zone; b. Basin of the Great Morava River with Šumadija; c. Western Serbia with Lim Valley; d. Timok Region with Đerdap Gorge; e. Southern Serbia with central Pčinja and the Kumanovo and Skopje Plains.

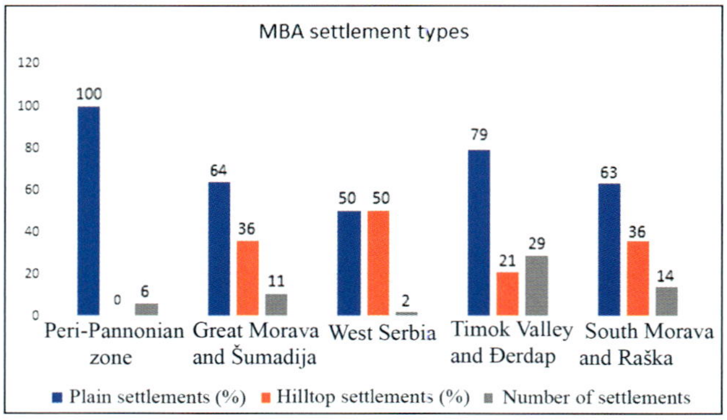

Plate 20. Types of Middle Bronze Age settlements.

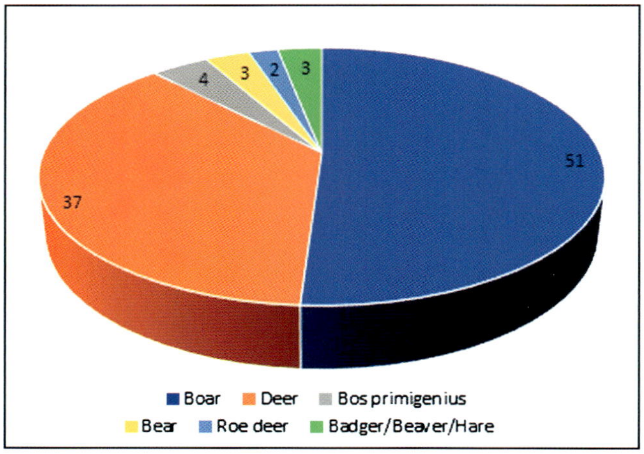

Plate 23. Ljuljaci, site of Milića Brdo: utilisation of wild animals (based on Greenfield 2006).

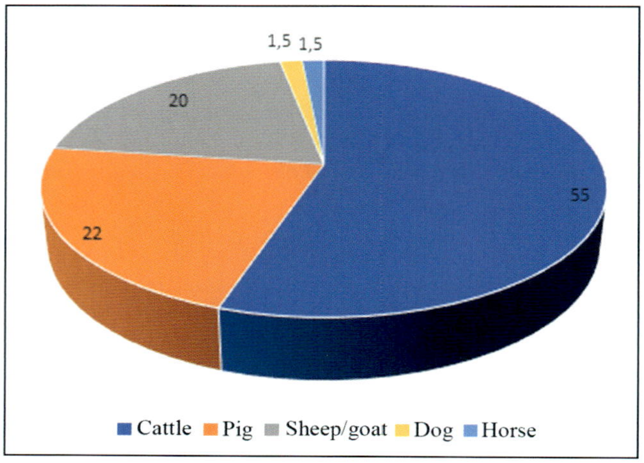

Plate 21. Cigansko Brdo site: structure 10a, utilisation of animal species (courtesy of D. Grujić).

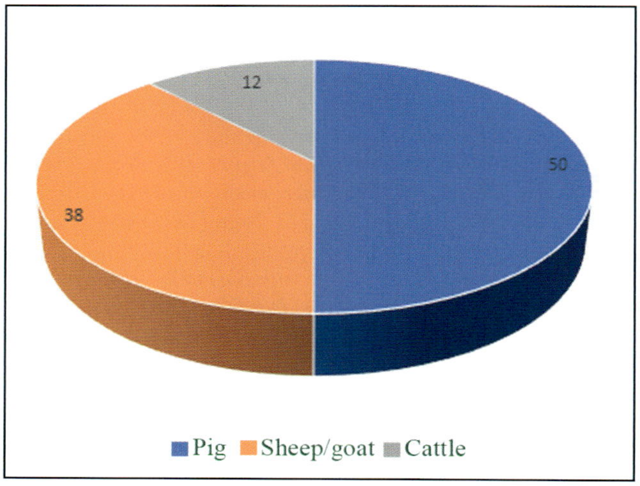

Plate 24. Svinjarička Čuka site: structure 1055, utilisation of animal species (courtesy of J. Bulatović).

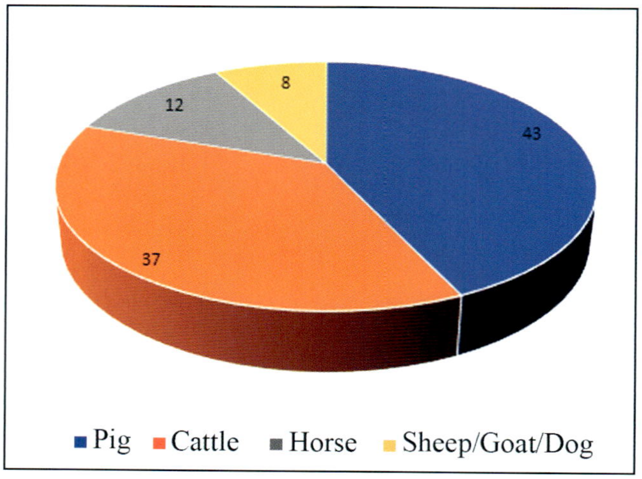

Plate 22. Ljuljaci, site of Milića Brdo: utilisation of domestic animals (based on Greenfield 2006).

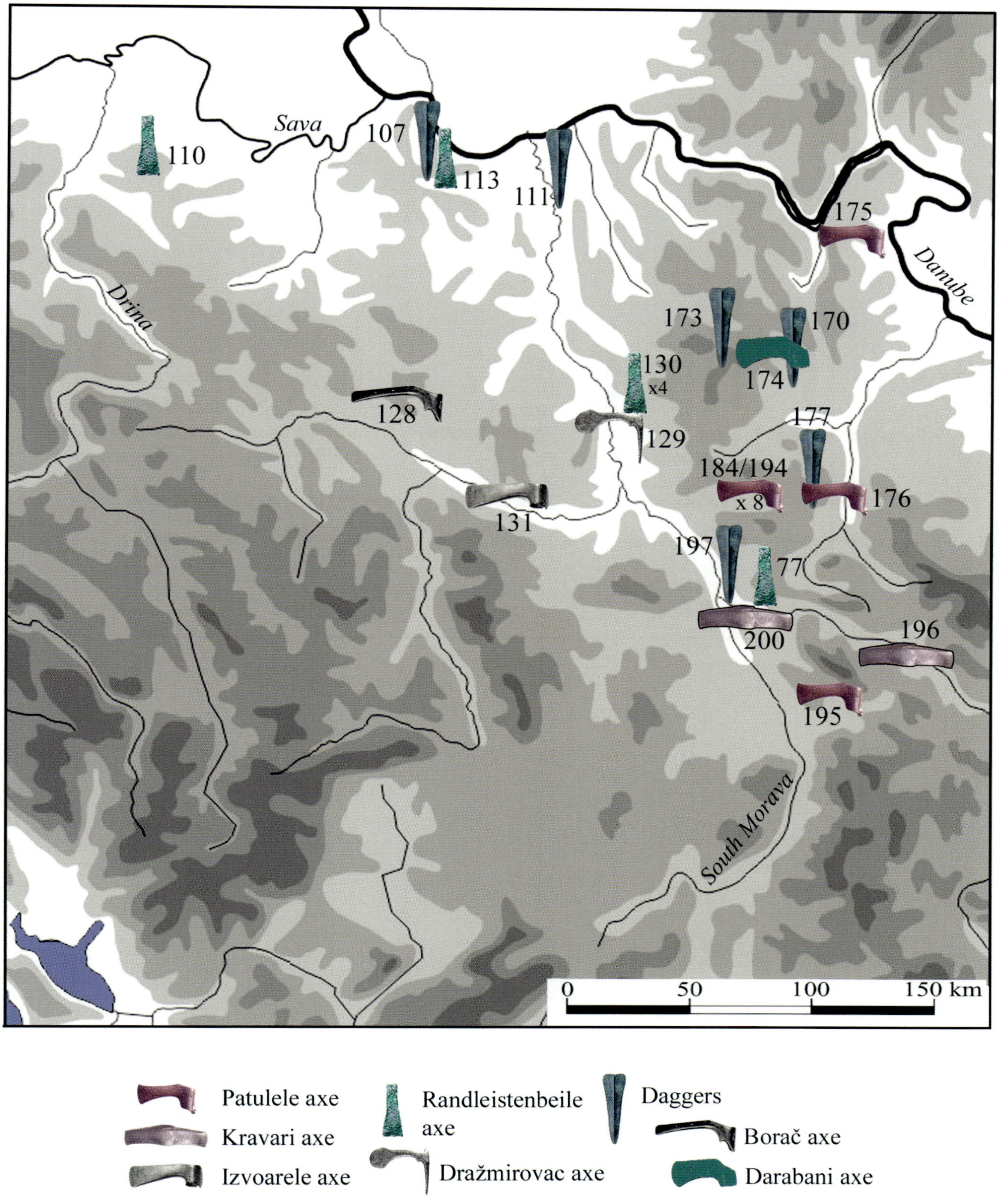

Plate 25. Distribution of Middle Bronze Age metal finds in the central Balkans.

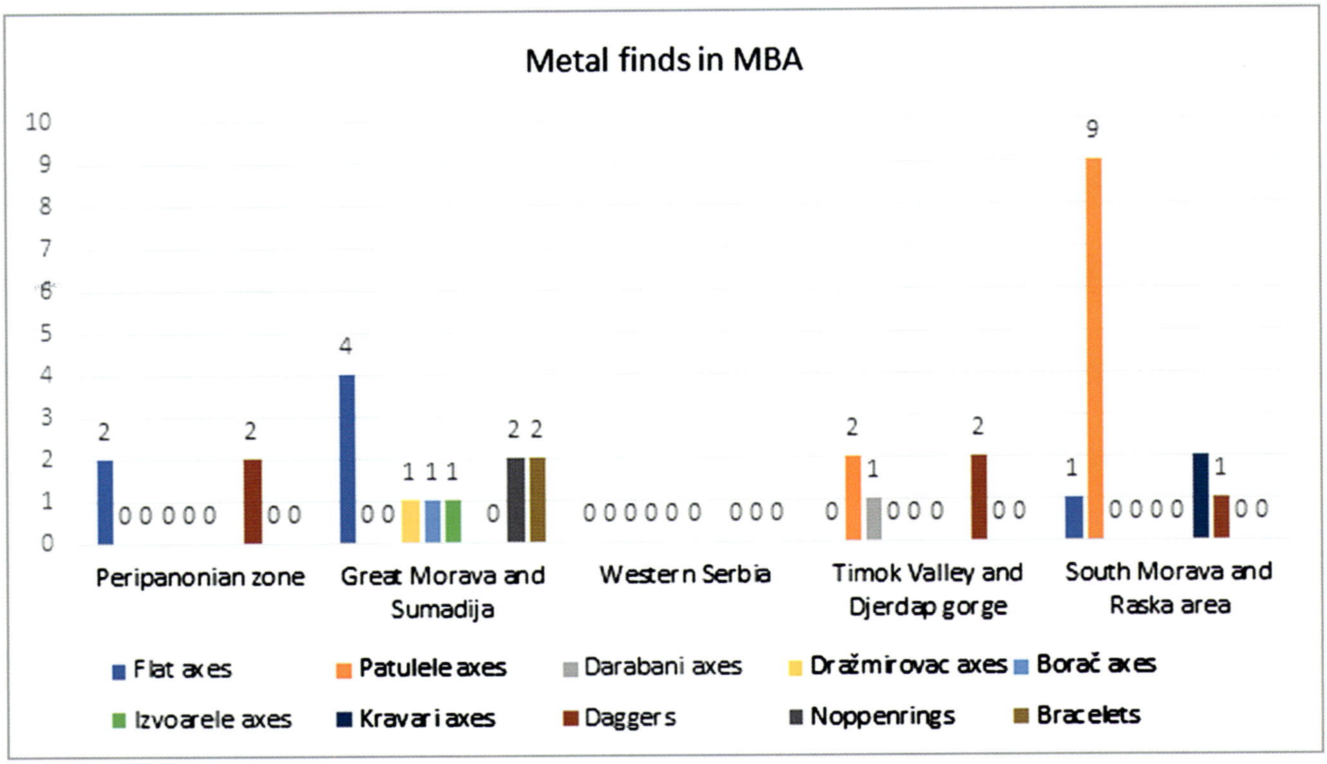

Plate 26. Middle Bronze Age metal finds in the central Balkans

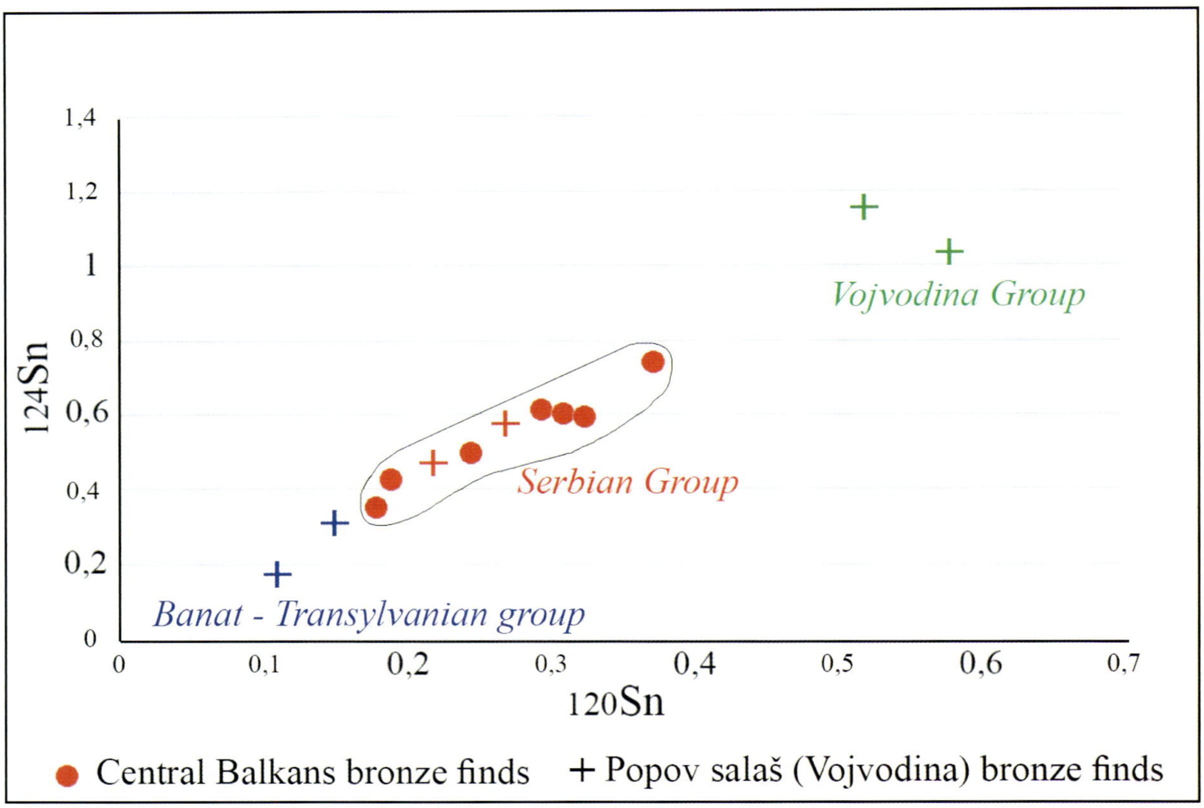

Plate 27. Tin isotopes of bronze artefacts from the central Balkans and the site of Popov Salaš in Vojvodina.

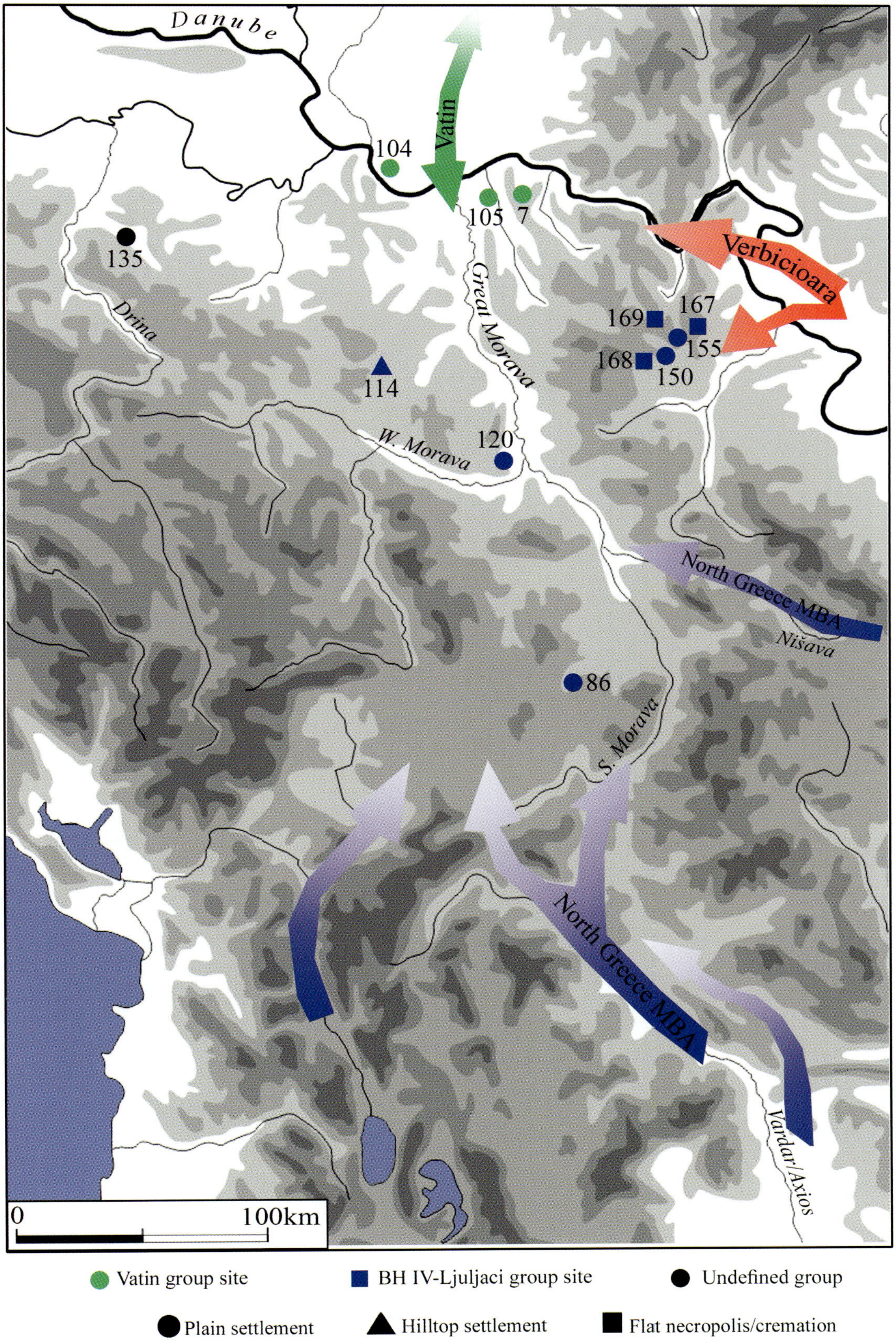

Plate 28. Cultural transmission of communities in the central Balkans and surroundings c. *1900–1600 cal BC.*

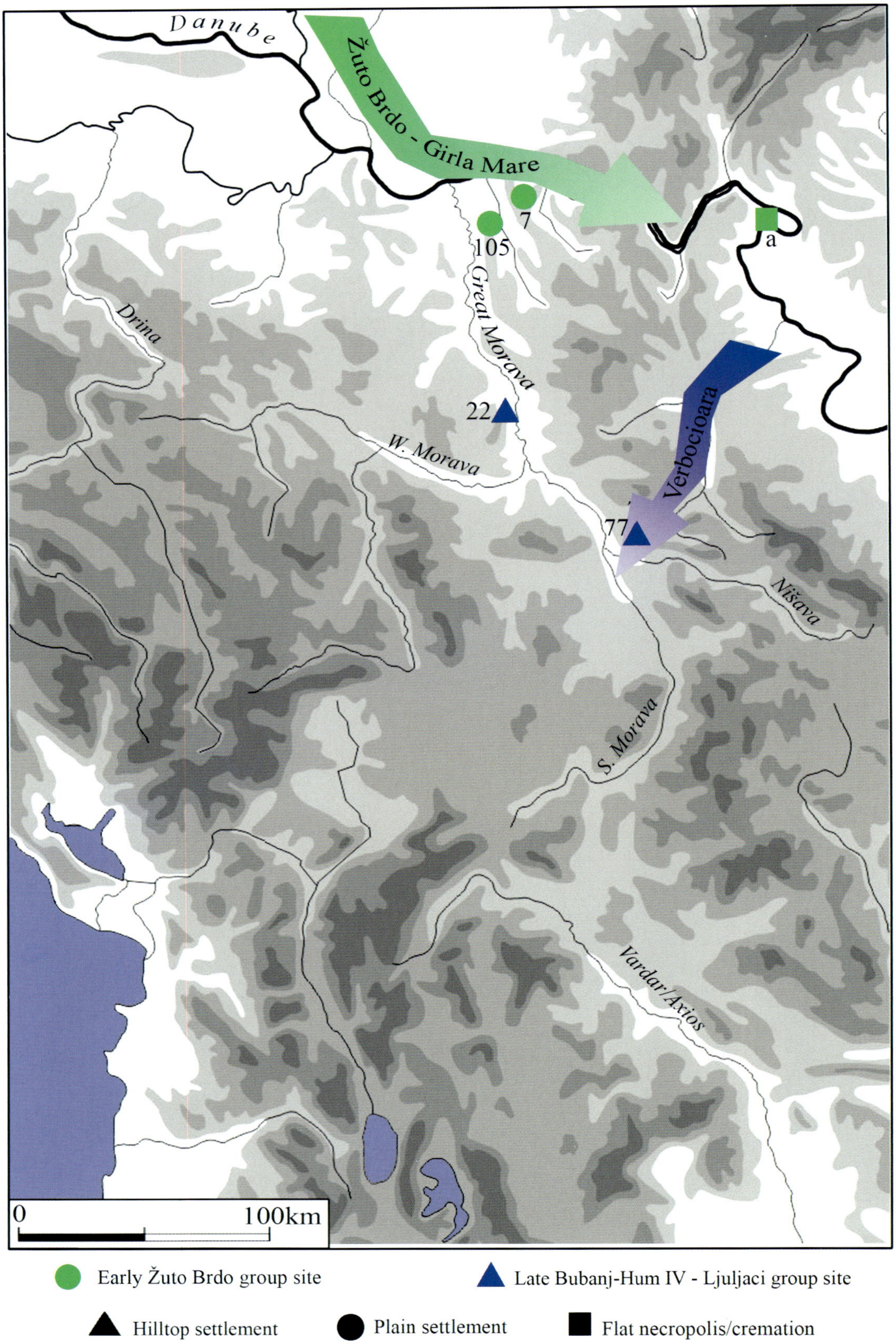

Plate 29. Cultural transmission of communities in the central Balkans and surroundings c. *1600–1550/1500 cal BC.*

3

The Middle Bronze Age

Following the Early Bronze Age, at the end of the 3rd and the beginning of the 2nd millennium BC, there was a stagnation in the previously intensive cultural interactions and development of cultural dynamics which became remarkably similar across nearly the entire territory of the central Balkans, with the exception of its far southern regions. This period, which would last approximately until the mid-2nd millennium, is referred to as the Middle Bronze Age.

3.1 The Peri-Pannonian zone

The geographical characteristics of this zone, as well as its natural resources and suitability for settlement, have already been discussed Chapter 2.

3.1.1 Settlement and dwelling

No hilltop settlements have been recorded in this zone but six settlements were identified in the flat terrain that predominates here. Site numbers refer to Plate 19.

List of settlements

6. The site of Nad Lugom in Drmno near Kostolac (Stojić and Jacanović 2008, 93–98, pl. xvii); 7. The site of Marjansko Brdo in Majilovac near Veliko Gradište;[1] 102. The site of Ušće Tumanske reke, Radoševac near Golubac (Stojić and Jacanović 2008, 122); 103. The site of Najeva Ciglana in Vojlovica near Pančevo (Radojčić 2013); 104. The site of Zlatica in Omoljica near Pančevo (Radojčić 2013); 105. The site of Cigansko Brdo in Bratinac near Požarevac;[2] 106. The site of Belo Brdo in Vinča (Tasić 1983, 61).

All recorded settlements in this zone are of the lowland type, situated on river terraces of the Danube at slightly higher elevations than in the previous period, between 70 m and 170 m, most commonly 75–80 m above sea level. The Tuman River confluence is located on the alluvial plain where the Tuman River flows into the Danube, at about 70 m above sea level, while Belo Brdo, Najeva Ciglana, Zlatica, Nad Lugom, and Cigansko Brdo are situated at the transition from alluvium to the river terrace of the Danube or Mlava, at altitudes between 75 m and 80 m. Only the Marjansko Brdo site is at a somewhat higher altitude, on a broad colluvial terrace above a larger natural depression, at about 170 m above sea level.

Unfortunately, architectural remains are preserved only at the Zlatica and Cigansko Brdo sites. At Zlatica, three above-ground houses, seven pits filled with pottery, and three storage pits were documented (Radojčić 2013, 8). However, limited information is available from these excavations; we know only that the houses lay at a relative depth of around 0.8 m, were rectangular in shape, and constructed using the wattle and daub technique. The floor was made of compacted earth, 20 cm thick, coated with a reddish layer, with traces of soot. One of the pits indicates the possible presence of a dugout dwelling at the site, while the others were smaller, filled with pottery, animal bones, soot, ash, and pebbles.

At Cigansko Brdo, a larger, irregularly shaped dugout dwelling with a reconstructed length of about 7.5 m and a width of about 5.5 m was excavated, consisting of a larger central oval depression and several smaller ones along the edges. The dugout contained remnants of carbonised wood, a significant amount of soot, animal bones, and pottery. Small and large bronze fragments (and/or copper ore?), slag, and several small fragments of bronze artefacts were found throughout the dugout, with the largest concentration in the western depression. Larger fragments of plaster were found and, in the north-western depression, remains of a stove base and a large covering slab were documented. Remnants of a stove, in the form of semi-spherical fragments, were recorded in the north-eastern depression, although the full dimensions of this stove were not determined, as it extended into the northern profile of the trench. In this part of the dugout, where the stove was located, daub and pottery with intense burning traces were noted. The dugout is dated to the 19th–18th centuries BC, with a cultural layer from the Late Bronze Age, specifically the Žuto Brdo-Girla Mare cultural group, dating to the 16th century BC, situated above it (see Table 1).

Despite extensive research in the surrounding area, no other residential structures from this period were discovered. A single grave was found, approximately 45 m west of the dugout dwelling, containing the remains of an individual in a crouched position, dating almost contemporaneously with the dugout.

At the well-known Neolithic site of Vinča–Belo Brdo near Belgrade, closed contexts, mostly pits, were identified that belong to the Middle Bronze Age Vatin group. Unfortunately, detailed information on the fill of these pits is lacking except that one of them was identified as a cremation grave.

During rescue excavations at the Marjansko Brdo site near Veliko Gradište in 2023, no remains of residential structures from the Middle Bronze Age were discovered but several smaller circular or oval pits, measuring 1.5–2.0 m in diameter/length and up to 1 m deep, were found. These were filled with pottery, soot, animal bones, daub, and similar materials. In structure 11, measuring 1.5 × 1.2 m and about 1 m deep, alongside burned pottery, daub, animal bones, and carbonised wood, parts of spindle whorls (Fig. 3.7/19, 20), a star-shaped fired clay object (Fig. 3.7/18), a lamp/altar with five receptacles (Fig. 3.7/16), slag fragments, and part of a bi-faced stone mould (Fig. 3.7/17) were discovered. This structure might represent a pit with a 'special', possibly ritual purpose related to metallurgy or a refuse pit for a household or metallurgical workshop, although in the latter case more metallurgical waste would likely be expected.

3.1.2 Necropolises and burial practices

Only two single graves from the Middle Bronze Age have been found in this geographical zone.

List of single graves

104. Omoljica, the site of Zlatica; 105. Bratinac, the site of Cigansko Brdo site (Tasić 1983, 61); 106. Vinča, the site of Belo Brdo site (Vasić 1936a, 137; 1936b, 129; Jovanović 1961, 9–10; Tasić 1984, 76).

During excavations at the Zlatica site in Omoljica between the two World Wars, a grave containing a body in a crouched position was discovered, suggesting the possible existence of a necropolis from the settlement period, i.e., the Middle Bronze Age (Radojčić 2013, 7, 8).

During rescue excavations in 2023 at the Cigansko Brdo site in Bratinac near Požarevac, a single grave was documented about 45 m east of the Vatin dugout dwelling discussed above. The grave contained an inhumed individual in a crouched position on their left side, oriented north–south (head to the north), with hands positioned beneath the head. A stone was placed on the skull and dark soil with a certain concentration of soot, more intense around the skeleton, was observed around the remains. Burn marks were evident on the pelvic bones and vertebrae. The burial pit is oval, measuring 1.62 × 0.9 m, with a depth of approximately 0.9 m. Large fragments of two vessels were found in the fill of the pit, one of which was reconstructed (Fig. 3.6/1), along with a grinding stone palette.[3] The grave is dated to the 19th/18th century cal BC, with minimal differences in BP dates between the dugout dwelling and this grave (Fig. 4.1).

One of the pits identified at the Belo Brdo site in Vinča, near Belgrade, has been defined as that of a cremated individual (Vasić 1936a, 137; Jovanović 1961, 9, 10). It consisted of a stone grave structure with an urn containing ashes and eight smaller vessels (Vasić 1936b, 129). However, only five artefacts from this grave have been published and M. Vasić mentions other similar structures that were destroyed by agricultural activities (Vasić 1936b, 129).

3.1.3 Portable finds

3.1.3.1 Pottery

The most numerous portable finds are, of course, fragments of vessels made from fired clay, which will therefore be the primary focus here. Understandably, it was not possible to present all ceramic finds in this book, especially from sites that were extensively excavated. Thus, we have represented the types of pottery in approximate proportion to their occurrence at each site, providing a reasonably reliable impression of the percentage distribution of individual types and sub-types of vessels at each site, as well as in relation to other sites in this zone. Information on texture, surface quality, and colour of the vessels is presented inconsistently, depending on the quality of data available in the literature and, for some sites, these details are entirely lacking.

A. BOWLS

The most common types of bowls in this zone are types 2a (Fig. 3.1/3; Fig. 3.2/7; Fig. 3.4/7), 3a (Fig. 3.4/6; Fig. 3.5/16), and 3e (Fig. 3.1/1, 4; Fig. 3.6/2, 5), which together comprise 70% of bowls. Less well represented are types 1a (Fig. 3.1/2; Fig. 3.5/1; Fig. 3.6/3, 6), 1b (Fig. 3.1/18; Fig. 3.2/11; Fig. 3.6/4), and 1c (Fig. 3.1/17). Unlike in the Early Bronze Age in this zone, when types 1a and 1b were predominant, these types are now less common, while types 2a and 3a, previously present but less frequent, now dominate. A new type not documented in the Early Bronze Age, appearing in the Middle Bronze Age, is type 3e – a mostly semi-circular bowl with a triangularly

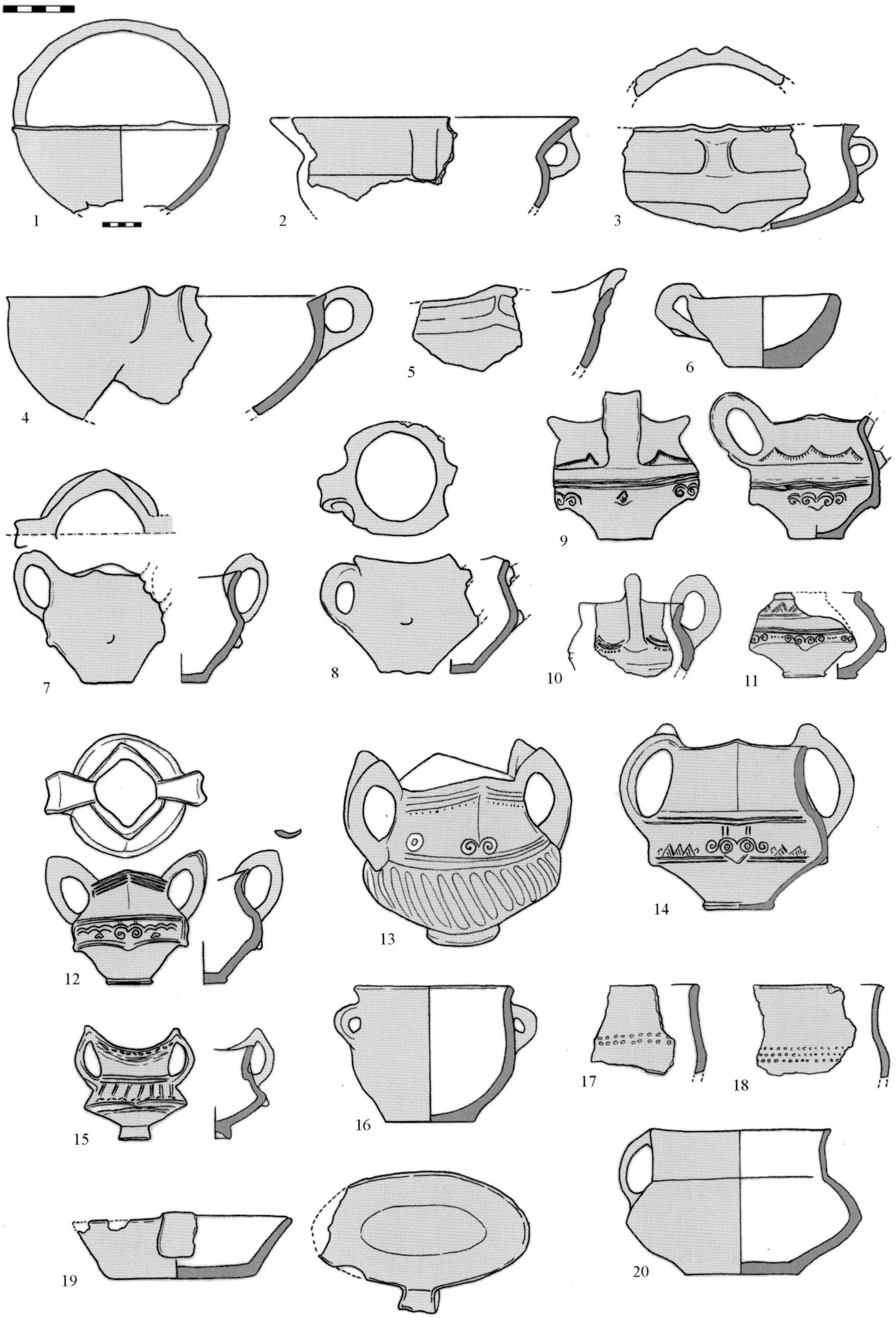

Figure 3.1. Omoljica: site of Zlatica.

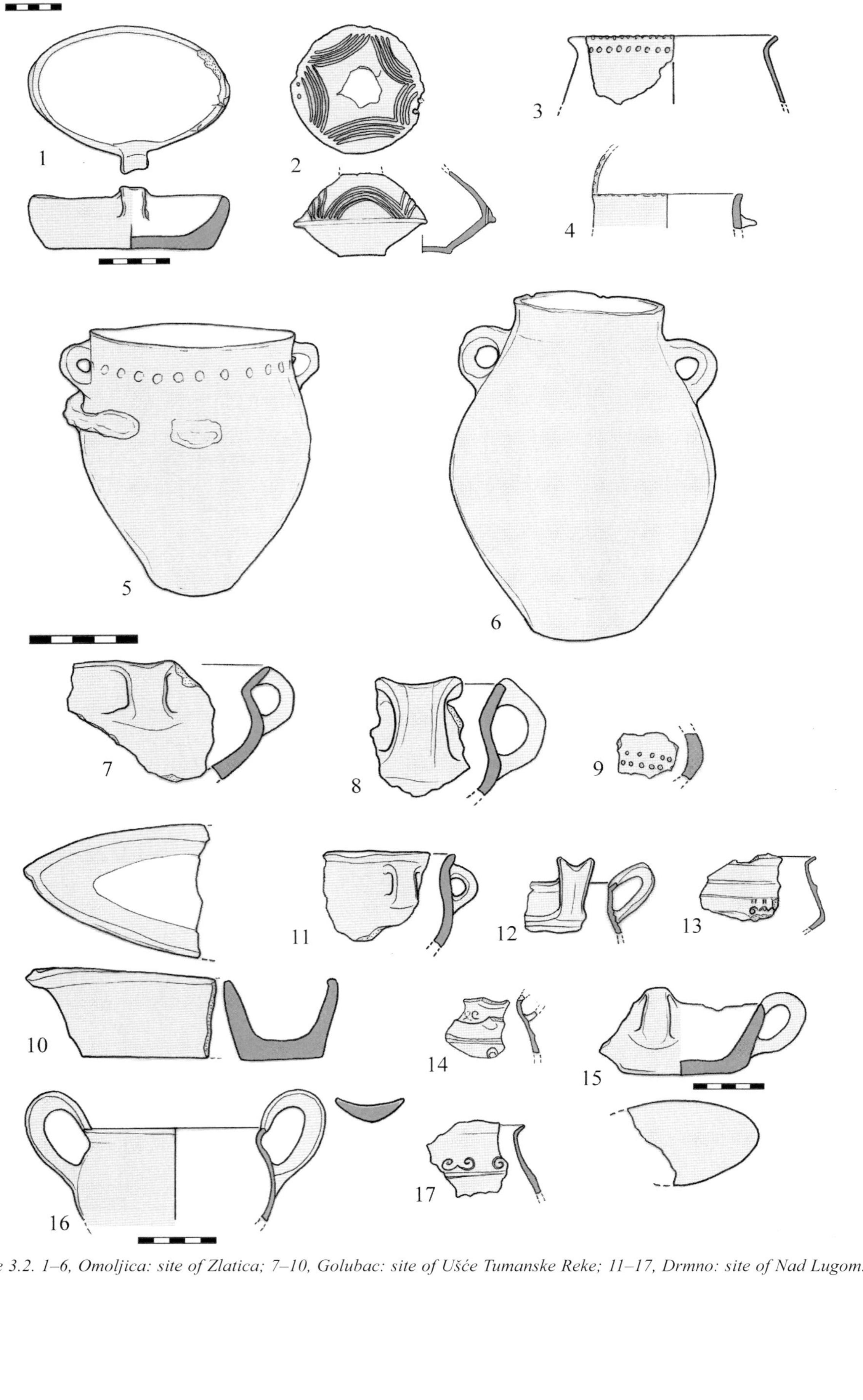

Figure 3.2. 1–6, Omoljica: site of Zlatica; 7–10, Golubac: site of Ušće Tumanske Reke; 11–17, Drmno: site of Nad Lugom.

Figure 3.3. Vojlovica: site of Najeva Ciglana.

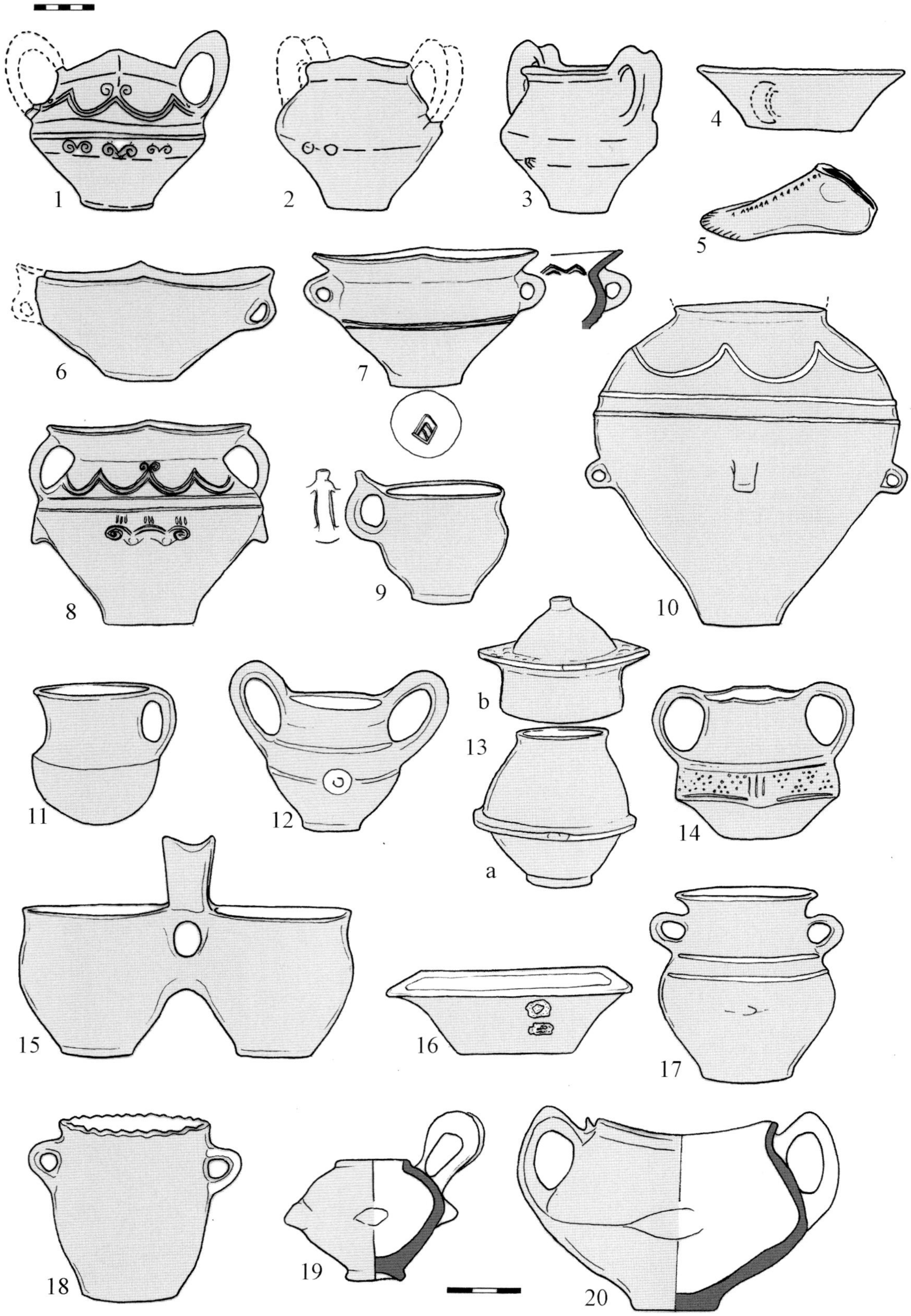

Figure 3.4. 1–5, Vinča: site of Belo Brdo, a grave of cremated individual; 6–18, Vinča: site of Belo Brdo, cultural layer; 19, Bratinac-Mlava, unknow site; 20, Požarevac, site of Živinarska Farma.

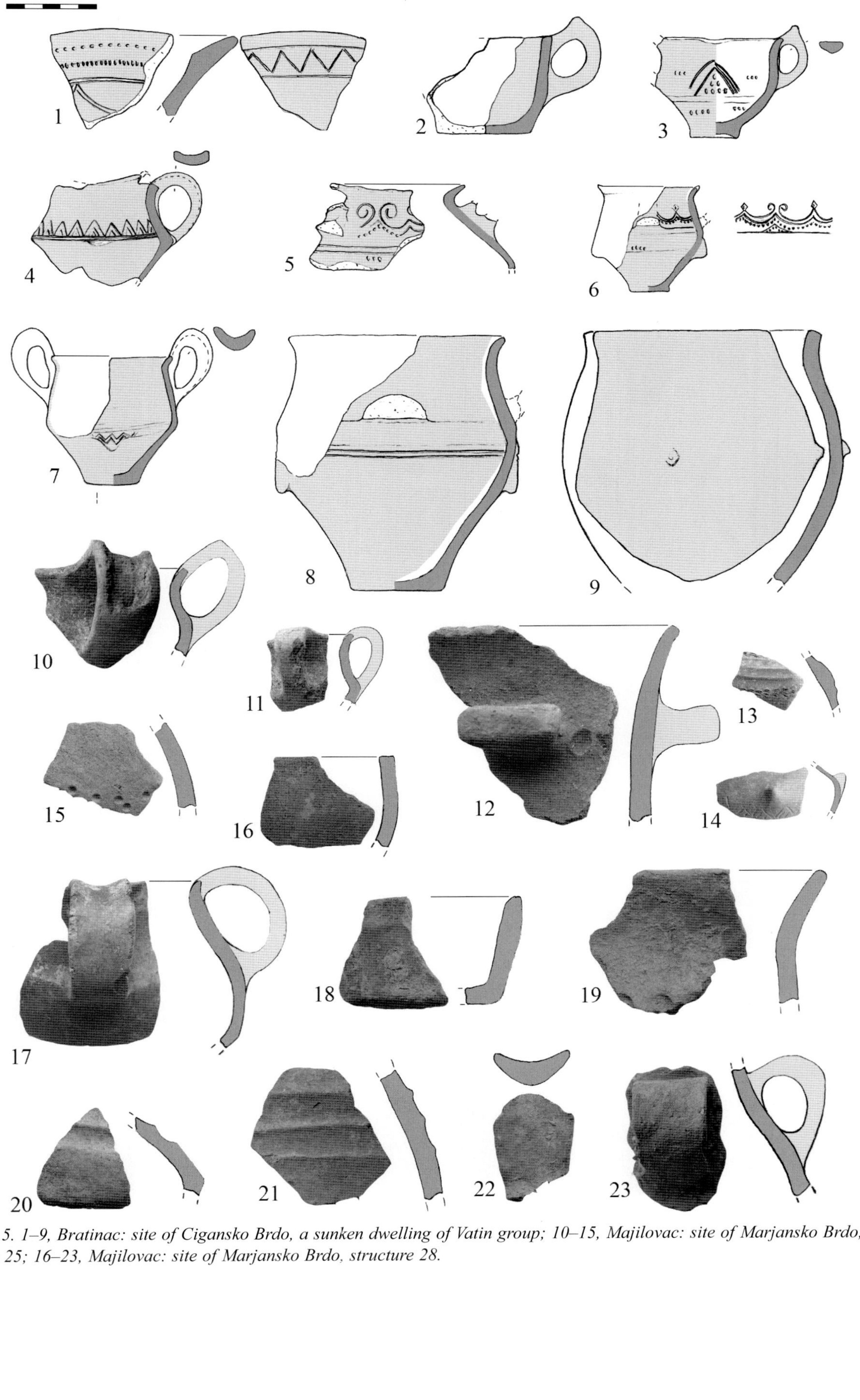
1 2 3 4 5 6 7 8 9 10 11 12 13 14 15 16 17 18 19 20 21 22 23

Figure 3.5. 1–9, Bratinac: site of Cigansko Brdo, a sunken dwelling of Vatin group; 10–15, Majilovac: site of Marjansko Brdo, block 3, structure 25; 16–23, Majilovac: site of Marjansko Brdo, structure 28.

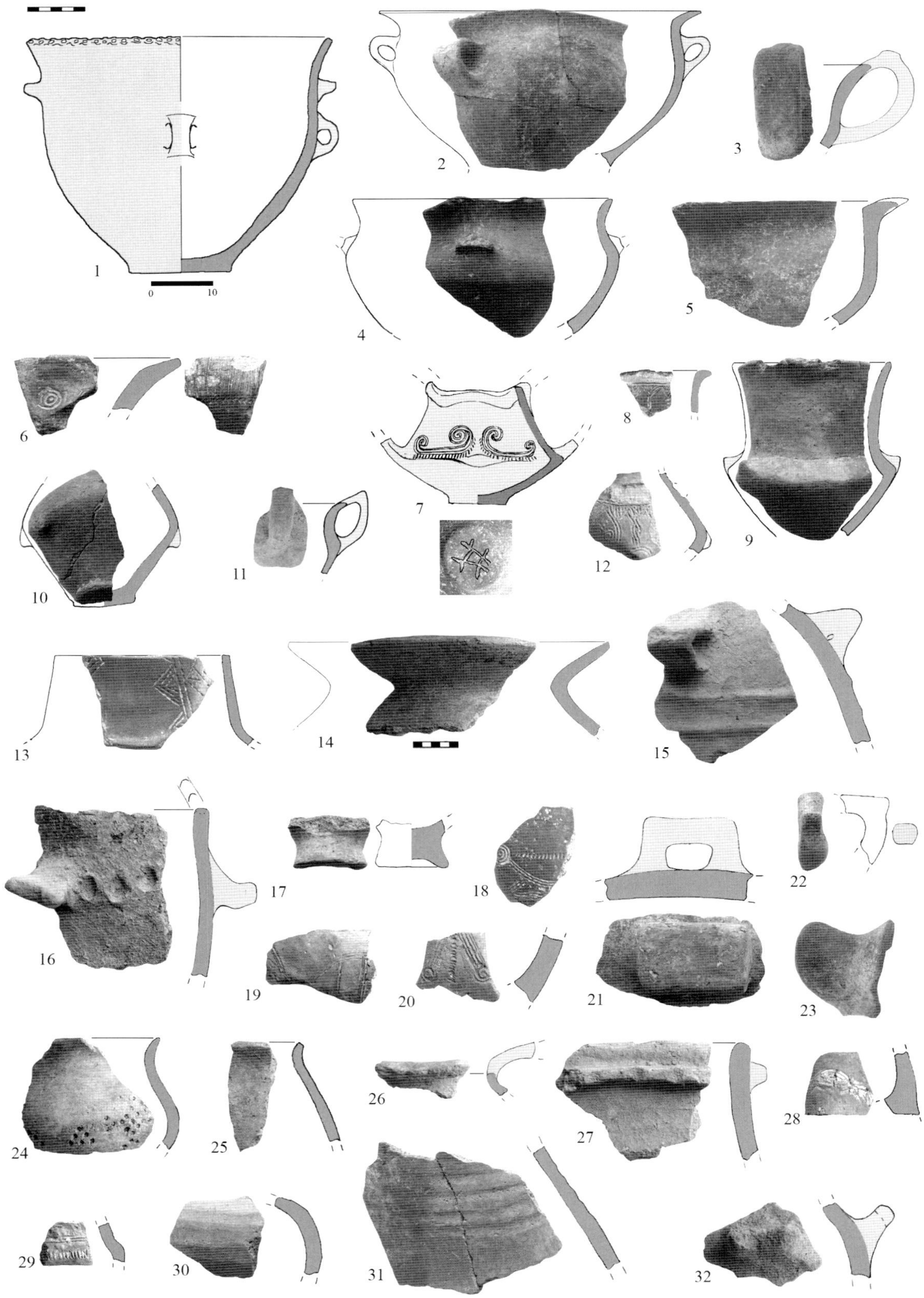

Figure 3.6. 1, Bratinac: site of Cigansko Brdo, grave 5; 2–32, Majilovac: site of Marjansko Brdo, 2–23,, structure 11; 24–32, structure 35 (the west part).

profiled rim, often sharply thickened on the inner side. This type is sporadically documented in the Middle Bronze Age across other central Balkan regions but is most abundant in Timok Valley.

The bowls are mostly undecorated with the exception of two examples of type 3e, which are decorated on both sides: one with incised zigzag, arched, and horizontal lines, sequences of notches, and dot punctures (Fig. 3.5/1), and the other with long vertical parallel incised lines bordered by rows of angular impressions and concentric circles (Fig. 3.6/6).

In Vinča, the bowls are fired in shades of grey-black and, more commonly, dark brown, with a polished, glossy surface (Vasić 1936a, 132). In Omoljica, bowls are finely crafted, typically fired in grey and brown hues, and most have a polished surface (Radojčić 2013, 37, 38). A similar situation is observed at Najeva Ciglana, where bowls are made in both fine and coarse textures in yellow-brown, grey, or grey-brown tones (Radojčić 2013, 63). The bowl from the Cigansko Brdo dugout dwelling is ochre-black and polished to a sheen. The bowls from Marjansko Brdo are fired in brown, grey, and reddish hues, with an external surface that is smoothed or polished.

B. Cups

In this zone during the Middle Bronze Age, cup types labelled 2b and 4b appear. While type 4b, known from the previous period, is predominant (three examples), type 2b appears in only one instance and is described in more detail in the section on special-purpose vessels, below.

Type 4b is documented at Vinča, Najeva Ciglana and Cigansko Brdo, with all examples featuring arched handles that extend above the vessel's opening and have a plastic extension on top (Fig. 3.3/2, Fig. 3.4/9, Fig. 3.5/2).

A conically profiled cup with a handle that rises above the vessel's opening, designated as type 5, appears for the first time (Fig. 3.3/3). This type will become characteristic of the following Late Bronze Age.

All recorded cups are undecorated. At Zlatica in Omoljica, the cups are mostly finely crafted, fired in shades of brown, grey, and red. The exception is thicker-walled cups (Fig. 3.1/6) of coarse texture, in yellow-brown or dark brown-grey (Radojčić 2013, 31, 32. This vessel is described below under Special purpose vessels At the Najeva Ciglana, the cups are mostly finely crafted, fired in grey (63%), brown (10%), or black (27%) shades (Radojčić 2013, 57–61) while that from Cigansko Brdo is fired in dark red-ochre-grey shades with a polished surface.

C. Beakers

The most prevalent types of beakers in the Middle Bronze Age in the peri-Pannonian zone are types 1f (Fig. 3.1/7, 8, 10; Fig. 3.2/12–14, 17; Fig. 3.3/9; Fig. 3.4/12; Fig. 3.5/11; Fig. 3.6/25), characterised by a globular or biconical body with a short, flared rim, and 7d (a beaker with either a short or long neck, which may be funnel-shaped, conical, or cylindrical, and a low, broad, squat body: Fig. 3.1/9, 11–15; Fig. 3.2/2; Fig. 3.3/4, 11; Fig. 3.4/1–3, 8, 14; Fig. 3.5/5; Fig. 3.6/7, 12), which together comprise over 60%. These are followed in frequency by type 1a, making up about 12% (Fig. 3.3/8; Fig. 3.5/6–9; Fig. 3.6/10). Other types, 1b (Fig. 3.6/8), 1c (Fig. 3.5/17; Fig. 3.6/24, 26), 1e (Fig. 3.5/10; Fig. 3.6/11), 1g (Fig. 3.4/20), 2a (Fig. 3.2/8), 3a (Fig. 3.2/16; Fig. 3.3/9, 10; Fig. 3.4/19), and 5a (Fig. 3.5/3), collectively make up about 25%. A richly decorated beaker resembling type 4a, with a semi-circular body but a much lower hollow foot than in the previous period, is also recorded (Fig. 3.3/7).

It should be noted that types 1f and 7d were unknown in the Early Bronze Age and appear for the first time in this period, characterising the Middle Bronze Age in the central Balkans, particularly the periPannonian zone and Timok Valley.

Beakers exhibit a variety of decoration techniques and motifs. Incising predominates, including arched, horizontal, or vertical lines that often terminate in spiral shapes (Fig. 3.1/9–11, 12, 14, 15; Fig. 3.2/2, 13, 14, 17; Fig. 3.3/4–7, 10; Fig. 3.4/1, 8, 14; Fig. 3.5/1, 3–6; Fig. 3.6/7, 12, 28). Other motifs include incised hatching (Fig. 3.1/14; Fig. 3.5/14), inscribed triangles (Fig. 3.5/4; Fig. 3.6/8, 13), and zigzag lines (Fig. 3.5/1, 7; Fig. 3.6/6, 28). Additionally, punctuated decorations appear, consisting of rows of small indentations that sometimes follow incised lines (Fig. 3.1/9–11, 13; Fig. 3.2/2, 9; Fig. 3.3/6, 10; Fig. 3.4/14; Fig. 3.5/1, 3, 5, 6; Fig. 3.6/24), as well as diagonal or horizontal grooves (Fig. 3.1/13; Fig. 3.2/13; Fig. 3.3/10; Fig. 3.4/1, 13, 20, 21; Fig. 3.6/15, 30, 31). This period and peri-Pannonian zone are notable for horn-shaped plastic extensions, usually oriented downward, predominantly found on the bodies of beakers and, less frequently, bowls (Fig. 3.1/3, 7–9, 11, 12, 14, 15; Fig. 3.2/2; Fig. 3.3/7, 6, 8, 10, 11; Fig. 3.4/2, 3, 8, 12, 14, 17, 19, 20; Fig. 3.5/4, 6–9, 14; Fig. 3.6/9, 10). Another novelty characteristic of the transitional zone for the Middle Bronze Age is the concave-profiled arched handles, or *ansa lunata* handles, on beakers (Fig. 3.1/12, 13; Fig. 3.2/8, 12, 16; Fig. 3.3/10; Fig. 3.4/1, 3, 19, 20; Fig. 3.5/4, 7, 10, 17, 22; Fig. 3.6/23), with concentric circles also appearing sporadically (Fig. 3.6/6, 18, 20).

It is interesting that ornamentation is most prevalent on beaker types unknown in the previous period, 1f and 7d, and consists mainly of incised straight lines or garland and spiral forms, often combined with rows of dot punctures. One example of type 7d is decorated with broad diagonal grooves on the body (Fig. 3.1/13). Other decorated types include 1a and 1g, primarily with straight and zigzag incised lines. Beaker type 4a is similarly decorated with horizontal lines and garlands, bordered by rows of short, obliquely incised lines (Fig. 3.3/7).

Regarding the texture and surface treatment of these vessels, M. Vasić describes so-called Pannonian pottery – defined at that time as Middle Bronze Age pottery from Vinča – as having a polished glossy surface, coated with clay suspended in water, showing the influence of metal vessels (Vasić 1936a, 137; 1936b, 119). The beakers are predominantly fired in black, although there are also examples fired in grey tones (Vasić 1936b, 120, 121).

In Omoljica, the beakers are mostly finely crafted, with one-third having a polished surface. They are fired in shades of brown (25%), grey (31%), or combinations of these (25%), with the remaining examples being black with a polished surface (Radojčić 2013, 15–25). Similarly, at Najeva Ciglana, most beakers are finely crafted, except for one coarsely crafted example, fired in grey-black (Radojčić 2013, 44–54). Finely crafted beakers frequently have a polished surface and are fired in grey (34%), brown (18%), black (31%), or combinations of these colours. Beakers from the Cigansko Brdo dugout dwelling are finely crafted, mostly black, and sometimes dark red-ochre in colour, with a polished or burnished surface. Beakers from Marjansko Brdo have smoothed (59%) or polished (42%) surfaces and are fired in shades of grey (65%), reddish (24%), or black (11%).

D. AMPHORAE

Amphorae are not recorded in large numbers in the peri-Pannonian zone during the Middle Bronze Age. A total of eight amphorae have been documented, six of which belong to type 1a, while the specimen from Cigansko Brdo belongs to type 3a (Fig. 3.6/1), and the amphora from Marjansko Brdo to type 3b. Amphorae in this zone are either undecorated or feature a sharply profiled horizontal rib around the entire body at belly height (Fig. 3.3/15; Fig. 3.4/13a) or horizontal plastic ribs with a semi-circular profile (Fig. 3.4/17). The vessel fragment from Marjansko Brdo, believed to be a type 1a amphora, is decorated with a horizontal row of fingertip impressions (Fig. 3.5/12), while the specimen from the grave at Cigansko Brdo has a row of fingertip impressions along the rim (Fig. 3.6/1). New to this period are type 3b amphorae with longer funnel-shaped necks (Fig. 3.6/14) and amphorae with wider, sharply profiled horizontal ribs on the belly, frequently found in Middle Bronze Age sites in southern Pannonia.

The amphora from Najeva Ciglana is finely crafted and fired in black (Radojčić 2013, 56). Amphorae from Marjansko Brdo have mostly smoothed (75%) or polished surfaces (25%) and are all fired in shades of grey.

E. JUGS

Jugs are even rarer in the Middle Bronze Age than in the previous period, not only in the peri-Pannonian zone but across the central Balkans. Three specimens have been recorded in Omoljica, Najeva Ciglana, and Vinča, with forms slightly different from types 1a and 2a of the previous period. These have been categorised as type 3a (Omoljica), type 2c (Najeva Ciglana), and type 4a (Vinča). The jug from Omoljica has a broader body, sharper profiling, and a squatter shape (Fig. 3.1/20), while the specimen from Vinča is taller, with a semi-circular profiled body and a longer, concavely profiled neck (Fig. 3.4/11). Type 4a resembles type 2a but is shorter with a more sharply profiled body. The jug from Najeva Ciglana has a long funnel-shaped neck and a low biconical body (Fig. 3.3/1). All jugs are undecorated.

The specimens from Omoljica are finely crafted, black with a polished coating, while those from Najeva Ciglana are also finely crafted, in grey-yellow or grey-black hues with a polished surface (Radojčić 2013, 36, 55).

F. POTS

Pots are larger vessels intended for cooking, and thus will not be extensively discussed. Due to their size, they are often preserved in fragments and are rarely restored, making it difficult to define different types. They are typically decorated with plastic bands featuring fingertip impressions or notches and have substantial tongue-shaped or rectangular handles (Fig. 3.2/3, 4; Fig. 3.3/12, 13; Fig. 3.4/18; Fig. 3.6/15, 26). A distinct type of pot is the one with a cooking pot also known as a *piraunos*. One such pot has been documented in Omoljica (Fig. 3.2/5). Most pots are of coarser texture with inclusions such as coarse sand or small pebbles.

G. SPECIAL-PURPOSE VESSELS

Special-purpose vessels include so-called fish-bowls (*Fischbute*), pouring spoons (ladles),[4] vessels with a rectangular base, strainers, double vessels, and so-called cinerary vessels. In the peri-Pannonian zone, the recorded special-purpose vessels consist of fish-bowls, pouring spoons, and double vessels.

Fish-bowls, shallow vessels with an oval base and typically one short arched handle with a ribbon-like cross-section, are very common in this zone, which somewhat confirms their designation as 'fish vessels'. They have primarily been recorded at sites along the Danube, such as Omoljica, Najeva Ciglana, Vinča, Drmno, and Golubac (Fig. 3.1/19; Fig. 3.2/1, 10, 15; Fig. 3.3/14; Fig. 3.4/4, 16), as well as Marjansko Brdo. Another example was found at Glameja in Đerdap, also along the Danube, while in the interior, during the Middle Bronze Age, these vessels are known only from Ljuljaci, Ostra, and Velika Humska Čuka, although the latter was found out of context so its chronological classification is uncertain (Bogdanović 1986, cat. no. 54; Stojić and Jocić 2006, T. CI/52). It should be noted that this type of vessel was not known in the Early Bronze Age, suggesting its appearance may be associated with the transitional geographic zone (peri-Pannonia), specifically the Danube area, during the Middle Bronze Age. At Vinča, these vessels are fired in grey-black, with either polished or coarse surfaces (Vasić 1936a, 121). In Omoljica, there are fine-textured examples fired in shades of brown, along with coarser ones in similar shades; a similar situation is seen at Najeva Ciglana, where they are either finely or coarsely crafted and fired in shades of grey (Radojčić 2013, 33–35, 62).

A ladle (or melting pot) was found at Zlatica; it is a semi-circular vessel resembling a type 1b cup from the Early Bronze Age, but with a significantly shallower body and much thicker walls, along with an arched handle extending above the vessel's opening (Fig. 3.1/6).

Among other special-purpose vessels, a double vessel was discovered in Vinča (Fig. 3.4/15), in grey-black with a polished, glossy surface (Vasić 1936b, 132). Double vessels were also recorded in the previous period in somewhat greater numbers than in the Middle Bronze Age.

An unusual item to mention here is a piece with five small, shallow connected receptacles made from fired clay, standing on four broken legs (Fig. 3.7/16). It is crafted from clay mixed with fine sand, with smoothed exterior walls. The purpose of this vessel is unclear, but it may have served as a lamp or a type of altar, similar to later *kernos* vessels. Similar items from this period have been found at sites in the Carpathian Basin (Bona 1975, pl. 261/2).

None of the three types of listed special-purpose vessels is decorated.

H. LIDS

In this zone, cylindrical lids with a circular base are characteristic of the Middle Bronze Age. These often feature a wide, sharply profiled plastic horizontal rib encircling the lid just above the opening. Such lids have been recorded at Najeva Ciglana (Fig. 3.3/16) and Vinča (Fig. 3.4/13b). The plastic rib of the lids is vertically perforated with eight smaller holes, grouped in pairs of four, likely serving to secure the lid to the vessel. The lids are undecorated.

The lid from Najeva Ciglana is finely crafted and black (Radojčić 2013, 65).

I. HANDLES

In this zone during the Middle Bronze Age, arched handles with a ribbon-like or oval cross-section are by far the most common. A new feature is the concave-profiled arched handles (*ansa lunata*), generally extending above the vessel opening on beaker types 1f and 7d (Fig. 3.1/12, 13; Fig. 3.2/12, 16; Fig. 3.4/1, 3, 15, 19, 20; Fig. 3.5/4, 7; Fig. 3.6/23, etc.). Shorter arched handles with various cross-sections also appear on bowls, typically below the rim, as well as on jugs, fish-bowls, pots, amphorae, and double vessels.

Tongue-shaped handles, sometimes with an indentation (Fig. 3.6/31), and rectangular handles are much less common, generally found on larger vessels such as pots and amphorae (Fig. 3.2/4; Fig. 3.3/12, 13, 15; Fig. 3.5/12; Fig. 3.6/1, 15, 20).

J. ORNAMENTATION

The predominant decoration techniques are incising and puncturing. Incised motifs primarily include garlands, as well as horizontal, arched, or vertical lines, which often end in spiral forms (Fig. 3.1/9–11, 12, 14, 15; Fig. 3.2/2, 13, 14, 17; Fig. 3.3/4–7, 10; Fig. 3.4/1, 8, 14; Fig. 3.5/1, 3–6; Fig. 3.6/6, 7, 12, 18–20). Other motifs include incised hatching or inscribed triangles and zigzag lines (Fig. 3.1/14; Fig. 3.5/1, 4, 7, 14; Fig. 3.6/5, 7, 12, 27).

Puncturing is achieved by pressing sequences of dot-like indentations, or less frequently notches, often following the incised lines (Fig. 3.1/9–11, 13, 17, 18; Fig. 3.2/2, 9; Fig. 3.3/6, 10; Fig. 3.4/14; Fig. 3.5/1, 3, 5, 6; Fig. 3.6/23), as well as diagonal or horizontal grooves (Fig. 3.1/13, 17; Fig. 3.2/13; Fig. 3.3/10; Fig. 3.4/1, 13, 20, 21; Fig. 3.5/1; Fig. 3.6/15, 29, 30). Notably, most of these decorations are found on beaker types that were not present in the Early Bronze Age (types 1f and 7d).

Among plastic decorations, a characteristic motif for this period is the horn-shaped plastic extension, usually pointing downward, mostly found on the belly of beakers, less frequently on bowls (Fig. 3.1/3, 7–9, 11, 12, 14, 15; Fig. 3.2/2; Fig. 3.3/7, 6, 8, 10, 11; Fig. 3.4/2, 3, 8, 12, 14, 17, 19, 20; Fig. 3.5/4, 6–9, 14; Fig. 3.6/8, 9). Wart-like appliqués on the belly of beakers are also very common, as are plastic extensions of various shapes on the handle tops or bowl rims (Fig. 3.1/5, 14; Fig. 3.3/2; Fig. 3.4/9; Fig. 3.5/2, 3; Fig. 3.6/3), which appear for the first time in this zone during this period. Another plastic decoration is the trapezoidal modelling of beaker openings documented in Omoljica, Vinča, Požarevac, and Bratinac, first appearing in the Middle Bronze Age (Fig. 3.1/8; Fig. 3.4/14, 20; Fig. 3.5/4) and representing one of the main cultural characteristics of this period.

Other sporadic decorations include sequences of hollowed indentations pressed directly onto the vessel wall or rim (Fig. 3.2/3, 5; Fig. 3.3/13; Fig. 3.5/12) or sequences of notches (Fig. 3.3/12; Fig. 3.6/7, 18, 20, 29), as well as concentric circles (Fig. 3.6/6, 18, 20) and double arched and vertical incised lines (Fig. 3.6/19), observed exclusively in the latest Middle Bronze Age structure at Marjansko Brdo (structure 11), dated to the 17th century BC, potentially hinting at the beginnings of the Žuto Brdo group, for which these decorations are characteristic.

3.1.3 Other finds

In addition to pottery and fired clay vessels, other portable finds have been uncovered in the peri-Pannonian zone, the most common being spindle whorls and clay weights, as well as a spoon. Metal artefacts such as an axe, daggers, and a stone mould for casting bronze objects have also been found.

List of sites with chance finds

107. Ritopek, unknown site, curved dagger (Fig. 3.7/14) (Vukmanović and Radojčić 1995, cat. no. 174); 108. Bratinac-Mlava, Požarevac, single-handled beaker (Fig. 3.4/19) (Stojić and Jacanović 2008, T. V/1); 109. Požarevac, the site of Živinarska Farma, two handled beaker with trapezoidal opening (Fig. 3.4/12) (Stojić and Jacanović 2008, T. LXXXVI/1); 110. Bela Reka, the site of Popovača, flat axe (Fig. 3.7/13) (Stojić and Cerović 2011, 63); 111. Petka near Požarevac, unknown site, dagger (Fig. 3.7/14) (Stojić and Jacanović 2008, Fig. 40); 112. Kurjače near Požarevac, unknown site, part of a beaker with an *ansa lunata* handle (Stojić and Jacanović 2008, T. LV/1); 113. Begaljica, unknown site, flat axe (Fig. 3.7/12) (Antonović 2014, 53).

The metal random finds include two axes and two daggers. These are flat axes with pronounced edges (*Randleistenbeile* type) from sites in Popovača in Bela Reka near Šabac and in Begaljica (Fig. 3.7/12, 13) (Stojić and Cerović 2011, 370). The axe from Begaljica is made of copper with traces of arsenic but no tin (Antonović 2014, 107 and table 1), while the axe from Popovača is made of tin bronze.[5] Tin isotopic analysis of this axe revealed a composition (δ^{124}Sn is 61 and δ^{120}Sn is 30), classifying it within the so-called Serbian group and indicating that the tin originated from Mount Cer (Mason *et al.* 2016, 115). This type of axes is mainly recorded in southern Pannonia and the peri-Pannonian zone in Serbia, though a cache with several bronze axes of this type was also found in Trućevac, in Great Morava Valley (Krstić *et al.* 1972, cat. no. 32). Notably, a tin bronze axe of this type was discovered in a closed context at the Velika Humska Čuka site near Niš (Fig. 3.49/12), currently the southernmost find of this axe type in the central Balkans.[6]

The curved dagger from Ritopek, resembling a knife in form, has two rivets at the top for securing the handle (Vukmanović and Radojčić 1995, cat. no. 174). Researchers have chronologically placed it at the end of the Early and beginning of the Middle Bronze Age, based on analogies by I. Kilian-Dilmeier (1975).

The double-edged dagger from Petka near Požarevac is similar to an example found during gas pipeline construction near Zaječar (Fig. 3.34/5) (Aleksić and Filipović 2020). This dagger has a thin blade with a pronounced central rib, an arched extension at the top of the riveting plate, and four perforations. This type resembles central European daggers from the end of the Early and Middle Bronze Age, originating from regions such as present-day Czech Republic, southern Germany, and France (Aleksić and Filipović 2020, 22, 23; Wels-Weyrauch 2015, 83–85, pl. 19–21, 49, 57). Analysis showed it is made of copper, without tin and with a very low arsenic content.[7]

A particularly significant find is part of a two-sided mould from a (waste/ritual?) pit at the Marjansko Brdo site. One side of the mould appears to hold impressions for several narrow, triangular, or rectangular cross-section objects (chisels, awls?) (Fig. 3.7/17), while the other side likely corresponds to a *Randleistenbeile* type flat axe. The mould's association with metallurgical activities at the site is supported by pieces of slag found in the same pit.

Among other finds from the excavated sites, spindle whorls of various shapes are the most common. Middle Bronze Age spindle whorls from this zone come in various forms, including biconical, conical, and discoid (Fig. 3.7/1, 3, 8–10, 20), wheel-shaped with a prominent axle (Fig. 3.7/2, 5, 7, 19), while weights are mostly pyramidal (Fig. 3.7/11). An intriguing find is a circular fired clay plate richly decorated on both sides with incised arched lines with coiled ends arranged in a circle, circular rows of dot indentations, concentric circles, and parallel lines filled with oval impressions, zigzag lines, and circles with a marked centre (Fig. 3.7/6). Similar plates have been recorded at several Vatin sites in southern Pannonia though their purpose remains unclear. A similar, smaller ceramic circular plate decorated with small dot impressions in concentric circular rows (Fig. 3.7/21) was found in a pit (structure 35-western half) at Marjansko Brdo. Structure 35-western half and structure 35-eastern half are actually two distinct pits, with the later one, designated as 35-eastern half, intruding into the earlier one (structure 35-western half). They were named as such because, at the observation level, they appeared as a single, larger pit.

An interesting star-shaped object (resembling a cog) with seven short arms or teeth was also discovered. Objects of this shape are known from Late Bronze and Iron Age sites in Pannonia (Kalicz-Schreiber 2010, pl. 9, 19, 39; Medović and Medović 2010, fig. 101/13), with some scholars suggesting it may symbolise the sun (Medović and Medović 2010, 112).

Some spindle whorls are exceptionally richly decorated with incised or impressed motifs such as heart-shaped designs (Fig. 3.7/2) or rows of dot indentations (Fig. 3.7/3). The most prominent part of a spindle whorl from Najeva Ciglana (Fig. 3.7/9) is decorated with parallel diagonal lines intersecting to create a small rhomboid grid, while the upper part is profiled as a flower with seven petals.

3.1.4 Cultural and chronological classification of the Middle Bronze Age in the peri-Pannonian zone

Even without detailed analysis of Middle Bronze Age pottery in the peri-Pannonian zone, based on their distinctive stylistic-typological characteristics, it can be suggested that they belong to one of the earliest defined cultural groups in the central Balkans, the Vatin group. However, it should be noted that almost all sites in this zone are located downstream from the confluence of the Sava and Danube rivers and, to date, no Middle Bronze Age sites have been found west of the Sava's confluence, with the exception of the Paulje site in Brezjak near Loznica. At this site, an

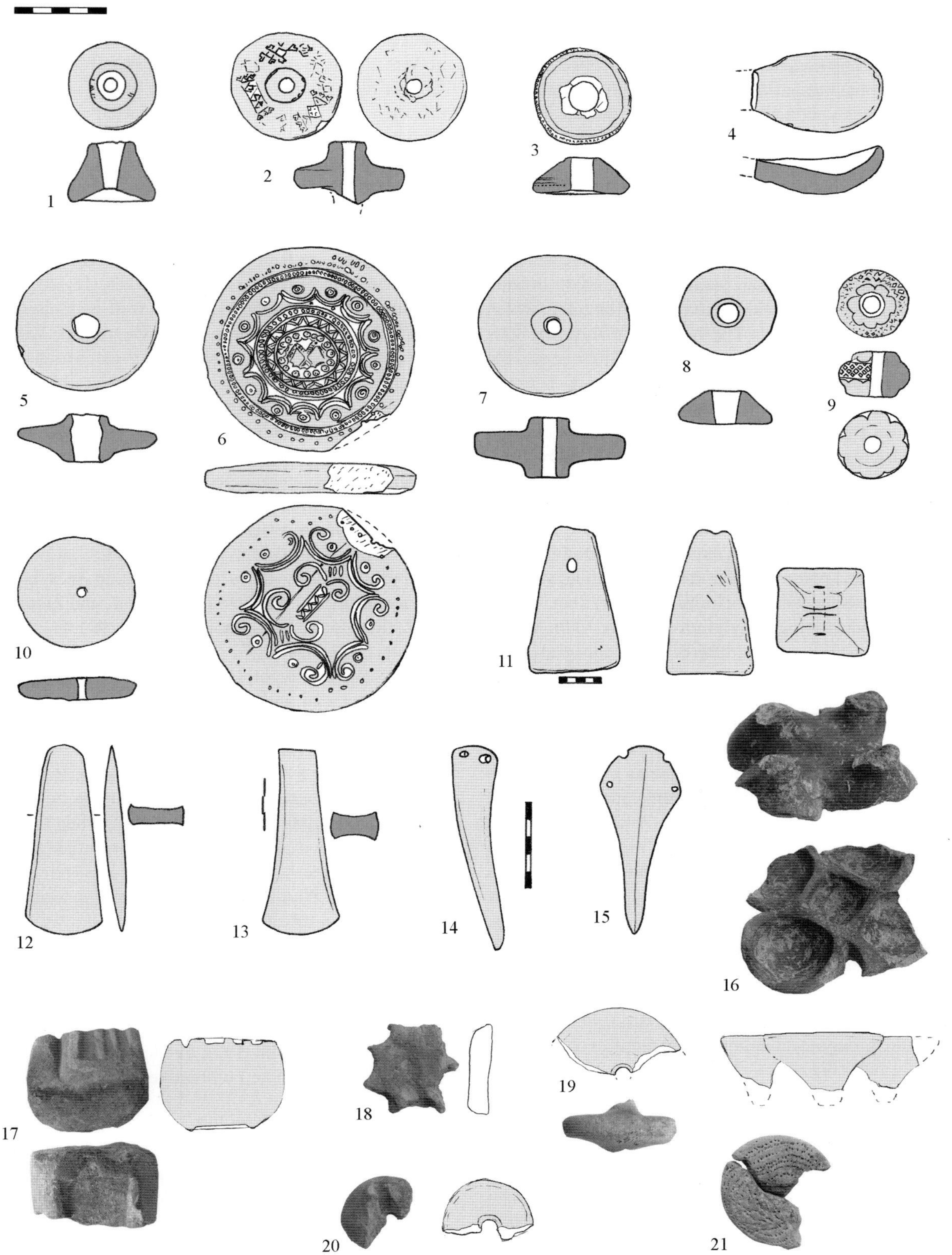

Figure 3.7. 1–4, Omoljica: site of Zlatica; 5–11, Vojlovica: site of Najeva Ciglana; 12, Begaljica, an unknown site; 13, Bela Reka: site of Popovača; 14, Ritopek, unknown site; 15, Petka near Požarevac; 16–21, Majilovac: site of Marjansko Brdo, 16–20, structure 11; 21, structure 35.

absolute date corresponding to the Middle Bronze Age was detected in a settlement pit near numerous tumuli, though the finds from this context belong to the so-called Brezjak group (a regional variant of the Belegiš I group), which is several centuries younger than the period indicated by the absolute date in the second half of the 19th and early 18th century cal BC.[8]

Pottery from other sites downstream from the Sava confluence primarily contain stylistic-typological elements characteristic of the Vatin group, such as two handled, segmentally profiled beakers (type 7d in our typology) or two handled, slightly biconical or globular beakers with a short, everted rim (type 1f), sometimes with a delta-shaped opening, which are often richly decorated. The handles of these beakers extend above the vessel's opening and are often concavely profiled (*ansa lunata*). A common decoration on beakers, and less frequently on bowls, is a small plastic wart-shaped protrusion on the belly or two horn-shaped protrusions on the belly, arranged in pairs facing downward.[9] Shallow oval-based vessels (*Fischbute*), double vessels, and cylindrical lids with horizontal ribs are also characteristic of the Vatin group (Ljuština 2022, 75–87, and the cited literature).

It is observed, however, that particularly in Omoljica and at Najeva Ciglana, pottery appear that may be either younger or older than typical Vatin ceramics, meaning they do not stylistically and typologically align with the Vatin group. These include a semi-circular beaker with a foot and richly decorated inner side (Fig. 3.3/7), resembling examples from the Mako-Kosihy–Čaka or Vinkovci–Somogyvár group; a jug with a funnel neck and low, squat body (Fig. 3.3/1); and a bowl with a plastic tongue-shaped thickening on the rim (Fig. 3.1/5), which resembles ceramics from the *Hügelgräber* complex at the end of the Middle and beginning of the Late Bronze Age (Tasić 1983, fig. 44; Milanović and Bulatović 2011, T. II/7; Kapuran 2019, pl. 1/6, 23/2; 25/2; 51/2; 70/1). It is possible, therefore, that Najeva Ciglana and Zlatica are multi-layered Bronze Age sites, but unfortunately, no additional data on potential closed contexts, stratigraphy, or absolute dates are available from these sites, except for one that dates the Vatin horizon in Omoljica from the mid-20th to mid-18th century cal BC (Table 1).

The situation is different at Cigansko Brdo, where numerous finds in a dugout dwelling correspond exclusively to the Vatin group (Fig. 3.5/1–9). This dugout is dated from the early 19th to the third quarter of the 18th century cal BC. Among other finds, a type 1g beaker with a trapezoidal opening (Fig. 3.5/4), very similar to the one from Omoljica (Fig. 3.1/8), was discovered in the dugout. Beakers with this type of opening are uncommon in the Vatin group and mainly appear in its early phase, but they are a defining feature of the Middle Bronze Age group in South Morava Basin (Bulatović 2020b). The date from this dugout is the earliest for the Vatin group and marks the initial developmental phase of this group in this area.

Ceramic forms resembling the inventory of the preceding Novačka Ćuprija–Pančevo group have also been identified at Vinča (Fig. 3.4/15) and Marjansko Brdo (Fig. 3.5/10, 11, 17; Fig. 3.6/4, 24), suggesting that the Vatin group in this area developed from the foundations of that group at the end of the Early Bronze Age, resulting in virtually no chronological hiatus between them.

In addition to Vatin pottery, other ornaments appear in closed contexts at the Marjansko Brdo site, such as stamped concentric circles, which are widespread in the Žuto Brdo group of the Late Bronze Age. This is observed in structure 11, where concentric circles (Fig. 3.6/6, 18, 20) joined by paired straight or arched lines, as well as incised circular lines (Fig. 3.6/19), appear alongside typical Vatin forms (Fig. 3.6/7, 8, 12, 15). This structure is dated to the mid-17th century BC, suggesting that minor changes in the material culture of the Vatin group might have begun by that time, eventually resulting in the dominance of the Žuto Brdo group in this area after the 16th century (Fig. 4.1).

Apart from pottery, other finds from this zone also point to the Vatin group. Decorated spindle whorls in various shapes, pyramidal weights, ladles, stone moulds for casting bronze objects, *Randleistenbeile* type axes, and daggers are common inventory items at Vatin group sites in southern Pannonia, such as Feudvar, Popov Salaš, and Židovar (Tasić 1983, fig. 24/a, b; Hansel and Medović 1991, pl. 11, pl. 24/8; Ljuština 2012, figs 62, 72, 89/18, 21, 91/5, 6, 21.92/14–18). The stylistic and typological characteristics of ceramics, as well as the metal finds, indicate an interconnection between peri-Pannonian zone communities with southern Pannonia, Šumadija, Great Morava Valley, and eastern Serbia.

Based on all available dates, the Middle Bronze Age in the peri-Pannonian zone (Vatin group) can be determined from the beginning of the 19th century, when the Novačka Ćuprija–Pančevo group transformed into the Vatin group, to the end of the 17th or beginning of the 16th century cal BC, when the Žuto Brdo group emerged, marking the Late Bronze Age in this area.

3.2 Basin of the Great Morava River and Šumadija

3.2.1 Settlement and dwelling

In this zone, four hilltop and five lowland settlements have been documented. Site numbers refer to Plate 19.

3.2.1.1 Hilltop settlements

22. The site of Đula in Ostrikovac (Stojić 1989); 114. The site of Milića Brdo in Ljuljaci (Bogdanović 1986); 115. The site of Gologlava in Stalać (Čađenović 2003; 2009, 168); 116. The site of Gradac in Novo Lanište (Stojić 1992).

Hilltop settlements were situated in Šumadija (Milića Brdo, Ljuljaci), in the basin of the Great Morava (Gradac in Novo Lanište and Đula in Ostrikovac), and the last one in the confluence area of the South and West Morava rivers (Gologlava in Stalać).

The Milića Brdo site in Ljuljaci near Kragujevac is a multi-layered Bronze Age site. It is situated on an oval plateau on a prominent, difficult to access elevation surrounded by several peaks of the Rudnik Mountain. It covers an area of *c.* 0.8 ha, with settlement activity concentrated on the western part of the plateau, while the eastern part remained open space. Systematic excavations conducted from 1965 to 1977 identified three stratigraphic horizons (Bogdanović 1986, 15–18). However, the chronological difference between these horizons is uncertain as although four absolute dates are available, they exhibit a high chronological variability of ±95 and ±100 years, resulting in an extensive chronological range when calibrated.

The Milića Brdo site is a compact, small settlement of approximately 65 × 25 m, with square-based above-ground houses partially enclosed by a wall. On the south-western side of the settlement, a rampart was uncovered, appearing as a larger mound and several embankments made of earth and small crushed stones. The mound's height is around 2 m, and the embankments extend 25–30 m in length. The chronological and stratigraphic relationship between the identified rampart and the settlement horizons has not been determined.

The earliest houses were built along the western edge of the plateau with the settlement gradually expanding toward the central part, while older houses were also periodically renewed. The house foundations are square, with dimensions of 4 × 4 m, 3.5 × 3.5 m, and 3 × 3 m, and the entrance is always on the south-east wall (Bogdanović 1986, 18, 29). The houses were constructed from wood, stone, and earth; wooden posts were deeply embedded in the ground, interwoven with branches and twigs, and coated with mud. The posts have diameters up to 0.2 m, spaced 0.2–2 m apart. The lower parts of some walls were re-inforced with stones. Floors were made of compacted earth, levelled and bordered with stones, and coated with a thin layer of mud. Some houses contained remains of domed ovens or open hearths and, in one, a large stone grinding mill was fixed to the floor with a low mud wall about 0.2–0.3 m high built around it on three sides. No architectural structures were found on the eastern side of the plateau, leading M. Bogdanović to suggest it was an open space where communal daily activities took place (Bogdanović 1986, 32).

In the oldest horizon, I, the house entrances were on the south-east side, with 2–3 m of space between structures. Crushed stone was used as a levelling base for the floors, covered by a layer of earth. Open hearths were present in the houses, and one house also contained a domed oven (Bogdanović 1986, 29–30, 62).

The settlement from Horizon II expanded slightly compared to Horizon I, as did the spacing between houses, while their shape, construction method, and dimensions remained unchanged. In the following Horizon III at Ljuljaci, the settlement reached its largest area (3600–4000 m^2), with new houses built along the northern edge of the plateau and older houses being renovated. The free space for movement within the settlement also increased, giving the impression that the settlement in Horizon III was much better organised than the previous two (Bogdanović 1986, 60–62). According to M. Bogdanović, the absolute dates originate from the first two settlements, while the youngest settlement at Ljuljaci remains undated (Bogdanović 1986, 70).

Two hilltop settlements in this zone are located within the Great Morava Basin. Gradac in Novo Lanište is positioned at the southern entrance to the Bagrdan Gorge, on one of the eastern slopes of Mount Crni Vrh descending into the Morava Basin. Known for its defensive architecture and Iron Age settlement, a small number of fragments attributed to the Middle Bronze Age were also found during excavations, displaying stylistic-typological traits similar to the Vatin group (Stojić 1992). No architectural information is available regarding the settlement or houses from this period, suggesting that any Bronze Age settlement may have been completely destroyed by Iron Age activity.

The second hilltop settlement in the Great Morava Basin is located in a dominant position on a tongue-shaped plateau of Mount Juhor, overlooking the Great Morava Valley. The plateau covered *c.* 1 ha but has been largely destroyed by a local quarry (Garašanin and Stojić 1986, 192; Stojić 1989, 171). Finds from a pit dated to the late Middle Bronze Age, specifically the second half of the 16th century BC, originate from this site.

The last hilltop settlement in this zone is situated on a flat plateau atop an elevation above the eastern outskirts of Stalać, overlooking the confluence of the South and West Morava rivers. Excavations conducted from 1985 to 1987 identified the foundations of two houses, approximately 2.5 × 3 m in size, constructed with river pebbles and crushed stone, as well as a larger pit (Tasić and Tomić 1987, 131; Tasić 2001, 10, 11). Due to erosion, it was not possible to obtain detailed information about the architecture and layout of the settlement but the quantity of portable finds led researchers to presume that life in this settlement was intense. Besides finds from the Late Bronze Age, some artefacts were identified based on stylistic-typological analogies as belonging to the Middle Bronze Age (Čađenović 2009, 168). However, it remains unknown whether the remnants of the two houses and the pit belong to the Late or Middle Bronze Age.

3.2.1.2 Lowland settlements

81. Rujište, the site of Crnokalačka Bara (Tasić and Tomić 1969; Stojić and Čađenović 2006, 188); 118. Stragari, the site of Reka/Šljivik, Kruševac (Stanković 1988; Stojić and Čađenović 2006, 217); 119. Šanac-Bošnjane, the site of Skela Kolarac, Kruševac (Stojić and Čađenović

2006, 234); 120. Maskare, the site of Bedem, Kruševac (Stojić and Čađenović 2006, 163; Stojić 2011, 313–327); 121. Kruševac, the site of Lazarev Grad (Jordović and Jurišić 1970 and the cited literature; Stojić and Čađenović 2006, 101); 122. Globoder, the site of Ivlje, Kruševac (Palavestra and Bankoff 1986, 67–68; Stojić and Čađenović 2006, 87–90); 125. Jagodina (formerly Svetozarevo), the site of Sarina Međa (Stojić 1980, cat. no. 39).

Lowland settlements are more numerous than hilltops and are mainly situated on terraces along major rivers. Such settlements have been identified in Bošnjane and Maskare, where they are positioned on a high terrace on the left bank of the West Morava River. These two settlements are about 2.5 km apart, and the distance from the Bošnjane settlement to Lazarev Grad, which is located on a high terrace on the right bank of the West Morava, is approximately 6.5 km in a straight line. The Ivlje site is nearby, about 8 km west of Lazarev Grad, on a high terrace of the right bank of the West Morava and the right bank of the Lipovac Stream. A similar topographic feature characterises the settlement at the Sarina Međa site on the south-eastern outskirts of Jagodina (Stojić 1986, 21, 22), situated on the terrace of the Lugomir River near its confluence with the Great Morava. Although this site has been published as a multi-layered settlement from the transition period and the Iron Age, it was evidently also inhabited during the Middle Bronze Age (Stojić 1980).

The multi-layered prehistoric settlements at Stragari near Trstenik on the Reka site (Stojić and Čađenović 2006, 217),[10] which S. Stanković suggests (1988, 95–97) may correspond to the site known as Šljivik, and at Crnokalačka Bara, exhibit a somewhat different natural environment. The Šljivik site is located on an elevated plateau surrounded by a meander of the Riljačka River, with the entire area situated between two hills (Nerezina and Belo Brdo) on a high terrace about 30 m above the West Morava River. This settlement, primarily Neolithic, has also yielded finds from the Copper, Iron, and Middle Bronze Ages. The Crnokalačka Bara site is situated on a gentle slope several kilometres from the South Morava alluvium, on a horseshoe-shaped elevation near a water source (Tasić and Tomić 1969, 10).

Unfortunately, little information is available about the layout, architecture, and residential or other structures of these settlements. Data from rescue excavations conducted about two decades ago on the multi-layered Bedem site in Maskare include a closed context, specifically an indeterminate-purpose pit dated to the Middle Bronze Age (19th/18th century cal BC).[11]

3.2.2 Necropolises and burial practices

No necropolises or graves from the Middle Bronze Age have been documented in this geographical zone to date.

3.2.3 Portable finds

3.2.3.1 Pottery

A. BOWLS

In contrast to the Early Bronze Age, when types 3a and 1a were the most prevalent, Middle Bronze Age bowls are typically deeper and larger, with biconical profiles, often featuring handles on the upper cone or belly (Fig. 3.8/1, 2; Fig. 3.9/18–20; Fig. 3.12/4 – type 3d), comprising one-third of all bowls. These are followed by biconical bowls with flared rims, or S-profiles (type 1b), making up about 25% of the total (Fig. 3.8/4; Fig. 3.9/1; Fig. 3.10/4, 18; Fig. 3.12/6). Types 3a (semi-spherical bowls with mostly unprofiled or slightly profiled rims – Fig. 3.8/3; Fig. 3.11/13; Fig. 3.12/1) and 1c (Fig. 3.12/2, 5) account for 17% and 11%, respectively. Additionally, type 1a (Fig. 3.8/5), type 3e (Fig. 3.10/19; Fig. 3.12/3), and type 3c (Fig. 3.9/23) have been recorded, though in much smaller percentages.

None of these bowl types is ornamented, and nearly all have vertical arched handles, with the exception of a type 3d bowl from Ljuljaci, which features two symmetrically arranged, vertically perforated, horizontally positioned trapezoidal handles on its belly (Fig. 3.8/2).

Available data indicate that bowls from Ljuljaci were produced in various grades, from coarse to medium and fine. According to M. Bogdanović, most fine quality bowls were recorded in the youngest settlement (Bogdanović 1986, 40–42, table 3). A similar situation exists at sites near Kruševac, where bowls were made in various textures, primarily in brown hues, with some fired in shades of brown and black (Stojić and Čađenović 2006, 112–115, 234). At Gologlava, all bowls are ochre-coloured and of medium quality (Čađenović 2009, 168).

B. CUPS

Cups are relatively common in this zone compared to other zones during the Middle Bronze Age. Interestingly, all cup specimens from this zone come from a single site, Milića Brdo in Ljuljaci, which is unsurprising given that it is the only systematically researched site in this region. Semi-spherical cups with a single handle extending over the rim, belonging to type 1a (Fig. 3.9/2; Fig. 3.10/21), and gently biconical cups of type 4a (Fig. 3.8/9) continued to be used during this period. Oval-shaped cups with a single handle extending over the opening (type 4b: Fig. 3.8/7, 8) have also been recorded. All cup types are approximately equally represented and, due to the small number of documented specimens, no dominant type can be identified.

None of the cups is ornamented, except for a type 4b specimen (Fig. 3.8/7), which features a wart-shaped plastic extension at the top of the handle. All cup types from Ljuljaci were produced in coarse, medium, and fine grades, except for type 4a, which is of fine quality with uneven firing, resulting in colour variations from grey to brown.

C. BEAKERS

The most prevalent beaker type in this geographical zone is type 1g (Fig. 3.8/14; Fig. 3.10/11, 13, 14, 16; Fig. 3.11/3, 14–17; Fig. 3.12/7), comprising approximately one-third of all beakers in this zone. Following this are type 7d, with 20% (Fig. 3.8/11, 16; Fig. 3.9/3, 5, 7, 9, 10); type 3a, with 15% (Fig. 3.9/4, 6; Fig. 3.8/15; Fig. 3.11/21); and type 1c, also with 15% (Fig. 3.8/13; Fig. 3.9/8, 11; Fig. 3.11/18). Less common types, including 1f (Fig. 3.10/15, 17), 1e (Fig. 3.8/12), 5a (Bogdanović 1986, figs 217, 226), and 2a (Fig. 3.11/1), collectively account for around 15%. It is clear that the beaker type dominant in the Early Bronze Age is no longer popular, making way for new types, namely 1f, 1g, and 7d, which are characteristic of the Middle Bronze Age in the central Balkans and collectively represent over two-thirds of all beakers in this zone. The beakers from Pit 1 at Ostrikovac cannot be confidently assigned a specific type (Fig. 3.10/20, 22).

In terms of decoration, only beakers of types 1g, 2a, 3a, and 7d are ornamented. Type 1g, a Middle Bronze Age product, is generally decorated with parallel rows of dot indentations, mostly placed above the most prominent line of the belly (Fig. 3.10/2, 11, 16; Fig. 3.11/2; Fig. 3.12/7), though undecorated examples also exist. Type 7d, which also emerged in this period, is the most intensely decorated vessel type of the Middle Bronze Age. These beakers are adorned on the neck and belly, primarily with incised spiral or garland-like lines (Fig. 3.9/5, 7). Similarly, type 3a beakers are decorated (Fig. 3.9/6), while type 2a is decorated with a row of notches along the rim (Fig. 3.11/1).

No specific data are available on the texture or surface treatment of pottery from Ljuljaci. Most beakers are of coarse or fine quality, with a minimal number of medium quality (Bogdanović 1986, table 3). There is also evidence that the quality of double-handled beakers made in coarse and medium textures declines in Horizons Ljuljaci II and III (Bogdanović 1986, 61, 62). At sites around Kruševac, beakers are mostly medium or fine quality, fired primarily in black, ochre, or shades of brown and grey. They frequently have a burnished finish, and one specimen from Lazarev Grad is polished to a shine (Fig. 3.12/7).

It is noteworthy that type 1g beakers, which were not documented in the previous zone, are quite prominent in this zone. This type is dominant to varying extents across other geographical zones of the central Balkans.

D. AMPHORAE

Amphorae are more frequently found in the Morava Basin and Šumadija than in other central Balkan regions, except in the Timok Region, where they are far more abundant. The most common type of amphora in this zone is type 2a, constituting more than half of all amphorae here (Fig. 3.10/5, 6; Fig. 3.11/5, 12, 21; Fig. 3.12/8–11). Next is type 5a (Fig. 3.9/14, 15; Fig. 3.11/13, 20), comprising approximately one-fifth of these vessels, while types 1a (Fig. 3.9/13; Fig. 3.10/12), 1b (Fig. 3.11/11), and 5b (Fig. 3.8/21) are much less common, each accounting for less than 10%.

Most amphorae are undecorated, with exceptions including specimens decorated with finger impressions along the rim (Fig. 3.9/13–15) or with plastic amorphous appliqués (Fig. 3.9/14). Depending on the type, they may feature tongue-shaped (often four) or triangular handles, as well as arched vertical handles.

In the lower West Morava Valley, amphorae are mostly of medium quality and brown in colour, with one example of lower quality also in brown (Stojić and Čađenović 2006, 113, 114, 234). In Šumadija, at the Milića Brdo site in Ljuljaci, amphorae vary by type: they are coarse in texture with sand inclusions and light brown in colour (3a); coarse or medium in texture, fired in shades of brown or grey (5a); or made in various textures and fired in shades of brown, reddish, or grey (5b) (Bogdanović 1986, 41–44).

While amphorae are relatively more common in the Morava Valley during the Middle Bronze Age compared to other zones, they are by far most numerous in the Timok Region. This can be attributed to the extensive excavations of necropolises with cremated remains from this period in the area, where urns, classified as amphorae in this book, served as urn vessels.

E. JUGS

In this zone, jugs have only been recorded at Ljuljaci, specifically types 1a and 2a (Fig. 3.8/10, 18). They are undecorated, made in coarse quality, fired in light brown tones with a slightly burnished coating (Fig. 3.8/10), or with thick walls and a high sand content in their composition (Fig. 3.8/18).

F. SPECIAL-PURPOSE VESSELS

Among the so-called special-purpose vessels in this zone, there are oval-based shallow vessels (*Fischbutte*), ladles, a miniature cone-shaped vessel, a square-based vessel with an arched handle on the rim, and strainers.

The shallow oval-based vessels, typically with one shorter arched handle of strap-like cross-section, are rare in this zone, recorded only at Ljuljaci (Fig. 3.9/16). This example is of coarse quality with a rough surface (Bogdanović 1986, 42).

A vessel with a hemispherical body similar to a thick-walled cup, featuring a single handle extending over the rim, is classified as a ladle or pouring spoon and is documented at Ljuljaci (Fig. 3.8/6).

An unusual vessel, a miniature vessel with an oval base, broad bottom and belly, and narrow opening, was recorded from the second settlement horizon at Ljuljaci (Fig. 3.8/17). It has two tongue-shaped, vertically perforated handles on the sides, resembling so-called milk churning

Figure 3.8. Ljuljaci: site of Milića Brdo, 1st and 2nd horizon.

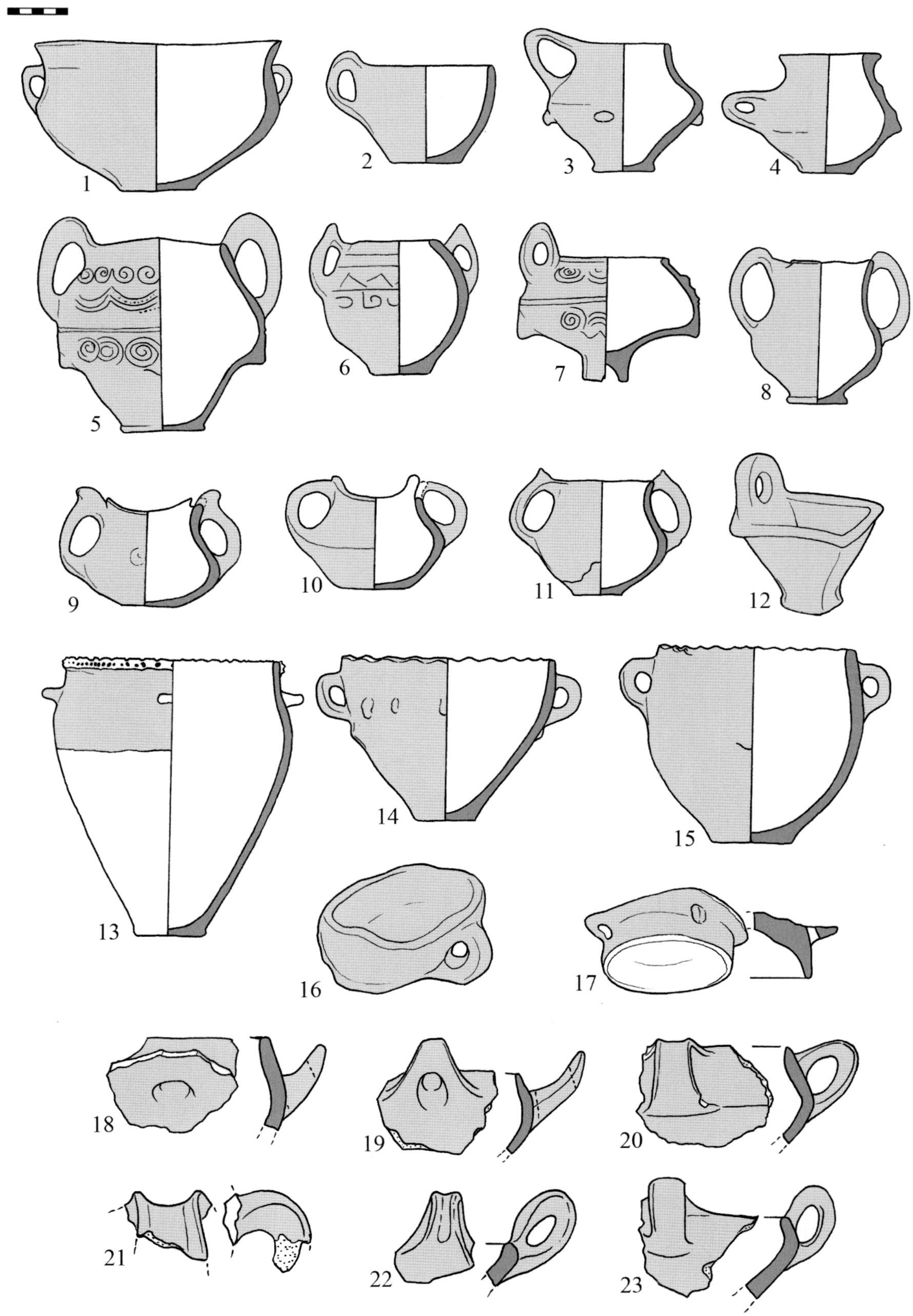

Figure 3.9. 1–16, Ljuljaci: site of Milića Brdo, 3rd horizon; 17–23, Stalać: site of Gologlava.

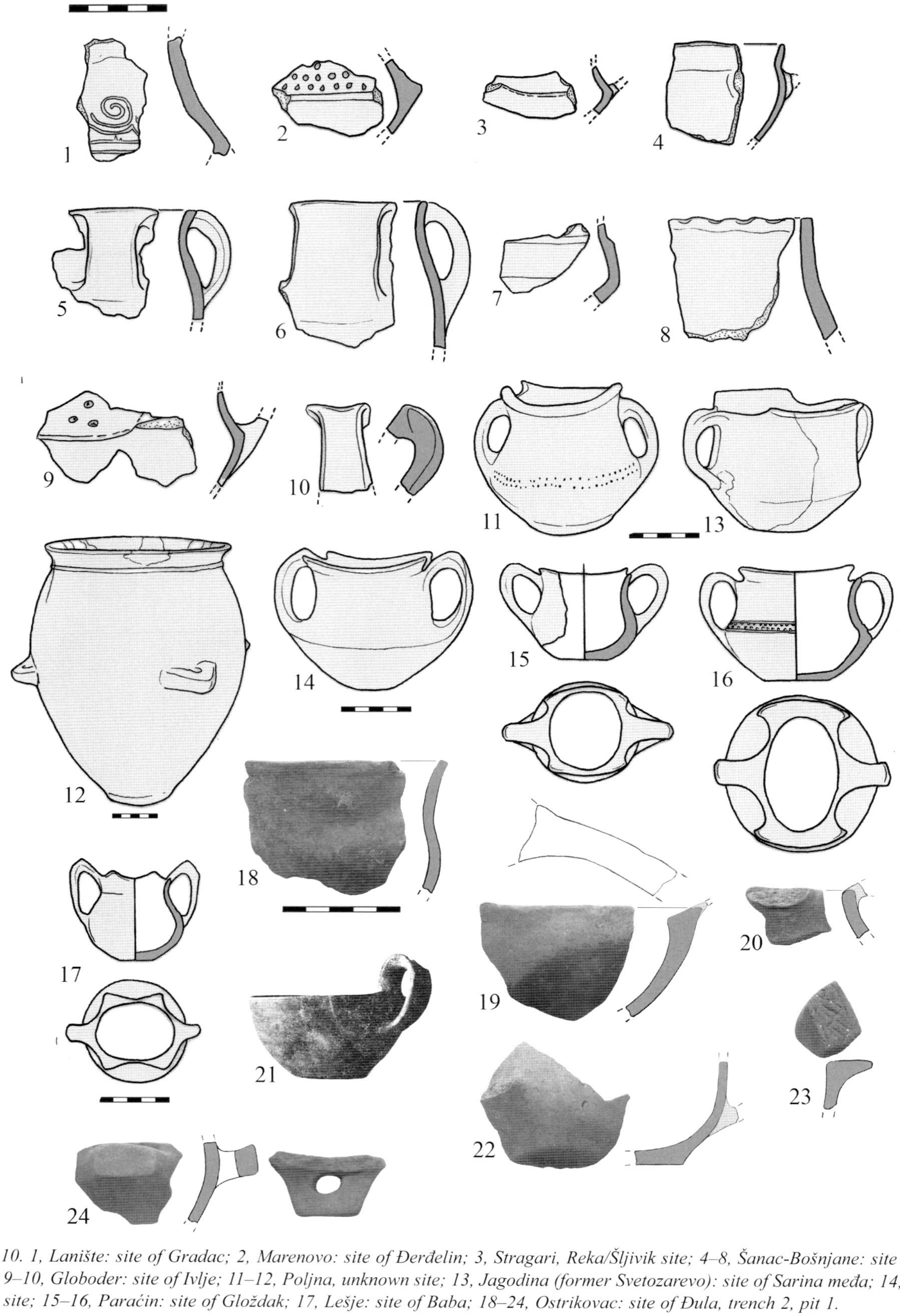

Figure 3.10. 1, Lanište: site of Gradac; 2, Marenovo: site of Đerđelin; 3, Stragari, Reka/Šljivik site; 4–8, Šanac-Bošnjane: site of Skela Kolarac; 9–10, Globoder: site of Ivlje; 11–12, Poljna, unknown site; 13, Jagodina (former Svetozarevo): site of Sarina međa; 14, Orašje, unknown site; 15–16, Paraćin: site of Gloždak; 17, Lešje: site of Baba; 18–24, Ostrikovac: site of Đula, trench 2, pit 1.

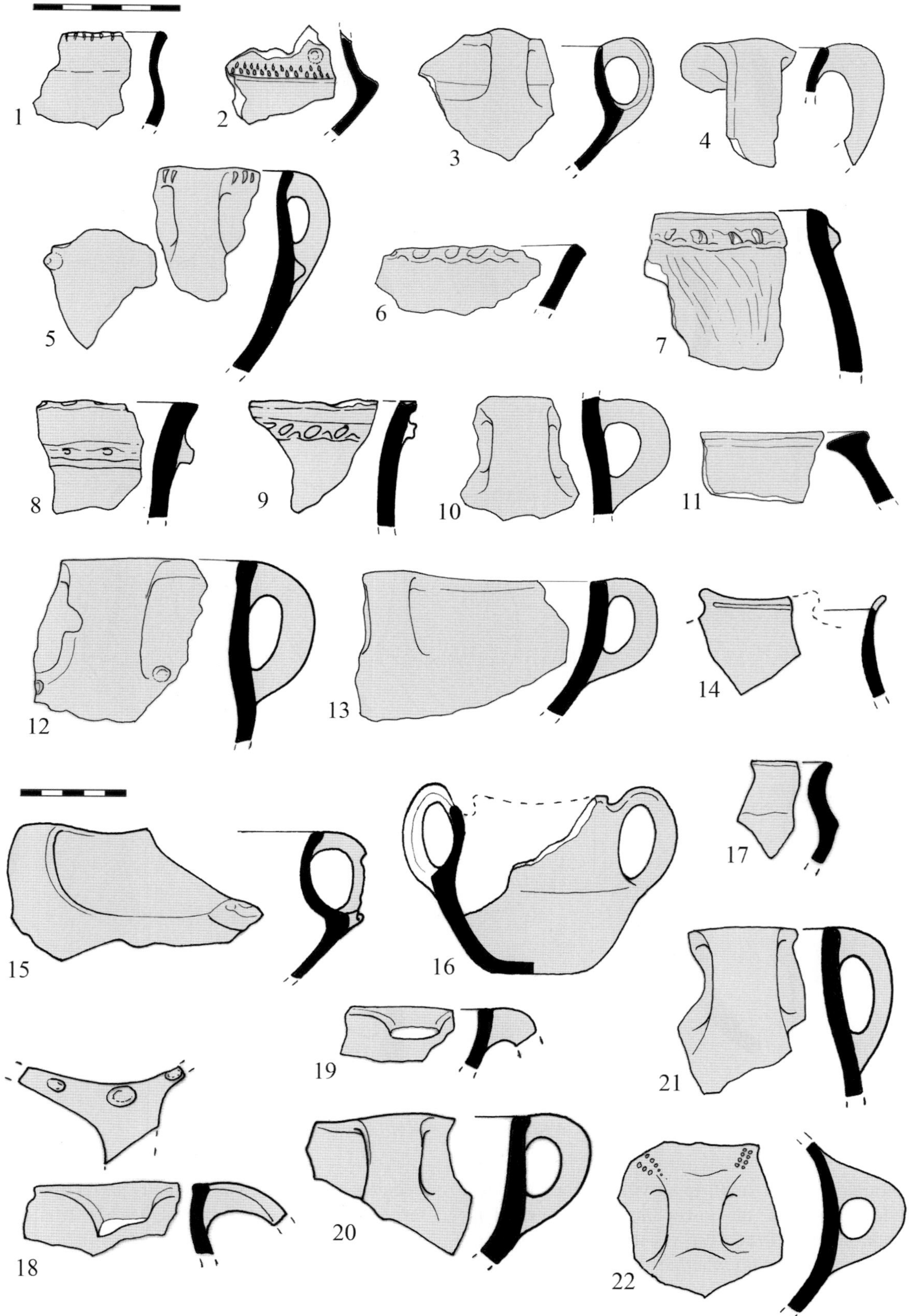

Figure 3.11. Maskare: site of Bedem: 1–10, Trench 13, pit; 11–13, Trench 13, cultural layer; 14–22, Trench 15, cultural layer.

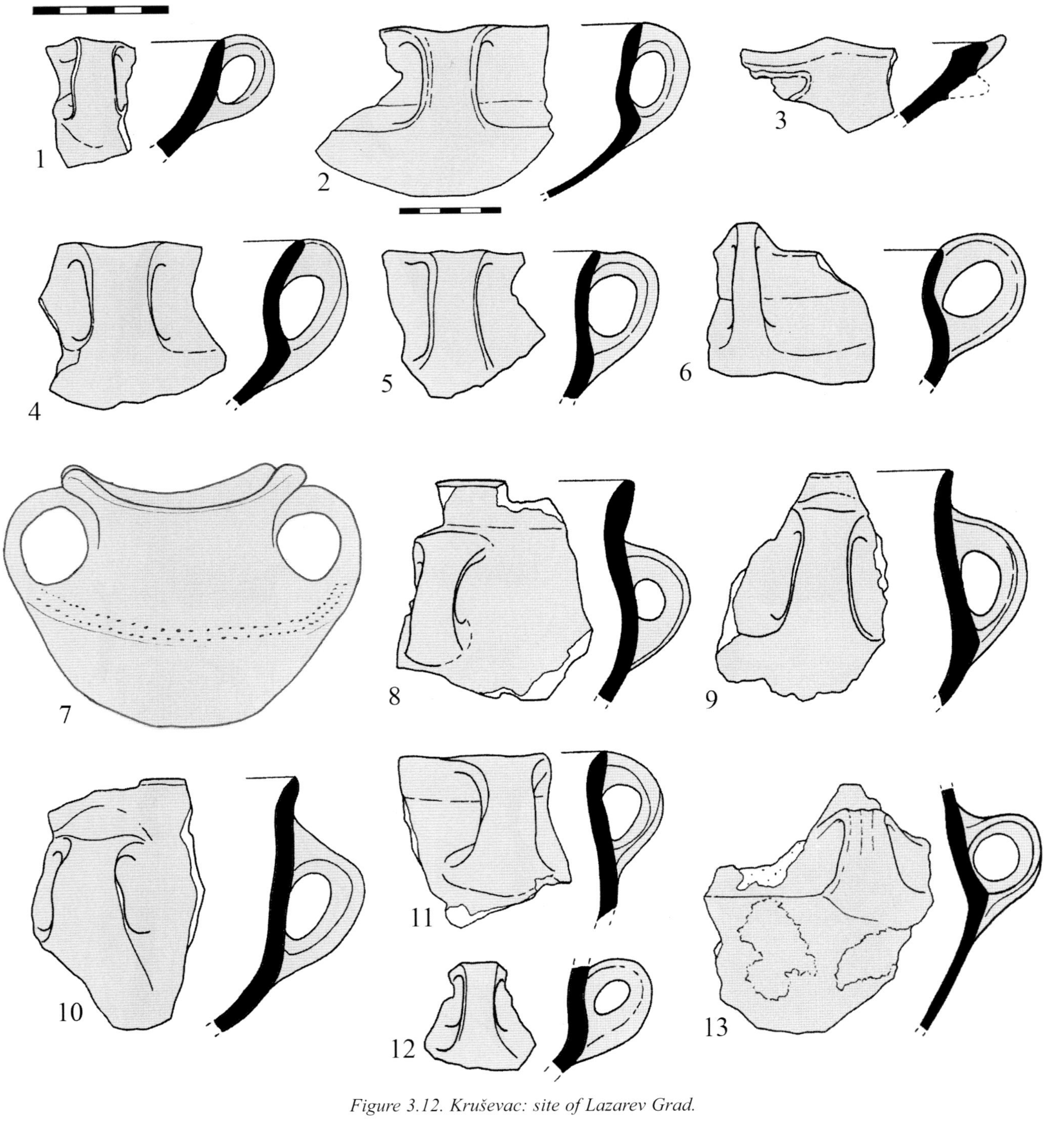

Figure 3.12. Kruševac: site of Lazarev Grad.

vessels, though it is too small to serve that function. M. Bogdanović states that 'the lower part of the vessel is oval and bottomless' (1986, 49), yet the drawing depicts a base, making it uncertain whether the vessel originally had a bottom. The vessel is of coarse quality with a rough wall surface.

Furthermore, at Ljuljaci, in the youngest settlement, a smaller, square vessel was recorded, with a square base, a conical profile, and a horizontally perforated arched handle set vertically on the rim (Fig. 3.9/12). It is made of fine quality material (Bogdanović 1986, 49).

Semi-circular vessels with a horizontal handle and body featuring several circular perforations, strain-type vessels, have also been documented at Ljuljaci (Fig. 3.13/13). None of these three types of special-purpose vessels is decorated.

G. POTS

Pots used for preparing or storing food are large and exhibit similar characteristics throughout prehistoric periods. They have a coarse exterior or are occasionally burnished, with coarse sand, chaff, and other inclusions often found in their composition.

The most common decorative elements are horizontal plastic bands with finger impressions, though they may also feature rows of notches along the rim, plastic bands with incisions, or tongue-shaped and arched handles located below the rim or on the belly of the vessel (Fig. 3.10/8; Fig. 3.11/7–9). *Piraunoi* are not documented in this zone.

H. LIDS

Lids are rare, but due to research at Ljuljaci where all the lids from this zone were found, three types have been identified for the Middle Bronze Age. The first, basic type is a lid made from a circular ceramic plate with a handle at the centre of the upper surface (Bogdanović 1986, 47, fig. 72). The second type is also a circular plate, with a solid, columnar handle sculpted on the upper surface (Bogdanović 1986, 48, fig. 74), and the third is a shallow cylindrical lid with a broad rectangular upper part, featuring a vertical perforation at each corner (Fig. 3.9/17). The lids are fired in shades of grey, reddish, or brown, with a medium quality and occasionally burnished surfaces. All are undecorated.

I. HANDLES

The most prevalent type of handle in this zone is the vertically positioned arched handle, usually with a strap or oval cross-section, mainly found on beakers and bowls. Unlike the Early Bronze Age, these handles are no longer predominantly strap-shaped but also appear in oval and, less commonly, circular forms. A notable addition is the handle with a pronounced concave cross-section, predominantly seen on beakers. These so-called *ansa lunata* handles, originating from the northern Vatin culture, are particularly significant. In addition, slightly concave arched handles, whose origins are unclear – whether as imitations of *ansa lunata* handles or as their prototypes – have also been recorded. Both handle types are frequently observed at Ljuljaci and sporadically at other sites in this zone (Fig. 3.8/8, 12; Fig. 3.9/3, 5, 7, 10, 20–22; Fig. 3.10/10, 13, 14). Interestingly, in the youngest horizon at Ljuljaci, arched handles with vertical ridges decorated with notches appear, characteristic of the Verbicioara culture in Oltenia, which is not the only similarity between this site's ceramics and the Verbicioara culture, as will be discussed later. For vertical arched handles on beakers, it is observed that, unlike the Early Bronze Age, these handles generally extend above the vessel's rim to varying degrees.

Tongue-shaped handles are also present in this zone but are much less common than arched handles. They are typically found on amphorae, positioned on the upper part of the vessel (Fig. 3.8/17, 21; Fig. 3.9/13; Fig. 3.10/12).

An interesting type of handle, positioned vertically beneath the rim of bowls, has been documented. These handles are triangular or trapezoidal, vertically perforated, and found at Ljuljaci, Stalać, and Ostrikovac (Fig. 3.8/2; Fig. 3.9/18, 19; Fig. 3.10/24). The Ljuljaci example features wart-shaped plastic extensions at the ends.

J. ORNAMENTATION

Compared to the previous transitional zone, ceramics in the Morava Basin and Šumadija regions are much less decorated. The most common decorative elements are plastic attachments at the top of the handle, which may be horn-shaped, button-like, wart-like, or volute-shaped (Fig. 3.8/2, 7; Fig. 3.9/6, 9, 11), and trapezoidal modelled openings on beakers (Fig. 3.8/11; Fig. 3.9/9, 10; Fig. 3.10/11, 13–17; Fig. 3.11/14, 16), which are more numerous in this zone than in the previous one, as well as plastic attachments on the bowl rim (Fig. 3.10/19).

Parallel rows of dot impressions, usually in pairs, are commonly found on beakers (Fig. 3.10/2, 11, 16; pl. 52/2, 22), sometimes combined with incised curved lines or spirals (Fig. 3.9/5, 7).

No cups are decorated except for a type 4b specimen (Fig. 3.8/7), which has a wart-shaped plastic extension at the top of the handle. Incised ornaments in the form of contiguous rhomb-shaped cross-hatching framed by two parallel incised lines are present on the upper rim surface of a vessel from Pit 1 in Ostrikovac (Fig. 3.10/23).

Only beakers from the youngest settlement in Ljuljaci (type 7d) display a combination of incised spirals, curved lines, and dot impressions, characteristic of the Vatin culture. These vessel forms also indicate intense contact between the population of Ljuljaci's youngest settlement and the population of the peri–Pannonian zone or the Danube region.

Less common decorations include plastic wart-like appliqués, mostly on the bellies of beakers, often oriented downward on type 7d beakers (Fig. 3.8/3, 20; Fig. 3.9/2–5, 7, 9, 14, 15; Fig. 3.11/5; Fig. 3.13/1), and pit impressions made directly on the vessel's surface (Fig. 3.11/12, 18) or on the rim (Fig. 3.8/19, 20; Fig. 3.9/13–15; Fig. 3.10/8).

3.2.3.2 Other and chance finds

Other recorded finds include bronze jewellery fragments, axes, various clay items such as weights and spindle whorls, bone tools, and stone axes. Most of these items were discovered at Ljuljaci, unsurprising given the extensive excavations conducted there.

The spindle whorls from Ljuljaci are conical or biconical, with vertical circular perforations along the axis (Fig. 3.13/11, 12, 14). The weights are of two main types: pyramidal with a circular horizontal perforation at the top (Fig. 3.13/16) and low conical with a horizontal groove and perforation in the middle (Fig. 3.13/15). Additional finds include various perforated bone tools (Fig. 3.13/21–23), stone grinding tools, amulets (Fig. 3.13/19, 20), and perforated stone axes-hammers (Fig. 3.13/17, 18). An interesting example is an axe with a blunt section shaped into three transverse ribs (Fig. 3.13/17).

LIST OF SITES WITH CHANCE FINDS

117. Marenovo, the site of Đerđelin, a fragment of biconical beaker; 123. Poljna, unknown site, beaker with trapezoidal opening and amphora (Fig. 3.10/11, 12) (Stojić and Čađenović 2006, 326, fig. 54);[12] 124. Paraćin, the site of Gloždak, beakers with trapezoidal opening (Fig. 3.10/15, 16) (Stojić 1998, pl. v/2, 6); 126. Orašje, unknown site, beaker with trapezoidal opening (Fig. 3.10/14) (Čađenović 2009, 167, fig. 2/3); 127. Baba, Lešje, beaker with trapezoidal opening (Fig. 3.10/17) (Stojić 1998, pl. v/7); 128. Borač, uknown site, Borač type axe (Fig. 3.13/8) (Krstić *et al.* 1972, cat. no. 27); 129. Dražmirovac, unknown site, Dražmirovac type axe (Fig. 3.13/10) (Stojić 1980); 130. Trućevac, uknown site, hoard/grave (Fig. 3.13/1–7) (Krstić *et al.* 1972, cat. no. 32); 131. Medveđa, uknown site, Izvoraele type axe (Vukmanović and Radojčić 1995).

Among the chance finds from sites in this zone, which lack detailed information on topography or precise location, are several whole vessels and three axes.

The axe from Dražmirovac near Jagodina features a thin, elongated blade that flares and rounds at the end, with a tubular haft that extends at the rear (Fig. 3.13/10) (Stojić 1980; Antonović 2014, 96). This belongs to the Dražmirovac type, dating to the Middle Bronze Age (Antonović 2014, pl. 60). A similar axe type is characteristic of the Middle Bronze Age in the Pannonian Plain (Bona 1975, pl. 182/1; Kiss 2012, 130–31, figs 28, 35).

The axe from Borač near Kragujevac has a thin, gracefully rounded blade. It is positioned at a slight angle relative to a tubular haft with an extended lower rear portion (Fig. 3.13/8) (Krstić *et al.* 1972, cat. no. 27; Antonović 2014, 95). Made of bronze with approximately 10% tin (Antonović 2014, table 2), this axe is classified as a Borač type, which dates to the Middle Bronze Age (Antonović 2014, pl. 60). The Medveđa axe is of the Izvoraele type (Fig. 3.13/9) (Vukmanović and Radojčić 1995, cat. no. 141) which, according to D. Antonović, dates to the Middle Bronze Age and is typical of the region now in south-western Romania (Antonović 2014, 93). This is the only example recorded in the central Balkans.

In this geographical zone of the central Balkans, one Middle Bronze Age hoard has been documented at Trućevac near Jagodina. This group of metal finds is characterised as either a hoard or grave goods and includes a smaller vessel, likely a beaker (Fig. 3.13/1), four flat axes with emphasised/re-inforced side edges (*Randleistenbeile* type) (Fig. 3.13/2, 3) (Antonović 2014, pl. 8/108–111), two bracelets (Fig. 3.13/4), two gold earrings (or hair ornaments?) (Fig. 3.13/7), a necklace, and seven fragments of spirally wound wire pendants (Fig. 3.13/5, 6) (Krstić *et al.* 1972, cat. no. 32). Such axes are commonly found in the Middle Bronze Age in the southern Pannonian Plain and the peri-Pannonian zone and, until the discovery of this axe type at Velika Humska Čuka in South Morava Basin (Fig. 3.49/12), the axes from Trućevac were the southernmost finds of this type (Antonović 2014, 53–55, Taf. 47). All axes from Trućevac are made of tin bronze, with tin content ranging from 1.5–10% (Antonović 2014, table 2). The beaker from the hoard is of type 1f or 7d, both of which emerged during the Middle Bronze Age and are characteristic of the Vatin culture area, as are the flat axes. The bracelets are open-type with flared ends, while the hair ring ornaments are triangular in cross-section, dating from the end of the Early to the Late Bronze Age (Aleksandrov 2009, 13, fig. 1/22).

Most vessels are two handled beakers with trapezoidal openings as described above, so further discussion will focus on the context of these finds. The beaker with a trapezoidal opening (Fig. 3.10/11) was initially published as originating from Lazarev grad (Čađenović 2009, 164, fig. 2/2) but was later attributed to Poljna along with a larger type 1a amphora (Stojić and Čađenović 2006, fig. 13, 54). The permanent exhibit at the National Museum in Kruševac lists it as originating from Lazarev grad, so the location of this beaker remains unclear and these data should be regarded with caution.

The beakers from the Gloždak site in Paraćin were also imprecisely located in publication (Stojić 1998, pl. v/2, 6). Upon visiting the Paraćin Museum, three such beakers were observed but with unclear locations. It is likely that they are from the Gloždak site (referred to as Gloždar in earlier literature), though it is uncertain whether they are from the Late Bronze Age necropolis with cremated remains at this site or an adjacent prehistoric settlement that also belongs to the Gloždak area (Čađenović 2009, 167).

A local resident of Orašje found a trapezoidal-opening beaker alongside an urn and a cup, but the urn was destroyed, while the beaker and cup were donated to the Kruševac Museum (Čađenović 2009, 167). The cup has not been published. The last Chance find, a trapezoidal-opening beaker, originates from the Baba site in Lešje near Paraćin, though no additional information about it is available (Stojić 1998).

3.2.4 Cultural and chronological determination of the Middle Bronze Age in the basin of the Great Morava and Šumadija

Only one systematically researched settlement has been attributed to the Middle Bronze Age in the geographical zone encompassing the Great Morava Basin along with Šumadija and the broader area around the confluence of the West Morava, extending west to the Grabovac Gorge, while other finds are either from surveys, smaller-scale excavations, or chance discoveries.

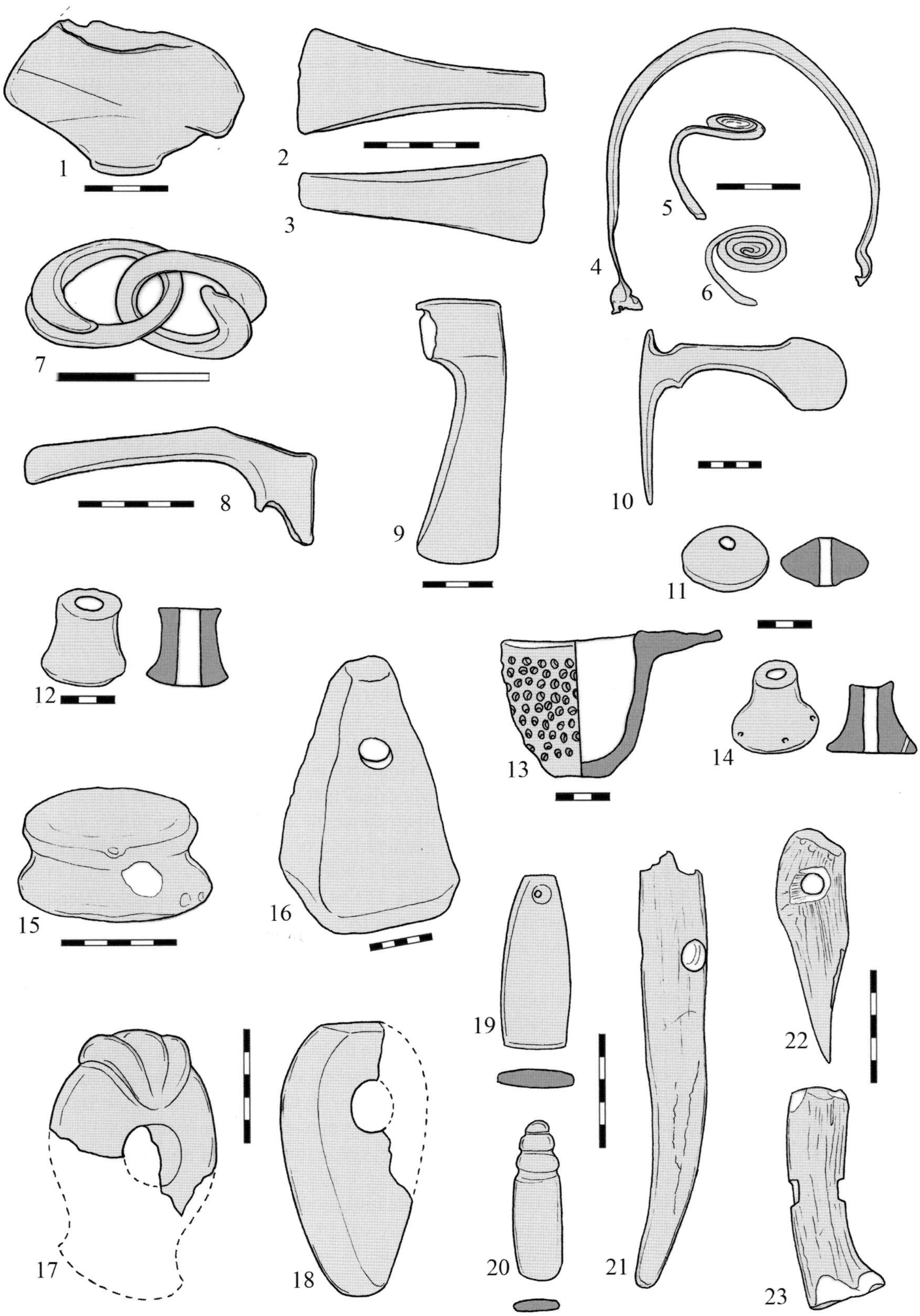

Figure 3.13. 1–7, Trućevac, hoard; 8, Borač, unknown site; 9, Medveđa, unknown site; 10, Dražmirovac, unknown site; 11–23, Ljuljaci: site of Milića Brdo.

The site of Milića Brdo in Ljuljaci, Šumadija, was excavated over several years, revealing three settlement horizons, including remnants of residential and defensive architecture (Bogdanović 1986). Absolute dates from this site derive from the oldest and middle settlements while, according to M. Bogdanović, dates from the youngest settlement are lacking. However, technical documentation shows the existence of two clear settlement horizons, with the third being harder to identify (Bogdanović 1986, figs 5 and 7). In any case, samples from two horizons have yielded absolute dates, although with a significant calibration range: three dates for the older horizon indicate a period of 1940–1630 cal BC (68.2% probability) (see Table 1), while a later date attributed to the middle horizon spans 1870–1520 cal BC (68.2% probability). Given the large margin of error, it is difficult to determine precisely when the oldest settlement was founded, though statistical probability suggests it originated in the 19th or 18th century cal BC. This settlement likely experienced architectural interventions observed during excavations, though these cannot be dated with precision within the defined chronological period. Additionally, the question remains whether the youngest date from the site indeed corresponds to the middle horizon or, perhaps inadvertently, belongs to the uppermost, youngest horizon, suggesting that all settlement horizons at Ljuljaci could span between the oldest and youngest dates, or from 1940–1520 cal BC, statistically most likely in the 19th–17th centuries cal BC.

Stylistically and typologically, finds from the youngest, third horizon at Ljuljaci are analogous to those recorded throughout Vojvodina and along the southern edge of the peri-Pannonian zone in the Danube Valley, where they are associated with the Vatin group. For instance, pottery found in a pit at Cigansko Brdo near Požarevac, roughly 80 km north-east of Ljuljaci, match those from Ljuljaci's youngest horizon, though this pit is dated to the 19th/18th centuries cal BC, approximately the same as Ljuljaci's oldest horizon. This further complicates the chronological framework for Ljuljaci, especially regarding the relative chronology of its habitation horizons.

In any case, ceramics from Ljuljaci's older settlement have analogies in Omoljica and other sites in the peri-Pannonian zone. The most indicative stylistic-typological element across all habitation horizons at Ljuljaci is the two handled beaker with a trapezoidal rim. These beakers, previously noted (Bulatović 2020), are widespread in the Middle Bronze Age from the area where the Mureș flows into the Tisza down to South Morava Basin, and they are most prevalent in central parts of the Central Balkans (Bulatović 2020, fig. 1). Absolute dates from multiple sites place them in approximately the same period as the settlements at Ljuljaci, spanning from the early 19th to the late 16th century cal BC.

Apart from these beakers, which mostly correspond to types 1g, 1f, and 7d, the oldest horizon includes beakers of type 1c known from the Early Bronze Age, as well as biconical cups with a single handle of type 4a, amphorae of type 1a, and others. The only significant novelty in this horizon is the trapezoidal-rimmed beakers, also found at Maskare in a cultural layer with a pit dated to the 19th–18th century cal BC, as well as at Poljna, Sarina Međa, Gloždak, Lešje, and Lazarev Grad. The oldest reliable date for these beakers comes from Maskare and Cigansko Brdo (19th–18th centuries cal BC), while the youngest is from Velika Humska Čuka (16th century cal BC). Culturally and chronologically, pottery from this zone belong to a single cultural area, defined about a decade ago based on stylistic-typological ceramic characteristics as the Bubanj-Hum IV–Ljuljaci group (Bulatović and Stankovski 2012, 337–347). Pottery from the second horizon at Ljuljaci resembles that from the preceding horizon but introduce some new forms, notably type 7d beakers (Fig. 3.8/16) and type 3d bowls (Fig. 3.8/1, 2). Only in the third horizon, according to M. Bogdanović, does the ceramic inventory at Ljuljaci change significantly; while beakers with trapezoidal opening remain, beaker forms evolve, with types 7d and 1f becoming dominant. In this horizon, beakers are richly decorated with incisions and punctures, while plastic ornaments on the tops of handles, which were sporadic in the previous horizon, become common. If stylistic-typological elements on pottery from older settlement horizons belonged to the Bubanj-Hum IV–Ljuljaci group, elements from the youngest settlement also share much in common with Vatin ceramics from the Danube Valley as well as with the Verbicioara group in Oltenia and Banat.

Contacts with the Verbicioara group are reflected in cylindrical lids and handles with a vertical rib and plastic ornament at the top (Bogdanović 1986, fig. 73, 183, 206), characteristic of this group and of Middle Bronze Age groups in Pannonia (Bona 1975, pl. 140, 141; Craciunescu 2004, 227, pl. lii/2, lvii/2, 3). Evidently, interactions between the population at Ljuljaci and the northern Danube Valley intensified during the 18th/17th centuries cal BC, significantly influencing the stylistic and typological characteristics of ceramics from that time, particularly in Šumadija and in the youngest settlement at Ljuljaci. These contacts are also visible in finds from the Trućevac hoard, especially type 7d beakers typical of the Vatin group and flat axes commonly associated with the Vatin group on the Balkans.

For the younger horizon, or the final phase of the Middle Bronze Age in this zone, we must mention the absolute date from pit 1 at Đula in Ostrikovac, which dates this pit to approximately the second half of the 16th or the early 15th century cal BC. The ceramics in the pit were mixed with Vinkovci–Somogyvár group ceramics discussed above, but due to the distinctiveness of these groups, it was possible to isolate indicative ceramics from the late Middle Bronze Age (Fig. 3.10/18–24). Stylistic-typological traits of these ceramics indicate the Bubanj-Hum IV–Ljuljaci group's tradition, as well as new stylistic elements such as rich incision decoration with motifs corresponding to the Verbicioara style.

3.3 Western Serbia and the Lim Valley

3.3.1 Settlements and dwellings

Site numbers refer to Plate 19.

List of settlements

132. Ostra, the site of Sokolica, hilltop settlement (Ljuština and Dmitrović 2009); 133. Gornja Gorevnica, the site of Slatina, lowland settlement (Nikitović 1995).

Unlike the Early Bronze Age, where no settlements were documented in this zone despite the presence of several necropolises, the situation in the Middle Bronze Age is notably different. During this period, the region of Western Serbia and the Lim Valley contains evidence of one hilltop and one lowland settlement, both located on the western edge of the West Morava Valley.

The sole hilltop settlement in this zone was identified at the Sokolica site in Ostra near Čačak, approximately 15 km south-west from the roughly contemporaneous site at Milića Brdo in Ljuljaci. Unfortunately, the Middle Bronze Age settlement has been extensively disrupted by later activities during the Iron Age and the Byzantine period, resulting in a significant loss of information regarding the settlement's size and the architecture of the dwellings and other structures.

About 20 km to the west-north-west of this hilltop, on the northern side of the western edge of the West Morava Valley, situated on the gentle slopes towards the Miokovac field, lies the site of Slatina in Gornja Gorevnica. The site was excavated in two campaigns confirming its primary Neolithic origins. However, one pit dating to the Middle Bronze Age was found dug into the Neolithic layer. This pit had a roughly oval base with a gently conical profile and rounded edges, measuring 2.4 × 2.6 m. Its fill consisted of loose soil mixed with ceramic fragments, plaster, animal bones, charcoal, ash, and scorched red earth. Based on the pit's shape and dimensions, K. Dmitrović suggests that it may have been a shallowly dug dwelling (Dmitrović 2009, 104, 105, fig. 2). However, it remains unclear whether Bronze Age ceramics were found throughout the site or only in this pit, which would indicate the nature and duration of the site's use during the Bronze Age.

3.3.2 Necropolises and burial practices

Necropolis

134. Jabuka, the site of Savin Lakat, tumulus (Lazić 2007).

The only necropolis from this geographical region potentially belonging to the Middle Bronze Age is located at the Savin Lakat site in Jabuka, near the border crossing between Serbia and Montenegro. The site is situated on the edge of a broad limestone plateau at an elevation of approximately 1100 m. Three mounds were identified at Savin Lakat, one of which has been excavated (Lazić 2007, 109). The mounds form an orderly row, with two almost touching, while the third is positioned a few metres away. The diameters of the mounds range between 15 m and 18 m and their heights vary from 1.5–2 m. The excavated mound, located centrally in the row, has a diameter of 15 m and a height of 1.5 m. It was built on a solid limestone foundation with remnants of a stone ring about 14 m in diameter still visible in places. A layer of dark brown clay with traces of ash formed a platform *c.* 11 m in diameter, atop which lay a circular stone platform with a diameter of 11 m and a thickness of 0.3 m.

The central structure of the tumulus comprised a cone of large stones, with a diameter of 5.5 m and a height of 1.5 m. Between the stones were loose dark soil, ash, scattered cremated human remains, fragments of bronze jewellery (including necklaces, pendants, and buttons), amber beads, flint artefacts, and pottery fragments. A layer of sandy soil mixed with clay lumps, 1.15 m thick, was then laid over this structure to form the mound, with a thin layer of stone, 0.25–0.3 m thick, applied to the surface. This outer layer also contained pottery fragments, chipped stone artefacts, and a bronze pendant.

The mound contained a total of seven inhumation graves, although M. Lazić suggests there may have been more based on the human remains found within and around the central structure. Cremated remains were also found in the mound, indicating at least one cremation burial, likely within the central structure.

The inhumation graves were distributed throughout the mound: beneath the central structure (graves 5 and 6), within the embankment above the stone platform (graves 1–4), and in the space between the mound's stone ring and the platform (grave 7). The inhumed deceased were buried in various ways but were all placed in a slightly flexed position. The peripheral graves (1–4 and 7) were shallowly dug, located beneath the stone surface layer, with two of them being double graves (grave 4 – two children; grave 7 – a child and an adult). Of the peripheral graves, only grave 4 had any burial structure and contained a bronze hair ornament made of spiral twisted wire.

The central graves, 5 and 6, are the most intriguing. Grave 5 lay on the limestone foundation at the centre of the mound beneath the dark clay layer, the stone platform, and the central stone structure. A slightly flexed skeleton of an adult female lay on her left side atop a rectangular base of finely laid stones, without grave goods. The other central grave, 6, was located beneath the central stone structure and platform, and according to M. Lazić, was likely dug into the platform after its formation. The slightly flexed skeleton of an adult male lay on his right side on a paved base surrounded by limestone fragments. A complete beaker was found near the abdomen and animal bones near the shoulder.

Human remains, mostly of children, were found scattered throughout the mound. All bronze objects found within the mound (buttons, pendants, spring wires), aside from the hair ornament in grave 4, were scattered throughout the central stone structure, along with five amber beads.

While the cremation burial within the central structure appears to belong to the Late Bronze Age, based on the types of jewellery found (Hänsel 1968, Taf. 14, 26; Bulatović *et al.* 2023; Cwalinski *et al.* 2023), the inhumation graves might represent an earlier period. These graves not only involve a distinctly different treatment of the deceased but are also largely devoid of metal or amber grave goods, except for grave 4, which contained a hair ring – a widely datable item, unlike the circular pendants with central spines, button-like decorations, and amber beads that are typically dated to post-15th century BC in this region (Bulatović *et al.* 2023; Cwalinski *et al.* 2023). However, the beaker found in grave 6 is strikingly similar to well-known two handled beakers with a trapezoidal shaped vessel opening. Although the beaker from Jabuka has a similarly shaped rim, only one side is modelled while the other is simply extended (Fig. 3.17/4). These beakers are characteristic of the Middle Bronze Age, leading to the assignment of this mound to that period.

3.3.3 Portable finds

3.3.3.1 Pottery

The quantity of ceramic finds in this zone is not as substantial as in other zones from the Middle Bronze Age; nevertheless, these are the most numerous among artefacts in this region.

A. BOWLS

The predominant bowl types include 1b, 3b, and 3e, though only marginally more frequent than type 1c. Types 1b and 3b are known from the Early Bronze Age in the central Balkans, with type 1b being especially characteristic of this zone. Types 1c and 3e represent new occurrences not recorded in the previous period. Type 1b is documented in Ostra (Fig. 3.14/1, 2), type 3b exclusively in the tumulus at Jabuka (Fig. 3.17/1, 2), and type 3e in Gornja Gorevnica (Fig. 3.16/2, 3), where type 1c is also found (Fig. 3.16/1). The latter type closely resembles beakers of type 2a but is wider in diameter. None of the bowls features ornamentation, except for one with rectangular, vertically perforated handles placed horizontally on the shoulder (Fig. 3.14/1) and another type 1b bowl adorned with brad-shaped appliqués on the belly (Fig. 3.14/2).

The bowls from Gornja Gorevnica are made from fine to medium fabric mixed with fine sand, with surfaces that are either smoothed or polished, and they range in light to dark brown hues (Dmitrović 2009, 106). The bowls from Jabuka are composed of well-purified clay mixed with fine sand, fired in reddish-brown tones (Lazić 2007, 119, 120). Similarly, the bowls from Ostra, like those from Gorevnica, are created from fine to medium fabric and are fired in light and dark brown shades (Dmitrović and Ljuština 2007, 13).

B. CUPS

Only one cup has been documented in this zone during the Middle Bronze Age. It is a semi-circular cup with a single handle extending over the rim (type 1a) (Fig. 3.14/12).

C. BEAKERS

The types of beakers identified in this zone during the Middle Bronze Age include 1a (Fig. 3.16/11), 1c (Fig. 3.16/15; Fig. 3.17/4), 1f (Fig. 3.14/7, 1; Fig. 3.16/7), 1g (Fig. 3.14/4–6, 8, 9; Fig. 3.16/4), 2a (Fig. 3.16/6, 9), and 5a. All types are approximately equally represented, each making up around 12–19%, except for type 1g, which accounts for over 25%. It should be noted that type 5a (Fig. 3.14/3; Fig. 3.16/13) was not recorded in this zone in the previous period. These beakers first appeared in the Western Morava Valley and Pčinja Region during the Early Bronze Age (Fig. 2.19/6; Fig. 2.41/8), and during the Middle Bronze Age, they also appear in South Morava Basin and the Timok Region (Fig. 3.20/24; Fig. 3.42/9). Notably, a stylistic element seen across other zones in the central Balkans appears in this geographic zone for the first time on beakers. This is the trapezoidal shaped rim (Fig. 3.14/4, 6, 9; Fig. 3.16/4; Fig. 3.17/4), found on various types of beakers depending on the region. In this zone, the trapezoidal rim is observed on types 1a, 1c, and 1g, appearing on both newly developed beakers (1g) and those inherited from the Early Bronze Age (1a and 1c).

The beakers in this zone are unornamented and generally have two strap handles that connect the rim and body of the vessel. Some specimens feature plastic protrusions on the body (Fig. 3.14/4, 9, 7, 13; Fig. 3.16/4) or dimple impressions on the upper surface of the rim (Fig. 3.16/5).

Beakers from Ostra were made from well-purified clay, sometimes with fine sand added, and were fired in shades of brown and grey. Some specimens have polished surfaces (Dmitrović and Ljuština 2007, 12). Beakers from Gornja Gorevnica were similarly made from refined clay with fine sand, often in medium fabric, and exhibit colours in shades of grey and brown. Some have polished surfaces, while others are only smoothed (Dmitrović 2009, 106). The beaker from Jabuka was made from refined clay mixed with sand of varying granulation. It is coarsely constructed, with a thin polished coating in greyish-brown tones (Lazić 2007, 120).

D. AMPHORAE

Amphorae are not commonly found in the inventories of Middle Bronze Age sites in western Serbia. Documented types include 1a (Fig. 3.14/16), 3b (Fig. 3.17/6), and 5a,

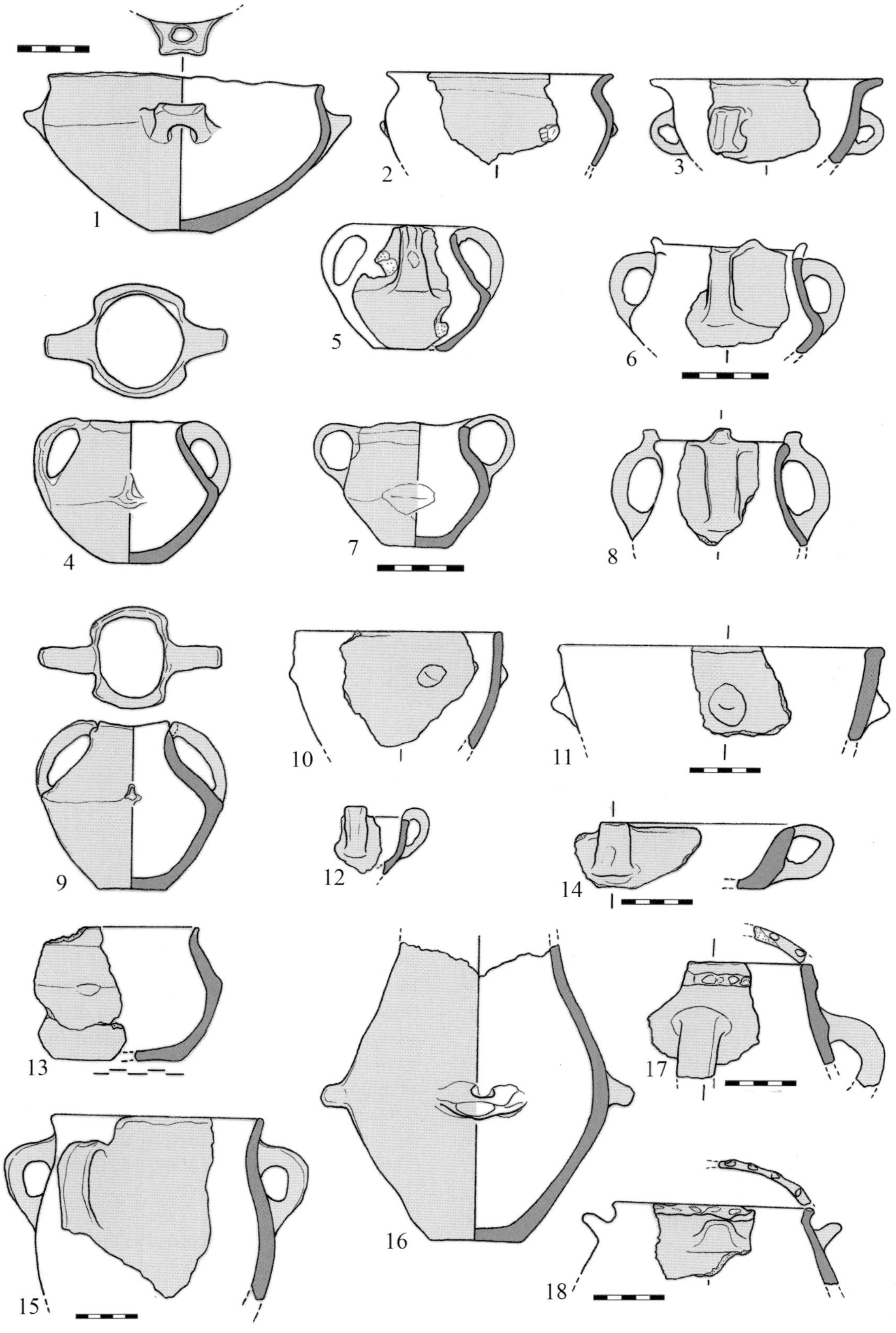

Figure 3.14. Ostra: site of Sokolica.

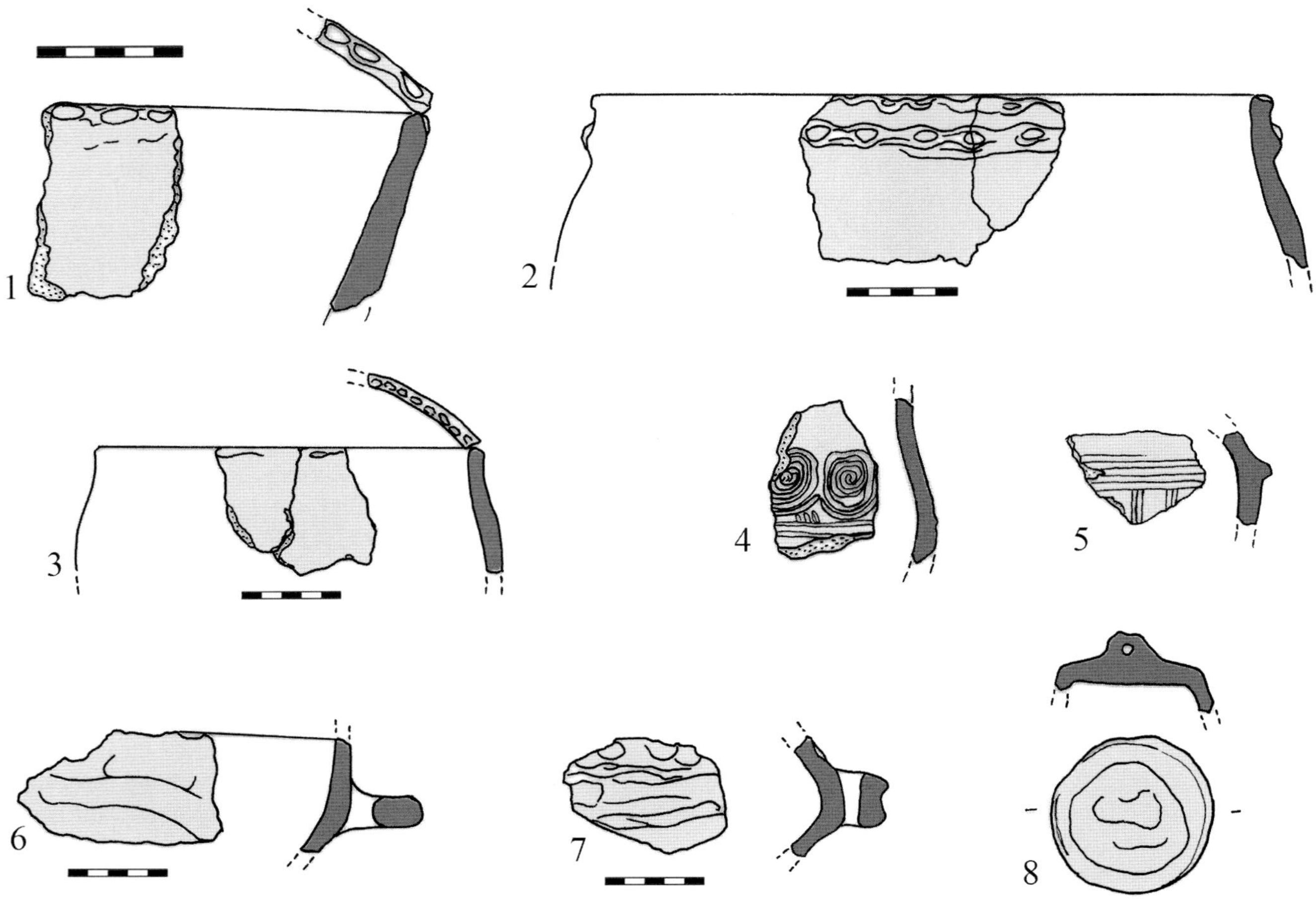

Figure 3.15. Ostra: site of Sokolica.

all equally represented. Type 5a (Fig. 3.16/8) only appears during the Middle Bronze Age, whereas the other two were already known in this zone during the Early Bronze Age. Notably, amphorae from this period are undecorated, unlike those from the previous period when one amphora was decorated with geometric motifs created by incising, grooving, and stamping (Fig. 2.23/15).

The amphora from Ostra is of medium fabric with fine sand inclusions and fired in shades of grey, orange, and brown (Dmitrović and Ljuština 2007, 14), whereas the specimen from Gornja Gorevnica is noted to be of rougher manufacture (Dmitrović 2009, 111). The amphora from Jabuka is made from well-refined clay, fired in grey tones with a thin polished reddish-brown coating visible (Lazić 2007, 120).

E. POTS

Pots are arguably the most abundant type of vessel in this zone, especially at sites in Ostra and Gornja Gorevnica, whereas no pots were found in the mound at Jabuka. A similar situation was observed in the Early Bronze Age, where pots were exceedingly rare due to the presence of only necropolises from this period in the region. Most pots are of type 1a (Fig. 3.14/17, 18; Fig. 3.15/1–3; Fig. 3.16/12, 16–18), with type 2a (Fig. 3.14/15) being less common. Decorations mainly consist of rows of finger impressions along the rim and plastic horizontal bands with finger impressions. Some of the larger pots could be classified as pithoi (Fig. 3.15/1–3; Fig. 3.16/16–18). These are made of coarse fabric with significant amounts of sand of varying granularity and are fired in shades of grey and brown (Dmitrović and Ljuština 2007, 14; Dmitrović 2009, 112).

F. LIDS

Only one lid has been recorded in this zone, found at Ostra, consisting of just the top with a small handle and remnants of the walls. This lid likely belongs to type 1b and is decorated with an incised circular line on the upper surface (Fig. 3.15/8). It is made from well-refined clay and fired in a light brown colour.

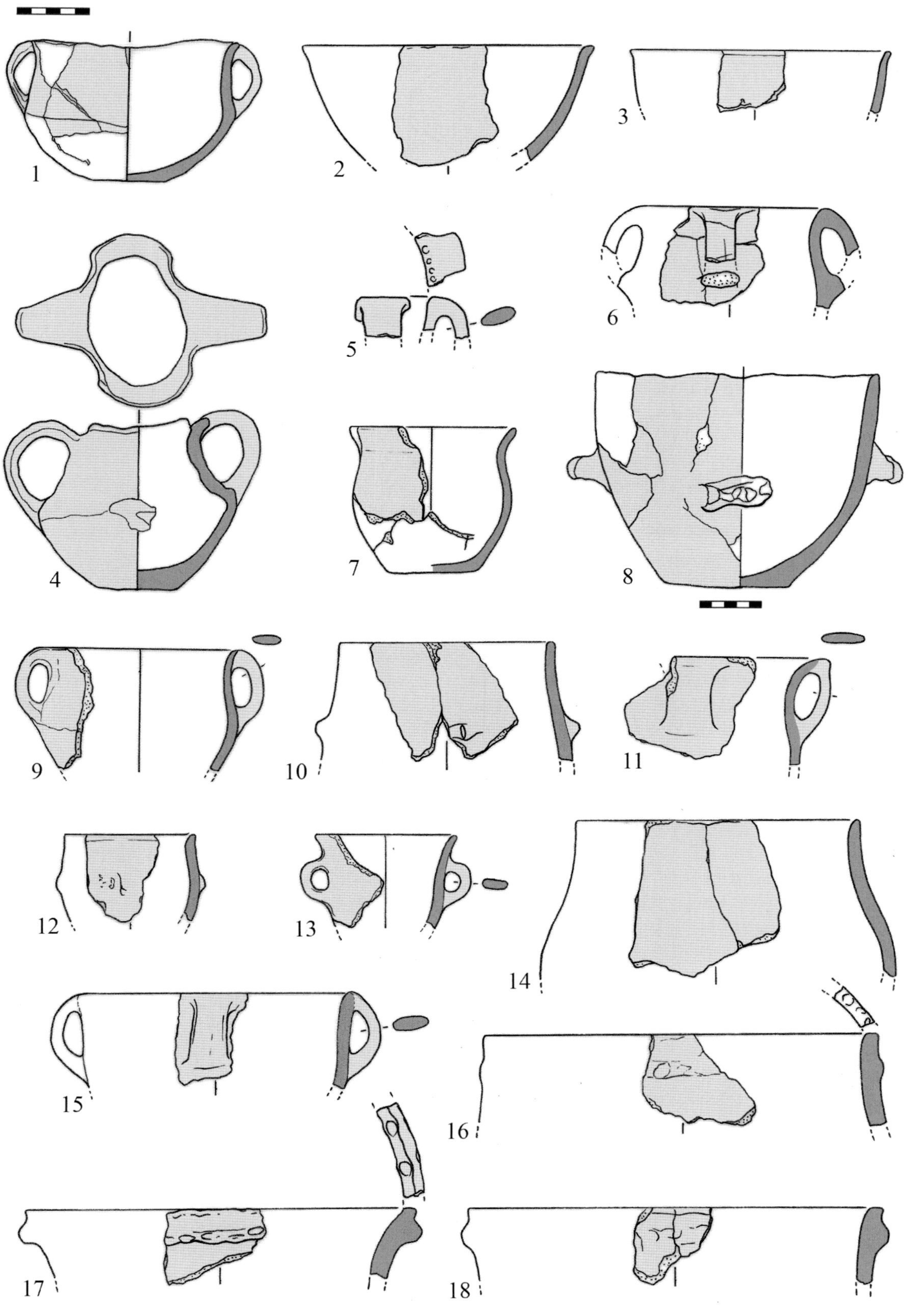

Figure 3.16. Gornja Gorevnica: site of Slatina.

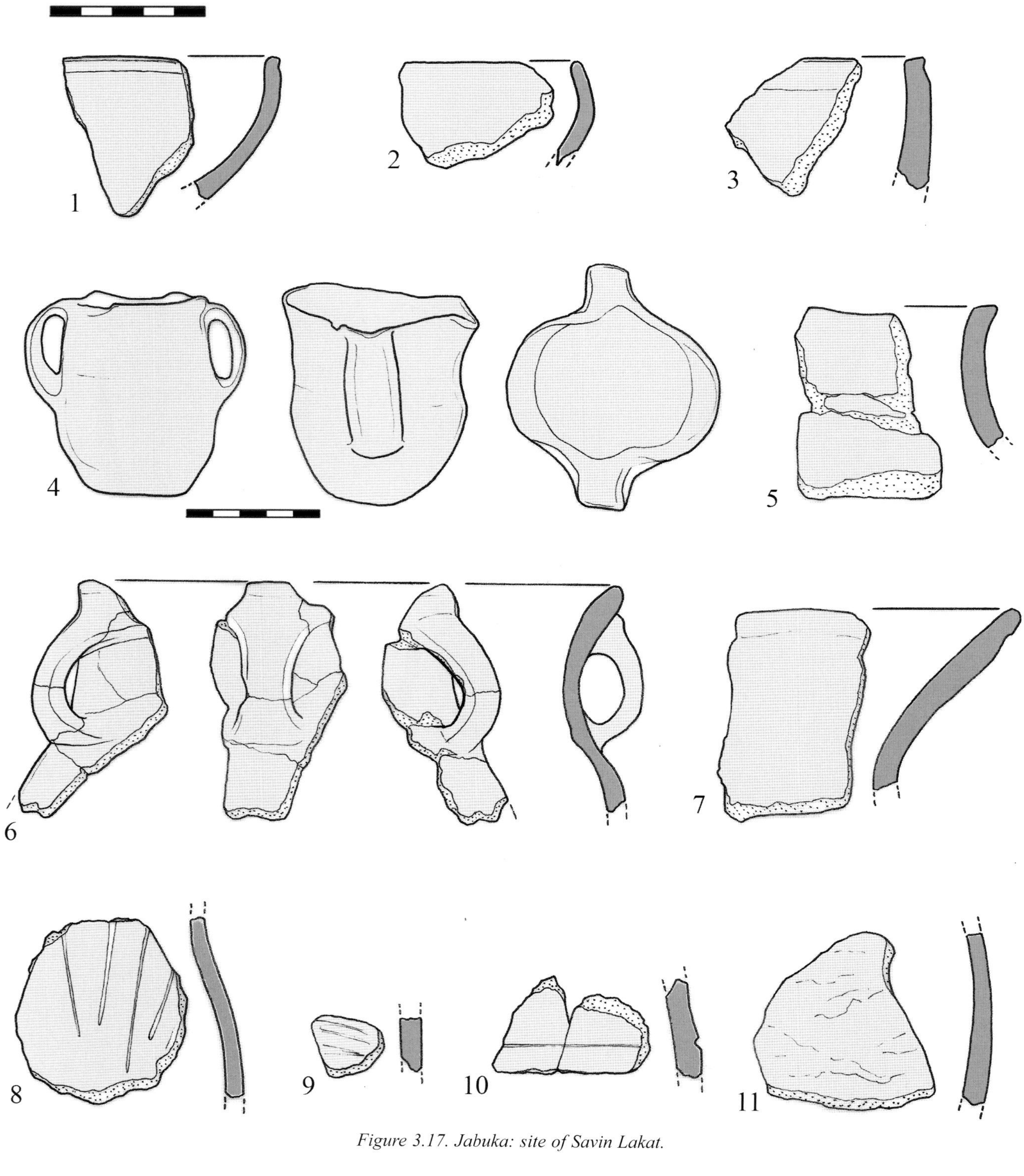

Figure 3.17. Jabuka: site of Savin Lakat.

G. SPECIAL-PURPOSE VESSELS

Among special-purpose vessels, a shallow vessel with an oval base and a handle extending above the rim has been discovered (Fig. 3.14/14). As discussed above, these vessels, known as fish platters (*Fischbutta*), are characteristic of the peri-Pannonian zone or the Danube Basin, appearing sporadically in the south. This vessel is of coarse fabric and dark brown in colour.

H. HANDLES

The most common type of handle remains the vertically positioned loop handle with a strap or, less frequently, oval cross-section, typically located between the rim and body of the vessel, most often on beakers and less frequently on bowls and cups. Shorter vertical loop handles are also found on the bodies of beakers and pots. Additionally, horizontally positioned tongue-shaped handles with vertical perforations are found mainly on the bodies of amphorae (Fig. 3.14/16; Fig. 3.15/6, 7; Fig. 3.16/8), as well as rectangular horizontal perforated handles on a type 1b bowl. Non-perforated tongue-shaped handles are also recorded (Fig. 3.14/18), and some loop handles have plastic extensions in various shapes, such as conical or horn-like (Fig. 3.14/8; Fig. 3.17/6).

I. ORNAMENTATION

Ornamentation on Middle Bronze Age vessels in this zone is modest. The most common features are wart-like or conical plastic extensions or thickened zones on the body of the vessel, along with rows of dimpled impressions (fingerprints?) pressed onto the fresh surface of the vessel or plastic bands. Only a few fragments show incisions, primarily forming metope fields, spirals, and circles (Fig. 3.15/4, 8) (Dmitrović and Ljuština 2007, T. III/5).

3.3.3.2 Other finds

This zone does not have many recorded finds aside from ceramic vessels. Only a ceramic spindle whorl, chipped stone tools, and bone tools have been documented. The spindle whorl was discovered in the mound at Savin Lakat in Jabuka and has a discoidal shape with a central circular perforation, fired in brown shades (Fig. 3.18/1). Three fragments of serrated blades made of chipped greyish-brown stone, one bone spatula, two bone awls, and two sewing needles with perforated tips were found in the pit at the Slatina site in Gornja Gorevnica (Fig. 3.18/2–7) (Dmitrović 2009, 112).

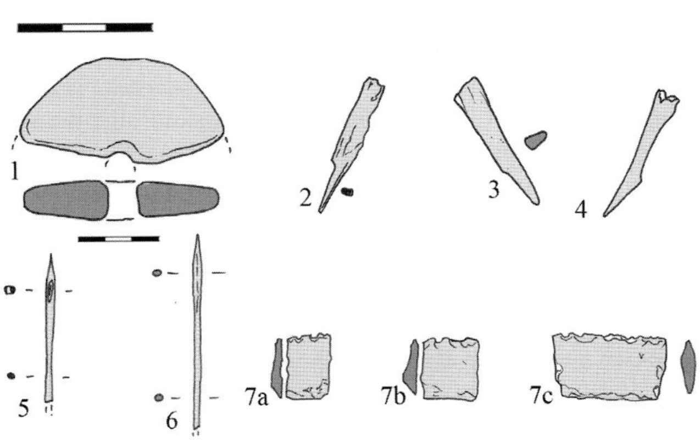

Figure 3.18. 1, Jabuka: site of Savin Lakat, mound 1; 2–9, Gornja Gorevnica: site of Slatina, pit 1.

3.3.4 Cultural and chronological classification of sites in western Serbia and the Lim Valley Region

In this geographic zone of western Serbia and the Lim Valley Region, there is only one absolute date from the Middle Bronze Age, yet the ceramic finds from this context do not correspond to this date. Specifically, this refers to a pit-house at the Paulje site in Brezjak near Loznica. Most material from this pit-house corresponds to the so-called Brezjak group of the Late Bronze Age, a regional variant of the Belegiš I group. One date from the pit-house suggests an early phase of habitation around the 19th–18th century cal BC, corresponding to the Middle Bronze Age (Table 1). The sample for AMS dating was carbonised wood, known for the 'old wood effect', but even with the maximum deviation of this effect considered, the date remains early for material from the Brezjak group, which is generally dated to the early 15th century cal BC (Bulatović *et al.* 2023). Notably, a similarly early date was obtained from a tumulus burial (Mound 38) at a nearby necropolis, containing a vessel typical of the Brezjak group.

There are two potential explanations for this phenomenon: either the Late Bronze Age necropolis and settlement were established on older habitation or burial grounds, or our understanding of the cultural-chronological characteristics of the Brezjak group needs revision. It is worth mentioning that, until now, no Middle Bronze Age sites have been recorded in this region encompassing Jadar, Rađevina, and Azbukovica, despite its known habitation during both the preceding (Early Bronze Age) and subsequent (Late Bronze Age) periods (Bulatović *et al.* 2017, 52).

A similar situation was observed further south, in the Čačak Region and Lim Valley. Following the Early Bronze Age and the numerous tumulus necropolises from that period, it appeared that habitation in this region ceased. However, it has since been demonstrated that the sites in Gornja Gorevnica and Ostra, as well as the mound in Jabuka, belong to the Middle Bronze Age, partially filling this apparent gap. The question then arises: to which cultural manifestation does the ceramic materials from these sites belong? Based on the stylistic and typological characteristics of the pottery, and lacking absolute dates, it could be posited that this geographic zone largely falls within the cultural domain of the so-called Bubanj-Hum IV–Ljuljaci group for several reasons.

First, the favourable orographic characteristics of the region, namely the geographic openness of the central part of the West Morava valley towards the west, include sites such as Slatina and Sokolica with only a minor natural barrier at the Trstenik Gorge. The Bubanj-Hum IV–Ljuljaci group characterises the Middle Bronze Age in the middle and lower West Morava valley, which is arguably part of the core territory of this group, suggesting probable contacts with contemporaneous populations inhabiting the western edge of this valley, located only about 60 km away.

Secondly, the stylistic and typological elements observed in the ceramics from Slatina and Sokolica are nearly identical to those of the Bubanj-Hum IV–Ljuljaci group. The most recognisable stylistic feature is the trapezoidal-shaped vessel openings, primarily on beakers, documented at Slatina and Sokolica and even in Jabuka in the Lim Valley Region, more than 80 km away. Additionally, type 1b bowls, although not exclusive to this cultural group, are prevalent. The type 5a beaker, which appears to be confined to sites of this group, ranges from the Timok Region in the east to the western edge of the West Morava valley and from Šumadija in the north to Pusta Reka in the south.

New ceramic features associated with this group include more pronounced biconical profiles of beakers, plastic projections on handle tops, and horizontally set, vertically perforated rectangular, semi-circular, or triangular handles. These elements are recorded on ceramics from Slatina and Sokolica, and some are even found at Savin Lakat, suggesting that this region should be included in the territory inhabited by the Bubanj-Hum IV–Ljuljaci group. The sole exception remains northwestern Serbia, specifically Jadar, Azbukovica, and Rađevina, where no pottery from this period have been confirmed based on current evidence.

3.4 The Timok Region with Đerdap Gorge

The geographic and natural characteristics of this zone, which includes eastern Serbia and the basins of the Svrljig Timok, Crni Timok, Beli Timok, and Trgoviški Timok rivers, along with the surrounding mountains and the Đerdap Gorge, have been discussed in detail in Chapter 2.

3.4.1 Settlement and dwelling

In this geographic zone, six hilltop and 23 plain or highland settlements, as well as two cave habitats, have been identified. Site numbers refer to Plate 19.

3.4.1.1 Hilltop settlements

LIST OF HILLTOP SETTLEMENTS (FIG. 3.19)

136. Mokranjske Stene, the site of Potkapina (Bulatović *et al.* 2013; Kapuran and Janjić 2015); 137. Bor, the site of Čoka Kazak (Kapuran *et al.* 2014, 89–91); 138. Bor, the site of Čoka Njica (Srejović and Lazić 1997, 226; Kapuran *et al.* 2014, 93; Mehofer *et al.* 2021); 139. Tanda, the site of Mali Vizak (Kapuran *et al.* 2014, 189, 190); 140. Gamzigradska Banja, the site of Banjska Stena (Srejović and Lazić 1997, 229, 230); 141. Podvis, the site of Bolvan (Jovanović 1987; Kapuran 2011; Kapuran and Bulatović 2012a).

This extensive geographic zone, stretching north to south and comprising several smaller sub-regions, has influenced the socio-cultural development of past communities. Of the five confirmed hilltops in this zone, none is located in the Đerdap Gorge; instead, they are all situated in the mountainous regions of the Svrljig Timok and Crni Timok valleys or on the southern slopes of the ore-rich Homolje Mountains.

All settlements are small in area, positioned on elevated, dominant, and restricted or difficult to access locations. The Potkapina (Kapuran and Janjić 2015),[13] Bolvan, and Banjska Stena settlements are situated just above watercourses, such as the Svrljig Timok (Bolvan), Crni Timok (Banjska Stena), and smaller rivers like the Sikolska Reka (Potkapina), or at the exit of a gorge (Bolvan). The Čoka Kazak, Čoka Njica, and Tanda hilltops are located in the interior of the ore-rich mountain mass, away from major watercourses, suggesting a possible connection to copper ore extraction, especially since a slag depot was identified at the Tanda site (Kapuran 2014, 109), and the Čoka Kazak and Čoka Njica sites are close to Ružana, where evidence of copper metallurgy has been recorded (Kapuran *et al.* 2016).

Unfortunately, none of these settlements has been excavated, so information about the size, appearance of the hilltops, and structures within them is minimal. During surveys at the Bolvan site, numerous ceramic fragments and house daub were found, but as the site is multi-layered, the period of the daub cannot be precisely determined (Kapuran and Bulatović 2012a, 110). More data come from the Crni Timok valley, particularly from the Banjska Stena site, where a defensive wall made of large stones and wooden palisades was discovered, but no information on residential structures within the settlement is available (Srejović and Lazić 1997, 229, 230; Lazić 1998, 150; 2010, 25).

3.4.1.2 Lowland settlements

LIST OF PLAIN SETTLEMENTS (FIG. 3.19)

142. Dobra, the site of Padina (Jovanović 1971b); 143. Dobra, the site of Gospođin Vir (Popović 1983, 151; Bulatović *et al.* 2013, 80); 144. Kladovo, the site of Donje Butorke (Bulatović *et al.* 2013, 91–93); 145. Mala Vrbica, the site of Livade (Vukmanović and Popović 1984; 1986); 146. Rtkovo, the site of Glameja (Vasić and Janković 1971; Bulatović *et al.* 2013, 172); 147. Brza Palanka, the site of Obala kod crkve (Bulatović *et al.* 2013, 63, 64); 148. Brza Palanka, the site of Egeta-block III (Bulatović *et al.* 2013, 61, 62); 149. Mali Krivelj, the site of Valja Mare-Ciglana (Kapuran *et al.* 2014, 175, 176); 150. Banjsko Polje, the site of Ružana (Kapuran *et al.* 2014, 103–105); 151. Brestovačka Banja, the site of Selište (Kapuran *et al.* 2014, 105, 106); 152. Brestovačka Banja, the site of Hajdučka Česma (Srejović and Lazić 1997, 227; Kapuran 2014, 101); 153. Čoka Kormaroš; 154. Bor, the site of Kučajna (Srejović and Lazić 1997, 227; Kapuran 2014, 97); 155. Brestovačka Banja, the site of Trnjane (Jovanović and Janković 1990, 1; Kapuran *et al.* 2014, 107–112); 156. Brestovac, the site of Dubrava (Kapuran *et al.* 2014, 94, 95); 157. Zvezdan, the site of Njive na ulazu u Zvezdan (Kapuran and Škundrić 2009; Kapuran 2014, 134); 158. Gamzigrad, the site of Basilica III (Srejović and Lazić

1997, 229; Kapuran 2014, 125); 159. Metovnica, the site of Kot 1 (Kapuran *et al.* 2014, 176–178); 160. Gamzigrad, the site of Potoci (Kapuran 2014, 134); 161. Grlište, the site of Osenje, Along the Gas Pipeline site; 162. Knjaževac, the site of Kadijski Krst (Srejović and Lazić 1997, 232; Peković and Jevtić 2006); 163. Knjaževac, the site of Boševo-Tina (Jovanović 1987; Kapuran and Bulatović 2012a); 164. Kalna, the site of Bojčin (Kapuran and Bulatović 2012a).

This group of settlements includes those located in the plains, on river terraces, loess plateaus, gentle slopes above rivers, as well as settlements situated in higher mountainous areas but on slopes, without natural or artificial defensive elements characteristic of hilltop settlements. In this zone, Timok Valley including the Đerdap Region, 23 plain settlements have been identified, seven of which are in the Đerdap area, and the remainder in the Timok Valley.

Plain settlements in the Đerdap Region were established in Danube coves (Gospođin Vir, Padina), on the Danube terrace (Donje Butorke, Egeta, Obala kod crkve, Livade), or on the loess plateau inland from the Danube (Glameja). In any case, they are located right by the Danube. This geostrategic position greatly influenced their economy and facilitated communication with neighbours on both the Romanian and local sides of the Danube, upstream and downstream. It should be noted, however, that while there are no absolute dates from Middle Bronze Age sites in the Đerdap Region, based on the stylistic and typological characteristics of pottery and other artefacts, these sites mostly date from the end of the Middle and the beginning of the Late Bronze Age, necessitating a different chronological perspective compared to most Middle Bronze Age sites in the Timok Valley.

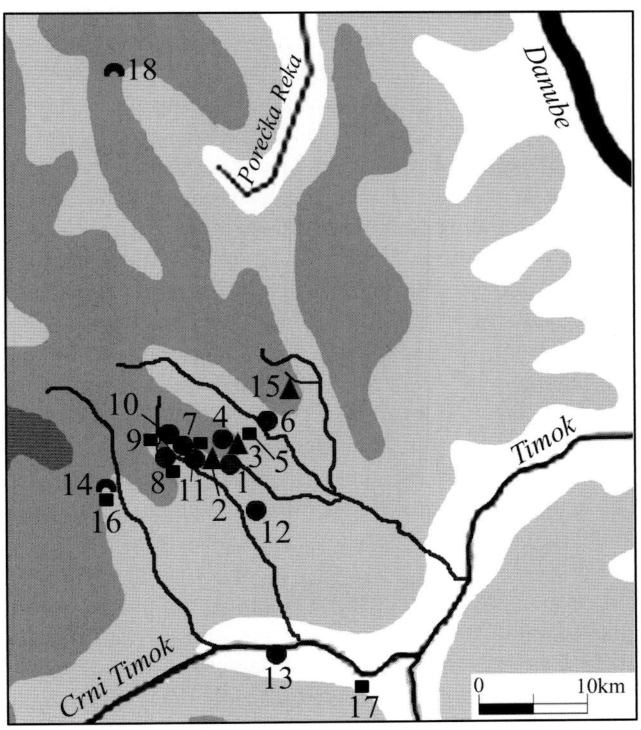

Figure 3.19. Map of the Middle Bronze Age sites in the Crni Timok and Timok Valley. Sites: 1. Kučajna (Pl. 19, 154); 2. Čoka Njica (138); 3. Čoka Kazak (137); 4. Čoka Kormaroš (153); 5. Kriveljski Kamen (167); 6. Valja Mare (149); 7. Trnjane (155, 170); 8. Hajdučka Česma (152, 171); 9. Borsko Jezero (169); 10. Selište (151); 11. Ružana (150); 12. Dubrava (156); 13. Kot 1 (159); 14. Zlotska Pećina (165); 15. Tanda (139); 16. Šoka Lu Patran (168); 17. Magura (172); 18. Kapetanova Pećina (166).

In the Timok Valley, the topographical situation of plain sites is entirely different, conditioned largely by the hilly relief that characterises this region. The only major river is the Timok, yet no sites from this period have been identified along it, which is surprising given earlier settlement patterns and those of other geographical zones. The settlement pattern in this region differed from others. Plain settlements were not located on terraces of larger rivers but on the fringes of mountainous areas rich in ore, particularly in the Bor area. The wealth of copper ore, which began to be intensively exploited and processed at the start of this period, dictated a completely different perception of the settlement system, seemingly tailored to mining and metallurgy activities. These settlements were located near smaller rivers or springs, as water was essential for daily life and potentially for copper processing. However, they are absent from the Timok Valley, where they might have been expected based on earlier settlement patterns.

Plain settlements in the Timok Valley were mostly situated on gentle slopes toward streams or smaller rivers (Ružana, Basilica III, Potoci), or on slopes toward the confluence of two streams or smaller rivers (Selište, Kučajna, Dubrava). Settlements were also built on slopes protected on one or two sides by steep cliffs (Čoka Kormaroš, Trnjane) or on river terraces of larger rivers (Zvezdan and Kot 1 on the Crni Timok, Kadijski Krst on the Svrljiški Timok, Boševo on the White Timok, Bojčin on the terrace of the Izvorska River which joins the Trgoviški Timok nearby). The smallest number of settlements was identified on terraces of smaller rivers at the base of hills (Mali Krivelj, Bojčin) or on slopes far from streams or rivers but near springs (Osenje, Hajdučka Fountain). Many of these settlements, such as Ružana, Settlement, Trnjane, and Valja Mare-Ciglana, were established near copper ore deposits (Kapuran 2014, 56), and remnants of metallurgical activities discovered during excavations at Ružana (Kapuran *et al.* 2016) indicate that this location for settlements was chosen deliberately. Some settlements were placed directly next to necropolises (Trnjane, Hajdučka Česma).

Most of these sites have not been archaeologically excavated, so there is limited information about the architecture of the settlements and structures. Residential structures with hearths and fireplaces were noted at the Kučajna site, but there are no further details on their dimensions and appearance (Kapuran 2014, 97). At older excavations at Trnjane, burned structures with floors covered with pottery, slag, and animal bones were discovered, and two bronze sewing needles were found on one of them. Recent excavations did not uncover similar structures, but a pit filled with Middle Bronze Age ceramics, plaster, and slag was identified (Kapuran *et al.* 2020, 56). Thus, while no new insights were gained about residential architecture, it can at least be confirmed that copper ore processing activities were conducted within the settlements.

Plaster and slag were discovered during surveys at Settlement in Brestovačka Banja, as well as at Dubrava and Potoci (Kapuran 2014, 102, 103, 134). Limited excavations were carried out at Osenje, where a small amount of plaster and pottery were found,[14] as well as at Kadijski Krst in Knjaževac, where a small amount of crushed plaster was also identified (Peković and Jevtić 2006, 114).

Based on the scant information available, it could be inferred that Middle Bronze Age residential structures in the Timok Valley were of an above-ground type, constructed using wattle and plaster, and likely featured compacted earth floors. Hearths were identified within the structures, as well as slag, indicating the possibility that copper ore processing took place within these structures.

3.4.1.3 Cave habitats

LIST OF CAVES (FIG. 3.19)

165. Zlot Cave, Zlot (Lazareva Pećina) (Tasić 1969, 36–39; Kapuran *et al.* 2014, 123–143); 166. Majdanpek, Kapetanova Cave (Kapetanova pećina) (Kapuran *et al.* 2014, 171, 172).

In this geographical zone, two caves have been identified, located in the vicinity of Bor and Majdanpek. Both caves have been archaeologically excavated but are multi-layered, with highly disturbed stratigraphy. Consequently, despite the discovery of residential structure remains, it is impossible to determine to which of the numerous layers they belong (Tasić 1980).

3.4.2 Necropolises and burial practices

In the Timok Valley and Đerdap zone, six necropolises have been identified, all located in the Timok Valley: five in the Bor Region and one in the Zaječar Region. All documented necropolises exclusively contained cremated remains.

List of necropolises (Fig. 3.19)

167. Bor, the site of Kriveljski Kamen (Kapuran *et al.* 2014, 152–154; 2022, 51); 168. Šoka lu Patran (Kapuran *et al.* 2022, ref. 53); 169. Brestovac, the site of Borsko Jezero (Kapuran 2011; Kapuran *et al.* 2014, 105, 106); 170. Brestovačka Banja, the site of Trnjane (Jovanović and Janković 1990, 1; Srejović and Lazić 1997; Kapuran *et al.* 2014, 107–112; 2020); 171. Brestovačka Banja, the site of Hajdučka Česma (Kapuran 2011; Kapuran *et al.* 2014, 112, 113; 2022, 51); 172. Zaječar, the site of Magura (Srejović and Lazić 1997, 228, 229; Kapuran 2014, 131).

The necropolis at Kriveljski Kamen consists of four circular stone burial structures, up to 3.5 m in diameter, with four graves containing cremated remains (Kapuran *et al.* 2014, 215). Besides the fractured grey sandstone used in the construction, chalcopyrite fragments, pebbles, and parts of stone querns were also noted. Each grave contained a pear-shaped urn with horizontally placed handles. The bones inside the urns were heavily fragmented and burnt at very high temperatures, with no remnants from the pyre found in the urns, although traces of copper slag were visible on the bones.

The necropolis at Šoka lu Patran is not precisely located due to missing documentation; however, according to the discoverer, it may be near Zlotska Pećina. Fragmented urns and cremated human bones were discovered at this site long ago but the exact number of urns is unknown (Kapuran *et al.* 2022, ref. 53).

In 1997 and 2002 excavations at the cremation necropolis were conducted during periods of low water levels at Borsko Lake. A total of 32 circular, stone burial structures made of fractured stone were uncovered, typically 2–3 m in diameter but some reaching up to 7 m (Kapuran *et al.* 2014, 213, 214). The outer ring of the these structures was composed of large sandstone pieces, while the interior was filled with smaller stones, occasionally mixed with pebbles. In the centre of each was an urn containing cremated remains, sometimes accompanied by artefacts such as spindle whorls, vessels, and pottery fragments. A beaker containing the cremated remains of an individual was found inside an urn, suggesting a possible double burial. As at Kriveljski Kamen, the bones were highly fragmented with a high degree of organic matter oxidation and traces of copper slag were noted on the bones.

The necropolis at Trnjane is the largest Middle Bronze Age necropolis in this region. It is in Brestovac near Bor and consists of 43 stone circular structures with diameters ranging from 1.5 m to 2.2 m, occasionally reaching up to 3 m (Kapuran *et al.* 2014, 208–210). Although it was used over a prolonged period, spanning 2–3 centuries, the structures do not overlap, suggesting that they might have had markers or been covered by smaller mounds, even though they appeared flat at the time of excavation, similar to other necropolises in the region. In the north-west part of the necropolis, several isolated stone structures were discovered containing numerous ceramic fragments, significant amounts of ash, charred wood, animal bone remnants, and slag, leading the authors to hypothesise that ritual activities related to the burial process might have taken place there (Jovanović and Janković 1990, 9). As observed in other necropolises, the structures consisted of an outer ring of large stones with the infill composed of smaller stones surrounding the urn holding the cremated remains, with the urns placed directly on the subsoil or slightly embedded within it. Notably, children were buried at the edges of the necropolis, while older individuals were buried in the central area. The urns were generally uncovered, except in one grave where the urn was topped with a bowl. Given that the urns showed traces of burning, and burn marks were found beneath them, it is assumed that cremation took place at the burial site itself. Grave goods were sparse and modest, with scattered ceramics across the stone structures and metallic slag found both within them and in the urns, a feature also observed at other necropolises. Additional grave goods included a bronze razor, fragments of a needle with an expanded and coiled head, fragments of a bronze strip, stone axes, and several ceramic spindle whorls. Anthropological analysis revealed, as in other necropolises, a high degree of bone fragmentation due to severe oxidation of organic materials, as well as significant amounts of slag in and around the urns, with traces of slag on the bones themselves (Kapuran *et al.* 2017). Although the burial ritual and methods were nearly identical to those at necropolises in the Bor Region, based on the metal artefacts and several absolute dates, this necropolis is believed to have originated at the end of the Early Bronze Age and continued into the Middle Bronze Age.[15]

Hajdučka Česma in Brestovac, about 1 km from Trnjane, is a partially excavated necropolis where 18 graves of cremated individuals have been found to date. In 1992, four graves were investigated during minor rescue excavations (Kapuran *et al.* 2014, 217) and, in 2018 and 2019, an additional 14 graves were excavated. These graves consisted of circular stone structures with an urn containing cremated remains at their centre, and geophysical surveys indicated that around 100 more such graves are present (Kapuran *et al.* 2022, 51). The burial rites and urn shapes were very similar to those at other necropolises in the region and anthropological analyses revealed the same characteristics: high bone fragmentation due to severe oxidation of organic materials and the presence of slag on the bones and in the urns.

At Magura near Zaječar, 82 graves containing cremated remains placed in urns were investigated. These urns were left at the centre of circular stone structures (Srejović and Lazić 1997, 228–229; Kapuran 2014, 131). Similar to the necropolises around Bor, these featured an outer ring of larger stones, with diameters up to 6 m, and urns at the centre. However, unlike the Bor necropolises, the infill within the outer ring was composed of grey marl (Kapuran *et al.* 2022, 54). In two cases, the urns had marl covers, and some marl fragments were decorated with incised motifs. Grave goods included ceramic vessels, spindle whorls, a bronze arrowhead, a spear tip, a fragmentary biconical needle head, and more.

According to absolute dates and metal grave goods, the necropolis at Magura is somewhat younger than the Bor Region necropolises and likely belongs, at least in part, to the Late Bronze Age. Thus, only some of the graves that might be older, potentially belonging to the Middle Bronze Age, are included here. Before the recent acquisition of absolute dates, some authors considered all these necropolises contemporaneous, dating them to the end of the Middle and the Late Bronze Age (Jovanović 1999, 69–71), which could indeed be the case for the Magura necropolis (Kapuran *et al.* 2022, 56). M. Lazić, however, proposed the existence of a distinct cultural group, which, together with D. Srejović, he named the Gamzigrad culture, believed to have developed in this region over several centuries, from the end of the Eneolithic to the Late Bronze Age (Srejović and Lazić 1997, 241, 242). The duration of this culture was later refined to the period between the 18th and 13th centuries BC (Lazić 2010, 24), similar to the Magura necropolis (Lazić 2016, 30, 31, fig. 15). The same author identified 14 graves at Magura that might belong to the Middle Bronze Age (18th–17th centuries BC), but he did not specify which graves these were. For this book, we have selected certain graves whose urns, based on stylistic characteristics, indicate this period. According to M. Lazić (Lazić 2016), there are three phases of the necropolis: late Early Bronze Age, Middle Bronze Age, and Late Bronze Age, but the urns are not categorised by period in the publication and are presented collectively in the plates. By analogy, it could be inferred that the oldest examples resemble those from Trnjane, Hajdučka Česma, Kriveljski Kamen, etc., while the youngest (or at least later) urns have cups or handles attached to their bodies.

3.4.3 Portable finds

The artefacts from the Timok Region and the Đerdap area during the Middle Bronze Age consist mainly of ceramic vessels and, to a much lesser extent, spindle whorls, weights, tools made of clay, bone, and stone, and very few metal items.

3.4.3.1 Pottery

In this geographical zone ceramic vessels include bowls, cups, beakers, amphorae, pots, double vessels, and so-called special-purpose vessels.

A. BOWLS

Bowls are significantly represented in this zone compared to other types of vessels. Seven different types have been identified, with type 3e (Fig. 3.21/1; Fig. 3.22/3; Fig. 3.23/6–10; Fig. 3.26/1, 2, 11, 13–15; Fig. 3.28/3, 4; Fig. 3.29/1; Fig. 3.31/2) comprising about 30% and type 3a (Fig. 3.20/3, 24; Fig. 3.25/1, 10; Fig. 3.26/3, 9, 10; Fig. 3.28/1, 2, 23–25; Fig. 3.32/2, 3; Fig. 3.33/7, 25; Fig. 3.34/9–12) also around 30% of all bowl types.

Next in prevalence are types 1b (Fig. 3.20/1, 14, 23; Fig. 3.25/12, 21; Fig. 3.27/3; Fig. 3.33/1, 8, 14, 15) and 2a (Fig. 3.21/14; Fig. 3.23/1; Fig. 3.25/9, 11, 25; Fig. 3.27/4), each representing approximately 14%, while types 1a (Fig. 3.20/4; Fig. 3.25/13; Fig. 3.29/14), 3b (Fig. 3.22/1; Fig. 3.27/2; Fig. 3.32/1), and 3d (Fig. 3.26/4; Fig. 3.28/21) are found in Middle Bronze Age sites in the Đerdap and Timok regions, each with about 3–4%.

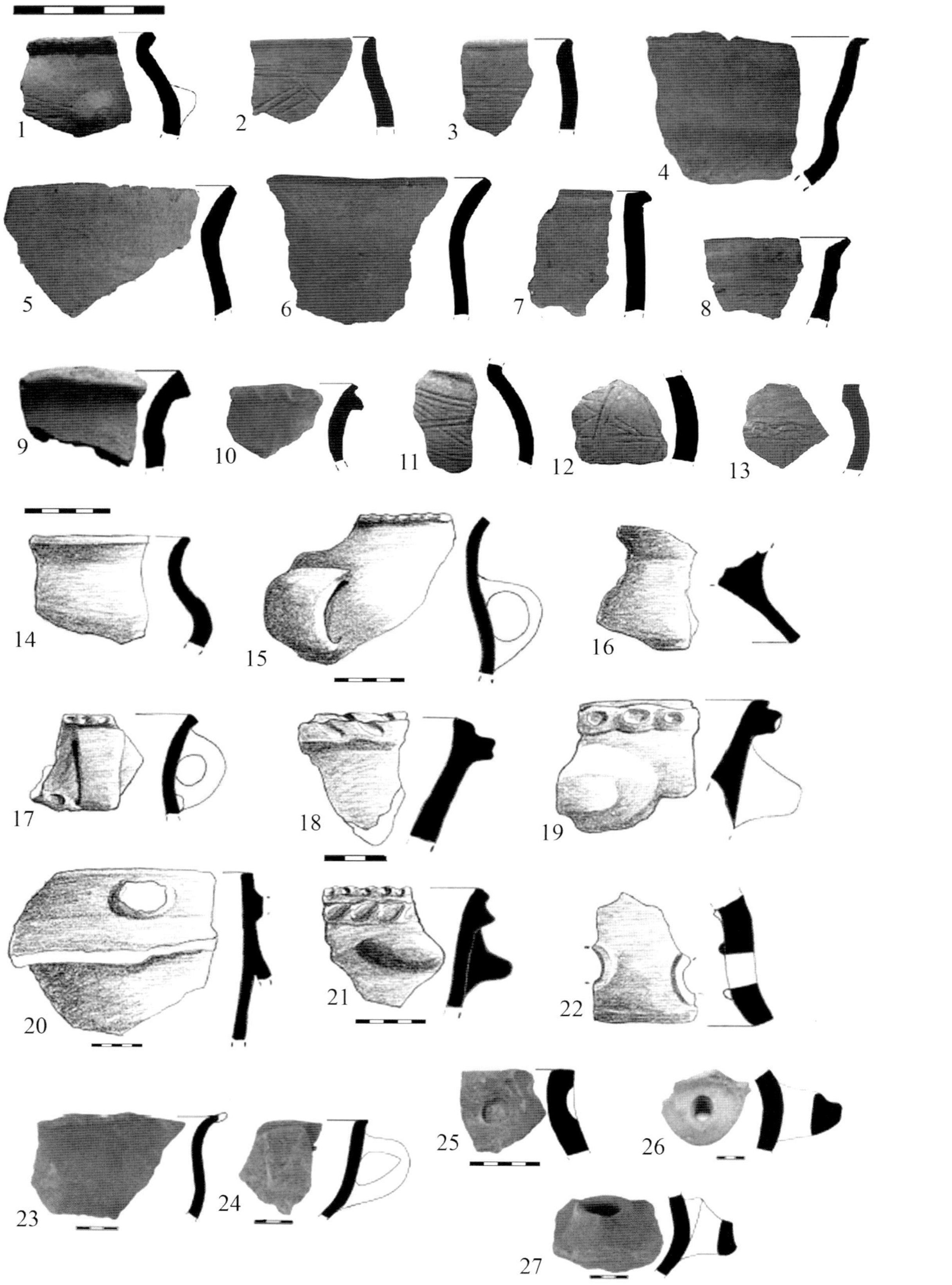

Figure 3.20. 1–13, Mokranjske Stene: site of Potkapina; 14–22, Bor: site of Čoka Kazak; 23–27, Bor: site of Čoka Njica.

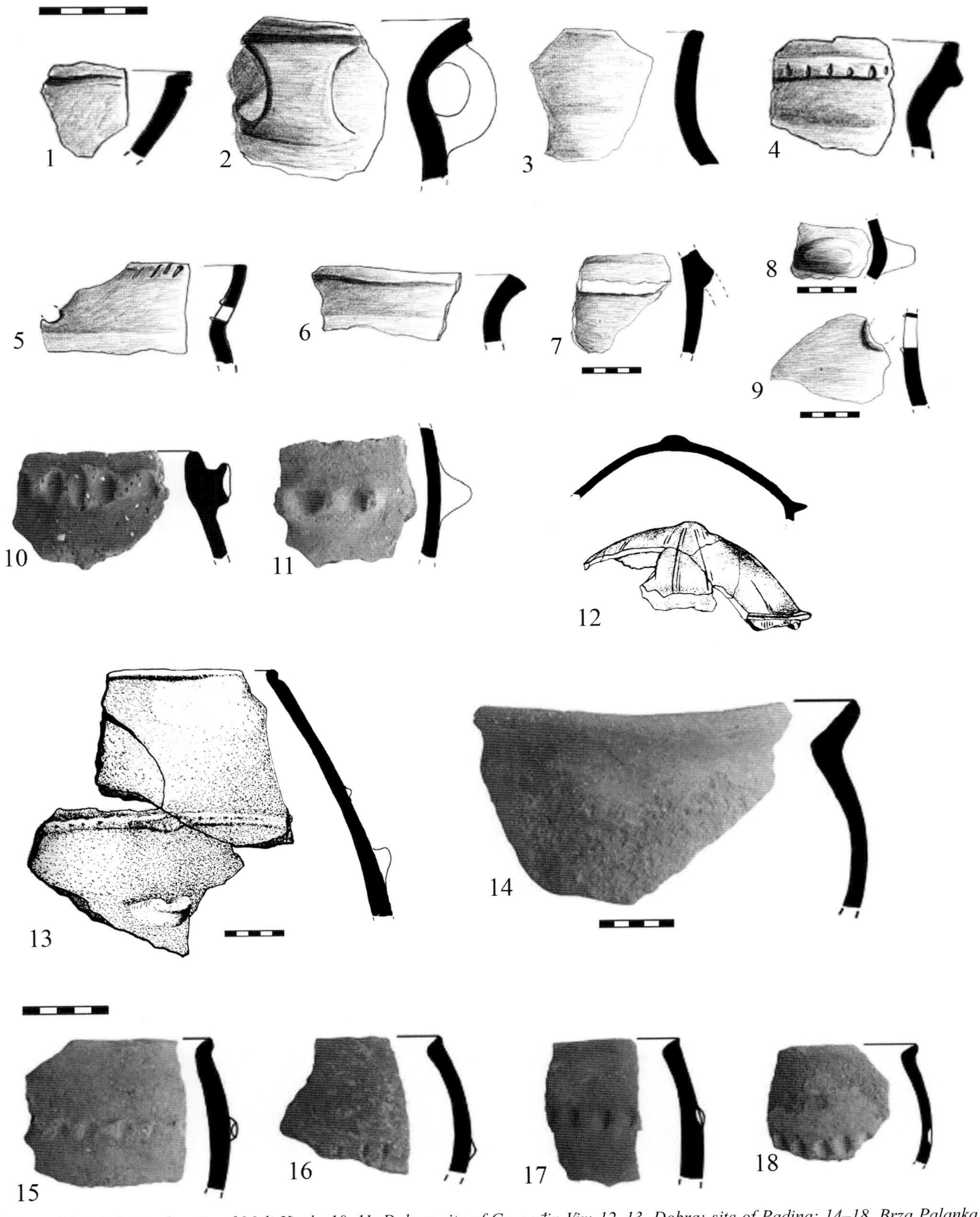

Figure 3.21. 1–9, Tanda: site of Mali Vizak; 10–11, Dobra: site of Gospođin Vir; 12–13, Dobra: site of Padina; 14–18, Brza Palanka: site of Obala kod crkve.

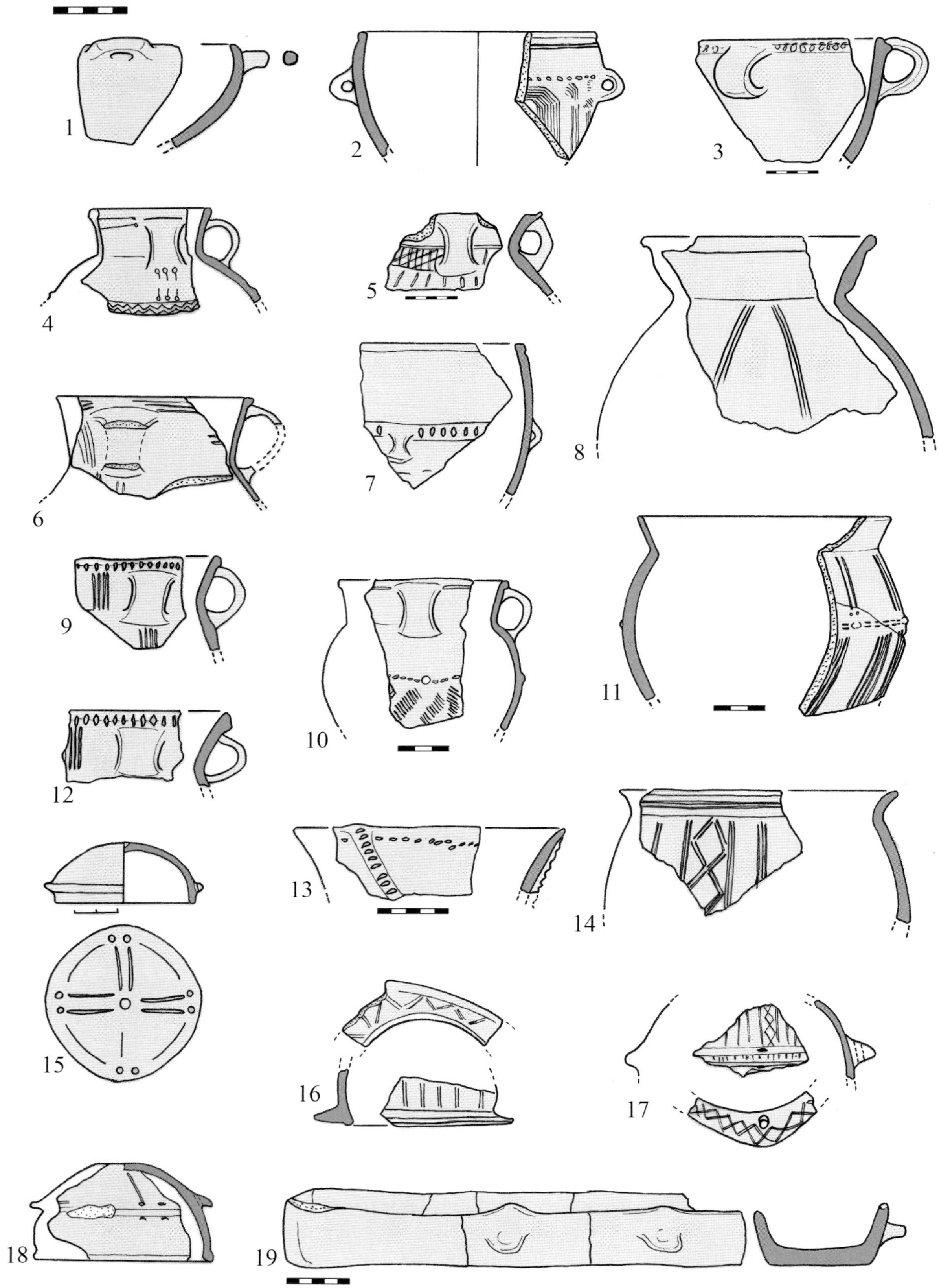

Figure 3.22. Mala Vrbica: site of Livade, 1st horizon.

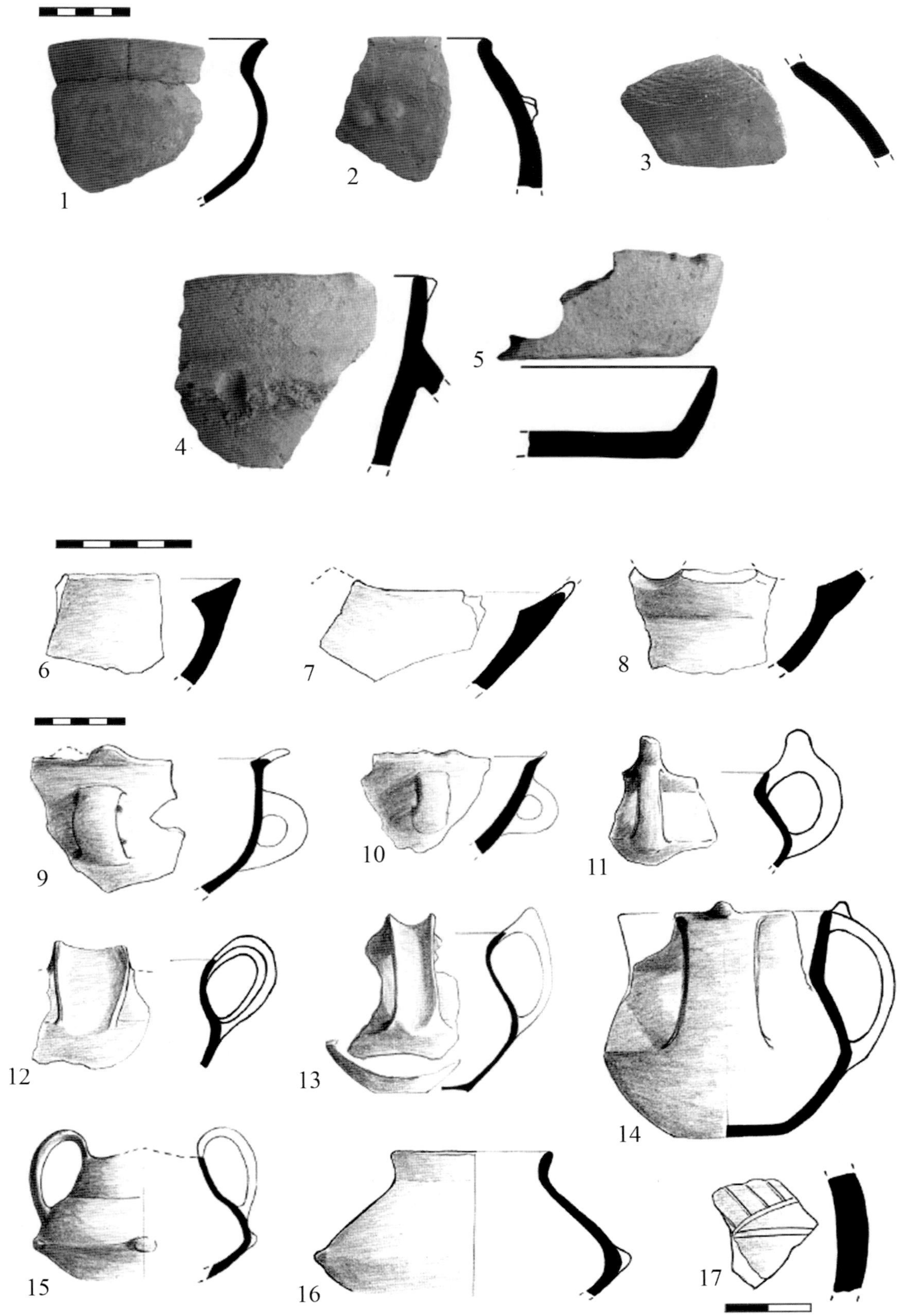

Figure 3.23. 1–3, Kladovo: site of Donje Butorke; 4–5, Rtkovo: site of Glameja; 6–17, Banjsko Polje: site of Ružana.

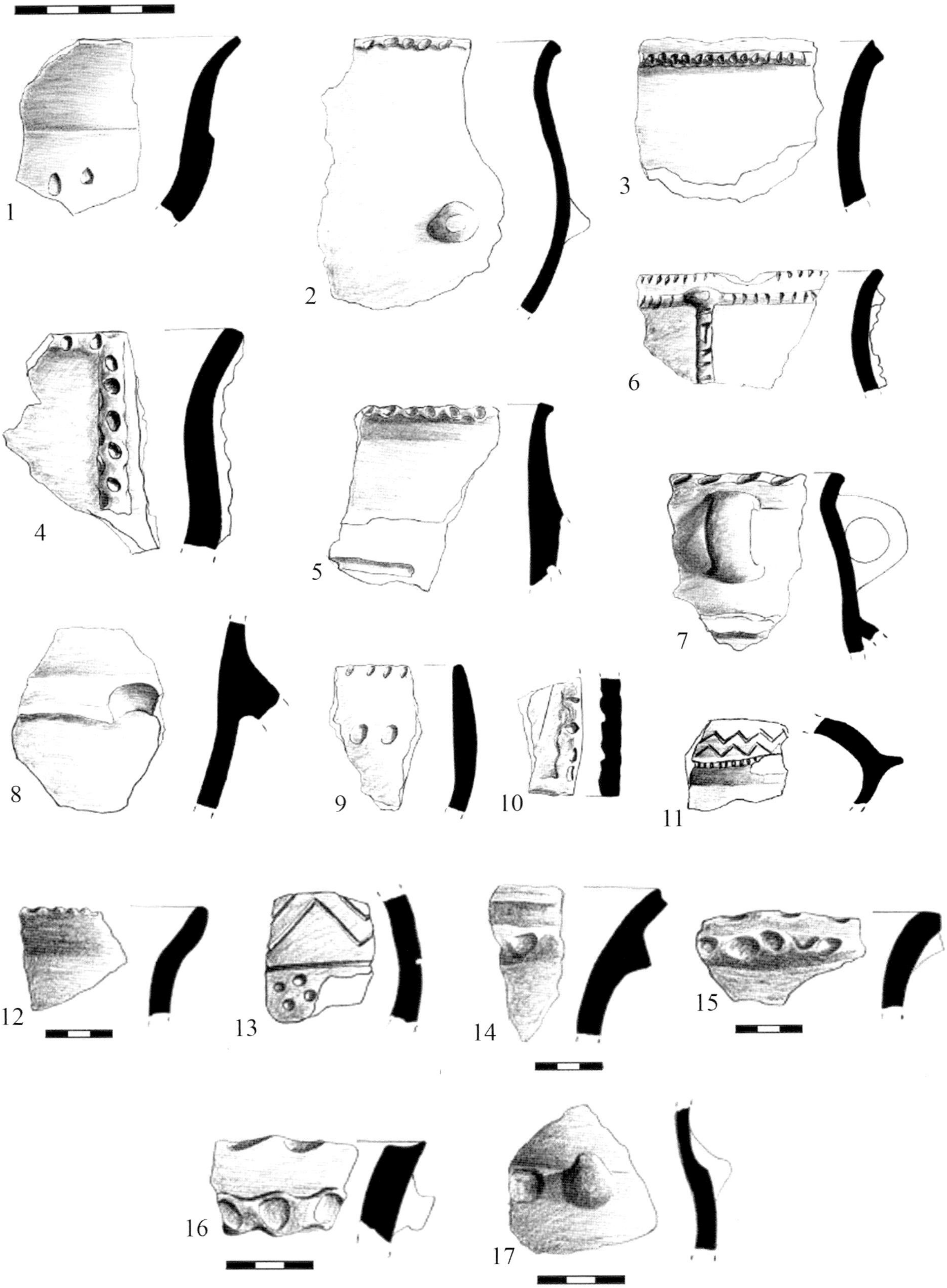

Figure 3.24. 1–11, Banjsko Polje: site of Ružana; 12–17, Brestovac: site of Dubrava.

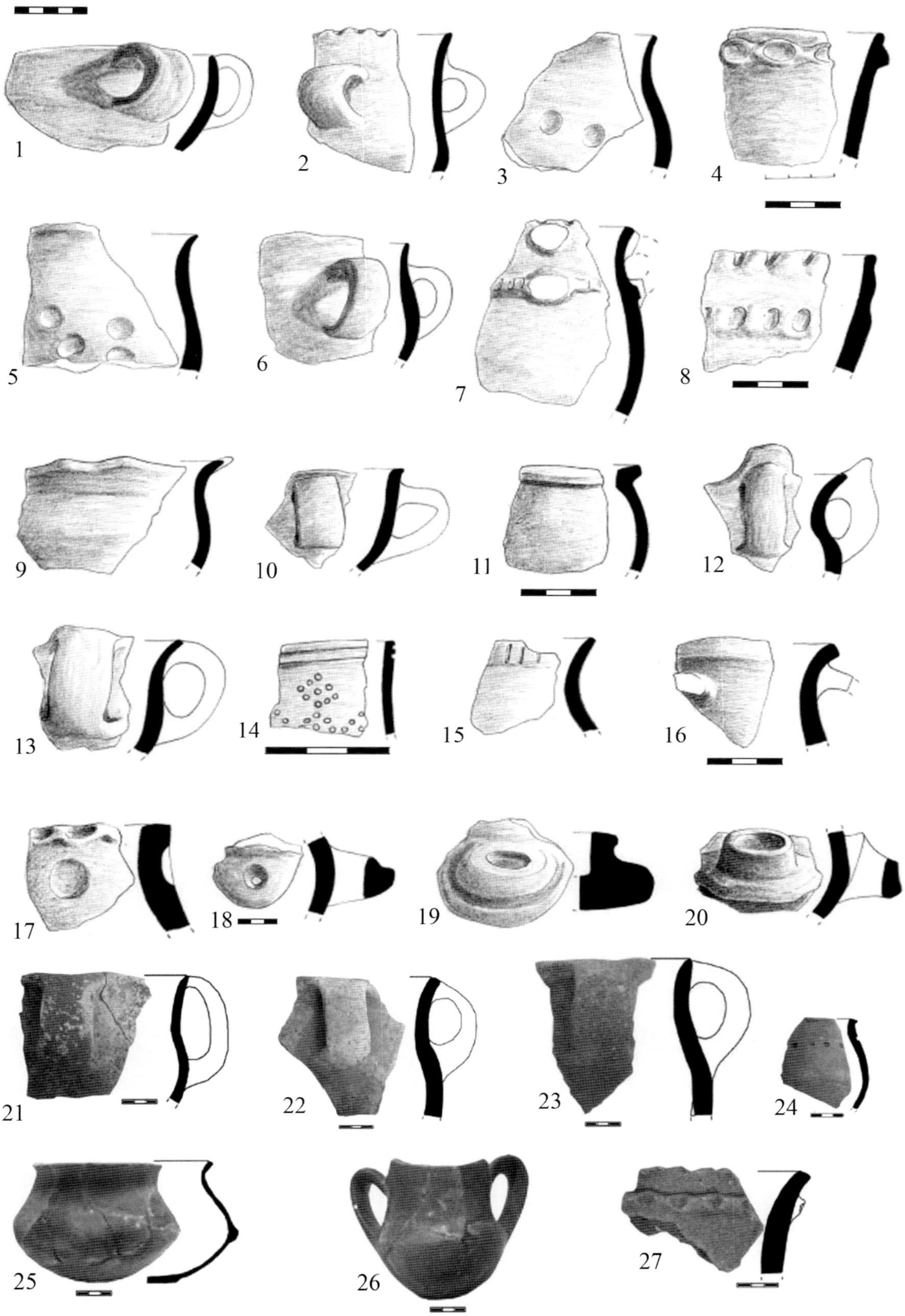

Figure 3.25. 1–8, Brestovačka Banja: site of Selište, 9–20; site of Čoka Kormaroš; 21–27, Bor: site of Kučajna.

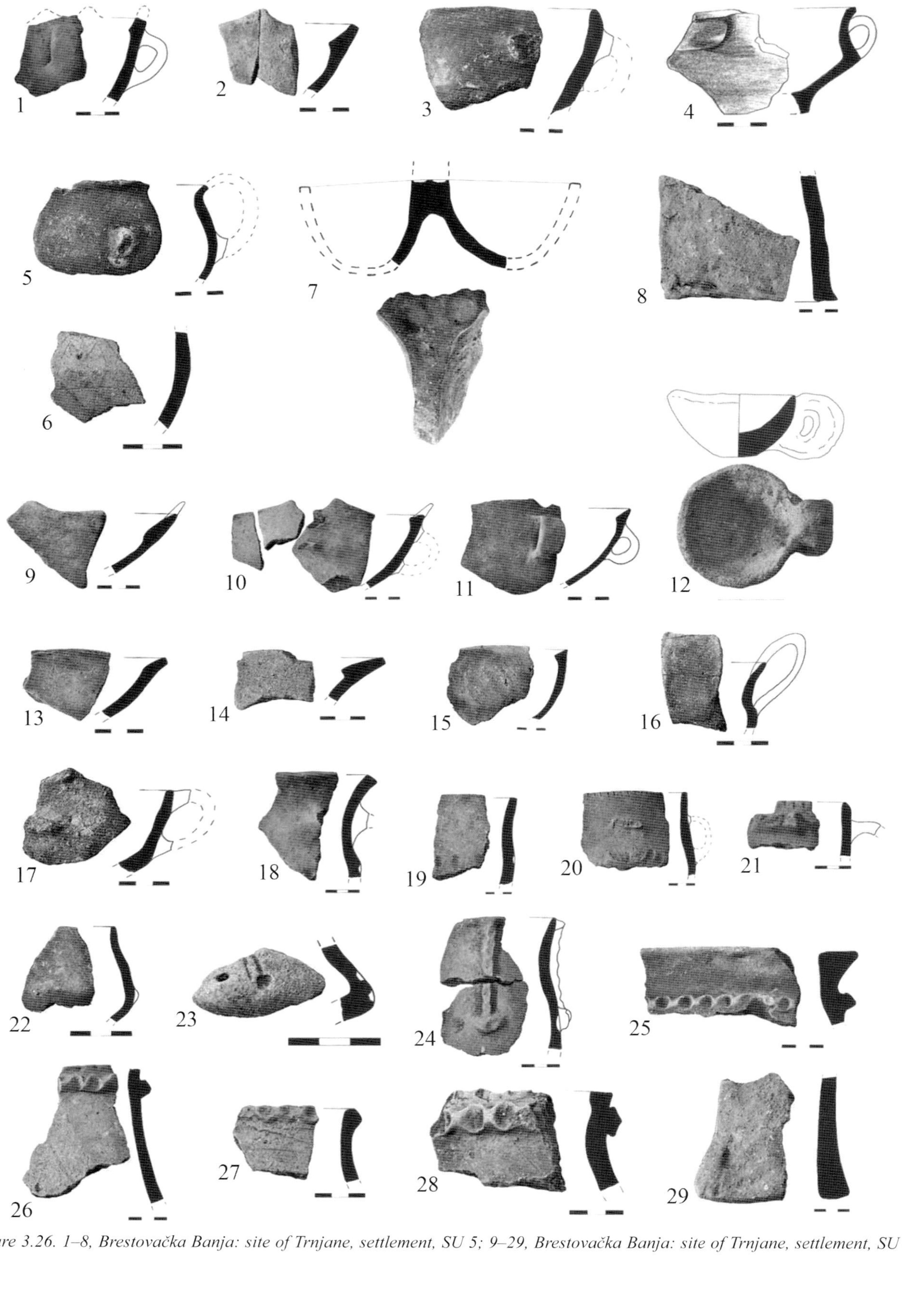

Figure 3.26. 1–8, Brestovačka Banja: site of Trnjane, settlement, SU 5; 9–29, Brestovačka Banja: site of Trnjane, settlement, SU 4.

Unlike the Early Bronze Age, from which only two bowls, both type 3a, originate from this zone, a large number of bowls were registered in this area in the Middle Bronze Age. Notably, the most common bowl type in the Timok Region is type 3e, which is only sporadically found in other central Balkan areas during this period. It appears in the Middle Bronze Age, emerging towards the end of the Early Bronze Age, and seems to draw traditions from the Eneolithic period, specifically the Coţofeni–Kostolac group, where similar bowls were typical (Kapuran and Bulatović 2012a, T. II/14; T. III/19, 27; T. VI/59; T. VII/84, 85; T. VIII/90; T. X/132; T. XI/146).

Bowls are generally undecorated, with the exception of those from Mokranje adorned with incised lines and several bowls featuring plastic projections of various shapes on the rim (Fig. 3.20/23; Fig. 3.23/9, 10; Fig. 3.25/9, 12; Fig. 3.26/1, 9, 10; Fig. 3.28/2–4, 23; Fig. 3.31/2; Fig. 3.34/12). Interestingly, some of these projections are trapezoidal in shape (Fig. 3.28/2, 23), a primary stylistic feature of Middle Bronze Age beakers in the central Balkans.

B. CUPS

Cups are recorded in very small numbers compared to other vessels in this zone, though they are more common here than in other central Balkan areas during the Middle Bronze Age. Two types are noted, 1a and 4b, with type 1a (Fig. 3.32/3; Fig. 3.33/9, 16, 17) making up over half of the total, while type 4b accounts for slightly less than 50% (Fig. 3.27/23; Fig. 3.33/18).

The cups are mostly undecorated, except for an example from Banjska Stena (type 4b) decorated with vertical incised lines, between which are shorter parallel horizontal lines (Fig. 3.33/18). Although most cups lack decoration, their handles often feature plastic projections at the top in the form of rectangles with pointed tips, fans, or double horns (Fig. 3.33/16, 17; Fig. 3.27/23). It appears that handles found without associated vessels likely belonged to cups or possibly beakers, as these handles often have plastic projections at the top, such as fans, cylinders, buttons, etc. (Fig. 3.28/26; Fig. 3.32/15, 18).

C. BEAKERS

Beakers are represented by seven types. The most common is type 1f (Fig. 3.23/11, 13, 14; Fig. 3.25/24; Fig. 3.26/5; Fig. 3.33/19, 21, 22), comprising about 26%, followed by type 1c (Fig. 3.25/26; Fig. 3.32/6; Fig. 3.33/2, 26) at 22%, type 1g (Fig. 3.27/6; Fig. 3.27/22a, 24; Fig. 3.31/11; Fig. 3.34/7, 8, 22) at 25%, and type 1a (Fig. 3.23/14) at 5%. Types 1e (Fig. 3.23/12; Fig. 3.26/16) and 7d (Fig. 3.23/15; Fig. 3.27/5; Fig. 3.33/20) collectively account for about 18%, and type 3a is represented by only one specimen (Fig. 3.27/1).

The most notable stylistic detail on the beakers in this zone is the appearance of trapezoidal openings, as seen in other parts of the central Balkans during this period. Such openings appear on different types of beakers, from 1a and 1c to 1g, sharing two vertical loop handles that are mostly aligned with or extend above the rim. On one beaker, the handles are located on the shoulder, although due to its dimensions, this vessel might also be classified as an amphora (Fig. 3.31/11).

Of the beaker types recorded during the Early Bronze Age, only type 1c persisted into the Middle Bronze Age. Types 1f, 1g, and 7a are characteristic of the Middle Bronze Age and do not appear in the previous period.

Beakers are generally undecorated, apart from a few examples, such as a beaker from Trnjane adorned with a series of horizontal and two parallel rows of vertical punctate impressions (Fig. 3.27/6), or examples from Banjska Stena – one decorated in the Vatin style with incised spirals accompanied by rows of punctuations (Fig. 3.33/20), and another with long incised hanging triangles (Fig. 3.33/21). A beaker from Podgorac is decorated with two horizontal rows of punctate impressions (Fig. 3.34/8), while others are either undecorated or have handles adorned with plastic projections at the top (Fig. 3.23/11, 14).

D. AMPHORAE

Amphorae are prevalent in the Timok Region due to the extensive number of cremation necropolises in this area, where urns are defined as amphora-type vessels serving as urns in this context.

The most common type is 4a, with ovoid or globular shapes featuring shorter cylindrical or funnel-shaped necks and two or more handles on the body, mostly horizontally aligned (Fig. 3.23/16; Fig. 3.24/12; Fig. 3.27/11–15, 17, 18, 22; Fig. 3.28/13; Fig. 3.30/1, 3, 4, 15, 16, 18, 20, 21; Fig. 3.31/5, 8, 9, 12, 13, 18), making up about 31%. The similar type 1b (ovoid with a very short, flared or subtly profiled rim) is also significantly represented at around 28% (Fig. 3.21/13–18; Fig. 3.22/2, 7, 14; Fig. 3.23/2; Fig. 3.24/2; Fig. 3.28/12; Fig. 3.29/11; Fig. 3.30/5–7, 10, 17; Fig. 3.31/2, 3, 6, 7, 14–16). Types 1a and 2a, inherited from the Early Bronze Age like the previous two, together constitute about 10% (Fig. 3.25/2, 3, 5–7; Fig. 3.28/14; Fig. 3.30/2) and around 3% (Fig. 3.25/22, 23), respectively. Other types appear for the first time in the Middle Bronze Age, such as types 3b (Fig. 3.21/2, 4, 5; Fig. 3.22/4–6, 8–13; Fig. 3.27/21), 4b (Fig. 3.30/13; Fig. 3.31/1), 5b (Fig. 3.27/16, 20), 5a (Fig. 3.33/23, 24), and 6a (Fig. 3.31/4), which collectively account for about 28%, with type 3b alone comprising about 16%. Type 3b is characteristic of this zone, with only one example found in the neighbouring peri–Pannonian zone (Fig. 3.6/14). The type 6a, an unusual form featuring a deeper conical vessel with four large triangular plastic projections on the rim (Fig. 3.31/4), is common in the Wietenberg culture of Transylvania (Borofka 1994, taf, 15/7, 8, pl. 19/9, pl. 21/8 etc).

Most amphorae, apart from type 6a, typically feature four short, arching, horizontally placed handles on the body and/or longer, arching vertical handles on the shoulder. Amphorae are generally undecorated, with a few exceptions that are decorated with incised lines or punctate impressions, or plastic bands with imprints (Fig. 3.21/4, 5, 13, 15–18; Fig. 3.25/2, 3). Some amphorae are noted to have wart-like projections (Fig. 3.23/2, 16; Fig. 3.24/2, 3, 5, 7; Fig. 3.28/14), and a few examples feature larger circular depressions above the handles (Fig. 3.27/13; Fig. 3.30/2, 4, 9, 19; Fig. 3.31/6).

E. POTS

Apart from the usual types of pots that appear throughout different periods across all geographical zones without specific discernible patterns, this zone is notable for the frequent presence of *piraunos* (Fig. 3.20/20, 22; Fig. 3.21/9; Fig. 3.23/4; Fig. 3.24/5, 7, 8, 10; Fig. 3.26/29; Fig. 3.29/6; Fig. 3.32/11). Some scholars suggest that these vessels were also used in metallurgical processes for heating ores (Jovanović and Janković 1990, 1).

F. LIDS

Lids are significantly more common in this zone compared to other geographical zones studied in this research. At the site of Livade in Mala Vrbica alone, several domed lids with horizontal plastic ribs above the opening and attachment holes were found (type 1a) (Fig. 3.22/15–18). The same type of lid was also documented at Padina (Fig. 3.22/12) and Ružana (Fig. 3.24/11). The lids are decorated with incised straight lines (Fig. 3.21/12; Fig. 3.22/15–17) and zigzag lines (Fig. 3.22/16–17; Fig. 3.24/11), paired zigzag lines forming a series of connected rhombuses (Fig. 3.22/17), and sometimes the edge of the rib is adorned with incisions (Fig. 3.24/11).

G. SPECIAL-PURPOSE VESSELS

Double vessels: Dual vessels, characterised by two containers connected by a massive handle, known as double vessels or salt cellars, were not previously known in this geographical zone as they were in the peri-Pannonian zone or Šumadija, associated with the *Novačka Ćuprija–Pančevo* group, dating to the late Early Bronze Age. However, in the Middle Bronze Age, one specimen was found at the settlement in Trnjane within a structure dated between the 19th and 17th centuries cal BC. Besides this zone, only two more examples from the Middle Bronze Age in the central Balkans have been recorded, from Vinča and Donja Brnjica, unlike the earlier period when more examples were found in the peri-Pannonian zone, Šumadija, and one in the South Morava valley.

Ladles/melting vessels(?): In this zone, several shallow, small vessels resembling cups but with thicker walls and a substantial handle have been documented, defined differently by various authors (Fig. 3.26/12). A. Kapuran and co-authors classify them as lamps or ladles (Kapuran *et al.* 2020, 59, 66), which is also suggested in this study. However, it may be worth considering the possibility that they served as some form of melting vessels in metallurgical processes, given that some examples reportedly showed signs of burning on the interior (Kapuran *et al.* 2020, 67). Smaller conical vessels with thick walls and rougher construction, noted at Gamzigrad (Fig. 3.33/28), could also have been used in metallurgical processes as melting vessels (Srejović and Lazić 1997, fig. 56).

Fischbute: Two *Fischbute* vessels were documented in this zone (Fig. 3.22/19; Fig. 3.23/5), specifically in the Ključ area on the Danube terrace. The vessel from Donje Butorke is of standard dimensions, while the specimen from Mala Vrbica measures over 25 cm in length and 8 cm in width.

Authors who have written about the Middle Bronze Age in the Timok Region and Đerdap typically described the method of pottery production, colour, and texture, as well as the general quality of the vessel surfaces without differentiating between types. Therefore, detailed descriptions of the pottery in this zone are omitted compared to previous geographical zones. Nonetheless, these general descriptions indicate that red pottery, or pottery in reddish-brown tones, is more frequently represented in this zone.

H. HANDLES

The most prevalent type of handle in this zone are the vertical arched handles, oval or strap-shaped in cross-section. On beakers, these handles extend from the rim to the body, not surpassing or only slightly surpassing the rim, while on bowls and amphorae, they are shorter and wider. This type of handle often has a concave profile, classified as the *ansa lunata* type (Fig. 3.23/12, 13; Fig. 3.27/6; Fig. 3.31/11; Fig. 3.33/20), sometimes featuring a plastic projection at the top (Fig. 3.23/11, 14; Fig. 3.27/20, 23; Fig. 3.28/10, 26; Fig. 3.31/3; Fig. 3.32/15, 17, 18; Fig. 3.33/16, 17). Short arched horizontal handles are also common, mainly strap-shaped and, less frequently, circular in cross-section, predominantly found on amphorae or urns (Fig. 3.27/11–15, 17–19, 22; Fig. 3.28/12; Fig. 3.30/1–4, 6, 8, 9, 12, 13, 15–19; Fig. 3.31/1, 2, 4–18), although they sporadically appear on other vessel types (Fig. 3.22/1; Fig. 3.33/14; Fig. 3.34/9). In some instances, these handles are spool-shaped, modelled as hollow cups or smaller receptacles (Fig. 3.20/26, 27; Fig. 3.25/18–20; Fig. 3.28/11; Fig. 3.30/10, 20; Fig. 3.33/13, 14).

Additionally, tongue-shaped handles (Fig. 3.20/19, 21; Fig. 3.21/8, 13; Fig. 3.22/19; Fig. 3.32/14, 16) were noted, some featuring semi-circular grooves on the upper surface (Fig. 3.32/16; Fig. 3.33/6), and others with a notch at the top (Fig. 3.32/14). Triangular handles with vertical perforations (Fig. 3.31/2) and plug-like handles, mainly on cooking pots (Fig. 3.20/19; Fig. 3.33/5), are present in smaller numbers.

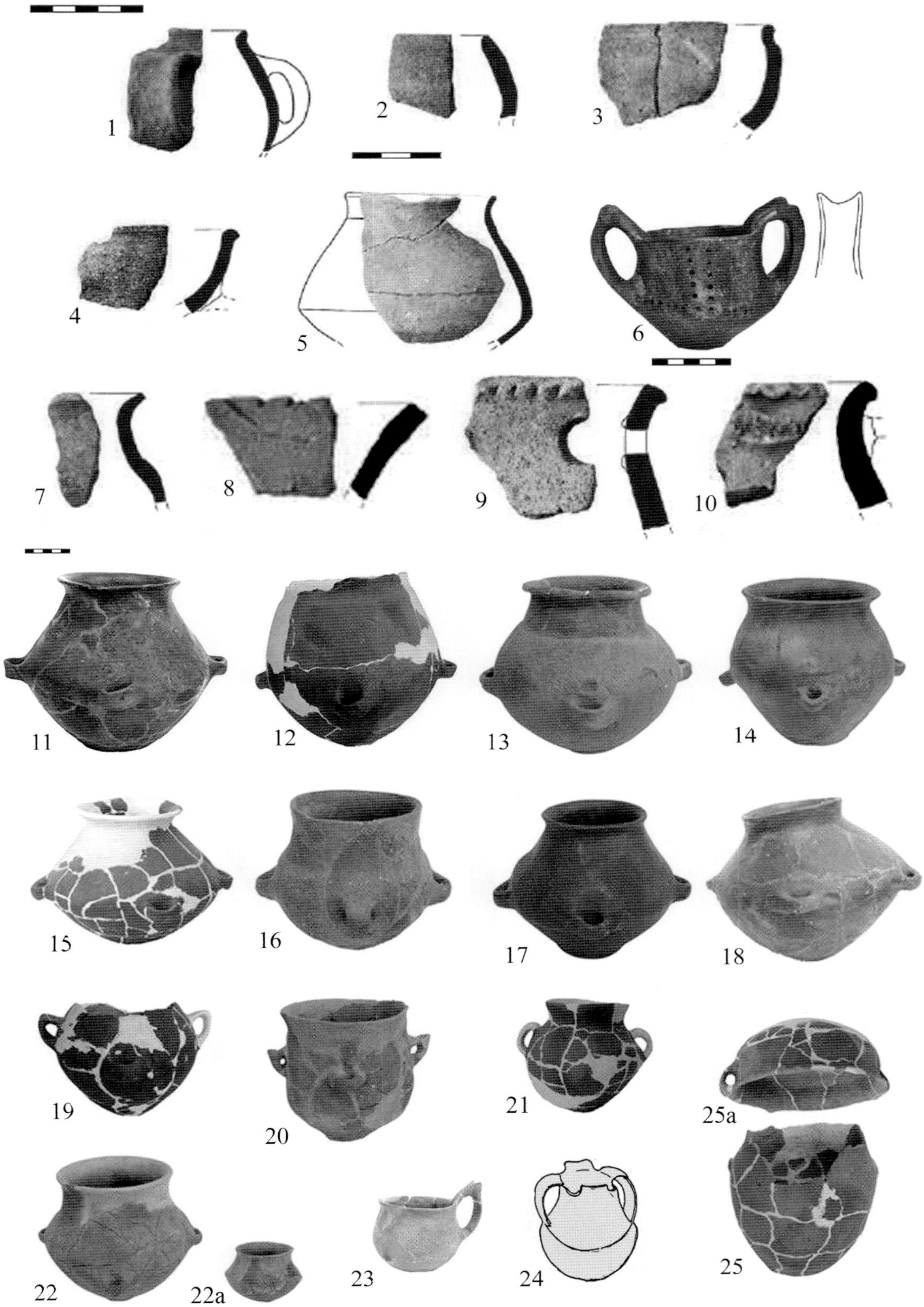

Figure 3.27. Brestovačka Banja: site of Trnjane: 1–3, settlement, SU 1; 4–10, settlement, SU 2; 11 grave 10; 12, grave 28; 13, grave 1; 14, grave 4; 15, grave 41; 16, grave 2; 17, grave 8; 18, grave 13; 19, grave 11; 20, grave 21; 21, grave 37; 22, grave 3 (two vessels); 23, grave 14; 24, grave 32; 25, grave 33 (two vessels).

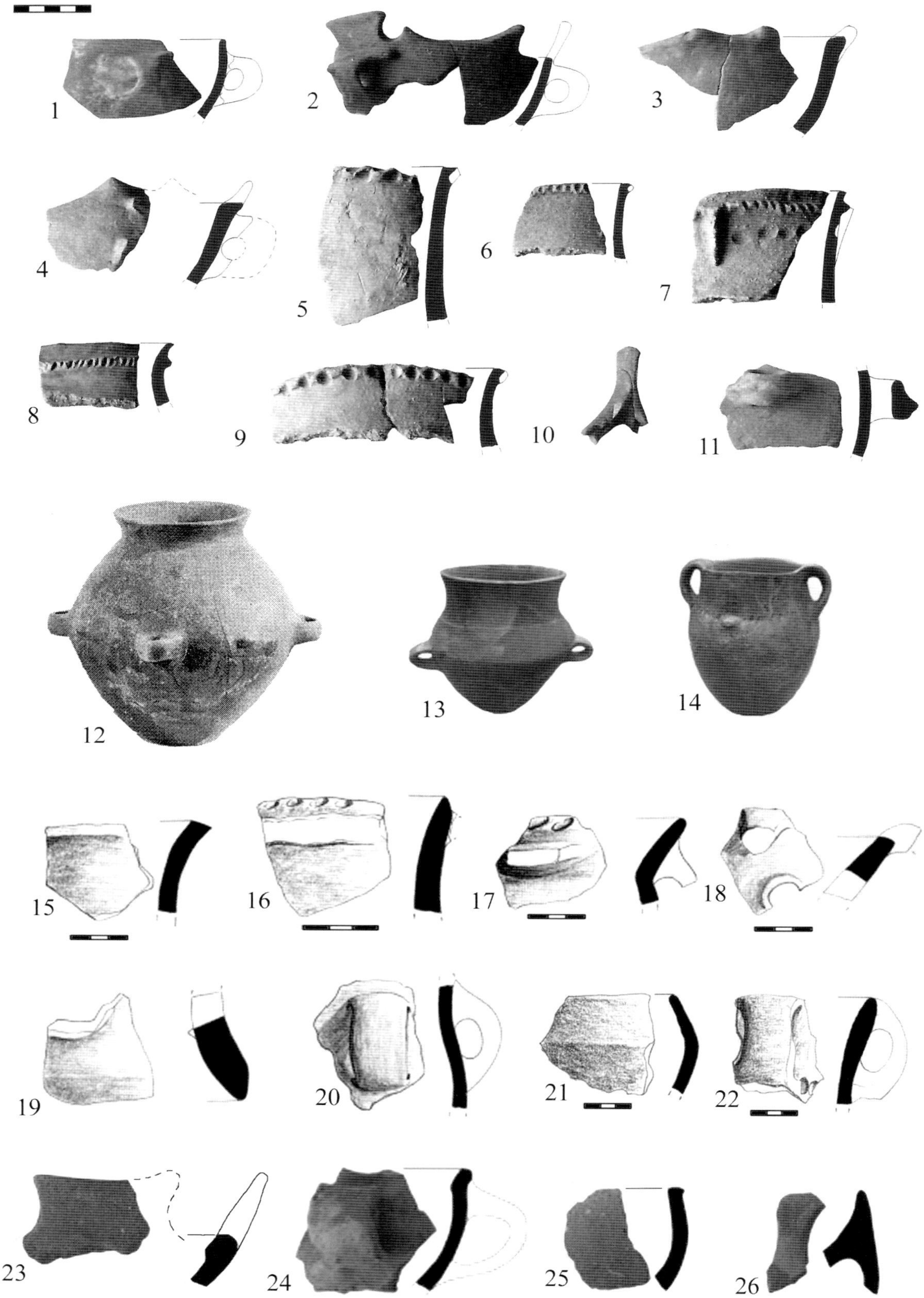

Figure 3.28. 1–11, Zvezdan: site of Njive na ulazu u Zvezdan, settlement; 12, Zvezdan, grave; 13–14, Knjaževac: site of Kadijski Krst; 15–20, Urovica: site of Valja Mare; 21–22, Gamzigrad: site of Bazilika III; 23–26, Gamzigrad: site of Potoci.

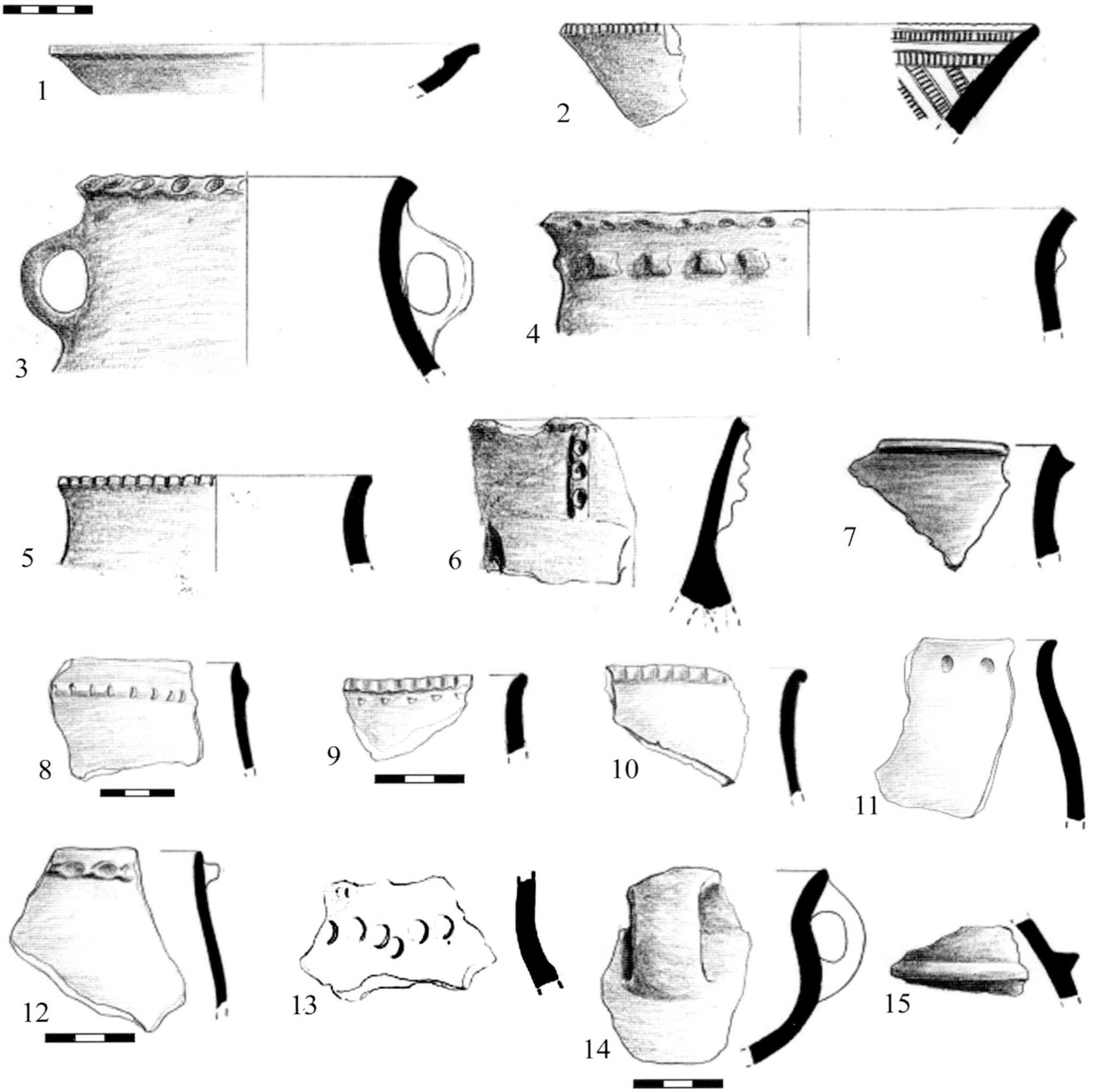

Figure 3.29. 1–6, Metovnica: site of Kot 1; 7–13, Zlot, Zlotska/Lazareva pećina (Zlot/Lazar Cave); 14–15, Majdanpek, Kapetanova pećina.

I. ORNAMENTATION

Ornaments are not frequently found on pottery in this zone during the Middle Bronze Age. A stylistic analysis of the pottery suggests that pieces with richer incised decoration belong mainly to the later phase of the Middle Bronze Age, unlike the earlier phase, where ornamentation is minimal and consists primarily of plastic decorations and impressions directly on the vessel surface.

All dated contexts, including graves from the 20th/19th to the 19th/18th century cal BC, feature pottery without incised ornaments, except for a few fragments from Ružana decorated in the style of the *Verbicioara* group (Fig. 3.23/17; Fig. 3.24/11). Ružana yielded three nearly identical absolute dates, placing it in the 19th/18th century cal BC. However, younger material seems to be present at the site (Kapuran *et al.* 2014, 176), so this dating may not necessarily apply to the 'Verbicioara' elements.

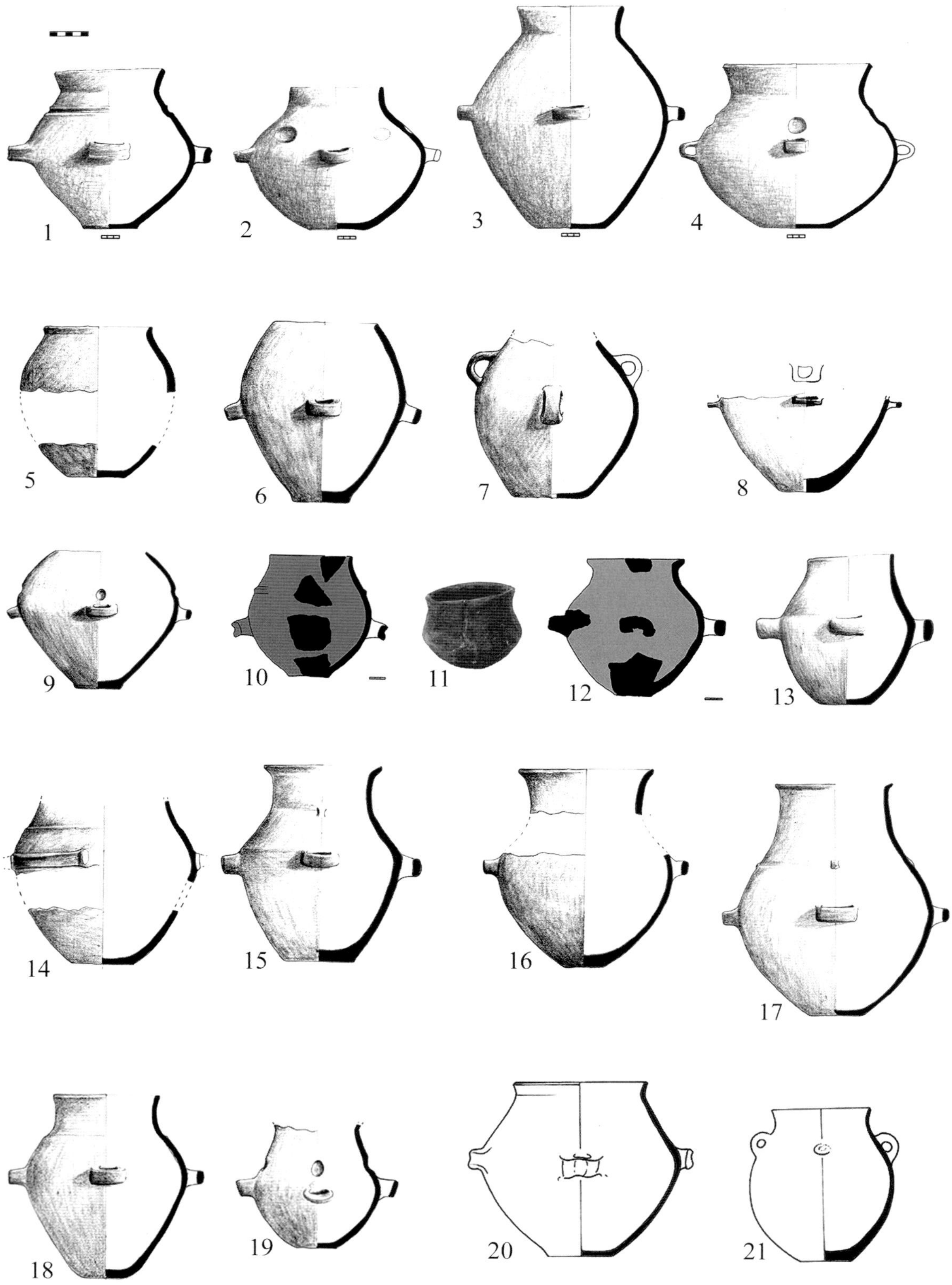

Figure 3.30. 1–4, Bor: site of Kriveljski kamen; 5–17, Brestovac: site of Borsko Jezero: 5 grave 5/2002; 6, grave 4/1997; 7, grave 5/1997; 8, grave 19/2002; 9, grave 10/1997; 10, grave 2/1997; 11, grave 2/2002; 12, grave 13/1997; 13, grave 12/1997; 14, grave 14/2002; 15, grave 12/2002; 16, grave 14/2002; 17, grave 18/2002; 18–19, Brestovačka Banja: site of Hajdučka Česma, excavation in 1992; 20–21, Brestovačka Banja: site of Hajdučka Česma, excavation in 2018.

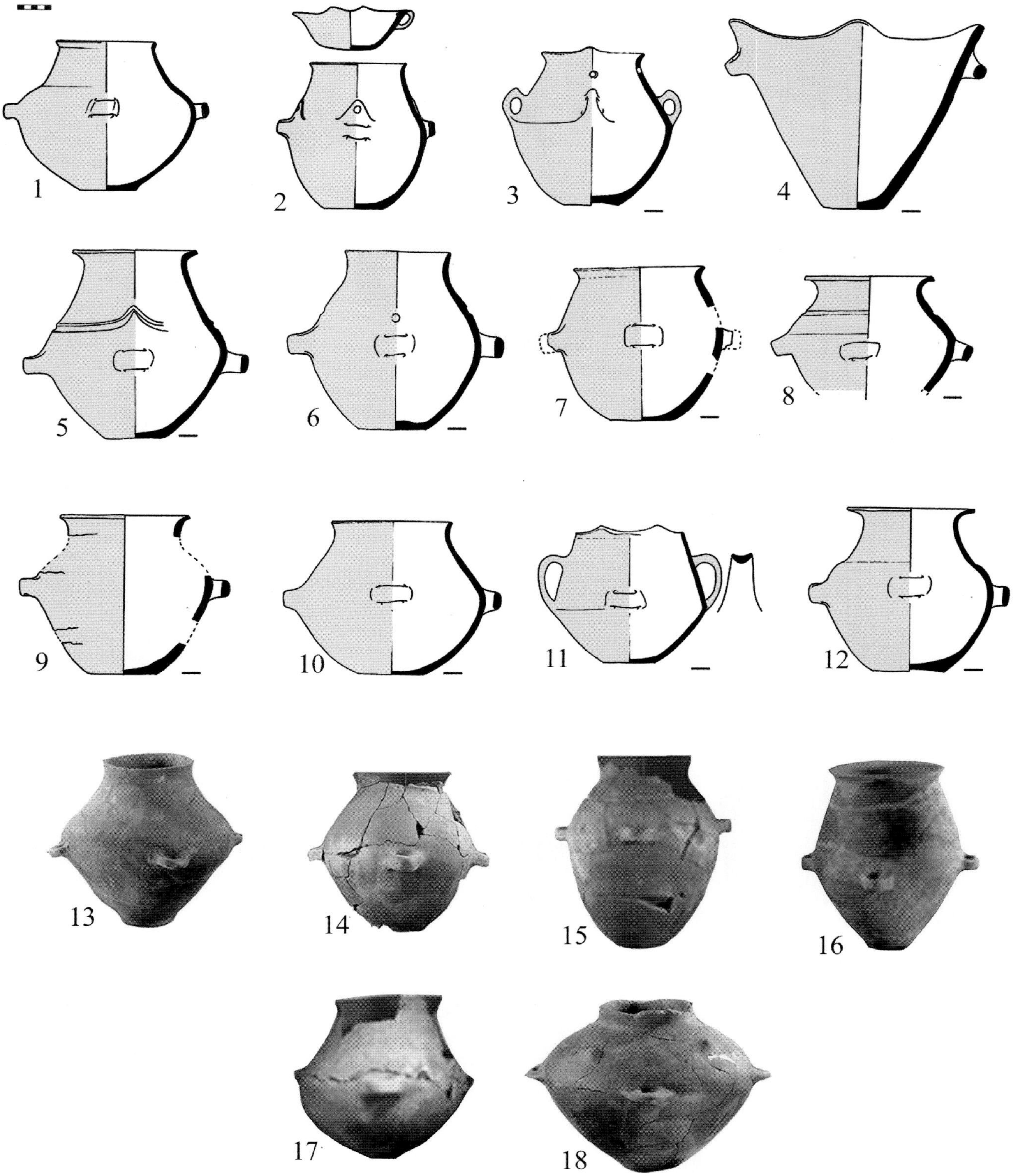

Figure 3.31. 1–12, Brestovačka Banja: site of Hajdučka Česma: 2, grave 1; 3, grave 5; 4, grave 6; 5, grave 7; 6, grave 8; 13–18, Zaječar: site of Magura.

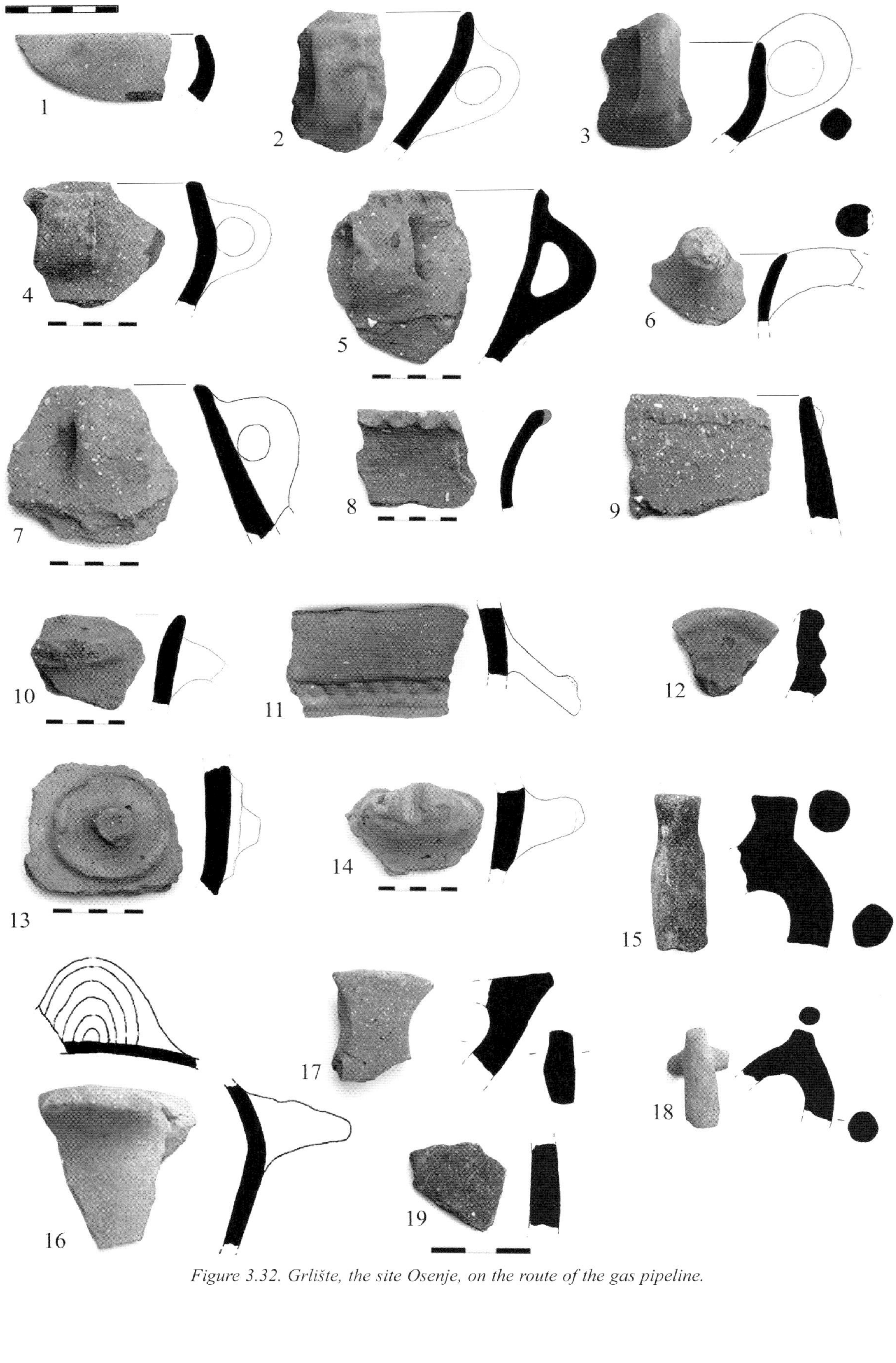

Figure 3.32. Grlište, the site Osenje, on the route of the gas pipeline.

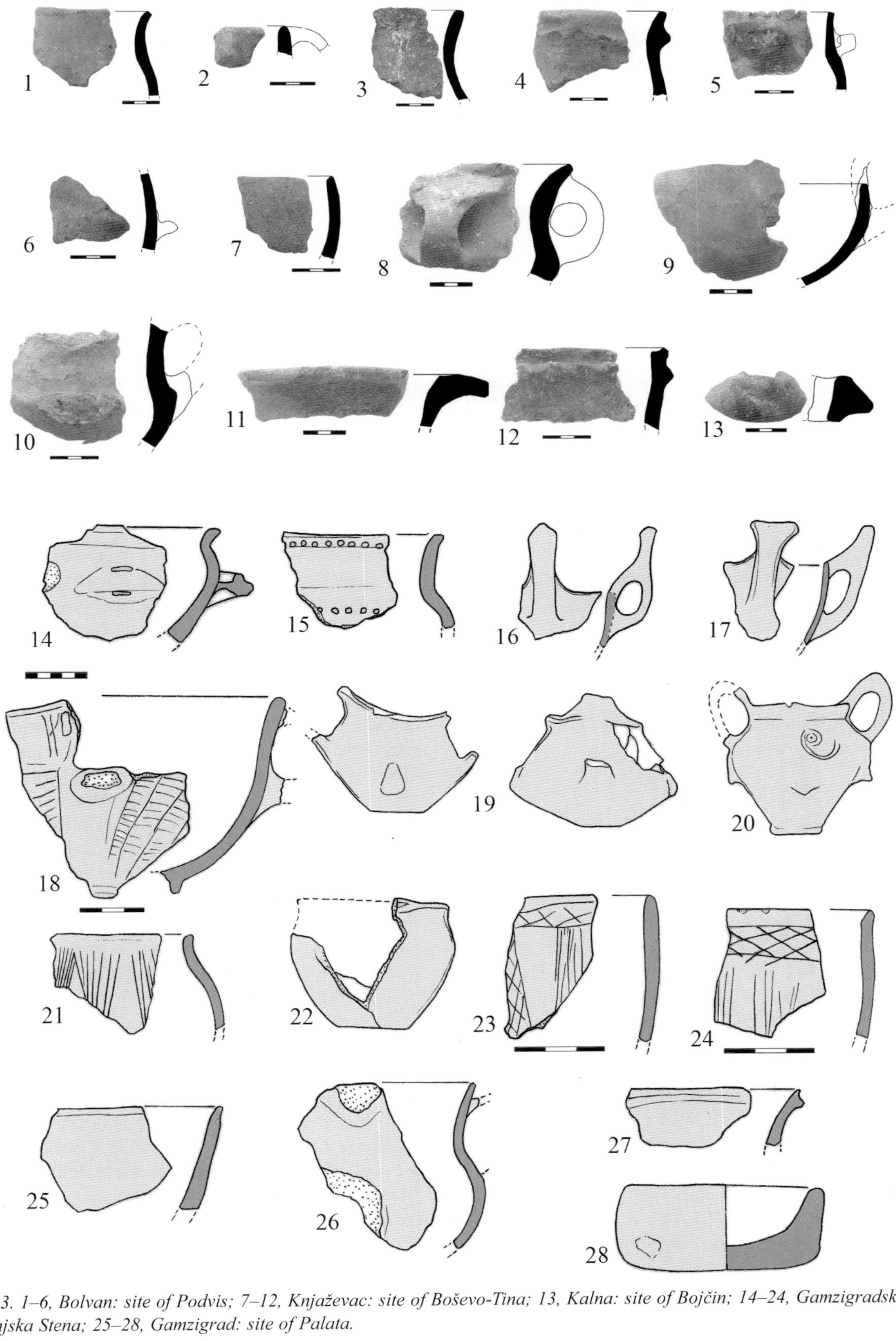

Figure 3.33. 1–6, Bolvan: site of Podvis; 7–12, Knjaževac: site of Boševo-Tina; 13, Kalna: site of Bojčin; 14–24, Gamzigradska Banja: site of Banjska Stena; 25–28, Gamzigrad: site of Palata.

Pottery from Ružana and Trnjane, dated to the 21st/20th–19th/18th centuries cal BC, is adorned with plastic projections on the vessel rim (Fig. 3.23/7–10; Fig. 3.26/1, 9, 10), rows of punctate impressions or dimples (Fig. 3.24/1, 9; Fig. 3.26/19, 23; Fig. 3.27/6), and plastic bands with finger impressions (Fig. 3.24/3–7, 10, 14, 16; Fig. 3.26/24–28). These ornaments persisted into later periods, as seen on pottery from Čokanjica, dated to the 18th/17th–16th century cal BC, where plastic projections on bowl rims are still present.

Incised ornaments are noted on pottery from Mokranjske Stene, Padina, Mala Vrbica, Metovnica, Osenje, and Banjska Stena, with occasional finds at Ružana and Dubrava. The motifs are mainly straight or zig-zag lines (Fig. 3.20/1–3, 11–13; Fig. 3.21/12; Fig. 3.22/6, 8, 9, 11, 12, 14–16; Fig. 3.23/17; Fig. 3.24/13; Fig. 3.32/19; Fig. 3.33/23, 24), zigzag lines sometimes forming sequences of rhomboids (Fig. 3.22/4, 5, 14, 16, 17; Fig. 3.24/11; Fig. 3.33/23, 24), inscribed hanging triangles (Fig. 3.33/21), dual parallel incised lines filled with vertical slashes (Fig. 3.29/2; Fig. 3.33/18), and combed lines (Fig. 3.22/2, 10). These ornaments are characteristic of the second and especially the third phase of the *Verbicioara* cultural group (Crăciunescu 2004), present from the Early Bronze Age in Oltenia, western Bulgaria, and southeastern Pannonia. The third phase is dated to 1600–1300 BC.

Noteworthy is a beaker whose form and decoration are identical to those typical of the *Vatin* group. It is decorated with paired curved lines ending in spirals, possibly explained by contacts between the Middle Bronze Age communities of the Timok Region and populations in the Danube Basin, where such beakers were common.

3.4.3.2 Chance and special finds

LIST OF SITES WITH CHANCE AND SPECIAL FINDS

173. Žagubica, the site of Straža, dagger (Filipović 2022); 174. Brestovac, unknown site, Darabani-type axe (Antonović 2014, 94); 175. Urovica, the site of Valja Mare, Patulele-type axe (Jovanović 1971a; Antonović 2014, 94); 176. Koželj, unknown site, Patulele-type axe (Stojić and Ilijić 2011, 79; Antonović 2014, 94); 177. Tromeđa of Lenovac, Leskovac, and Gornja Bela Reka, the site of Gas Pipeline Route, dagger (Aleksić and Filipović 2020); 178. Podgorac, the site of Strmljeno, beaker with a trapezoidal rim (Kapuran 2014, T. 15/11); 179. Bor, unknown site, beaker with a trapezoidal rim (Stojić 1998); 180. Džanovo Polje, unknown site, vessel fragments (Kapuran 2014, 57); 181. Gornja Bela Reka, the site of Suvi Peć, amphora parts with horizontal handles (Srejović and Lazić 1997, 230); 182. Gornja Bela Reka, the site of Česma, amphora parts with horizontal handles (Srejović and Lazić 1997, 230); 183. Kamenica, unknown site, two handled beaker (Stojić and Ilijić 2011, 70).

A Darabani-type axe, containing 2.5% arsenic, was discovered as a chance find in Brestovac near Bor (Fig. 3.34/1). The material classifies it as an arsenical copper object (Antonović 2014, table 2), which is a rare find since items made from arsenical copper are uncommon in the central Balkans. Another similar find from the Early Bronze Age is a Kozarac-type axe from the Negotin area (Pernicka *et al.* 1993, table 3), as discussed in Chapter 2. Such arsenical copper finds in the central Balkans are predominantly linked to the Timok Region, though they are more frequently encountered in Pannonia, particularly in Banat. Darabani-type axes are mainly distributed in the valleys of the Siret and Prut rivers on the border of present-day Romania and Moldova (Vulpe 1970, pl. 46 A), making this example relatively isolated within the central Balkans.

Urovica yielded a Patulele-type copper axe (Fig. 3.34/2) (Antonović 2014, table 5), and a similar example from Koželj near Knjaževac (Fig. 3.34/3) has an unknown composition. Patulele-type axes are primarily found in the central Balkans, particularly east of the Morava River, in the Timok Region and South Morava Basin. Their origin is uncertain, potentially traceable to Oltenia and Transylvania or the Bulgarian Danube Region, where most of these axes have been recorded (Vulpe 1970, pl. 44 B).

A smaller single-edged bronze knife/dagger or razor (Fig. 3.34/4) with a high tin content of 10.7% was found in grave 28 at the Trnjane necropolis, dated between the mid-18th and mid-17th centuries cal BC (Table 1) (Jovanović and Janković 1990, 1; Srejović and Lazić 1997; Kapuran *et al.* 2014, 107–112; 2020). Interestingly, another bronze item from Trnjane, a piece of bronze sheet metal, also had a high tin content of 8.8%.[16] An eye needle, likely found on a house floor in the settlement based on its description (Jovanović and Janković 1990), was also made of bronze. The Sn^{124}/Sn^{120} tin isotope analysis revealed that these items belong to the so-called 'Serbian group' tin source (Mason *et al.* 2016, 115; 2020, data supplementary table, 35–37). While no direct analogies for the knife/dagger were found, similar forms have been discovered in the Aegean (Kapuran *et al.* 2020, 67). The eye needle is a standard form that appears throughout all Bronze Age phases, providing limited value for tracing its origin by form.

A double-edged dagger was discovered during the exploration of sites impacted by the 'Turski tok' gas pipeline at the confluence of Lenovac, Leskovac, and Gornja Bela Reka near Zaječar. It features a pronounced central rib and an expanded rivet plate that is damaged (Aleksić and Filipović 2020). The blade is considerably worn, possibly from use or frequent sharpening (Fig. 3.34/5). This type of dagger resembles those found in Central Europe from the end of the Early and into the Middle Bronze Age, from present-day Czechia, southern Germany, France, etc (Aleksić and Filipović 2020, 22, 23; Wels-Weyrauch 2015, 83–85, Taf. 19–21, 49, 57).

A chance find from the area of the Mlava River springs at Straža in Žagubica was a double-edged dagger about 16.5 cm long, with a trapezoidal rivet plate and four perforations

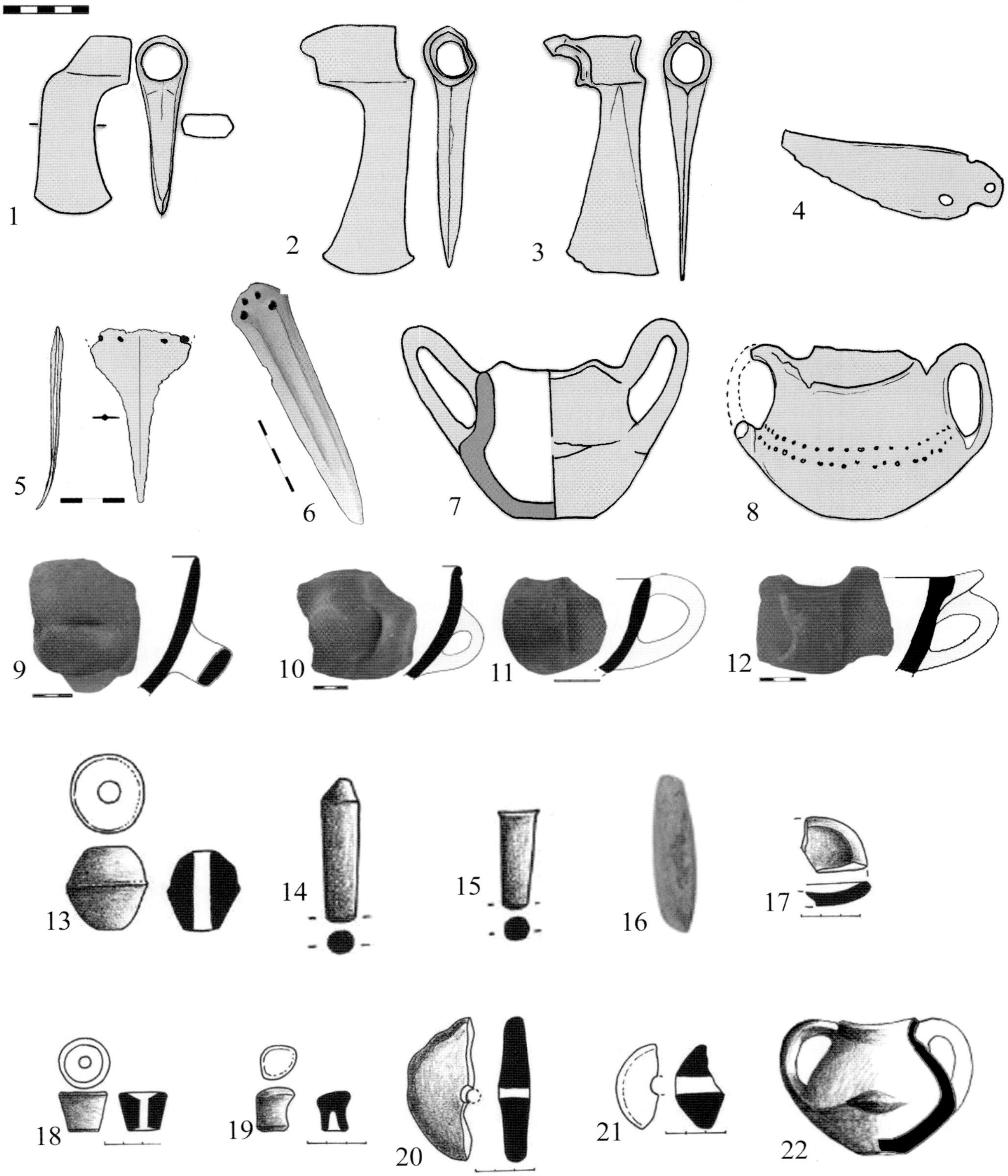

Figure 3.34. 1, Brestovac, unknown site; 2, Urovica, unknown site; 3, Koželj, unknown site; 4, Brestovačka Banja: site of Trnjane, grave 28; 5, Zaječar area, unknown site; 6, Žagubica: site of Straža; 7, Bor, unknown site; 8, Podgorac: site of Strmljeno; 9–12, Džanovo Polje, unknown site; 13–21, Brestovačka Banja: site of Trnjane: 13–15, settlement, SU 2; 16, grave 33; 17–21, settlement, SU 4; 22, Kamenica, unknown site.

for rivets (Fig. 3.34/6) (Filipović 2020, 39, 40). Based on numerous analogies, mainly from Central Europe, this dagger can be dated to 1650–1450 BC (Filipović 2020, 41).

Notable chance finds include two beakers with trapezoidal rims, one from Podgorac and another from Bor (Fig. 3.34/7, 8). The example from Podgorac is decorated with two horizontal rows of punctate impressions on the shoulder, while that from Bor features a plastic oval protrusion on the body. Intriguing finds were uncovered at Džanovo Polje from an unspecified site, comprising deep hemispherical bowls of type 3a with wide vertical handles and, in one case, a horizontal handle (Fig. 3.34/9–12). One example has triangular plastic projections on the rim near the handle, all stylistically and typologically consistent with Middle Bronze Age pottery from this zone.

Significant special finds from the Trnjane settlement include biconical, conical, and discoid spindle whorls (Fig. 3.34/13, 18–21), a spoon (Fig. 3.34/17), a stone axe or chisel from grave 33 (Fig. 3.34/16), cylindrical stone objects, likely remnants from making stone axes or sockets (Fig. 3.34/13, 14), as well as grinding stones and stone axes (Kapuran *et al.* 2020, pl. vi–vii). These provide insight into the daily life of the Middle Bronze Age populations inhabiting the Timok Region.

These metal finds highlight the intense direct or indirect interactions of the Middle Bronze Age Timok populations with those in the wider region, including the Aegean, the Lower Danube, and Transylvania. Pottery evidence, particularly the distinctive Vatin culture beaker from Banjska Stena (Fig. 3.33/20), further supports these connections, showcasing cultural transmission in the Middle Bronze Age.

3.4.4 Cultural and chronological attribution of Middle Bronze Age communities in the Timok Region and Đerdap Gorge

Several decades ago, when the first necropolis in this zone was excavated in Trnjane near Bor, researchers classified it within the Paraćin group of the Late Bronze Age, primarily based on the appearance of the urns and the architecture of the graves (Jovanović and Janković 1990, 9). Later, B. Jovanović expanded on this thesis, referring to this manifestation as the Timok group of the Paraćin culture, which was reasonable given the lack of analogies or similar sites, as well as the appearance of the stone grave structures and urns, which were very similar to the necropolises and urns of the Paraćin group (Jovanović 1999, 69–70). At the same time, D. Srejović and M. Lazić systematised and presented, alongside Trnjane, a larger number of sites and finds from the Timok Region, extending the lower chronological boundary and attributing them to multiple phases of the Bronze Age, defining them as a new cultural phenomenon – the Gamzigrad culture (Srejović and Lazić 1997, 241, 242). However, in the meantime, more settlements and necropolises belonging to this group were excavated, significantly increasing the number of portable finds, allowing for a stylistic-typological analysis of the ceramics.

A. Kapuran, in a critique of Srejović and Lazić's work, noted that it was premature to speak of a new culture based on an insufficient number of finds, especially since these finds resemble existing groups – such as the Verbicioara group, the Crvenka-Gornești group, and the Vatin culture, among others. Moreover, the narrow distribution of these sites would only allow for the definition of a local cultural phenomenon rather than an entire culture (Kapuran 2009, 59, 60). Later, A. Bulatović and J. Stankovski, in their analysis of Bronze Age ceramic material from the central Balkans, observed a certain cultural unity in the pottery of the Middle Bronze Age from the Morava Valley and the Timok Region. They defined this Middle Bronze Age cultural phenomenon in the central Balkans as the Bubanj-Hum IV–Ljuljaci group, or the Morava-Timok variant of the Vatin culture (Bulatović and Stankovski 2012, 337–347).

A decade later, with the emergence of the first absolute dates from the Timok Region, the hypothesis proposed by Srejović and Lazić, and later supported by Bulatović and Stankovski, about the older origin of these finds proved accurate. Most of the dates indicated that this cultural group existed as early as the 20th/19th century cal BC (see Fig. 4.11), suggesting that it was not exclusively linked to the Late Bronze Age (Kapuran *et al.* 2020; 2022; Mehofer *et al.* 2021).

In terms of the cultural aspects of this group, it becomes evident that a certain cultural unity prevailed in the Timok Region from the end of the Early Bronze Age, i.e., from the late 3rd–early 2nd millennium cal BC, though exclusively in the northern part of the basin, particularly in the Bor Region. The necropolises shared uniform features, consisting of circular stone structures containing cremated remains in urns that were nearly identical. Settlement ceramics also displayed similar stylistic and typological characteristics, all pointing to a cohesive cultural group. A comparable burial practice involving circular stone structures and cremated remains, unprecedented at that time, was documented earlier in the southern Morava Valley at the Meanište site in Ranutovac near Vranje (Bulatović *et al.* 2016). This necropolis was dated to between the 22nd and 19th centuries cal BC (Bulatović 2020, 81–83). Almost identical funerary architecture with similar ceramic forms, occasionally featuring urns with lids, was observed in northern Greece, on the middle prong of Chalkidiki, at Sykia, which is notably older, broadly dated to the second half of the 3rd millennium BC (Asouchidou *et al.* 1998, fig. 8). It can be speculated that the cremation burial custom involving circular stone structures characteristic of the Timok Region came from the south. However, why this custom was readily adopted, or if the Middle Bronze Age population of the Timok Region itself originated from the south bringing the funerary practice with them, remains uncertain. Cremation graves were mentioned in the Early Bronze Age Glina culture in neighbouring Oltenia but they were few and lacked detailed documentation, with inhumation being the dominant practice (Machnik 1991, 16, 17; Schuster 2003, 138), making it unlikely that this rite was adopted from that area.

It is clear that during the Early Bronze Age, according to current findings, there are no significant settlement traces in the Timok Region, unlike the Late Eneolithic period when life flourished (Kapuran and Bulatović 2012b). This implies that during the Early Bronze Age this territory was somewhat of a demographic vacuum. Supporting the theory of a southern origin for the population inhabiting the Timok Region in the Middle Bronze Age is the pottery found at the Sykia necropolis, particularly urns with arched or tunnel-like vertical perforated handles, closely resembling examples from the Timok Region (Asouchidou *et al.* 1998, fig. 7). These urns at the Chalkidiki necropolis, along with similar pottery and identical burial structures as seen in the Timok Region, were dated to the first half of the 3rd millennium BC.

Beyond a few scattered ceramic finds, mainly beakers and bowls from Kučajna and Gamzigrad, which stylistically and typologically may belong to the Middle Bronze Age, and two stray finds of axes of the Kozarac-type from Laznica and Osnić, no significant Early Bronze Age finds have been documented in the Timok Region. The situation is somewhat more favourable in the Đerdap Region, where two Early Bronze Age necropolises or graves have been found, with evidence suggesting cultural contacts with the peri-Pannonian zone west of Đerdap. Thus, it appears that the Timok Region was either uninhabited or sparsely populated during the Early Bronze Age, which seems unusual given its significant habitation in both the preceding (Late Eneolithic–Coţofeni-Kostolac group) and subsequent (Middle Bronze Age) periods.

Some explanations for this phenomenon propose that nomadic communities engaged in mobile pastoralism may have lingered in these areas until the Middle Bronze Age (Kapuran 2014, 52). Alternatively, it is believed that this region was a sparsely populated part of a broader cultural complex encompassing Bulgaria, south-eastern Serbia, and north-eastern Macedonia, from which regional cultural groups crystallised during the Early Bronze Age (Kapuran *et al.* 2014, 38). Regardless, unlike other regions of the central Balkans, the Timok Region lacked a known cultural foundation upon which the Middle Bronze Age cultural group emerged, characterised by cremation deposits in urns placed within circular stone structures and distinct ceramic forms.

The ceramics from Ružana and Trnjane, as well as those from the necropolises at Hajdučka Česma, Kriveljski Kamen, Borsko Jezero, and Trnjane – the oldest Middle Bronze Age ceramics dated to the 20th/19th–19th/18th centuries cal BC – feature semi-circular bowls with a triangularly thickened inner rim (types 3e or 3a) or bowls with an inset rim (type 3b) (Fig. 3.23/6–10; Fig. 3.26/1–3, 5, 9–15; Fig. 3.27/1–3; Fig. 3.31/2), as well as pear-shaped beakers with two arched vertical handles aligned with or extending above the rim (Fig. 3.23/11–15; Fig. 3.26/10; Fig. 3.27/6). Various types of amphorae, most commonly 1b, 3b, and 4a, featuring horizontal or occasionally vertical short arched ribbon-shaped handles, primarily served as urns (Fig. 3.27/11; Fig. 3.30/15, 21; Fig. 3.31/2, 5, 6). The most common decorative feature in this period includes triangular or tongue-shaped plastic projections on the vessel rim, especially on bowls (Fig. 3.23/7–10; Fig. 3.26/1, 2, 8, 9), and rows of punctate and dot impressions (Fig. 3.24/1, 9; Fig. 3.26/7, 19, 20, 23, 24; Fig. 3.27/6). Notably, one of the most indicative ceramic forms in the Middle Bronze Age, not only in the Timok Region but throughout the central Balkans, is the beaker and, less frequently, the bowl, with a trapezoidal rim. This form, as already established, is one of the primary indicative elements of the Bubanj-Hum IV–Ljuljaci group and frequently appears in ceramic inventories from the Timok Region (Fig. 3.25/26; Fig. 3.27/24; Fig. 3.28/2; Fig. 3.31/11; Fig. 3.34/7, 8).

The ceramic elements mentioned above, characteristic of the earlier phase of the Middle Bronze Age in the Timok Region, have also been identified at other undated sites. These include locations such as Obala kod Crkve (Fig. 3.21/15–18), Selište (Fig. 3.25/3, 5), Čoka Kormanc (Fig. 3.25/9, 10, 12, 14), Kučajna (Fig. 3.25/21–26), Zvezdan (Fig. 3.28/2–4, 12), Potoci (Fig. 3.28/23, 24), Metovnica (Fig. 3.29/1), Zlotska Pećina (Fig. 3.29/11, 13), and Džanovo Polje (Fig. 3.34/9–12) (Kapuran and Bulatović 2012b, T. II/14; T. III/19, 27; T. VII/84, 85; T. X/132; T. XI/146; Bulatović and Milanović 2020, fig. 199/4, 5; fig. 206/7, 10; fig. 207/3; fig. 208/4; fig. 209/2). The bowls with triangularly thickened inner rims may have direct analogies with the preceding Coţofeni–Kostolac group, where such bowls were a common ceramic form in this region and beyond. These bowl profiles also appear sporadically in the Early Bronze Age of the peri-Pannonian zone (Fig. 2.3/3), the Great Morava Valley (Fig. 2.17/10), and the South Morava Valley (Fig. 2.33/10, 23; Fig. 2.37/8; Fig. 2.38/4; Fig. 2.39/15, etc.), interpreted as survivals from the previous period (Late Eneolithic), when the Coţofeni–Kostolac group populated not only the Danubian region but also the Great Morava and the Southern Morava valley territories (Kapuran and Bulatović 2012b, 76; Bulatović and Kapuran 2017).

The stylistic and typological characteristics of the pottery from the earlier phase of the Middle Bronze Age in the Timok Region bear a strong resemblance to the Bubanj-Hum IV–Ljuljaci group, which was spread across the Morava Valley and western Serbia. This group evolved from the cultural foundations of the Bubanj-Hum III group from the Early Bronze Age which, alongside sites in western Bulgaria and northern Macedonia, formed a broader complex known as the Bubanj-Hum III–Pelince–Pernik during the second half of the 3rd millennium. It seems that the cultural group of the Middle Bronze Age in the Timok Region developed on these foundations, aligning with the Bubanj-Hum IV–Ljuljaci group, at least in its earlier phase. Later, after the 18th/17th century BC, new cultural trends emerged, most prominently observed in the Timok Region but also visible in other areas of the Bubanj-Hum IV–Ljuljaci group.

However, the origins of this group in the Timok Region remain unresolved. Current research suggests that this zone was uninhabited for unknown reasons during the Early Bronze Age, i.e., during the second half of the 3rd millennium, and only became settled at the end of this period by a population from the southern Morava Valley. This is supported by Božilova and Tonkov's view that significant climatic changes in the last quarter of the 3rd millennium BC affected the Balkans' population (Božilova and Tonkov 2007). The hypothesis that the Coţofeni–Kostolac group persisted until the end of the 3rd millennium lacks sufficient evidence, as more characteristic elements of this group would have been retained beyond the bowls with thickened inner rims. Additionally, in EBA 2 connections between the southern Morava communities and Oltenia were noted, which are absent in the Timok Region. P. Roman documented Oltenian pottery matching the Bubanj-Hum III group alongside pottery featuring Vinkovci–Somogyvár traits (Roman 2006, 459), indicating interactions through the peri-Pannonian zone and the Danube region toward Đerdap rather than the closer Timok Region.

The depopulation of the Timok Region during the Early Bronze Age and the avoidance of it as a natural corridor may be attributed to the region's topographical features and likely reforestation of mountainous and marshland areas following the Eneolithic Coţofeni–Kostolac group's disintegration.

The data from Ružana indicate that by the 19th/18th century cal BC, this population was already familiar with copper metallurgy, a knowledge that requires long-term development and generational transmission. Given that copper metallurgy was not present in this zone during the Late Eneolithic and considering the distinct burial practices in the Middle Bronze Age unfamiliar in the Eneolithic, the hypothesis of direct continuity from the Late Eneolithic does not seem well-founded. Furthermore, part of the copper ore used in Ružana's metallurgical process came from outside the region, specifically northern Italy, suggesting an established metallurgical system involving diverse resources and contact with distant regions for raw material procurement.

Based on currently available data, the Middle Bronze Age in the Timok Region developed from the Early Bronze Age culture of the central Balkans (Bubanj-Hum III–Pelince–Pernik), potentially influenced by populations from Đerdap bearing a blend of this complex and Pannonian cultures like the Vinkovci–Somogyvár and Novačka Ćuprija–Pančevo groups, with strong connections to southern central Balkan communities that may have ethnically filled this zone by the end of the Early Bronze Age. One reason for these movements from the south to the north might have been the incursion of the Armenochori group from northern Greece through the Vardar Valley. The increased mobility of the central Balkan population at that time was likely facilitated by the domestication and intensive use of horses. Namely, horse remains have been discovered at several Early Bronze Age sites, such as Rit in the peri-Pannonian zone, Novačka Ćuprija in Šumadija, and Bubanj in the South Morava Valley. All contexts where the bones were found date to the 21st/20th centuries BC.

At a certain point during the Middle Bronze Age, the presence of Verbicioara group elements from the north or north-east becomes noticeable in Đerdap and the Timok Region. However, it remains unclear exactly when they appeared, whether they emerged simultaneously across all micro-regions of the Timok Region and Đerdap, or if they were absent in some areas. The situation at the Livade site in Mala Vrbica is particularly intriguing, where three occupation horizons have been documented: the oldest, Horizon I, associated with the Verbicioara group; Horizon II, characterised by finds of the Žuto Brdo group; and the youngest, Horizon III, featuring artefacts from the Gava group (Vukmanović and Popović 1986, 12–14). This unique stratigraphy has helped to clarify the stratigraphic and chronological relationship between the Verbicioara and Žuto Brdo cultural groups in Đerdap. The earliest date for the Žuto Brdo group in Đerdap currently comes from the village of Mala Vrbica, specifically from grave 12/1986 at the Konopište site, dating to the second half of the 16th century cal BC. This suggests that the Verbicioara group at sites in Đerdap likely dates to before the second half of the 16th century, corresponding to the end of the Middle Bronze Age, aligning with the dating of the Verbicioara group's II/III phase as outlined by researchers defining the stratigraphy and chronology at Mala Vrbica (Vukmanović and Popović 1986; Crăciunescu 2004, 227). It is possible that the displacement of the Žuto Brdo group's population triggered the movement of the Verbicioara group's bearers southward, whose elements are also noted in the southern Morava Region at the beginning of the Late Bronze Age, as will be discussed in the following chapter. Verbicioara elements are also present in ceramics from the Timok Region, seen at Mokranjske Stene, Ružana, Banjska Stena, and other sites. The layer containing pottery with Verbicioara elements at Banjska Stena has been dated approximately to the 15th century.[17] Therefore, it is clear that Verbicioara elements were certainly present at these sites in the 16th century, raising the question of when and why they initially appeared.

Some researchers suggest that the 'shift' of the Verbicioara group's bearers may be related to changes in the distribution of Wietenberg group settlements in Transylvania during the Verbicioara group's II/III phase. These contacts between the Wietenberg and Verbicioara groups can be evidenced by the ornamental motifs of spirals and meanders characteristic of the B–C phases of the Wietenberg group (Boroffka 1994, 288–290, table 16, 22, 26, pl. 13), which became dominant motifs in Oltenia within the Verbicioara group during phases III/IV (Crăciunescu 2004, pls lxi, lxiii). During Phase II, Verbicioara settlements were densely distributed along the Danube in the Ključ area on both the Romanian and Serbian sides. In Phase III, these settlements disappear (Crăciunescu 2004, pls xcvi, xcvii), possibly moving westward and southward at the end of Phase II and the beginning of Phase III, approximately in the 17th/16th century BC (Crăciunescu 2004, 227). This might explain the increased presence of Verbicioara elements in the younger phase of the Middle Bronze Age in the Timok Region, from the 17th/16th century onwards.

In summary, based on available data, the Middle Bronze Age in the Timok Region and Đerdap can be viewed in two phases. The older phase, beginning in the 21st/20th century and lasting until the 17th/16th century, saw the presence of the Bubanj-Hum IV–Ljuljaci group, which might have settled this area from the south, with some survivals of the preceding Late Eneolithic Coţofeni–Kostolac elements. From the 17th/16th century, in the younger phase of the Middle Bronze Age, there were significant contacts with the communities of Verbicioara group and possible migrations of this population into Đerdap and the Timok Region. However, these interactions did not reach a degree or intensity sufficient to erase the foundational elements of the previous phase, the Bubanj-Hum IV–Ljuljaci group. Instead, these elements persisted and even influenced the formation of Late Bronze Age cultural groups in the central Balkans.

3.5 Southern Serbia with Middle Pčinja and Kumanovo and Skopje plains

This geographic zone encompasses the basin of the South Morava, Middle Pčinja, and Skopje Plain. The Raška area is not included in this analysis as no sites from this period have been documented there.

3.5.1 Settlements and dwelling

Within this geographic region during the Middle Bronze Age, there are records of four hilltop settlements, eight lowland settlements, and two ritual sites known from the earlier period. Site numbers refer to Plate 19.

3.5.1.1 Hilltop settlements

LIST OF HILLTOP SETTLEMENTS

77. Hum, the site of Velika Humska Čuka (Bulatović and Milanović 2021); 79. Skopje, the site of Kale (Mitrevski 2016); 184. Sokobanja, the site of Popovica (Milojević and Kapuran 2023); 185. Semče, the site of Pusto Semče (Stojić 2001, 27; Bulatović and Jović 2010, 282); 186. Gornje Krnjino, the site of Česma-Provalija (Bulatović and Stankovski 2012, 43, T. XVII).

Hilltop settlements in this zone were strategically positioned along the edges of significant valleys, such as Velika Humska Čuka at the northern rim of the Niš Plain at approximately 450 m above sea level, and Kale in Skopje, located on a dominant plateau in the middle of the Skopje Plain near the Vardar River. Additionally, three hilltops were noted in areas distant from main natural communication routes, on Suva Planina and in the Moravica Valley within the Sokobanja Basin. The sites of Česma-Provalija and Pusto Semče on Suva Planina may not have been built for overseeing major communication routes but possibly served to secure and manage copper ore resources, which are still visible as malachite and azurite deposits. This theory is further supported by three incidental metal finds in this geostrategically passive micro-region, including a Middle Bronze Age Patulele-type axe and a mould and axe of the Kilindir-type, although the latter two may be linked more to the Late Bronze Age.

Popovica, located on a prominent elevation above the Moravica River opposite Sokograd, also yielded seven Patulele-type axes as incidental finds, indicating that these hilltops may have been linked to copper ore exploitation or an alternative communication route that bypassed the South Morava Valley. Excavations at Popovica revealed Late Eneolithic, Middle Bronze Age, and Iron Age cultural layers (Milojević and Kapuran 2023); however, only two ceramic assemblages and a severely disrupted Middle Bronze Age cultural layer were identified.

Of these settlements, only those at Skopje, Hum, and Popovica have been investigated. However, the excavations did not provide significant results concerning the Middle Bronze Age. At Kale, evidence of an earthen embankment with a wooden structure was found, preserved over a length of 75 m (Mitrevski 2016, 127–130). The embankment's core was constructed of earth and stones framed by wooden beams made up of two rows of massive posts spaced approximately 3 m apart. A trench ran outside the embankment, following the terrain and reaching a depth of about 2 m. Due to the site's intensive occupation in later periods, no additional architectural structures were found.

Excavations at Velika Humska Čuka uncovered several damaged features from this period (ceramic assemblages, pits, cultural layers) but no architectural structures that could shed light on the construction methods, appearance, or scale of the settlement and its dwellings. In 2009, excavations on the northeastern edge of the site revealed remnants of a structure composed of a stone foundation damaged by a Roman-era pit. Within it, two nearly complete beakers, several large ceramic fragments (mostly pots and amphorae), and a flat bronze axe of the *Randleistenbeile* type (Fig. 3.36; Fig. 3.49/12) were found (Bulatović and Stankovski 2012, 69), dating the structure to the Middle Bronze Age (Br A2–B2 according to Central European chronology) (Bulatović and Milanović 2015, 177). A similar situation was observed in 2021 when trench 2/21 revealed a Middle Bronze Age ceramic assemblage damaged by a medieval pit (Fig. 3.37/1–7). In 2022, trench 2/22 on the northern periphery, approximately 30 m south-west of structure 8/09, revealed a group of pottery, several animal bones, two stone grinding slabs, and a few chipped stone tools (Fig. 3.38), dating to the latter half of the 16th century cal BC, marking the end of the Middle Bronze Age.

Finds from Velika Humska Čuka offer limited insight into the lives of the Middle Bronze Age inhabitants beyond indicating their use of tin bronze tools, continued reliance on chipped stone tools, and evidence of cereal consumption, likely processed with hand-operated mills.

3.5.1.2 Lowland settlements

LIST OF LOWLAND SETTLEMENTS

83. Niš, the site of Bubanj (Bulatović and Milanović 2020); 187. Niš, the site of Mediana (Garašanin 1973; Jevtić 1975; Bulatović and Stankovski 2012, 41); 188. Čekmin, the site of Kućište (Ercegović Pavlović and Kostić 1988, 12; Bulatović and Stankovski 2012, 43); 189. Bobište, the site of Izvorište–Sastanci (Stojić 2001, 27; Bulatović and Stankovski 2012, 45); 190. Trnava, the site of Trnavska Reka (Bulatović and Stankovski 2012, 53); 191. Lopate, the site of Pribovce (Sanev 1999, 127–136; Bulatović and Stankovski 2012, 53); 86. Štulac, the site of Svinjarička Čuka (Horejs *et al.* 2018); 192. Karagač, the site of Valač (Srejović 2002, 151–199); 193. Donja Brnjica (Srejović 2002, 151–199).

Lowland settlements during the Middle Bronze Age in this geographical zone were primarily established on terraces of larger rivers such as the Nišava (Bubanj and Mediana), the South Morava (Bobište), the Ibar (Karagač), or on terraces of smaller rivers along the edges of fields, near their confluences (Čekmin, Lopate, Trnava, Donja Brnjica). One settlement was located far from the main natural communication route of the South Morava valley, on the terrace of a smaller river at a site where it once meandered in the past. That is the site of Svinjarička Čuka and palaeo-geological research has established that the former riverbed surrounded the site on the eastern, southern, and southwestern sides (Horejs *et al.* 2018).

Remains of architecture or other structures from this period were discovered only at the site of Svinjarička Čuka near Lebane. Here, besides a large pit in the northern part of the site (SU 1055), remains of a structure with stone, daub, numerous pottery fragments, and animal bones were uncovered in the central part of the exploration zone. This structure was damaged by agricultural activities as it was close to the surface (Horejs *et al.*2022, 303–306). The stylistic and typological characteristics of the pottery from this structure indicate both the Middle and Late Bronze Age, at least according to current knowledge. Therefore, it remains uncertain whether the ceramic forms from the structure, characteristic of the Late Bronze Age, originated in the Middle Bronze Age and persisted, or if the materials from the two periods were mixed due to agricultural work and erosion. In any case, the structure, which likely represents the remains of an above-ground residential building constructed using wattle and daub techniques, has been dated to the 18th/17th century cal BC, similar to the pit.

This pit was located in the northern part of the site, approximately 15 m north-east of the residential structure. It was roughly circular in shape, with a diameter of about 2.5 m and a depth of about 1.2 m, and it was damaged by subsequent burials from the Iron Age (Horejs *et al.* 2022, 303–304). It was filled with loose grey soil containing a significant amount of soot, ash, animal bones (burned and unburned), pottery fragments, pieces of daub, as well as fragmented baked clay weights and bone tools. Judging by its contents, it was probably a refuse pit, possibly related to the residential structure mentioned nearby.

3.5.2 Necropolises, burial practices, and ritual spaces

In the South Morava Basin and northern Macedonia, no necropolises or single graves from the Middle Bronze Age have been recorded. However, the ritual spaces at Tatićev Kamen and Dve Mogili appear to continue being used during this period.

LIST OF RITUAL SPACES

93. Pelince, the site of Dve Mogili (Trajkovska 1995; 1999; 2003; Bulatović and Stankovski 2012); 94. Kokino, the site of Tatikev Kamen (Stankovski 2002; 2003; 2007; 2010; Mitrevski 2003; Bulatović and Stankovski 2012).

The ritual spaces at Kokino Selo and Pelince were extensively discussed Chapter 2. It was noted that the stone ritual structures at Kokino Selo primarily belonged to the Early Bronze Age population, while the finds from the Middle and Late Bronze Ages came mainly from layers or scattered contexts, complicating their attribution. The continuation of ritual activities throughout the Bronze Age is supported by astronomical calculations, which indicate that the ritual space was used in the 19th and 18th centuries BC (Cenev 2009, 9, table 2), during the Middle Bronze Age. However, it is difficult to specifically identify these finds due to the absence of absolute dates for the contexts, and because the architecture of the ritual structures and the stylistic-typological features of the pottery did not change. The argument for the continuity of ritual activities throughout the Bronze Age at both sites is further re-inforced by the confirmed ritual contexts from the Late Bronze Age, validated through ceramic typological features and an absolute date from Dve Mogili, which dated the youngest zone to the 12th century cal BC (Bulatović *et al.* 2018a). An absolute date from another Early Bronze Age context at Pelince dated it to the 24th/23rd century cal BC, making it unusual for the site to not have been used during the Middle Bronze Age while being active in both the Early and Late periods, especially given the architectural changes in the ritual structures and the new, smaller pyre protected by a retaining wall south of the main large pyre, which could belong to the Middle Bronze Age. However, the stylistic-typological features of the pottery from the site, aside from those from the Late Bronze Age, are uniform, making it difficult to distinguish pieces that might belong to the Middle Bronze Age.

Thus, analysing the architecture of the ritual contexts at the site rather than the stylistic-typological features of the pottery reveals that a new, smaller pyre was established south of the main large circular pyre at some point, secured by a low retaining wall. Surrounding it are contexts which, according to Bulatović and Stankovski 2012), belong to zone 3 of the sanctuary. The problem is that one context from this zone has been dated to the Early Bronze Age, so the same could be presumed for the other contexts in this zone.

Nevertheless, based on the stylistic-typological characteristics of the ceramics, it has been noted that zone 3 lacks two handled beakers typical of zones 1 and 2, and that whole vessels are rare, with fragments mostly being deposited. It is also observed that other ceramic elements, such as plastic attachments on the rim of recessed-rim bowls (triangular, rectangular, horn-shaped, trapezoidal), one-handled jugs, pots decorated with plastic ribs and bands, and decorations in the form of incised lines and punctures, remain in use as in zones 1 and 2. On the other hand, the site lacks ceramic forms characteristic of Middle Bronze Age northern Macedonia, as found at sites like Kale in Skopje or Pribovce in Lopate, making it scientifically irresponsible to attempt defining Middle Bronze Age ceramics at the Pelince sanctuary without absolute dates. Since the only three animal bones found at the site were used for AMS analysis,[18] thermoluminescence dating of ceramic fragments is the only remaining option for further dating the sanctuary and establishing whether there was continuous use throughout the Bronze Age.

The situation is similar for the ritual space at Kokino Selo, with the difference being that no radiocarbon absolute date exists for this site, apart from the aforementioned astronomical ones, making the attribution of Middle Bronze Age ceramics or contexts even more challenging.

3.5.3 Portable finds

3.5.3.1 Pottery

A. BOWLS

The most common type of bowl in this geographic zone is type 1b, comprising about one-third of the total bowls. These have a gentle or sharper S-profile, seemingly equally represented in both the South Morava Basin and northern Macedonia (Fig. 3.35/1; Fig. 3.39/6; Fig. 3.41/1, 2, 4; Fig. 3.45/1–3; Fig. 3.46/2–4, 9). The second most common type is 1a, accounting for approximately 16% of the total number of bowls, found exclusively at the sites of Velika Humska Čuka in the Niš Plain and Pribovce in the Kumanovo Plain in Macedonia (Fig. 3.38/2; Fig. 3.46/6, 7, 11–14). This is followed by type 2a (Fig. 3.37/2; Fig. 3.42/3; Fig. 3.46/8) at around 11%, and types 1c (Fig. 3.39/7; Fig. 3.42/1; Fig. 3.45/4), 3a (Fig. 3.38/3; Fig. 3.41/3; Fig. 3.42/2, 5, 11; Fig. 3.43/3), and 3d (Fig. 3.40/1; Fig. 3.42/7), each at about 9%, and 3c (Fig. 3.37/1, 8, 9; Fig. 3.46/10; Fig. 3.48/1, 2) at approximately 12%. The least represented types of bowls are 1b (Fig. 3.46/1) and 3e (Fig. 3.35/11).

None of the bowls is decorated, but some examples feature cylindrical, conical, or biconical plastic projections at the top of the handle (Fig. 3.37/1, 8; Fig. 3.41/8; Fig. 3.43/1–3).

B. CUPS

Several cups have been recorded in this zone, all of which were discovered at Karagač. All specimens have hemispherical bodies (Fig. 3.43/4–6) and belong to type 1a. The cups are undecorated.

C. BEAKERS

During the previous period, the Early Bronze Age, the prevalent type of beaker in this zone was type 1c, now represented by only about 10% (Fig. 3.35/12; Fig. 3.37/5; Fig. 3.39/9; Fig. 3.41/5; Fig. 3.43/1). The most common type in the Middle Bronze Age is type 1g, making up over 60% (Fig. 3.36/1, 2; Fig. 3.37/3; Fig. 3.39/1–5, 10, 11; Fig. 3.41/6; Fig. 3.42/8; Fig. 3.43/2, 4–9, 12; Fig. 3.47/1, 12). This is followed by type 1e at around 17% (Fig. 3.39/8; Fig. 3.47/2, 4; Fig. 3.48/7, 9, 10), with type 1c making up about 9%. Types 3a (Fig. 3.46/5; Fig. 3.43/8) and 5a (Fig. 3.42/9) are together represented by approximately 7%. Like type 7d in the northern central Balkans, type 1g emerged in the Middle Bronze Age, primarily in the south, appearing less frequently in the northern central Balkans or the peri-Pannonian zone, where no examples have been recorded. Interestingly, both specimens of type 3a beakers were found in the southern part of this zone, in Kosovo and northern Macedonia. The beakers are generally undecorated, except for one from Vitkovac, whose shoulder is adorned with two rows of punctate impressions arranged in metopes and bordered by two parallel horizontal incised lines (Fig. 3.46/12). Other beakers are often 'decorated' with trapezoidal-shaped rims (Fig. 3.36/1, 2; Fig. 3.37/3; Fig. 3.38/6, 7; Fig. 3.39/1–5, 10; Fig. 3.41/6; Fig. 3.43/13; Fig. 3.46/12), triangular plastic projections on the rim that mimic trapezoidal opening (Fig. 3.43/2–4, 7, 9, 11), or plastic projections at the top of the handles (Fig. 3.36/1; Fig. 3.38/12; Fig. 3.41/7; Fig. 3.43/5; Fig. 3.44/13). A beaker

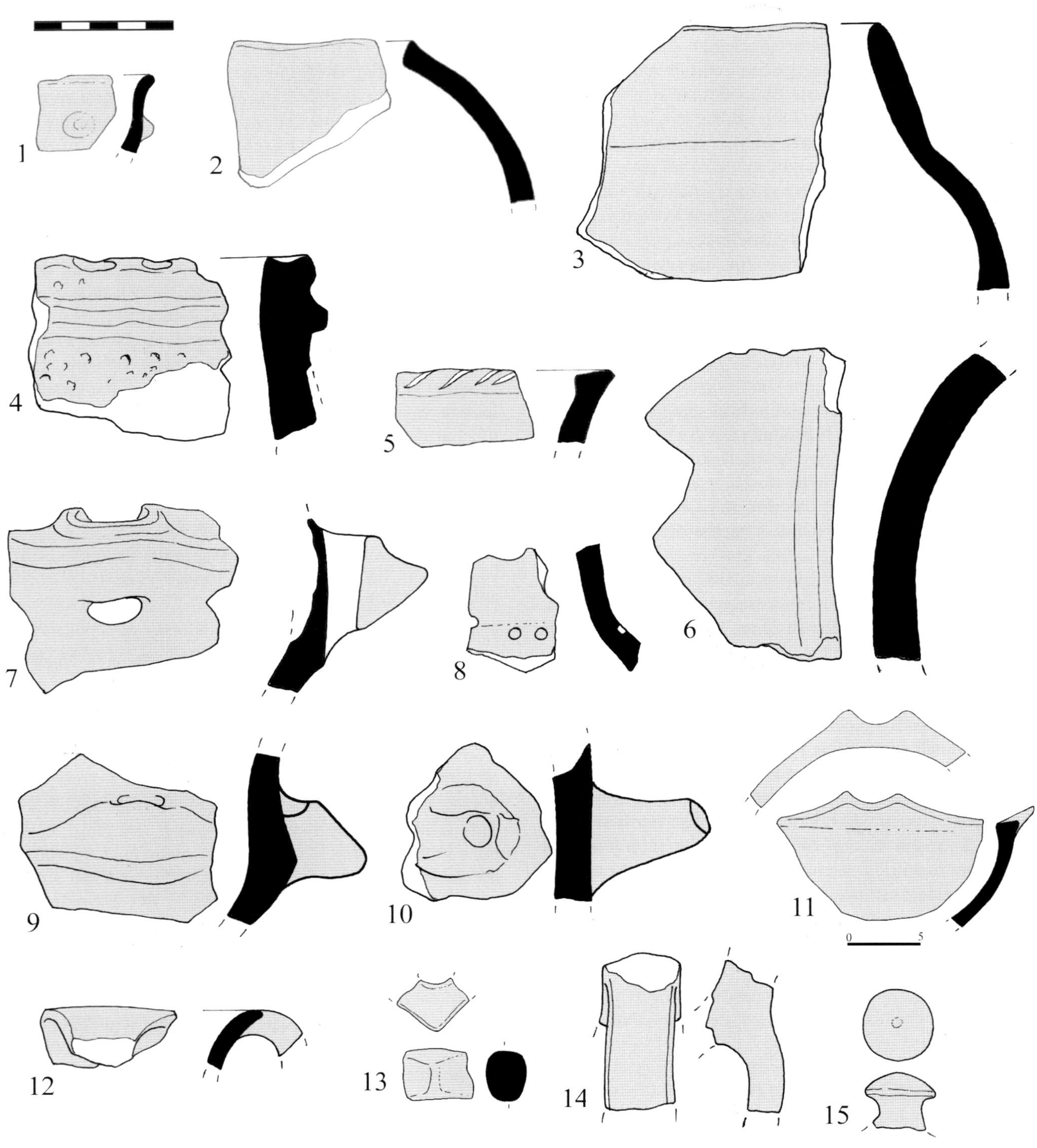

Figure 3.35. Sokobanja: site of Popovica: 1–3, Trench 2, structure 2; 4–10, Trench 2, pottery accumulation; 11–15, cultural layer.

from Lopate has a punctate impression at the base of the handle (Fig. 3.46/4), and the handle of a type 3a beaker has a fan-shaped top (Fig. 3.46/5), which will become characteristic of the Late Bronze Age in this zone.

D. AMPHORAE

As in the previous period, amphorae were rarely present in this zone during the Middle Bronze Age. Types 1b (Fig. 3.35/2; Fig. 3.38/5), 2a (Fig. 3.37/4), 3a (Fig. 3.35/5), 4b

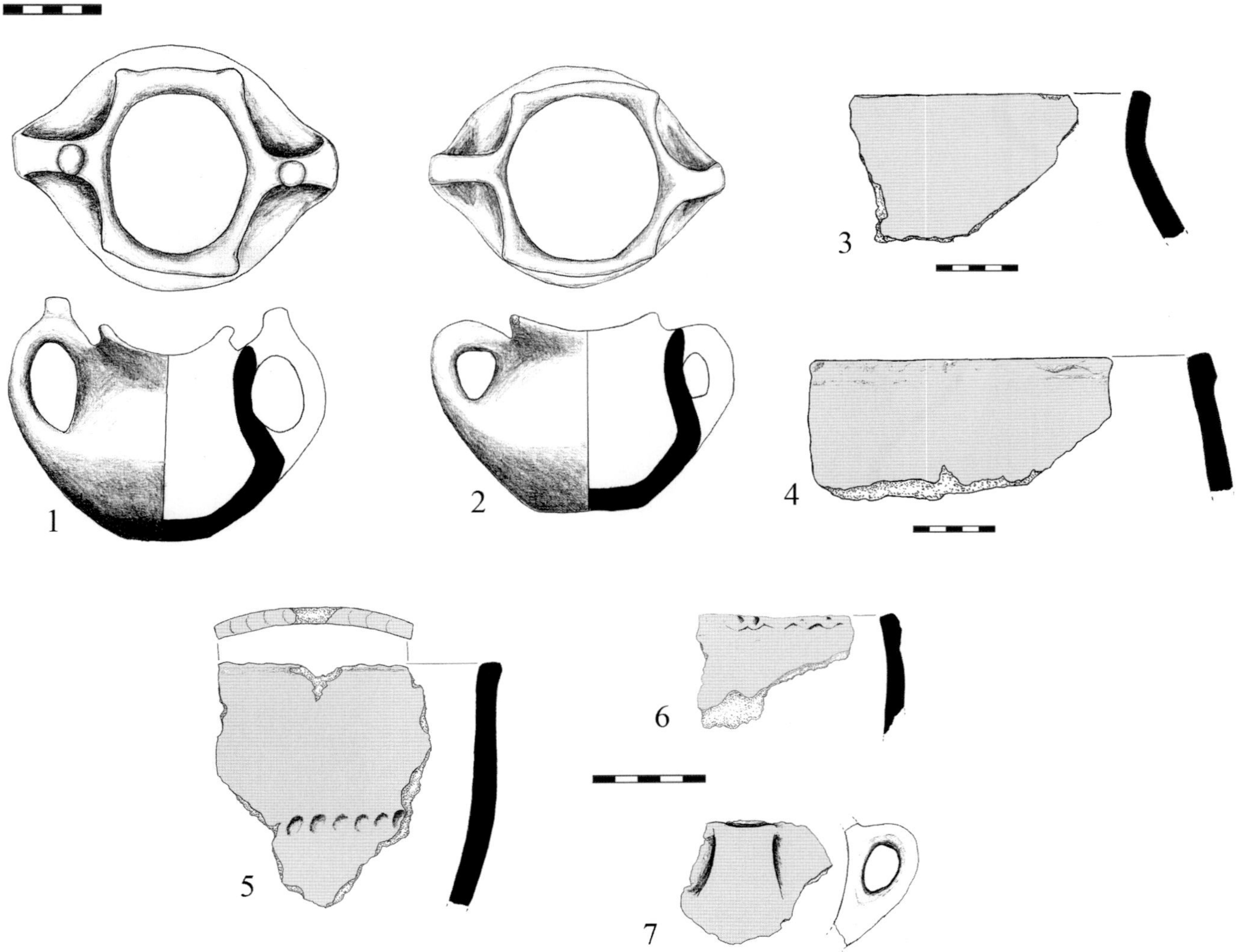

Figure 3.36. Hum: site of Velika Humska Čuka, Trench 1/09, structure 8.

(Fig. 3.35/3), 5a (Fig. 3.36/5; Fig. 3.44/3), and 5b (Fig. 3.38/1) were each found only once. All specimens originate from the sites Velika Humska Čuka and Popovica, with only two being decorated – one with a series of punctate impressions on the body and rim (Fig. 3.36/5) and the other with a series of slanting notches on the rim (Fig. 3.35/5).

E. SPECIAL-PURPOSE VESSELS

Ember containers: Two ember containers come from this zone, both from northern Macedonia, one from the Kumanovo plain and another from the ritual site Tatikev Kamen in Kokino Selo (Fig. 3.46/10, 11). The container from Lopate has an elongated cylindrical neck, with the front opening styled in a 'spatula' shape, and a small arched handle on the rear side. The container from Kokino Selo is simpler, featuring a semi-circular upper and front opening with a slightly larger missing handle. The front side between the two openings includes a small circular perforation, likely for enhanced airflow. These containers have been known in this region, as well as in northern Greece and southern Albania, since the end of the Early Bronze Age.

Double vessels: On the site in Donja Brnjica, Kosovo, the only recorded double vessel with a hemispherical container and an arched transverse handle (Fig. 3.43/12) was found. Another fragment from the same site and layer could represent a double vessel, indicated by a part of a globular container and a handle fragment without a visible root on the container, suggesting it is a double vessel (Fig. 3.43/11).

Pyraunoi: The *pyraunoi* were found at Velika humska čuka and Popovica. The specimen from Velika Humska Čuka, dated to the late Middle Bronze Age (Fig. 3.38/16), and similar ones from Popovica (Fig. 3.35/4, 6) date similarly.

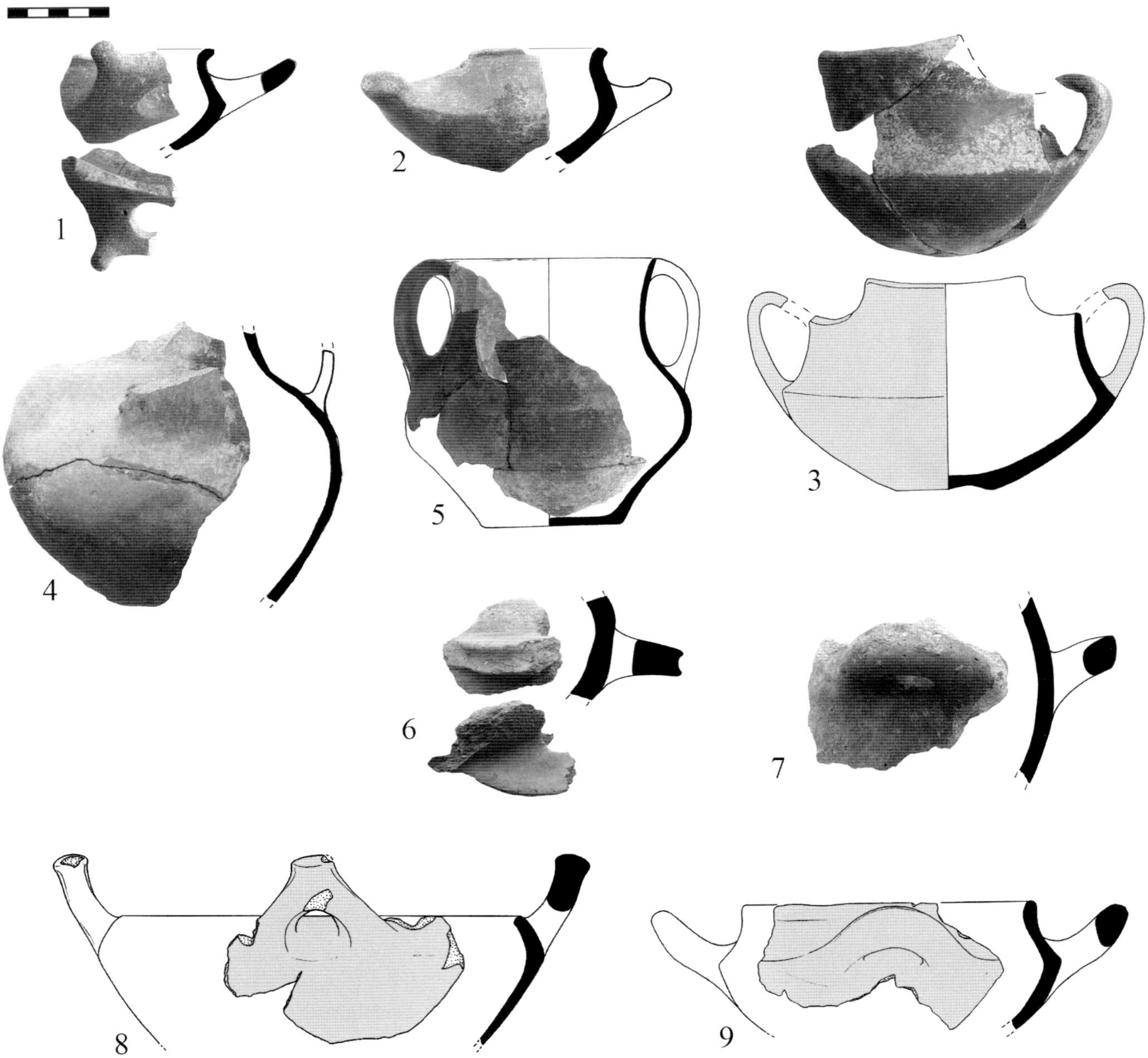

Figure 3.37. Hum: site of Velika Humska Čuka: 1–7, Trench 2/21, pottery accumulation in Middle Bronze Age layer; 8, Trench 1/16s; 9, Trench 3/16.

The Velika Humska Čuka example has a hemispherical profile, with a nearly vertical and low hearth barely separating the vessel's bottom from the hearth level. It features a tongue-shaped handle on the body, and the rim is decorated with a series of punctate impressions. The two examples from Popovica might belong to the same vessel, as both a rim and a part of the arched hearth with an opening were found. The Popovica rim is also decorated with a series of punctate impressions.

Ladles (dippers): A so-called dipping ladle or scoop, a shallow vessel with thin walls and a massive handle extending beyond the vessel's dimensions (Fig. 3.42/12), was found in this zone. Based on its form and wall thickness, it likely served for scooping granular or liquid food.

F. HANDLES

As in the previous period, the most common handle type is the arched, vertically placed handle, which, unlike in

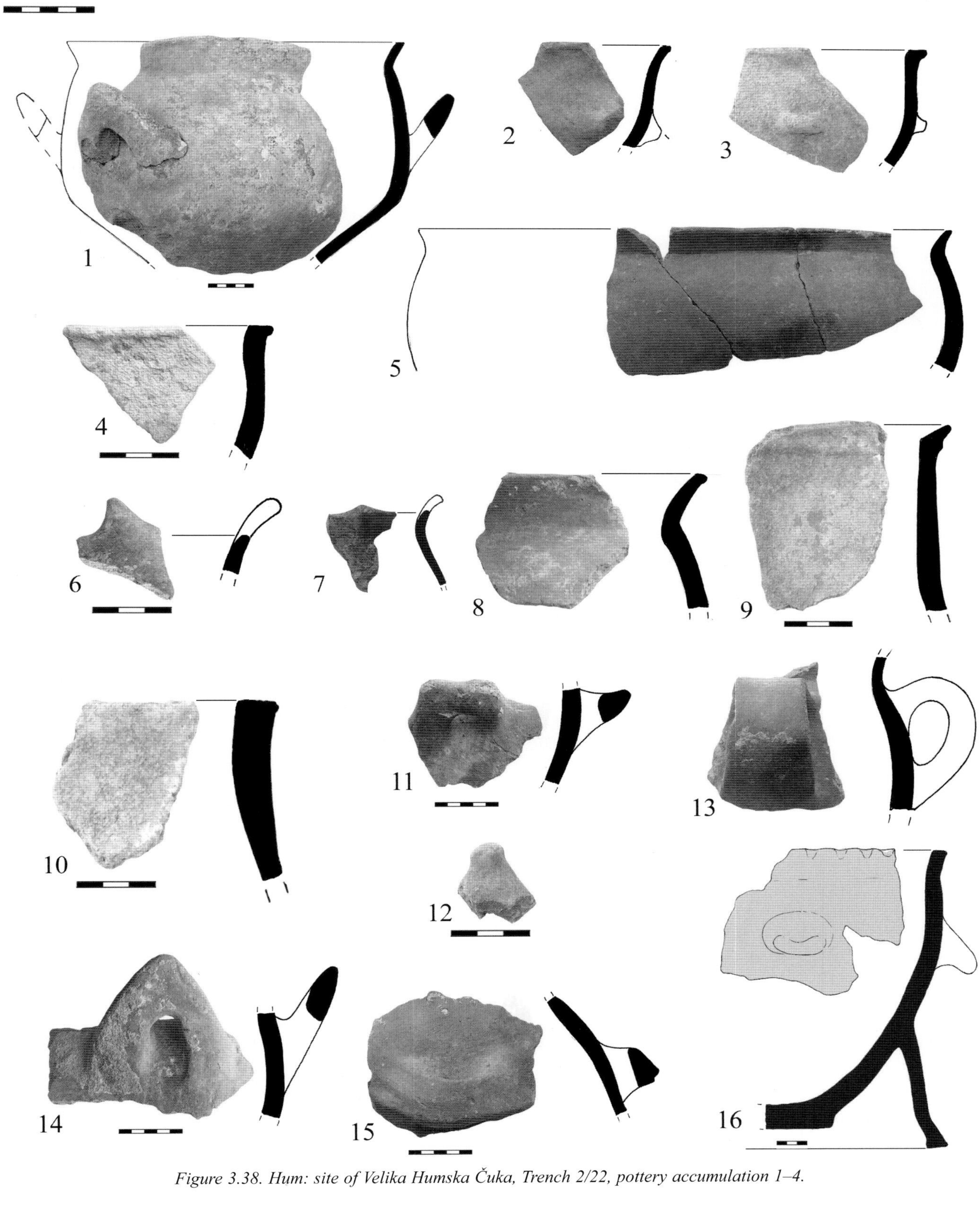

Figure 3.38. Hum: site of Velika Humska Čuka, Trench 2/22, pottery accumulation 1–4.

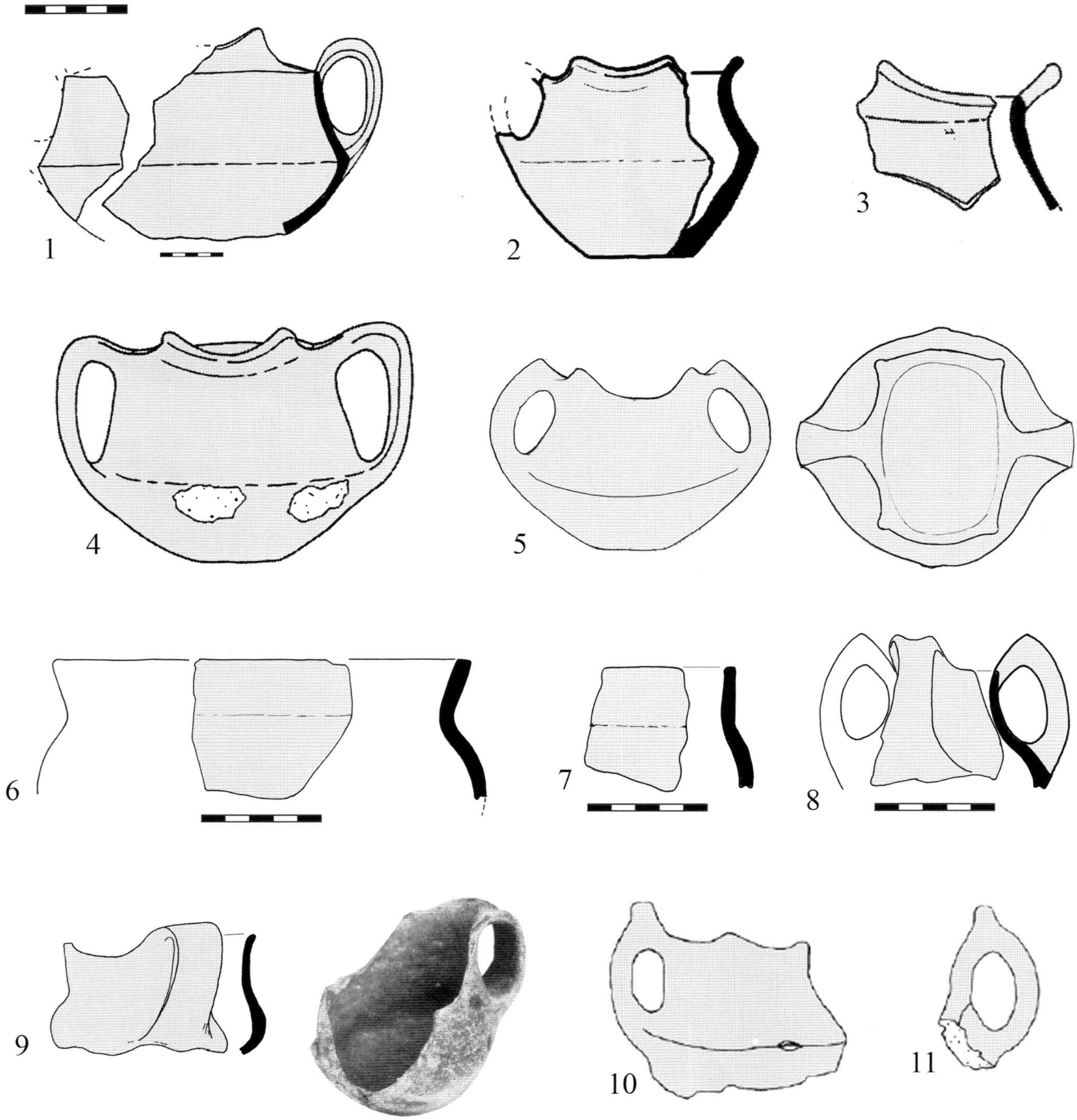

Figure 3.39. 1–4, Novo Selo: site of Bubanj; 5–7, Kaštavar: site of Novo Groblje; 8, Čekmin: site of Sastavci; 9, Čekmin: site of Kućište; 10–11, Niš: site of Medijana.

earlier periods, often extends above the vessel's rim on beakers. These handles are mostly found on beakers, from rim to body, but also appear on bowls (Fig. 3.42/8; Fig. 3.46/3; Fig. 3.43/1–3), cups (Fig. 3.43/4–6), amphorae (Fig. 3.36/7; Fig. 3.38/13; Fig. 3.40/3; Fig. 3.44/3), funerary urns (Fig. 3.46/10, 11), and double vessels (Fig. 3.43/11, 12). On beakers and bowls, these handles often feature a plastic projection at the top or vertical shallow grooves (Fig. 3.45/12; Fig. 3.46/3). Most are strap-shaped, with some concave profiled (pseudo- *ansa lunata*), and less commonly, oval or triangular in cross-section, with circular being sporadic.

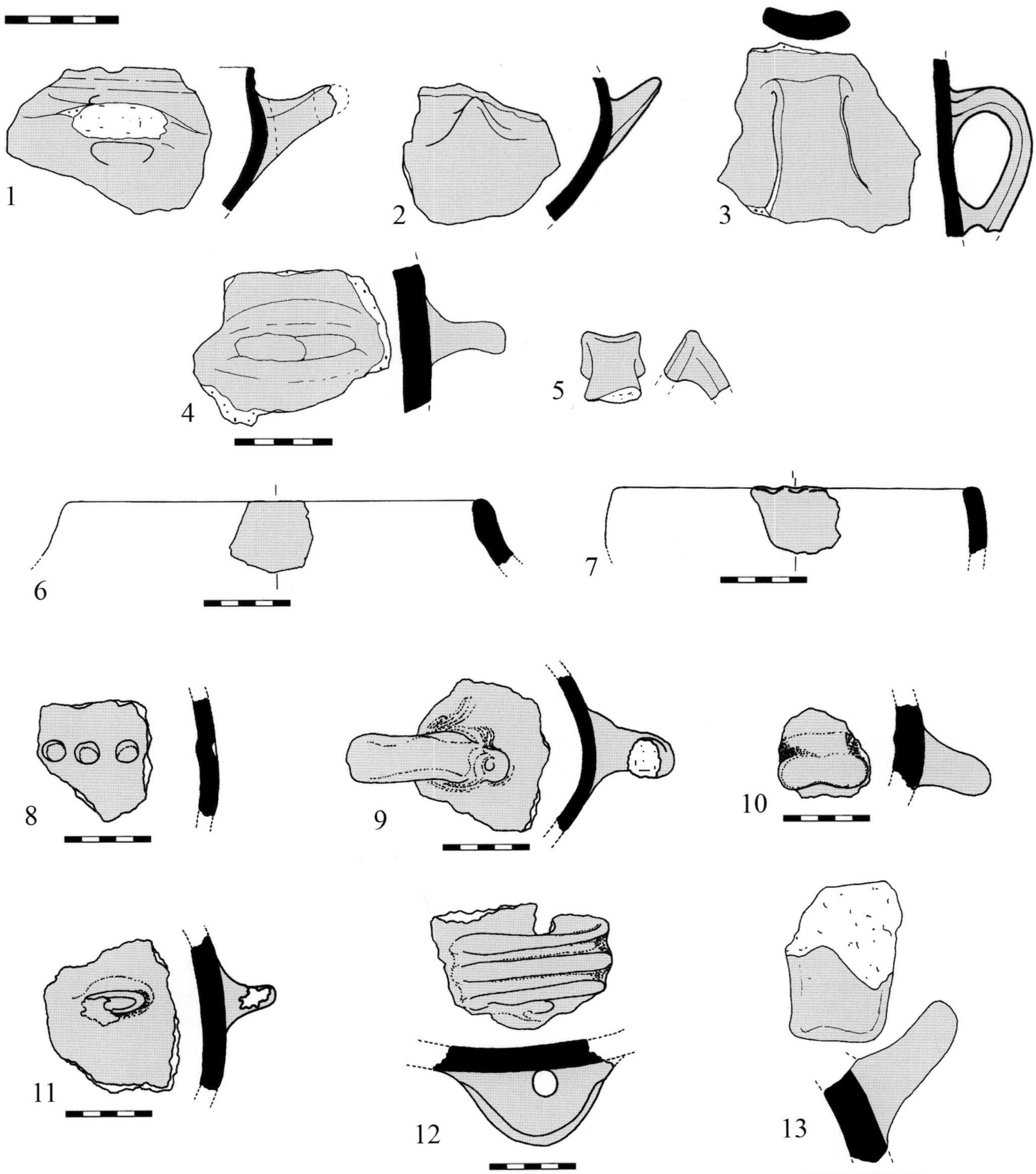

Figure 3.40. 1–5, Semče: site of Pusto semče; 6–13 Gornje Krnjino: site of Česma-provalija.

Arched horizontal handles, primarily on amphorae (Fig. 3.35/7; Fig. 3.37/6, 7; Fig. 3.38/15; Fig. 3.40/9, 12; Fig. 3.41/9) and bowls (Fig. 3.37/9; Fig. 3.41/4; Fig. 3.45/1, 2), are also found and often decorated with deeper grooves on the outer side (Fig. 3.37/6; Fig. 3.38/15; Fig. 3.40/12). These handles are mostly rectangular, ribbon-shaped, or circular in cross-section. One example from Popovica is modelled as a hollow cup (Fig. 3.35/7), characteristic of the Timok Region.

Rectangular, vertically perforated horizontal handles are less common, found mainly on the bodies of bowls (Fig. 3.37/1) and amphorae (Fig. 3.38/11; Fig. 3.44/12), sometimes with plastic projections at the top (Fig. 3.37/1). Non-perforated rectangular horizontal handles (Fig. 3.35/10; Fig. 3.40/4, 10, 13) and one vertical rectangular handle (Fig. 3.45/13) were also recorded.

Triangular, vertically perforated handles, typically angled on the rim or body of bowls, were found at several sites (Fig. 3.35/13; Fig. 3.38/1, 14; Fig. 3.40/1; Fig. 3.41/1, 3, 8). A few triangular non-perforated handles (Fig. 3.40/2) were also documented, one adorned with a biconical plastic projection (Fig. 3.41/8) and another with a rectangular projection (Fig. 3.37/8). These handles are known as 'wishbone' handles in northern Greece and will be further discussed.

Tunnel-shaped handles were mainly found at the Pribovce site in Lopata (Fig. 3.46/4, 9, 10, 12, 13), with plastic expanded ends on all specimens.

Other handle types include tongue-shaped (Fig. 3.35/9; Fig. 3.38/3, 16; Fig. 3.40/11; Fig. 3.42/1; Fig. 3.44/11; Fig. 3.45/8), elbow-shaped (Fig. 3.40/5), and horn-shaped handles (Fig. 3.37/2).

G. ORNAMENTATION

As in other geographical zones of the central Balkans, except the peri–Pannonian zone, the least represented decorative technique is incising combined with punctation, noted only on a beaker from Vitkovac (Fig. 3.46/12), with a simple linear motif observed on pottery from Trnava (Fig. 3.45/6, 9). On one specimen from Popovica, a pair of punctate impressions made with a blunt cylindrical tool was recorded (Fig. 3.35/8).

Conversely, the most common decoration is plastic appliques or projections, which can be located on the vessel's body (Fig. 3.46/1, 2, 10), rim (Fig. 3.35/11; Fig. 3.43/2, 7, 9, 11, 14; Fig. 3.44/1, 2), or at the top of the handle (Fig. 3.35/14, 15; Fig. 3.36/1; Fig. 3.37/1; Fig. 3.38/12; Fig. 3.41/7, 8; Fig. 3.44/13; Fig. 3.43/1–3, 13, 14).

Less frequently represented techniques include impressions made with fingertip-like depressions directly on the vessel's surface (Fig. 3.36/5; Fig. 3.40/8; Fig. 3.44/4, 8, 11; Fig. 3.46/4, 8, 9), or on the upper side of the rim (Fig. 3.35/4; Fig. 3.36/6; Fig. 3.38/16; Fig. 3.44/4, 8; Fig. 3.47/8), plastic ribs (Fig. 3.45/7), and horizontal grooves on arched handles (Fig. 3.37/6; Fig. 3.38/15; Fig. 3.40/12; Fig. 3.45/12; Fig. 3.46/3).

One of the most significant features of the Middle Bronze Age in this zone, as well as in most geographical areas of the central Balkans, is the trapezoidal-shaped vessel opening, mostly on beakers. These beakers can vary in type, but type 1g is most common here, appearing throughout the zone, except in northern Macedonia and Kosovo (Fig. 3.36/1, 2; Fig. 3.37/3; Fig. 3.38/6, 7; Fig. 3.39/1–5, 10; Fig. 3.41/6; Fig. 3.43/13; Fig. 3.46/12).

3.5.3.2 Chance and other finds

LIST OF SITES WITH CHANCE AND OTHER FINDS

184. Sokobanja, Popovica site, hoard of axes of the Patulele type (Mitrović and Filipović, in preparation); 194. Sokobanja, unknown site, axe of the Patulele type (Garašanin *et al.* 1971, cat. no. 245); 195. Štrbovac, Čuka site, axe of the Patulele type (Garašanin *et al.* 1971, cat. no. 246); 196. Staničenje, unknown site, axe of the Kravari type (Garašanin *et al.* 1971, cat. no. 230); 197. Lipovac, Lipovac Fortress, dagger (Filipović and Milojević 2015; Milojević and Trajković-Filipović 2017, 129–132, fig. 66); 198. Vitkovac, unknown site, beaker with trapezoidal rim (Stojić and Jocić 2006, 297, fig. 8); 199. Kaštavar, Novo Groblje site, beaker with trapezoidal rim (Stojić and Jocić 1993); 200. Niš, unknown site, axe of the Kravari type (Garašanin 1954, 48).

On the southeastern periphery of Sokobanja at the hilltop of Popovica above Moravica, opposite Sokograd, seven axes were found accidentally a few years ago (Fig. 3.49/3–9). According to the discoverers, the hoard was found slightly below the settlement at Popovica, near the river and a thermal spring.[19] These were axes of the Patulele type, six made of bronze and one of copper (Mitrović and Filipović in preparation). The tin content in the bronze axes varied from 1.3% to 11.6%, with traces of use observed through microscopic analysis. Based on analogies, the axes were dated to the Middle Bronze Age, a hypothesis somewhat supported by excavations at the site confirming a cultural layer from this period (Milojević and Kapuran 2023). Interestingly, another Patulele-type copper axe was found in the Sokobanja area several decades earlier, though the exact location is unknown (Fig. 3.49/2) (Garašanin *et al.* 1971, cat. no. 245). This axe contained about 0.64% arsenic (Antonović 2014, table 2), and three axes from Popovica also showed arsenic levels above 0.5%. It seems that most of these axes from Sokobanja contained some arsenic in their copper composition, not enough to classify them as arsenic copper, but enough to indicate a common copper ore source for these axes. A Patulele-type axe was also recorded several decades ago at the site of Čuka in Štrbovac (Fig. 3.49/1) (Garašanin *et al.* 1971, cat. no. 246), near hilltop settlements in Semče and Gornje Krnjino. Judging by the site name, this might also be a hilltop or a hoard site.

Apart from Patulele-type axes, Chance finds include one Kravari-type axe each from Staničenje near Pirot in the Nišava Valley and the area near Niš (Fig. 3.49/10, 11). D. Garašanin mentions another axe with parallel blades from Jelašnica near Niš, specifically from the Radosinj site (Garašanin 1954, 48; Garašanin *et al.* 1971, cat. no. 230). Analysis of the Staničenje axe showed that it was made of tin bronze, with a tin isotope imprint of 124Sn 0.60/120Sn 0.32, matching the so-called Serbian group of tin sources (Mason *et al.* 2016), while the copper isotope value (δ^{65}Cu) was similar to findings in Stig, Timok Region, and Srem

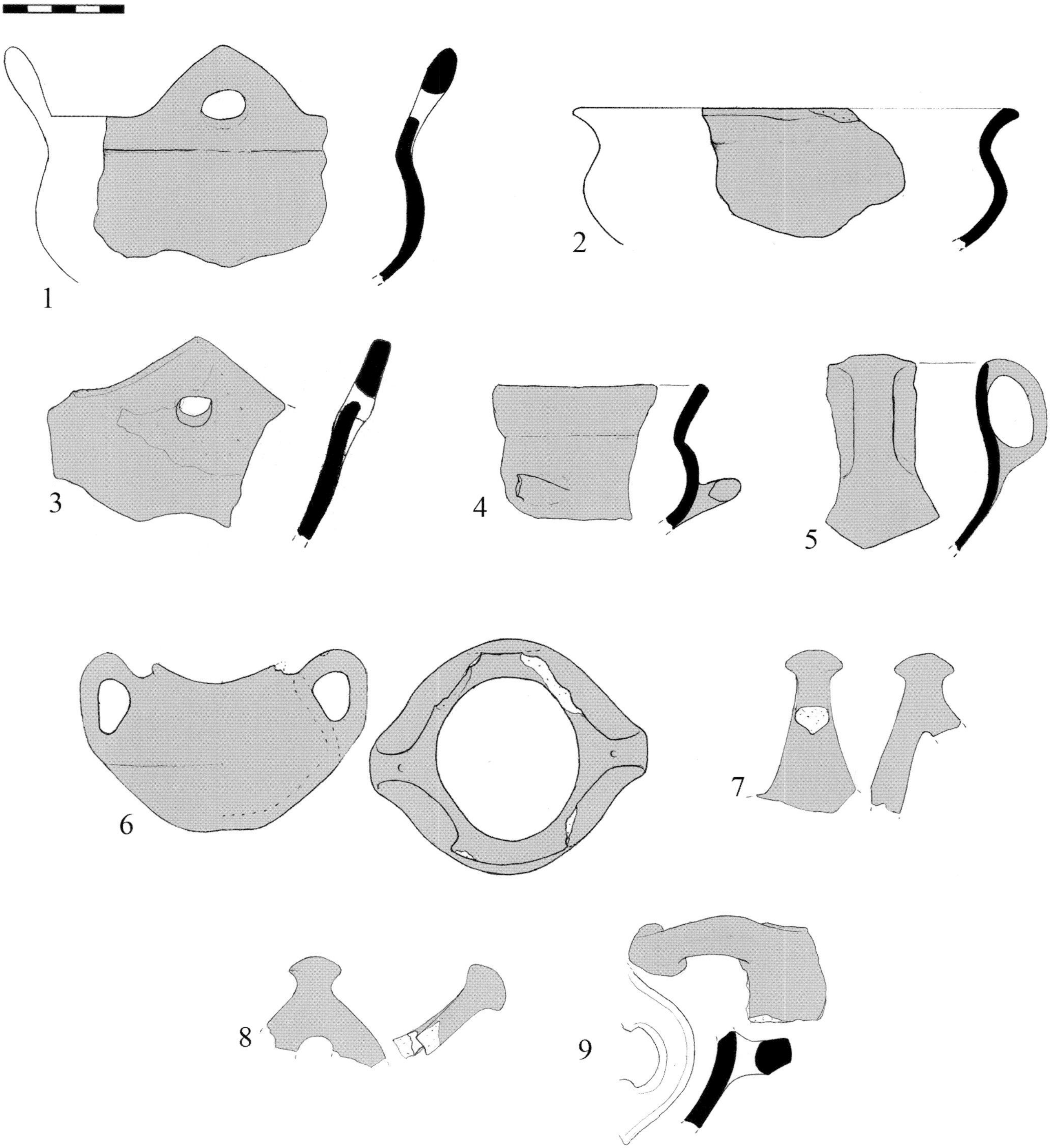

Figure 3.41. Štulac: site of Svinjarička Čuka, Middle Bronze Age structure in trench N1.

(Powell *et al.* 2017). No further details are available for the axe from the Niš area. This type of axe was found in Kravari near Bitola, along with a Patulele-type axe and double-handled beakers typical of the late Early and Middle Bronze Ages (Bulatović and Stankovski 2012, 119; Antonović 2014; Mitrović and Filipović in preparation).

In addition to the accidental axe finds, one axe was found during an excavation in an archaeological context. This was a flat axe of the *Randleistenbeile* type (Fig. 3.49/12), discovered in a damaged complex composed of a stone structure made of medium-sized stones, two complete beakers, and several larger ceramic fragments, mostly pots and amphorae

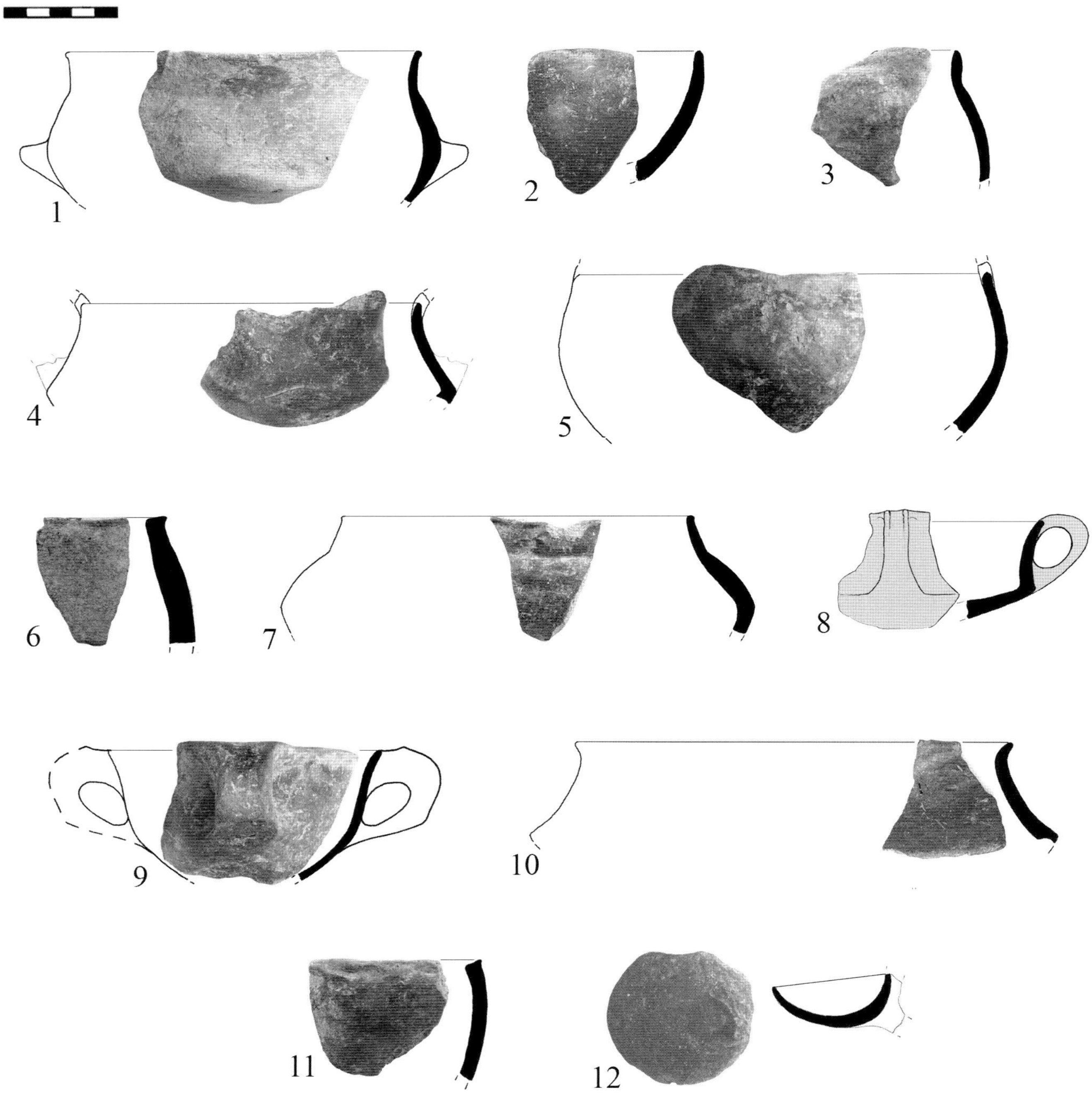

Figure 3.42. Štulac: site of Svinjarička Čuka, SU 1055.

(Bulatović and Stankovski 2012, 69). Based on analogies, the axe was dated to the Middle Bronze Age (Br A2–B2, according to Central European chronology), consistent with the ceramic stylistic and typological features (Bulatović and Milanović 2009, 177). The axe was made of bronze with a tin content between 5% and 7% (Bulatović and Milanović 2009), with a tin isotope imprint of 124Sn 0.74/120Sn 0.37, also matching the Serbian group of tin sources (Mason *et al.* 2016). The copper isotope value (δ^{65}Cu) matched contemporary findings from the Timok Region and Banat (Powell *et al.* 2017).

In Lipovac, where a medieval monastery and fortress are located, a bronze double-edged dagger with a central rib and an expanded, heart-shaped upper part, of rhomboid cross-section, was found accidentally (Fig. 3.49/13). Authors have dated this dagger to the end of the Early and middle Minoan periods (Filipović and, Milojević 2015). The dagger contained about 10% tin (Filipović and Milojević 2015, Ref. 58).

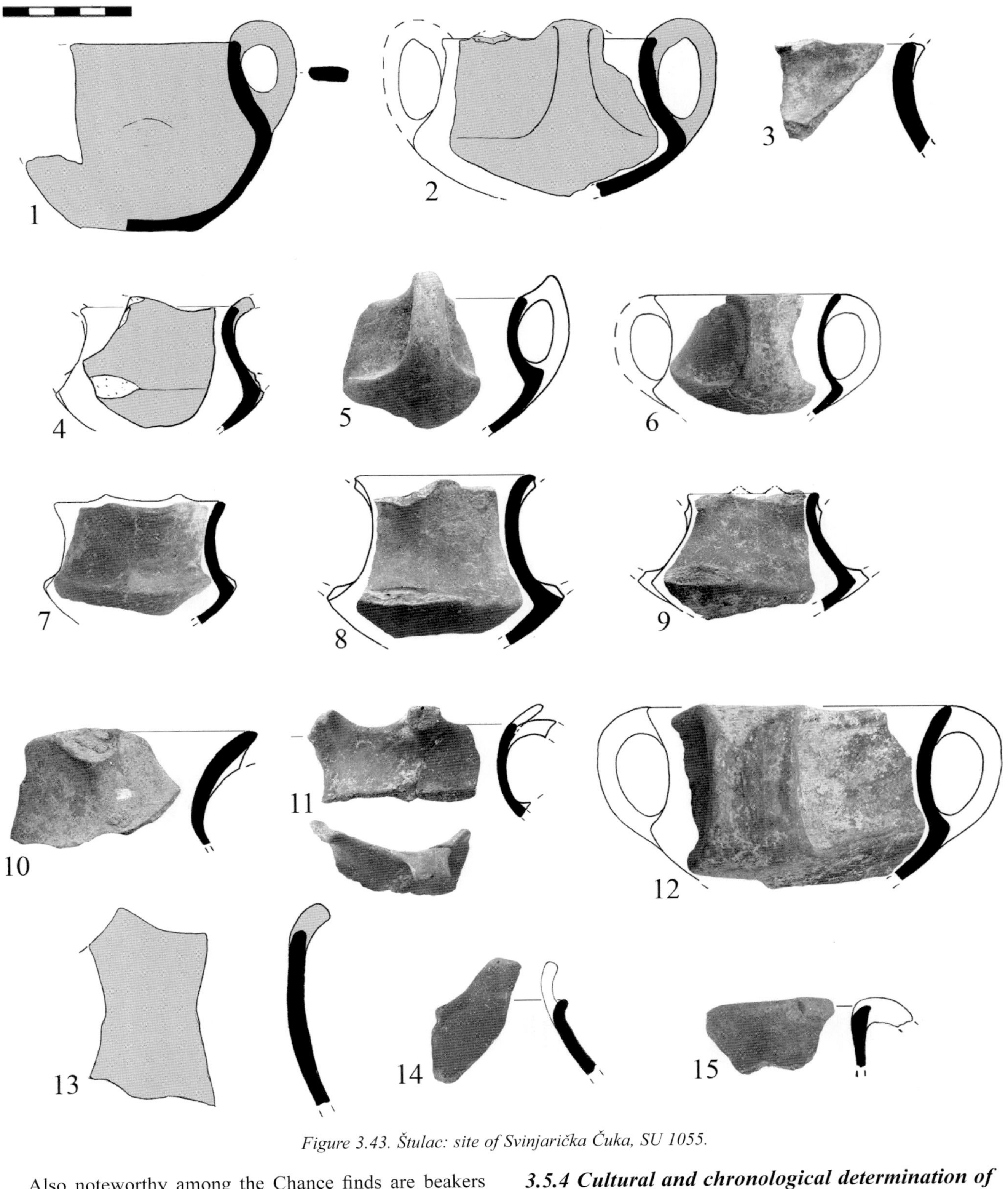

Figure 3.43. Štulac: site of Svinjarička Čuka, SU 1055.

Also noteworthy among the Chance finds are beakers with trapezoidal rims from Vitkovac near Aleksinac and Kaštavar near Leskovac (Fig. 3.39/5; Fig. 3.46/12) (Stojić and Jocić 1993; 2006), which have been previously discussed in the pottery section.

3.5.4 Cultural and chronological determination of southern Serbia with Middle Pčinja and Kumanovo and Skopje plains cultures

Several absolute dates from the Middle Bronze Age have been obtained from this geographical zone but they come

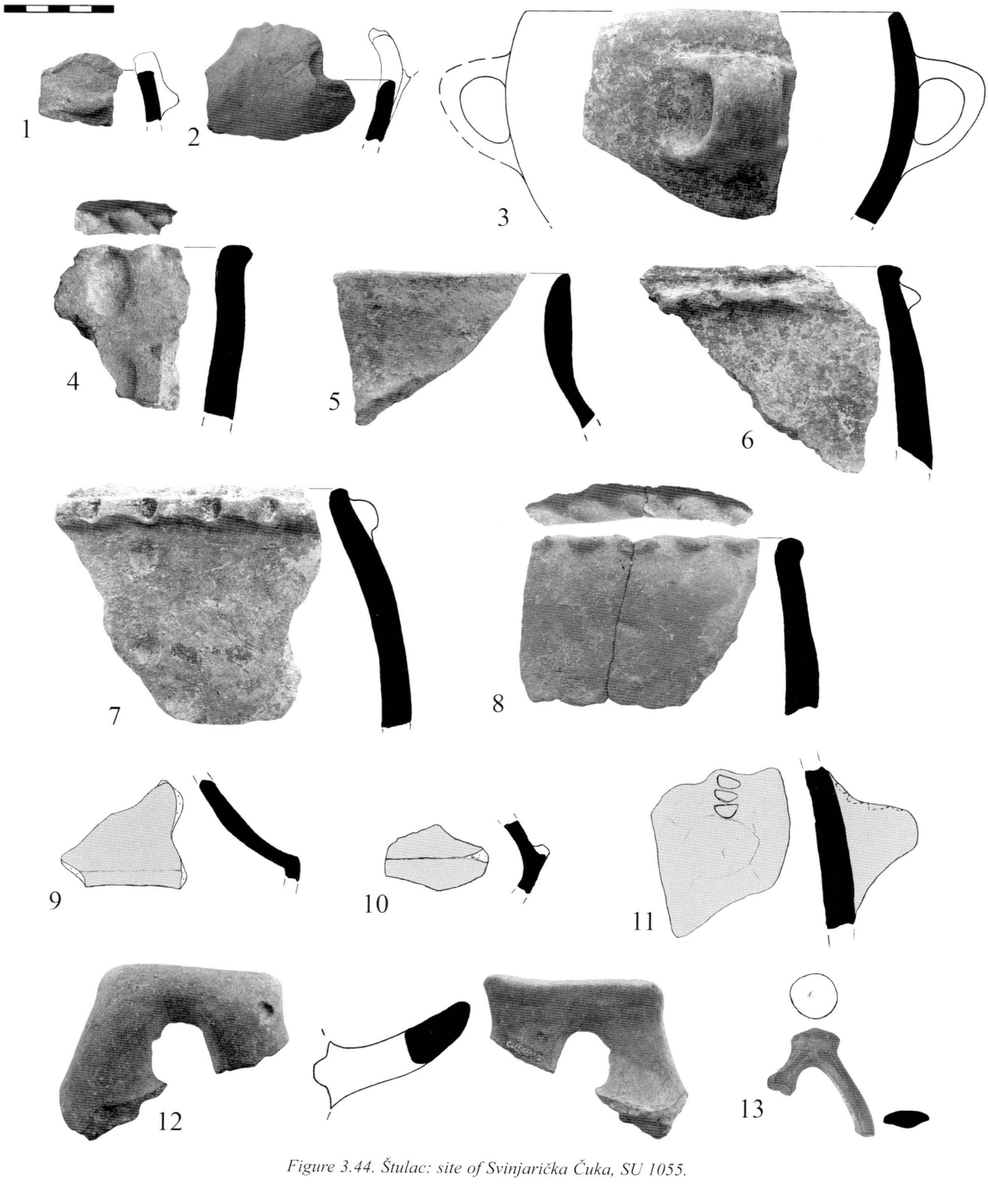

Figure 3.44. Štulac: site of Svinjarička Čuka, SU 1055.

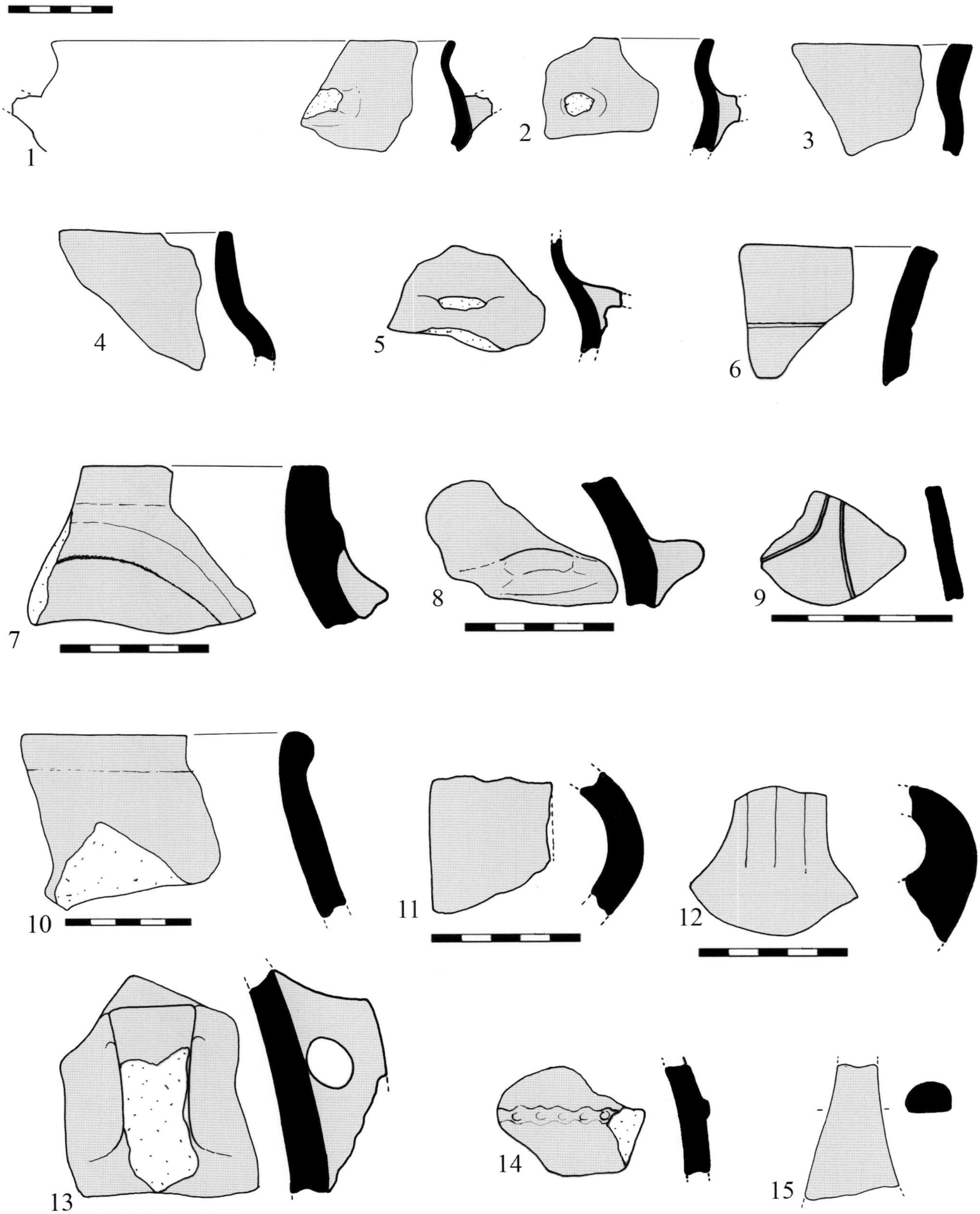

Figure 3.45. Trnava: site of Trnavska Reka.

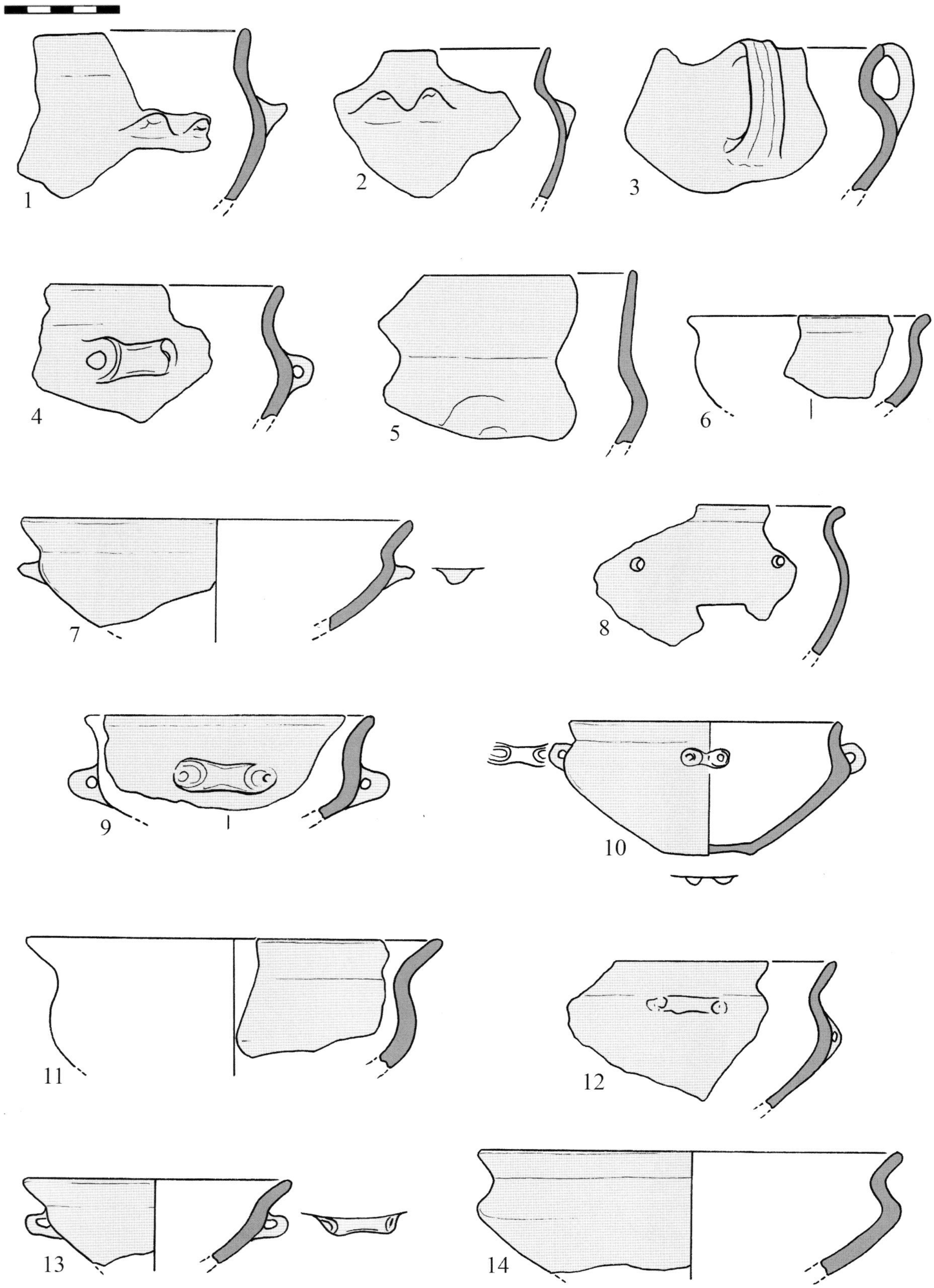

Figure 3.46. Lopate: site of Pribovce.

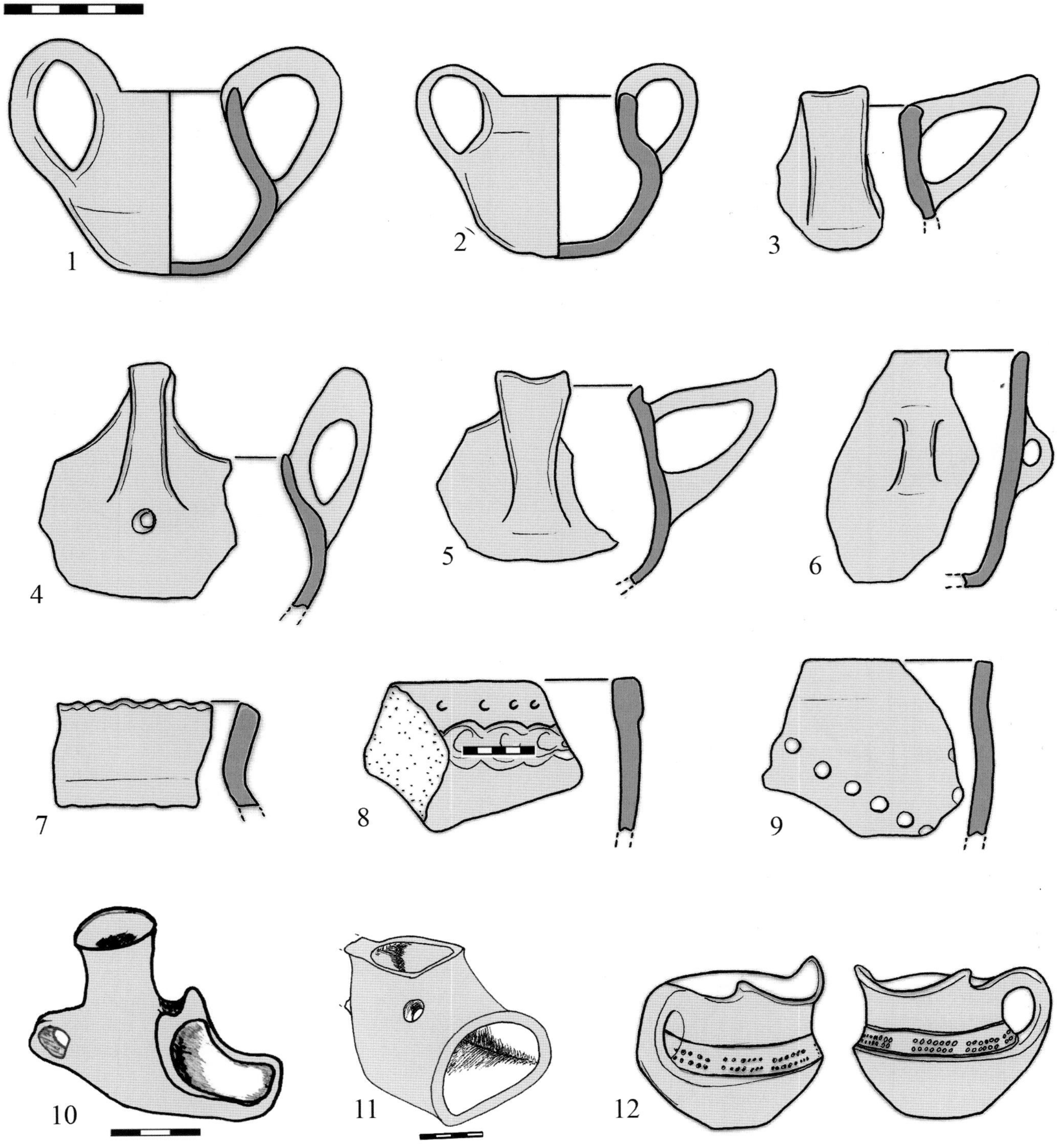

Figure 3.47. 1–10, Lopate: site of Pribovce; 11, Kokino Selo: site of Tatikev Kamen; 12, Vitkovac, unknown site.

from only two sites: Svinjarička Čuka near Lebane and Velika Humska Čuka near Niš. Fortunately, these dates correspond to different phases of the Middle Bronze Age, which greatly aided in determining the chronology of this period in the southern central Balkans.

The dates from Svinjarička Čuka, are from a large pit described above. Two almost identical dates place it in the period from the mid-19th to the early 17th century, with the highest statistical probability dating to the 18th century cal BC (Table 1). The second date is from the same site, from a

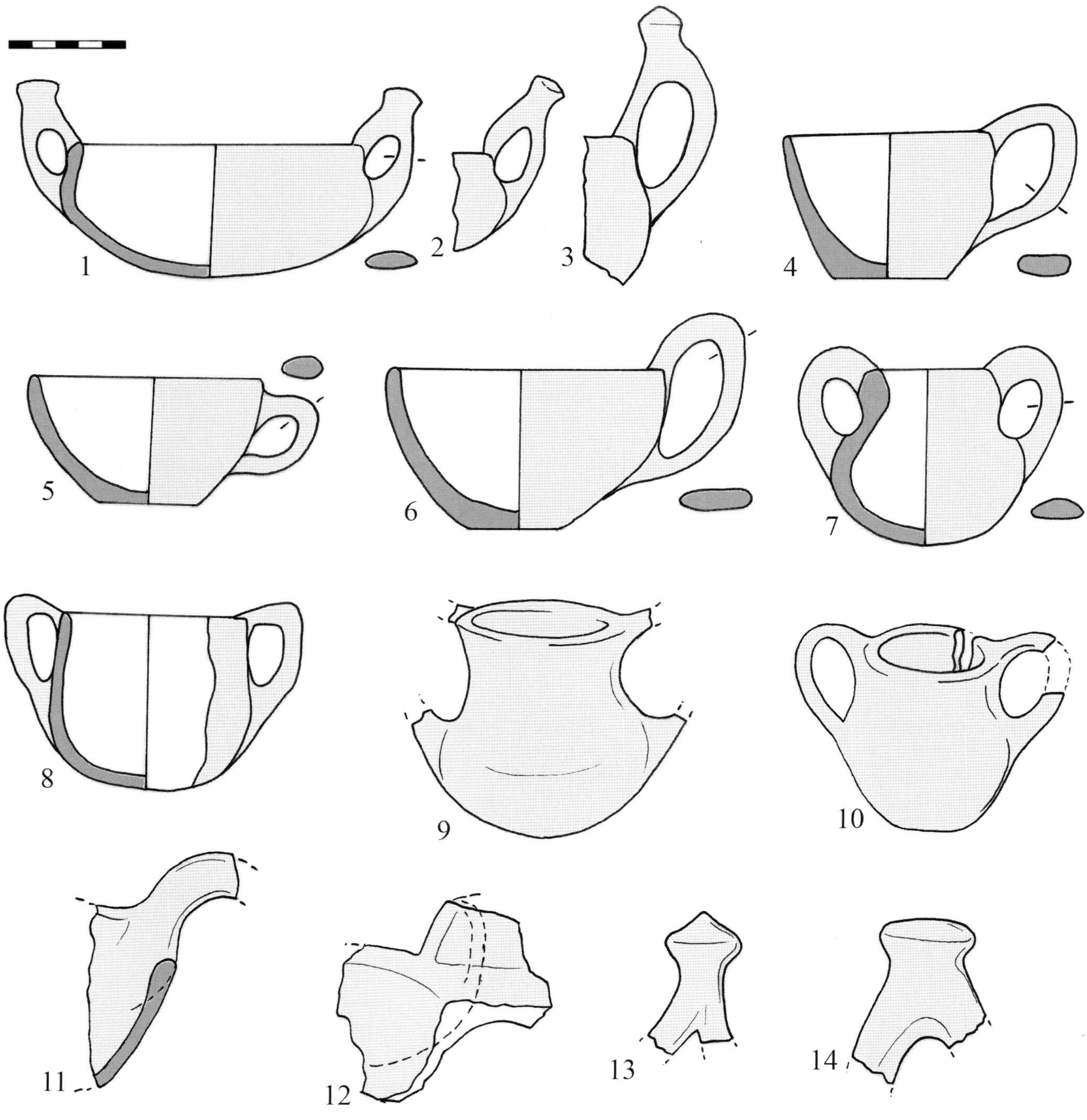

Figure 3.48. 1–8, Karagač: site of Valač, cultural layer II; 9–14, Donja Brnjica, cultural layer I.

damaged structure also described in the previous section on habitation. This date is somewhat later, covering the period from the mid-18th to the mid-17th century, with the highest statistical probability dating to the 18th century. Comparing the absolute values of these dates in BP and their deviations, it could be said with reasonable confidence that the older dates from this site indicate the first half, and the second date the latter half of the 18th century.

The next and last date comes from Velika Humska Čuka, from a larger group of pottery at the base of the Middle Bronze Age layer. In addition to the artifacts, animal bones were found, one of which was dated to the period from the mid-16th to the early 15th century, which quite precisely places this structure in the second half of the 16th century.

The ceramic finds from these structures at two different sites, approximately 50 km apart, are very similar and certainly belong to the previously mentioned Bubanj-Hum IV–Ljuljaci group. The main characteristic of pottery in this zone, which applies generally to this group, is the beakers (and sometimes other vessels) with trapezoidal shaped openings. Additionally, type 1c beakers or their later variant 1e (with handles extending above the rim), type 1g and 5a beakers, and bowls of types 1b and 3a are common. Among the decorations, plastic extensions on the rims of the bowls, which can take various forms, are the most frequent, followed by plastic attachments (button-shaped, conical, biconic, etc.) on the tops of handles, decorations in the form of rows of pit impressions directly on the vessel wall (without bands), horizontally placed arched handles, as well as diagonally set triangular and rectangular handles. Incised decorations combined with punctation are rare but interestingly appear in at least a few specimens across the geographical zones of this cultural group, mostly on beakers.

During the previous period, the Early Bronze Age, a unified cultural manifestation known as Bubanj-Hum III–Pelince–Pernik existed throughout the southern Morava Basin, including western Bulgaria. According to absolute dates, it lasted through the third quarter of the 3rd millennium and was succeeded by the Bubanj-Hum III group, named so due to the reduction in the territory previously covered by the Bubanj-Hum III–Pelince–Pernik group, which persisted in this area in the last quarter of the 3rd millennium and the beginning of the 2nd millennium.

Absolute dates from the Early Bronze Age cemetery in Ranutovac in the South Morava valley indicate that by the end of the Early Bronze Age (end of the 3rd and beginning of the 2nd millennium cal BC), cultural elements of the Armenochori group dominated this region. This contrasts with the earlier period and shows that the interconnections between the population of this part of the South Morava valley and the Vardar valley were very intense during this time. The elements are so dominant that, when interpreting the cultural-chronological picture, possible migrations of this population from the south to the north, i.e., from the Vardar valley to the South Morava valley, should not be ruled out.

Although these contacts were intense, they do not appear to have been long-lasting or were geographically limited only to this part of the South Morava valley, as the stylistic-typological features of Middle Bronze Age ceramics in other parts of this zone exhibit almost no elements of the Armenochori group. Instead, they evolved from the Bubanj-Hum III–Pelince–Pernik manifestation that preceded it. This is most evident in the gradual evolution of plastic triangular extensions on vessel rims from the Early Bronze Age into vessels (mainly beakers) with trapezoidal shaped rims characteristic of the Middle Bronze Age (Bulatović 2021, 135, 136).

For the Middle Bronze Age, which, according to the absolute dates for the Early Bronze Age and the earliest dates for the Middle Bronze Age, could have begun in this zone at the end of the 20th and the beginning of the 19th century BC, the stylistic-typological elements of the Bubanj-Hum IV–Ljuljaci group, which have already been mentioned and defined, are characteristic. It is interesting that these elements are present in this zone in dated units from the beginning of the Middle Bronze Age, but also in units from the end of the Middle Bronze Age (second half of the 16th century cal BC), such as the 'group of pottery 1–4' at Velika Humska Čuka. Thus, at Svinjarička Čuka, in a pit dated to approximately the first half of the 18th century and the remains of a structure dated to approximately the second half of the 18th century cal BC, as well as in the mentioned unit at Velika Humska Čuka, dated to the second half of the 16th century, beakers with trapezoidal shaped openings, arched handles with plastic attachments at the top, diagonally placed triangular or rectangular perforated handles, horizontally placed arched handles, etc., are present (Figs 3.38, 3.41–44).

There are, however, certain differences in the ceramic material from dated units at Velika Humska Čuka and Svinjarička čuka. Noticeable, for example, are the triangular vertically perforated handles, which are recorded at both sites, but at Velika Humska Čuka, they are on the vessel body, while at Svinjarička Čuka, they are on the rim of bowls, and at Svinjarička Čuka, they date almost two centuries earlier. These handles are known from northern Greece, where arched handles placed diagonally on the rim of bowls first appear in the Early Bronze Age, at sites such as Kastanas (from layer 24), Kritsana (from layer IV), Axiochori (pit S30, 31, and 33/34), which are approximately contemporary and date to the last century of the 3rd millennium BC (Aslanis 1985, 221–319; Hansel and Aslanis 2010, Abb. 22). These handles are also recorded in Troy during the Early Bronze Age, from settlement II (approximately mid-3rd millennium) (Blegen *et al.* 1950, pl. 308, 412/16-21-23; Blum 2016, fig. 9), as well as in Hagios Mamas, Malionpirgo, Servia, and Axiochori, where wishbone handles, or handles shaped like a wishbone, often with a plastic rectangular extension at the top, also appear in the Early Bronze Age (Heurtley 1939, cat. no. 178, 209, 218, 220, 310, 311, figs 45, 52(ii), 56).

Looking at the form of the wishbone handle, it is observed to be very similar to triangular handles with the only difference being the rectangular attachment at the top, which gives it a completely different appearance. These handles evolved from diagonally placed arched handles at the end of the Early Bronze Age (Aslanis 1985, pl. 89/7, 15, pl. 90/4, pl. 104/2) and in the Middle Bronze Age wishbone handles are a common ceramic element at sites in northern Greece (Heurtley 1939, cat. no. 374, 381, 385–388, figs 71,

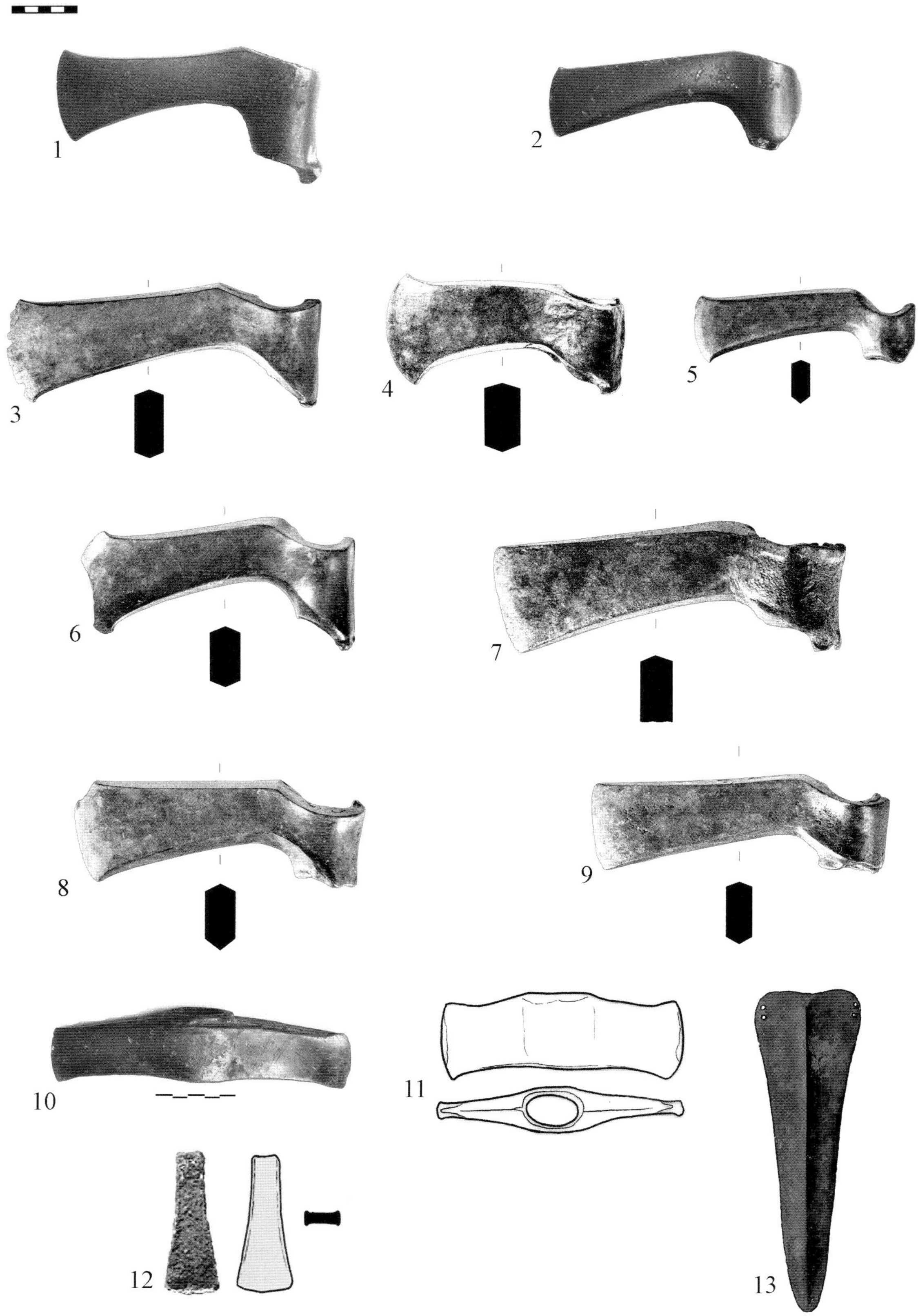

Figure 3.49. 1, Štrbovac: site of Čuka; 2, Sokobanja, unknown site; 3–9, Sokobanja: site of Popovica (hoard); 10, Staničenje, unknown site; 11, Niš area, unknown site; 12, Hum: site of Velika Humska Čuka, structure 8/09; 13, Lipovac: site of Lipovički Grad.

76), and remain in use in the Late Bronze Age, although, alongside them, triangular vertically perforated handles are still occasionally used (Heurtley 1939, cat. no. 404, 406, 452, 456, figs 71, 76).

Interesting examples of these handles are found in units S31, S30, and S28 from Axiochori and from horizon V at Kritsana. Examples from Kritsana and unit S31 from Axiochori (Aslanis 1985, pl. 89/15, 104/2), which are approximately contemporary and date to the 22nd/21st century cal BC (Aslanis 1985, abb. 130; Hansel and Aslanis 2010, abb. 22), are intermediate types between arched and triangular (wishbone) handles, while the example from S30 at Axiochori (21st century cal BC) already represents a true wishbone handle, even with a small plastic button-like attachment at the top (Aslanis 1985, pl. 89/7). The example from Axiochori from unit S28 (19th century cal BC) is already a fully formed wishbone handle with a characteristic rectangular attachment at the top (Aslanis 1985, pl. 90/4).

The form that represents a transitional phase between arched and triangular vertically perforated handles was also recorded in layer 22a at Kastanas (Aslanis 1985, pl. 74/18, 21), dated to the 19th century cal BC. Although wishbone handles with rectangular (sometimes trapezoidal) extensions at the top (Hansel and Aslanis 2010, Abb. 22) appear in this area as early as the 19th century, this type of handle only appeared at Kastanas in layer 18 (Hochstetter 1984, pl. 8/3), which, according to Hansel and Aslanis, can be dated to the 16th century (Hansel and Aslanis 2010, Abb. 22).

In any case, the very concept of forming diagonally placed horizontal handles on the rim or body of a vessel was not recorded in the central Balkans until the Middle Bronze Age. There were sporadic finds of horizontally placed arched handles in this zone during the Early Bronze Age, on the body of the vessel (Davidovac, Skopje: Fig. 2.31/11, Fig. 2.35/5), while such handles (arched or triangular) on the rim of bowls only appeared in the Middle Bronze Age, and only at one site in this zone (Fig. 3.41/1, 3).[20] Interestingly, a bowl of identical form with the so-called wishbone handle, which is known to appear at the end of the Early and last through the Late Bronze Age but is most prevalent during the Middle Bronze Age of northern Greece, was recorded at Velika Humska Čuka (Fig. 3.37/8) (Heurtley 1939, cat. no. 374, 381, 385–388, 406, 450, 452, figs 52(ii), 56, 71, 76). Unfortunately, it was found in a disturbed layer, outside a clear archaeological context. Another similar bowl of type 3c, almost identical to the example on Figure 3.37/1 but lacking the plastic extensions at the top of the handle, was recorded in a disturbed layer at Velika Humska Čuka (Fig. 3.37/8). Given that this concept of placing horizontal arched or triangular handles diagonally on the vessel wall evidently originates from the south, specifically northern Greece, it is quite certain that there were contacts between the population of South Morava Basin and the population of Vardar Macedonia, and possibly even Chalkidiki. Regarding the direction or natural communication routes of these contacts, based on the distribution of these finds, two possible routes can be assumed – the Struma Valley, followed by the Nišava Valley to the north and Strumica Valley to the west; and the Vardar Valley, with the White Drim Valley as another potential route (Pl. 19). Namely, wishbone handles have been recorded at Middle Bronze Age sites in Pelagonia (Gagić 1984, fig. 11; Simoska 1984, fig. 9; Sanev 1999, pl. iv/4), suggesting that this could also have been one of the communication routes through which contacts were made. Further north, handles have been recorded around Strumica (Rujak 2020, table 16), Štip (Nacev 2009, fig. 66, 70), in Skopje Plain, Kumanovo Plain (Mitrevski 2016, T. XCIII/3, XCIX/1), and the Moravica Valley (Fig. 3.45/1, 2). These handles have also been recorded on ceramics from Horizon II (end of the Middle Bronze Age) at Koprivlen in the Struma Valley (Alexandrov 2002, fig. 11/9; fig. 22/4, 5), and then at the site of Mađilka in the Nišava Valley (beginning of the Late Bronze Age) (Jevtić 1990; Lazić 1996; Kapuran *et al.* 2022), indicating continued contact during this period. However, it seems, at least based on the distribution of the finds and the established chronology, that the oldest route of communication through which these contacts occurred was: Pelagonia – Vardar Valley – Kumanovo Plain – Moravica – South Morava.

Vessels of very similar form to the example from Velika Humska Čuka (Fig. 3.38/1), with a triangular vertically perforated handle on the body, have been recorded at the cremation necropolis at Mađilka in Ponišavlje (Jevtić 1990; Lazić 1996, T. XXX/7–9), which dates to the period between the 15th/14th and 13th/12th centuries cal BC.[21] Additionally, although these handles appear in the Middle Bronze Age in this geographical zone, they are very common on the bowls of the Brnjica group in the Late Bronze Age (Lazić 1996, T. XVII/8, T. XIX/7, 8; T. XXVI/6. Bulatović and Stankovski 2012, T. XXX/105, 106; T. LXVI/79).

Although the ceramic group 1–4 at Velika Humska Čuka, with triangular handles and beakers with fan-shaped rims (Fig. 3.38), is dated to the second half of the 16th century cal BC, based on other finds from this site, particularly from object 8/09 (beakers with fan-shaped rims, an axe of the *Randleistenbeile* type: Fig. 3.36), as well as from the group of pottery from trench 2/21 and finds from the layer (Fig. 3.37), which include bowls of type 3c with diagonally placed arched or triangular handles (in the form of a wishbone), it can be assumed that life at this settlement also occurred during the earlier phases of the Middle Bronze Age. Particularly indicative are the stylistic-typological characteristics of a type 3c bowl with a wishbone handle with a rectangular extension on the rim (Fig. 3.37/8), which is almost identical to the forms of bowls and handles from Axiochori (Aslanis 1985, pl. 89/11, 14, 90/4), dated to the period between the 21st and 19th centuries, or handles from Kilindir, Molinopirgos, and other Middle Bronze Age sites in northern Greece (Heurtley 1939, fig. 71, cat. no. 374, fig. 76/e).

In any case, triangular handles in this area are associated with the end of the Middle and Late Bronze Age, but according to the findings from the object at Svinjarička Čuka (Fig. 3.41/1, 3), they may have been present in this area somewhat earlier. Other characteristic elements include beakers with trapezoidal openings, bowls of types 1c, 2a, and 3a, as well as beakers of types 1c, 1g, 5a, ornaments in the form of a series of punctate impressions directly on the vessel surface, arched vertical handles with a plastic biconical extension at the top, etc. Particularly interesting is a wishbone-shaped handle with a wide rectangular modelled end (Fig. 3.44/12) from a dated pit at Svinjarička Čuka, which dates such handles in the central Balkans to at least the first half of the 18th century cal BC (Table 1). Identical handles have been recorded at the Middle Bronze Age site of Molinopirgos on Chalkidiki (Heurtley 1939, cat. no. 386–388).

From the above, it can be concluded that the bearers of the Bubanj-Hum IV–Ljuljaci group inherited the stylistic-typological elements of pottery from their predecessors, the bearers of the Bubanj-Hum III–Pelince–Pernik group, or the Bubanj-Hum III group, and that they inhabited the South Morava Basin as early as the 18th century cal BC, and probably earlier, judging by the absolute dates of this group from the Timok Region and the Great Morava Basin. It is also certain that they maintained contacts with their neighbours in the Vardar Region and probably the Struma valley, possibly even with Pelagonia and Chalkidiki, resulting in new ceramic elements in this group unique to the sites of this group within this geographical zone. These contacts are also confirmed by axes of the Kravari and Patulele types, found distributed at sites in Pelagonia as well as in northern Greece (Gori 2015, fig. 73). Based on the distribution of Patulele axes in the central Balkans, contacts between this population and the population in the Timok Region can be assumed, as well as with the population in the Morava Region and the Danube Basin on the territory of the Vatin group, as suggested by the flat axe of the *Randleistenbeile* type.

It is notable that at some sites, such as Popovica in Sokobanja, Semče, Gornje Krnjino, sites in Kosovo, and northern Macedonia, basic stylistic-typological characteristics of the Bubanj Hum IV–Ljuljaci group, such as beakers with trapezoidal openings, are missing but have been included in this group based on other elements and analogies with finds from this group at other sites. Exceptions are the sites in the far south of this zone, in the Moravica valley (Trnava River) and northern Macedonia (Lopate, Kokino), whose ceramic characteristics correspond to the Armenochori (Karamani) group of the Vardar Region and, judging by the analogies with dated units in Ranutovac, date from the end of the Early and beginning of the Middle Bronze Age (Bulatović and Stankovski 2012; Bulatović 2020).

Interesting finds come from Kosovo, specifically from the sites of Karagač and Donja Brnjica. Finds from Karagač (Fig. 3.48/1–8), according to D. Srejović, who relied on the thesis of M. Garašanin, were placed in the period between the Bubanj-Hum III and the so-called Slatina group (Srejović 2002, 154). Although the Slatina group, like the Bubanj-Hum III group, was determined to belong to the Early Bronze Age, this interpretation seems accurate as it was later established that the Slatina group actually referred to settlement ceramics of the Brnjica group of the Late Bronze Age, which until then had been known mainly from necropolis ceramics (Bulatović 2000, 39, 40). In the case of Karagač, when this pottery was classified as between the Bubanj-Hum III and Slatina (actually Brnjica) groups, it was assigned to the Middle Bronze Age, likely in the later phase, as indicated by ceramic analogies from other sites in this zone. The same can be said for the finds from layer I in Donja Brnjica (Fig. 3.48/9–14).

At Velika Humska Čuka, a large number of finds with stylistic-typological characteristics of the Verbicioara group were recorded in the Late Bronze Age layer, which, unfortunately, was disturbed and without enclosed units. Regarding the period when these contacts between the population of the South Morava valley and the bearers of the Verbicioara group were established, an absolute date from the ceramic group 1–4, dated to the second half of the 16th century cal BC, can serve as a *terminus post quem*. No pottery with Verbicioara group characteristics were found in this unit, so it can be assumed that these contacts likely occurred shortly after this date. In any case, these elements played an important role in the genesis of the Brnjica group of the Late Bronze Age, as evidenced by the Svinjarička Čuka site, where Verbicioara ceramic stylistic-typological elements were recorded from the end of the 15th or the beginning of the 14th century cal BC (Horejs *et al.* 2022; Bulatović *et al.* 2023, 41).

Thus, in this zone, the bearers of the Bubanj-Hum IV–Ljuljaci group, enriched in its late phase with Verbicioara elements, created the so-called Brnjica cultural group during the 15th century cal BC, which characterised the Late Bronze Age in the regions of Kosovo, the Raška area, the South Morava Basin, Nišava Valley, and northern Macedonia.

3.6 Discussion on the Middle Bronze Age in the central Balkans

The diversity of the terrain and its orographic characteristics in the central Balkans, along with social factors, had a significant impact on the emergence and development of cultures during the Middle Bronze Age. The following discussion addresses all aspects of the origin and development of the cultural groups of the Middle Bronze Age as well as their decline, to better understand their cultural and chronological relationship with the communities of the preceding and subsequent periods, as well as their interactions with neighbouring communities.

3.6.1 Sites topography, settlements, and dwelling structures

Unlike the Early Bronze Age, when a single hilltop settlement was recorded in the peri-Pannonian zone, no such settlements were noted during the Middle Bronze Age in this region. The highest percentage of hilltop settlements compared to lowland ones was observed in the second and third zones (Great Morava Valley with Šumadija and western Serbia), where four and one hilltop settlement were recorded respectively. However, the highest number of hilltop settlements, six in total, was recorded in the Timok Region, although the percentage of lowland settlements there was much higher than that of hilltops. In West Morava Valley only two settlements were recorded, unlike the Early Bronze Age which saw only one but a large number of necropolises. In South Morava Basin and Skopsko Polje, four hilltop settlements were identified, two of which were already inhabited during the Early Bronze Age (Velika Humska Čuka and Kale) while, in other geographical zones of the central Balkans, hilltop settlements were not occupied in the preceding period. The total number of settlements in the Middle Bronze Age amounts to 62, with slightly over 70% being lowland settlements and just under 30% being hilltop type settlements. When comparing the ratio of hilltop to lowland settlements in this period with that of the Early Bronze Age, it can be concluded that the percentage ratio is similar, with a slightly lower percentage of hilltop settlements (Pl. 20).

Hilltop settlements, as in the previous period, were constructed along the main communication routes at the edges of the Great Morava, South Morava, and Vardar valleys (Gradac, Lanište; Đula, Ostrikovac; Gologlava, Stalać; Velika Humska Čuka; Kale, Skopje). However, these settlements mostly belong to the late phase of the Middle Bronze Age, while the hilltop settlements from the earlier phase were largely located away from these main communication routes, in the valleys of smaller rivers within local communication networks (Šumadija and western Serbia – Milića Brdo and Ostra; Bor Region – Čoka Kazak, Čoka Njica, and Mali Vizak; Babušnica – Semče and Gornje Krnjino). Defensive architecture was noted only at the settlements in Skopje, Ljuljaci, and Gamzigrad Banja, although the horizon in Skopje may also belong to the late phase of the Early Bronze Age, as discussed in detail in the previous chapter. In any case, the defensive structure at this location consisted of an earthen rampart 75 m long, with a core made of earth and stone framed by a wooden superstructure. The rampart in Ljuljaci comprised an embankment made of earth and small broken stones, about 2 m high and preserved for approximately 25–30 m, protecting the south-western part of the plateau where the settlement was built. It is not known, however, to which phase or settlement this rampart belonged. The rampart at Banjska Stena in Gamzigrad Banja was made of larger stones and a palisade of wooden construction.

It seems that during the Middle Bronze Age in addition to the main communication line along the Great Morava, South Morava, and Vardar valleys, which was used in the Early Bronze Age, other smaller mountainous areas also became important and were protected by hilltops for specific reasons. A careful look at the map, combined with geological and archaeological information, reveals that these areas were ore-rich regions around Bor and Babušnica, where metallurgical activities have been recorded (Ružana near Bor) and where a significant number of bronze items and moulds for their production were found (Sokobanja, the vicinity of Babušnica). It is noteworthy that all these hilltops recorded outside the main communication routes are in the eastern part of south-eastern Serbia and the Timok Region, known for its ore-bearing mountains rich in copper. This suggests that this region of the central Balkans became a sort of 'metallurgical zone' during the Middle Bronze Age, characterised by increased activities in copper extraction and processing, as well as the production of copper artefacts.

Residential architecture from the Middle Bronze Age at hilltop settlements was recorded only at the site of Milića Brdo in Ljuljaci. Here, three stratigraphic horizons with small above-ground houses of a square base were noted, with an entrance in the south-eastern part of the house. The houses were built by deeply embedding wooden posts into the ground which were then interwoven with branches and twigs and coated with clay.[22]

Plain settlements during the Middle Bronze Age in the central Balkans were predominantly constructed on river terraces, with the river valleys serving as the main communication routes of that time. Settlements were thus identified on terraces of the Danube (Najeva Ciglana, Omoljica, Marjansko Brdo, Golubac, Gospođin Vir, Mala Vrbica, Glameja, Obala Kod Crkve, Egeta), in the Great Morava valley (Sarina Međa), the West Morava (Ivlje, Lazarev Grad, Bošnjane, Maskare), the Nišava Valley (Bubanj, Mediana), the South Morava Valley (Čekmin, Bobište), the Timok Valley (Kot 1, Gamzigrad, Zvezdan, Boševo, Kadijski Krst, Bojčin), and the Ibar Valley (Karagač). Only exceptionally were settlements established outside these routes, on elevated positions in mountainous terrain, such as in the vicinity of Bor or near Čačak (Gornja Gorevnica). In the Bor area, an entire system of settlements was constructed in the valleys of smaller rivers, tributaries of the Crni Timok and Timok (Kučajna, Valja Mare, Trnjane, Hajdučka Česma, Selište, Ružana, etc.), which can primarily be explained by the metallurgical activity recorded in that region during this period.

Architecture in plain settlements was not recorded at many sites. At the site of Zlatica, above-ground rectangular houses were registered, built using wattle and daub techniques, with earthen floors approximately 20 cm thick, covered with a reddish coating. One of the pits discovered at the site indicates the existence of semi-subterranean structures.

A larger, irregularly shaped semi-subterranean structure, reconstructed to be about 7.5 m long and 5.5 m wide, consisting of a larger central oval depression and several smaller peripheral depressions, was documented at the Cigansko Brdo site near Požarevac. This structure was filled with carbonised wood remains, a significant amount of ash, animal bones, and pottery, with small and large bronze fragments (and/or copper ore?), slag, and fragments of small bronze items scattered throughout the structure, most abundantly in the western part. Larger fragments of plaster were found, while in the north-western and north-eastern depressions, parts of the furnace base and dome fragments were noted. This structure was dated to the 19th–18th century cal BC.

In western Serbia, one oval pit with gently sloping sides and rounded edges, measuring 2.4 × 2.6 m and dug into a Neolithic layer, was discovered as part of Middle Bronze Age architectural remains. In eastern Serbia, there are references to residential structures with hearths and furnaces, sometimes with burned floors, but detailed data on these structures are lacking. Notably, slag is mentioned as part of the inventory of these structures, suggesting potential metallurgical use. Remains of an above-ground structure built using wattle and daub techniques, with a stone foundation and dated to the 18th/17th century cal BC, were found at the Svinjarička Čuka site near Lebane in south-eastern Serbia. However, the pottery from this structure is characteristic of the Late Bronze Age (Brnjica group, dated to the early 15th century cal BC), casting uncertainty on its chronological classification.

From the sparse data on settlements and residential architecture during the Middle Bronze Age, it can be concluded that people lived in small settlements, primarily using small, above-ground rectangular houses with hearths and ovens inside. On the other hand, there are indications that small semi-subterranean structures were used, at least in western Serbia, but this information is not entirely reliable and should be considered cautiously. The large pit at the Cigansko Brdo site near Požarevac in the peri-Pannonian zone may have been a structure solely intended for copper or bronze metallurgical processes, so it cannot be treated definitively as a residential building.

3.6.2 Necropolises, burial practices, and ritual activities

Based on the available data on burial practices during the Middle Bronze Age in the central Balkans, a preliminary conclusion can be drawn that cremation of the deceased and the deposition of remains in urns was the only burial practice prevalent in the Timok Region, where urns were surrounded by smaller circular stone structures, forming necropolises resembling so called Stone fields. This practice was also noted in the Vatin culture at the site of Vinča. From the Vatin culture, but at the site of Cigansko Brdo near Požarevac, comes a grave of an inhumed individual in a crouched position, indicating diverse approaches to burial practices within this culture. Inhumed individuals in slightly contracted positions were found in a mound necropolis in western Serbia in the Lim Valley Region and, by all accounts, belong to the Middle Bronze Age (Savin Lakat).

This varied burial rite within different geographical zones of the central Balkans, even within the same zone and culture, points to changes that began in the Early Bronze Age when cremation necropolises appeared for the first time in this region, as discussed in Chapter 2. It is interesting that Middle Bronze Age necropolises in the Timok Region, dated to the period after the 20th century cal BC, are almost identical to the necropolis at Ranutovac, which absolute dates place in the 22nd/21st–19th/18th century cal BC. These sparse data suggest that in the Middle Bronze Age cremation was the dominant burial practice, while inhumation persisted, albeit in isolated cases or in less active regions of the central Balkans.

No necropolises from the Middle Bronze Age have been recorded in the basin of the South Morava and the upper Vardar. However, two ritual spaces from this geographical zone, discussed Chapter 2, indicate continued use into the Middle Bronze Age. Nevertheless, this horizon is difficult to recognise as there are no dates from Tatićev Kamen, and from Pelince, only two dates exist, one for the Early and one for the Late Bronze Age (see Table 1). Based on ceramics with characteristic stylistic and typological features,[23] they appear almost identical until the Late Bronze Age, when changes occur, such as the appearance of oblique channels on vessel bodies, characteristic so-called Brnjica rims (obliquely flared rims with ring-like profiles on the inner edge), knee-profiled handles with fan-shaped tips, and other elements typical of the Late Bronze Age (Bulatović *et al.* 2018b). An argument for the use of Tatićev Kamen during the Middle Bronze Age is the date obtained through astronomical calculations for the initial operation of the megalithic observatory at this site, which could have been used to observe certain known astronomical phenomena, dated to the 19th–18th century BC, i.e., the Middle Bronze Age (Cenev 2009, 9. Table 2). Additionally, ritual units (pits with offerings) from the Early and Late Bronze Age identified at both sites suggest continuous use, making it unlikely that these sites were not used during the Middle Bronze Age; rather, the stylistic and typological features of the ceramics may have gradually evolved, making them difficult to identify and define.

A similar situation was recorded in the geographical zone of western Serbia, where a significant number of sites (mostly tumulus necropolises) were documented in the

Early and Late Bronze Ages, but despite relatively extensive research, only one site from the Middle Bronze Age (Savin Lakat in Jabuka) has been documented. Although a hiatus in settlement activity is noted in western Serbia during the Middle Bronze Age, the tradition of burial under tumuli resumed in the Late Bronze Age.

3.6.3 Vessel typology in the Middle Bronze Age in the central Balkans

As mentioned in Chapter 2, this typology is based on the form and profile of the vessel, the method and style of production, decorative features, proportions of certain vessel elements, and other indicative characteristics. All vessels present in the Middle Bronze Age period in the central Balkans can be classified into several types: bowls, beakers, amphorae, and pots, as well as a category of 'other vessels', which includes double vessels, so-called fish-bowls, vessels with a quadrilateral base, strainers, lids, and others. The chronology of the pottery typology is summarised in Figure 3.55, below.

3.6.3.1 Bowls (Fig. 3.50)

With regard to the bowls, type 1, types 1a and 1b remain in use, but a new type of bowl appears, with a deeper container and a longer cylindrical or slightly conical neck and a gently rounded body, typically with handles extending from the rim to the shoulder, defined as type 1c.[24] Type 2a bowls also remain in use, while type 2b has not been recorded in the Middle Bronze Age in the central Balkans.

Perhaps the most common type of bowl in the Middle Bronze Age is type 3, encompassing all subtypes or variants that were in use during the Early Bronze Age (3a, 3b, and 3c), with the addition of two new types:

Type 3d: deeper, larger biconical bowls, often with handles on the upper cone or body, and

Type 3e: semi-circular or conical bowls with a form similar to type 3a; however, unlike type 3a, which features a semi-circular interior rim, type 3e has a triangularly modelled inner rim and a variety of outer rim profiles: an expanded rim with a levelled horizontal top surface; an expanded slightly inverted rim with a flattened slanted

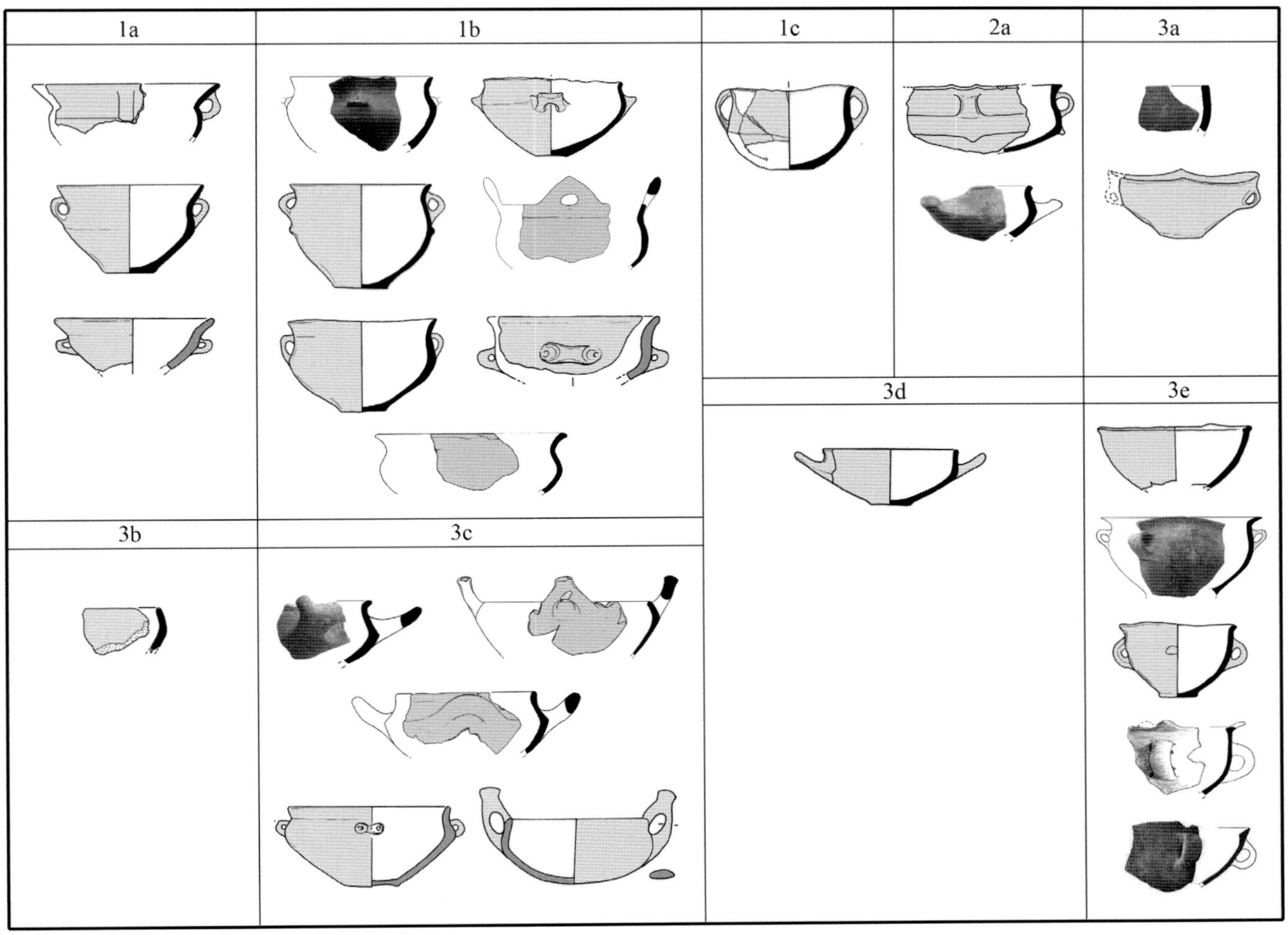

Figure 3.50. Middle Bronze Age bowls in the central Balkans.

top surface; an open rim with a flattened slanted top surface; semi-circular or triangularly thickened inner rims, among others, as well as a triangularly modelled inner rim profile.

Type 4a is not recorded during this period.

3.6.3.2 Cups (Fig. 3.51)

The types of cups appearing in the Middle Bronze Age in the central Balkans are 1a, 2b, 4a, 4b, and 5, with types 2b and 5 being new to this period. These are shallow, smaller, semi-circular vessels with a single handle, resembling type 1a beakers but with a significantly shallower body and generally thicker walls (2b) or a conical, shallow form, usually with one handle (type 5). Type 2b, in fact, also resembles type 2a, but it features thicker walls and an arched handle rather than an elongated, tongue-like handle aligned with the vessel's opening. This type of beaker has been recorded in the peri-Pannonian Region, as well as in the Timok Valley and Great Morava Valley regions, including Šumadija. Based on its characteristics, it appears that its function differed from other beaker types and may have served as a 'pouring scoop' or possibly as a 'melting pot' although physical-chemical analyses of the vessel walls are required for definitive confirmation. This type of vessel will henceforth be treated in this book as a vessel of specific purpose.

3.6.3.3 Beakers (Fig. 3.52)

In addition to the types of beakers documented in this territory during the Early Bronze Age (1a, 1c, 1e, 2a, 3a, and 5a), new forms of beakers emerged. Early Bronze Age beaker types 1b, 1d, 3b, 4a, 4b, 6a, 7b, 7c, and 8a were no longer in use. New types in the Middle Bronze Age included:

Type 1f: a beaker with a globular body and a short, flared rim or a conical neck;

Type 1g: a deeper biconical beaker with a less defined rim and a more sharply or gently profiled shape, typically with handles that do not extend above the vessel's opening;

Type 7d: a beaker with either a short or long neck, which may be funnel-shaped, conical, or cylindrical, and a low, broad, squat or tiered body.

3.6.3.4 Amphorae (Fig. 3.53)

Among the amphorae used during the Early Bronze Age, types 1a, 3a, and 4a continued into the Middle Bronze Age, with new types emerging as 1b, 4b, 5a, 5b, and 6a.

Type 1b: amphorae primarily of ovoid form, with an extremely short, flared rim or a minimally defined rim;

Type 3b: larger, ovoid or globular amphorae with a longer funnel-shaped neck, often featuring an arched handle from rim to shoulder;

Type 4b: very similar to type 4a, being a low amphora with a wide opening, a biconical or globular body, and a broad belly, but differing from type 4a with a longer conical neck;

Type 5a: deeper, wide-mouthed vessels with one or two handles, resembling large semi-circular beakers;

Type 5b: deeper, wide-mouthed vessels with a longer cylindrical neck and a gently rounded belly;

Type 6a: a deeper conical vessel with four large, triangular plastic extensions on the rim.

3.6.3.5 Jugs (Fig. 3.54)

In addition to jug types 1a and 2a, known from the Early Bronze Age, new types appeared in the Middle Bronze

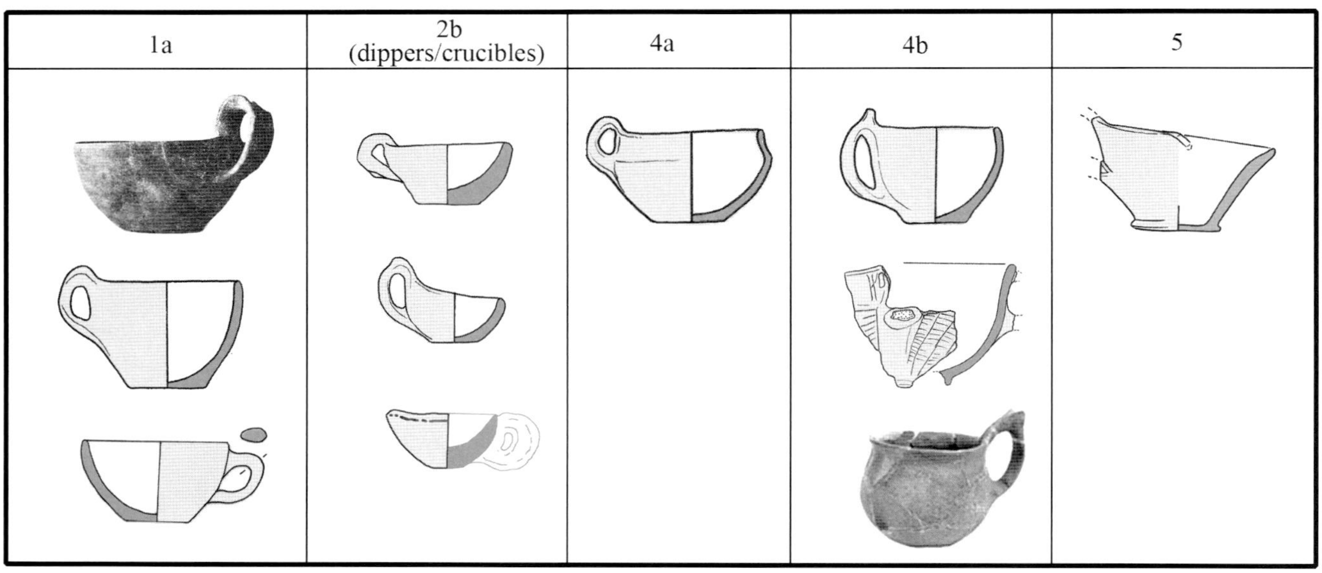

Figure 3.51. Middle Bronze Age cups in the central Balkans.

Age, similar in form to type 2a. The first type (2b) is a biconical jug with a concavely profiled neck, a semi-circular body, and a single arched handle on the neck, while type 2c is a jug with a funnel-shaped neck and a low biconical body.

3.6.3.6 Pots

This group includes vessels generally of larger dimensions, with thicker walls, coarser texture, and surface, typically decorated with plastic bands and equipped with larger tongue-shaped or arched handles. It should be noted that these vessels are mostly preserved in fragments, making it challenging to determine their exact form and classify them into specific types.

There are slightly more types of pots in the Middle Bronze Age than in the previous period.

Type 1a: ovoid or wide, almost globular pots with a wide opening, often decorated with finger impressions on the rim and a plastic band with impressions on the neck;

Type 2a: ovoid or globular pots with a narrowing opening, sometimes with handles below the rim or on the shoulder.

A pot with a distinctly funnel-shaped neck, designated as type 1b, also appears in the Middle Bronze Age. *Piraunos* pots are more frequently recorded at Middle Bronze Age sites in the central Balkans, especially in eastern Serbia, compared to the previous period, where they are exceptionally rare. These are designated as pots of type 3.

3.6.3.7 Pithoi

No vessel from this period can be definitively identified as a pithos.

3.6.3.8 Double vessels (Fig. 3.54)

Double vessels are also recorded in the Middle Bronze Age in the central Balkans, albeit very rarely, and their form resembles examples from the previous period.

3.6.3.9 Ember containers (Fig. 3.54)

These unusually shaped vessels are also recorded in the Middle Bronze Age but, as in the late Early Bronze Age, are found exclusively in the southern part of the central Balkans, specifically in zone 5, in the Kumanovo Plain. Their form does not differ from those of the previous period; they typically have two openings, one at the front and another on the top, along with a small carrying handle. The top opening is often shaped like a chimney or funnel while the front opening resembles a wide spatula.

3.6.3.10 Oval-based vessels

This vessel type has an oval base with a conical profile, most often featuring a short, arched handle with an oval cross-section. Interestingly, these vessels are defined as fish bowls, which could be supported by their distribution, as all examples have been found exclusively in zone 1, in settlements along the Danube's banks, with only sporadic finds in Šumadija and western Serbia.

3.6.3.11 Quadrilateral-based vessels (Fig. 3.54)

Only one vessel with a rectangular base and conical profile has been recorded, with an arched handle positioned on the vessel's rim.

3.6.3.12 Strainers (Fig. 3.54)

A semi-circular vessel with a longer horizontal handle on the rim and numerous perforations on the body is classified as a strainer.

3.6.3.13 Lids (Fig. 3.54)

Lids appear more frequently in the Middle Bronze Age than in the previous period, mostly recorded in the northern part of the central Balkan region. Lids can be divided into two types, 1a and 1b. Both types have deep bodies and circular bases, but type 1a has a dome shape with a horizontal rib above the rim and can be either undecorated or decorated with various incised or impressed motifs. Type 1b is also deep but has a more conical profile, with handles near the top or directly at the top of the lid.

3.6.3.14 Handles

Handles on vessels, particularly certain types, can be a highly indicative element for the cultural-chronological interpretation of a vessel and are thus treated as an essential component. Based on the form, shape, and cross-section of handles observed on Middle Bronze Age vessels in the central Balkans, they can be divided into several types with sub-types or variants.

The most common handle type is the arched handle, which can vary in cross-section: ribbon-like, rectangular, oval, circular, rhomboidal, triangular, and, in the Middle Bronze Age, also saddle-shaped or lunate-type. Arched handles are longer than they are wide, forming an arc, and may be located anywhere on the vessel, although they most often extend from the rim to the shoulder or body. Unlike the previous period, arched handles in this period rise above the vessel's opening and often have plastic extensions on the top, such as cylindrical, button-like, or wart-like forms.

Tongue-shaped handles, modelled as plastic projections resembling a tongue – flat at the base and rounded at the tip – are also widespread, as in the previous period. They are typically horizontally positioned on the vessel wall, most frequently on the body but occasionally on the rim. Some tongue-shaped handles are vertically perforated (Fig. 3.14/16; Fig. 3.15/6) or have a central indentation (Fig. 3.16/8).

Rectangular handles, flat at the base with a rectangularly modelled top, appear relatively frequently, as in the previous period, and are located on the vessel's neck

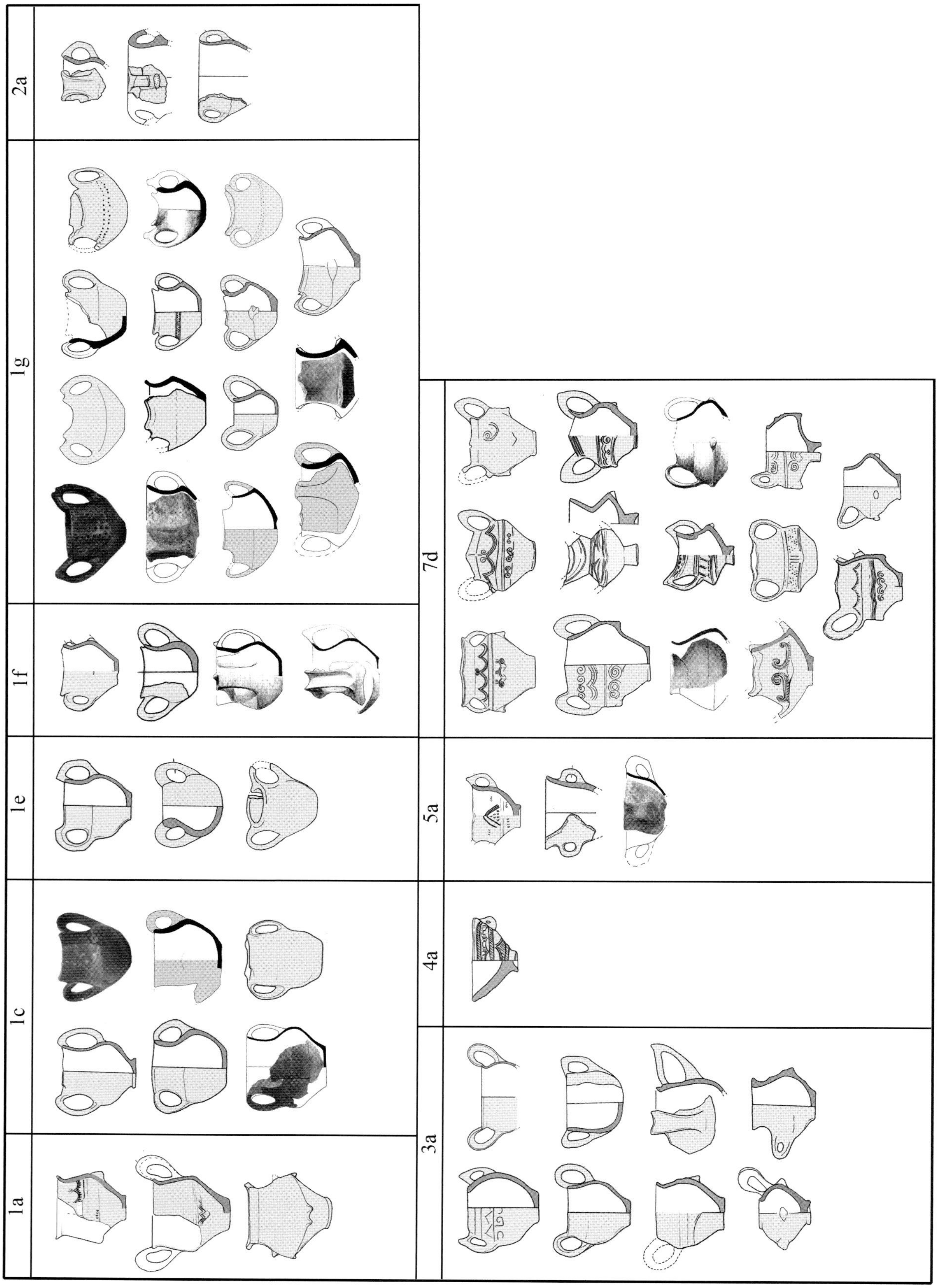

Figure 3.52. Middle Bronze Age beakers in the central Balkans.

(Fig. 3.3/12–13; Fig. 3.8/21). These handles sometimes feature a central indentation but often exhibit vertical perforations with symmetrical plastic appliqués on the tips (Fig. 3.8/2; Fig. 3.14/1; Fig. 3.37/1, 6, 7).

Triangular handles are more commonly found than in the previous period, especially examples with vertical perforations set obliquely or horizontally on the vessel body (Fig. 3.10/12; Fig. 3.9/19; Fig. 3.31/2; Fig. 3.38/1, 14; Fig. 3.40/1, 2).

Unlike in the previous period, tunnel-shaped handles are rare in the Middle Bronze Age. These are arched handles, usually with a saddle-shaped cross-section, although they have a shorter height than width. They are documented on one lid from Ljuljaci (Fig. 3.8/17) as well as on bowls from Lopate (Fig. 3.46/4, 9, 12, 13), generally located on the vessel body.

Handles with proportions similar to tunnel-shaped ones are documented more frequently on amphorae used as urns in eastern Serbia; however, they have a slightly greater height than width and are thus classified as arched handles. They may be positioned horizontally or vertically and are notably recorded on ceramics from eastern Serbia and South Morava Basin (Fig. 3.27/11–18; Fig. 3.30; Fig. 3.31, etc.).

One prominent feature on Middle Bronze Age pottery is the use of wart-like and horn-shaped plastic appliqués on vessels, recorded across all geographical zones, especially on bowls and beakers. Another element frequently found on ceramics is plastic extensions on the rim, which can take various forms – fan-shaped, triangular, horn-shaped, etc. Characteristic of this period are trapezoidal modelled beaker openings, almost throughout the entire central Balkan territory, which will be discussed in more detail later. Among typological elements appearing for the first time in this period are cup-shaped handles, particularly prevalent in eastern Serbia (Fig. 3.20/26, 27; Fig. 3.25/18–20).

3.6.4 Subsistence and economy

There is very limited data on the diet and economy of the communities that inhabited the central Balkans during the Middle Bronze Age. In the peri-Pannonian Region at the site of Cigansko Brdo, within the pit dwelling already discussed, the presence of five domestic animals and one freshwater shell was identified while no wild animals were noted. The most prevalent remains were of cattle (55%), followed by pig (22%), and sheep/goat (20%), with smaller representations of dog and horse (1.5% each). When the prevalence of animal species at this site is compared to nearby Early Bronze Age sites (Nad Klepečkom, Rit, Marjansko Brdo), significant similarities are observed, as cattle were the most common species in that period too, followed by pigs and sheep/goats, though wild species were also present at that time (Pl. 21).

In Šumadija, at the site of Milića Brdo in Ljuljaci, a large number of animal species were found during excavations, with domestic animals making up about 59%, while wild animals were also present in significant numbers (41%) (Bogdanović 1986, 78; Greenfield 2006, 234, table 7). Among domestic animals, pig and cattle were most common (43% and 37%, respectively), followed by horse (12%), with sheep, goat, and dog appearing in smaller numbers (*c.* 8% in total) (Pl. 22). Among wild animals, wild boar (51%) and deer (37%) were predominant, with wild cattle (around 4%), bear (around 3%), and roe deer (around 2%) following in smaller numbers, while badger, beaver, and hare were recorded in much smaller numbers (*c.* 3% in total) (Pl. 23). Wild animals, particularly deer and wild boar, were used for food and for making tools and implements. It is noteworthy that the domesticated horse was recorded at a high percentage (12%) compared to other domestic animals at this site, as well as relative to the proportion of horses at other Middle Bronze Age sites in the central Balkans. This, among other reasons, supports the theory that this site had a higher social status, possibly as an elite settlement with a superior role in the region (Renfrew and Bahn 1991; Webster *et al.* 1997; Greenfield 2006, 240–242).

When the representation of animal species from Ljuljaci is compared with the nearby Early Bronze Age site of Novačka Ćuprija, significant similarities are evident, with cattle and pig being the most common. However, the representation of sheep/goat was much higher (around 28%), while the percentage of horse was much lower (around 2%) (Greenfield 1986). The presence of horses in this region and the peri-Pannonian area south of the Danube from the Early Bronze Age, and in greater numbers during the Middle Bronze Age, may indicate the existence of some early centres or points for the gathering, taming, or breeding, and possibly the distribution of horses in the central Balkans.

In the southern Morava Basin, archaeo-zoological analysis has been conducted at only one site, a large pit at Svinjarička Čuka dated to the period from the mid-19th to the early 17th century cal BC. Unfortunately, the pit contained only a few animal bones but a rough idea of the distribution of species during this period in the southern part of the central Balkans can be gleaned. Pig was the most common species at 50%, followed by sheep/goat at 38%, and cattle at 12%, although these data should be taken with extreme caution due to the very small sample size (Pl. 24).[25] However, from the same pit came a single grain each of einkorn and emmer wheat, seven barley grains, two lentil seeds, one pea seed, a cornelian cherry pit, and a black elder seed,[26] indicating the types of plant species and cereals used in the Middle Bronze Age in this region.

From these sparse data it can be concluded that hunting continued as a supplementary source of food and raw materials in the Middle Bronze Age, similar to the Early Bronze Age. The proportions of domestic animals at individual sites and between regions are also very similar to those of the Early Bronze Age, indicating a consistent and continuous

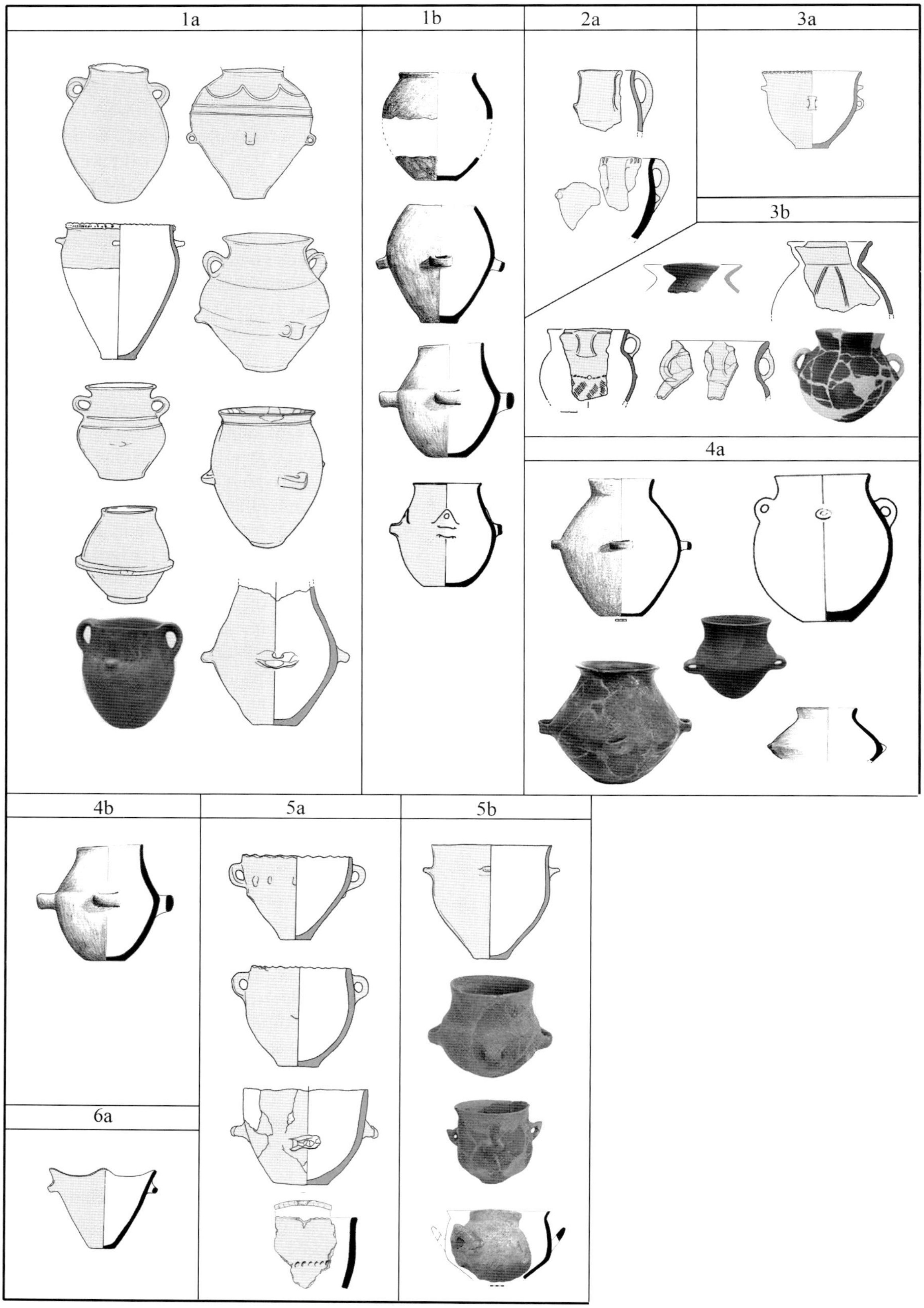

Figure 3.53. Middle Bronze Age amphorae in the central Balkans.

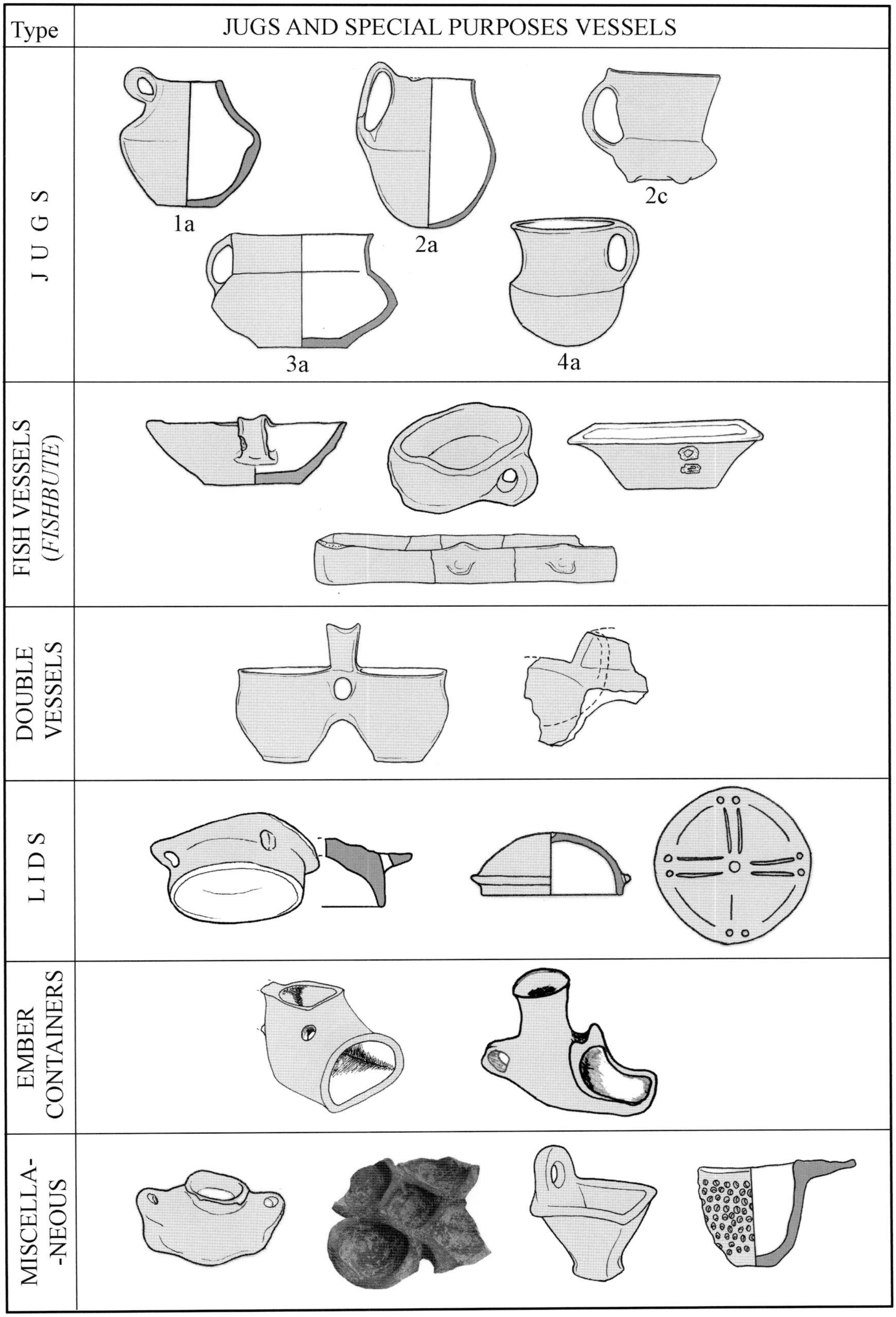

Figure 3.54. Middle Bronze Age jugs and special purpose vessels in the central Balkans.

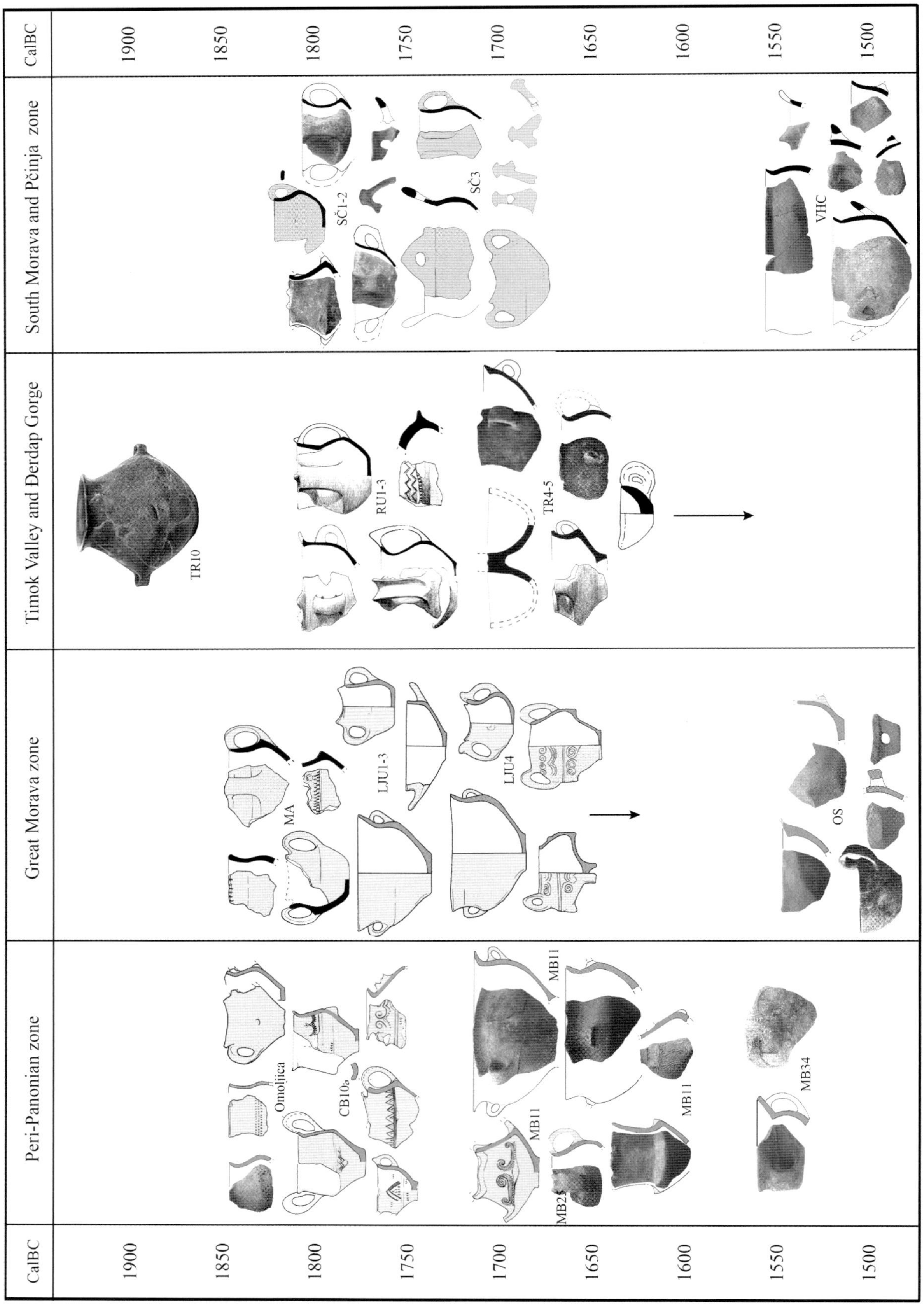

Figure 3.55. Chronology of Middle Bronze Age pottery in the central Balkans.

strategy for food gathering and subsistence from the last quarter of the 3rd millennium to the first half of the 2nd millennium BC. The only notable difference is the significantly higher percentage of domesticated horses (*Equus caballus*) compared to the previous period, especially at sites in Šumadija and the southern peri-Pannonian zone (Novačka Ćuprija, Rit, Nad Klepečkom, Vinča–Belo Brdo, Ljuljaci), suggesting that this area may have served as a centre for breeding, taming, or distributing horses from the Early to the Middle Bronze Age.

3.6.5 Mining and metallurgy

In the Middle Bronze Age in the central Balkans, tin bronze artefacts became much more prevalent compared to the Early Bronze Age, although objects made of pure copper, sometimes with traces of arsenic, still appeared. The theory that the lack of metal (copper) artefacts in the Late Eneolithic and Early Bronze Age (based on absolute dates, approximately 3500–2000 BC) was due to the complete exploitation of oxidised, surface copper ores in the preceding period has been largely confirmed at Middle Bronze Age sites in the Timok Region. It was discovered that copper metallurgy in this period was based exclusively on the use of sulphide copper ores (Jovanović and Janković 1990, 9). Other researchers reached similar conclusions (Powell *et al.* 2017; Mehofer *et al.* 2021), although some sources indicate that in addition to local copper in the Timok Region, copper from the south-eastern Alpine ore deposits in present-day northern Italy was also used. If accurate, this would imply certain indirect or direct interactions between the central Balkan communities and those in southern Central Europe during the first half of the 2nd millennium BC.

Artefacts made of 'pure' copper have been recorded across all zones of the central Balkans, occasionally with traces of arsenic (e.g., an axe from Begaljica (Antonović 2014, 107 I, table 1), a dagger from the Zaječar gas pipeline,[27] a Patulele-type axe from Urovica (Antonović 2014, table 5), and a Patulele axe from Sokobanja) (Antonović 2014, table 2). It is interesting those axes of types Darabani, Patulele, and Izvoarele have been dated in Romania in the Early Bronze Age (Bajenaru 2014, 239–242). A chance find from Brestovac near Bor includes an axe of the Darabani-type with 2.5% arsenic content, classifying it as arsenical copper (Antonović 2014, table 2). This is a rare find, as arsenical copper artefacts are not common in the central Balkans. The Early Bronze Age also produced an axe of arsenical copper, but of the Kozarac-type, which was discussed earlier in the book in the chapter on the Early Bronze Age. It appears that arsenical copper finds on the central Balkans are mainly recorded in the Timok Region, with the highest frequency in Pannonia, particularly in Banat, which falls outside the geographical scope of this book.

Other more numerous metal finds are made of tin bronze and are more-or-less represented across all geographical zones of the central Balkans, except in western Serbia, where no metal artefacts have been recorded (Pls 25 and 26). The highest percentage of tin is found in an axe from the Popovica hoard (11.6%) (Mitrović and Filipović in preparation), a single-edged knife/dagger (or razor) from Trnjane (10.7%),[28] and axes from Borač and Trućevac (Antonović 2014, table 2), as well as a dagger from Lipovac (Filipović and Milojević 2015, ref. 58), all containing about 10% tin. Other tin bronze items had tin content ranging from 1.3–10% (e.g., a needle from Trnjane, hoards from Trućevac, axes from Popovica, a flat axe from Velika Humska Čuka, and a Patulele axe from Staničenje).

One piece of evidence confirming metallurgy in this region is a fragment of a double mould found in a Middle Bronze Age pit (17th century cal BC) at the Marjansko Brdo site in the peri-Pannonian zone. The mould featured a negative of a *Randleistenbeile*-type flat axe on one side and negatives of several narrow items (chisels, awls) on the other. Copper slag pieces were also found in the same pit. Another site that directly confirms copper metallurgy is Ružana in the Timok Region, where traces of melting sulphide copper ore were discovered.

As for the origin of the tin used for making bronze items, the few analyses of tin isotopes 120 and 124 (δ^{120}Sn and δ^{124}Sn) have shown that tin used in the Middle Bronze Age in the central Balkans mostly came from this region (Pl. 27). The flat axe from Popovača, based on its isotope profile, belongs to the so-called Serbian group, with the Cer Mountain believed to be the source of this tin (Mason *et al.* 2016, 115). Other analysed bronze artefacts, such as those from Trnjane (a needle with an eye, a dagger/razor, and sheet metal), a Patulele-type axe from Staničenje, and a flat axe from Velika Humska Čuka, are also classified within this group. It should be noted that in the following Late Bronze Age period, more groups with different tin isotope signatures appear, though the Serbian group remains present, suggesting intensified contacts between central Balkan communities and neighbouring or more distant regions, such as Central Europe or the Carpathians. When the tin isotope analysis results of bronze artefacts from the central Balkans are compared with those from the contemporaneous Popov Salaš site in Vojvodina, belonging to the Vatin group, it is observed that the tin in these artifacts falls into three groups: Serbian, Vojvodinian, and Banat–Transylvanian (Pl. 27) (Mason *et al.* 2016, supplementary data). A similar situation was noted at the Middle Bronze Age site in Ostojićevo, Banat, where tin isotope signatures belonged to two groups: Serbian and Banat-Transylvanian. Clearly, the Vatin group communities in Vojvodina had intensive contacts with central Balkan communities, sourcing tin from the Serbian group (Mason *et al.* 2016, supplementary data), while mutual contacts are evidenced by the stylistic-typological features of ceramics and metal artifacts in Vojvodina and northern central Balkans.

Regarding the copper isotope values ($\delta^{65}Cu$), very few analyses have been conducted for Middle Bronze Age objects from the central Balkans. The results indicate that these values are similar across all analysed artefacts, corresponding to those from the Timok Region, suggesting that the copper originated from this mining area.

In the Middle Bronze Age, hoards of metal artefacts also appear, becoming more widespread during the Late Bronze Age. Unlike those from the following period, Middle Bronze Age hoards are smaller, containing only a few items, at least in the central Balkans. For instance, the Trućevac hoard, which some authors suggest may represent a grave (though no bones were found), comprised a small vessel (Fig. 3.13/1), four flat axes with accentuated thickened sides (*Randleistenbeile*) (Fig. 3.13/2, 3), two bracelets (Fig. 3.13/4), two gold earrings (or hair ornaments?) (Fig. 3.13/7), a necklace, and seven fragments of spiral wire pendants (Fig. 3.13/5, 6) (Krstić *et al.* 1972, cat. no. 32). Based on the context, this could indeed be a grave, but it is a chance find with limited information, so certainty about its context is lacking.

Another hoard was found at Popovica near Sokobanja, consisting of seven Patulele axes. The hoard was buried near a thermal spring not far from a Middle Bronze Age settlement (Milojević and Kapuran 2023). Of the seven axes, six are made of tin bronze, and one of copper (Mitrović and Filipović in preparation). Notably, three axes from the hoard, and one found previously in the Sokobanja area (Garašanin *et al.* 1971, cat. no. 245), contained more than 0.5% arsenic.

It is notable that the highest number of bronze artefacts was recorded in the Timok Region and the wider Nišava Valley area (Pls 25 and 26), including the Popovica hoard. In the mountainous areas of the South Morava Basin, Suva Planina, and the Moravica Valley in the Sokobanja Basin, a greater number of hilltop settlements have been observed, located far from main natural communication routes. These hilltops (Česma–Provalija and Pusto Semče on Suva Planina) were not likely established for controlling important communication routes but may have served for monitoring and securing mineral resources, most likely copper, as known deposits still exist. This geo-strategically passive micro-region, apart from these hilltops, also yielded three incidental 'metal' finds: a Middle Bronze Age Patulele axe, a Kilindir-type axe mould, and a Kilindir-type axe (although axes of the Kilindir-type are more likely associated with the Late rather than the Middle Bronze Age), further indicating the region's importance as a copper resource. The hilltop at Popovica, where an axe hoard was found, is situated on a prominent hill above the Moravica River, across from Sokograd. Here too, seven Patulele axes were found by chance, further supporting the idea that these hilltops were connected to copper ore exploitation.

A similar situation was noted in the Timok Region, particularly around Bor, where copper metallurgy was registered. At Ružana near Bor in the Timok Region, a structure was discovered where sulphide copper ore was melted in a furnace that was essentially a small pit. The ore was melted multiple times until a metallic copper state was achieved (Mehofer *et al.* 2021). This method differs significantly from the previous period, where only oxidised or oxidised-sulphide ore was used and smelted in a single step, indicating advancements in copper smelting technology and more sophisticated metallurgical skills during the Middle Bronze Age. However, the question arises as to how these more sophisticated metallurgical skills were acquired by the Middle Bronze Age communities in the Timok Region, where copper metallurgy traces were first recorded in the Early Eneolithic of the 5th millennium and then not again until the Middle Bronze Age, over three millennia later. The suggestion by M. Mehofer and colleagues that, in addition to local copper, copper from the Alps (Mehofer *et al.* 2021, 11) was also used in the Middle Bronze Age in the Timok Region could indicate the region or one of the regions from which new metallurgical skills arrived.

3.6.6 Cultural-chronological overview of the Middle Bronze Age in the central Balkans

Material and spiritual culture and relations with neighbouring cultural groups

The cultural landscape of the central Balkans during the Middle Bronze Age is fairly uniform. The first impression when examining ceramic material is that all cultural groups present in the region at this time emerged from a similar cultural foundation. This is true to some extent as, even in the preceding period, at the end of the Early Bronze Age, uniformity and noticeable similarities between cultural groups in various zones of the central Balkans were becoming evident.

Starting from the north, from the first, peri-Pannonian zone, it can be observed that the so-called Novačka Ćuprija–Pančevo group evolved into the Vatin group (or culture).[29] The term 'evolved' is most suitable here as many ceramic elements are shared, making it sometimes difficult to determine which group is actually represented. The best example of this is the site of Marjansko Brdo near Veliko Gradište on the Danube, where, in structure '35/western half' dated to the 19th-17th century cal BC, pottery with stylistic-typological features of both groups were found (Fig. 3.6/24–32). However, this phenomenon is only recorded on the southern periphery of the Vatin group, in the territory of the previous Novačka Ćuprija–Pančevo group while, in the southern central Balkans during the Middle Bronze Age, the so-called Bubanj-Hum IV–Ljuljaci group dominated (Pl. 28).

The Vatin group thus appeared in the territory of the previous Novačka Ćuprija–Pančevo group, in the northern central Balkans, i.e., in the peri-Pannonian zone, and the recognisable style of this group extends south to Šumadija (Ljuljaci), Western Serbia (Ostra), and the Timok Region

(Banjska Stena). The earliest date for the Vatin group in the peri-Pannonian zone falls between the mid-20th and mid-18th centuries cal BC (Omoljica), although this date comes from an unknown context and has a relatively high variability of 60 years, so it should be taken with caution. The next date from this zone comes from a Vatin dugout dwelling at Cigansko Brdo, dated to between the last quarter of the 19th century and the last quarter of the 18th century cal BC (Table 1). Interestingly, the beginning of the Vatin group, in general, including its main territory in Banat and south-eastern Bačka, is dated by the aforementioned date from Omoljica. Thus, starting from the 19th century, and probably somewhat earlier, this group was present in the peri-Pannonian zone (Fig. 3.1–3.6), with typical pottery bearing Vatin stylistic-typological characteristics, discussed in earlier sections of the book. The end of the Vatin group in the peri-Pannonian zone, according to limited available dates, falls in the 17th century, and soon, by the end of the 17th or the beginning of the 16th century cal BC, a material culture partly derived from the Vatin, with elements of incrusted ceramics from the north, known as the Žuto Brdo-Girla Mare group, emerged in this region (Pl. 29).[30] This absolute chronology for the Žuto Brdo–Girla Mare group is based on dates from Cigansko Brdo and Marjansko Brdo and is confirmed by the vertical stratigraphy at Cigansko Brdo, where above the Vatin dugout dwelling dated to the 19th/18th century, a cultural layer of the Žuto Brdo–Girla Mare group was recorded, dated to the second half of the 16th century cal BC. A similar stratigraphic relationship was noted at the site Livade in Mala Vrbica on the Danube (Vukmanović and Popović 1986, 12–14) where, beneath the layer of the Žuto Brdo–Girla Mare group, a layer with Verbicioara findings was documented, whose cultural-chronological relationship with the Vatin group is still not entirely clear (for a more detailed discussion on this issue, see: Tasić 2004, 29; Kapuran 2009; Bulatović 2021, 138–144). However, chronologically speaking, if the oldest date for the Žuto Brdo–Girla Mare group is placed in the second half of the 16th century cal BC (Konopište, Table 1), it can be assumed that, judging by the stratigraphy at the nearby site of Livade, the layer with Verbicioara finds is somewhat older than this date and could be dated no later than the first half of the 16th century, and likely earlier, judging by the established chronology of this group in nearby Oltenia (Crăciunescu 2004, 227–230).

Stylistic and typological characteristics of the Verbicioara group were recorded, alongside those of the Vatin group, in the youngest layer at Ljuljaci, in the heart of Šumadija (Bulatović 2021, 140, 141), which dates to the 18th/17th century cal BC, suggesting that this pottery arrived together with the Vatin ceramics through contacts with the Vatin population to the north. Apart from Đerdap, Verbicioara pottery was also present in the Timok Region, where at the Banjska Stena site, this pottery was dated to the 15th century BC.[31] Based on stratigraphic conditions and limited dates, it can be inferred that intense contacts between central Balkan communities and the Verbicioara group were not established before the 18th/17th century BC, most likely in the 17th century (Pl. 29). At the Velika Humska Čuka site on the edge of the Niš Plain, a layer with pottery exhibiting stylistic and typological features characteristic of the Verbicioara group was identified. This layer has not been dated; however, a group of pottery on the north-eastern edge of the site, dated to the second half of the 16th century, contained pottery of the late phase Bubanj-Hum IV–Ljuljaci group, without a single fragment characteristic of the Verbicioara group, which might indicate that this pottery appeared at the site after this period, earliest at the end of the 16th century or more likely in the 15th. From the above it can be concluded that contacts between central Balkan communities and the bearers of the Verbicioara group were first established in the Timok Region in the 18th/17th century, then gradually expanded southward through the Svrljiški Timok valley toward the Niš Plain and further south, forming one of the bases for the genesis of the Brnjica group of the Late Bronze Age in the southern central Balkans.

Simultaneously with the Vatin group in the north, the material culture defined as the Bubanj-Hum IV–Ljuljaci group existed in other zones of the central Balkans, named after the eponymous sites Bubanj, Velika Humska Čuka, and Milića Brdo in Ljuljaci. It is quite uniform, with certain regional differences, as discussed earlier. The oldest confirmed date for this group (between the beginning of the last quarter of the 20th and the middle of the 18th century BC) comes from Maskare, and it is almost identical (in BP) to the earliest date for the Vatin group from Omoljica. It should be noted that there are older dates from the Timok Region that could belong to this group, but they come from graves or contexts containing ceramics that cannot be definitively attributed to the Bubanj-Hum IV–Ljuljaci group. The oldest date from the Timok Region that can be confidently associated with this group comes from Ružana, dating to the period between the early 19th and mid-18th century cal BC. This group practically extended over most of the regions where the Bubanj-Hum III group and partially the Novačka Ćuprija–Pančevo group were present in the Early Bronze Age, covering the area between southern Šumadija and the Grdelica Gorge, and the basins of the Western Morava and Ibar to the Timok Region. From the orographic perspective of site distribution for this group, it is observed that its settlements are mainly concentrated in the mountainous zone of South Morava Basin and the Timok Region, and in the wider basin zones of the South Morava and Western Morava, with a few sporadic sites in West Morava Valley and the south-western part of the Central Balkans.

Although the material culture of this group is quite uniform, with some regional characteristics as seen in the Timok Region, the burial practices differ. However, there are not enough necropolises within this group's territory to make an adequate comparison, as the Timok Region contains several cremation necropolises while, outside this zone, there is only one burial, located in the far west of the central Balkans at Jabuka near Prijepolje, where the deceased was buried by inhumation under a tumulus, with a beaker exhibiting characteristics typical of the Bubanj-Hum IV–Ljuljaci group. Apart from burial practices, other distinctive ceramic elements have been recorded in the Timok Region, such as handles shaped like small vessels, with similar elements appearing in western Bulgaria (Lazić 2016, 42). Copper smelting metallurgy has also been confirmed in this region, which could explain why it was the most densely populated area in the central Balkans during the Middle Bronze Age. For these reasons, it might be necessary to distinguish this zone within the Bubanj-Hum IV–Ljuljaci group and define it as the Timok variant of this group.

However, a stylistic element found throughout the entire territory of the Bubanj-Hum IV–Ljuljaci group, including the Timok Region and beyond, is the beakers with trapezoidal shaped rims, which deserve full attention as the most indicative typological element of the Bubanj-Hum IV–Ljuljaci material culture.

3.6.6.1 Beakers with trapezoidal shaped opening

These beakers were defined about 10 years ago as one of the main stylistic-typological indicators of the Bubanj-Hum IV–Ljuljaci group but, due to a lack of absolute dates, they were broadly placed in the Middle Bronze Age (Bulatović and Stankovski 2012, 337–347). They originated, like this cultural group, on the foundations of the Bubanj–Hum III group from the Early Bronze Age. Their evolution from bowls with double horn-like plastic projections on the rim can be traced back to the Early Bronze Age (Bulatović 2021, 138, fig. 5). Interestingly, these beakers have been sporadically recorded in the territory of the Vatin group in southern Banat and in the Danube region, but more frequently at sites in the broader zone of the Mureş and Tisza rivers, indicating intensive mutual, indirect or direct, interactions between communities in the central Balkans and those in the southern part of the Carpathian Basin (Fig. 3.56) (Bulatović 2021, fig. 1). The oldest absolute date for a site where these beakers have been recorded comes from Omoljica, although the dated context is unknown, so it is not clear whether it pertains to a layer or context where these beakers were found. The reliable date for dating these beakers is from Maskare (20th–18th century cal BC), with slightly later dates coming from Ljuljaci. It is noteworthy that a beaker (Fig. 3.5/4), aside from Omoljica, was recorded in the Vatin dugout dwelling, featuring typical Vatin ceramics at the Cigansko Brdo site, dated to the 19th/18th century cal BC. The 'popularity' of these beakers, therefore, did not remain confined to local communities in the central Balkans but was also recorded, in greater numbers, far to the north, in the zone of the Mureş and Tisza rivers at several sites. These beakers, however, are decorated in the style of the local communities' culture and are somewhat younger (18th/17th century), but the beaker's opening is distinctly shaped in a trapezoid form (Bulatović 2021, 134, figs 1, 3). One such beaker was dated to a grave in Szoreg to the period 1885–1694 cal BC (Bona 1975, Taf. 112/10; O'shea *et al.* 2019, table 1), which pushes the dating of this type of beaker back to the 18th century and indicates very early interactions between Middle Bronze Age populations from this part of the Carpathian Basin and the Central Balkans.

It has been observed that the chronology of beakers with trapezoidal shaped rims is synchronous with the chronology of the Bubanj-Hum IV–Ljuljaci group (Figs 4.14 and 4.15) although it is worth noticing however the model's performance was poor, as indicated by corresponding low A-model values, and results should then be taken with caution. The youngest date for these beakers comes from the site of Velika Humska Čuka (Fig. 3.38/6, 7), corresponding to the second half of the 16th century cal BC. The survivals of these beakers can be recognised in the triangular and horn-like plastic projections on the rims of vessels, mainly bowls, in Late Bronze Age groups of the central Balkans,

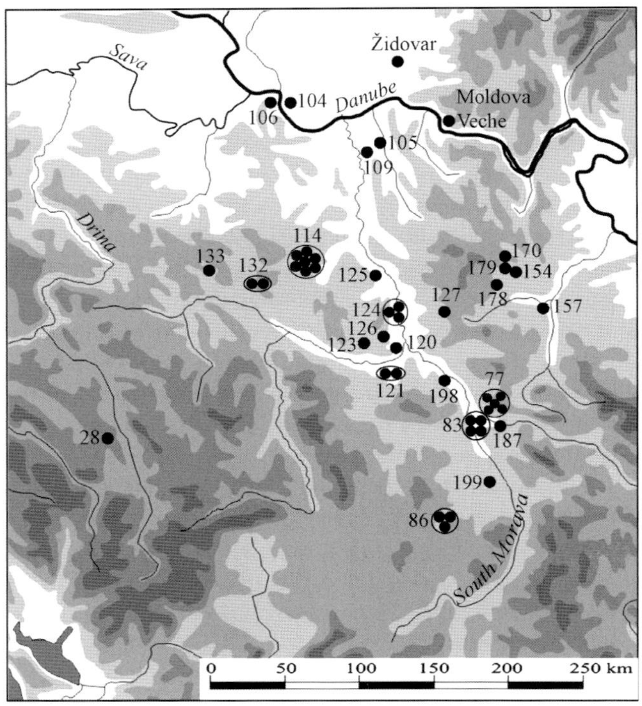

Figure 3.56. Distribution map of sites with beakers with trapezoidal mouth in the central Balkans: 1. Vinča; 2. Omoljica; 3. Židovar; 4. Moldova Veche; 5. Požarevac; 6. Bratinac; 7. Gornja Gorevnica; 8. Ostra; 9. Ljuljaci; 10. Sarina Međa; 11. Gloždak; 12. Orašje; 13. Poljna; 14. Maskare; 15. Lazarev Grad; 16. Trnjane; 17. Kučajna; 18. Bor; 19. Hajdučka Česma; 20. Podgorac; 21. Zvezdan; 22. Vitkovac; 23. Velika Humska Čuka; 24. Bubanj; 25. Medijana; 26. Kaštavar; 27. Svinjarička Čuka; 28. Jabuka.

such as the Paraćin and Brnjica groups, which 'inherited' the Bubanj-Hum IV–Ljuljaci group.

However, one ceramic element from this group that, among others, persisted significantly in the Late Bronze Age group mentioned s is the arched handles with plastic projections at the top, a distinctive ceramic element of the Bubanj-Hum IV–Ljuljaci group (Fig. 3.9/9, 11; Fig. 3.14/8; Fig. 3.23/11, 14; Fig. 3.27/23; Fig. 3.32/15, 18; Fig. 3.33/16, 17; Fig. 3.36/1; Fig. 3.38/12; Fig. 3.39/10, 11; Fig. 3.41/7, 8; Fig. 3.44/13; Fig. 3.48/1–3, 13, 14).

It should be noted that some stylistic-typological elements of the Bubanj-Hum IV–Ljuljaci group are also recognisable on the eastern edge of the central Balkans, in the western periphery of the Sofia Basin in present-day Bulgaria, at a Middle Bronze Age site in the village of Slivnitsa, which is dated to the 19th/18th century cal BC, approximately concurrent with the development of this group in the western part of the central Balkans (Mutafchieva *et al.* 2024). It is assumed that this reflects the synchronous development of this group in both regions, based on the interaction of these communities, as both groups are founded on the preceding Bubanj Hum III–Pelince–Pernik complex, which encompassed the southern part of the Central Balkans, including western Bulgaria.

According to the oldest known dates so far, the Brnjica group, which succeeded the Bubanj-Hum IV–Ljuljaci group in South Morava Basin, emerged during the second half of the 15th century BC, while the beginnings of the Paraćin group in Great Morava Valley and Timok Valley date somewhat earlier. The Paraćin group is considered the true successor of the so-called Timok variant of the Bubanj-Hum IV–Ljuljaci group, retaining many of its survivals.[32]

In the southernmost part of the central Balkans, south of the Grdelica Gorge, the situation is somewhat different. At several sites in the Skopje and Kumanovo Plains, the Moravica valley, and the Pčinja valley, the material culture is based on changes observed in this area at the end of the Early Bronze Age, influenced by elements of the Armenochori group. Certain ceramic forms from this region, such as bowls with gentle S- or biconical profiles (types 1b, 3c, and 3d), are also found in the Bubanj-Hum IV group, indicating the participation of the Armenochori group in its genesis. Unfortunately, the absolute chronology of this group in the southern central Balkans is unknown beyond the end of the Early Bronze Age, specifically the youngest graves at Ranutovac, dated to the 19th century cal BC. According to the stylistic-typological features of pottery from Kale (Fig. 2.31), Trnava (Fig. 3.45), and Lopate, these sites could be placed at the end of the Early and the beginning of the Middle Bronze Age, that is, in the period of the 20th–19th/18th centuries. It is interesting that these communities seemed to have inhabited only the lowland part of this territory, as sites of this group have not been recorded in the hilly-mountainous areas of this zone.

Due to the lack of archaeological data, it is not entirely clear what happened in this area in the interim. D. Mitrevski notes that there is insufficient information about the Middle Bronze Age in this area but suggests that the Armenochori (or Pelagonian group, according to Macedonian periodisation) likely persisted into the Middle Bronze Age (Mitrevski 2013, 180, 181), which aligns with our own view. During the Late Bronze Age, this region was also part of the Brnjica cultural group, more precisely, its southern periphery.

Notes

1 The Institute of Archaeology, Belgrade, conducted excavations at this site in the spring of 2023; however, the results have not yet been published.

2 The excavation of this site was conducted by the Institute of Archaeology, Belgrade, in the autumn of 2022 and spring of 2023, with results yet to be published.

3 I extend my thanks to the director of the research, O. Mladenović, for providing the data.

4 Described in more detail in Chapter 3.4.3.1/G.

5 The analysis was conducted by W. Powell from Brooklyn College, New York, and I would like to extend my gratitude to him for this information.

6 For further details on this axe and the conditions of its discovery, see Section 3.5, below.

7 The analysis was conducted by W. Powell from Brooklyn College, New York, to whom I extend my gratitude for the information provided.

8 The absolute dates were obtained from the Isotoptech Zrt. Laboratory in Debrecen, Hungary. I thank my colleague R. Gligorić for the information.

9 These forms and ornaments are one of the main characteristics of Middle Bronze Age pottery, especially in the northern parts of the central Balkans (Peri-Pannonia and the Great Morava Valley).

10 During the topographic analysis of map 1:25,000, section 531.3.2, and the site description, it was established that the broader area where the site Šljivik is located is called Reka.

11 I extend my thanks to my colleague G. Čađenović for the information and to my colleague M. Miladinović from the National Museum in Kruševac for providing the sample for dating.

12 In G. Čađenović's study (2009, fig. 2/2), this beaker is noted as having been discovered at Lazarov grad in Kruševac.

13 The site is actually situated immediately above 'Potkapina' on a narrow, oval, elevated prominence overlooking the Sikolska River, where no excavations have been conducted. Excavations were carried out at the Potkapina site, at the base of the elevation on its eastern side, where, among other things, fragments of Middle Bronze Age pottery were found.

14 This refers to rescue archaeological research conducted by the Institute for the Protection of Cultural Monuments in Niš in 2019. I take this opportunity to thank the project manager, A. Aleksić, for the information and for granting access to the material. Unfortunately, the trenches had to be opened along the gas pipeline route, which is located on the periphery of the settlement, yielding very few finds and no architectural remains.

15 Verbal communication with A. Kapuran, co-author of the excavation.

16 I extend my gratitude to W. Powell from Brooklyn College in New York, USA, for providing the analysis results.
17 The dates are in the process of publication. I thank one of the authors, A. Kapuran, for the information.
18 Of the three AMS analyses conducted, only two were successful (Table 1).
19 I extend my thanks to P. Milojević for the information provided.
20 This object is indeed dated to the second half of the 18th century; however, the material was partially mixed with finds from the Late Bronze Age, so it cannot be ruled out that these bowls (Fig. 3.41/1, 3) belong to that period. On the other hand, this type of handle has been dated at Velika Humska Čuka to the second half of the 16th century, indicating that it was in use as early as the Middle Bronze Age.
21 There are two dates from this necropolis. For the earlier date, see Kapuran *et al.* 2022. The later date is unpublished and dates grave 2 to the 13th/12th century.
22 For a more detailed discussion of residential architecture across specific stratigraphic phases, see the section on hilltop settlements of the Middle Bronze Age within the second geographical zone (the Great Morava Basin with Šumadija) in this book.
23 For an in-depth examination of ceramics, see the section on ritual spaces in the Early Bronze Age in this book.
24 Compare with the bowl typology of the Early Bronze Age (Chapter 2.1).
25 The analysis was conducted by J. Bulatović from the University of Gothenburg, Sweden, to whom I extend my gratitude for sharing the results.
26 The analysis was conducted by D. Filipović from the Institute for Pre- and Protohistory, Kiel University, Germany, to whom I express my gratitude for sharing the results.
27 The analysis was conducted by W. Powell from Brooklyn College, New York, to whom I extend my thanks for the information.
28 I extend my thanks to W. Powell from Brooklyn College, New York, USA, for the analysis results.
29 The term 'culture' has been used for decades to describe the Vatin group; however, in this book, the term is generally avoided as it is deemed overly pretentious and inadequate.
30 In recent Serbian literature, the term 'Žuto Brdo group' is increasingly used, while in Bulgaria and Romania, this group is treated terminologically in different ways.
31 Verbal communication from colleague A. Kapuran, to whom I extend my thanks.
32 The mentioned absolute dates for Brnjica and Paraćin group will be published soon.

Bibliography

Alexandrov, S. 2002. The late Bronze Age Settlement at Koprivlen. In: *Koprivlen* 1, eds A. Bozkova and P. Delev, 63–82. Sophia: NOUS.

Aleksandrov, S. (Александров, С.). 2009. Украшения за коса от злато и сребро през бронзовата епоха в Северна Блгария. *Археология* 50(1–2), 7–20.

Aleksić, A. and Filipović, V. (Алексић, А., Филиповић, В.). 2020. Бронзани бодеж и нож са трасе магистралног гасовода из околине Зајечара. *Етно-културолошки зборник* 23, 19–26.

Antonović, D. 2014. *Kupferzeitliche Äxte und Beile in Serbien.* Stuttgart: Prähistorische Bronzefunde 9(27).

Aslanis, I. 1985. *Kastanas, die Fruhbronzezeitlichen Funde und Befunde.* Berlin: Wissenschaftsverlag Volker Spiess.

Asouchidou, S. Mantazi, D. and Tsolakis, S. 1998. Tafikos tymvos P.E.H. sto Kriaritsi Sykias, N. Chalkidikis. Thessaloniki: *To Archaiologiko Ergo sti Makedonia kai sti Thraki* 12.

Bajenaru, R. 2014. *Sfârşitul Bronzului timpuriu în regiunea dintre Carpaţi şi Dunăre.* Cluj-Napoca: Editura Argonaut.

Blegen, C., Caskey, J., Rawson, M. and Sperling, J. 1950. *Troy: General introduction the first and second settlements.* Princeton NJ: Princeton University Press.

Blum, S. 2016. The final stages of the Early Bronze Age at Troy: Cultural development, chronology, and interregional contacts. In: *Early Bronze Age Troy: Chronology, cultural developments and interregional contacts*, eds E. Pernicka, S. Ünlüsoy and W. E. Blum, 89–122. Bonn: Habelt.

Bogdanović, M. (Богдановић, М.). 1986. *Љуљаци, насеље протовантинске и ватинске културе.* Крагујевац: Народни музеј, Крагујевац

Bona, I. 1975. *Die Mittlere Bronzezeit Ungarns und ihre Südöstilchen Beziehungen.* Budapest: Archaeologia Hungarica, NS 49.

Boroffka, N. 1994. *Die Wietenberg-Kultur* 1(2). Bonn: Habelt.

Božilova, E. and Tonkov, S. 2007. Paleoecological evidence of the main postglacial vegetation and climate changes in southwestern Bulgaria from the Neolithic to modern times. In: *The Struma/Strymon river Valley in Prehistory*, eds H. Todorova, M. Stefanovich and G. Ivanov, 531–534. Sofia: Gerde Henkel Stiftung.

Bulatović, A. (Булатовић, А.). 2000 Налазишта брњичке културне групе у Врањско - бујановачкој и Прешевској котлини. *Гласник Српског археолошког друштва* 15–16, 23–42.

Bulatović, A. 2020. *Ranutovac, an Early Bronze Age Necropolis in Southeastern Serbia.* Oxford: British Archaeological Report S2978.

Bulatović, A. Gori, M. and Vander Linden, M. 2020. Radiocarbon dating the 3rd millennium BC in the Central Balkans: A re-examination of the Early Bronze Age sequence. *Radiocarbon* 62(5), 1163–1191.

Bulatović, A. 2021. Beakers with trapezoidal mouth as one of the most specific types of Middle Bronze Age vessel in the Central Balkans. In: *Crafting Pottery in Bronze Age Europe*, eds V. Vučković, V. Filipović, B. Stojanović and R. Rich, 121–148. Paraćin: National Museum of Paraćin.

Bulatović A, Kapuran A. 2017. Cultural contacts between communities of southwestern Romania and the central Balkans in the fourth millennium BC, in: Cristian I. P. (ed.), The Carpathian Basin and the Northern Balkans between 3500 and 2500 BC: Common Aspects and Regional Differences, Annales Universitatis Apulensis: Series Historica, 20/II (2016), 183–201.

Bulatović, A. and Milanović, D. (Булатовић, А., Милановић, Д.) 2015. Велика хумска чука, истраживања 2009. године - прилог проучавању стратиграфије енеолита и бронзаног доба у југоисточној Србији, Гласник Српског археолошког друштва 30, Српско археолошко друштво, Београд, 163–188.

Bulatović, A. and Milanović, D. 2020. *Bubanj, the Eneolithic and the Early Bronze Age Tell in Southeastern Serbia.* Vienna: Mitteilungen der Prahistorischen Kommission 90.

Bulatović, A. and Milanović, D. 2021. The cultural and chronological context of sites of Bubanj and Velika Humska Čuka near Niš (southeastern Serbia) and their significance for understanding the emergence and development of the Central Balkans Eneolithic. *Циркумпонтика/Circumpontics* 2021(5), 36–64.

Bulatović, A. and Stankovski, J. (Булатовић, А., Станковски, Ј.). 2012. Бронзано доба у басену Јужне Мораве и у долини Пчиње/*Бронзено време во басенот на Јужна Морава и долината на Пчиња*. Куманово: Археолошки институт Београд и НУ Музеј,

Bulatović, A., Kapuran, A. and Janjić, G. (Булатовић, А., Капуран, А., Јањић, Г.). 2013 *Неготин, културна стратиграфија праисторијских локалитета у Неготинској Крајини*, Београд-Неготин: Археолошки институт, Београд, Музеј Крајине, Неготин.

Bulatović, A., Bizjak, D. and Vitezović, S. 2016. Early Bronze Age necropolis at the site of Meanište near Vranje. In: *Archaeological Investigations Along the Route of the E 75 Highway, 2011–2014,* eds S. Perić and A. Bulatović, 71–89, Belgrade: Institute of Archaeology.

Bulatović, A., Filipović, V. and Gligorić, R. (Булатовић, А., Филиповић, В., Глигорић, Р.). 2017. *Лозница, културна стратиграфија праисторијских локалитета у Јадру, Рађевини и Азбуковици*. Лозница: Археолошки институт, Београд, Центар за културу.

Bulatović, A., Gori, M. and Vander Linden, M. 2018a. New AMS dates as a contribution to the absolute chronology of the Early Eneolithic in the central Balkans. *Старинар* н.с. 68, 19–32.

Bulatović, A. Gori, M. and Vander Linden, M. 2018b. New absolute dates as a contribution to the study of the Late Bronze Age chronology in the Central Balkans. *Гласник САД* 34, 121–132.

Bulatović, A., Kapuran, A., Mladenović, O. and Milojević, P. 2023. Set of bronze jewellery from the site of Velika Humska Čuka near Niš, SE Serbia: A contribution to the study of interactions between Bronze Age communities of Central Europe and the Central Balkans. *Старинар* 73, 27–51.

Čađenović, G. (Чађеновић, Г.). 2003. Гологлава код Сталаћа, градинско насеље из металног доба. *Крушевачки зборник* 9/10, 44–72.

Čađenović, G. (Чађеновић, Г.). 2009. Налазишта ватинске културне групе у зони става Јужне Мораве и Западне Мораве. *Крушевачки зборник* 14, 161–179.

Cenev, G. 2009. The role of the Kokino megalith in the life of the Bronze age agricultural community. In: *The Role of Astronomy in Society and Culture*, eds. D. Valls-Gabaud and A. Boksenberg, 1–15. Cambridge: Cambridge University Press

Crăciunescu, G. 2004. *Cultura Verbicoara în jumătatea vestică a Olteniei*. Craiova: Bibliotheca Thracologica Craiova: Editura MJM.

Cwaliński, M., Filipović, V., Bulatović, A., Kaur, S., Stout, E. and Gligorić, R. 2023. Paulje, mound XI (mound K): New AMS dates and provenience of the earliest amber finds in Serbia. *Prilozi Instituta za arheologiju u Zagrebu* 40(1), 75–97.

Dmitrović, K. (Дмитровић, К.). 2009. Насеље раног бронзаног доба на налазишту Слатина у Горњој Горевници код Чачка. *Зборник Народног музеја* 19(1), 103–117.

Dmitrović, K. and Ljuština, M. (Дмитровић, К., Љуштина, М.). 2007. Керамика из бронзаног доба на локалитету Соколица у Остри код Чачка. *Зборник радова Народног музеја* 337, 11–34.

Ercegović Pavlović, S. and Kostić, D. (Ерцеговић-Павловић, С., Костић, Д.). 1988. *Археолошки споменици и налазишта лесковачког краја*. Београд: Археолошки институт, Београд, Народни музеј, Лесковац.

Filipović, V. (Филиповић, В.). 2022. Бронзани бодеж са локалитета Стража код Жагубице. *Етно-културолошки зборник* 25, 37–42.

Filipović, V. and Milojević, P. 2015. A Minoan (?) dagger from Lipovačko Gradište (Central Balkans). *Караџић* 7, 16–25.

Gagić, G. (Гагиќ, Г.). 1984. Археолошки комплекс Суводол, локалитет Анови – II. *Зборник на трудови* 4–5, 21–32.

Garašanin, D. (Гарашанин, Д.). 1954. *Каталог метала* 1. Београд: Народни музеј.

Garašanin, M. (Гарашанин, М.). 1973. *Праисторија на тлу Србије*. Београд: Српска књижевна задруга.

Garašanin, M. and Stojić, M. (Гарашанин, М., Стојић, М.). 1986. Ђула у Остриковцу – градинско насеље из металног доба. *Гласник Српског археолошког друштва* 3, 192–194.

Garašanin, M., Ajdić, R. and Dejanović, D. (Гарашанин М., Ајдић Р., Дејановић, Д.). 1971. *Праисторијске културе Поморавља и источне Србије*. Ниш: каталог изложбе, Народни музеј.

Gori, M. 2015. *Along the Rivers and Through the Mountains*. Bonn: Habelt.

Greenfield, H. 1986. Summary report on the Vertebrate fauna from Novačka ćuprija, *Зборник Народног музеја* 12(1), 63–74.

Greenfield, H. 2006. The social and economic context for domestic horse origins in southeastern Europe. In: *Horses and Humans: The evolution of human-equine relationships*, eds S. Olsen, S. Grant, A.m M. Choyke and L. Bartosiewicz, 221–244. Oxford: Archaeopress.

Hänsel, B. 1968. *Beiträge zur ur- und frühgeschichtlichen archäologie des mittelmeer–kuturraumes*. Bonn: Habelt.

Hänsel, B. and Aslanis, I. 2010. *Das Prahistorische Olynth, ausgrabungen in der Toumba Agios Mamas 1994–1996*. Rahden/Westfahlen: Marie Leidorf.

Hänsel, B. and Medović, P. 1991. *Vorbericht uber die jugoslawich-deutschen Ausgrabungen in der Siedlung von Feudvar bei Mošorin (Gem. Titel, Vojvodina) von 1986–1990.* Mainz am Rhein: Sondedruck aus Bericht der Romisch-Germanischen Kommission 72.

Heurtley, W. A. 1939. *Prehistoric Macedonia*. Cambridge: Cambridge University Press.

Hochstetter, A. 1984. *Kastanas, die Handgemachte Keramik*. Berlin: Prähistoriche Archaeologie in Sudosteuropa 3.

Horejs, B., Bulatović, A., Meyer, C., Milić, B., Schneider, S., Schlöffel, M. and Stevanović, V. 2018. Prehistoric landscapes of the Pusta Reka river (Leskovac), new investigations along the Southern Morava River. *Гласник САД* 34, 23–51.

Horejs, B., Bulatović, A., Bulatović, J., Brandl, M., Burke, C., Filipović, D. and Milić, B. 2019. New insights into the later stage of the Neolithisation process of the Central Balkans. First excavations at Svinjarička Čuka 2018. *Archaeologia Austriaca*, 175–226.

Horejs, B., Bulatović, A., Bulatović, J., Burke, C., Brandl, M., Dietrich, L., Filipović, D., Milić, B. Mladenović, O., Schinnerl, N., Schroedter, T. and Webster, L. 2022. New multi-disciplinary data from the Neolithic in Serbia. The 2019 and 2021 excavation at Svinjarička Čuka. *Archaeologia Austriaca* 103, 175–226.

Jevtić, M. 1975. Trasa puta motel Medijana, Niška Banja – eneolitsko i bronzano doba. *Arheološki pregled* 17, 26–28.

Jevtić, M. (Јевтић, М.). 1990. Праисторијска некропола у Пироту. Прилог познавању брњичке групе. *Гласник САД* 6, 92–103.

Jordović, C. and Jurišić, A. (Јордовић, Ч., Јуришић, А.). 1970. Резултати археолошких испитивачких радова у Крушевцу (период 1961–1962. године), *Саопштења* 9, 3–12.

Jovanović, B. 1961. Pojava keramike vatinskog tipa na vinčanskom naselju. *Vesnik* 1–2, 5–14.

Jovanović, B. 1971a. *Metalurgija eneolitskog perioda Jugoslavije*. Beograd: Arheološki institut.

Jovanović, B. (Јовановић, Б.). 1971b. Праисторија Горњег Ђердапа. *Старинар* н.с. 22, 1–18.

Jovanović, B. 1999. Funerary rites and tomb constructions in necropoles of the Paraćin and Donja Brnjica Cultures. In: *Macedonia and the Neighbouring Regions from 3rd to 1st Milenium* [sic] *b.c.*, ed. E. Petrova, 62–72. Skopje: Museum of Macedonia

Jovanović, B. and Janković, I. 1990. Nekropola paraćinske grupe u Trnjanima kod Brestovačke banje. *Zbornik radova muzeja rudarstva i metalurgije u Boru* 5/6, 1–20.

Jovanović, S. (Јовановић, С.). 1987. Праисторијски локалитети књажевачког краја. *Гласник Српског археолошког друштва* 4, 120–124.

Kalicz-Schreiber, R. 2010. *Ein Gräberfeld der Spätbronzezeit von Budapest-Békásmegyer.* Budapest: Institut für Archäologische Wissenschaften Eótvós Loránd Universität Budapest.

Kapuran, A. (Капуран, А.). 2009. О утицајима Ватина и Вербичоаре на налазима гамзиградске културне групе. *Старинар* н.с. 59, 53–69.

Kapuran, A. 2011. Relationship between settlements and necropolis of the Bronze Age in eastern Serbia. In: *Bronze Age Rites and Rituals in the Carpathian Basin*, eds S. Berecki, R. Nemeth and B. Rezi, 9–20. Targu Mureş: Editura MEGA.

Kapuran, A. 2014. *Praistorijski lokaliteti u severoistočnoj Srbiji.* Beograd: Arheološki institut.

Kapuran, A. 2019. *Velebit, Tumulus Culture Necropolis in the Southern Carpatian Basin (Vojvodina, Serbia).* Oxford: British Archaeological Report S2942.

Kapuran, A. and Bulatović, A. (Капуран, А., Булатовић, А.). 2012a. Праисторијски локалитети у долинама Сврљишког Тимока, Трговишког Тимока и Белог Тимока. *Гласник Српског археолошког друштва* 28, 107–132.

Kapuran, A. and Bulatović, A. (Капуран, А., Булатовић, А.). 2012b. Културна група Коцофени-Костолац на територији источне Србије, *Старинар* н.с. 62, 63–94.

Kapuran, A. and Janjić, G. (Капуран, А., Јањић, Г.). 2015. Стратиграфија археолошког комплекса Мокрањске стене. У: *Мокрањске стене, културна баштина Неготинске Крајине, Зборник радова*, ур. А. капуран и А. Булатовић, 9–22. Неготин: Музеј Крајине.

Kapuran, A. and Škundrić, J. (Капуран, А., Шкундрић, Ј.). 2009. Резултати систематских рекогносцирања локалитета Ромулијана 2008/9. Године. *Саопштења* 41, 245–263.

Kapuran, A., Bulatović, A. and Jovanović, I. (Капуран, А., Булатовић, А., Јовановић, И.). 2014. *Бор и Мајданпек, културна стратиграфија праисторијских локалитета између Ђердапа и Црног Тимока.* Београд-Бор: Археолошки институт, Београд Музеј рударства и металургије, Бор.

Kapuran, A., Gavranović, M. and Jovanović, I. 2022. Bronze Age burials within the Morava, Nišava and Timok basins. *Starinar* n.s.72, 45–71.

Kapuran, A., Gavranović, M. and Mehofer, M. 2020. Bronze age settlement and necropolis of Trnjane, near Bor – revision and new researche results. *Старинар* 70, 51–84.

Kapuran, A., Miladinović-Radmilović, N. and Vuković, N. 2017. Funerary traditions of the Bronze Age metallurgical communities in the Iron Gates Hinterland. In: *Late Urnfeld Culture Between the Southern Alps and the Danube*, ed. D. Ložnjak-Dizdar, 131–141. Zagreb: Institute of Archaeology.

Kapuran, A., Živković, D. and Štrbac, N. 2016. New evidence for prehistoric copper metallurgy in the vicinity of Bor. *Старинар* н.с. 66, 173–191.

Kilian-Dilmeier, I. 1975. *Gürtelhalken, Gürtelbleche und Blechgürtel der Bronzezeit in Mitteleuropa.* München: Prähistorische Bronzefunde 12(2).

Kiss, B. 2012. *Middle Bronze Age Encrusted Pottery in Western Hungary.* Budapest: Archaeolingua.

Krstić, D., Stalio, B., Garašanin, D., Galović, R., Pavlović, K. and Miletić, M. (Крстић, Д., Сталио, Б., Гарашанин, Д., Галовић, Р., Павловић, К., Милетић, М.). 1972. *Бронзано доба Србије.* Београд: каталог изложбе, Народни музеј.

Lazić, M. (Лазић, М.). 1996. *Култура Доња Брњица – генеза, развој и хронологија.* (Unpublished PhD dissertation) непубликована докторска дисертација одбрањена на Филозофском факултету у Београду.

Lazić, M. (Лазић, М.). 1998. Гамзиградска култура, последње откриће Драгослава Срејовића. У: *Рад Драгослава Срејовића на истраживању праисторије централног Балкана*, ур. Н. Тасић, 147–158. Крагујевац: Центар за научна истраживања САНУ у Крагујевцу.

Lazić, M. (Лазић, М.). 2007. Хумка из бронзаног доба на локалитету Савин лакат код Пријепоља. *Археика* 1, 109–130.

Lazić, M. 2010. Prehistoric settlements and necropoles at Gamzigrad and in its surroundings. In: *Felix Romuliana Gamzigrad*, ed. I. Popović, 21–27. Belgrade: University of Belgrade.

Lazić, M. 2016. Magura – la Nécropole de l'Âge du Bronze â Gamzigrad à l'Est de la Serbie. In: *Funerary Practices During the Bronze and Iron Ages in Central and Southeast Europe*, eds V. Sirbiu, M. Jevtić, K. Dmitrović and M. Ljuština, 29–42. Beograd-Čačak: University of Belgrade.

Ljuština, M. 2012. Stratigrafija naselja i periodizacija vatinske kulture u Vojvodini. (Unpublished PhD dissertation) neobjavljena doktorska disertacija odbranjena na Filozofskom fakultetu u Beogradu.

Ljuština, M. (Љуштина, М.). 2022. *Изазови средњег бронзаног доба: ватинска култура и балкански суседи.* Београд: Филозофски факултет.

Ljuština, M. and Dmitrović, K. 2009. The Bronze age Vatin culture in the West Morava basin – case study of Sokolica in Ostra. *Studia Archaeologiae et Historiae Antiquae*, 53–63.

Machnik, J. 1991. *The Earliest Bronze Age in the Carpathian Basin.* Bradford: Bradford University.

Mason, A. H., Powell, W. G., Bankoff, H. A. Mathur, R., Bulatović, A., Filipović, V. and Ruiz, J. 2016. Tin isotope characterization of bronze artifacts of the central Balkans. *Journal of Archaeological Science* 69, 110–117.

Mason, A., Powell, W., Bankoff, H. A., Mathur, R., Price, M., Bulatović, A. and Filipović, V. 2020. Provenance of tin in the

Late Bronze Age Balkans based on probabilistic and spatial analysis of Sn isotopes. *Journal of Archaeological Science* 122, 1051–1081.

Medović, P. and Medović, I. 2010. *Gradina na Bosutu, naselje starijeg gvozdenog doba.* Novi Sad: Platoneum.

Mehofer, M., Gavranović, M., Kapuran, A., Mitrović, J. and Putica, A. 2021. Copper production and supra-regional exchange networks – Cu-matte smelting in the Balkans between 2000 and 1500 BC. *Journal of Archaeological Science* 129 (105378).

Milanović, D, and Bulatović, A. (Милановић, Д., Булатовић, А.). 2011. Хоризонт бронзаног доба на налазишту Песак код Пригревице. *Рад Музеја Војводине* 53, 9–90.

Milojević, P. and Kapuran, A. (Милојевић, П., Капуран, А.). 2023. Резултати истраживања праисторијске градине на Поповици код Сокобање. *Зборник Народног музеја Србије-археологија* 26(1), 65–92.

Milojević, P. and Trajković-Filipović, T. (Милојевић, П., Трајковић-Филиповић, Т.). 2017. *Праисторијска налазишта у Алесиначкој котлини.* Алексинац: Завичајни музеј/Ниш: Народни музеј.

Mitrevski, D. 2003. Prehistory in Republic of Macedonia-F.Y.R.O.M. In: *Recent Research in the Prehistory of the Balkans*, ed. D.V. Grammenos,13–72. Thessaloniki: Archaeological Institute of Northern Greece.

Mitrevski, D. (Митревски, Д.). 2013. Праисторија на Република Македонија. Y: *Македонија, миленијумски културно-историски факти,* ур. Е. Димитрова, Ј. Донев, П. Кузман, 83–266. Скопје: Медиа принт Македонија и Евробалкан.

Mitrevski, D. 2016. *Skopje Fortress – Kale, from Prehistory to the Early Ancient period.* Скопје: ПНВ Публикации.

Mutafchieva, Y., Dimitrova, V. and Ilieva, D. (Мутафчиева, Я., Димитрова, В., Илиева Д.). 2024. Обект от средната бронзова епоха в землището на град Сливница, Област София. *Известия на Регионален исторически музей – Перник*, 123–147.

Nacev, T. (Нацев, Т.). 2009. *Трите керамитки-резултати од заштитните археолошки истрашувања Злетовица 2007–2009.* Штип: Национална установа Завод за заштита на споменициte на културата и Музеј Штип

Nikitović, L. (Никитовић, Л.). 1995. Археолошки локалитети старијег неолита у околини Чачка. *Археолошка радионица* 2. Параћин. Завичајни музеј, Параћин.

O'Shea, J., Parditka, G., Nikodemus, A., Kristiansen, K., Sjögren, K.-G., Paja, L., Pálfi, G. and Milašinović, L. 2019. Social formation and collapse in the Tiza-Maros region: Dating the Maros Group and its Late Bronze Age successors. *Antiquity* 93(369), 604–623.

Palavestra, A. and Bankoff, A. 1986. Pozlatska reka. *Arheološki pregled* 26, 67–68.

Peković, M. and Jevtić, M. (Пековић, М., Јевтић, М.). 2006. Сондажна археолошка истраживања налазишта Кадијсаки крст код Књажевца. *Гласник САД* 22, 111–122.

Pernicka, E., Begemann, F., Schmitt-Strecker, S. and Wagner, G. A. 1993. Eneolithic and Early Age copper artefacts from the Balkans and their relation to Serbian copper ores. *Praehistorische Zeitschrift* 68(1), 1–19.

Popović, P. (Поповић, П.). 1983. Манастир-Господјин вир, праисторијско налазиште, *Старинар* н.с. 33–34, 151.

Powell, W. G., Mathur, R., Bankoff, H. A. Mason, A. H., Bulatović, A., Filipović, V. and Godfrey, L. 2017. Digging deeper: Insights into metallurgical transitions in European prehistory through copper isotopes. *Journal of Archaeological Science* 88, 37–46.

Radojčić, N. (Радојчић, Н.). 2013. *Златица у Омољици и Најева циглана у Војловици код Панчева, керамички налази бронзаног доба.* Београд: Народни музеј.

Renfrew, C. and Bahn P. 1991. *Archaeology: Theories, methods and practice.* London: Thames and Hudson.

Roman, P. 2006. Preuves concernant les mouvements ethno-culturels de l'est á l'ouest et du sud au nord, dans la haute période de l'age du bronze, résultées des recherches faites á Ostrovul Corbului. In: *Homage to Milutin Garašanin*, ed. N. Tasić, 455–468. Belgrade: Serbian Academy of Sciences and Arts.

Rujak, Z. 2020. *Carevi Kuli, From Prehistory to the Roman Empire.* Strumica: National Institution for Protection of Cultural Monuments and Museum.

Sanev, V. 1999. Pottery in favour of designating the cultural borders of the Early Bronze Age in Macedonia. In: *Macedonia and the Neighbouring Regions from 3rd to 1st Milenium* [sic] *b.c.*, ed. E. Petrova, 127–136. Skopje: Museum of Macedonia

Schuster, C. 2003. Zur Bestattungsweise in Südrumäniem in der Bronzezeit. In: *Sahranjivanje u bronzano i gvozdeno doba*, ed. R. Vasić, 109–130. Čačak: Narodni muzej; Arheološki Institut

Simoska, D. (Симоска, Д.). 1984. Висок рид, праисториjска повекеслојна населба (прелиминарен извештај). *Зборник на трудови* 4–5, 5–20.

Srejović, D. (Срејовић, Д.). 2002. *Илири и Трачани.* Београд: Српска књижевна задруга.

Srejović, D. and Lazić, M. (Срејовић, Д., Лазић, М.). 1997. Насеља и некрополе бронзаног доба у Тимочкој крајини, У: Археологија источне Србије, 225–247. Београд: Универзитет у Београду.

Stanković, S. 1988. Šljivik – Stragari, Trstenik. In: *The Neolithic of Serbia,* ed. D. Srejović, 95–97. Belgrade: Belgrade University.

Stankovski, J. (Станковски, Ј.). 2002. Татикев Камен – мегалитска опсерваторија и светилиште. *Музејски гласник* 7–9, 29–48.

Stankovski, J. (Станковски, Ј.). 2003. Три мегалитни споменици во кумановскиот регион. *Пирајхме* 2, 229–262.

Stankovski, J. (Станковски, Ј.) (ed.). 2007 *Кокино, тврдина на сонцето*, каталог изложбе. Куманово: Национална установа Музеј Куманово.

Stankovski, J. (Станковски, Ј.). 2010. Прилог кон проучување на обредната практика на локалитетот Татиќев Камен, село Кокино. *Macedoniae Acta Archaeologica* 19, 115–125.

Stojić, M. (Стојић, М.). 1980. *Старе културе и народи на тлу средњег Поморавља.* Светозарево: Завичајни музеј Светозарево.

Stojić, M. (Стојић, М.). 1986. Праисторијско насеље Вецина мала у Мајуру код Светозарева. *Старинар* н.с. 37, 145–152.

Stojić, M. (Стојић, М.). 1989. Праисторијско налазиште Ђула у Остриковцу код Светозарева. *Balcanica* 20, 171–183.

Stojić, M. (Стојић, М.). 1992. Налазишта ватинске културне групе у средњем Поморављу. *Зборник Народног музеја* 14(1), 213–220.

Stojić, M. (Стојић, М.). 1998. Lieux de trouvaille de la ceramique de type Vatin en Serbie au sud de la Save et du Danube. In:

Die Kulturen der Bronzezeit in dem Gebiet des Eisernen Tores, 81–104. Bukarest: S. C. Vavila Edinf SR.

Stojić, M. (Стојић, М.). 2001. Брњичка културна група у басену Јужне Мораве. *Лесковачки зборник* 41, 15–94.

Stojić, M. 2011. Maskare, Bedem Site. Contribution to the research of foundations of cultures: Of ostrikovac and two-handled beakers. Y: *Златното пето хилядолетие*, ред. Я. Бояджиев, С. Игнатова, 313–327. София: Българска Академия на науките, Национален Археологически институт с Музей.

Stojić, M. and Cerović, M. (Стојић, М., Церовић, М.). 2011. *Шабац, културна стратиграфија праисторијских локалитета у Подрињу.* Београд–Шабац: Археолошки институт, Београд Народни музеј, Шабац.

Stojić, M. and Čađenović, G. (Стојић, М., Чађеновић, Г.). 2006. *Крушевац, културна стратиграфија праисторијских локалитета у зони става Западне Мораве и Јужне Мораве.* Београд–Крушевац: Археолошки институт, Београд Народни музеј, Крушевац.

Stojić, M. and Ilijić, B. (Стојић, М., Илијић Б.). 2011. *Књажевац, културна стратиграфија праисторијских локалитета књажевачког краја.* Београд: Археолошки институт Београд, Завичајни музеј Књажевац.

Stojić, M. and Jacanović, D. (Стојић, М., Јацановић, Д.). 2008. *Пожаревац, културна стратиграфија праисторијских локалитета у Браничеву.* Београд: Археолошки институт Београд, Народни музеј Пожаревац.

Stojić, M. and Jocić, M. (Стојић, М., Јоцић, М.). 1993. Метално доба у Лесковачкој котлини. *Лесковачки зборник* 33, 291–306.

Stojić, M. and Jocić, M. (Стојић, М., Јоцић, М.). 2006. *Ниш-културна стратиграфија праисторијских локалитета у нишкој регији.* Београд-Ниш: Археолошки институт, Београд Народни музеј, Ниш.

Tasić, N. 1969. Zlotska pećina – višeslojno praistorijsko nalazište. *Arheološki pregled* 11, 36–39.

Tasić, N. 1980. Metalni nalazi izZlotske pećine. *Zbornik muzeja rudarstva i metalurgije* 1, 43–61.

Tasić, N. (Тасић, Н.). 1983. *Југословенско Подунавље од Индоевропске сеобе до продора Скита.* Нови Сад-Београд: Матица Српска и Балканолошки институт САНУ.

Tasić, N. 1984. Die Vatin-Kultur. In: *Kulturen der Fruhbronzezeit des Karpatenbeckens und Nordbalkans*, ed. N. Tasić, 59–81. Beograd: Balkanološki institut SANU

Tasić, N. (Тасић, Н.). 2001 *Праисторијске културе и налазишта на подручју.* Крушевца. *Археолошка налазишта Крушевца и околине*, 7–19. Народни музеј, Крушевац Балканолошки институт САНУ, Београд.

Tasić, N. 2004. Historical picture of development of Bronze Age cultures in Vojvodina. *Старинар* н.с. 53–54, 23–34.

Tasić, H. and Tomić, E. 1969. *Crnokalačka bara, naselje starčevačke i vinčanske kulture.* Kruševac-Beograd: Narodni muzej, Kruševac, Arheološko društvo Jugoslavije.

Tasić, H. and Tomić, E. (Тасић, Н., Томић, Е.). 1987. Археолошка ископавања у долини доњег тока Западне Мораве и проблеми етногенезе Дарданаца. *Гласник Српског археолошког друштва* 4, 129–136.

Trajkovska, L. (Трајковска, Л.). 1995. Рано бронзено светилиште кај селото Пелинце. Y: *каталог изложбе*, ур. Б. Таневски. Куманово: Народни музеј у Куманову.

Trajkovska, L. (Трајковска, Л.). 1999. Градиште-Пелинце, истражување на секторот Две Могили. *Macedoniae acta archaeologica* 15, 47–61.

Trajkovska, L. (Трајковска, Л.). 2003. Светилиште од раното бронзено доба на лок. 'Градиште' во село Пелинце кај Куманово. *Пирајхме* 2, 289–297.

Vasić, M. (Васић, М.). 1936a. *Преисториска Винча* 2. Београд: Državna štamparija

Vasić, M. (Васић, М.). 1936b. *Преисториска Винча* 4. Београд: Državna štamparija

Vasić, R. and Janković, Đ. 1971. Desna obala Dunava od Kladova do Prahova. *Arheološki pregled* 13, 107–116.

Vukmanović, M. and Popović, P. (Вукмановић, М., Поповић, П.). 1984. Ливаде, Мала Врбица. *Ђердапске свеске* 2, 85–92.

Vukmanović, M. and Popović, P. 1986. Recherches archeologiques sur la localite 'Livade' pres de Mala Vrbica. *Đerdapske sveske* 3, 7–25.

Vukmanović, M. and Radojčić, N. (Вукмановић, М., Радојчић, Н.). 1995. *Каталог метала* 2. Београд: Народни музеј.

Vulpe, A. 1970. *Die Äxte und Beile in Rumänien.* München: Prähistorische Bronzefunde 9(2).

Webster, D., Evans, S. T. and Sanders, T. W. 1997. *Out of the Past: An introduction to archaeology*, London: Mayfield.

Wels-Weyrauch, U. 2015. *Die Dolche in Bayern.* Frankfurt am Main: Prahistorische Bronzefunde 6(15).

4

Absolute chronology of the Early and Middle Bronze Age of the central Balkans

In the introductory section to this book, on the chronology of the Bronze Age in the Balkans, some chronologies used in Serbian literature over the past few decades were mentioned. Unfortunately, there were almost no absolute dates and for the few that existed, the margin of error was too large, up to 300 years, making these dates, with outdated calibration, of little help. Today, after decades of studying the Bronze Age, thanks to several scientific projects the situation has drastically changed, with more than 100 absolute dates from the Early and Middle Bronze Age available. This has enabled the creation of a periodisation for this period, based not on relative but absolute chronology. Some of these dates are not presented here due to copyright restrictions, as they are already in the process of publication in a relevant journal. The absolute dating was facilitated through numerous projects, a few of which are highlighted here: *THE FLOW – Interactions-Transmission-Transformation: Long-distance connections in Copper and Bronze Age of the Central Balkans*, funded by the Science Fund of the Republic of Serbia (Program IDEAS, Grant no. 7750074); *Prehistoric Landscapes of the Pusta Reka Region (Leskovac)*, funded by the Austrian Archaeological Institute, Vienna; *New Insight in Bronze Age Metal Producing Societies*, funded by the Austrian Science Fund (FWF-Project 32096_G25); *Archaeological Research of the Site of Velika Humska Čuka, in Hum near Niš (SE Serbia)*, funded by the Ministry of Culture of the Republic of Serbia; *Rewriting Early Bronze Age Chronology in the southwestern Balkans: Evidence from large-scale radiocarbon dating*, funded by the Fritz Thyssen Fund, among others.

The AMS absolute dates come from different laboratories, the most numerous being from the Isotoptech ZRT Laboratory in Debrecen (lab code DeA) and the Curt-Engelhorn-Zentrum Archäometrie gGmbH laboratory (l MAMS). However, dates from many other laboratories are also represented, such as: Oxford Radiocarbon Accelerator Unit (OxA); Institut Royal du Patrimoine Artistique, Brussels (RICH); Institut für Isotopenforschung und Kernphysik, University of Vienna (VERA); Christian-Albrechts-Universität, Kiel (KIA); Beta Analytic Inc., Miami (Beta); Scottish Universities Environmental Research Centre (SUERC); and Centre de Datation par le RadioCarbone, Lyon (Ly). Older dates from decades ago, conducted using classical radiocarbon analysis, come from the Brooklyn College Radiocarbon Dating Laboratory (BC) and the Ruđer Bošković Institute in Zagreb (Z).

All sets of dates for individual phases of the Bronze Age within the geographical zones and specific cultural groups presented in this chapter (Table 1). Calibration and further Bayesian modelling were performed using OxCal 4.4, with a probability of 68.3% (Bronk Ramsey 2009), using Intcal 20 (Reimer *et al.* 2020).

4.1 Absolute dating of the Early Bronze Age by geographical zones

4.1.1 The peri-Pannonian zone

According to absolute dates and the cultural characteristics of communities during the Early Bronze Age in the peri-Pannonian zone, this period can be defined through three chronological phases. The first would be defined by communities with Eneolithic traditions in material and spiritual culture; the second by the bearers of the Vinkovci–Somogyvár cultural group; and the third phase would consist of communities of the so-called Novačka Ćuprija–Pančevo group.

Absolute dates and Bayesian modelling have shown that in the Early Bronze Age, the peri-Pannonian zone had communities with traditions of Eneolithic cultures

Table 1. Absolute dates for the Early and Middle Bronze Ages sites in the Central Balkans (Key: PP peri-Pannonian zone; GM Great Morava Valley with Šumadija; WS West Serbia zone; ES Timok Valley with Đerdap Gorge and SM South Morava Valley with Pčinja)

No	Village/Site	Context	Lab. code	Date BP	Date cal BC	Date cal BC (95.4%) (OxCal 4.4.)	Sample	Reference	Zone	Map No.	Plot code
	EARLY BRONZE AGE										
a	Vojlovica, Rafinerija	grave 1	Poz-88701	4290±35	2920–2885 (68.2%)	3012–2875	Human bone	Koledin *et al.* 2020	PP	*a*	VO
b	Jabuka, Tri humke	grave 1	Poz-93213	4100±45	2851–2578 (68.2%)	2872–2496	Human bone	Koledin *et al.* 2020	PP	*b*	JA
c	Pančevo, Livade	grave 12	Poz-81208	4050±40	2828–2491 (68.2%)	2847–2469	Human bone	Koledin *et al.* 2020	PP	*c*	PA
1	Jančići, Veliko polje	mound 1, central grave, inhumation	MAMS 31474	4119±15	2849–2627 (68.2%)	2859–2581	Human bone	Bulatović *et al.* 2020	WS	42	VP1
2	Hum, Velika Humska Čuka	sonda I/16s, structure 6a	MAMS 31475	4103±16	2696–2578 (68.5%)	2850–2577	Animal bone	Bulatović *et al.* 2020	SM	77	VHC6a
3	Jančići, Dubac	mound 1, grave 6	OxA-41189	4018±20	2576–2472 (95.4%)	2577–2472	Human bone	Dmitrović & Molloy 2021	WS	43	DU6
4	Krstac, Ivkovo Brdo	mound 1, stone cist, incineration	RICH 24515	3958±31	2570–2400 (68.2%)	2572–2345	Cremated human bone	Bulatović *et al.* 2020	WS	54	KR6
5	Majilovac, Marjansko brdo	structure 45	DeA 44839	3906±20	2466–2339 (93.7%)	2467–2304	Animal bone	This study	PP	7	MB45
6	Štulac, Svinjarička čuka	inhumation	VERA-8173	3898±31	2469–2288 (95.4%)	2469–2289	Human tooth	Horejs *et al.* forthcoming	SM	86	SCgr
7	Dučalovići, Ruja	mound 12, inhumation	MAMS 31473	3892±16	2455–2348 (68.2%) 2464–2335 (89.2%)	2462–2299	Human bone	Bulatović *et al.* 2020	WS	50	RU12
8	Ostrikovac, Đula	E2, trench 3, pit III	DeA-32271	3886±26	2411–2342 (61.4%)	2465–2288	Animal bone	This study	GM	22	OS
9	Hum, Velika Humska Čuka	layer with exclusively BH III pottery	MAMS 31477	3885±16	2454–2344 (68.2%) 2462–2332 (84.2%)	2459–2297	Animal bone	Bulatović *et al.* 2020	SM	77	VHC
10	Braljina, Smrdan	material from modern clay pit	DeA-32273	3871±24	2350–2293 (51.7%)	2461–2211	Bone awl	This study	SM	80	BR
11	Štulac, Svinjarička Čuka	SU 20	MAMS 40139	3857±21	2434–2236 (68.2%)	2456–2208	Emmer grain	Horejs *et al.* 2019	SM	86	SC20
12	Pelince, Dve Mogili	ritual space, zone III, sq. Б28	MAMS 31472	3843±22	2344–2211 (68.2%) 2351–2204 (80.8%)	2452–2203	Animal bone	Bulatović *et al.* 2020	SM	93	PE
13	Lučani, Suva Česma	mound, incineration	RICH 24503	3831±30	2340–2200 (68.2%) 2460–2190 (94.2%)	2453–2149	Cremated human bone	Bulatović *et al.* 2020	WS	49	SC1
14	Štulac, Svinjarička Čuka	SU 140	MAMS 54201	3814±23	2289–2204 (68.2%)	2343–2146	Seed	Horejs *et al.* 2022	SM	86	SC140

(Continued)

No	Village/Site	Context	Lab. code	Date BP	Date cal BC	Date cal BC (95.4%) (OxCal 4.4.)	Sample	Reference	Zone	Map No.	Plot code
15	Grčac, Novačka ćuprija	pit 2 (semi-pithouse)	Beta 2572	3800±330	2860–1765 (68%) 3105–1436 (94.3%)	3318–1436	?	Krstić *et al.* 1986; Nikolova 1999	PP	8	NĆ2
16	Štulac, Svin-jarička Čuka	SU 45	MAMS 46942	3785±22	2281–2146 (68.2%)	2289–2141	Seed	Horejs *et al.* 2022	SM	86	SC45
17	Majur, Vecina mala	trench 1/86, pit in W sector	DeA-42050	3778±47	2240–2138 (70%)	2401–2035	Animal bone	This study	GM	27	VM
18	Hum, Velika Humska Čuka	E 203/2, trench 1/22, feature 16	DeA-42046	3772±34	2209–2139 (70%)	2296–2040	Animal bone	This study	SM	77	VHC2
19	Štulac, Svin-jarička Čuka	SU 1024	MAMS 46945	3770±22	2274–2142 (68.2%)	2287–2062	Seed	Horejs *et al.* 2022	SM	86	SC1024
20	Novo Selo, Bubanj	structure 91	MAMS 31461	3718±22	2191–2044 (68.2%)	2199–2033	Animal bone	Bulatović *et al.* 2020	SM	83	BU91
21	Ranutovac, Meanište	Trench 8, grave 3	RICH -24516	3701±31	2140–2030 (68.2%) 2200–2010 (93.1%)	2200–1979	Cremated human bone	Bulatović *et al.* 2020	SM	92	RA3
22	Jančići, Dubac	mound 2, grave 4	OxA-41292	3679±20	2140–2016 (87.4%)	2140–1977	Human bone	Dmitrović & Molloy 2021	WS	43	JA4
23	Viminacium, Nad klepečkom	Trench 77, structure 9	DeA-14239	3652±30	2040–1965 (79.6%)	2137–1940	Animal bone (Bos taurus)	Kapuran *et al.* 2019	PP	5	NK9
24	Novo Selo, Bubanj	structure 20: garbage pit	SUERC 61530	3648±32	2120–1950 (68.2%)	2137–1931	Animal bone (Equus Sp.)	Bulatović & Vander Linden 2017	SM	83	BU20
25	Ranutovac, Meanište	Trench 13, grave 21	RICH -24542	3644±31	2040–1950 (62.7%)	2136–1924	Cremated human bone	Bulatović *et al.* 2020	SM	92	RA21
26	Prijevor, Ada	mound, central grave, incineration	RICH 24502	3638±30	2035–1945 (68.2%)	2134–1900	Cremated human bone	Bulatović *et al.* 2020	WS	44	ADA
27	Novo Selo, Bubanj	1: shallow pit	SUERC 69298	3632±34	2035–1942 (68.2%)	2133–1895	Animal bone (Sus sp.)	Bulatović & Vander Linden 2017	SM	83	BU1
28	Majilovac, Mar-jansko brdo	E120, sonda 6, obj. 12 (jama)	DeA 45287	3597±34	1978–1918 (67%)	2116–1826	Charcoal	This study	PP	7	MB12
29	Ranutovac, Meanište	Trench 13, grave 17	RICH-24543	3594±31	2020–1900 (68.2%)	2034–1828	Cremated human bone	Bulatović *et al.* 2020	SM	92	RA17
30	Viminacium, Rit	trench 18, pit 1	DeA-14236	3593±28	1977–1907 (91.6%)	2031–1882	Animal bone (*Equus* Sp.)	Bulatović *et al.* 2019	PP	4	Rit1
31	Grčac, Novačka Ćuprija	pit 1	BC 84	3590±100	2160–1850 (68%)	2276–1641	?	Krstić *et al.* 1986; Nikolova 1999	PP	8	NĆ1

(Continued)

No	Village/Site	Context	Lab. code	Date BP	Date cal BC	Date cal BC (95.4%) (OxCal 4.4.)	Sample	Reference	Zone	Map No.	Plot code
32	Ranutovac, Meanište	Trench 6, grave 9	RICH -24513	3584±32	1980–1890 (68.2%) 2031–1877 (91.3%)	2031–1782	Cremated human bone	Bulatović *et al.* 2020	SM	92	RA9
33	Brestovačka Banja, Trnjane	grave 10	DeA 18164	3567±27	1947–1886 (68.2%)	2020–1778	Charcoal	Kapuran *et al.* 2020	ES	170	TR10
34	Brezjak, Paulje	Mound 38, grave 1	DeA 31445	3567±25	1979–1876 (84.6%)	2019–1779	Charcoal	This study	WS	135	BR38
35	Ranutovac, Meanište	Trench 8, grave 1	RICH -24544	3548±33	1950–1780 (68.2%)	2014–1769	Cremated human bone	Bulatović *et al.* 2020	SM	92	RA1
36	Majilovac, Marjansko brdo	trench 8, structure 24	DeA 44840	3546±19	1930–1879 (83%)	1949–1775	Animal bone	This study	PP	7	MB24
37	Ranutovac, Meanište	Trench 8, grave 7	RICH -24514	3543±33	1940–1870 (46.9%) 1940–1780 (68.2%)	2012–1754	Cremated human bone	Bulatović *et al.* 2020	SM	92	RA7
38	Majilovac, Marjansko brdo	trench 8, structure.35 (eastern part)	DeA 44841	3534±19	1849–1773 (53%)	1936–1773	Animal bone	This study	PP	7	MB35
	MIDDLE BRONZE AGE										
39	Omoljica, Zlatica	Settlement	BC 2	3530±60	1960–1760 (68.2%)	2030–1691	?	Gogaltan 1999	PP	104	Omoljica
40	Maskare, Bedem	trench 13, pit 1	DeA 44857	3522±19	1853–1768 (68%)	1927–1768	Animal bone	This study	GM	120	MA
41	Brezjak, Paulje	SU 7, pit 5	DeA 33888	3506±31	1849–1771 (82.7%)	1924–1743	Charcoal	This study	WS	135	
42	Banjsko Polje, Ružana	settlement	MAMS 39765	3484±24	1886–1742 (93.9%)	1886–1701	Charcoal from surface of copper slag	Mehofer *et al.* 2021	ES	150	RU1
43	Banjsko Polje, Ružana	Settlement	MAMS 38020	3482±28	1886–1740 (92.1%)	1886–1698	Animal bone	Mehofer *et al.* 2021	ES	150	RU2
44	Ljuljaci, Milića Brdo	settlement, 1st horizon (?)	Z 546	3480±100	1940–1680 (68.2%) 2037–1533 (94.6%)	2116–1533	Charcoal	Gogaltan 1999	GM	114	LJU1
45	Banjsko Polje, Ružana	level with copper slag	Lyon 13837	3480±35	1896–1732 (88.0%)	1896–1690	Animal bone	Mehofer *et al.* 2021	ES	150	RU3
46	Brestovačka Banja, Trnjane	settlement, SU 5	DeA 19121	3477±27	1877–1749 (68.2%)	1884–1698	Charcoal	Kapuran *et al.* 2020	ES	155	TR5
47	Bratinac, Ciganbrdo	inhumation	DeA 44856	3468±20	1828–1738 (61%)	1881–1696	Human tooth	This study	PP	105	CB56
48	Bratinac, Cigansko brdo	settlement, structure 10a	DeA 42035	3463±31	1884–1730 (86.1%)	1884–1689	Animal bone	This study	PP	105	CB10a

(Continued)

No	Village/Site	Context	Lab. code	Date BP	Date cal BC	Date cal BC (95.4%) (OxCal 4.4.)	Sample	Reference	Zone	Map No.	Plot code
49	Ljuljaci, Milića Brdo	Settlement	Z 548	3460±100	1930–1670 (68.2%)	2028–1519	Charcoal	Gogaltan 1999	GM	114	LJU2
50	Bor, Čoka Njica	Settlement	DeA 23585	3439±38	1826–1627 (78.8%)	1879–1627	Burnt animal bone	Mehofer *et al.* 2021	ES	138	COK
51	Štulac, Svinjarička Čuka	SU1055	MAMS 46947	3438±29	1869–1689 (68.2%)	1878–1631	Seed	Horejs *et al.* 2022	SM	86	SČ1
52	Štulac, Svinjarička Čuka	SU 1055	MAMS 46940	3430±22	1863–1689 (68.2%)	1873–1633	Animal tooth	Horejs *et al.* 2022	SM	86	SČ2
53	Ljuljaci, Milića Brdo	Settlement	Z 545	3425±95	1890–1630 (68.2%)	2008–1504	Charcoal	Gogaltan 1999	GM	114	LJU3
54	Majilovac, Marjansko brdo	trench 8, structure 35 (W part)	DeA 45283	3423±31	1775–1623 (87%)	1874–1623	Charcoal	This study	PP	7	MB35
55	Brestovačka Banja, Trnjane	Settlement, SU 5	MAMS 42796	3418±24	1747–1688 (68.2%)	1868–1626	Seed from vessel	Kapuran *et al.* 2020	ES	155	TR5a
56	Štulac, Svinjarička Čuka	SU 1016	MAMS 40140	3412±20	1743–1688 (68.2%)	1862–1626	Emmer grain	Horejs *et al.* 2019	SM	86	SČ3
57	Brestovačka Banja, Trnjane	settlement, SU4	DeA 19119	3404±30	1774–1662 (68.2%)	1868–1617	Animal bone	Kapuran *et al.* 2020	ES	155	TR4
58	Majilovac, Marjansko brdo	trench 5, 1.55–1.6 m	DeA 45288	3403±32	1741–1631 (1σ)	1871–1613	Charcoal	This study	PP	7	MB
59	Brestovačka Banja, Trnjane	grave 28	DeA 18174	3403±27	1742–1664 (68.2%)	1862–1619	Charcoal	Kapuran *et al.* 2020	ES	170	TR28
60	Ljuljaci, Milića Brdo	settlement	Z 549	3370±100	1870–1520 (68.2%)	1919–1441	Charcoal	Gogaltan 1999	GM	114	LJU4
61	Majilovac, Marjansko brdo	trench 3, structure 28	DeA 45291	3359±33	1689–1611 (83%)	1740–1536	Charcoal	This study	PP	7	MB28
62	Majilovac, Marjansko brdo	trench 3, structure 11	DeA 45290	3357±33	1689–1610 (80%)	1740–1536	Charcoal	This study	PP	7	MB11
63	Bratinac, Cigansko brdo	trench 4/22, 3rd spit	DeA-42036	3302±32	1612–1573 (52.4%)	1668–1501	Animal bone	This study	PP	105	CB
64	Majilovac, Marjansko brdo	trench 9, structure 34	DeA 45286	3284±33	1545–1507 (55%)	1624–1458	Charcoal	This study	PP	7	MB34
65	Hum, Velika Humska Čuka	trench 2/22, pottery group 1-4	DeA-39101	3269±19	1548–1498 (78.4%)	1611–1462	Animal bone	This study	SM	77	VHC
66	Mala Vrbica, Konopište	grave 12/1986	DeA-42815	3254±42	1544–1493 (61.7%)	1616–1437	Cremated bone	This study	ES	a	KON
67	Ostrikovac, Đula	trench 2, pit 1	DeA-43021	3248±22	1522–1498 (66%)	1600–1444	Animal bone	This study	GM	22	OS

(Continued)

('steppe' tumuli in Jabuka, Pančevo, and Vojlovica) that existed during the first half of the 3rd millennium, approximately until the middle of that millennium (3080–2886 to 2610–2410 cal BC; Table 1), while the earliest date for the beginning of the next phase of the Early Bronze Age in this zone, culturally defined by the Vinkovci–Somogyvár group, is approximately the third quarter of the 3rd millennium (2458–2346 cal BC), albeit based on only one date, making it possible that these two manifestations overlapped at some point (Fig. 4.1). Thus, the earliest modelled dates for the appearance of the so-called steppe tumuli in this zone, but on the left bank of the Danube near Pančevo, fall within the first quarter of the 3rd millennium, although most of these steppe tumuli are found in eastern Bačka and Banat (Šajkaš, Padej, etc.) (Koledin *et al.* 2020).

The second phase of the Early Bronze Age began in the third quarter of the 3rd millennium (2458–2346 cal BC), and due to the presence of only one date, it is currently not possible to determine its duration in this zone. The earliest modelled date for the third, youngest phase of the Early Bronze Age in this zone, defined by the Novačka Ćuprija–Pančevo group, falls at the beginning of the 20th century (2061–1931 cal BC), with the end of this phase in this zone being at the end of the 20th and the beginning of the 19th century (1921–1840 cal BC).

Unmodelled dates for the first phase of the Early Bronze Age in the peri-Pannonian zone are somewhat more recent, but they still place the beginning of this phase at the end of the 1st quarter of the 3rd millennium (2920–2884 cal BC) and its end between 2629 and 2488 cal BC. According to unmodelled dates, the duration of the second phase falls between 2461 and 2349 cal BC, but this is based on only one date, while the third phase is placed between 2830– 1778 cal BC and 1919–1779 cal BC. It is observed that the oldest unmodelled date for the third phase is quite extreme, due to the exceptionally high variability, i.e., the deviation of the oldest date from Novačka Ćuprija by as much as ±300 years (see Fig. 4.16).

Based on the dates for the Vinkovci–Somogyvár group in the Great Morava Valley Region and western Serbia (Belotić–Bela Crkva group), where it disappears at the transition from the third to the last quarter of the 3rd millennium, it can be assumed that it similarly ceased in the peri-Pannonian zone. However, this raises the question of what happened in this zone until the emergence of the Novačka Ćuprija–Pančevo community, which would be almost three centuries. There are several possible answers to this question – either the Vinkovci–Somogyvár group persisted longer in this zone, until the beginning of the 20th century, or the Novačka Ćuprija–Pančevo communities settled this zone much earlier, with no existing dates yet to confirm this. A third possibility is that the peri-Pannonian zone was uninhabited for some reason during the last quarter of the 3rd millennium, which is the least acceptable answer.

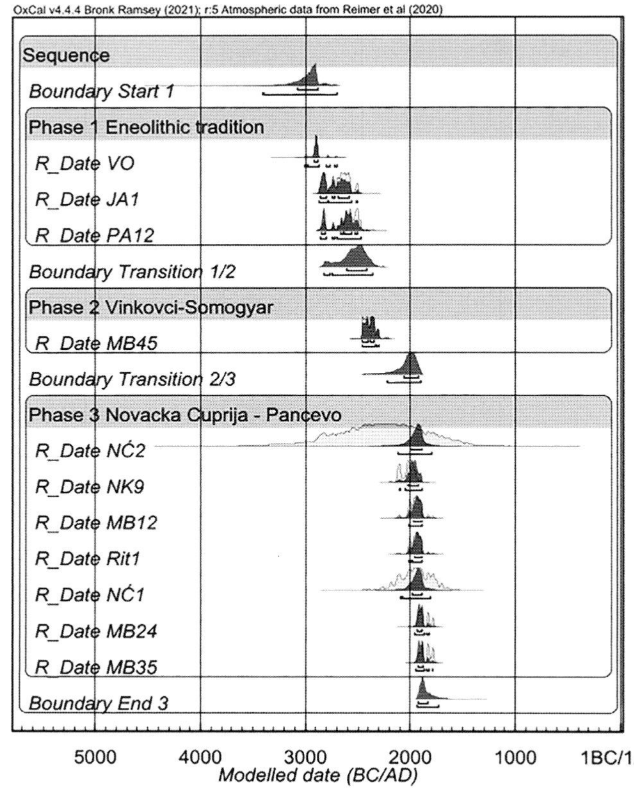

Figure 4.1. Modelled dates for the Early Bronze Age sites in peri-Pannonian zone.

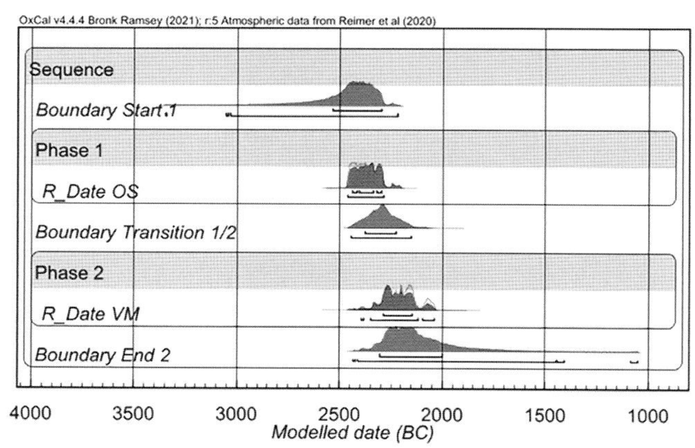

Figure 4.2. Modelled dates for the Early Bronze Age sites in Great Morava Valley with Šumadija zone.

4.1.2 The basin of the Great Morava River with Šumadija

In the next zone, the central (Great) Morava Basin with most of Šumadija, the first phase of the Early Bronze Age is also evident (tumuli in Rogojevac and Bara) (Srejović 1976). However, absolute dates are lacking, so, based on the dates of tumuli in Banat and western Serbia, it can only be roughly assumed that this phase in the Morava Basin and Šumadija chronologically belongs to the first half of the 3rd millennium BC.

For the second phase in this zone, defined by the culture of the Vinkovci–Somogyvár group communities, there is only one date which, according to Bayesian modelling, falls in the period 2440–2300 cal BC (Table 1 and Fig. 4.2). However, this model based on two dates, is not really valid so it should be accepted with certain caution. The date from Vecina Mala, marking the third phase of the Early Bronze Age in this zone, is somewhat later (2291–2144 cal BC), with the material mostly belonging to the Novačka Ćuprija–Pančevo group, featuring elements of the Bubanj-Hum III–Pelince–Pernik group, its southern neighbour.

Since only two dates are available, one for each group, the unmodelled dates do not significantly differ from the modelled ones, yielding 2456–2310 cal BC for Ostrikovac and 2288–2138 cal BC for Vecina Mala.

Based on the chronology and the stylistic and typological characteristics of pottery, it is noted that in this transitional area between the Bubanj-Hum III–Pelince–Pernik group and the Novačka Ćuprija–Pančevo group, the ceramic finds from the third phase of the Early Bronze Age, which belong to the last quarter of the 3rd millennium, represent a unique mix of both groups. This is not surprising considering that this is a contact zone between these groups. Given that the Bubanj-Hum III–Pelince–Pernik group is considerably older, it is assumed that its presence in the Morava Basin and the peri-Pannonian zone, whether through intensive contacts with these communities or population movements in that direction, partially laid the foundation for the formation of the Novačka Ćuprija–Pančevo group.

4.1.3 Western Serbia with Lim Valley

In the third zone, western Serbia, sites with certain Eneolithic traditions similar to those in the previous zones, have also been recorded. This is defined as the first phase of the

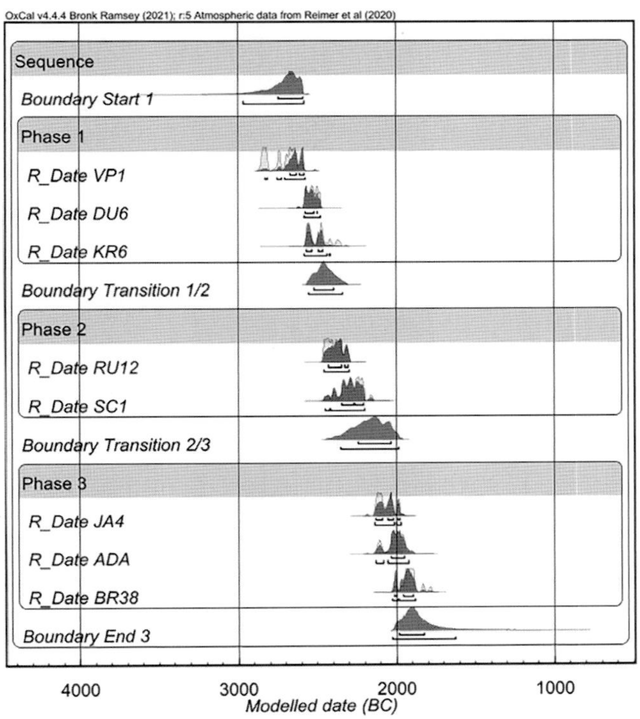

Figure 4.3. Modelled dates for the Early Bronze Age sites in West Serbia zone.

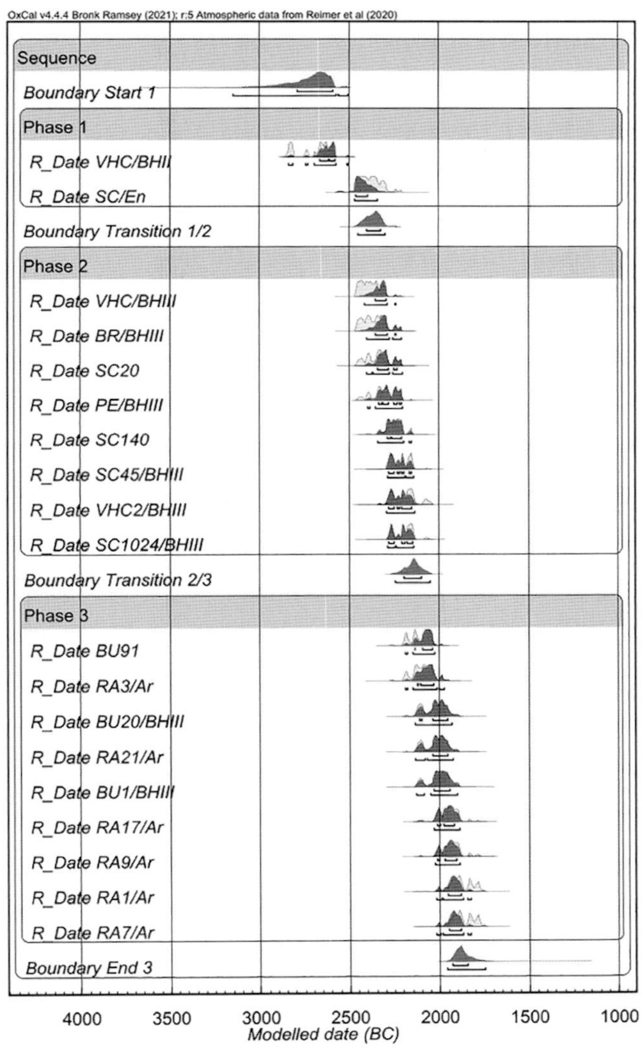

Figure 4.4. Modelled dates for the Early Bronze Age sites in Southern Serbia with central Pčinja and the Kumanovo and Skopje Plains.

Early Bronze Age in this zone. Tumuli with inhumation burials and ceramic vessels with Eneolithic stylistic and typological characteristics, as well as traces of ochre on the deceased, were registered at the sites of Veliko Polje, Dubac, and Ivkovo Brdo. According to Bayesian modelling, this phase is dated to the period between 2741–2588 cal BC and 2517–2394 cal BC (Fig. 4.3).

The next phase is characterised by communities of the Belotić–Bela Crkva group, which is actually a regional variant of the Vinkovci–Somogyvár group. Based on two dates, this phase is set in the period between 2426–2303 cal BC and 2242–2033 cal BC, approximately concurrent with the Vinkovci–Somogyvár group in the first two zones.

The last phase in this zone, based on three modelled dates, is roughly placed between 2127–1982 cal BC and 1987–1826 cal BC, i.e., the last quarter of the 3rd and first century of the 2nd millennium. This phase partially overlaps with the previous one, indicating their chronological continuity. This phase is characterised by a material culture based on the stylistic and typological features of pottery, which, similar to the previous zone, correspond to the Novačka Ćuprija–Pančevo group but with noticeable elements of the Bubanj-Hum III–Pelince–Pernik group. This seems to be a characteristic of the early phase of the Novačka Ćuprija–Pančevo group, which can be dated to the last quarter of the 3rd millennium.

Unmodelled dates suggest that the first phase lasted between 2847–2627 cal BC and 2567–2363 cal BC, the second phase is placed between 2456–2345 cal BC and 2341–2204 cal BC, and the third between 2133–2027 cal BC and 1949–1885 cal BC (Fig. 4.16).

4.1.4 Timok Region with the Đerdap Gorge

There are no absolute dates from this zone that belong to the Early Bronze Age.

4.1.5 Southern Morava Basin with Middle Pčinja and Kumanovo and Skopje plains

In the last and southernmost geographic zone, the Southern Morava Basin, the first phase of the Early Bronze Age, which chronologically corresponds to the first phase in the previous zones, was also observed. A modelled date from Velika Humska Čuka, from the remains of a house with pottery corresponding to the Bubanj–Hum II group, which preceded the Bubanj-Hum III–Pelince–Pernik group, places it in the period 2662–2579 cal BC (Fig. 4.4). Another date, chronologically closer to the second phase of the Early Bronze Age (2466–2397 cal BC), culturally corresponds to the first phase, i.e., the Eneolithic culture, as it pertains to the grave of an inhumed individual in a crouched position, with grave goods in the form of a gold hair ring and tubes made of coiled gold wire, which are common offerings in steppe tumuli in the Lower Danube region (Alexandrov 2009; 2021). This grave was found in the geographically passive region of Jablanica at the foot of Radan, where orographic isolation may have contributed to the prolonged presence of these traditions. Based on the model of these two dates, the first phase could be set in the period between 2792–2588 cal BC and 2405–2322 cal BC.

The second phase, modelled with a set of eight absolute dates, is defined as the period between 2405–2322 cal BC and 2197–2101 cal BC and consists of the culture of the Bubanj-Hum III–Pelince–Pernik group. The third phase is marked by the continued development of this group, which, due to the reduced territory of the previously mentioned group (contracting in the south and east while expanding north), was named after the eponymous sites in the Southern Morava Region, the Bubanj-Hum III group. This phase also includes the necropolis in Ranutovac, featuring finds from the Armenochori group, which expanded northward into the southern part of the Southern Morava Region at the end of the 3rd millennium at the expense of the

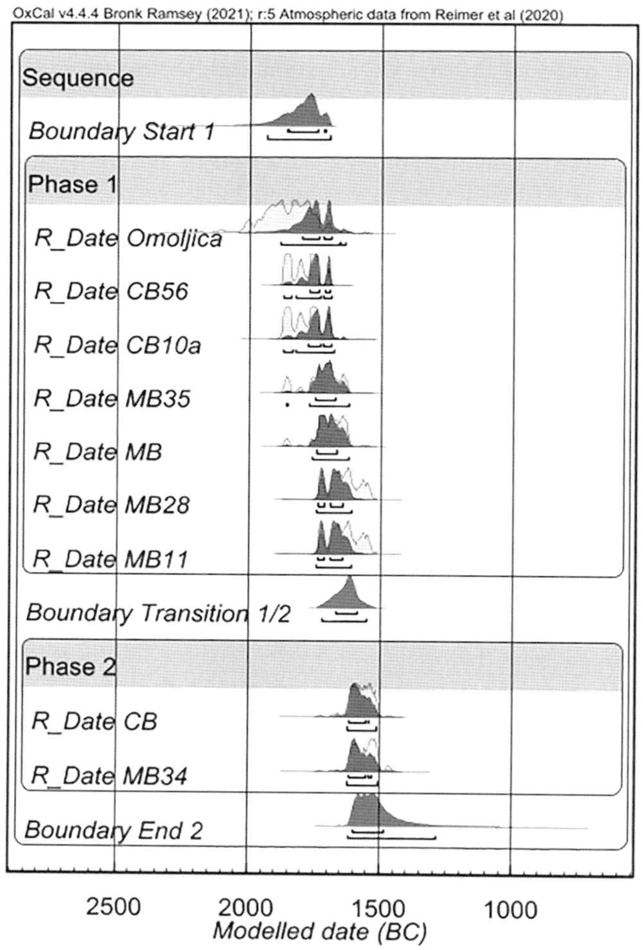

Figure 4.5. Modelled dates for the Middle Bronze Age sites in peri-Pannonian zone.

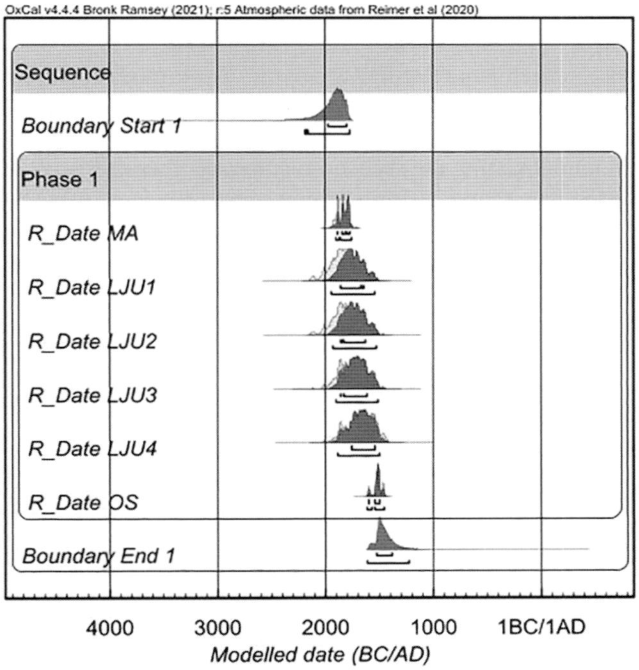

Figure 4.6. Modelled dates for the Middle Bronze Age sites in Great Morava with Šumadija zone.

Bubanj-Hum III–Pelince–Pernik group. The third phase is set between 2137–1944 cal BC -(Bubanj-Hum III group) and 2124–1882 cal BC (Armenochori group, based on six dates from the necropolis), with an overall duration falling between 2197–1846 cal BC.

Unmodelled dates for the first phase are slightly higher, from 2839–2583 cal BC to 2461–2344 cal BC; for the second phase, from 2454–2342 cal BC to 2275–2141 cal BC; and for the third phase, from 2192–2042 cal BC to 1937–1779 cal BC (Fig. 4.16).

4.2 Absolute dating of the Middle Bronze Age by geographical zones

4.2.1 The peri-Pannonian zone

Unlike the Early Bronze Age, the culture of the Middle Bronze Age is quite uniform and is not defined through multiple cultural-chronological phases. In the peri-Pannonian zone, the Middle Bronze Age is defined by the Vatin group, formed on the basis of the preceding Novačka Ćuprija–Pančevo group, which, as a reminder, lasted until around the mid-19th century BC. The Vatin group, and thus the Middle Bronze Age, according to a set of modelled dates, begins in the first half of the 18th century BC (between 1863 and 1714 cal BC), and the latest date for this group is 1671–1590 cal BC (Fig. 4.5).

The unmodelled date for the Middle Bronze Age in this zone is slightly higher, at 1945–1767 cal BC. However, the modelled date fits much better into the chronological framework of the Early and Middle Bronze Age in this zone, making it more likely (Fig. 4.16).

According to the modelled date from Cigansko Brdo, already by the end of the 17th or the first half of the 16th century (1615–1540 cal BC), settlements of the Žuto Brdo group, which emerged from the local Vatin group and the incrusted pottery culture from the north-west, appeared in this zone, marking the beginning of the Late Bronze Age. The unmodelled date from Cigansko Brdo does not differ significantly and is 1612–1532 cal BC.

4.2.2 Basin of the Great Morava River with Šumadija

In this zone, the Middle Bronze Age is characterized by the so-called Bubanj-Hum–Ljuljaci group, formed on the cultural basis of the Bubanj-Hum III group. According to a set of six dates, the model showed that the duration of the Middle Bronze Age in this zone is between 1966–1798 cal BC and 1531–1390 cal BC (Fig. 4.6).

Unmodelled dates seem to provide a more acceptable chronology, defining the Middle Bronze Age in this zone between 1891–1776 cal BC and 1533–1464 cal BC (Fig.

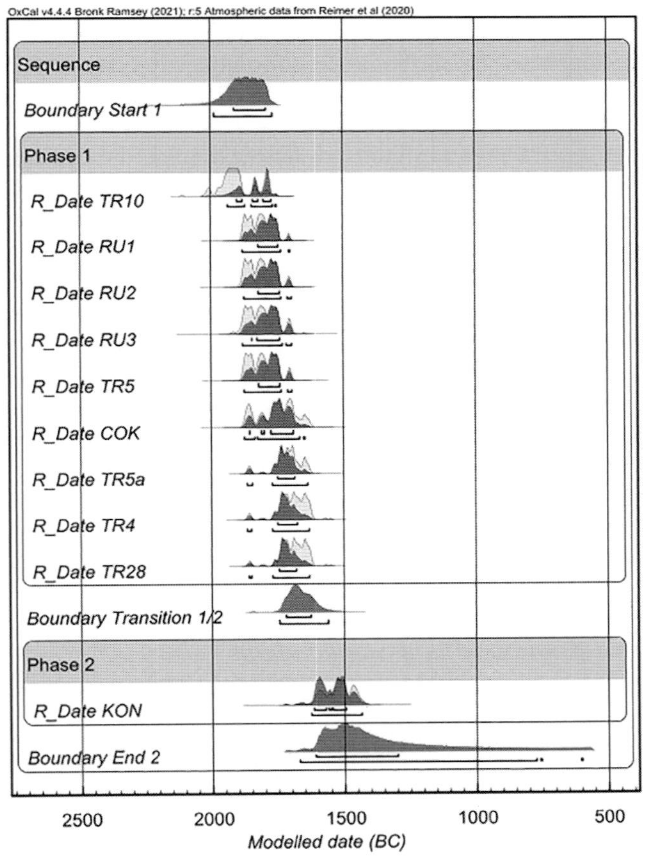

Figure 4.7. Modelled dates for the Middle Bronze Age sites in Timok basin and Đerdap Gorge zone.

4.17). It should be noted that the modelling provided quite extreme dating limits, likely due to the larger number of dates from Ljuljaci with a high variability of ±100 years.

The date from Đula in Ostrikovac (1599–1496 cal BC), whose pottery still has some parallels with the Bubanj-Hum IV–Ljuljaci group, probably belongs to its end and possibly the beginnings of the Late Bronze Age, which would later be represented in this zone by the Paraćin cultural group. This date can currently be accepted as a *terminus ante quem* for the Bubanj-Hum IV–Ljuljaci group in this zone.

4.2.3 Western Serbia and the Lim Valley

There are no absolute dates from this zone that belong to the Middle Bronze Age.

4.2.4 Timok Region with the Đerdap Gorge

In the Timok Region, the Middle Bronze Age saw the existence of communities that can be defined as bearers of the so-called Timok variant of the Bubanj-Hum IV–Ljuljaci group. According to a chronological model based on a set of nine dates, this group, i.e., the Middle Bronze Age in this zone, falls between 1913–1795 cal BC and 1720–1627 cal BC (Fig. 4.7), suggesting that the Timok variant of the Bubanj-Hum IV–Ljuljaci group, according to available dates, could be placed between the mid-19th and mid-17th centuries BC. According to the absolute dates from Timok Valley, currently in the process of publication, this group extends its duration into the Late Bronze Age.[1]

Unmodelled dates are significantly higher in terms of the upper limit and slightly so for the younger limit, ranging between 1955–1882 cal BC and 1740–1634 cal BC (Fig. 4.16). However, based on the similarities of the material culture of the Timok variant of the Bubanj-Hum IV–Ljuljaci group with the culture of the Paraćin group, which would succeed it in the Late Bronze Age, it is assumed that this group lasted longer than the mid-17th century, similar to the Bubanj-Hum IV–Ljuljaci group in the Morava Basin.

There is one absolute date from Đerdap, but it belongs to the Late Bronze Age, specifically the Žuto Brdo group (1615–1496 cal BC) (Table 1 and Fig. 4.7), which is particularly significant as it indicates an early presence of this group's communities in Đerdap and provides a *terminus ante quem* for the Verbicioara group in Đerdap.

4.2.5 Southern Morava Basin with Middle Pčinja and Kumanovo and Skopje plains

In this zone, the Middle Bronze Age comprises the culture of the Bubanj-Hum IV–Ljuljaci group. According to a modelled set of four dates, this group, and thus the Middle Bronze Age in this zone, falls within the period 1874–1707 cal BC and 1601–1441 cal BC (Fig. 4.8). It is worth noticing however the model performance was poor, as indicated by corresponding low A-model value, and its results should then be taken with caution. However, unmodelled dates give an almost identical upper limit, with a slightly narrower lower range (1869–1689 cal BC and 1539–1503 cal BC), which supports the accuracy of the modelled dates (Fig. 4.16).

The youngest date comes from Velika Humska Čuka from a unit containing the stylistic-typological characteristics of the Bubanj-Hum IV–Ljuljaci group, but also some new stylistic elements that herald the next phase in the development of the Bronze Age, the Late Bronze Age. However, the oldest

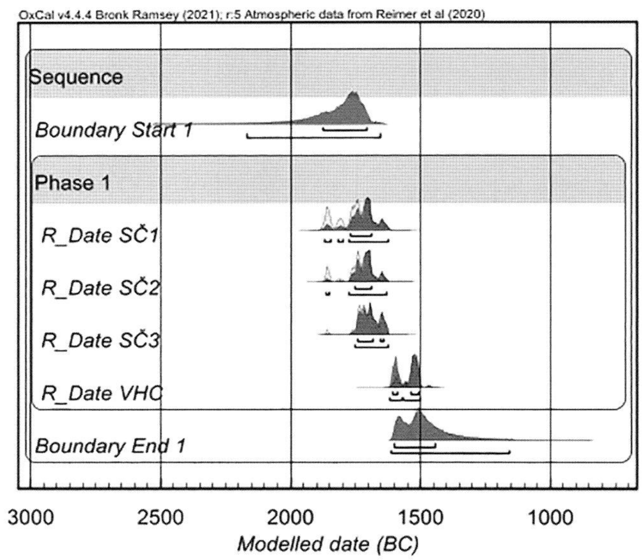

Figure 4.8. Modelled dates for the Middle Bronze Age sites in Southern Serbia with central Pčinja and the Kumanovo and Skopje Plains.

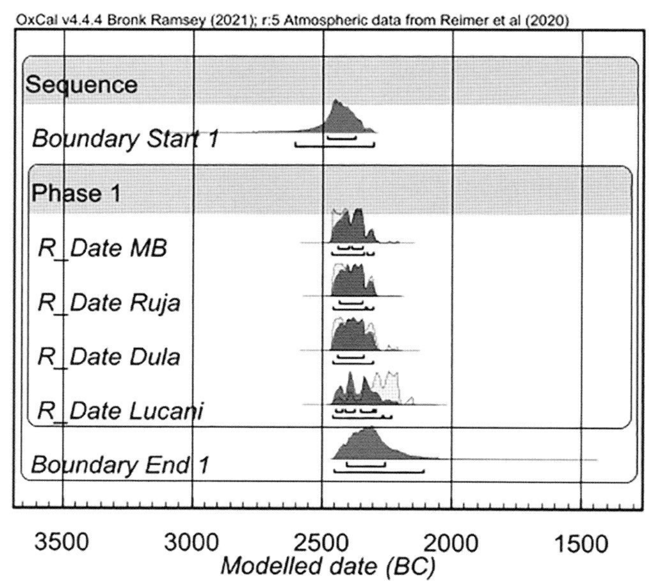

Figure 4.9. Modelled dates for the Vinkovci–Somogyvár group in the Central Balkans.

known date for the Late Bronze Age cultural group in the Southern Morava Basin, the Brnjica group, is from the first half of the 15th century cal BC, raising the question of what occurred during those few decades: whether older dates for the Brnjica group or younger dates for the Bubanj-Hum IV–Ljuljaci group should be expected, or simply a future chronological definition of a transitional phase containing elements of both groups.

4.3 Absolute chronology of cultural groups of the Early and Middle Bronze Age in the central Balkans

Regarding individual groups of the Early Bronze Age, Bayesian modelling has shown that the Vinkovci–Somogyvár group, including its Belotić–Bela Crkva variant, according to all available dates in the central Balkans, began in the period 2482–2372 cal BC, which is slightly later than the earliest dates in Slavonia on the core territory of this group (Durman and Obelić 1989; Kalafatić 2006). According to a set of four available dates from the central Balkans modelled using the Bayesian method, it lasted until 2405–2259 cal BC (Fig. 4.9). In any case, all dates for this group in the central Balkans are quite close, while in Slavonia and the Carpathian Basin, there is a wide chronological spectrum of dates, indicating that communities in the Balkans did not retain the characteristics of this group for long, but through symbiosis with the Bubanj-Hum III–Pelince–Pernik group from the south, they contributed to the formation of the Novačka Ćuprija–Pančevo group. Unmodelled dates are slightly earlier, suggesting the group lasted between 2461–2349 cal BC and 2341–2204 cal BC (Fig. 4.16).

The Bubanj-Hum III–Pelince–Pernik group is dated between 2432–2310 and 2184–2095 cal BC, while its later phase (Bubanj-Hum III) is dated between 2184–2095 and 2111–1911 cal BC (Fig. 4.10), which aligns well with the chronological models of the second and third phases of the Early Bronze Age in the Southern Morava Basin. Unmodelled dates provide a slightly earlier chronological framework from 2454–2342 cal BC to 2275–2141 cal BC for the Bubanj-Hum III–Pelince–Pernik group, while the range for the Bubanj–Hum III group is similar (from 2192–2042 cal BC to 2110–1941 cal BC) (Fig. 4.16).

The Armenochori group, which appeared in the southern central Balkans at the end of the Early Bronze Age, is dated using modelled dates from the Ranutovac necropolis to between 2112–1980 cal BC and 1939–1829 cal BC (Fig. 4.11), while unmodelled dates provide a slightly different range of 2138–2036 cal BC to 1937–1779 cal BC (Fig. 4.16). The highest dates for the Armenochori group in Ranutovac are almost three centuries later than the earliest dates for this group in northern Greece, which is the original territory of the group (Bulatović *et al.* 2020, 1179–1184, fig. 8).

The Novačka Ćuprija–Pančevo group, spread across the peri-Pannonian zone, the Great Morava Basin, Šumadija,

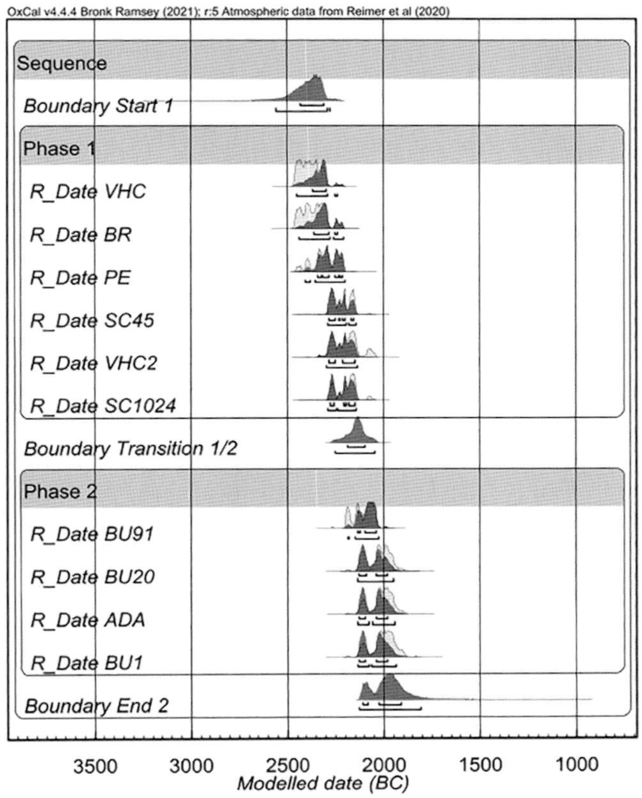

Figure 4.10. Modelled dates for the Bubanj-Hum III–Pelince–Pernik and Bubanj-Hum III groups.

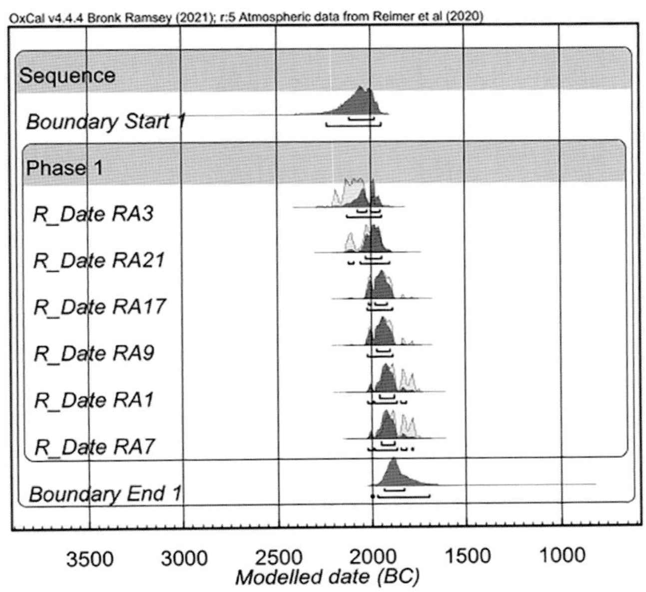

Figure 4.11. Modelled dates for the Armenochori group in the Central Balkans.

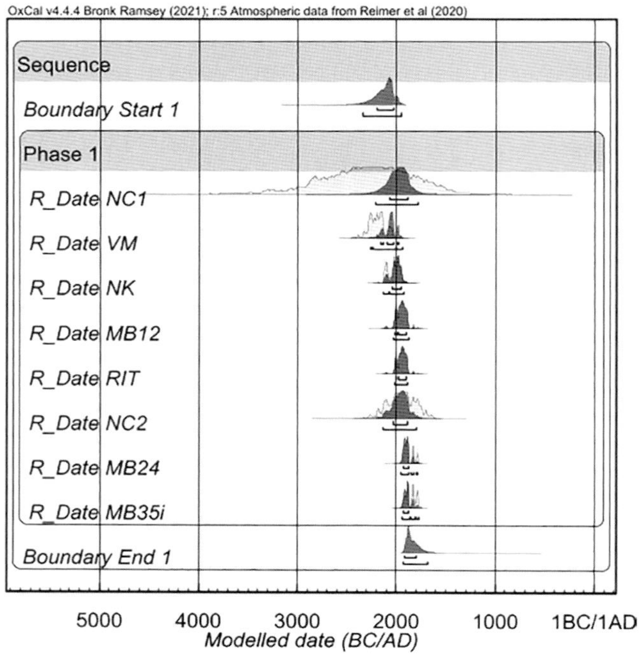

Figure 4.12. Modelled dates for the Novačka Ćuprija–Pančevo group.

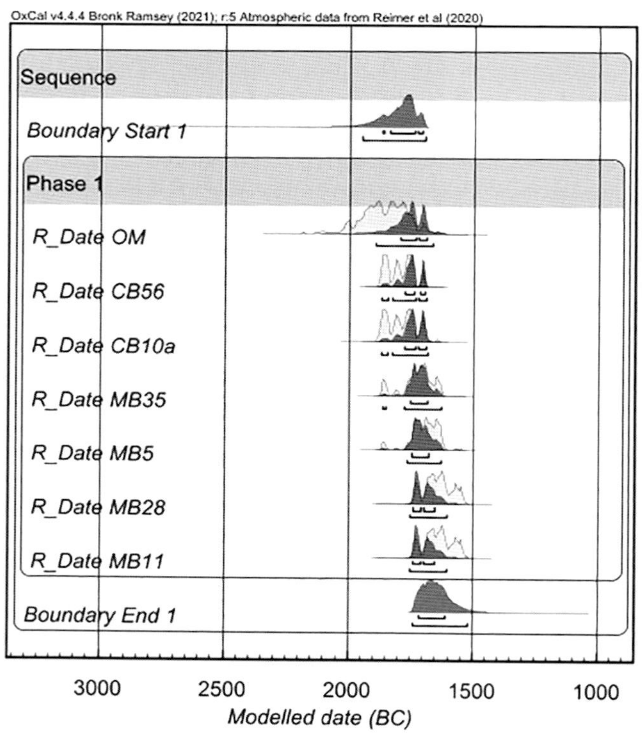

Figure 4.13. Modelled dates for the Vatin group in the Central Balkans.

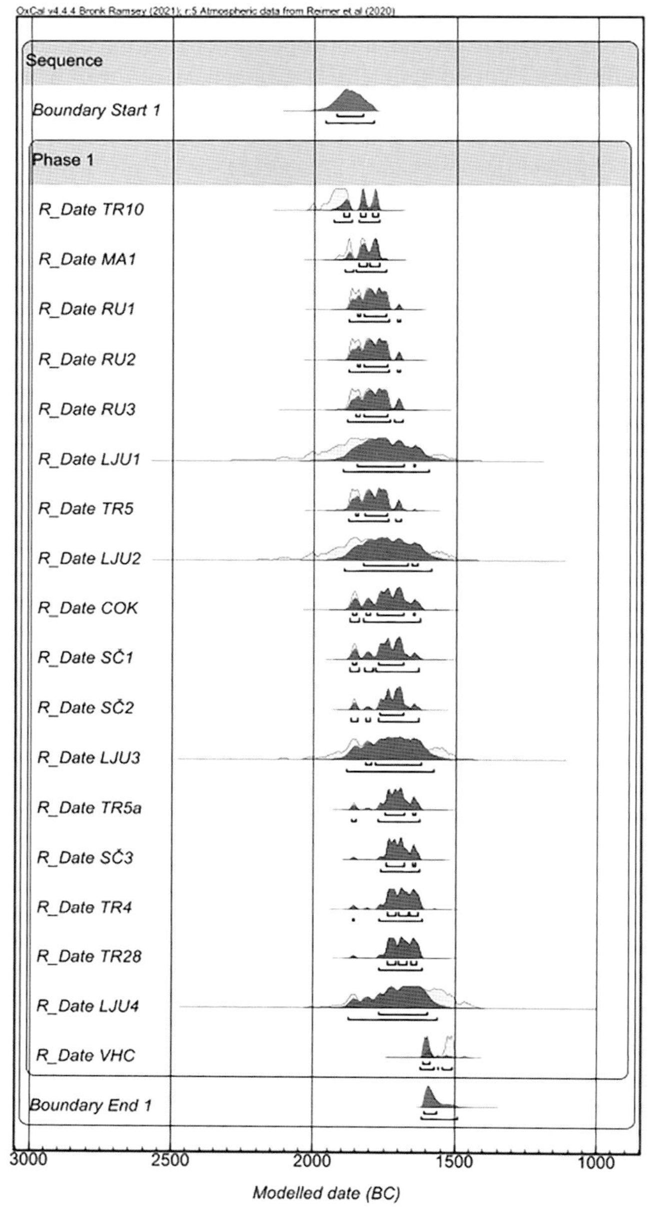

Figure 4.14. Modelled dates for the Bubanj-Hum IV–Ljuljaci group.

and the eastern edge of Western Serbia, has a modelled chronological range of 2206–2036 cal BC to 1910–1801 cal BC (Fig. 4.7), while unmodelled dates place this group between 2841–1774 cal BC and 1919–1779 cal BC (Fig. 4.12). The dates indicate that it chronologically follows the Vinkovci–Somogyvár group with short hiatus in between and ends with the formation of the Vatin group in the peri-Pannonian zone. It is noted that the Bayesian models (Figs 4.1 and 4.13) for the third phase of the Early Bronze Age in the peri-Pannonian zone and the Novačka Ćuprija–Pančevo group do not align, likely because the earliest dates for this group, based on currently available absolute dates, originate from Šumadija and the Morava Basin, while it only expanded north into the peri-Pannonian zone in the second half of the 21st century BC.

***

When discussing the Middle Bronze Age, according to a modelled set of seven dates, the Vatin group, which defines this period, spans from 1870–1710 cal BC to 1716–1611 cal BC (Fig. 4.13). According to unmodelled dates, which show higher values for the upper boundary and lower for the lower boundary of this group, the timeframe falls between 1945–1767 cal BC and 1732–1547 cal BC (Fig. 4.16). The earliest modelled date for the Vatin group from the peri-Pannonian zone, which is also the oldest date for this group overall, originates from Omoljica and places the beginnings of the Vatin group at 1797–1693 cal BC (Table 1), thus not before the start of the 18th century (Gogaltan 1999, 224, 225, pl. 16). It should be noted, however, that the unmodelled date is somewhat higher at 1945–1767 cal BC, and that dates from Cigansko Brdo, which are not modelled, also indicate slightly higher ranges of 1874/1875–1744/1699 cal BC, suggesting that these could represent an upper boundary for this group in the peri-Pannonian zone. The Vatin group in this zone, according to the youngest modelled date from Marjansko Brdo, continues until 1653 cal BC, while by the late 17th or early 16th century cal BC, settlements of the Žuto Brdo–Girla Mare group begin to appear. Conversely, in Pannonia, the Vatin group persists somewhat longer, into the 15th century cal BC (Gogaltan 1999, 224, 225, pl. 16). Thus, the span of this group in the peri-Pannonian zone can be defined approximately from the second half of the 19th century to the end of the 17th century cal BC.

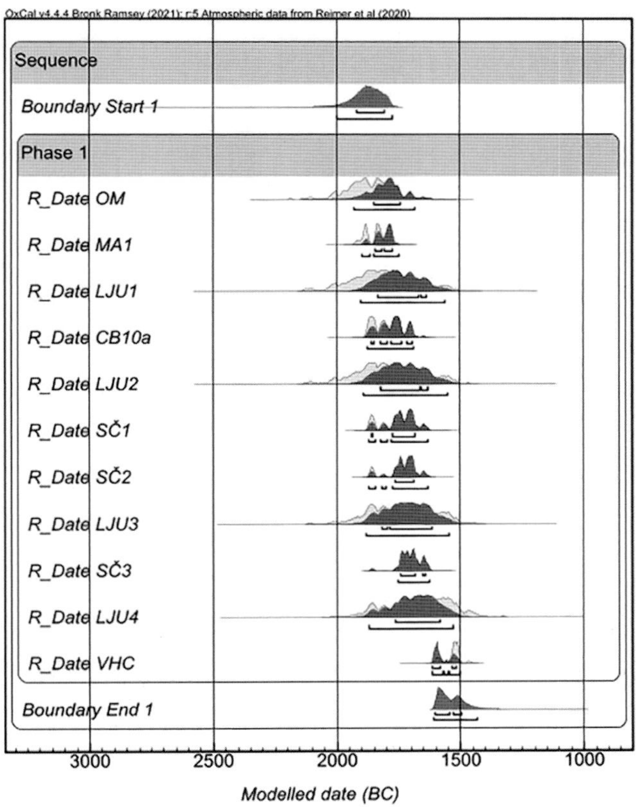

Figure 4.15. Modelled dates for the sites with beakers with trapezoidal mouth in the Central Balkans.

The Bubanj-Hum IV–Ljuljaci group marked the Middle Bronze Age over most of the central Balkans, spanning four zones except for the peri-Pannonian. Although most stylistic and typological ceramic elements in the Timok Region correspond to this group, certain specific traits led to its definition as the Timok variant of the Bubanj-Hum IV–Ljuljaci group. Dates from the Timok Region align with those from other zones where this group is present, suggesting it is a unified cultural group. The duration of this group, based on a modelled set of 18 dates, spans from 1923–1832 cal BC to 1609–1561 cal BC, while unmodelled dates place the group from 1955–1882 cal BC to 1539–1503 cal BC (Figs 4.14 and 4.16). However, results of modelling for the Bubanj-Hum IV–Ljuljaci group should be taken with caution since model performance was poor.

The earliest date comes from Trnjane in the Timok Region, falling between 1901–1777 cal BC, overlapping mostly with the date from Maskare in the broader region of the South Morava and West Morava basins (1844–1774 cal BC). The latest date for this group comes from Velika Humska Čuka and is 1613–1588 cal BC. Thus, according to the Bayesian model, the group's duration can be defined from the start of the 19th century to the first half of the 16th century. When comparing the duration of this group to the Vatin group, it becomes apparent that the Bubanj-Hum IV–Ljuljaci group begins slightly earlier and ends somewhat later, but the chronological frameworks of these two neighbouring groups largely overlap.

A few years ago, a group of authors established a Bronze Age chronology for the central Balkans that aligns with the chronologies of neighbouring regions, such as Romania, Bulgaria, and Greece (Bulatović *et al.* 2020). This compatibility reflected the mutual cultural influences of that period, as communities across these areas engaged in close contact, which contributed significantly to the genesis and development of Bronze Age cultural groups in the central Balkans and vice versa. However, at that time, only a limited number of dates were available. In this study, which benefits from a substantially larger set of dates, that chronology has been partially refined.

According to the modelled absolute dates, the first phase of the Early Bronze Age in the central Balkans would have begun in the first quarter of the 3rd millennium BC and lasted until around the middle of the millennium. The start

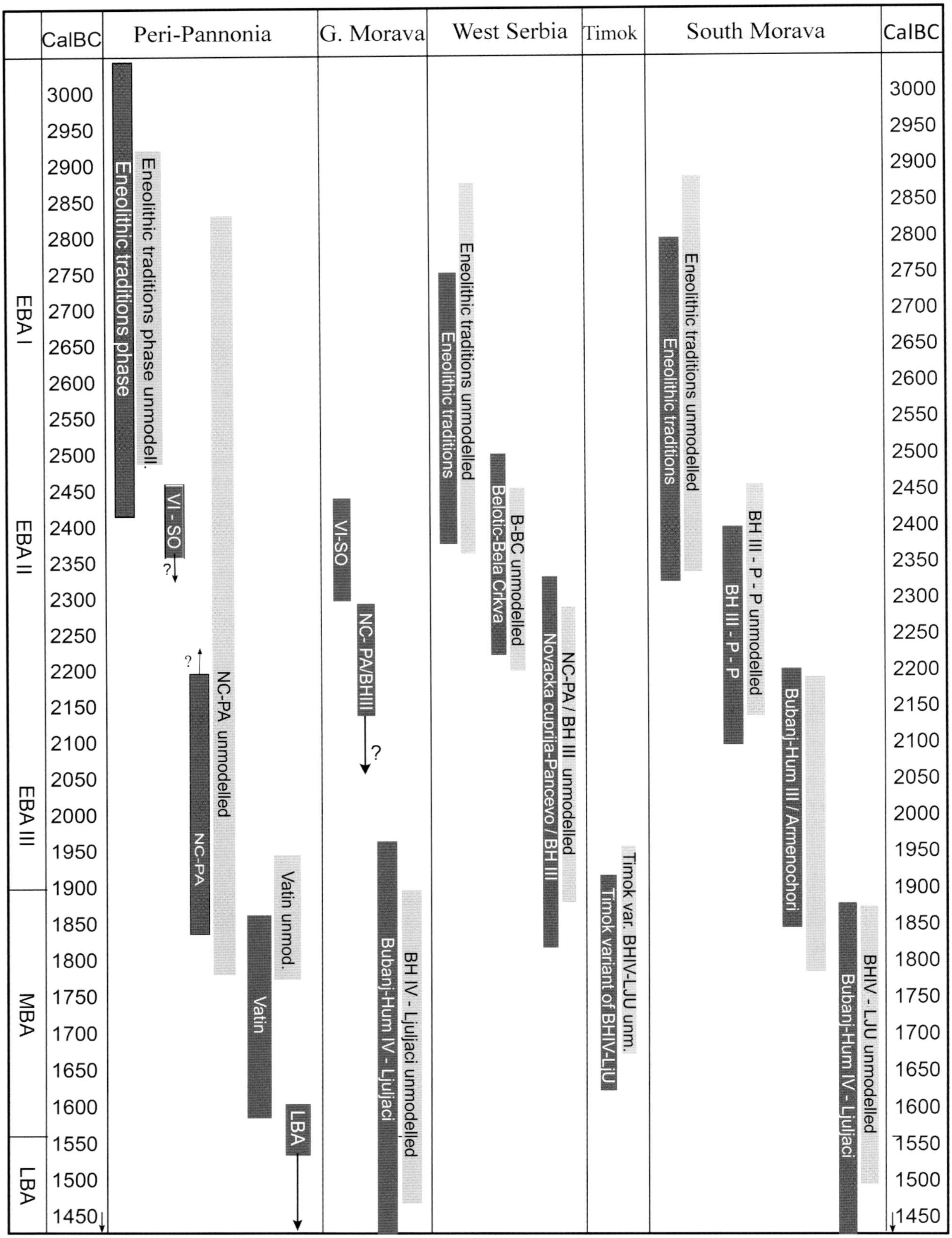

Figure 4.16. Chronology of the Central Balkans Early and Middle Bronze Ages (modelled and unmodelled).

BC	Centr. Europe (Reinecke)	Carphatian Basin (Kiss et al.)	Centr. Europe (Gerloff)	Greek mainland (Manning)	Troy (Blum)	Kastanas	Banat (Gogaltan)	Voivodina (Tasić)	Serbia (Garašanin)	Bulatović (this study)	BC
										LCA	
3000											3000
		LCA		EH I	I					EBA I	
2800							LC				2800
		Transitional period					LC/EB I	Late Copper Age	Late Copper Age		
2600				EH II			EB I				2600
		EBA I	Glocken-becher		II	28					
2400						27	EB II			EBA II	2400
		EBA II			III	26					
2200						25	EB III				2200
			Br A1	EH III	IV	24		EBA I		EBA III	
						23					
2000	Br A1	EBA III							I		2000
				MH I	V	22b	MB I				
						22a	MB II				
				MH II				EBA II			
1800			Br A2								1800
						21					
	Br A2	MBA		MH III		20	MB III	EBA III	II	MBA	
1600	Br B1			LH I		19					1600
	Br B2		Br A3		VI	18	LB I	MBA			
				LH II		17					
1400	Br C		Br B			16		LBA	III	LBA	1400
			Br C								

Figure 4.17. Comparative chronology of the Early and Middle Bronze Ages in the Central Balkans and surroundings areas.

of the second phase would fall at the beginning of the third quarter, while the end of this phase would be at the start of the last quarter of the 3rd millennium. The final phase of the Early Bronze Age would have lasted from the beginning of the last quarter of the 3rd millennium until the beginning of the 19th century BC.

The Middle Bronze Age in the central Balkans, according to the Bayesian model, starts in the 19th century BC, likely in the first half, and ends at the close of the third quarter of the 2nd millennium, marking the start of a new era in the central Balkans – the Late Bronze Age.

In comparison to neighbouring and more distant regions, the EBA 1 phase of the central Balkans would chronologically correspond to the Late Eneolithic and EBA I in Banat (Gogaltan 2015) and the Carpathian Basin (Kiss *et al.* 2015), as well as Troy I (Blum 2016) and EH I in Greece and Asia Minor (Manning 1995) (Fig. 4.17). The EBA 2 phase is parallel to the EBA II phase in Banat and the Carpathian Basin, the Bell Beaker culture in Central Europe (Gerloff 1993), Troy II–III, EH II, and horizons 28–26 at Kastanas (Aslanis 1985). The EBA III phase in the central Balkans would chronologically align with BrA1 in Central Europe (Reinecke 1965), EBA III in the Carpathian Basin and Banat, Troy III–V, EH III, and MH I in Greece (Greek mainland), and horizons 25–22 at Kastanas.

The Middle Bronze Age in the central Balkans would parallel chronologically the BrA2–B2 phases in Central Europe (according to Gerloff 1993, Br A2–A3), the MH II–LB I phases in Helladic world, Troy V, Kastanas, horizons 21–19, and the Middle Bronze Age in the Carpathian Basin and Banat.

Note

1 I thank one of the study's authors, A. Kapuran, for providing the data.

Bibliography

Alexandrov, S. (Александров, С.). 2009. Украшения за коса от злато и сребро през бронзовата епоха в Северна Блгария. *Археология* 1(1–2), 7–20.

Alexandrov, S. 2021. Fourth/third millennium BC barrow graves in North-East Bulgaria (120 years of investigations). In: *Yamnaya Interactions*, eds V. Heyd, G. Kulscár and B. Preda-Bălănică, 271–314. Budapest: Archaeolingua 44.

Aslanis, I. 1985. *Kastanas, die Fruhbronzezeitlichen Funde und Befunde.* Berlin: Wissenschaftsverlag Volker Spiess.

Blum, S. 2016. The final stages of the Early Bronze Age at Troy: Cultural development, chronology, and interregional contacts. In: *Early Bronze Age Troy: Chronology, cultural developments and interregional contacts*, eds E. Pernicka, S. Ünlüsoy and W. E. Blum, 89–122. Bonn: Habelt.

Bronk Ramsey, C. 2009. Bayesian analysis of radiocarbon dates. *Radiocarbon* 51(1), 337–360.

Bulatović, A. Gori, M. and Vander Linden, M. 2020. Radiocarbon dating the 3rd millennium BC in the Central Balkans: A re-examination of the Early Bronze Age sequence. *Radiocarbon* 62(5), 1163–1191.

Durman, A. and Obelić, B. 1989. Radiocarbon dating of the Vučedol culture complex. *Radiocarbon* 31(3), 1003–1009.

Gerloff, S. 1993. Mittelmeerländische Kontakte und absolute Chronologie der Frühbronzezeit. *Praehistorische Zeitschrift* 68(1), 58–102.

Gogâltan, F. 1999. *Bronzul timpuriu şi mijlociu în Banatul românesc şi pe cursul inferior al Mureşului. I. Cronologia şi descoperirile de metal.* Timişoara: Orizonturi Universitare.

Gogaltan, F. 2015. The Early and Middle Bronze Age chronology on the eastern frontier of the Carpathian Basin. Revisited after 15 years. In: *Bronze Age Chronology in the Carpathian Basin*, eds R. Németh and B. Rezi, 53–96. Târgu Mureş: Bibliotheca Mvsei Marisiensis Seria archaeologica 8.

Kalafatić, H. 2006. Žarni grob vinkovačke kulture s lokaliteta Vinkovci-Duga ulica 40. *Prilozi Instituta za arheologiju u Zagrebu* 23, 17–28.

Kiss, V., Fábián, S., Hajdu, T., Köhler, K., Kulscár, G., Major, I. and Szabó, G. 2015. Contributions to the relative and absolute chronology of the Early and Middle Bronze Age in western Hungary based on radiocarbon dating of human bones. In: *Bronze Age Chronology in the Carpatian Basin*, eds R. Németh and B. Rezi, 23–36. Târgu Mureş: Bibliotheca Mvsei Marisiensis Seria archaeologica 8.

Koledin, J., Bugaj, U., Jarosz, P., Novak, M., Przybyla, M., Podsiadlo, M., Szczepanek, A., Spasić, M. and Wlodarczak, P. 2020. First archaeological investigations of barrows in the Bačka region and the question of the Eneolithic/Early Bronze Age barrows in Vojvodina. *Praehistoriche Zeitschrift* 2020, 1–26.

Manning, S. W. 1995. *The Absolute Chronology of the Aegean Early Bronze Age: Archaeology, radiocarbon and history.* Sheffield: Sheffield Academic Press.

Reimer, P., Austin, E.N.W., Bard, E., Bayliss, A., Blackwell, G.P., Bronk Ramsey, Ch., Butzin, M., Cheng, H., Edwadrs, L., Friedrich, M., Grootes, P.M., Guilderson, Th.P., Hajdas, I., Heaton, T.J., Hogg, A.G., Hughen, K.A., Kromer, B., Manning, S.W., Muscheler, R., Palmer, J.G., Pearson, Ch., Van der Plicht, J., Reimer, R.W., Richards, D.A., Scott, E.M., Southon, J.R., Turney, Ch.S.M., Wacker, L., Adolphi, F., Büntgen, U., Capano, M., Fahrni, S.M., Schulz, A.F., Friedrich, R., Köhler, P., Kudsk, S., Miyake, F., Olsen, J., Reinig, F., Sakamoto, M., Sookdeo, A. and Talamo, S. 2020. The IntCal20 northern hemisphere radiocarbon age calibration curve (0–55 cal kBP). *Radiocarbon* 62(4), 725–757.

Reinecke, P. 1965. *Mainzer Aufsatze zur Chronologie der Bronze- und Eisenzeit.* Bonn: Habelt.

Srejović, D. 1976. Humke stepskih odlika na teritoriji Srbije, Godišnjak XIII. *Centar za balkanološka ispitivanja* 11, 117–129.

5

Conclusion

The fundamental task of an archaeologist is the interpretation of the past. Unlike historians, archaeologists have the unique opportunity to not only use historical sources but also to delve into the past by uncovering layers of soil, thus revealing remnants left unintentionally by our ancestors. This privilege, however, carries significant responsibility for those who interpret the past, as any poorly reasoned interpretation based on unreliable or insufficiently reliable arguments can do more harm than good to the academic world. Additionally, the interpreter must remain free from scientific bias, tractability, political dogma, national inclination, or other human frailties.

In this book, an attempt has been made to construct a cultural–chronological image of life in the communities of the central Balkans during the Early and Middle Bronze Age, considering all available information, which at times was sparse or incomplete. This work also seeks to explore their inter-relations within the central Balkans and their interactions with neighbouring communities.

It is evident that a specific community of people creates a group of uniform customs, characteristic details on pottery, a particular style of decorating vessels, practises similar ritual activities, burial customs, and other distinctive details of material and spiritual culture that can, in the absence of a perfect archaeological approach, be defined by the technical term 'cultural group'.

This definition, of course, does not depend on the ethnic, genetic, political, or other affiliations of the community, which are impossible or only partially possible to define from this historical perspective. Rather, it relies primarily on the material culture and, if present, the visible and tangible aspects of spiritual culture, such as necropolises or ritual sites.

Interdisciplinary analyses, such as ancient DNA studies and strontium isotope analysis, are undoubtedly significant. However, their major limitation is the small number of samples available, preventing definitive conclusions about the movements and origins of prehistoric populations. Thus, they should still be approached with a degree of caution.

Artefacts, especially pottery, along with absolute dating methods that are increasingly precise, continue to form the majority of the evidence used for interpreting the past. Pottery, as the most prevalent form of material culture, is undoubtedly a human product, involving selection and preparation of raw materials, vessel formation, firing, decoration, and finally use and distribution. In this process, the individual as part of a community applied their knowledge, experience, tradition, mythical thinking, sense of aesthetics, possibly certain community rules regarding the appearance or shape of vessels, interactions with other community members or those from neighbouring settlements, and much more.

In this context, a person is indeed reflected in the pottery, not in the way theoretical archaeologists might claim, such as saying 'pots don't mean people', but rather in a way that should read 'pot doesn't mean a nation or ethnicity'. The individual, as part of a community, embodies the vessel, and the vessel embodies the individual. A group of people creating similar pottery forms a community, not in an ethnic or political sense, but in a cultural sense that can be technically defined as a cultural group in the absence of a more adequate term. For this reason, a cultural-historical approach has been used in the manuscript to provide a view of past information through the material culture of the communities over time.

A certain change in the cultural, social, economic, and other aspects of life within a broader community is archaeologically treated as a new period or phase – and if the change is more significant, it is defined as a new epoch or era. This is the case with the prehistoric period in the central Balkans, marked by the disintegration of the Eneolithic cultures, such as the Vučedol and the Coţofeni–Kostolac groups, and their shift southward, probably by chain reactions, to the Adriatic coast in the case of the Vučedol group, and the Aegean coast for the Coţofeni–Kostolac group. During this time of intense social upheaval, tumuli with steppe characteristics emerged in the peri-Pannonian zone, as well as in the zones of Western Serbia and Šumadija, signalling a new era in the development of prehistoric communities in the central Balkans – the Bronze Age. Moreover, the interactions among communities in this period were significantly influenced by natural features of the terrain, particularly its orographic openness, which facilitated easier and quicker contacts. Socio-cultural interactions were also affected by climatic factors, especially climate crises, one of the most severe of which occurred in the last quarter of the 3rd millennium BC. Natural catastrophes, such as volcanic eruptions in Iceland and Santorini (2354 cal BC and 1627 cal BC), also impacted these interactions, with these dates roughly aligning with the end of Early Bronze Age 2 and the beginning of Late Bronze Age in the central Balkans.

In the earliest, first phase of the Early Bronze Age in the central Balkans, which began in the first quarter of the 3rd millennium BC, material culture was based on survivals from the preceding Eneolithic period, while spiritual culture was reflected in the distinctive burials under tumuli with ochre in the graves – customs originating from the east, from the steppe regions, and adopted in the northern central Balkans, Šumadija, the peri-Pannonian zone, and western Serbia, where the tradition of burial under tumuli persisted throughout the Bronze Age. The orographic openness of the terrain certainly facilitated this east-to-west spread of tumuli, following the valleys of the Danube and Sava, and then the smaller rivers southward toward Great Morava Valley and western Serbia. Besides this east–west interaction, similar interconnections occurred in the south-east of the region, where the zones of interaction were South Morava Basin and Timok Valley, although these interactions were one-sided, likely involving population movements of late Coţofeni–Kostolac communities from Timok Valley toward the Niš Plain and further south.

Some elements of steppe culture, such as characteristic gold jewellery, were also observed in the southern central Balkans, in the area of southern Serbia, but these date somewhat later, to the third quarter of the 3rd millennium BC, which chronologically belongs to the second phase of the Early Bronze Age, but culturally to the first phase, often called the 'phase of steppe traditions'. Not much is known about this phase, so the economy, metallurgy, and other aspects of life in the first half of the 3rd millennium BC in the central Balkans remain largely unknown. A number of silver and gold finds have been discovered in steppe tumuli in the central Balkans but no evidence of metallurgy from this period has been documented in this region. According to some analysed finds in neighbouring areas (e.g., Velika Gruda in the Montenegrin littoral), it seems that raw materials for metal objects were sourced from outside the Balkans. On the other hand, it is unusual that the copper-rich mountains of this part of the Balkans, particularly in the eastern region, remained unnoticed in the first half of the 3rd millennium, especially since they were proven to be exploited from the later phases of the Early Bronze Age (e.g., Prljuša). During this period, finds of tin bronze with clumsily made alloys containing a high iron content are mentioned in neighbouring regions (e.g., Slavonia), suggesting that this period might be characterised as a time of experimentation in metallurgy, with intensive interactions and exchange of metallurgical knowledge and skills between the populations of the Balkans and Central Europe.

Already in the second phase of the Early Bronze Age in the central Balkans, roughly dated to the third and the beginning of the fourth quarter of the 3rd millennium, material culture was based on an indigenous culture partially rooted in the Eneolithic survivals of the Vučedol group in the north and the Bubanj-Hum II group in the south. This phase is defined by two regional groups: the Vinkovci–Somogyvár group in the peri-Pannonian zone and Great Morava Valley, with its regional variant, the Belotić–Bela Crkva group in western Serbia, and the Bubanj-Hum III–Pelince–Pernik group in the southern central Balkans. The spiritual culture of this phase continued in the north and west to be influenced by steppe traditions, with burials under tumuli, but without ochre in the graves. A grave containing a contracted individual in the interior of the South Morava basin, though lacking a tumulus, included gold jewellery characteristic of the steppe Yamnaya culture, indicating an enduring steppe legacy in the third quarter of the 3rd millennium in the interior of the Balkan Peninsula.

Unlike the first phase of the Early Bronze Age, where the direction of intensive interactions in the northern part of the central Balkans followed an east–west axis, at the beginning of the second phase, the interaction shifted to a north–south–north and an west–east axis. From the mid-3rd millennium BC onward, strong cultural interconnections were observed between communities in the peri-Pannonian zone south of the Danube and Sava and those in the south-western Carpathian Basin. The symbiosis of Eneolithic traditions and the culture of the Pannonian Basin led to the emergence of the Vinkovci–Somogyvár group, which characterised the second phase of the Early Bronze Age. These interactions likely introduced daggers, which began appearing in this phase in the central Balkans, and possibly domesticated horses, although absolute dating for the latter is only confirmed in the subsequent, third phase of the Early Bronze Age. During this period, interactions were also recorded between the communities of the peri-Pannonian zone and Great Morava Valley, and further downstream along the Danube with communities in Đerdap and Oltenia.

Available data on the economy during this period is insufficient for a comprehensive understanding of diet and subsistence, as zooarchaeological data comes from only one pit in the peri-Pannonian zone. According to this data, cattle were the primary livestock (64%), followed by sheep/goats (12%), domestic pigs (16%), and dogs (8%), with no evidence of wild animals. Regarding metallurgy, there are no traces of copper exploitation or metallurgical activity in this phase, although axes of the Kozarac- and Lozane-types are commonly found across the entire central Balkans. Among the few finds whose physical-chemical composition has been analysed, most were made of copper or copper with a low arsenic content up to 1%, with only one axe made of arsenic copper containing 3.5% arsenic.

By the end of the third and the beginning of the last quarter of the 3rd millennium BC, cultural changes as well as economic shifts occurred among these communities, defining what is referred to as the Early Bronze Age 3 phase in the central Balkans. The stylistic and typological characteristics of pottery in the north no longer matched those of the Vinkovci–Somogyvár group; instead, a new cultural phenomenon emerged, built upon this group and elements of the Bubanj-Hum III group from the south, which was already expanding northward at that time. This new cultural entity, with its specific features, was named the Novačka ćuprija–Pančevo group, after the eponymous sites. This group occupied the peri-Pannonian zone, then spread into Šumadija and the Great Morava Basin. These changes occurred at a micro-regional level within the central Balkans, with certain interactions with communities from the southern Carpathian Basin.

At the same time, the Bubanj-Hum III group continued to exist in the South Morava Basin, albeit with a reduced territory (hence the absence of Pelince and Pernik in the group's name), as these communities retreated northward during the last quarter of the 3rd millennium (no later than the 21st century cal BC, as indicated by grave 3 from Ranutovac) due to the expansion of the Armenochori group from the south, from Pelagonia and Vardar Basin. These changes were of a macro-regional nature, affecting regions beyond the central Balkans, as evidenced by the defensive architecture observed at the hilltop settlement of Kale in Skopje.

Additionally, given the scope of these changes, which included not only stylistic and typological features of pottery but also the practice of cremation under so-called 'Stone fields', it is assumed that population movements occurred alongside cultural interactions between these regions and the southern central Balkans.

As mentioned, while cremation practices emerged in the southern central Balkans during this period, encompassing the last century of the 3rd millennium, the north and west retained the biritual burial practices noted in the second phase of the Early Bronze Age, with burials under tumuli persisting only in western Serbia. Ritual offerings to higher powers and the deposition of gifts in rock crevices or shallow pits, recorded in the Pčinja basin (Pelince) in the southern central Balkans, continued throughout the second and third phases of the Early Bronze Age but seemingly ceased with changes in population structure, only to re-appear several centuries later in the Late Bronze Age.

Based on limited palaeo-botanical data, single-grain and two-grain wheat and barley were cultivated in the southern central Balkans during this phase (e.g., Bubanj), while more extensive archaeo-zoological data is available. In the north, at the Marjansko Brdo site in the peri-Pannonian zone, cattle, sheep, goats, and pigs continued to be raised, with the proportion of sheep and goats increasing compared to the second Early Bronze Age phase at this site, while the prevalence of cattle decreased significantly and the proportion of pigs remained constant. Similar livestock compositions were recorded at nearby Viminacium sites, where cattle were the most numerous, followed by sheep/goats, pigs, and dogs, with some wild animals also present. Slightly further south in the same zone (Novačka ćuprija), pigs were the most common, followed by cattle, dogs, with sheep/goats being minimally represented, and a small presence of wild animals.

In the southern central Balkans (e.g., Bubanj) during this phase, cattle were the most common, followed by sheep/goats and pigs, but wild animals were more prevalent than in the north. This suggests that the strategy of domestic animal husbandry and hunting in the last two centuries of the 3rd millennium varied according to local conditions and community preferences for certain livestock species. The most significant development in this Early Bronze Age phase, however, was the domesticated horse, whose remains have been identified both in the north (e.g., Rit, Nad klepečkom, Novačka ćuprija) and in the south (e.g., Bubanj) by the end of the 3rd and the beginning of the 2nd millennium BC, which would greatly alter the way of life during the Bronze Age.

Unfortunately, horse remains from the central Balkans have not undergone genetic analysis, leaving questions unanswered as to whether they belong to the DOM2 lineage or perhaps a local lineage, which would greatly clarify uncertainties regarding the origins and movement of domesticated horses in South-eastern Europe.

Copper oxide ore exploitation (e.g., Prljuša) has been confirmed for this phase, although traces of metallurgical activities have not yet been identified. The only reliably dated metal artefact from this phase is a copper needle without traces of arsenic or tin, found in a pit dated to the 20th century cal BC at Marjansko Brdo. Only from the 19th century BC, with the beginning of the Middle Bronze Age, can we speak of a more widespread use of tin bronze artefacts in these areas. Gold finds from the Early Bronze Age are scarce, but based on their type and form, they appear to be the result of interactions with the Lower Danube and the Carpathian Basin. Currently, there is no scientific evidence to confirm that, besides cultural transmission, there were migrations from these directions, although this remains a possibility.

At the start of the 19th century BC significant changes occurred across the central Balkans, except in the Skopje and Kumanovo Plains in the south, where the Armenochori communities retained the stylistic-typological characteristics of their ceramics from the end of the Early Bronze Age. In the northern central Balkans, in the peri-Pannonian zone and parts of the Great Morava Basin, ceramics with distinct stylistic-typological traits emerged, forming the basis for defining the Vatin group. Meanwhile, in the southern central Balkans, a culture identified as the Bubanj-Hum IV–Ljuljaci group developed from the Bubanj-Hum III group. This period in the evolution of the Bronze Age in the Balkans is marked as the Middle Bronze Age, lasting until the appearance of Late Bronze Age cultures, around the mid-16th or early 15th century cal BC.

During the Middle Bronze Age, burials in the northern central Balkans were performed in a biritual manner, whereas in the east (Timok Region), cremation was practised exclusively, with remains placed in urns laid in circular stone structures. It is noteworthy that no Early Bronze Age sites were found in the Timok Region, while numerous sites from both the preceding (Late Eneolithic) and subsequent Middle Bronze Age periods were recorded. This population hiatus may have been due to depopulation caused by a climatic crisis. Interestingly, during the Middle Bronze Age, a culture similar to that of the Great Morava Valley region existed in the Timok area, with certain Eneolithic survivals and elements reminiscent of Early Bronze Age communities in the Aegean. This similarity is evident in cremation practices, with urns placed in circular stone structures, and in certain stylistic-typological features of the pottery, especially urns.

Additionally, it is likely that by the end of the 3rd millennium BC, communities of the Bubanj-Hum III group moved north from the southern central Balkans in response to the expansion of Armenochori communities from the south. This northward movement might explain the intensive resettlement of the Timok Region after the Early Bronze Age depopulation, with settlers coming from South Morava Basin, who had already been in contact, directly or indirectly, with the Armenochori group.

In the Timok Region, along with numerous settlements and cemeteries of cremated individuals, a metallurgical workshop with an underground small-mouth furnace was discovered, used to smelt copper sulphide ore multiple times until full metal purity was achieved. This sophisticated metallurgical technology might be linked to the copper ore's partial origin from the Alpine region, as suggested by isotope analyses. The distribution of settlements exclusively in mountainous ore-rich areas, rarely found in major river valleys, points to mining and metallurgy as key economic activities for these communities. The presence of copper slag traces on the bones from many graves suggests that cremation was performed in metallurgical furnaces, highlighting the intensive use of copper metallurgy in this zone.

The Middle Bronze Age in the central Balkans featured a higher number of tin bronze artefacts, found relatively equally across all geographic zones, except in western Serbia, where Middle Bronze Age settlements were few. Copper and, occasionally, arsenic copper artefacts continued to be used, along with stone moulds for object casting, indicating established casting technology from at least the 17th century cal BC (based on a pit dated at Marjansko Brdo) and likely earlier. The distribution of settlements, metal artefacts, and moulds suggests that the Timok Region and the eastern part of the South Morava Basin led in copper exploitation and bronze production. Isotope analysis of tin (120 and 124) showed that the tin in all analysed artefacts originated from the Central Balkans, probably from Mount Cer. The most common metal artefacts were Patulele-type axes, daggers, and flat axes, mainly found in the eastern and south-eastern central Balkans. These interactions are further evidenced by the nearly identical cultural identity of the populations in the northern central Balkans (peri-Pannonian zone) and the southern Carpathian Basin, supported by the central Balkan origin of tin in the bronze artefacts of the Vatin group in Vojvodina.

Information on cereal and other plant usage during this period is lacking. According to zooarchaeological results from the well-explored Ljuljaci settlement in Šumadija, pigs and cattle were predominant, with sheep/goats and dogs present in smaller numbers. A similar domestic animal ratio was found in the peri-Pannonian zone, with no wild animals reported in the small sample from the Cigansko Brdo site. In the southern central Balkans, although the sample was very small, pigs were the most common, followed by sheep/goats, with cattle in fewer numbers. Horses were slightly more common in the peri-Pannonian zone, reaching 12% at Ljuljaci, significantly higher than at Early Bronze Age sites in the region. Similar to the Early Bronze Age, economic strategies were based on breeding the same domestic animals, with their ratios and the intensity of hunting influenced by local natural conditions and community preferences for specific livestock.

The culture remained relatively uniform across the central Balkans without major changes until the 17th/16th century, when ceramics with stylistic-typological characteristics of the Verbicioara group from Oltenia and north-western Bulgaria appeared in the Timok Region and Đerdap. These intense cultural interactions were also felt, to a lesser extent, in Šumadija, the peri-Pannonian zone, and the basins of the Great Morava and South Morava, where similar ceramic elements were noted. During the 16th century (evidenced in the second half and possibly the first half), significant cultural changes in the peri-Pannonian zone and Đerdap Gorge were triggered by contacts between indigenous communities and those associated with encrusted ceramics from the west and north. This cultural phenomenon is known in Serbian Danube as the Žuto Brdo–Girla Mare group, confirmed in this area during the second half of the 16th century, marking the beginning of the Late Bronze Age.

In the south, the Bubanj-Hum IV–Ljuljaci group communities, with minor interactions with the Verbicioara group and cultural influences from the Aegean, gradually transformed within the central Balkans into Late Bronze Age groups, such as the Brnjica group in South Morava Basin, Kosovo, and Raška, and the Paraćin group in the Great Morava Basin and the Timok Region. The most recent date for the Bubanj-Hum IV–Ljuljaci group comes from Velika Humska Čuka and is placed in the second half of the 16th century cal BC, while the Late Bronze Age groups have not been dated earlier than the second half of the 15th century, leaving the intervening period still open to future clarification.

This study confirmed the validity of all previously recognised cultural phenomena defined as cultural groups or cultures in the central Balkans from the first quarter of the 3rd millennium to the mid-2nd millennium BC. However, due to previous chronologies and limited information, this study has revised their timelines and introduced some new cultural phenomena or groups, which could not have been identified with the previously available data.